Court, household, and itinerary of King Henry II

Instancing also the chief agents and adversaries of the King in his government, diplomacy, and strategy

R. W. Eyton

Alpha Editions

This edition published in 2019

ISBN : 9789353928995

Design and Setting By
Alpha Editions
email - alphaedis@gmail.com

PREFACE.

Facts; simple facts; where they were accomplished; when they were accomplished; who accomplished them; and what was said as to how they were accomplished at the time of their coming to pass; these are the primary and most essential elements of pure history.

Estimates of causes and consequences, physical or moral; of personal intellect, mind, or character; of individual feelings, motives, or principles; of social forces or influences; of national or party creeds, whether religious or political; these indeed all belong to real history, but they are not its primary elements: they are its superstructures, they are deductions, they are calculations from, or upon, those elements. They subsist on facts, on facts analysed, facts pluralized, facts combined. Rightly conceived they form the philosophy of history, wrongly conceived they exhibit only the bigotry of prejudice or the folly of opinion. Broadly and honestly worked-out, such estimates will endure for all time as the credentials of the true Historian: garbled or narrowly dealt-with, they will obtain but an ephemeral currency. Posterity will regard them only as the badges of the essayist, the sophist, or the partisan.

The following pages claim nothing more than to be the diligent and honest work of a mere Indicator, or Registrar, or compiler of facts. They are not intended to propagate, recommend, or even announce any form of political theory or metaphysical opinion as entertained by the compiler. In other words, he does not aspire to, he carefully avoids, the domains of historical philosophy and of political science; he will never willingly enter upon any discussion of moral questions, or any debate as to personal qualities or conduct. He only affects to supply a broad basis of facts, references, dates, places, names, and documents, for the use of some genuine and impartial Historian who may come hereafter to review the reign and biography of Henry Fitz Empress; and who may prefer rather to take his stand of observation among the things and doings themselves, than to contemplate the twelfth century through the haze or halo of the nineteenth.

The late Deputy Keeper of the Public Records, editing, many years since, the Patent Rolls of King John, appended thereto a

Tabular Itinerary of that King. The merit and value of the work have been too widely acknowledged to need any testimony here. For all previous and many subsequent reigns, a good Itinerary of the reigning King will be the one auxiliary most likely to be prized by the Historian. The topography and chronology necessarily embodied in an Itinerary are not only in themselves of intrinsic historical value, but they are tests, verifying or correcting, the facts alleged by chroniclers.

Now, the Itinerary of King John, being compiled almost exclusively from dated documents, was capable of being condensed and simplified in the form adopted by Sir Thomas Hardy. But for no earlier reign is the same simple method available; summarily, because no diurnally dated Rolls, like those used by Sir Thomas Hardy, exist for any earlier reign. It follows that any Itinerary of any earlier reign than that of John must needs be a composite structure; incapable of uniform precision, and consequently unfit for the Tabular Form. In the case of John's reign, authentic dates were ready at hand to the compiler; in the case of other and earlier reigns, the few dates which are supplied have still to be verified, the many dates which are not supplied must be found. And thus it comes to pass that, in constructing the best practicable Itinerary of any King, earlier than John, the Constructor will have to import a great variety of matter, not indeed relevant to an ordinary Itinerary, but very relevant to the facts which it is the chief use of an Itinerary to verify and to test.

But apart from the Itinerary, or Record of time and place, facts can seldom be outlined, seldom portrayed, never established, without due mention of agency and attestation. In other words, to entitle alleged facts to full credit and import, it is always desirable to ascertain who enacted them, who knew best about them, which of them was deposed to at the time, and whether by the actors or by spectators. Thus, to make a mere Itinerary subservient to its object, viz. the ascertainment of fact, we must add to it all that is ascertainable, and at the same time important, of the chief actors of the day, especially of the King and the members of his Household, Court, and Government; all that is relevant, as to his allies, his enemies, and his diplomatic correspondents.

And again, one whose broad object is the ascertainment of facts, will be compelled to advert occasionally to yet another class of evidence. For indeed there are some important facts, the very existence and knowledge of which would never have dawned on posterity had they not been hinted at by letter-writers, news-mongers, and politicians, in support of some argument or opinion, and which are attested by no better evidence. Such facts can be proved or estimated only by the introduction of controversial and tedious matter. Nevertheless, and even at such a cost, any addition to the realm of fact is worthy of purchase; at all events it is necessary to the completion of the undertaking now professed.

And now having sufficiently declared the object and programme of his compilation, the author would fain say something as to the relations between chronology and fact.

To dated facts, wherever discoverable, great deference is due, in respect of their intrinsic, though, it may be, not of their historical value individually. For a dated fact is not merely a fact doubly authenticated in itself, but it usually gives the means of approximating to the dates of other facts.

These proximately dated facts may be of great historical import; at all events they are of more value than facts that are altogether undated.

Lastly, we find many important facts, not undated indeed, but wrongly dated; and these too, if their true dates can be discovered, become, by so much, more authentic and more valuable: and alleged facts whose dates can neither be found nor rectified, and which are chronologically impossible, need not therefore to be always discarded. Sometimes, their alleged conditions being rectified, they may become both possible and valuable.

Some instances of the mutual rectifications which are exchangeable between date and fact are as follows:—

I. We are told as a fact bearing upon the history of the law and practice of judicial evidence, that in the reign of King Henry II. a protracted suit was determined by the Chief Justice of England vouching himself as a personal witness in regard to the main points at issue; and that the king gave sentence accordingly and at once, declaring that such testimony ought to over-ride all others.

On examining the Chief Justice's recorded testimony, it appears that he will have alleged himself to have been an eye-witness and recollector of things which took place some five years before he was born, probably ten years before he could read, and at least fifteen years before he could have apprehended the mode and ratio of the matters on which he deponed. What follows? That the monk who drew this record imagined or invented the whole story? Not so. At a time when those were considered the most eligible jurors who had most previous knowledge of the fact at issue, it is quite likely that King Henry considered his Chief Justice a first-class witness. The gist of the monk's story was not an entire falsehood. He only invalidated his own testimony as a law-reporter by putting a false chronology into the mouth of the Chief Justice.

A corollary, of course false, follows on false premises. The monk's story would make Robert, Earl of Leicester, the justiciar in question, to have lived to be at least 78. From a mass of contradictory statements made by the Chroniclers as to the date of his death, we evolve the fact that he died at about the age of 64.

II. Again, in regard to King Henry's "Ten Ordinances," the date of their issue is in itself of great importance, and affects many side questions also. One historian, dating their issue as A.D. 1165, adds the plausible circumstances that they were despatched from Normandy to England by the hands of two High Sheriffs, whom he names. But these two Sheriffs happen not to have entered office till Easter, 1170.

The question being disencumbered of all false conditions, it appears that the "Ten Ordinances" were transmitted to England about November, 1169; so that, *as sheriffs*, these two envoys can have had nothing to do with their issue. Nevertheless, as individuals, they very probably were so concerned.

III. Another historian learns from the very letter of the same "Ten Ordinances," that the lands of the *Earl of Chester* had been illegally interdicted, and the Earl's person excommunicated by two Anglican Bishops. Thus a very remarkable episode, in which, however, the Earl of Norfolk was the principal actor, was blotted from the page of authentic history merely because the historian did not know that another Earl, contemporary with him of Chester, was named Hugh.

IV. This same Earl of Chester is made the subject of yet another antiquarian craze, misleading, if it were not a craze, as to the date of the *Liber Niger*, and as to the dignity and franchises of a Palatine Earl. It has been said or strongly suggested that the reason why the said Earl neglected to make return of his fief to the Feodary now known as the *Liber Niger*, was because he was secretly disaffected to the Crown. So then the date of these returns being, as we shall hereafter show, *circa* February, 1166, the Earl's disaffection will have slumbered miraculously till April, 1173.

Now the real reason why the Earl of Chester heeded not to make any such return is highly instructive. It was because his dignity was Palatinate. The same reason operated in discharging all the Barons of Chester from a similar obligation. Nay, the King's Writ ordering any such return, *could not*, as the phrase was, *run* in a Palatinate.

A cognate reason exempted the Barons of the Welsh Marches from making these returns. So there is no return in the collection of the Fief of Strigoil, none of the Marcher Knights holding under the See of Hereford, none of the Fiefs of Mortimer of Wigmore, or Corbet of Caux.

V. Again it has been said (by the writer, he is bound to confess) that William Longespee, King Henry's son by Rosamond Clifford, was born before the King's accession to the throne. This was on the very natural presumption that Longespee was older than Geoffrey Fitz-Roy, who was put into the Church and became eventually a Bishop: and that again was on the mistaken assumption that Geoffrey was son of Rosamond Clifford. But Geoffrey, it transpires, was not Rosamond's son. His mother was a common harlot. He was older than William Longespee—perhaps fifteen years older.

VI. Again it has been taught us at school, or at least we have read in unexceptionable school-books about the 'Labyrinth at Woodstock,' and how 'Fair Rosamond' was poisoned by 'jealous Queen Elianor.' Chronology disproves the latter story. Rosamond was in the hey-day of her influence when Elianor had entered on the prison, which still held the Queen when Rosamond quitted her bower at Woodstock for her grave at Godstow.

About the 'Labyrinth' nothing is here said to impugn the story, because these are dated facts which are in some consistency with such a legend.

Another misleader about the age of William Longespee is that, under the sobriquet of *Manzer*, he led the Royalists who captured the King of Scots at Alnwick on July 13, 1174.

But this story is susceptible of an explanation which is far more consistent with chronology. Geoffrey of Vigeois, alone among the Chroniclers, tells of "a son of King Henry" as having achieved the said success. The messenger, into whose mouth Vigeois puts the news thereof, attributes it to the King's son "Manzer." In course of time certain commentators on Vigeois' story discovered in the sobriquet 'Manzer,' that son of King Henry who was afterwards called William Longespee. But the 'Manzer' of Vigeois' narrative was undoubtedly Geoffrey Fitz-Roy—he whom other Chroniclers show to have been active elsewhere in the suppression of the Rebellion of 1174, though none of them tell of his presence in the affair of Alnwick. (It will be seen in the sequel not only how Geoffrey Fitz-Roy comported himself on the other occasions in question, but how the Chroniclers, generally, attribute the capture of the King of Scots to six Royalists, of whom Robert de Stuteville and Ranulf de Glanville were the chief.)

Another allegation connected with the same subject is a marvel of itinerary impossibilities. It is that the news of the fight at Alnwick reached King Henry at Canterbury the day it happened.

VII. An alleged letter of Pope Alexander III, is proved to be a forgery, not merely by its extravagant absurdities but by its date. This date being constructively 2 Dec. 1159, the Letter orders the deposition and incarceration of Thomas Archbishop of Canterbury, who was elected to that dignity in May, 1162.

Yet this letter, being evidently a nearly coeval forgery, has its use, in that it shows what certain impostors or partizans of a later day thought, or wished to be thought, or cared to circulate. The Historian may learn hence how to estimate the evidence of more cautious and less suspected writers who have said similar things without belying themselves by absurdities or anachronisms.

Of the five Reigns which followed on the Norman Conquest of England, that of Henry Fitz Empress is the most difficult to deal with in matters of Itinerary and Chronology. This will be better evident in what should now be said about the chief authorities for the ensuing collections. The said authorities are—

I. Chronicles, which in respect of the said Reign are sparing in their statements of diurnal date, often indefinite on larger questions of chronology, often contradictory of one another, both as to facts and the sequence of facts.

II. Pipe-Rolls, which indeed are first-rate evidence as to the year of the few historical matters to which they allude, but which supply little or nothing as to months or days; which tell much of the *personnel* of the King's Household, Court, and Government, but little indeed of men's actions and still less of their ways.

III. Norman Exchequer Rolls, analogous to the English Pipe-Rolls in regard to matter, but preserved only for two years of the thirty-eight during which Henry Fitz Empress held the Dukedom.

IV. The Liber Niger Scaccarii, a Feodary, purporting to contain the names, and containing most of the names of the contemporary Tenants-in-capite and of their Sub-Tenants by Knights' Service. This Record is undated in itself and has been misdated by Antiquaries; but, its date being ascertainable and ascertained, its evidence as regards Fiefs and persons is doubly valuable. Of topography it contains little, of events nothing.

V. The Rotuli de Dominabus et pueris et puellis de donatione Regis in XII Comitatibus,—a record of Wardships, Reliefs, and other Sovereign rights in the Eastern Counties, as ascertained by four justices-in-eyre. This Record is of some personal and some topographical interest, but contains little to our present purpose. It will be quoted in its place. It is misdated, by its Editor, but only by a year. It belongs to the year 1186 rather than 1185.

VI. Royal Charters, auxiliary to one's purpose chiefly in respect of the *personnel* of their Testing-clauses. These Records, valuable as they are when studied, can be used only hypothetically and after being so studied. Of all the Kings who have reigned since the Conquest, Henry Fitz Empress was the one King who was least careful to add chronological dates to his Manifestoes. Therefore, before we can use his Charters for the present purpose, we must first establish their dates, or qualify ourselves to form a reasonable judgment on that matter.

VII. Epistolary Correspondence: a class of document of which the Reign of the Second Henry furnishes a redundancy. Few of these Letters are dated and those are Papal. Again, of dated Papal Letters, few are dated of the year or of more than the place, month, and day. Yet these, their year being discovered and their month and day already declared,—these imply the proximate dates of wholly undated letters, to which they were replies, or which they called forth in reply. Charters, when their dates are elaborated, supply much knowledge as to agents and persons. Epistles, whose dates are ascertained, supply numberless facts of great historical importance, yet not otherwise recorded.

It has been found impossible to introduce Epistolary documents for the mere purpose of dating the said documents and others with which they are associated, without at the same time expressing more or less of the theoretical or argumentative or political matter which they happen to contain. But this has been done unwillingly, the object (we repeat) being simply to fix or to make reference to every fact, date, place, action, and personage, which is of importance to an historical estimate of a particular reign.

VIII. LAW-REPORTS, of which but few are extant, happen to embody some curious particulars of Royal Itinerary and of the *personnel* of the King's Curia and Council. As to what took place in Court one finds that the Law-Clerks must have reported many things as said, which they only thought might have been, or ought to have been, said; and that many things which they heard said, they failed to understand themselves, and consequently to make intelligible to posterity.

IX. ENGLISH HISTORIES. To these, wherever the author is indebted to them, he will make reference in his notes; but one group of such references requires special explanation. The present compilation of evidences (or rather nine-tenths thereof) was many years ago ready for the press and was offered to more than one Archæological Society for publication. No publication ensued, and it was much later that the author became aware of an "Outline Itinerary of King Henry II." appended to Professor Stubbs' edition of Benedict of Peterborough. This, and other discoveries induced the author to rewrite some portions of the former MS. In doing so he has been anxious to acknowledge by referential notes his obligations to Professor Stubbs' work; but, if he should have anywhere failed to do so, he here desires to make his apology and to repeat his acknowledgment of a great assistance.

INTRODUCTORY NOTICES AND EXPLANATIONS.

The full style of Henry of Anjou was "Henry, King of England, Duke of Normandy and Aquitaine and Comte of Anjou." Colloquially he was, in his lifetime, spoken of as Henry Fitz Empress, sometimes as King Henry the Second.

"Henry son of the King" was usually so spoken of till his

Coronation, when he was called "Henry the younger King" or sometimes "King Henry the Third."

So with K. Henry's son, Richard, the titles of Duke of Aquitaine and Comte of Poitou accrued to him while yet his Father was using them.

As to Geoffrey, he became Duke of Bretagne by his marriage; but he was usually called only Comte of Bretagne, the superior title being asserted indeed by himself but not generally recognized. He was also Earl of Richmond.

The King's son John, Comte of Moretain, also had the Title of "Lord," sometimes expressed "Prince," "of Ireland": which Title was not at any time assumed by King Henry himself.

In the following pages it is convenient to speak of the sons and daughters of Kings as 'Princes' and 'Princesses,' not that any of them, except John, were ever so called in their day. The style of "Fitz-Roy," though more in keeping with the usage of the twelfth century, has a sinister sound in the ears of the nineteenth. It is used therefore of William Longespee or of the Chancellor Geoffrey. For any of the King's legitimate sons the appellation of Prince is preferred, not as implying any Title, but as a concise, intelligible, and non-pedantic expression.

So too if the writer should apply to Thomas the Chancellor, to Thomas Archbishop of Canterbury, to St. Thomas Martyr, the briefer and more familar name of Becket, no disrespect will be intended to the memory of the individual, no disregard of the usages of antiquity; conciseness only will be the object.

In the following volume the writer adopts a division by Fiscal, as well as the ordinary division by Dominical, years. The Pipe-Rolls, ending as they do at Michaelmas in each year, and therefore not containing evidences quite parallel with those of the Dominical year, necessitated this arrangement. At the same time the Dominical and Regnal year of each event or document is left as clear as it would have been under any other arrangement.

As to Regnal years, the first year of King Henry II.'s reign commenced with his coronation, on 19 Dec. 1154, and ended 18 Dec. 1155; a circumstance which, barring 13 days, brings each Regnal year of the reign into strict parallellism with some specific Dominical year. However, there are one or two cases whére the regnal years of K. Henry II. seem to have been computed from the death of Stephen, which took place 25 October 1154, that is 55 days before Henry's Coronation at Westminster.

With regard to the spelling of proper names, the writer does not affect to copy the original in all cases. He will be particular to do so in cases where there is any doubt about accuracy or significance.

The Chronicle Authorities usually relied on in the following pages are Gervase, Diceto, Hoveden, Benedictus (Hearne's Edition), and the Chronicon Normanniæ. Where these or any of them are the sole authority for any statement, special reference in the notes has not been considered as always necessary.

Monastic Charters, where special references are not made in the notes, may be found in the Six-Volume Monasticon under the history of the Monastery concerned.

References to the Pipe-Rolls of the 2nd, 3rd and 4th years of the Reign are to the pages of the printed edition.

SIGNS AND ABBREVIATIONS.

In the right-hand Margin, where a place has not been identified, or where its insertion in a particular sequence is conjectural, its name is bracketed thus (   ).

Where such name, or its insertion in due sequence, is not only doubtful but questionable, a note of Query is added; thus (?).

c., in the left-hand margin, or elsewhere, denotes *circa*.

G.S. or Gall. Script. signifies Rerum Gallicarum et Francicarum Scriptores.

S.T.C. signifies "Sancti Thomæ Cantuariensis Vita et Epistolæ" (Giles).

L.N. signifies Liber Niger Scaccarii (Hearne's printed Edition, MDCCLXXIV).

R.D. signifies "Rotulus de Dominabus et Pueris et Puellis" (Grimaldi's Edition, MDCCCXXX).

COURT, HOUSEHOLD, AND ITINERARY OF K. HENRY II.

FROM MICHAELMAS, 1154, TO MICHAELMAS, 1155.

1154. Oct. 10. Roger, Archdeacon of Canterbury, was consecrated Archbishop of York at Westminster, by Theobald Archbishop of Canterbury, in the presence of Richard Bishop of London, Robert Bishop of Lincoln, Gilbert Bishop of Hereford, Walter Bishop of Rochester, Robert Bishop of Bath, Nigel Bishop of Ely, William Bishop of Norwich, and John Bishop of Worcester.[1]

Oct. 25. Stephen, King of England, died at Canterbury.[2]

Dec. 2. Pope Anastasius IV. died.

" 3. Adrian IV elected to the Papacy.

" 7. Henry, Duke of Normandy, embarked at Barfleur for England. The 'Duchess Alianora' accompanied[3] him, as did his two brothers, Geoffrey and William. Barfleur.

" 8. Duke Henry landed near the New Forest.[4] Hampshire.

Duke Henry next proceeded to Winchester, where several Nobles met him, to do fealty. Winchester.

" 19. King Henry crowned at Westminster by Theobald Archbishop of Canterbury. There were present Roger Archbishop of York, Richard Bishop of London, Robert Bishop of Lincoln, Walter Bishop of Chester, Gilbert Bishop of Hereford, Robert Bishop of Bath, John Bishop of Winchester (*read* Worcester), Robert Bishop of Exeter, Hilary Bishop of Chichester, Joceline Bishop of Salisbury, Walter Bishop of Rochester, Nigel Bishop of Ely, William Bishop of Norwich, Hugh Bishop of Durham, Adelulf Bishop of Carlisle, Hugh Archbishop of Rouen, Philip Bishop of Westminster.

[1] Gervase, p. 1376.

[2] Gervase, sub anno.

[3] So says a French Chronicle (Gall. Script. xii. 482), adding, with less knowledge of subsequent facts, that he was 'consecrated King at *Winchester* on Dec. 19.'

[4] Diceto, p. 529. Gervase says that the Duke landed at Hostreham. Hostreham was a sea-port of Normandy, elsewhere called Ostrea and Oisterham. I conceive the place to be now represented by Estreham, a village at the mouth of the river Orne. I am by no means sure that there was not also an Ostreham on the English coast, which may have led to Gervase's misapprehension. Certainly there was such a place somewhere in Kent, and its very name would suggest a juxta-marine position. There are independent reasons for thinking that it was in the vicinity of Sandwich or Deal. But K. Henry, embarking at Barfleur, was more likely to disembark at Southampton, and so, near the New Forest, than at a place east of Dover; and his going *first to Winchester* is still more decisive evidence in favour of Diceto's statement.

1154. c. Dec. 19. Baieux, Arnulf Bishop of Liseux, Herbert Bishop of Avranches, and Theodoric Comte of Flanders.[1] Westminster

At Westminster, and (as presumed) immediately after his coronation, K. Henry expedited the Charter whereby he *gives* to William, Earl of Arundel, the Castle and Honour of Arundel and the *tertium denarium* of Sussex. Witnesses, Theobald, Abp of Canterbury; Hilary, Bishop of Chichester; Nigel, Bishop of Ely and Chancellor;[2] William, the King's brother; Roger (*read* Reginald), Earl of Cornwall; Hugh, Earl of Norfolk; Henry de Essex, Constable; Richard de Humez, Constable; Richard de Lucy; Warin fitz Jerold, Chamberlain; Josceline de Bailliol; Robert de Dunestanvill; Robert de Curci.[3]

At Westminster also, by another charter (of apparently the same date), K. Henry confirms to William, son of Robert fitz Walter of Windsor, the lands of his late father. Witnesses, Earl Reginald (of Cornwall); Robert, Earl of Leicester; Hugh, Earl of Norfolk; Henry de Essex, Constable; Richard de Humez, Constable; Joceline de Bailliol.[4]

Dec. 25. K. Henry held his Court at Bermondsey.[5] Bermondsey.

1155.

A.D. 1155.

c. Jan. 4. The King, now at Oxford, confirms the recent election of William de Walterville to the Abbacy of Peterborough.[6] Oxford.

" 13. The King, still at Oxford, and attended by Archbishop Theobald, grants franchises to his Burgesses of Wallingford; "et hoc pro servitio et labore magno, quem pro me sustinuerunt in acquisitione hereditarii juris mei in Angliâ."[7]

We may assign to this period a Royal Charter to Trentham Priory, dated at *Oxford*, and attested by Philip, Bp of Baieux; Arnulf, Bp of Liseux; Robert Earl of Leicester; Rainald, Earl of Cornwall; William fitz Hamo; and Master Alvered.

[1] Chron. Normann. p. 990.

[2] Teob. Archiep'o Cant'; Hil. Ep'o Cic.: N. Ep'o de Ely et Canc; Willo fr'e R. So runs the testing-clause in the best authority (Rot. Cart. 5 Edw. III. m. 1.).

Hence we learn that, for a few days at least after his accession, Nigel, Bishop of Ely, was Henry's Chancellor. Consistently with this, Wendover dates Becket's appointment to the office in 1155. Other authorities, ancient and modern, seem to concur in the notion that Henry II.'s first appointment to the Chancellorship was of Becket. I should except Dean Hook, who, judging from a passage in his Lives of the Archbishops (Vol. ii. pp. 364–5), suspected the correctness of the said notion.

[3] Selden's Titles of Honour, p. 539.

[4] Harl. Charters, 43, c. 22.

[5] Gervase, p. 1377. At this Council a general demolition of castles erected during the late reign, and the expulsion of the Flandrian adventurers who had overrun the kingdom, were agreed upon.

[6] Monast. I. 352. b. Sax. Chron. p. 373.

[7] Hearne's Liber Niger, pp. 816–818. This Charter is dated *Apud Oxeneford primo idus Januarii.*

1155. Jan. 13. Also a certificate of a trial (*placitum*), held at *Oxford* before the King and Robert Earl of Leicester, "then the King's Chief Justice for all England" (*tunc temporis Capitali justiciâ meâ totius Angliæ*); which trial resulted in a *Quit-claim* to Abbot Bernard and the monks of St. Ebrulf (Uticum), as attested by the King himself; H., Bp of Winchester; Hillary, Bp of Chichester; Robert, Earl of Leicester; Richard de Lucy; and Ernald de Bosco.[1] Oxford.

From Oxford the King seems to have gone northwards.
Jan. It was now probably that he passed through *Silverston* (Selvest'), whence he addresses a certificate to Hilary, Bp. of Chichester, and the lieges of Sussex; the document being attested by Thomas the Chancellor; Manasser Biset, Dapifer; Fulqueius Painel; and Geoffry Le Moine (Monacus).[2] Silverston.

Northampton was perhaps the next place of the King's sojourn. There he expedites a Charter whereby he *makes* Hugh Bigot Earl of Norfolk, and concedes to him the Stewardship of his father, Roger. Witnesses, Theobald, Abp of Canterbury; Henry, Bishop of Winchester; Philip, Bp of Baieux; Arnulf, Bp of Liseux; Nigel, Bp of Ely; Thomas the Chancellor; Reginald, Earl of Cornwall; Henry de Essex, Constable; Richard de Humez, Constable; Richard de Luci; Warin fitz Gerold, Chamberlain; Manasser Biset, Dapifer; William fitz Hamo; Robert de Dunstanvill; and Josceline de Baillol.[3] Northampton.

To the same period may be assigned the five following Charters of the King, all dated at Northampton.

1. To Pagan de Monte Dublelli, restoring (reddidi) totam terram et tenementum quod fuit Patricii de Caducis avi sui per totam Angliam. Witnesses, Arnulf, Bp of Liseux; Thomas the Chancellor; Geoffrey the King's brother; William the King's brother; Reginald, Earl of Cornwall; Richard de Humez, Constable; William fitz Hamo, and Manasser Biset, Dapifer.[4]

2. To the Archbishop of Rouen and his successors. Witnesses, Philip, Bishop of Baieux; Rothroc, Bp of Evreux; Thomas the Chancellor; William fitz Hamo; and Warin fitz Gerold, Chamberlain.[5]

[1] Cartæ Antiquæ, W.
[2] Cartæ Antiquæ, S. 23.
[3] Collectanea Topographica et Genealogica, viii. 67.
[4] Original Charter in the Office of the Duchy of Lancaster.
[5] Cart. Antiq. P. 20.

1155. Jan. 3. To St. James's Priory at Northampton. Witnesses, Thomas the Chancellor; Richard de Hummet, Constable; Manaser Biset, Dapifer; Warin fitz Gerold, Chamberlain.[1] Northampton.

4. To Laund Priory (Leicestershire). Witnesses, Thomas, the King's Chancellor; the Earl of Cornwall; Richard de Humet, Constable; Gwarin fitz Gerald, Chamberlain.[2]

5. To Wykes Nunnery, Essex. Witnesses, Roger, Abp of York; Richard, Bp of London; Thomas the Chancellor; and Reginald, Earl of Cornwall.[3]

A Charter, dated *Apud Clium*, probably passed at Kingscliff (Northamptonshire) during this progress of the King. It is to Thorney Abbey (Cambridgeshire), which we know that he visited about this time;[4] and is attested by Thomas the Chancellor; Reginald, Earl of Cornwall; and Henry de Essex, Constable.[5] King's Cliff.

The King visited the Monastery of Peterborough on this journey.[6] Hence we have a Charter in favour of Daventry Priory, dated *Apud Burgum* (Peterborough), addressed to Robert, Bp of Lincoln, and Earl Simon (of Northampton), and attested by the said Bishop, by Thomas the Chancellor, and by Richard de Humet, Constable.[7] Peterborough.

The King also visited the Monasteries of Ramsey (Huntingdonshire), Thorney (Cambridgeshire), and Spalding (Lincolnshire), at this period.[8] Ramsey. Thorney. Spalding.

It is probable that he also visited Lincoln, and that the following Charters, all dated at Lincoln, belong to the occasion. Lincoln.

Charter to Lincoln Cathedral, attested by Theobald, Abp of Canterbury and Legate of the Romish Church; by Philip, Bishop of Baieux, and Ernulf, Bp of Liseux.[9]

Charter in favour of the See of Lincoln and Robert its Bishop, attested by Philip and Arnulf, Bishops of Baieux and Liseux, and by Thomas the Chancellor.[10]

Charter, restoring to Robert fitz Herbert the Chamberlainship of his father and grandfather. Witnesses, Philip, Bishop of Baieux; Ernulf, Bishop of Liseux; Thomas the Chancellor; Rainald, Earl of Cornwall; Richard de Humez, Constable; and John Marescall.[11]

[1] Monasticon, vi. 116.
[2] Monasticon, vi. 189.
[3] Transcript penes mei.
[4] Saxon Chronicle, p. 374.
[5] Cart. Antiq. A. A. 10.
[6] Saxon Chronicle, p. 374.
[7] Monasticon, v. 179, iv.
[8] Saxon Chronicle, p. 374.
[9] Monasticon, vi. 1276. Num. lxi.
[10] Ibidem, Num. lvi.
[11] Cart. Antiq. R. 33. See Antiquities of Shropshire, vol. vii. pp. 149–150.

1155. c. Jan. Charter to Croyland Abbey, attested by Theobald, Abp. of Canterbury; Philip, Bishop of Baieux; and Thomas the Chancellor.[1] Lincoln.

c. Feb. The King at York, where he accords with William, Earl of Albemarle.[2] York

Hence we have the following three Charters, dated at York.

(1.) Charter to Christ Church Monastery at Canterbury, and to Archbishop Theobald. Witnesses, Philip, Bp of Baieux; Arnulf, Bishop of Liseux; Thomas the Chancellor; Reginald, Earl of Cornwall; R., Earl of Leicester; and Henry de Essex, Constable.[3]

(2.) Charter to Selby Abbey (Yorkshire), attested by Theobald, Abp of Canterbury; Robert, Bishop of Lincoln; Hugh, Bishop of Durham; Adalwald, Bishop of Carlisle; Thomas the Chancellor; Rainald, Earl of Cornwall; Richard de Humez, Richard de Luci, Henry de Essex, and William, Earl of Albamarle.[4]

(3.) Charter to the Priory of Plessis Grimould (a Norman house in the diocese of Bayeux), attested by Arnulf, Bishop of Liseux; Philip, Bishop of Bayeux; Robert, Bishop of Lincoln; Thomas the Chancellor; and Richard de Humet.[5]

(4.) A Charter to the Yorkshire Priory of Nostell is undated, but it probably passed while the King was in that county. It is attested by Theobald, Abp of Canterbury; Roger, Abp of York; Robert, Bishop of Lincoln; Hugh, Bishop of Durham; Thomas, the King's Chancellor; Reginald, Earl of Cornwall; William, Earl of Albemarle; Robert, Earl of Leicester; Earl Hugh (of Norfolk); Henry de Essex, Henry de Suili (perhaps Oilli), William de Percy, and Eustace fitz John.[6]

From York the King appears to have gone to Scarborough.[7] Scarborough.

Feb. The King was next in Nottinghamshire.[8] William Peverel, of Nottingham, who had poisoned the late Earl of Chester, fled when he heard of the King's approach.

[1] Cart. Antiq. R.
[2] Chron. J. Bromton, p. 1046.
[3] Cart. Antiq. T. See Monast. I. p. 111, Num. xxxix.
[4] Cart. Antiq. P.
[5] D'Anisy's Extrait de Chartes, vol. ii. p. 62.
[6] Monasticon, vi. 93, iv.
[7] My authority for the King's visit to Scarborough is Professor Stubbs's 'Outline Itinerary of Henry II.,' printed among the Appendices to his edition of Benedict of Peterborough (vol. II. p. cxxix). In this instance W. Newburgh is the Professor's authority.
[8] Gervase, p. 1377.

1155. c. Feb. At *Nottingham* the King expedited three Charters; one to the city of Lincoln, which is now nearly illegible;[1] another to the Abbey of St. Hilda of Whitby. This is attested by Reginald, Earl of Cornwall; Richard de Luci, Manasser Biset, and William de Perci;[2] a third to Guy le Strange, which is attested by Walter, Bp of Chester; Richard de Humet, Constable; Manasser Biset, Dapifer; Richard de Luci; Richard de Campvill; and Henry de Oilli, Constable.[3] Nottingham.

The King seems next to have visited some of the Western counties.[4] Hence perhaps a Charter to Burton Abbey, dated at *Burton*, and attested by Walter, Bishop of Chester; Burton upon Trent Thomas the Chancellor, and William fitz John: also a Charter to Lilleshall Abbey (Shropshire), dated "apud Alrewas in exercitu," and attested by R. Bishop of Lincoln; Alrewas. (Staffordshire.) R. Bishop of London; Thomas the Chancellor; Manasser Biset, Dapifer; Warin fitz Gerold, Chamberlain; Robert de Dunstanville; and Joceline de Baliol:[5] also a Charter to Fairwell Nunnery (Staffordshire), dated at Radmore, and Radmore. (Staffordshire.) attested by Manasser Biset, Dapifer; Froger, Archdeacon (of Derby); Richard Peche, Archdeacon (of Coventry); Peter de Bermingham, and Falcheius the forester.[6]

Feb. 28. Prince Henry born at London, and baptized by Richard de Belmeis, Bishop of London.[7]

c. March 27. The King held a great Council at London, at which many London. Bishops and Abbots sought renewal and confirmation of their Charters.[8]

We may assign to this occasion the following four Charters, dated at London, and the following seventeen Charters, dated at Westminster.

(1.) To Bromfield Priory (Shropshire). Witnesses, Hillary, Bishop of Chichester; Reginald, Earl of Cornwall; William, Earl of Gloucester; and Richard de Humet, Constable.[9]

(2, 3.) Two Charters to the Canons of the Holy Trinity, London,[10] and to Christ Church, London, each attested by Queen Eleanor; Herbert, Bp of Avranches; Thomas the

[1] Cartæ Antiquæ Q. 21. A transcript in the Fœdera (Vol. I. p. 40) gives as witnesses, E. Episcopo Lexov. Thomâ Cancellario. H. Constab. (? Henry de Oilli), H. de Essex, Constab.
[2] Cart. Antiq. D. D.
[3] Cart. Cotton, xi. 14.
[4] Gervase, p. 1377.
[5] Lilleshall Chartulary.
[6] Monasticon, iv. 111, iii.
[7] Diceto, p. 530.
[8] Palgrave's British Commonwealth, Appendix, p. xxxii.
[9] Monast. iv. p. 155.
[10] Fœdera, p. 41.

1155. c. March 27. Chancellor; Richard de Lucy; Humphrey de Bohun, Dapifer; and Ralph de Hastings.[1] [2] London.

(4.) Charter to the citizens of Exeter, addressed to the Bishop of Exeter,[3] and attested by Arnulf, Bp of Liseux; Reginald, Earl of Cornwall; and Thomas the Chancellor.[4]

1. Charter to Montacute Priory (Somerset). Witnesses, Thomas (*read* Theobald), Archbishop of Canterbury; Henry, Bishop of Winchester; Philip, Bp of Baieux; Arnulf, Bp of Liseux; Richard, Bp of London; Joceline, Bp of Sarum; Robert, Bp of Bath; Gilbert, Bp of Hereford; William, Earl of Gloucester; R. Earl of Leicester; Warin fitz Gerold, Chamberlain; Manasser Biset, Dapifer; William fitz Hamo; and Joceline de Baillol.[5] Westminster.

2. Charter to the Abbey of St. Florant at Saumur. Witnesses, Philip, Bp of Baieux; Arnulf, Bp of Liseux; William fitz Hamo; and Robert de Dunestanvill.[6]

3. Charter to the Norman Abbey of Lire. Witnesses, Philip, Bp of Baieux; Ernulf, Bp of Liseux; Robert, Earl of Leicester; William, Earl of Gloucester; Richard de Humet, Constable; Manasser Biset, Dapifer; Warin fitz Gerold, Chamberlain; and Robert de Dunstanvill.[7]

4. Charter to the Abbey of the Holy Trinity at Caen. Witnesses, Philip, Bp of Baieux; Ernulf, Bp of Liseux; Thomas the Chancellor; and William fitz Hamo.[8]

5. Charter to Alcester Abbey (Warwickshire). Witnesses, Theobald, Abp of Canterbury; John, Bishop of Worcester; Robert, Earl of Leicester; and Richard de Luci.[9]

6. Charter to Chertsey Abbey. Witnesses, Richard, Bp of London; Thomas the Chancellor; and Humphrey de Bohun.[10]

[1] Fœdera, p. 41.

[2] Monast. vi. 157, Num. 14.

[3] Robert Chichester. He died March 28, 1155.

[4] Hearne's Liber Niger, p. 813.

[5] Cartæ Antiquæ F. F. The attestation of the Bishop of Winchester, not very frequent at the time, affects another question, which will be treated of in the sequel.

Here we should notice an undated Charter which probably passed on the same day as that to Montacute Priory. Thereby the King concedes and confirms to Henry, Bishop of Winchester, and his successors, the Manor of Sudton, which was once (first) of the Honour of Boulogne, and which King Stephen gave (to the Bishop) in exchange for Mordon. Witnesses, Philip, Bishop of Baieux; Arnulf, Bishop of Liseux; Thomas the Chancellor, Robert de Novo Burgo, and Richard de Luci (Cart. Orig. in Offic. Ducat. Lancast.).

And there is another undated Charter, which may here be noticed as having probably passed at Westminster, and on this occasion. It is in favour of Taunton Priory (Somersetshire), and is attested by Richard, Bishop of London; Nigel, Bishop of Ely; Robert, Bishop of Lincoln; Thomas the Chancellor; Robert, Earl of Leicester; and William, Earl of Gloucester (Monast. vi. 166, II.).

[6] Monast. vi. 1083.

[7] Monast. vii. 1092.

[8] Cart. Antiq. F. m. 2.

[9] Monasticon, iv. 177. vi.

[10] Cartæ Antiquæ D. No. 17.

1155. c. March 27. 7. Charter to Nigel, Bishop of Ely. Witnesses, Theobald, Abp of Canterbury; Walter, Bp of Chester; Thomas the Chancellor; and Reginald, Earl of Cornwall.[1] Westminster.

8. Charter to Thame Abbey (Oxfordshire). Witnesses, Philip, Bp of Baieux; Arnald, Bp of Liseux; T. Chancellor; Richard de Hument, Constable; Warin fitz Gerold, Chamberlain; Manasser Biset, Dapifer; and Robert de Dunestanvill.[2]

9. Charter to Hulm Abbey (Norfolk). Witnesses, Thomas the Chancellor; Reginald, Earl of Cornwall; Richard de Humez, Constable; and Warin fitz Gerold, Chamberlain.[3]

10. Charter to the Norman Abbey of Fecamp. Witnesses, Arnulf, Bp of Liseux; Philip, Bp of Baieux; Richard, Bp of London; William, the King's brother; Thomas the Chancellor; Richard de Humet; Guarin fitz Gerold; Manasser Biset, Robert de Newburgh, Robert de Dunstanvill, Joceline de Baillol, and Nicholas de Stuteville.[4]

11. Charter, confirming the agreement which Henry, Abbot of Fecamp, the King's cousin (cognatus meus), had made with William de Braose, concerning grants of Philip and William, father and grandfather of the said William de Braose. Witnesses, Gilbert, Bishop of London (*read* Hereford); Arnulf, Bp of Liseux; Philip, Bp of Baieux; Richard de Humet, Constable; Nicholas de Stutevill; Robert de Novo-burgo; and Warin fitz Gerold.[5]

12. Charter to Hugh de Mara. Witnesses, Earl Reginald; Earl Robert of Leicester; Manser Biset; and Warin fitz Gerold.[6]

13. Charter to the Burgesses of Gloucester. Witnesses, R. Earl of Cornwall; Manasser Biset, Dapifer; Warin fitz Gerold, Chamberlain; and Hugh de Longchamp.[7]

14. Charter addressed to the Bishop of Winchester, and confirming to William Briewerr the lands and tenures which he had in time of K. Henry, the King's grandfather.

[1] Cartæ Antiquæ, B. No. 29.
[2] Cartæ Antiquæ, K. No. 4.
[3] Cartæ Antiquæ, O & C C.
[4] Cartæ Antiquæ, S.
[5] Ibidem :—The first witness's name makes the genuineness of this Charter doubtful. At all events, these witnesses' names were not contemporarily added. Perhaps some transcriber, copying the original deed years after it passed, thought it well thus to record his own knowledge, that Gilbert Foliot, formerly Bishop of Hereford, had since been translated to London.
[6] Cartæ Antiquæ, Z.
[7] Cartæ Antiquæ, D D.

1155. c. March 27. Witnesses, Manasser Biset, Dapifer; Robert de Dunestanvill; and Josceline de Baillol.[1] Westminster.

15. Charter to Godstow Nunnery, confirming the grants thereto of Rainald fitz Count and Emelina his wife, and their sons. Witnesses, Robert, Bp of Lincoln; Nigel, Bp of Ely; Reginald, Earl of Cornwall; Robert, Earl of Leicester; Warin fitz Gerold; William de Caisneto; and Richard de Camvill.[2]

16. A Charter which probably passed at Westminster, whereby the King grants to Ralph Purcell, his Usher, the office of Robert Burnell, the said Ralph's uncle. Witnesses, Nigel, Bishop of Ely; Thomas the Chancellor.[3]

17. Charter to the Norman Abbey of St. Sauveur le Vicomte (Coutances Dioc.), confirming the donation which Queen Adeliza and William Earl of Chichester (her second husband) had made thereto. Witnesses, Theobald, Archbishop of Canterbury; Henry, Bp of Winchester; Reginald, Earl of Cornwall; William, Earl of Chichester; Richard de Humeto; Manasser Biset; and Garin fitz Gerold.[4]

c. March 20–27. Roger, Earl of Hereford, previously disaffected, places the Castles of Hereford and Gloucester at the King's disposal; and this by negotiation of Gilbert, Bishop of Hereford, the Earl's kinsman.[5]

We may presume that the King's Charter to the said Earl Roger passed immediately, and while the Court was still at Westminster. It is undated as to place, but is attested by Thomas the Chancellor; William, the King's brother; Reginald, Earl of Cornwall; Earl Patric (of Salisbury); John Marescall; Richard de Humez, Constable; William fitz Hamo; Richard de Sancto Remigio; Warin fitz Gerold, Chamberlain; and Josceline de Bailloil.[6]

March 28. On this day Archbishop Theobald was presiding in his own Court at Canterbury.[7]

April 10. The King holds a great Council at Wallingford, whereat Wallingford.

[1] Cartæ Antiquæ, E. E. See Dugdale's Baronage, fol. 700.

[2] Godstow Chartulary, fol. 3.

[3] Cartæ Antiquæ, F. 19. The testing-clause has been wrongly transcribed in the Fædera (p. 42), and would lead to the false assumption that Becket had in one instance attested a Royal Charter, under his style of Archdeacon of Canterbury. The reading of the Charter is *Toma Canc.* not *Tom. Cantuar.*

[4] D'Anisy's Transcripts, iii. 47.

[5] Gervase, of Canterbury, p. 1378.

[6] Rot. Chart. 1 John, memb. 6.

[7] Madox, Formulare, page 75.

1155. April 10. the Nobles recognize the successional rights of the Princes, William and Henry.[1] Wallingford.

The following three Charters, dated at Wallingford, doubtless belong to this occasion.

1. Charter to Glastonbury Abbey, attested by Reginald, Earl of Cornwall.[2]

2. Charter to Norton Priory (Cheshire), attested by T., Abp of Canterbury; Richard, Bp of London; Joceline, Bp of Salisbury; and R., Earl of Cornwall.[3]

3. Charter to the Abbey of St. Edmundsbury. Witnesses, Theobald, Abp of Canterbury; Joceline, Bp of Sarum; Richard, Bp of London; Thomas the Chancellor; R., Earl of Cornwall; Richard de Humetis, Constable; Warin fitz Gerold, Chamberlain; Manasser Biset, Dapifer; and William fitz Hamo.[4]

c. May. Immediately after the Council of Wallingford, the King went to suppress the rebellion of Hugh de Mortimer. The sieges of Cleobury, Wigmore, and Bridgnorth, occupied most of the summer.[5] Cleobury-Mortimer. Wigmore.

It was during the last siege, that the King expedited a Charter to Stoneley Abbey (Warwickshire). It is dated *Apud Brugiam in obsidione;* and is attested by Theobald, Abp of Canterbury; Roger, Abp of York; John, Bp of Worcester; Walter, Bp of Chester; Thomas the Chancellor; Reginald, Earl of Cornwall; Robert, Earl of Leicester; Richard de Humet, Constable; Warin fitz Gerold, Chamberlain; William de Beauchamp; and Maurice de Ambresley.[6] Bridgnorth.

June 4. Baldwin de Redvers, died at Quarr Abbey.[7] Now also, according to one account, died William, the eldest son of the King.[8] If so, he was under three years of age, having been born on August 17, 1153.

June 5. Archbishop Theobald is now at Canterbury, where he consecrates Robert Warlewast, Dean of Salisbury, to be Bishop of Exeter. The attending Bishops were Hillary of Chichester; Josceline of Salisbury; Nigel of Ely; and Walter of Rochester.[9]

July 7. A great Council was summoned to Bridgnorth, whereat the terms of the "King's Peace" with Mortimer were

[1] Chron. Normann. p. 991.
[2] Monast. i. 44. lxx.
[3] Monasticon, vi. 314, ii.
[4] Cartæ Antiquæ, P.
[5] Chron. Normann. p. 991.
[6] Monasticon, v. 447, vii.
[7] Monast. v. 381. See also Monast. vi. 54.
[8] Chron. Normann. p. 989.
[9] Gervase of Canterbury, p. 1378. See also Chron. Normann. p. 991.

1155. July 7. settled. It is incidentally mentioned that Reginald, Earl of Cornwall; Richard de Humez, Richard de Lucy, and Walter de Lucy, Abbot of Battle, were there.[1] Bridgnorth.

The five following Charters, dated at *Brug*, will further illustrate the subject.

1. Charter to Mereval Abbey (Warwickshire), attested by Theobald, Abp (of Canterbury); W. Bishop of Chester; Thomas the Chancellor; Earl Rainald (of Cornwall); Roger, Earl of Hereford; Goceline de Balliol; and Manasser Byseth.[2]

2, 3, 4. Three several Charters to Shrewsbury Abbey, attested by Archbishop Theobald; Gilbert, Bp of Hereford; Walter, Bp of Chester; John, Bp of Worcester; Thomas the Chancellor; Reinald, Earl of Cornwall; William, Earl of Bristol (*alias* Gloucester); Roger, Earl of Hereford; Hugh, Earl of Chester; William fitz Alan; Robert de Dunstanvill; Walcheline Maminoth; and Roger Corbeth.[3]

5. Charter to Robert Pinzun, addressed to William fitz Alan (now Sheriff of Shropshire), and attested by Reginald, Earl of Cornwall; Richard de Humez; and Hugh de Mortimer.[4]

Here intervenes a period of between two and three months, during which neither Chronicle nor Pipe-Roll records any movement of the Court. Some Charters, which conjecturally passed in the interval, must fill up the hiatus.—

July to September. One is dated at Worcester, whither the King may well have gone after the siege of Bridgnorth. It is in favour of the Norman Abbey of St. Martin at Troarn (Diocese of Bayeux). It is attested by Theobald, Archbishop of Canterbury; John, Bishop of Worcester; Gilbert, Bishop of Hereford; Thomas the Chancellor; William, the King's brother; Robert, Earl of Leicester; William, Earl of Gloucester; Reginald, Earl of Cornwall; Henry de Essex, Constable; Richard de Humez, Constable; Richard de Luci; Robert, son of the Earl of Leicester; Manasser Worcester.

[1] Palgrave's British Commonwealth, Appendix, page xxxv.

[2] Monasticon, v. 483, ii.

[3] Chartulary of Shrewsbury Abbey, Nos. 36, 45, and 46.

[4] Ibidem, No. 162.

1155. July to September. Biset, Dapifer; Warin fitz Gerold, Chamberlain; Robert de Dunstanvill; Gosceline de Baillol; Henry de Oilly; William de Lanvalein; and William de Beauchamp.[1] Worcester.

One, dated at Salisbury, is in favour of the borough of Wilton. It is attested by Thomas the Chancellor; Roger, Earl of Hereford; William, Earl of A. (probably Arundel); Richard de Humets, Constable; Warin fitz Gerold, Chamberlain; Robert de Dunstanvill; and Joceline de Baillol.[2] Salisbury.

One undated charter in favour of Seiher de Quinci, attested by Robert, Bishop of Lincoln; Thomas the Chancellor; Earl Reginald (of Cornwall); the Earl of Hereford; and Henry de Essex.[3]

Sept. 29. The King held a great Council at Winchester. He proposed to conquer Ireland, and give it to his brother, William. The Empress was present, and opposed the plan.[4] Winchester.

The five following Charters appear to belong to this occasion. They are all dated at Winchester.

1. Charter in favour of Archbishop Theobald. Witnesses, Thomas the Chancellor; Reginald, Earl of Cornwall; William, the King's brother; Richard de Humez, Constable; and Robert de Dunstanvill.[5]

2. Charter to Shrewsbury Abbey. Witnesses, Theobald, Abp of Canterbury; Thomas the Chancellor; Reginald, Earl of Cornwall; William, Earl of Bristol; Roger, Earl of Hereford; and Roger Corbet.[6]

3. Charter to the Cell of Sudbury (Suffolk), addressed to William, Bp of Norwich; and attested by Thomas the Chancellor; and Reginald, Earl of Cornwall.[7]

4. Charter to St. Peter's Hospital at York. Witnesses, T., the Chancellor; Richard de Humet, Constable; Richard de Luci; William fitz Hamo; and Richard de Chanvill.[8]

5. Charter to the Knights Hospitallers, expressed to be "for the health of the Grantor; of his mother the Empress;

[1] D'Anisy's Normandy Transcripts iii. 337. The King's first recorded visit to Worcester was in April, 1158; but, at that date, John, Bishop of Worcester, was dead.

[2] Journal of the Archæological Institute, No. 61, p. 312.

[3] Cartæ Antiquæ, K. 10.

[4] Chron. Normann, p. 991.

[5] Cartæ Antiquæ, F. 24.

[6] Salop Chartulary, No. 43.

[7] Monasticon, iii. 459, ii.

[8] Cartæ Antiquæ, D. D.

1155. c. Sept. 29. of A., the Queen, and of their children."[1] It is dated Apud Wintoniam in Concilio, and is attested by Thomas the Chancellor; R., Abp of York; Richard, Bp of London; R., (Bp) of Lincoln; G., (Bp) of Hereford; William, the King's brother; R., Earl of Leicester; R., Earl of Cornwall; W., Earl Warren; W., Earl of Gloucester; H., Earl of Norfolk; Earl Patric (of Wiltshire); R. de Novo burgo; H. de Essex, Constable; Richard de Humez, Constable; Guarin fitz Gerold, Chamberlain; Manasser Biset, Dapifer; William fitz Hamo; Richard de Luci; and Richard de Campevill.[1] Winchester.

The Pipe-Roll of Michaelmas, 1155, being that of the first regnal year of K. Henry II., is not extant, and therefore its evidence as to the events of that year is not available. The extracts from the said Roll, which have been preserved in the Red Book of the Exchequer, are too meagre for such a purpose.

MICHAELMAS, 1155, TO MICHAELMAS, 1156.

October 9. The King dispatches the Bishops of Le Mans, Liseux, and Evreux, with Robert Abbot of St. Alban's, on a mission to Rome.

Oct. Nov. Dec. In the last quarter of the year 1155, we gather from the Pipe-Rolls, or infer from Charters, that the King visited Cricklade, Woodstock, Newbury, and Windsor. Chricklade, etc.

The Pipe-Roll of the fiscal year ending Michaelmas, 1156, contains entries which serve our present purpose in two ways, viz., to indicate the names of certain Officers, who were in close attendance on the King, and to adumbrate (though not to arrange in chronological sequence) the movements of the Court. These entries are as follows:

YORKSHIRE. A certain debtor has paid ten merks *in Camerâ Regis* to *Stephen the Chamberlain*. Another debtor has paid £16. 13*s.* 4*d.* to *Geoffry Monk* in the *Camerâ Curiæ*.[3]

STAFFORDSHIRE. William de Beauchamp, fermor of Trentham, has paid £15 to *Geoffry Monk* in the *Camerâ Curiæ*.[3]

[1] Cartæ Antiquæ, C. C.
[2] Matth. Paris (Wats). vol. ii. p. 71.
[3] Rot. Pip. 2 Hen. II. pp. 27, 29, 52. The two first entries are inserted for the sake of the Official personages designated therein; not as indicating any movement of the Court. The debtor and the Fermor possibly travelled far from Yorkshire or Staffordshire to find the Court.

1155. Oct. Nov. Dec. WINCHESTER. The Fermor has paid £4. 10*s*. 8*d*. in the hire of two carts and horses, to convey the King's treasure to Cricchelade.[1] Cricklade.

OXFORDSHIRE. The Sheriff (Henry de Oilli) has paid 40*s*. in escort of the King's cousin (*cognatæ*), from 'Wudestoch' to London.[1] Woodstock.

WINDSOR. Richard de Luci, Fermor of Windsor, charges £4. 15*s*. 5*d*. *in corredio Regis* (a certain proof that the King had visited the Castle).[2] Windsor.

The Charter evidence which seems to belong to the same period of three months, is as follows :—

A Charter to St. Giles's Hospital (Salop), dated at Woodstock, addressed to Walter, Bp of Chester; and attested by Manasser Biset, Dapifer; and Warin fitz Gerold, Chamberlain.[3] Woodstock.

A Charter to Ralph de Hastyngs (the Queen's Dapifer), dated at Newebery; and attested by R., Earl of Leicester; R., Earl of Cornwall; William, Earl of Gloucester; Richard de Lucy; Manasser Biset; Josceline de Bailliol; and Wido de Sanford.[4] Newbury.

A Charter to Dunstaple Priory, dated at Windsor, and attested by Theobald, Abp of Canterbury; Herbert, Bp of Avranches; Thomas the Chancellor; Earl Reginald; Richard de Humet, Constable; Manasser Biseth, Dapifer; Warin fitz Gerold, Chamberlain; and Joceline de Bailiol.[5] Windsor.

Dec. 25. The King held a Council at Westminster.[6] Possibly some of the Charters, which have been assigned to the Westminster Council of March, 1155, belong rather to the Council of December. Westminster.

Among the important but not precisely dated events of the year 1155, are the flight of the late King Stephen's brother, Henry, Bishop of Winchester, and the demolition of his Castles by K. Henry.[7]

[1] Rot. Pip. p. 36.

[2] Ibidem, p. 19.

[3] Monasticon, vii. 640.

[4] Brakelond's Chronicle (Camden Soc.), Note, p. 119.

[5] Cartæ Antiquæ, S. S.

[6] Palgrave (ut supra), p. xxxvi.

[7] Diceto, p. 530. The occurrence was probably late in the year, for the charge for demolishing the Bishop's Castles is on the Pipe-Roll of the year ending Michaelmas, 1156. Diceto further indicates (p. 532) that the Bishop remained in exile at Clugni after the death of Archbishop Theobald (Apl. 18, 1161). This is very problematical. The best authority, that of the Pipe-Rolls, would suggest that at Michaelmas, 1157, the Bishop was still unreconciled to the King, but that at Michaelmas, 1158, his disgrace was at an end (*Vide* printed Rolls, pp. 105, 117, 118, 162).

There is another contradiction of evidences as to the duration of the Bishop's exile. We are told (Monasticon, iii. 104) that Hugh, Prior of West-

1155. Also the demolition by Royal Order of no less than 140 English Castles.

A.D. 1156.

1156. c. Jan. 1. The King probably went to Canterbury, after the Council of Westminster. Hence a Charter, dated at Canterbury, to the Church and Abbot of Saint Jean d'Angeli, and attested by R., Bishop of Lincoln; T., the Chancellor; Earl Reginald; Hugh, Earl of Norfolk; Roger, Earl of Clare; Richard de Humet, Constable; Manasser Biset, Dapifer; Warin fitz Gerold, Chamberlain; Walcheline Maminot; and Ralph de Hasting.[1] Canterbury.

Jan. 2-10. The King now goes to Dover.[2] Dover.

Hence the Sheriff of Kent pays £10 in the *Camerâ Curiæ* to Warin fitz Gerold.[3] Also the Sheriffs of London charge 2 merks for conveying the King's treasure to Shoreham.[3] Also the Sheriff of Southampton charges for sending treasure over sea by hand of William Cumin; and for sending the King's hawks and falcons over sea.[3]

We have also three Charters dated at Dover, and which undoubtedly passed on this occasion, viz.

(1.) To Christ Church, Canterbury, and Abp Theobald, attested by Roger, Abp of York; Nigel, Bp of Ely; Robert, Bp of Lincoln; Thomas the Chancellor; John, Treasurer of York; Roger, son of the Earl of Gloucester; Richard Peche, Archdeacon (of Coventry); Froger, Archdeacon (of Derby); Nicholas de Hamtune; Earl Reginald, (of Cornwall); Earl Hugh (of Norfolk); Henry de Essex, Constable; Richard de Humet; Robert de Dunstanvill; Manasser Biset, Dapifer; William de Beauchamp; Henry de Pomeray; and John Marescall.[4]

(2.) To St. Mary's Abbey at Leicester, attested by Roger, Abp of York; Robert, Bp of Lincoln; Nigel, Bp of Ely; Thomas the Chancellor; Robert, Earl of Leicester;

minster, was confirmed to be Abbot of St. Edmunds in 1157 by the Bishop of Winchester, *then Legate* of the Pope; but Gervase (p. 1378) declares that Abbot Hugh received the benediction in 1157 at Colchester, and at the hands of Archbishop Theobald; and it is certain that the latter was Papal Legate at the time. Two thoroughly ascertained dates may serve further to illustrate this curious question.—Between March 6 and April 10, 1160, the Bishop of Winchester occurs as being at Fareham (near Portsmouth), (Palgrave *ut supra*, Appx. p. xvi), and on May 23, 1162, he was at the election of Becket to the See of Canterbury.

[1] Cartæ Antiquæ, X.

[2] Diceto, p. 531.

[3] Rot. Pipe, 2 Hen. II, pp. 65, 3, 53.

[4] Monasticon, iv. 538, Num. ix.

1156. Jan. 2–10. Reginald, Earl of Cornwall; Richard de Humez, Constable; Henry de Essex, Constable; Richard de Lucy; and Warin fitz Gerold.[1] Dover.

(3.) The third Charter, being dated "Apud Dover in transitu Regis," shows the King's object in coming thither. He was going to Normandy and he grants the Earldom of Oxford to Earl Alberic. Witnesses, Thomas the Chancellor; Hugh, Earl of Norfolk; Roger, Earl of Clare; Earl Patric (of Wiltshire); Richard fitz Gilbert; Henry de Essex, Constable; Richard de Humez, Constable; Richard de Lucy; Walter fitz Robert; M. Biset, Dapifer; Warin fitz Gerold, Chamberlain; Richard de Canvill; William de Lanvall; and Hamo Peche.[2]

Jan. The King embarks from Dover, and lands at Witsand, in Picardy.[3] Witsand.

It is evident that, for the first six months of the King's absence, the Queen remained in England, and in a position of considerable trust. Her Writs were of Regal exigence, and related not only to her own household and expenditure, but to general matters of Royal revenue. One such Writ was in her name and that of the Justiciar of England; another was tested by Earl Reginald.[4] Her Corrodies or other expenses were furnished as follows:—by the Sheriffs of London two several sums of £3. 8*s.* 4*d.* and £40; by the Sheriff of Surrey, £70; by the Sheriff of Essex, £111. 6*s.* 8*d.*; by the Sheriff of Buckinghamshire, £30; by the Sheriff of Hampshire, £41. 8*s.* 7*d.*; and by the Sheriff of Kent, £70. 2*s.* 9*d.*[5] Most of these corrodies were paid through the hands of Ralph de Hastings, whom we have seen to have been the Queen's Dapifer.

Jan. From Witsand the King seems to have gone to St. Omer. Hence a Charter, dated *Apud Sanctum Audomarum*, to Santingfield Hospital (near Witsand). Witnesses, Thomas the Chancellor; William, the King's brother; Richard de Humez, Constable; Warin fitz Gerold, Chamberlain; and Manasser Biset, Dapifer.[6] St. Omer.

Feb. 2. The King is at Rouen.[7] Rouen.

The following Charters, dated at Rouen, may be assigned to this period.

1. To Woburn Abbey (Bedfordshire); attested by Philip, Bp of Baieux; Arnulf, Bp of Liseux; Thomas the

[1] Monasticon, vi. 467, xix.
[2] Selden's Titles of Honour, p. 539.
[3] Diceto, page 531.
[4] Rot. Pip. 2 Hen. II. pp. 4, 9, 23, 30, 53, 54, 57, 60, 63.
[5] Ibidem, pp. 4, 11, 17, 21, 54, 65.
[6] Monast. vi. 639, Num. i.
[7] Chron. Normann.

1156. Feb. 2. Chancellor; Froger, Archdeacon (of Derby); Richard de Humet, Constable; Robert de Novo Burgo; Warin fitz Gerold, Chamberlain; Manasser Biset, Dapifer; Walter de Hereford; and Robert de Dunstanvill.[1] Rouen.

2. To the Nuns of Godstow (Oxfordshire), attested by My Lady the Empress; Philip, Bp of Baieux; Arnulf, Bp of Liseux; Thomas the Chancellor; Robert de Newburgh; Richard de Humet, Constable; Warin fitz Gerold; Manasser Biset, Dapifer; and Robert de Dunstanvill.[2]

3. To St. Mary's Abbey at Leicester; attested by Thomas the Chancellor; Philip, Bp of Baieux; Richard de Humet; and Manasser Biset.[3]

4. To the Canons of Merton (Surrey); attested by T., the Chancellor; Robert de Novo-burgo; and Manasser Biset, Dapifer.[4]

Feb. 5. K. Henry holds a conference with Louis VII. on the borders of France and Normandy: and does homage to the French King for Normandy, Anjou, Touraine, Maine, and Aquitaine.[5] Marches of Normandy.

c. Feb. The King holds a conference with his brother Geoffrey, as to the claims of the latter to Anjou, Touraine, and Maine. This, as well as a conference with Theodoric, Comte of Flanders, was at Rouen. Rouen.

Geoffrey goes into Anjou, dissatisfied. The King follows him. Anjou.

Geoffrey expels Hoel Comte of Bretagne, and takes Nantes.

King Henry besieges Mirebeau (in Poitou) and Chinon, (in Touraine). Mirebeau. Chinon.

Hence we have a Writ-royal in favour of Philip, Bishop of Bayeux, attested by Robert de Novo-burgo (Justice of Normandy); and dated *Apud Mirabel in obsidione.*[6]

And a Writ in favour of D'Aunay Abbey (Bayeux Dioc.), attested by Richard de Humet, Constable; and dated *Apud Chinonem in exercitu.*[7]

[1] Monasticon, v. 479, iii.
[2] Godstow Chartulary, fol. 164.
[3] Cartæ Antiquæ, X.
[4] Ibidem, O. O. The Chancellor, Thomas a Becket, had been educated at Merton.
[5] Chron. Normann. p. 991.
[6] Extraits des Chartes (D'Anisy, ii. 442).
[7] D'Anisy's Transcripts, i. p. 7.

1156. c. Feb. Hence, too, we have a Charter to Henry de Oxeneford, dated *Apud Chinonem in exercitu*, and attested by William, the King's brother; Richard de Humet, Constable; Robert fitz Roy; Reginald de St. Walery; Warin fitz Gerold, Chamberlain; Mannasser Biset, Dapifer; Henry de Oilli, Constable; Robert de Dunstanvill; William de Lanvalay; Richard de Sancto Remigio; Philip de Columberiis; and Robert de Watevill.[1] Chinon.

c. May. The King reduces Mirebeau and Chinon, after long sieges. Loudun (in Touraine) is surrendered to him.[2] Loudun.

c. June. Death, according to one authority, of William, the King's eldest son. The Princess Matilda, born at London.[3] These two events, and the Queen's continuance in England, are well illustrated by an entry in the Sheriffs of London's accounts at Michaelmas, 1156. They charge £40 for the Queen's corrody; £24 for the corrody of Henry, the King's son, his sister, and his aunt (*Amitæ suæ*); and £7 for wine; and £6. 6*s*. for further corrody of the same persons, supplied by hand of Ralph de Hastings.[4]

June 10. Hugh, Abp. of Rouen; Robert, Bp of Evreux; Richard, Bp of Coutances; and Herbert, Bp of Avranches, meet at Mortain.[5]

c. July. The King and his brother Geoffrey come to terms.

Hence we have a Charter to Chertsey Abbey, dated *Apud Chinonem post pacem factam inter Regem et fratrem suum*, attested by R. (it should be H.) Archbp of Rouen; Thomas, the Chancellor; and Richard de Luci.[6] Chinon.

About this time the Queen crosses to Normandy. Hence, at Michaelmas, the Sheriffs of London charge £4. 0*s*. 4*d*. for certain expenses of the King's children *ante transfretationem Reginæ*.[7]

c. July. Stephen, Abbot of St. Florant, succeeds Alan, Bishop of Redon, in that See.[8]

Conan, Earl of Richmond, passes from England to Little Brittany, besieges Redon and expels his stepfather, the Vicomte Eudo. The Bretons accept Earl Conan as their *Duke*.[9]

Aug. 29. The Abbot of Battle, having crossed the sea, finds the King at Saumur (in Anjou). The Queen is there also, and Richard de Luci, the Abbot's brother.[10] Saumur.

[1] Cartæ Antiquæ, D. No. 42.
[2] Chron. Normann. p. 992.
[3] Bromton, p. 1047.
[4] Rot. Pipe, 2 Hen. II. p. 4.
[5] Chron. Normann. p. 992.
[6] Cartæ Antiquæ, D. No. 16. Another copy of this Charter (Cartæ Antiquæ, O. O.), purports to have been attested by "R., *Bishop* of Rouen;" a double error, falsifying both the name and title of the attesting Prelate.
[7] Rot. Pipe, 2 Hen. II. p. 5.
[8] Chron. Normann. p. 992.
[9] Chron. Normann. ibidem. Another authority (Gall. Scriptores, xii) seems to imply that Conan left England in September, 1155.
[10] Palgrave (ut supra), p. xxxvi.

1156. Sept. 29. The King is assumed to have been still in Anjou. Anjou.

Some persons, who, in the fiscal year now ended, appear to have administered occasional justice in the provinces may be here mentioned. These were the Chancellor (Thomas a Becket); the Earl of Leicester (implied in one instance by the mere title *Justiciarius*); the Archbishop of York (in his province); the Bishops of Chichester and Lincoln (quite incidentally); Wido fitz Tece (in London); one Gregory (in Surrey and Bucks); Ralph Picot (in Surrey); and Henry de Pomerai (in Cambridgeshire). Several of the above acted probably on special commissions. The only and regularly constituted Justice-in-eyre seems to have been Henry de Essex, who had held pleas singly in no less than six counties, and who had officiated in two (Kent and Essex) as Colleague of the Chancellor.[1]

MICHAELMAS, 1156, TO MICHAELMAS, 1157.

Sept. 30. Within the next six months and during the King's stay on the Continent, his places of sojourn must be partly concluded from Deeds.

1. A Charter to Eynesham Abbey is dated at Domfront (between Maine and Normandy), and attested by Nigel, Bp of Ely; Thomas the Chancellor; Manasser Biset, Dapifer; and Warin fitz Gerold.[2] Domfront.

2. A Charter, giving the Ushership of the Exchequer to Roger de Warenguefort, a King's Serjeant, is dated at Pont Audemer (in Normandy), and attested by Warin fitz Gerold; Manasser Biset; William fitz Hamo; and Master Alvered.[3] Pont Audemer.

3. A Charter to the Abbey of St. Saviour, in the Diocese of Coutances, is dated at Caen, and attested by Richard de Humet, Jordan Tessy, William fitz John, Nicholas de Vayens, and William fitz Hamo.[4] Caen.

October. In this month the King visited Limoges. He adjusted some differences between the Convent of St. Martial and the Citizens of Limoges, and levied procurations on both Abbey and City.[5] Limoges.

[1] Rot. Pip. 2 Hen. II., passim.

[2] Monast. iii. 20, xxxviii. Nigel, Bishop of Ely, was at this time much employed with re-organizing the Royal Exchequer. A payment by the Sheriff of Kent of one merk to Roger Ostiarius (Usher of the Exchequer) was authorized by the Bishop (Rot. Pip. 2 Hen. II.).

[3] Cartæ Antiquæ, i. 25. Roger de Warengefort, *alias* Roger Serviens, *alias* Roger Ostiarius, occurs with marks of favour in the Pipe Roll of 1156. In one instance, Gervase and John, Sheriffs of London, allege the following disbursement. "In liberatione Rogerii Ostiarii de Thesauro 28*s*. 8*d*. per breve Regis."

[4] Monast. vi. 1105.

[5] Gaufr. Vosiensis (Gall. Scrip. xii. 439).

1156. October. The King (as Suzerain in right of his wife as Duchess of Aquitaine), took in hand the lands of Ademar (v.) the "Boy-Vicomte" of Limoges: and committed them *for nearly three years* to Geoffrey de Newburgh and to William, surnamed Pandolf.[1] Limoges.

A Diploma of King Henry, dated at Limoges (apud Limovicum), and attested by Thomas the Chancellor, seems to belong to this occasion. It is a Writ of '*facias recognosci*' and '*habere facias*' in behalf of Philip, Bishop of Baieux. It is addressed for execution to William fitz John, or in his default to Robert de Newburgh (then Chief Justice of Normandy).[2] Limoges.

After his visit to Limoges, K. Henry, to please the Queen, sent a force to occupy Thouars, and to expel the Vicomte Geoffrey, who had assisted Prince Geoffrey at the siege of Chinon.

Oct. 28. Robert, Abbot of St. Albans; Robert, Bp of Lincoln; Richard, Bp of London; Hugh, Bp of Durham; and Gilbert, Bp of Hereford; meet at St. Neots (Huntingdonshire).[3]

c. Nov. 11. Hillary, Bp of Chichester, crosses to Normandy, and remains there with the Court till April, 1157.[4]

In this interval, therefore, we may date a Charter whereby the King, then at Argentan (in Normandy), gives the Manor of Linton (Herefordshire) to Richard Talbot, except 60 solidates of land, which Hugh de Longchamp had. Witnesses, Hilary, Bp of Chichester; R., Bishop of Evreux; Thomas the Chancellor; William, the King's brother; Manasser Biset, Dapifer; Warin fitz Gerold, Chamberlain; Richard de Canvill; Henry de Essex, Junior; William de Lanvalei; and Hugh de Periers.[5] Argentan.

Dec. 25. Peter, Abbot of Clugny, died.

Dec. 25. The King is said, on one authority,[6] to have kept Christmas at Bourdeaux. If this be correct,— Bourdeaux.

Dec. 31. The King probably remained in Guienne till the end of the year. Guienne.

[1] Chron. Anon. inter Gall. Scriptores (xii. 121, 417). Gaufr. Vosiensis (ibm. xii. 439). The former authority dates Henry's visit to Limoges as two years after his succession. The latter calls Geoffrey de Newburgh "brother of Rotrou, Comte of Perche." (As to date, see below, October, 1159, Note.)

[2] D'Anisy's Extraits de Chartes, vol. ii. p. 440.

[3] Matth. Paris. (Wats), ii. p. 72.

[4] Palgrave (ut supra) p. xxxvi.

[5] Cartæ Antiquæ, T.

[6] Chronicon Anon. inter Rerum Gallicarum Scriptores.

1156. Among the less precisely dated events of the year 1156, are :—

(1.) The death of Gilbert de Gant, sometimes styled Earl of Lincoln, whose sole daughter and heir is married to Simon, son of Earl Simon (of Northampton).[1]

(2.) A great Synod held at London between May and October, whereat Archbishop Theobald presided, and Archbishops, Bishops, Abbots, Earls and Barons attended; though Robert, Bishop of Lincoln, refused to attend.[2]

(3.) A grant by Margaret, Countess of Warwick, to the Order of Templars, dated 'in the Chapter-House of St. Stephen,' and 'in Normandy,' and attested by Rotrode, Bishop of Evreux (who was her son); Philip, Bishop of Baieux[3]; Henry de Novo Burgo (also her son); Robert de Novo Burgo, (also her son, and now seneschal of Normandy); Geoffrey de Novo Burgo; Roger, a Chaplain; and Walleran, Comte of Mellent (who was her late husband's[4] nephew).[5]

A.D. 1157.

1157. c. Jan. Early in this year the King is stated to have visited Mortain.[6] Mortain.

A royal Charter, of Franchises and rights, to the Abbey of Mont St. Michel, is dated *apud Moritonum*, and attested by Robert de Novoburgo.

In the year 1157, Assizes were held at Caen, whereat judgment was given between Robert, Abbot of Mont St. Michel, and Jordan de Sackville. This judgment was sanctioned by Robert de Novoburgo, *Dapifer et Justicia totius Normanniæ*, by Philip, Bishop of Baieux; Arnulf, Bishop of Lisieux; Richard, Bishop of Coutances; William Tallevac, Earl of Ponthieu; Ingerger de Bohun (written *Boura*); and Philip fitz Ernise.[7]

There is a Royal Charter, expressly dated A.D. 1157, and at Falaise, in which Henry, *divinâ miseracione Rex* Falaise. *Angliæ*, etc., *pro statu et incolumitate regni*, grants to the Church of St. John the Baptist of the Hospital of Falaise. Witnesses, Bishops—Philip of Baieux; Ernulf of Lisieux; Girard of Seez; and Rotrou of Evreux; Thomas the Chancellor; Richard (de Humez), the Constable; Guarin fitz Gerold; Manasser Biset; Robert de

[1] Chronicon Normanniæ, with the marginal date corrected.

[2] M. Paris, ii. 72.

[3] His name was Harcourt. He became Bishop in 1141, being elevated from the Deanery of Lincoln. He was deceased in 1165.

[4] Henry de Newburgh, the Countess's husband died in 1123. Her eldest son Roger died in 1153, leaving Gundred, his widow, and a son, William, now (1156) Earl of Warwick.

[5] Monasticon, viii. 1268. The Charter probably passed at Caen, where was St. Stephen's Abbey.

[6] Professor Stubbs's Itinerary (p. cxxx), quoting D'Anisy MS. i. 277, 280. But we cannot substantiate the reference.

[7] D'Anisy, Normandy Transcripts, ii. 280.

1157. c. Jan. Novoburgo; Richard de Luci; Henry de Pomerai; William Patric; Robert de Courci; and William de Ongiervill (Angervill).[1] Falaise.

Also a Writ Royal, dated at Falaise, addressed to Hugh, Archbishop of Rouen, in behalf of the See of Bayeux, is attested by Warin fitz Gerold; William fitz Hamo; and Manasser Biset.

There are several Charters which probably passed either in the last three months of the year 1156, or the first three months of 1157. I quote them, with no assumption as to their exacter date or relative sequence. Jan. to March.

1. A Charter to St. Stephen's Abbey at Caen, dated at Caen, and confirming the grants of the following persons or their progenitors, viz. William, Comte of Ponthieu; Robert, Earl (of Leicester, perhaps); G. (Gualeran), Comte of Mellent; Symon, Comte of Evreux; William de Romara; Richer de Aquila; and Walcheline de Ferrars. The witnesses of the Deed are the King himself (*Teste meipso*); Arnulf, Bishop of Liseux; Richard de Humet, Seneschal (read Constable) of Normandy; Robert de Vaus; and Godard de Vaus.[2] Caen.

(2.) A Charter to the same Abbey, dated at Caen, and attested by Rotroc, Bp of Evreux; Philip, Bp of Baieux; Arnulph, Bp of Liseux; Thomas the Chancellor; Geoffrey Ridel; Geoffrey, Chaplain; William fitz Martin; Richard de Homet; Manessier Bizet; William fitz John; Godard de Vaux; Jordan Tesson; and Richard de Haia.[3]

(3.) A Charter to the same Abbey, dated at Bayeux, and attested by Rotroc, Bp of Evreux; Philip, Bishop of Baieux; Arnulf, Bp of Liseux; Thomas the Chancellor; Geoffrey Ridel; William fitz John; and Jordan Taixun. Bayeux.

4. A Certificate as to the foundation of the Abbey of Mortimer, being the joint work of the King himself and his mother the Empress. This Deed is dated at Baieux, and attested by Arnulf, Bp of Liseux; Philip, Bp of Bayeux.

[1] D'Anisy, MS. ii. p. 7.
[2] D'Anisy's Transcripts, i. 211.
[3] Neustria Pia, p. 628. There is another version of this Charter in D'Anisy's Transcripts (vol. i. p. 154). It styles Bishop Rotrou of Evreux, 'Justiciar of Normandy,' (which was the style of his brother, Robert), and instead of *Tesson*, writes one witness's name *Taixun.*

1157. Jan. to March. Baieux; Rotrode, Bp of Evreux; Robert de Novo Burgo; Baieux. and William fitz Hamo.[1]

5. A Certificate by the Empress Matilda, that she and her son K. Henry, had founded the Abbey of St. Mary de Voto.[2] This Instrument is dated at Rouen, and attested by Rouen. Hugh, Abp of Ronen; Philip, Bp of Baieux; Arnulf, Bp of Liseux; Rotrode, Bp of Evreux; Guillelm (it should be Gualeran), Comte of Mollent; Gualter, Earl Giffard; Robert de Novo Burgo; Godo de Vals; and Guillelm de Herlouin.[3]

6. A Charter by the same Empress, in favour of Silly Abbey,[4] dated at Rouen, addressed to the Abp of Rouen, Rouen. and attested by Rotroc, Bp of Evreux; William, son of the Grantress; Godard de Valle; Robert fitz Emeric; Rosceline fitz Clarembald; William de Angervill; Laurence Chaplain; Hugh Chaplain; Eustace de Scotia; and Galter des Geneis.[5]

7. A contemporary Charter to the same Abbey, by K. Henry II., in which he mentions his mother; Thomas the Chancellor; and his two brothers, Geoffrey and William, as being present.[6]

8. A Royal Charter, dated (somewhat problematically) at Valognes, whereby the King grants to Blanche- Valognes. lande Abbey, a right of market and fair, and confirms all donations which Richard de Haia, his knight, had made to the said Abbey both in England and in Normandy. Witnesses, Jordan Taisson; William de Aureavalle; Robert de Novoburgo; Engelger de Bohon; and Reginald de St. Walery (*de Sancto Valeriano.*) [7]

During the King's stay in Normandy, Louis seems to have held a Court at Orleans, whereat he publicly recognized the right of Henry II., as Comte of Anjou and Seneschal of France, to custody of the Abbey of St. Julian at Tours. Among the witnesses of Louis's declara-

[1] D'Anisy, ut supra. Neustria Pia, p. 779.

[2] Notre Dame de Voeu, at Cherburgh. The first Abbot of this House was confirmed on June 11, 1157.

[3] Neustria Pia, p. 852.

[4] The Abbey of Silly, otherwise called *De Bosco*, in the Forest of Gouffer, near Argentan.

[5] Neustria Pia, p. 830.

[6] Stapleton's Rot. Normaun, i. lxxxix. The learned Writer's observation, that Becket was *first* in office as Chancellor in 1157, is erroneous.

[7] D'Anisy's Transcripts, i. 65. The Charter affects to be dated not only as to place, but time, viz., *Teste etiam meipso anno regni mei* xxix (*i.e.* 1182–3). That date is dissonant with the testing clause. It possibly refers to a renewal of the Charter in the year 1183 at instance of John, Comte of Moretain, the king's youngest son.

1157. Jan. to March. tion were, Joscius, Archbishop of Tours (who appears to have contested the matter previously); Philip, brother of the French King; William fitz Hamo; Robert de Novo Burgo; and Hugh de Cleeriis.[1] Valognes.

c. Feb. The Queen and her children leave Normandy, land at Southampton, and proceed to London. Hence at Michaelmas, 1157, the Fermor of Southampton charges: *In corredio Reginæ quando venit de Normanniâ*, 27*s*. 2*d*. Also the Fermor of Winchester charges: *In corredio Reginæ xv libras per Warinum filium Geroldi, post transfretationem Reginæ usque Lundon.* Also the Fermor of Windsor charges: *Pro Ruscâ portatâ Lundoniam ad opus filii Regis*, 44*s*. *per breve Regis.* Also the Sheriff of Surrey charges: *In liberacione filii Regis et filiæ et suorum.*[2] Hence also, in 1158, the Sheriffs of London accounting for the year ending Michaelmas, 1157, (*de firma anni præteriti*) charge:—*In pannis puellæ, Sororis Regis*, 52*s*. *Et pro pannis Sororis Regis et liberorum Regis*, £12. 3*s*. *Et pro patellis et Bacinis et Tualliis ad opus Reginæ*, 13*s*. *Et in corredio Reginæ per breve Regis*, £60. Lastly, in 1158, the Sheriff of Huntingdonshire, accounting for the year 1157, charges: *In corredio Reginæ per Henricum de Pomerei*, £40. 10*s*. 6*d*.[3]

A Royal Charter, dated *apud Valonias*, confirms to Blanchelande Abbey a certain Church *quam Robertus de Novoburgo, Decanus Ebroicensis, et Henricus de Novo-burgo frater suus dederunt, sicut carta Ricardi Constanciensis Episcopi testatur.* Witnesses, Richard, Bishop of Coutances; Stephen, Elect of Redon; Richard de Monteburg; Jordan Taisson; and William Malet, Dapifer.[4] Valognes.

c. March. A Royal Charter, dated *apud Cæsaris-burgum*, extends the King's protection to the Abbey of St. Sauveur (le Vicomte) in the Cotentin. Witnesses, Richard, Bishop of Coutances; Jordan Taxon; William de Vernon; Richard de Haia; Hugh de Bohon; Richard de Humet; and Robert de Hosa.[5] Cherbourg.

A Writ, dated *apud Barfleur in transfretatione Regis*, is in favour of Philip, Bishop of Bayeux, and is attested by Robert de Novoburgo (Seneschal of Normandy). Barfleur.

[1] Gallici Scriptores, xii, 494, *n*. The Editors confuse this Charter with the service sometime rendered by Henry's father, Comte Geoffrey le Bel, as Seneschal of France, at a Coronation held at Orleans.

[2] Rot. Pip. 3 Hen. II. pp. 107, 71, 94.

[3] Rot. Pipe, 4 Hen. II. pp, 111, 112, 141-2.

[4] D'Anisy's Transcripts, i. 64. Robert de Novoburgo, Dean of Evreux, here spoken of, was more usually called Rotrou, to distinguish him from his brother, Robert de Novoburgo, the Seneschal of Normandy. The former having been Dean, was now (1157) Bishop, of Evreux.

[5] D'Anisy's Transcripts, iii. 34.

1157. c April 1. The King, being at Barfleur, expedites a Charter to Hambie Abbey (in the Diocese of Coutances). Witnesses, Arnulf, Bp of Liseux; and Philip, Bp of Baieux.[1] Barfleur.

A Writ, dated *apud Barbefleu in transfretacione Regis*, and attested by Manasser Biset, Dapifer, is in favour of the Abbey of Montebourg. It is addressed to Richard de Redvers, and says that the Abbey is to have what Richard de Redvers *primus* gave and what the present Richard's father (Baldwin) confirmed. And if the present Richard should neglect execution, William de Vernon[2] or his subordinates (*ministri*) were to execute the Writ and do justice. *Et non remaneat pro passagio meo*, adds the King.[3]

Another Writ, dated *apud Barbefluctum in transfretatione* Regis, is addressed to the King's Bailiffs of the Bessin and the Foresters of Verney, in support of the rights of Philip, Bishop of Baieux. It is attested by Robert de Novo Burgo.[4]

c. April 8. The King embarks at Barfleur, lands at Southampton, and proceeds to London.[5] Hence at Michaelmas, 1157, the Fermor of Southampton charges—*In transfretatione Regis* £14. 13*s*. 4*d*.[6] Southampton. London.

c. April. A Royal Charter in favour of Godstow Nunnery is dated at London and, very conjecturally, passed about this time. It is attested by Robert, Earl of Leicester, Richard de Camvill, Warin fitz Gerold, and Henry fitz Gerold.[7]

The King is next heard of at Richard de Lucy's Castle of Ongar in Essex.[8] Ongar.

It was probably about this time that William, Earl of Warren and Moretain, surrendered the Castles of Norwich and Pevensey to the King, and that Hugh Bigot, Earl of Norfolk, surrendered his Castles.[9]

To the same period may be referred the following Charters of the King:—

[1] Neustria Pia, p. 822.

[2] William de Vernon was uncle to Richard de Redvers, Earl of Devon. He was living nine years after this deed. The introduction of his name in this writ is clearly in his official capacity. He was one of the Justices of Normandy.

[3] D'Anisy's Norman Transcripts, ii. 180.

[4] Archives de Calvados, ii. 442.

[5] Chron. Normann. p. 993.

[6] Rot. Pipe, 3 Hen. II. Tit. *Hantona*.

[7] Godstow Chartulary, fol. 163.

[8] Palgrave's British Commonwealth. Appendix of Proofs and Illustrations, p. xliii.

[9] Chron. Normann. p. 993.—Hence perhaps, it was that, at Michaelmas, 1157, Earl Hugh accounts for the ferm of Norfolk up to Easter previously; but William de Caisneto accounts for the half year last ended (Rot. Pipe, 3 Hen. II. pp. 75, 76).

1157. c. April and May. 1. Dated at Norwich, to the Cathedral Priory of Norwich, attested by Robert, Bp of Exeter; Nigel, Bp of Ely; William, Bp of Norwich; Hilary, Bp of Chichester; Thomas the Chancellor; Earl Hugh (of Norfolk); (Warin fitz Gerold) Chamberlain; Manasser Biset, Dapifer; William Martel; and Richard de Humez.[1] Norwich.

2. Dated at Thetford, to Thetford Priory. Witnesses, Nigel, Bp of Ely; R., Bp of Exeter; Hillary, Bp of Chichester; Thomas the Chancellor; H., Earl of Norfolk; Richard de Humez, Constable; Manasser Biset, Dapifer; William de Caisham (probably Wm. de Caisneto, Sheriff of Norfolk, April, 1157, to Sept., 1163); Robert de Dunstanvill; and Josceline de Baillol.[2] Thetford.

On May 10th died Nicholas Adelulf, Bishop of Carlisle, and his See remained vacant nearly 29 years.[3]

On May 12th, Pope Adrian, *apud Lateran*, writes to Robert, Bishop of Bath.[4]

May 19. The King was crowned at Bury St. Edmunds, Archbishop Theobald, Hillary, Bp of Chichester, etc. being present.[5] Bury St. Edmunds.

Hence at Michaelmas, 1157, the Fermor of Winchester charges—*Pro portandis coronis Regis ad Sanctum Edmundum, 2s.*[6]

May 23–28. These six days the King was at Colchester. His Court was attended by Theobald, Abp of Canterbury; Roger, Abp of York; Richard, Bp of London; Robert, Bp of Lincoln; Robert, Bp of Exeter; Silvester, Abbot of St. Augustine's (Canterbury); Geoffrey, Abbot of Hulm; Thomas (a Becket), the King's Chancellor; Robert, Earl of Leicester; Patric, Earl of Salisbury; Henry de Essex, Constable; Richard de Luci; Reginald de Warren; Guarin fitz Gerold; Hillary, Bp of Chichester; Walter de Luci, Colchester.

[1] Monast. iv. 17, vii.

[2] Monast. v. 150, viii.

[3] Benedictus (Stubbs), i. 349, calls the Bishop, *Adelwald*, and says that he died on the morrow of Ascension Day, 1157, that is on May 10. But he calls the year 1157 "the 5th year of Henry II," which is erroneous.

[4] The date of the letter is "4° id. Mai. Indie V. A.D. 1156, *pontificatûs* (*Adriani*) *anno tertio*:—all which is consistent, except the Dominical year, which should be 1157. This then is an instance of Pope Adrian having adopted the Pisan æra in his Bulls, which æra differed from the common æra by one year.

[5] Palgrave (ut supra, p. xliv).

[6] Rot. Pipe, 3 Hen. II. p. 107.

1157. May 23-28. Abbot of Battle; William, the King's brother; Richard de Humez; Radulf the Physician; and Nicholas de Sigillo.[1] Colchester.

At Colchester the King expedited a Charter to Faversham Abbey. It is attested by T., Abp of Canterbury; Robert, Bp of Lincoln; Hillary, Bp of Chichester; Thomas the Chancellor; William, Earl Warren; Henry de Essex, Constable; Reginald de Warren; Richard de Lucy; Richard de Humet, Constable; William Martell; Manasser Biset, Dapifer; Warin fitz Gerold, Chamberlain; Faramuse; and William de Kaisneto.[2]

c. June. At this period the King probably visited Waltham (in Essex). A Charter, there dated, is to Bridlington Priory (Yorkshire), and is attested by Roger, Abp of York; Hillary, Bp of Chichester; Thomas the Chancellor; John, Treasurer of York; William, the King's brother; Hugh Bigot, Earl of Norfolk; Manger Biset, Dapifer; Warin fitz Gerard, Chamberlain; Eustace fitz John; Richard de Campvill; Robert de Dunstanvill; and Simon fitz William.[3] Waltham.

Also a Charter, dated at Writtle, in Essex (*apud Writelam*), is to Woodham Priory (Essex), and is attested by Thomas the Chancellor; Earl Hugh (of Norfolk); H. de Essex, Constable; Richard de Lucy; Warin fitz Gerold, Chamberlain; and Humphrey de Barenton (probably Bohun).[4] Writtle.

An undated Writ, addressed to Ralph fitz Salomon, concerning the custody of the Park of Haveringes (Havering atte Bower, Essex), may here be noticed. It is attested by Warin fitz Gerold, and by Manasser Biset, Dapifer.[5]

July 17. The King holds a Great Council at Northampton.[6] Northampton. Silvester, Abbot of St. Augustine's, makes his profession to Archbishop Theobald, in the presence of the Bishops of

[1] Palgrave (ut supra), pp. xliv—lxiv.

[2] Cartæ Antiquæ, N. No. 39. The Transcript in the Monasticon (vol. iv. p. 573) erroneously dates the Deed *apud Glocester*. It is an interesting document. The King expedites it, "*prece et petitione Willielmi Comitis Warrene cognati mei.*" The Earl was K. Stephen's surviving son. It speaks also of Faversham Abbey as the place "*ubi requiescunt cognati mei videlicet Rex Stephanus et Matilda Regina uxor ejus et Eustachius filius eorum.*

[3] Monast. vi. 286, v. The Transcript of this Deed in the *Great Coucher* of the Duchy of Lancaster gives but three of the witnesses.

[4] Monast. vi. 446, i.

[5] Rymer's Fœdera, p. 42, iv.

[6] Gervase, p. 1380.

1157. July 17. Evreux, Bath, Norwich, Chichester, Lincoln, and Hereford. Northampton. Hence at Michaelmas, 1157, the Sheriffs of London charge—*Pro 1000 libris ceræ et pro conductu ejus ad Norhanton* £10. 5*s.*[1]

c. July. It was now probably that Malcolm, King of Scots, surrendered Bamborough, Newcastle, and Carlisle to the King. Malcolm seems to have passed through Yorkshire, Lincolnshire, and Nottinghamshire, and to have awaited King Henry at Peak Castle, in Derbyshire, and thence to Peak Castle. have accompanied the King to Chester. The following entries on the Pipe-Roll of Michaelmas, 1157, are pertinent to this subject:—

YORKSHIRE. The Sheriff charges—*In corredio Regis Scotiæ* £123. 0*s.* 9*d.*, xvi. *dierum.*

LINCOLNSHIRE. The Sheriff charges—*In corredio Regis Scotiæ* £72. 19*s.* 10*d. per Cancellarium et Comitem Legrecestriæ.*

NOTTINGHAMSHIRE AND DERBYSHIRE. The Sheriff charges—*In Camerâ Regis Radulfo filio Stephani* £17. *Et in adquietatione corredii Regis Scotiæ de Notingeham et de Pech* £37. 12*s.* 3*d. per breve Regis. Et in adquietatione corredii Regis apud Pech per Nigellum de Broc* £10. 1*s.* 4*d. Et in Camerâ Curiæ Warino filio Geroldi* 20 *marcas.*[2]

Malcolm, King of Scots, does homage to K. Henry at Chester.

The King invades North Wales.[3] The English army Chester. falls into an ambuscade near Basingwerk (at Counsylth).[4] Counsylth. Eustace fitz John and Robert de Courci were slain. Henry de Essex, Constable of England, disgraced himself (as was afterwards alleged) by personal cowardice.

With reference to this Welsh expedition, there are many entries on the Pipe-Roll of the following Michaelmas; e. g.—

SHROPSHIRE. The Sheriff charges—*In liberatione Archi-*

[1] Rot. Pipe, 4 Hen. II. (*De anno præterito*), p. 112. The conveyance of a large quantity of wax to any Royal residence indicates the King's intention of holding a Council their.

[2] Rot. Pipe, 3 Hen. II. pp. 85, 83, 90, 91.

[3] Curiously recorded in the Chronicle of Fécamp (Gall. Scrip. xii. 783). viz., *Anno MCLVII. Henricus Rex duxit exercitum in Gravelinges.* Some French or Flandrian, transcribing the original Chronicle, thus, according to his lights, rendered the word *Gualenses.* Gravelines was a town, then in Flanders, now in France.

[4] Brut y Tywysogion, sub anno 1156. Counsylth is diversely called Coleshulle and Cennadlog.

1157. c. July. *ariorum Regis in exercitu* 47*s*. *In Soltis pro* xxx. *baconibus et quater* xx. *et* vi. *summis frumenti liberatis Gaufrido Monacho* £8. 0*s*. 4*d*. North Wales.

WORCESTERSHIRE. The Sheriff charges—*Pro frumento et baconibus et aliis negotiis Regis* £12. 8*s*.

LONDON. The Sheriffs charge—*Pro* 500 *baconibus et in conductu eorum ad Waliam* £52.

OXFORDSHIRE. The Sheriff charges—*Pro thesauro conducendo ad Waliam* £1. 11*s*. 8*d*.

STAFFORDSHIRE. The Sheriff charges—*Pro* cxl. *baconibus* £15. 5*s*.

GLOUCESTERSHIRE. The Sheriff charges—*Pro picoiis et frumento et furnis ferreis* £12. 1*s*. 2*d*.

WINCHESTER. The Fermor charges—*In locand unâ navi ad portanda corredia Regis usque Pembroc, Rogero Constabulario* £4.[1]

c. Aug. The King penetrates as far as Snowdon, exacts homage from Prince Owen, and obliges him to give hostages. Hence in their account of Michaelmas, 1158, the Sheriffs of London charge—*Pro pannis obsidum Oeni Regis* 72*s*.[2] The King, on his way homeward, fortifies the Castles of Rhudlan and Basingwerk; and between them establishes a House of Templars.[3] Snowdon. Rhudlan. Basingwerk.

It was now probably that the King, being again at Chester, grants a Charter to Basingwerk Abbey (in Flintshire). Witnesses, Thomas the Chancellor; Richard de Humez, Constable; R. de Dunstanvill; Joceline de Bailoil; and William fitz Hamo.[4] Chester.

The King is supposed to have been now at Tamworth.[5] (Tamworth.)

c. Sept. About this time the King was in Wiltshire. Visiting Malmesbury Abbey, he, by Charter, released the Abbot and Convent from an annual payment of £6. 10*s*. which they had been used to pay to the Exchequer for quittance of County and Hundred Courts. Witnesses, Thomas the Chancellor; Richard de Humet, Constable; Humphrey de Malmesbury.

[1] Rot. Pipe, 3 Hen. II. pp. 89, 91, 112, 82, 97, 100, 103.

[2] Rot. Pipe, 4 Hen. II. p. 114.

[3] Chron. Normann. p. 993.

[4] Monast. v. 262, i.

[5] Stubb's Itinerary, quoting Rot. Pip. (3 Hen. II.) p. 87. The entry in question is a charge by the Sheriff of Warwickshire, viz., *Et in conductu Prisonum ad Oxineford et ad Tamewordam* 72*s*. 2*d*. Tamworth lay probably in the King's route.

1157. c. Sept. Bohun, Dapifer; Manasser Biset, Dapifer; and Fulk fitz Warin.[1] At Michaelmas, 1157, the Sheriff of Wiltshire acknowledges this immunity of the Abbey as follows:—*In Elemosynis constitutis. Et Monachis de Malmsberiâ £6. 10s. pro Sciris et hundredis.*[2] Malmesbury.

c. Sept. A Royal Writ, ascribed to this year, and probably belonging to the month of September, is addressed to Richard de Camvill, Sheriff of Berkshire (whose term of office expired at Michaelmas, 1157). It is in favour of Abingdon Abbey. It is dated at Windsor, and attested, singly, by Earl Reginald (of Cornwall).[3] A Royal Charter, dated at Woodstock, confirms an agreement made between William fitz Gilbert and the Monks of Furness Abbey (Lancashire). The witnesses (chiefly north-countrymen) are Hugh, Bishop of Durham; Robert, Bishop of Lincoln; Robert, Earl of Leicester; Richard de Luci, William de Vesci,[4] Geoffrey de Valoniis, William de Agremont, Aubert de Grellei, John Constable, Henry fitz Suan, Gospatric fitz Orm, Richard fitz Ivo, and Richard Pincerna. This Charter is expressed to be expedited '*per manus Stephani Capellani*,'—a Vice-Chancellor, who will afterwards appear in a like capacity as '*Magister Stephanus de Fulgeriis, Præcentor of Moretain.*' Windsor. Woodstock.

Sept. 8. Queen Eleanor gives birth to a son, Richard, at Oxford.[5] Hence at Michaelmas, 1157, the Sheriff of Oxfordshire charges—*In corredio Reginæ 20s.*[6] Oxford.

The Record of Law proceedings during the above fiscal year, indicate nothing in the shape of organized visitation of the provinces. The Chancellor and the Earl of Leicester seem to have been twice associated in judicial or quasi-judicial functions, viz., in Shropshire and in Lincolnshire. Other entries of amercements are on the Pipe-Roll, but they indicate only arrears of the previous year.

There is Record of the King being at Woodstock, and probably in this year. There he refers a question of Law to these Justiciars following, viz. Gregory of London, William fitz John, and Nigel de Broc.[7] Woodstock.

[1] Cartæ Antiquæ, Q. V. Another Royal Charter to Malmesbury Abbey is dated at Malmesbury, and attested singly by Thomas the Chancellor (Malmesbury Chartulary, No. 51.)

[2] Rot. Pipe, 3 Hen. II. p. 77.

[3] Chron. Abingdon, ii. 233.

[4] Monast. v. 248, x. William de Vesci, was son and heir of Eustace fitz John, who fell at Counsylth in July. 'John Constable,' that is John Constable of Chester, was grandson of the same Eustace fitz John. The latter had been Constable of Chester, in right of his second wife, the heiress of Fitz-Nigel of Halton. This lady was still living, and after her husband's death she re-married with Robert Fitz Count. Her Grandson and apparent heir, the above witness, though he is styled "Constable," was probably at this time in ward to the Crown, as was also his Suzerain, Hugh Kevelioc, the young Earl of Chester.

[5] Chron. Normann. p. 993, Diceto, p. 531. Annals of Waverley. The Chronicle of St. Albans gives the exact day, viz., September 8th.

[6] Rot. Pipe, 3 Hen. II. p. 82.

[7] Hist. Abingdon, ii. 186.

MICHAELMAS, 1157, TO MICHAELMAS, 1158.

1157. October. Within this fiscal year, the Pipe-Rolls suggest that the King and Queen were at Oxford and at Woodstock, and that the King visited Brill (in Buckinghamshire). Oxford. Woodstock. Brill.

OXFORDSHIRE. At Michaelmas, 1158, the Sheriff charges —*In corredio Regis per Warinum filium Geroldi* £10 *per breve Regis. Et in conductu Hernesii Reginæ ad Wudestoch et retro* 3*s*. *Et pro molendino quod Regina habuit* 20*s*. *Et in conductu pedicarum Regis ad Bruhullum* 3*s*.

HAMPSHIRE. The Sheriff charges—*In robâ Reginæ portandâ de Winton ad Oxineford* 8*s*.

WILTSHIRE. The Sheriff charges—*Ad Gantas Regis portandas ad Wudestoch* 12*s*. 8*d*.; *et in venatione Regis portandâ ad Wudestoch* 5*s*.

LONDON. The Sheriffs charge (at Michaelmas, 1157)— *In conductu Papilionis Regis ad Wudestoch* 60*s*. 10*d*.[1]

We have two Deeds, dated at Brill, which perhaps belong to the same period, viz.

1. *Apud Bruhellam in forestâ*, to Robert, Bp of Lincoln, attested by Thomas the Chancellor; Henry de Essex, Constable; Warin fitz Gerold, Chamberlain; William fitz Hamo; and H., fitz Gerold.[2]

2. *Apud Brehell*, to Lincoln Cathedral, attested by Thomas the Chancellor; Manasser Biset, Dapifer; and Warin fitz Gerold.[3]

c. Dec. A Charter dated at Stamford, belongs probably to the last month of 1157. It is in favour of the "Lepers of St. Lazarus of Jerusalem," and is attested by Earl Reginald, Richard de Luci, and Richard de Cauvill. Stamford.

c. Dec. 25. The King was crowned at Wikeford, a suburb of the City of Lincoln.[4] Hence at Michaelmas 1158, the following charges appear on the Pipe-Rolls:— Lincoln.

[1] Rot. Pipe, 4 Hen. II. pp. 149, 171, 115, 112.

[2] Monast. viii. 1276, lvii. lviii.

[3] Monast. iii. 435. v.

[4] Hoveden, p. 282. Diceto, p. 531. Collect. Topog. et Geneal. ii. 248. This is a good instance of where the errors and discordances of the Chroniclers may be most certainly adjusted by the Pipe-Rolls. Neubrigensis places the King's coronation at Lincoln in the 5th year of the King (that is after December 18, 1158)! And Neubrigensis further states that the event was at Christmas, and that Pope Adrian died in the next year. Now Pope Adrian IV. died undoubtedly on August 30th, 1159. Therefore, Neubrigensis is consistent with himself. He intends to date the Lincoln Coronation at Christmas, 1158. Nevertheless, it is clear that the said Coronation took place, as stated above, at Christmas 1157.

1157. c. Dec. 25. NOTTS AND DERBYSHIRE. *In conductu venacionis Regis usque ad Lincoliam 21s. per breve Regis.*[1] Lincoln.

WORCESTERSHIRE. *Ad conducendam venacionem Regis de Wirecestria ad Lincoliam £2. 4s. 8d. per breve Regis.*[1]

ESSEX AND HERTFORDSHIRE. *In conductu venacionis Regis ad Lincoliam 18s.*[1]

LINCOLNSHIRE. *In reparatione Hospicii Regis in Lincoliâ £8. 15s. per breve Regis. Et Warino filio Geroldi £30, ad faciendas liberaciones venatorum et armigerorum Regis, per breve Regis. Et in corredio Regis ad Natale £79. 6s. 8d. Et in camerâ Curiæ Gaufrido Monacho 100 marcas argenti per breve Regis.*[2]

The following three Charters probably belong to the same occasion, all being dated at Lincoln. Lincoln.

1. To Lincoln Cathedral, attested by Roger, Archbishop of York; Thomas the Chancellor, Warin fitz Gerold, Robert de Dunstanvill, Joceline de Bailiol, Richard de Luci, and William fitz Hamo.[3]

2. To Richard fitz Osbert, attested by Warin fitz Gerold, and Manasser Biset, Dapifer.[4]

3. To the Canons of Thornton (*Torenton*), attested by Thomas the Chancellor, Manasser Biset, Henry Biset, Richard de Humez, Hugh de Beauchamp, Walkeline Maminot, Ralph de Kaemes, William de Colevill, Robert Bertram, and Philip de Columbariis.[5]

The events not exactly dated (as to month or day) of the year 1157, are:

(1.) The departure of Theodoric, Comte of Flanders, on a Crusade.[6]

(2.) The death of Gerard, Bishop of Seez.[7]

A.D. 1158.

1158.

c. Jan. The King at Carlisle, grants the honour of knighthood to William Earl Warren, but refuses it to Malcolm, King of Scots.[8] Hence in the Pipe-Roll of Michaelmas 1158, the Sheriff of Carlisle charges—*In corredio parato contra* Carlisle.

[1] Rot. Pipe, 4 Hen. II. pp. 153, 155, 132, 136.
[2] Rot. Pipe, 4 Hen. II. (printed) p. 175.
[3] Monast. viii. 1276, Num. 55.
[4] Cartæ Antiquæ, OO.
[5] Cartæ Antiquæ.
[6] Chron. Normanniæ, p. 993.
[7] Chron. Normann., ibidem. Ordericus, v. 162. Gerard was succeeded in 1159 by Froger, the King's Almoner,—of whom more in the sequel.
[8] Chron. Normann. p. 993. Chron. Mailros. Professor Stubbs dates the King's visit to Carlisle on January 24.

1158. c. Jan. *adventum Regis, quod dedit Huberto de Vallibus* £11. 3*s*. *per breve Regis*. Also the Sheriff of Hampshire charges—*In summariis et conductu thesauri de Wintoniâ ad Carloillium* £13. 10*s*. *per Comitem Legrecestriæ*.[1] Carlisle.

The King fortifies the Castle of *Werc, i.e.*, Wark in Northumberland.[2] Hence, at Michaelmas following, the Sheriff of Northumberland charges—*Et in operacione Castelli de Werch* £21. 8*s*. 11*d*.[3] Wark, or Werk.

The King also visited Newcastle upon Tyne, and there expedited a Charter to Hubert de Vallibus above mentioned. The Charter is attested by R., Abp of York; R., Bp of Lincoln; H., Bp of Durham; Hugh, Earl of Norfolk; Earl Alberic (of Oxford); Earl Geoffrey (of Essex); Richard de Luci; Manasser Biset, Dapifer; Henry de Essex, Constable; Hugh de Morevill; Robert de Dunstanvill; William fitz John; Simon fitz Peter; Nigel de Broch; William Malet; Roger fitz Richard; Robert de Stutevill; and Turgise de Russedal.[4] Newcastle upon Tyne.

On his way southward the King probably passed through Yorkshire and Nottinghamshire. Hence, at Michaelmas, 1158, the Sheriff of Yorkshire charges—*In camerâ curiæ Radulfo filio Stephani* £18. 18*s*. And the Fermor of Doncaster charges—*Et in camerâ curiæ, Henrico filio Geroldi* £14. *Et Radulfo filio Stephani* £23. Also the Sheriff of Nottinghamshire charges—*In corredio Regis apud Pech* £36. 5*s*. *per breve Regis*. *Et in custamento venationis Regis conducendæ ad mare* £3. 6*s*. 8*d*.[5] Doncaster. Peak Castle.

The contemporary evidence of Charters is as follows, viz.:—

Three Charters dated at York: (1.) to Little Mareis Nunnery (Yorkshire), attested by Nicholas de Sigillo and John, Treasurer of York;[6] (2.) to Lincoln Cathedral, attested by Richard de Luci, Nicholas de Sigillo, and William fitz John;[6] (3.) to St. Leonard's Hospital at York, attested by William fitz John and Henry fitz Gerold.[6] York.

A Charter to Blythe Priory (Nottinghamshire), dated at Blythe.

[1] Rot. Pipe, 4 Hen. II. pp. 119, 175.
[2] Hoveden, p. 282.
[3] Rot. Pipe, 4 Hen. II. p. 177.
[4] Cartæ Antiquæ, DD.
[5] Rot. Pipe, 4 Hen. II. pp. 146, 179, 152.
[6] Monast. iv. 275, ii; viii. 1276, lxii; vii. 612.

Blythe, and attested by Thomas the Chancellor; Roger,
1158. c. Jan. Earl of *Guar* (probably Clare); Robert de Dunstanvill; and Ranulph de Broc.[1]

A Charter, dated at Nottingham, and addressed to Robert, Bishop of Lincoln; whereby the King certifies that he has restored *Ricardo de Haia Constabulariam suam de Lincolscira et custodiam castelli mei de Lincoln' et terram quæ fuit patris ejus.* Witnesses, Thomas the Chancellor; Reginald, Earl of Cornwall; William, the King's brother; Richard de Humez, Constable; Robert de Novo-burgo; R., de Sancto Remigio.[2] Nottingham.

A Charter, dated at Nottingham in favour of Furness Abbey, attested by Earl Reginald (of Cornwall); Robert, Earl of Leicester; Warin fitz Gerold, Chamberlain; and Manasser Biset, Dapifer.[3]

c. Feb. March. During these two months the King probably visited Oxfordshire, Hampshire, and Wiltshire. The Charters which we may refer to this period, are:—

One, dated at Woodstock, whereby the King gives "to William Malduit, son of William Malduit, my Chamberlain, the Barony which was his father's on the day that he became the King's man at Wudestoc, to wit, Hameslape and Maneton, which I gave to his father at Nottingham." Witnesses, Robert, Bishop of Lincoln; Thomas the Chancellor; Richard de Haia; Robert de Montfort; William de St. John; William de Caisneto; Hugh de Piris; William de Lanval; and William de Watevill.[4] Woodstock.

Two, dated at Brokeherst (Hampshire), viz. (1.) to Lenton Priory (Nottinghamshire), attested by Warin fitz Gerold, Chamberlain; Robert de Dunstanvill; and Master Alvered;[5] and (2.) to Plymton Priory (Devonshire), attested by Robert de Newburgh; Richard de Humez, Constable; Manasser Biset, Dapifer; Henry de Oilli, Constable; Robert de St. Mary-Church; and Hugh de Pireriis.[6] Brockenhurst.

Five, dated at Salisbury, viz. (1.) to Salisbury Cathedral, Salisbury.

[1] Monasticon, iv. 623. ii.
[2, 3] Original Charters in Offic. Ducat. Lancast. Quite possibly one or both of these Charters passed when the King was at Nottingham, in February 1155 (supra, page 6).
[4] Dugdale's MSS. (in Bibl. Ashmol.), L. fo. 41.
[5] Monasticon, v. 112, No. 3.
[6] Monasticon. vi. 53, No. iii.

1158. c. Feb. March. attested by Theobald, Archbishop of Canterbury; Roger, Abp of York; Hilary, Bp of Chichester; Robert, Bp of Lincoln; Thomas the Chancellor; Robert, Earl of Leicester; Earl Patric; Richard de Humet, Constable; Manasser Biset, Dapifer; Warin fitz Gerold, Chamberlain; Humphrey de Bohun, Dapifer; Engelger de Bohun; Richard de Haia; Robert Bertram; William fitz Hamo; Robert de Dunstanvill; and John fitz Hamo.[1] (2.) To the same, attested by the six first witnesses of the last Deed, and also by Nigel, Bp of Ely.[2] (3). To Rumsey Nunnery (Hampshire), attested by T., Abp of Canterbury; Roger, Abp of York; R., Bp of Lincoln; Thomas the Chancellor; Master Alvered; R., Earl of Leicester; William fitz Hamo; and Hamo Boterell.[3] (4.) To the Abbey of St. Remigius at Rheims, attested by Thomas the Chancellor; Richard de Humez, Constable; and Warin fitz Gerold, Chamberlain.[4] (5.) To Geldwin and Savaric, sons of Savaric; attested by Thomas the Chancellor; Warin fitz Gerold; Manasser Biset, Dapifer; Joceline de Baillol; and William fitz Hamo.[5] Salisbury.

Some entries on the Pipe-Roll of 1158 may refer to the above movements of the Court, *e.g.*:

The Fermor of Southampton charges—*In corredio Regis apud Brochehurst* £16 *per breve Regis.* And the Sheriff of Hampshire charges—*In conductu* 100 *modiorum vini ad Saresburiam et in tonellis emendis* 5 *marcas argenti.* And the Sheriffs of London charge—*In conductu ceræ Regis ad Clarendon* 13*s.* 4*d.*[6] Clarendon.

April 13. Alured, a Chaplain of the King, was enthroned Bishop of Worcester.[7]

April 20. This being Easter Day, is probably the date when the King and Queen were crowned at Worcester.[8] Hence at Michaelmas, 1158, we have the following entries on the Pipe-Rolls. Worcester.

WINCHESTER. *In conducendis coronis Regis ad Wirecestre*

1 Monast. vi. 1296, v.
2 Cartæ Antiquæ, OO.
3 Rot. Patent, 8 Edw. I. m. 27.
4 Rot. Patent, 6 Edw. III. p. 1. m. 8.
5 Stapleton's Rot. Normanniæ, ii. p. xxxiii
6 Rot. Pipe, 4 Hen. II. pp. 179, 172, 113.
7 Monasticon, vol. i. p. 572.

8 Hoveden, p. 282 (corrected as to date). The coronation at Worcester was notably the last of King Henry's coronations. Hoveden places it at Easter, 1159, when the King was over sea. Matthew Paris and others place it at Christmas, 1157, when we know that the King was at Lincoln. The intervening year (1158) is doubtless correct.

1158. April 20. *de Wintoniâ* 14*s*. 8*d*. *Et ad conducendam archam cum talliis, duobus itineribus* 23*s*. 8*d*.[1] Worcester.

WORCESTERSHIRE. *Et Stephano de Turonis* £54 *in camerâ Regis per breve Regis*.[1]

The four following Charters are dated at Worcester :—

(1.) To Buckfastre Abbey (Devonshire). Witnesses, Theobald, Abp of Canterbury; Thomas the Chancellor; Humphrey de Bohun, Dapifer; Roger de Novant; Warin fitz Gerold, Chamberlain; and William fitz Hamo.[2]

(2.) To Westwood Priory (Worcestershire). Witnesses, Thomas the Chancellor; Richard de Lucy; Manasser Biset, Dapifer; Bernard de St. Walery; and William de Beauchamp.[3]

(3.) Precept to Hugh, Earl of Chester; and M(atilda) Countess of Chester; attested by Thomas the Chancellor.[4]

(4.) Grant of Liberties and Fair to Malmesbury Abbey, attested by Robert, Earl of Leicester.[5]

And from Worcester, it is probable that the King passed to Tewkesbury. A Writ, there dated, and attested by Gregory (perhaps a clerk of the King), admonishes the tenants of the Abbey of Malmesbury that they perform due services to the Abbey.[6] Tewkesbury.

c. April to August. This year is distinguished as one in which the King is said to have made a summer progress.[7] The following entries on the Pipe-Roll of Michaelmas, 1158, may possibly relate to some such movements of the Court, but the significance of several of them, and the order of all cannot be certainly fixed.

SALOP. *In camerâ curiæ Radulfo filio Stephani* 40 *marcas argenti per breve Regis*.[8] Shropshire.

GLOUCESTERSHIRE. *In camerâ curiæ Radulfo filio Stephani* £16. 6*s*. 7*d*. *blanc' ad combustionem aliorum denariorum per breve Regis. Et in Picosiis* 13*s*. 5*d*. *per breve Regis. Et in camerâ curiæ Radulfo filio Stephani et Stephano de Turonis* £33. 6*s*. 6*d*. *Et in corredio Regis per* Gloucestershire.

[1] Rot. Pipe, 4 Hen. II. pp. 175, 155.
[2, 3] Monast. v. 385. i. and vii. 100.
[4] Munimenta Decani et Capituli Herefordiæ.
[5, 6] Malmesbury Chartulary, Nos. 55, 56. The last-named Writ commences 'Henricus Dei Gratiâ Rex Angliæ,' etc. We have doubts about its genuineness, but we have other evidence of official position held by the witness, Gregory, (infra, p. 37).
[7] Carte i. 368.
[8] Rot. Pipe, 4 Hen. II. p. 170.

1158. c. April to August. *breve ipsius* £5. 17*s*. 10*d*. *Et Manassero Biset ad corredium Regis* £4. 13*s*. *per breve Regis*.[1] Gloucestershire.

SOMERSETSHIRE. *Et in corredio Regis apud Well, et Cedre* (Wells and Chedder), £13. 4*s*. 5*d*.[2] Wells. Cheddar.

DEVONSHIRE. *In cerâ ad servitium Regis* 41*s*. 8*d*. *per breve Regis*.[3] *Vicecomes liberavit* 100*s*. *Radulfo filio Stephani in camerâ Regis*.[4]

DORSETSHIRE. (*In corre*)*dio Regis* £4 *per Manasserum Biset*.[5]

KENT. *Et in camerâ curiæ Warino filio Geroldi* £53 *per breve Regis*. *Et Gaufrido Monacho* £100.[6]

SUFFOLK. *Abbas de Hulmo liberavit* 10 *marcas argenti in camerâ curiæ Radulfo filio Stephani per breve Regis*. *Vicecomes (liberavit* 20 *marcas argenti) in camerâ Regis per breve Regis*.[7]

LONDON AND MIDDLESEX. *Et in conductu ceræ Regis ad Clarendon* 13*s*. 4*d*. *Et in custamento Girardi Probatoris Regis, ad conducendum eum ad Wintoniam et Wudestoch* £6.[8] Clarendon. (Winchester.) Woodstock.

NORFOLK. *In camerâ Regis Gaufrido Monacho* £36. 10*s*. *per breve Regis*. *Et Radulfo filio Stephani et Stephano de Turonis* £31. 3*s*. 4*d*.[9]

RUTLANDSHIRE. *In camerâ curiæ Radulfo filio Stephani* £18. *Et in liberacione ursorum et ursariorum* £4. 13*s*. 6*d*.[10]

NORTHAMPTONSHIRE. *In corredio Regis per Gaufridum Monachum* 37*s*. *Et portatoribus brevium Regis propter Monetarios* 9*s*. *per Gregorium*.[11]

The above extracts from the Pipe-Rolls are parallelled by equally irregular evidence from Charters, viz.:—

Charter, dated at Evesham, to Flexley Abbey (Gloucestershire). Witnesses, Richard de Humet, William de Crevecor, Philip de Columbariis, and William de Angervill.[12] Evesham.

Charter, dated at Evesham, to Dene Abbey (Gloucestershire). Witnesses, the three first witnesses of the last Deed.[13]

Charter to Thorney Abbey, attested by 'T., my Chancellor,' at Hereford.[14] Hereford.

1, 2 Rot. Pipe, 4 Hen. II. pp. 168, 120.
3, 4, 5 Rot. Pipe, 4 Hen. II. pp. 158, 160, 157.
6, 7, 8, 9, 10, 11 Ibidem, pp. 180, 127, 113, 125, 136, 141.
12 Monasticon, v. 590, ii.
13, 14 Cartæ. Antiquæ Q. Q. and Y.

1158. c. April to August. Charter, dated at Gloucester, to Eynsham Abbey (Oxfordshire). Witnesses, Thomas the Chancellor; Richard de Humez, Constable; Henry de Essex; Warin fitz Gerold, Chamberlain; Hugh de Piris; and Geoffrey de Bruere.[1] Gloucester.

Charter, dated at Gloucester, to Tewkesbury Abbey, attested by Humphrey de Bohun.[2]

Charter to Haughmond Abbey (Shropshire), dated *Apud Newa'* (probably Newnham in Gloucestershire), and attested by Richard de Humet, Constable; M. Biset, Dapifer; Warin fitz Gerold, Chamberlain; Robert de Dunstanvill; Walter Hosatus; and William fitz Alan.[3] Newnham (Gloucestershire.)

Charter to Richard de Luci, dated at Niweham. Witnesses, Thomas the Chancellor; Robert, Earl of Leicester; Richard de Humez, Constable; Warin fitz Gerold; and Manasser (Biset), Dapifer.[4] Newnham.

Writ, dated at Windsor, certifying the Bp of Lincoln of a mortgage given by Waleran fitz Walter to Robert fitz Sawin. Witnesses, Man. Biset, *Dur* (*dapifero*, perhaps), Hugh de Broc, Peter de Beauchamp, Hugh de Pirariis, and G. de Bruere.[5] Windsor.

Charter, dated at Reading in favour of Hurley Priory (Berks). Witnesses, William fitz John, Nigel de Broc, Robert de Dunstanvill.[6] Reading.

Charter to the Lepers of Herting (Sussex), dated at Patmer (Hertfordshire). Witnesses,—The Chancellor; William, the King's brother; William de Lanvalei; and William Malet.[7] Patmer.

And again, there is some probability that between April and August of this year, the King visited London.—

A Charter, dated at Westminster, is in favour of Bermondsey Priory, and is attested by Theobald, Archbishop of Canterbury; Thomas the Chancellor; and Manasser Biset, Dapifer.[8] Westminster.

[1] Monasticon III. p. 21. Num. xl.

[2] Monasticon III. p. 66.

[3] Haughmond Chartulary, fol. 77. Newnham is on the Severn, S.W. of Gloucester. Here was a frontier castle in the twelfth century.

[4] Cartæ Antiquæ, OO.

[5] Cartæ Antiquæ, P.

[6] Cartæ Antiquæ, KK. Madox's Formulare Angl. No. lxxxij. This confirmation includes mention of a grant by Agnes fitz Nigel and her husband, 'Robert,' to Hurley. Now, Eustace fitz John, elder brother of the first witness, and first husband of Agnes, was slain at Counsylth c. July, 1157.

[7] Cotton MSS. Vesp. E. xxiii. fol. 2. b.

[8] Monast. v. 101. vii. We ascribe this charter to the year 1158, because that date is the nearest possible approximation to the year 1159, to which the Bermondsey Chronicle (Monast. v. 97. a) assigns it. The King, it will be seen, was not in England during any part of the year 1159. The Bermondsey Chronicle is found in other instances to be a most unsafe guide in matters of date.

1158. June 24. There is problematical reason for supposing that on this day the King was at Carlisle.[1] (Carlisle.)

July 27. Geoffrey, the King's brother died at Nantes.[2]

August. c. July, August. It would seem from the Welsh accounts that K. Henry, just before his transfretation to Normandy, was engaged in hostilities with Rese, Prince of S. Wales, from whom he received hostages.[3] The year 1158 must be assigned to this fact (if such it was), not the year 1157, as the Welsh Chronicle has it. (South Wales.)

The Pipe-Roll of Michaelmas, 1158, only countenances the above story by a single entry in the account of the Sheriff of Winchester, viz., *In liberacione Radulfi Vituli* £19. 17*s*. 6*d*. *de Itinere de Waliâ*.[4]

August. In this said month of August, the King must have been at Winchester. The Pipe-Roll of the next month contains the following charges:

WINCHESTER. *In cerâ in camerâ Regis per Radulfum filium Stephani* £5. 3*s*. *Et in pane ad corredium Regis* £2. 3*s*. *per Gaufridum Anglicum*.[5] Winchester.

SOUTHAMPTON. *In conductu vini Regis de Hantuna ad Wintoniam* 18*s*.[6]

A Charter to Malmesbury Abbey, dated at Winchester, evidently belongs to this occasion. It is attested by Theobald, Abp of Canterbury; A., Bp of Worcester; Hillary, Bp of Chichester; R., Earl of Leicester; R., Earl of Cornwall; William, Earl of Gloucester; Richard de Luci; Manasser Biset, Dapifer; H. fitz Gerold, Chamberlain; Joceline de Baillol; Hugh de Gundevill; and R. de Dunstanvill.[7]

An undated Charter to Lewes Priory, perhaps passed at Winchester and on this occasion. Its witnesses will perhaps

[1] Stubbs' Itinerary, quoting R. de Monte (Struve), 890. Hoveden, 281. Pipe-Rolls, pp. 119, 175.

[2] Lobineau, Hist. de Bretagne, i. 153.

[3] Brut-y-Tywysogion, p. 193.

[4] Rot. Pipe, 4 Hen. II. p. 175.—It is quite possible that the entry relates to the autumn of 1157. Radulf Vitulus was a ship-master of Southampton, whence in case of Welsh invasions, provisions, etc., were occasionally shipped to Pembroke or Milford. From another authority, we learn that in the year 1158, William, Earl of Gloucester and his wife, Hawyse, were made prisoners by the Welsh at Cardi (Annals of Margan, p. 7). The circumstance indicates some Welsh outbreak at the time, and tallies well with the King's appearance in the Western Counties, though it by no means implies his actual entry on Prince Rese's territory. When we find the Earl in the King's court at Winchester about August, that phenomenon hardly affects the uncertainties of the question.

[5, 6] Rot. Pipe, 4 Hen. II. pp. 175, 179.

[7] Cartæ Antiquæ, V.

1158. August. have been A., Bishop of Worcester; Reginald, Earl of Cornwall; R., Earl of Leicester; Richard de Luci; H. fitz (Gerold); and G. (? R.) de Camvill.[1] Winchester.

Aug. 14. In the same month of August the King crossed the sea to Normandy.[2] He probably embarked from Portsmouth or Southampton, leaving the Queen at Winchester. The following entries on the Pipe-Roll of Michaelmas, 1158, are suggestive of such facts :— Portsmouth or Southampton. Normandy.

WILTSHIRE. *In portandâ venacione Regis ad Portesmuam* 4*s*.[3]

WINCHESTER. *In liberacione Sciprorum in passagio Regis* £7. *Et in corredio Reginæ per Comitem Legrecestriæ* £26. 13*s*. 4*d*. *Et ad opus Reginæ* 40*s*. *per breve ipsius : teste Joscelino de Baillol. Et in passagio Sororis Regis* 2 *marcas argenti per breve Reginæ. Et pro incenso ad opus Reginæ et pro Bacinis* 5*s*. 6*d*. *Et pro pipere et Cumino et Canellâ, et Amandis ad opus Reginæ* 15*s*. 3*d*. *Et in operacione Castelli et Ballivi et in minutis negociis Reginæ* £2. 5*s*. 3*d*.[4]

The following entries on the Pipe-Roll of Michaelmas, 1158, give some idea as to the Queen's movements and the *personnel* of her household during the previous year :—

HAMPSHIRE. *In corredio Reginæ per Warinum filium Geroldi* £76. 10*s*. *Et eidem per Nicholaum de Hanton* £26. 13*s*. 4*d*. *Et ad soltam Henrici filii Regis faciendam per Hugonem de Plucchenoi* £33. 10*s*. *Et in soltâ Reginæ per Manasserum Biset et per Radulfum de Hasting* £146. 13*s*. 4*d*. *Et ad perficiendam eandem soltam* 100*s*. *per eosdem. Et in corredio Reginæ et in Robbâ ad opus ipsius per eosdem* £16. 2*s*. 10*d*.[5]

WINCHESTER. *In corredio Reginæ per Radulfum de Hastinges et Bernardum de Chavigni* £6.[6]

DEVONSHIRE. *Reginæ per breve ipsius* £80. *blanc' et* £17. 10*s*. *numero*.[7]

DORSETSHIRE. *In corredio Reginæ per breve Reginæ* £18.[8]

BERKSHIRE. *Et in corredio Reginæ* £4. 5*s*. 8*d*. *Et in corredio Reginæ* 63*s*. *pro dimidiâ marcâ auri. Et in corredio Reginæ* £13. 2*s*. 10*d*. *Et in corredio Reginæ* 18*s*. 2*d*. *per Radulfum de Hasting*.[9]

WILTSHIRE. *Hugoni de Gundovill* 20 *marcas argenti per Comitem Legrecestriæ in corredio filii Regis. Et in corredio Reginæ per Radulfum de Hastinges* 40*s*.[10]

c. Sept. A Writ of the Queen which, probably issued at this period, shows her with Viceregal powers and resident at Westminster, where it is dated. Thereby Alianora the Queen enjoins on the Military tenants of Malmes-

[1] Cartæ Antiquæ, K. dorso. The Record is much defaced.
[2] Chron. Normann. p. 994.
[3, 4] Rot. Pipe, 4 Hen. II. pp. 115, 175.
[5, 6] Rot. Pipe, 4 Hen. II. pp. 171, 176.
[7] Ibidem, p. 158. This was a fixed charge on the Royal Revenues of Devon.
[8, 9, 10] Ibidem, pp. 157, 123–4, 115–6.

1158. bury Abbey, that they render to the Abbey such service as had been determined (*recognitum*) before the King and the Justiciar at Worcester. Witness, Robert Earl of Leicester.[1]

August. King Henry holds a conference with Louis VII. on the River Epte. They agree on a marriage between Prince Henry of England and the Princess Margaret of France.[2] Inter Gisors and Neufmarché.

Sept. 8. King Henry at Argentan summons the army of Normandy to muster at Avranches at Michaelmas, against Earl Conan who had invaded Nantes.[2] Argentan.

Sept. 19. Ingulf, Abbot of Abingdon, died.

King Henry visits Paris. The Princess Margaret confided to his care. He consigns her to Robert de Newburg (then Seneschal of Normandy). Paris.

The King is said to have been now at Mantes.[3] Mantes.

Sept. 23. Queen Eleanor, being in England, gives birth to a son, Geoffrey.[4]

Sept. 29. King Henry at Avranches. Earl Conan appears before him, and surrenders Nantes. Henry makes Conan a Duke. Avranches.

The Chancellor (Becket) and Henry de Pomerai appear in the above year, acting exceptionally and in three counties, as judicial functionaries. There was no regular *Iter* in the English provinces.

MICHAELMAS, 1158, TO MICHAELMAS, 1159.

c. Oct. The King visits Mont St. Michael.[5] Mont St. Michael.

The King visits St. Jacques.[6] St. Jacques.

The King visits Pont Orson. Pont Orson.

About this time a Vow of Crusade for three years was taken by many in St. Mary's Church, Mayenne.—

William, Bishop of Le Mans, signed the Votaries with the cross, he returning from *St. Michael in periculo maris* (where he had probably been attending K. Henry).—

Audoenus, a Priest, Dean of St. Julian's at Le Mans, officiated. Juhel de Meduana became trustee for the affairs of the intended Crusaders for the period of their vow.—

Among the Devotees were Geoffrey de Meduana, knight, son of Juhel;

[1] Malmesbury Chartulary (penes Remem. Regin.) No. 56.
[2] Chron. Normann. p. 994.
[3] Professor Stubbs' Itinerary, quoting Bouquet, xiii. 300.
[4] Chron. Normann. p. 994.
[5] Mount St. Michael,—a Norman town, near Avranches, on the borders of Bretagne (Lyttelton, vol. ii. p. 87).
[6] Professor Stubbs' Itinerary (ut supra) quoting D'Anisy's Normandy-Transcripts, i. 286, 'Chartulary of Mt. S. Michel.'

1158. Hamo, son of Geoffrey, knight; Walter, William, and Guy, brothers of Geoffrey; Geoffrey de Fougeres, son of William; Humfrey de Meduana; Henry de Vitrey; Pagan Coörsus (perhaps De Cadurcis); Hugh de Valletort; and Robert Avenell.[1]

c. Oct. 9. The King goes to Nantes, in Bretagne. He is armed with additional powers against the disaffected Bretons in virtue of his office as Seneschal of France.[2] Nantes.

The King besieges and takes Thouars (Castrum Toarcii). Thouars.

The King goes to Le Mans,[3] and there meets Louis of France. Le Mans.

Nov. 23. The King accompanies Louis VII. visiting the Norman Abbey of *St. Michael in periculo maris* (Mont St. Michael). Mont St. Michael.

Both Kings adjourn to Avranches.[4] Avranches.

K. Henry is next found at Baieux with Louis. Baieux.

Then at Caen. Caen.

Then at Rouen,[5] still entertaining Louis. Rouen.

Another authority[6] seems to trace a nearly co-temporary progress of the King through Normandy as bringing him successively to Pacey. Pacey.

And to Evreux. Evreux.

And to Neufbourg. Neufbourg.

And to Bec. Bec.

Nov. 29. The Queen is now at Salisbury. Richard de Luci is acting as a Justiciar in England.[7]

We have a Precept of "Alianore, Queen of England, Duchess of Aquitaine and Normandy, and Countess of Anjou," in behalf of Matilda, Countess (dowager) of Chester. It is dated at Salisbury, and attested by Joceline de Bailol.[8]

Also we have a Certificate whereby "A., Queen of England, etc.," confirms a quit-claim given in her presence by Robert Flambard to Warner de Lusoriis. Witnesses, Gosceline, Bp of Sarum; Earl Reginald

[1] Gallici Scriptores, xii. 556, n. These names are associated with K. Henry's dominions, both English and foreign. Of the whole number of Crusaders, 35 only returned, and that not till Nov. 7, 1162. The rest, says the Record, "died for the Faith, on Sinai."

[2] One Chronicle misdates the death of Prince Geoffrey and the surrender of Nantes as in 1159.—It says, (alluding to Prince Geoffrey), "*Obiit G. Martel.*" And then, "*In eodem anno Comes Conanus de Richemont recepit Nannetensem Civitatem, sed paucis diebus tenens eam Henrico Regi Angliæ dimisit illam circa festum Dionysii,*" (October 9).

[3] The siege of Thouars occupied 3 days. The King banished the Vicomte, destroyed the walls, and garrisoned the Castle (Chron. St. Albin. G. S. xii. 482. Gervase (p. 1380) says that after the reduction of Thouars-Castle, Henry conducted (*deduxit*) the King of France from Le Mans to Mont St. Michael, and thence to Baieux, Caen, and Rouen.

[4] Chron. Normann. p. 994.

[5] Gervase of Canterbury, p. 1380, as quoted above, under Note 3.

[6] R. de Monte (Pistorius, Ed. Struve, p. 891) quoted by Stubbs (Appendix p. cxxxij). But Stubbs seems to place this visit to Normandy in October.

[7] Palgrave (ut Supra), Appendix p. xi.

[8] Muniments of the Duchy of Lancaster.

1158. of Cornwall; Reginald de Warren; Josceline de Baillol; and Robert de Dunestanvill. Dated at Sarum.[1]

The Pipe-Roll of 1159 (5 Hen. II.) has further entries indicating many circumstances connected with the Queen's Court between Michaelmas and December, 1158, when she joined the King in Normandy.

HAMPSHIRE.— *In corredio Reginæ* £57. 13*s*. 8*d*. *per breve ipsius. Et Johanni de Dol* £16. 13*s*. 4*d*. *per breve Reginæ de dono. Et pro pannis liberorum Regis* 42*s*. 2*d*. *per breve Regis. Et Hugoni de Plugenai* £70 *ad corredium filii Regis. Et Girardo medico Henrici filii Regis.*

KENT. — *Et Radulfo de Hasting* £30 *ad corredium Reginæ per breve ipsius. Et Hugoni de Plugenoi* £25. 10*s*. *ad corredium Henrici filii Regis.*

BUCKS AND BEDFORDSHIRE.—*Et Radulfo de Hasting* 50 *marcas ad corredium Reginæ per breve ipsius.*

BERKSHIRE.—*In corredio Reginæ per breve ipsius Radulfo de Hasting* £7. 6*s*. 8*s*.

LONDON.—*Pro roba ad opus Reginæ*, £80. 6*s*. 8*d*. *In conductu ejusdem robæ* 20*s*. *In conductu probatorum Regis ad Saresburiam* 53*s*. 4*d*.

WARWICKSHIRE.—*In conductu Castanearum Reginæ ad Saresberiam* 3*s*. *per breve ipsius.*

WILTSHIRE.—*Et Radulfo de Hastings* 20 *marcas ad corredium Reginæ, per breve Regis.*

DORSETSHIRE.—*Radulfo de Hasting* £6. 13*s*. 4*d*. *ad corredium Reginæ per breve ipsius. Et Hugoni de Plugenoi et Joscelino* £11. 6*s*. 8*d*. *ad corredium filii Regis per breve Reginæ.*

c. Dec. DEVONSHIRE.—*Et in corredio Reginæ* 60*s*. *per breve ipsius. Et in liberacione Sneccæ* £7 *in transfretatione ipsius.*

On the Queen's passing to Normandy, the Earl of Leicester seems to have been left as Viceroy or Chief Justice of England. The Pipe-Roll of 1159 quotes his Writs as Quasi-regal in their nature and exigence.

Dec. Theobald, Comte of Blois, surrenders to K. Henry two castles, viz., Ambaxium (Amboise) and Fracta Vallis (Fréteval). Amboise. Fréteval.

Rotroc, Comte of Perch, whose wife was a sister of the said Comte Theobald, surrenders to the King the two Castles of Moulins and Bon Moulins. The King concedes Belesme (*Bellissimum Castrum*), to the said Comte Rotroc.[2] Moulins. Bon Moulins.

Dec. 25. The King and the Queen (who had lately crossed to Normandy) are at Cherbourg.[3] Cherbourg.

[1] Cartæ Antiquæ, N. 25.

[2] Chron. Normann. p. 994. Professor Stubbs (quoting R. de Monte, p. 892) entitles these compositions as "Peace with Champagne." Theobald was Comte of Blois, not of Champagne.

[3] Chronicon Normanniæ, p. 995.

A.D. 1159.

1159. c. January. About this time we incline to date a Charter of the King, then at Rouen, whereby he appoints Walcheline, a Monk of Evesham, to the Abbacy of Abingdon. The Charter is attested by the Bishops of Evreux (Rotroc); of Baieux (Philip); and by William de Caisneto.[1] Rouen.

A Charter, dated at Argentan, is in favour of the Abbey of St. Andrew in Gouffern (Coutances Dioc.). It is attested by Thomas the Chancellor; Manasser Biset, Dapifer; Richard de Luci; Robert de Dunstanvill; and Stephen de Beauchamp.[2] Argentan.

An ill-transcribed Charter, also dated at Argentan, is in favour of the Norman Abbey of Fontenay. Its witnesses seem to have been, Thomas the Chancellor; Manasser Biset, Dapifer (written as *juniolibet Dapifer*); and Humphrey de Bohun.[3] Argentan.

Another Charter, dated at Rouen, is a Royal Confirmation to the Abbey of Silly, a Præmonstratensian House in the Diocese of Seez. It is attested by Thomas the Chancellor; Stephen de Beauchamp; Manasser Biset, Dapifer; and Richard the Scribe (Scriptor). Rouen.

January–March. In the first three months of this year we incline to date several Charters of the King, given at Rouen, in behalf of Walcheline, the newly-appointed Abbot of Abingdon. One is addressed to Richard de Lucy, probably as being at the time Custos or Fermor of Windsor. These Charters are attested by Rotroc, Bishop of Evreux; Philip, Bishop of Baieux; Arnulf, Bishop of Liseux; William de Caisneto; William Fitz John; Hubert de Vaux; William de Hastings; and Manasser Biset, Dapifer; or by some of them.[4]

c. March 1. The Bishop of Winchester (Henry of Blois) is incidentally mentioned as being in England.

March 22. Robert Warelwast, Bishop of Exeter, is said to have died.[5]

c. March 22. (Midlent). K. Henry advertises his intended expedition to Toulouse.—

[1] Hist. Monast. de Abingdon, vol. ii. p. 216.—Walcheline's predecessor, Ingulf, died Sept. 19, 1158. (Vide supra, p. 41).

[2] D'Anisy's Transcripts, ii. 30, 31.

[3] Neustria Pia, p. 15.

[4] Hist. Abingdon, ii. pp. 217, 218, 219, 220–222.

[5] Chron. Normanniæ. But the 'Annals of Winton' give 1160 as the year of this *obit*.

1159. c. March. Levies were to be made in England, Normandy, Acquitaine, and other provinces. The King claimed the Fief against Raymond, Comte of St. Giles, and in right of his wife, Eleanor, Duchess of Acquitaine. Eighteen years previous, viz., in 1141, Louis VII. of France, being then husband of Eleanor, had claimed the Fief in the same right.[1] Normandy.

April. From one chronicle we should derive an impression that, thus early in the year, K. Henry went into Guienne and held conference with Raymond Berenger, Comte of Barcelona, at Blaye (*apud Castrum Blavium*). They agreed that in due time Prince Richard should marry Raymond's daughter, and that Henry should cede to them the Duchy of Acquitaine.[2] Blaye Castle (Guienne.)

There is also an alleged visit of Henry to Poictiers at this time, which would be quite intelligible as connected with his journey to or from Guienne. Otherwise we should incline to think that both the visits, to Poictiers and to Blaye, took place later in the year. Poictiers.

May 18. Summonses for foreign service in the Army of Toulouse were alleged by way of 'Essoign' in the English Law-courts.[3]

May 21–23. King Henry is for three days at Bec Hellouin.[4] Bec Hellouin.

May 24. The King is at Rouen.[5] Rouen.

May 28. Theobald, Comte of Blois, "frater Henrici" (brother of Henry of Troyes, must be meant), returning from a visit to the Shrine of St. James of Compostella, was received and lodged in the Abbey of St. Martial at Limoges. The Comte offered a gift of 10 merks "on the Sepulchre of the Apostle." Henry, King of England, by his Deputy (*per principatum*) or by his order (reading *per præceptum*), royally provided the Comte's entertainment, though the Comte did not wish it (*invitus fuit*).[6]

May 28. On the same day, one Geoffrey was admitted a Monk of St. Martial of Limoges, by Peter, Abbot of that House.[6] This Geoffrey was he, who, afterwards, becoming Prior of Vigeois, was known as Geoffrey de Vigeois, and from whose Chronicle we extract some of these particulars.

June 6–8. King Henry at Hilliricourt.[7] Hilliricourt.

June 24. King Henry at Poictiers.[7] Poictiers.

[1] Palgrave (ut supra), p. xii. Gallici Scriptores, xii–121 *n*. The expression of the Norman Chronicle (p. 995) with regard to the army of Toulouse, viz., "*Rex fecit submoveri*," is too early for the date given by the same authority, viz., Midlent. Midlent fell on March 22, in the year 1159.

[2] Stubbs, quoting Bouquet, xiii. 302.

[3] Palgrave (ut supra), p. xiv.

[4] Stubbs, quoting Bouquet, (xiii. 302).

[5] Palgrave (ut supra), p. xv.

[6] Gaufr. Vosiensis (G. S. xii. 440).

[7] Stubbs, quoting Bouquet, xiii. 302.

1159, June 24. A King's Writ, dated at Poictiers (apud Pictav') possibly belongs to this occasion. It certifies that the Church and Canons of Briweton (Bruton, Somerset) are in the King's hand and protection. It is attested by Richard de Luci. The Transcript purports it to be addressed "*Vicomiti et Ministris de Reiesmo*";[1]—a misreading which we do not venture to amend. Poictiers.

The King's progress southwards from Poictiers is not traced by the Chronicles.—

We venture to suggest one step thereof on the evidence of a Charter, dated "*apud Santoniam*" (Saintes in Saintonge). It is a grant by the King to Herbert Rufus. It is attested by Thomas the Chancellor; Richard de Luci; Henry fitz Gerold, Chamberlain; Richard de Camvill; and Robert de Dunstanville.[2] Saintes.

c. June 30. At Perigueux, in the 'Bishop's Meadow,' K. Henry conferred the honour of knighthood on Malcolm, King of Scots. Malcolm followed the King's arms, accompanied by thirty sons of nobles (*Heroüm*), who had been his associates in his late estate of tutelage (*recentis tyrocinii consocii*).[3] A Welsh Prince was also in the King's host.[4] It is in this connection, probably, that the Pipe-Roll of 1159 contains a charge by the Sheriff of Buckinghamshire, viz., of £17. 10*s*., which he had paid to the Knights. Perigueux.

June 30. "On the Feast-day of St. Martial," and coincidently in point of time with the knighting of Malcolm, Peter, Abbot of St. Martial of Limoges, at summons of the King of England, sent his military contingent in aid of the King's arms. The Abbot himself, already suffering from an optical disease which, within three years, ended in total blindness, after pronouncing benediction on his retainers, was scarce able to lead their outset (*processionem*) towards the King's camp.[5]

July 1–3. Muster of the King of England's forces at Agen (*apud Agennense Castrum*). Agen (Guieune).

A Diary of the period tells us incidentally of the King being at Auvilar (in Gascony).[6] The precise day of the King's being there is not definitely fixed by the Diary, but the end of May is suggested by the context. However, such a date is impossible; and we are obliged to Auvillards (Gascony).

[1] D'Anisy's Transcripts, iii. 344.
[2] Cartæ Antiquæ, P.
[3] Gaufr. Vosiensis (G. S. xii. 439).
[4] Gervase, p. 1381. Chron. Normanniæ.
[5] Gaufr. Vosiensis (G. S. xii. 439).
[6] Palgrave (ut supra), Appendix p. xiv.

1159. c. July 1-3. conclude that the King took Auvilar in his march from Agen towards Toulouse. Auvillards (Gascony.)

In curious parallelism with this extract from a Diary, we have a Charter of the King in favour of the Bishop of Rochester. It is attested singly by the Chancellor (Becket). It is dated, "*apud Auvilar in Castris.*" [1]

July. The King occupies the passes (*Saltus*) of Toulouse.

The siege of Toulouse now begins, and lasts till the end of September. Toulouse (Languedoc).

August 1. Robert de Newburgh, Steward and Chief Justice (*Dapifer et Justiciarius*) of Normandy is shorn a Monk at Bec-Hellouin.[2]

August 30. Robert de Newburgh dies, in Cloister at Bec.[3]

August 30. On the same day (rather than on September 1) died Pope Adrian IV.

Sept. 7. Roland Bandinelli, Cardinal of St. Mark, elected Pope.

Sept. 20. Roland Bandinelli crowned as Pope Alexander III.

In this year, Theodoric, Comte of Flanders, returned from Jerusalem.[4]

The King of England is still before Toulouse, when Louis of France throws himself into the town, adopting the cause of its defender, the Comte of St. Giles, because the Comte had married Constance, the French King's sister. Toulouse.

K. Henry, pressed by the Chancellor, Becket, to seize a favourable opportunity for assaulting the town refused, "*præsentis domini sui reverentiâ vetante*";[5]—such an act would be in defiance of the obligations and fealty which Henry owed to Louis, as regarded *the person* of the Suzerain.

c. Sept. 26. King Henry breaks up the siege of Toulouse.

The King goes first to Cahors, which he fortifies, and entrusts to Thomas the Chancellor.[6] Cahors (Guienne).

[1] Cartæ Antiquæ, F.
[2] Chron. Normann. p. 996.
[3] Gervase, p. 1381.
[4] Chron. Normann. p. 996.
[5] Gall. Script. xii. 121 *n.*
[6] R. de Monte (Struve), 894. Chron. Norm.

MICHAELMAS, 1159, TO MICHAELMAS, 1160.

1159. c. October. King Henry, after dismissing his army, arrives at Uzerche; the King of Scots being still in his company.[1] Uzerche (Limousin).

In the retreat from Toulouse died William, Comte of Boulogne and Moretain and *jure uxoris*, Earl of Surrey, son and heir of the late King Stephen.

October. King Henry next reaches Limoges. Here the King renders up to his late ward, Ademar V., Vicomte of Limoges, his paternal inheritance, marrying the youth to Sara, one of the three daughters of Reginald, Earl of Cornwall (the King's uncle).[1]

October. King Henry, having arrived in Normandy, invades Louis's territory about Beauvais (*pagum Belvacensem*).[2] Beauvoisis.

c. Nov. King Henry destroys the Border Fortress of Guerberoi.[2] Guerberoi.

In this sequence King Henry is at Estrepagni.[2] Estrepagni.

At this crisis of the conflict between Henry and Louis, Simon, Comte of Evreux, makes over his fortresses of Rochefort (*Rupem fortem*), Epernon (*Espernonem*), and Montfort (*Montem fortem*) to K. Henry. This was a great blow to Louis, inasmuch as it gave Henry command of the communications between Paris, Orleans, and Etampes. A truce was the result, to last till the octaves of Pentecost (May 22nd, 1160.)[3]

Nov. 29–Dec. 6. In the first week of Advent commenced a Winter of intense severity. Gerold, Bishop of Limoges, and Peter, Abbot of St. Martial (Limoges), set out for Rome.[4]

Dec. 7. Walter Durdent, Bishop of Chester, died.[5]

[1] Gaufr. Vosiensis. (G. S. xii. 439). The King, says the same authority, had now been nearly three years in possession of Limoges (See Oct. 1156, supra, page 20). His cousin, Sara de Dunstanvill, was now (1159) about 15 years of age. An Interpolator of Geoffrey of Vigeois' narrative says that she was buried "*apud S. Aredium*" (at Ared de la Perche) on the feast day of St. Columbanus (November 21) in the year 1216,—and that she left three sons, Guy, William, and Ademar. She will have died therefore at the age of about 72. It is of her son Guy V. that the same Interpolator is speaking when he says, alluding to the time of her death (1216):—*Tunc Guido Vicecomes obsederat Axiam.*

[2] Stubbs' Itinerary (p. cxxxiij) quoting "Normandy Transcripts," No. 137, and "Bouquet," xiii. 302.

[3] Chronicon Normanniæ, p. 996.

[4] Gaufr. Vosiensis (G. S. xii. 439). This is introduced here chiefly to show how well we may depend on the dates given by Geoffrey of Vigeois in his Chronicle. The persons who administered the affairs of St. Martial's Abbey during its Abbot's absence in Rome, were Peter, Abbot of St. Augustin (Limoges), and Martin, Prior of Vigeois. The Writer, Geoffrey, was at this moment a monk of St. Martial, but eventually succeeding Martin in the Priorate of Vigeois, he thus obtained his *cognomen* of *Vosiensis*.

[5] Hardy's Fasti, i. 54.—Possibly this Prelate died Dec. 7, 1160 (see Fasti ibidem, note 73).

1159. Dec. 25. The King and Queen keep Christmas at Falaise.[1]

c. Dec. 31. Queen Eleanor crosses to England.

Some time in the year 1159, Froger, the King's Almoner, was made Bishop of Seez. He was probably identical with Froger, previously Archdeacon of Derby (Chester Dioc.).

A.D. 1160.

1160. Some time in the first half of this year, the King would seem to have been at Argentan. A Charter, there dated, is in favour of the Cistercian Abbey of La Trappe in the Diocese of Seez. It is attested by Hugh, Archbishop of Rouen; Arnulf, Bishop of Liseux; Froger, Bishop of Seez; Richard de Humet, Constable; Geoffrey de Bonmoulin; and Herbert de Sanctâ Scolasticâ.[2] Argentan.

A nearly contemporary Charter, in favour of the same Abbey, is also dated at Argentan. It is attested by the Bishops of Liseux and Seez; by Robert, son of the Earl of Leicester; Richard de Humet, Constable; Geoffrey de Bruecort; Gilbert, his brother; and Herbert de Sanctâ Scolasticâ.[3]

c. Jan. The Empress, in declining health, makes many eleemosynary grants, and is warmly seconded by her son.

Baieux Cathedral burnt. Philip, its Bishop, energetically engages in its restoration.[4]

May. Peace between K. Henry and Louis, whereof the articles are preserved in a Charter which purports to be attested by the Bishops, Peter of Paris, Hugh of Soissons, Robert (Rotroc) of Evreux, Ernald (Arnulf) of Exe (Liseux, probably), Philip of Baieux, Roger (usually called Froger) of Seez, and Hugh of Durham; also, by Thomas the Chancellor, the Comte of Flanders, Comte Theodoric, Henry, Comte of Soissons; the Comte of Bellomonte, Teodor' Wileriann, William Pavet, the Master of the Temple, and the Brethren,—Otto de St. Ludonir, Gilbert de Laci,[5] Richard Normandy.

[1] Chronicon Normanniæ, p. 996.

[2, 3] D'Anisy's Transcripts, iii. 310, 311. Both deeds passed between 1159 and January, 1163.

[4] Chron. Normann. p. 996.

[5] That Gilbert de Lacy, Baron of Ludlow, Weobley, and Ewias, became a Templar, I have elsewhere (Antiquities of Shropshire, v. 252-3). presumed. Here is proof positive of the fact.

1160. May. de Hastings, Peter Bishop, and Robert de Piro; also by William, brother of the King of England; the Comte of Mellent, Richard de Humet, and Jordan Taxo.— Normandy.

The treaty concerns the settlement of the Norman Vexin; the demolition of the Castle of Stipennei; the restoration to France of the fealty of Simon, Comte of Evreux; the surrender to France of the fealties of Goceline Crispin and Goell de Vaudemonte; the retention by Henry of his acquisitions in the Honour of Toulouse, and Cahors, and the Quercy (*Cadurco et Cadurcino*);—a year's truce from Pentecost (May 22) to be conceded by Henry to the Comte of St. Giles; and further conditions for the marriage to be had between Henry's son and Louis's daughter.[1]

In the year 1160, and probably in May or June, a dispute between the Church of Avranches and the Abbey of St. Michael de Monte was settled at Rouen in the presence of K. Henry. There were in attendance on the Court, Hugh, Archbishop of Rouen; Philip, Bishop of Bayeux; Rotrou, Bishop of Evreux; Herbert, Bishop of Avranches; Hugh, Bishop of Durham; Thomas the Chancellor; Richard, de Humet, Constable; and William fitz Hamo.[2] Rouen.

Matthew, son of the Comte of Flanders, marries Mary, Abbess of Romsey (daughter of K. Stephen), and so becomes Comte of Boulogne.

July. Henry and Louis assemble the Bishops, Abbots, and Barons of Normandy and Beauvais in Council at Neufmarch. They agree in reprobating Victor, the Anti-Pope, and in favouring Alexander. Neufmarché.

Sept. Constance, Queen of France, dies in child-bed; her child, a daughter, surviving.

Herbert, Bishop of Avranches, dies.

Queen Eleanor, Prince Henry, and the Princess Matilda cross to Normandy.

c Sept. 15. William of Pavia, Legate of the Holy See, wishes to send Peter, Abbot of St. Martial at Limoges, to convert Hugh, Abbot of Clugni, to the cause of Pope Alexander. Hereupon, the Abbot of St. Martial resigns office.

Sept. 29. The Pipe-Roll made up at this date contains many entries allusive to the King's continuous absence in Normandy;—also to the Queen's arrival in England (Dec. 31, 1159);—to her Regency in England; to her return

[1] Lyttelton, vol. iv. p. 174. The Document is inadequately transcribed, as is usual with the Transcripts of this Historian.

[2] D'Anisy's Normandy Transcripts, ii. 287.

to Normandy (Sept. 1160); and to the movements of others of the Royal family, *e. g.*—

LONDON AND MIDDLESEX.—*Pro vino Reginæ* £4. 16*s*. 4*d*. *per breve ipsius. Et pro* ii *unciis auri ad deaurandas cuppas Regis* 2 *marcas argenti. Et pro* ii *tonellis vini* 34*s*. *ad opus Reginæ. Et pro* iv *modis vini ad opus Reginæ* 30*s*. *Et in liberacione filii Regis* £13. 4*s*. 7*d*. *per Willielmum filium Aldelini.*

DONCASTER.—*Robertus de Ross debet* £533. 6*s*. 8*d*., *sed sunt in respectu donec Rex redeat in Angliam per breve Regis de ultra mare.*

WILTSHIRE.—*Et Reginæ per breve ipsius* £20 *ad corredium. Et pro conducendo vino Reginæ ad Warengefordiam* 4*s*.

BERKSHIRE.—*Et in corredio Reginæ per breve ipsius* £6. 13*s*. 4*d*.

SOUTHAMPTON.—*Et in passagiis thesauri* £6. 13*s*. 8*d*. *Et in corredio Reginæ per breve ipsius* 33*s*. 3*d*. *Et in conductu vini Reginæ et onerando et deonerando* 7*s*. 3*d*. *Et pro vino Reginæ empto* 61*s*. 1*d*. *Et in conductu vini ad Warengeford per breve Reginæ* 4*s*. 6*d*. *Et in conductu vini de Britanniâ* 104*s*. 2*d*. *Et in passagio Reginæ extremo* £16. 12*s*. 6*d*. *Et in passagio Ricardi de Camvill et Austrucariorum et Falconariorum Regis* (*et*) *pro hugiis* £6. 14*s*.

HAMPSHIRE.—*Et in corredio Reginæ per breve ipsius* £226. 3*s*. 9*d*. *in* xiii *talliis. Et in corredio Henrici filii Regis* £56. 13*s*. *in* iv *talliis. Et in vassellâ filiæ Regis* £7. 16*s*. 4*d*. *Et in minutis negociis Reginæ* 26*s*. 8*d*. *Et in liberacione hominum Sneccæ de passagio Reginæ et Henrici filii Geroldi cum thesauro, et Nicolai de Sigillo* £30. 10*s*.[1] *Et in passagio cum thesauro ad festum Sancti Johannis* £7. 10*s*.[2] *Et in passagio Reginæ extremo*, £7. 10*s*.[3] *Et pro conducendo thesauro ad Pascham et ad festum Sti Michaelis* 13*s*. 4*d*.

WORCESTERSHIRE. — *Et in corredio Reginæ per breve ipsius* £13. 6*s*. 8*d*.

SURREY, CAMBRIDGE AND HUNTINGDONSHIRE.—*Et Reginæ* x. *marcas argenti per breve ipsius.*

DORSETSHIRE.—*Et Reginæ per breve ipsius* £25. 4*s*. 7*d*.

WINCHESTER.—*Pro conductu robæ Reginæ et vini sui et incensi et coffrorum capellæ et scutis puerorum* 31*s*. *Et pro camerâ Reginæ et cheminatâ et cellario* £22. 13*s*. 2*d*. *In corredio Reginæ per breve ipsius* £36.

MICHAELMAS, 1160, TO MICHAELMAS, 1161.

Oct. K. Henry and Louis renew peaceful engagements. (Marches of Normandy.)

Prince Henry does homage to Louis for the Duchy of Normandy.[4]

[1] This, so far as we can judge from the usual significance of the words used, can hardly allude to any arrival of the Queen in England, such as that about the end of the year 1159. We rather prefer to suppose that the Queen went to, and returned from Normandy in the first and second quarter of the year 1160; but such facts are elsewhere unchronicled. Henry fitz Gerold, who was at Saintes in May, 1159, seems subsequently to have been attached to the Queen's suite.

[2] The Feast of St. John, as a Pipe-Roll, or Exchequer date, is, we believe always, the Nativity of John Baptist (June, 24).

[3] This alludes to the Queen's *Transfretation* circa September, 1160.

[4] Diceto, p. 532. Chron. Normann. p. 997.

1160. c. Oct. Louis of France marries a sister of Theobald, Comte of Blois.[1]

Nov. 2. Prince Henry espoused to the Princess Margaret at Neufbourgh (Novum Burgum), with consent of the Cardinal Legates, Henry of Pisa, and William of Pavia.[2] Neufbourg.

K. Henry builds the three Castles of Gisors, Néaupple (Niafliam), and Château-neuf-sur-Epte (*Novum Castellum*). Rupture between K. Henry and Theobald, Comte of Blois. Henry takes Chaumont (*Calvum montem*),[3] and gives it to Hugh de Amboise. He also fortifies Amboise and Fretteville (*Fractam Vallem*). Gisors. Neaufle. Neufchâtel. Chaumont Amboise. Fréteval.

Dec. 25. K. Henry and Queen Eleanor spend Christmas at Le Mans. A Charter, probably of this period, bears date at Le Mans (*apud Cenoman'*). It is in favour of Walden Abbey (Essex), and is attested by Roger, Earl of Clare; Earl Alberic; William, Earl of Arundel; Richard de Humez, Constable; Henry de Essex, Constable; Richard de Luci; and William fitz Hamo.[4] Le Mans.

In the above year (1160), Robert, a monk of Bec, was made Abbot of St. Evroul of Uticum.

A.D. 1161.

1161. c. Jan. The King seizes and entrusts to his own lieutenants the Castles of the Comte of Mellent and other Norman Barons. He strengthens Gisors and other Border Castles. Gisors.

He builds a Palace and makes a Park (*apud Cheruleium*) near Rouen.

To this period may be attributed K. Henry's Charter to the Norman Abbey of St. Barbe-en-Auge. It is dated at Rouen. It mentions Froger, Bishop of Seez, as a benefactor to the Abbey, and it is attested by Thomas the Chancellor; Richard de Humet, Constable; and Richard de Luci.[5] Rouen.

At this same period we are told that Achard, Abbot of St. Victor at Paris, was made Bishop of Avranches[6]; and we have another Charter dated at Rouen and attested by

[1, 2] Diceto, p. 532. Chron. Normann. p. 997.

[3] Now the *Chateau de Chaumont*, on the Loire, just below Blois.

[4] Monasticon, iv. 152, xviii.

[5] Monasticon, vii. p. 1113.

[6] His predecessor at Avranches was Herbert.

1161. c. Jan. that very Prelate. This is a Charter to the Canons of St. Bartholomew, London. The witnesses are Rotroc, Bp of Evreux; A., Bp of Avranches; Thomas the Chancellor; William, Earl of Albemarle; Earl Hugh (of Norfolk or Chester?); the Earl of Arundel; the Earl of Clare; Richard de Humet, Constable; Manasser Biset, Dapifer; William de Keisneto; and Stephen de Turonis, Chamberlain. This Charter is expedited—*per manum Stephani de Fulgeriis*.[1] Rouen.

Jan. 5. Peter del Barri, Abbot of St. Augustine (Limoges), elected Abbot of St. Martial (Limoges). The Legate, William of Pavia, approved the election, but King Henry opposed it. Hereupon the Abbot Elect went to the King; as did also Peter, the late Abbot of St. Martial, now seeking reappointment.[2]

Feb. 12. (On "*Circumdederunt*" or *Septuagesima* Sunday). An eclipse of the moon.[3]

The King founds a Leper-house at Caen. Caen.

The King builds a Castle at Osmanville (*Amandivillam*) on the River Vire. Osmanville.

March 1. The King was at the Abbey of Mortimer-en-Lions; and (it being the first day of Lent) Peter of Tarentaise, the Papal Legate, celebrated Mass before the King in that Monastery.[4] Mortimer-en-Lions.

c. March. Perhaps at this time the King visited Leons, or Lions-la-Forêt, in the same district. A Charter to the Canons of Herting (Sussex) bears date at Leon, and is attested by Thomas the Chancellor, William de Braose, William de Lanvalein, W. Aguilon, Hugh de Morevill, and Robert de St. Mary-Church.[5] Lions-la-Forêt.

Another Charter to William Pistor is dated *apud Leon*, and attested by Hugh de Perers, William de Crevecor, Hugh Prior, and Robert de Ivingney.[6]

A grant of Franchises to the Abbey of St. Mary of

1 Cartæ Antiquæ, L.

2 Geoffrey of Vigeois.

3 Gallici Scriptores, xii. 284. The verification of eclipses is important, as showing the method or accuracy of any given Chronicler. The alleged day of this eclipse is so far credible as that the moon was full on Feb. 12.

4 Neustria Pia, p. 775. Tarentaise was a district of Savoy.

5 Cotton, MSS. Vespas. E. xxiii. fol. 1, b.

6 Formulare Anglicanum, p. 44. This Charter is one of a series. The argument that it passed after the decease (7 December, 1159, or perhaps 7 December, 1160) of Walter Durdent, Bishop of Litchfield, is given in a note on that Bishop's obit, in Hardy's Le Neve. The Charter also appears to have passed before the death of Archbishop Theobald (April 18, 1161). Within the limits, thus ascertained, the dating at *Leon*, coupled with the King's *whereabout* on March 1, guide us to the month if not the very day of the King's Charter.

1161. Lonlay, a Benedictine House in the Diocese of Le Mans, is dated at Lyons and attested by Richard de Lucy.[1] Lions-la-Forêt.

c. March. In the beginning of Lent the King was at Le Mans, where Hugh, Archbishop of Dol, resigned his See[2]; the Legates, Henry of Pisa and William of Pavia, being present. Le Mans.

April 9. (*In Ramis Palmarum*). Peter del Barri, Abbot elect of St. Martial, returns to Limoges, with Kings Henry's assent to his election. The King had refused to sanction the reappointment of Peter, the late Abbot.

c. April 16. Richard Peche is consecrated Bishop of Chester by Walter, Bp of Rochester, and in the presence of Abp Theobald, then in his last illness, but who was carried into his chapel to witness the ceremony.

April 18. Theobald, Abp of Canterbury, died.[3] Soon afterwards Bartholomew Iscan was consecrated Bp of Exeter; and Walter, Bp of Rochester, officiated, because the See of Canterbury was vacant, and because the Bp of London was paralytic, and the Bp of Winchester was at Clugni.[4]

c. May. Henry and Louis are campaigning, first in the Vexin (in Vilcasino), and then in the Dunois (in Dunensi pago.)[5] The Vexin. The Dunois.

About this time we have a Charter, dated at *Andele*, which I take to be Andeli, by which the King confirms to Ralph de Wili, son of Ailward, certain lands at Briweton, which came in marriage with Agatonia, daughter of Henry de Caravill, and which the said Henry held at the time of his death, under Rabel the Chamberlain, and which had been confirmed by Charter of William the Chamberlain, son of Rabel. Witnesses, Robert de Dunstanvill; Manasser Biset, Dapifer; Walter de Dunstanvill; Alan, his brother; Baldwin de Frettevill; and Henry de Winton.[6] Andeli.

c. June 30. Henry and Louis make truce. Henry goes into Aquitaine and besieges a castle called Castellion, above the town of *Aden*.[7] Guienne.

Aug. 10. Henry takes Castellion. Châtillon.

Aug. 13. Obit of Maurice, Bishop of Bangor.

c. Sept. The Princess Elianor, born at Domfront,[8] and baptized by Henry

[1] D'Anisy's Transcripts, ii. 92.

[2] Chron. Normann.

[3] Gervase, p. 1381. Robert de Monte dates Archbishop Theobald's death on April 17.

[4] Diceto, p. 532. If correct, this indicates repeated visits to Clugni by Henry of Blois (vide supra, pp. 14–15, *note;* and p. 44).

[5] The district about Châteaudun.

[6] Cartæ Antiquæ, Q.

[7] There is some doubt about this locality. Elsewhere (Benedictus i. 101) it is called *Castelloneum supra Agiens*. Professor Stubbs identifies the latter with *Castillon on the Dordogne*. We take it, however, that the Châtillon, besieged by K. Henry, was on the Garonne, rather than the Dordogne, and was near the town of Agen.

[8] Diceto, incomprehensibly dates the Princess Elianor's birth as in 1165, (Ymag, Hist. p. 539). There was some talk of a contract for her marriage in that year, which perhaps misled the Historian.

1161. c. Sept. of Pisa, the Cardinal Legate; Achard, Bishop of Avranches; and Robert, Abbot of Mount St. Michael-de-periculo-maris, were present.

Sept. 21. Obit of Samson, Archbishop of Rheims.[1]

Sept. 29. The PIPE-ROLL made up to this date contains very few entries illustrative of Court-history during the previous year. The following are all that seem worth quotation :—

LONDON. *Et Reginæ* £12. 13*s*. 4*d*.

HAMPSHIRE. *Et Cancellario et Ricardo de Luci* £102. 10*s*. 10*d*. *ad liberacionem militum et navium in* ii. *talliis*. *Et Nicolao de Sigillo* £7. 10*s*. *in custamento Esneccæ*. *Et hominibus de Esneccâ* 30*s*. *de liberacione* iii. *dierum per breve Regis*. *Et in liberacione* iii. *navium ad portandas Damas Regis ultra mare* £15 *per visum Nicolai de Sigillo*. *Et in liberacione navium Quinque portuum quæ perrexerunt cum thesauro* £34. 18*s*. *per Henricum filium Geroldi*. *Et ad conducendam Arcam de Wintonia ad Lundoniam* 5*s*. 8*d*.

WINCHESTER. *Pro thesauro conducendo ad Hantoniam* 10*s*. 2*d*.

MICHAELMAS, 1161, TO MICHAELMAS, 1162.

c. Oct. A peace between Henry and Louis negotiated at Fréteval.[2] Fréteval.

Dec. 25. The King and Queen keep Christmas at Baieux. Baieux.

During the above year, as one Chronicle relates, Comte Theobald, son of Comte Theobald, besieged the castle of Vendome. John, Comte of Vendome, with his sons Burchard and Lanceline, defended the fortress successfully.

A.D. 1162.

1162. Jan. 14. Succession of Henry, brother of Louis VII., to the Archiepiscopate of Rheims.[3]

Feb. 25. K. Henry holds a Council at Rouen, which was adjourned to Lillebone (*Julia bona*). Rouen. Lillebone.

Henry, at Fecamp, orders the disinterment and reburial of Richard I. and Richard II., Dukes of Normandy. Fecamp.

Perhaps a Charter to Bordesley Abbey (Worcestershire) belongs to this occasion. It purports to be dated *apud Fissam* (*Fiscannum* perhaps), and is attested by Richard de Luci, William fitz Hamo, Robert de Dunestanville, Hugh de Claeris, and William Malet, Dapifer.[4]

[1] Gallici Scriptores, xii. 275.

[2] Diceto, p. 533. It is the last fact named by the Historian, under the year 1161. He says that the two Kings were about to engage in battle.

[3] Gallici Scriptores, xii. 275.

[4] Formulare Anglicanum, No. lxxviii.

1162. c. April 8. Pope Alexander visits Montpellier (Montem Pessulanum), in France.

About this time we know that Robert, Bishop of Lincoln, and Hillary, Bishop of Chichester, visited Normandy.[1] There are two Royal Charters in favour of the former Prelate. Both are dated at Rouen, and both are attested by Roger, Abp of York; Hillary, Bp of Chichester; Hugh, Bp of Durham; and Thomas the Chancellor.[2] Rouen.

May 4. Richard de Belmeis, Bishop of London, died.

c. May. K. Henry is at Falaise, and there, at the solicitation of Robert, Bp of Lincoln, executes a judicial precept addressed to Robert, Earl of Leicester, who was then acting as Chief Justice of England.[3] Falaise.

It was also at Falaise that the King and the Cardinal, Henry of Pisa,[4] pressed the Chancellor Becket to accept the Primacy of England.[5] Becket reluctantly assented and crossed to England.[6] It must have been at this crisis c. May 23. that the Bishops and Abbots assembled in London, and followed Thomas the Chancellor in rendering fealty to Prince Henry. It is further probable that the King himself intended to cross the Channel at this period. The following entries from the Pipe-Roll of 1162 bear upon the occasion.[7]

BERKSHIRE. *Et in soltis per breve Regis Willielmo Cade £38. 6s.; pro auro ad coronam filii Regis et Regalia paranda.*

LONDON. *Et Willielmo Constabulario 20s. ad summonicionem faciendam contra adventum Regis ad Pentecostem* (viz. May 27, 1162).

The King remaining in Normandy, the following persons were sent as his messengers to the Monks of Christ Church, Canterbury, to enjoin the election of Becket to the Pri-

[1] M. Paris (Wats), ii. 75. Gervase, p. 1382.

[2] Monast. viii. pp. 1275-6, Nos. liv. lx.

[3] M. Paris (Wats), ii. 75.

[4] It will have been at or soon after the Council of Rouen that Roger, Archbishop of York, made some Præbendal gift or arrangement in the presence of "Henry, Priest-Cardinal of the Holy Roman Church and Legate of the Apostolic See," and of Robert, Bishop of Lincoln, Henry (read Hugh), Bishop of Durham; and of the Bishops of Liseux, Evreux, and Seez.—

The ill-transcribed document, from which we venture to deduce thus much, is of no further interest than that it shows certain English Prelates to have been in Normandy at the time of the visitation of the Cardinal Legate, Henry of Pisa, and so far illustrates other documents quoted in the text.

[5] Lingard, vol. ii. p. 204.

[6] Diceto, p. 533.—

Gervase of Canterbury (p. 1382), adds that the King sent Becket to England on other national affairs, not relative to the Primacy.

[7] Rot. Pipe, 8 Hen. II.

1162. c. May. macy. They were Hillary, Bp of Chichester; Bartholomew, Bp of Exeter; Walter, Bp of Rochester; the Abbot of Battle; and Richard de Luci.[1] Normandy.

The said monks, the Bishops and Clergy of the Province of Canterbury, and the Justiciars of England assembled before Prince Henry, at London, and unanimously elected Becket.[1]

May 23. Henry, Bishop of Winchester, published the said election in the Refectory of Westminster Abbey.[1]

June 2. Becket was ordained Priest by Walter, Bishop of Rochester, at Canterbury.[2]

June 3. Becket was consecrated Archbishop by Henry, Bp of Winchester in the presence of the Bps of Ely, Bath, Salisbury, Norwich, Chichester, Chester, Exeter, Lincoln, Rochester, Llandaff,[3] St. Davids, St. Asaph, and Hereford.

Messengers went to the Pope at Montpellier, to obtain the Palliumfor the new Archbishop. They returned to Canterbury on August 10. They were John, Treasurer of York; Adam Abbot of Evesham; John of Salisbury; Jordan of Chichester; Simon, a monk of Canterbury; and Master Arnulf.

c. June. About this time, the King, being at Chinon, addresses Thomas, Archbishop of Canterbury, and all his lieges of Kent, on behalf of the Monks of St. Peter of Gant and their manorial rights at Lewisham and Greenwich. Witnesses, Reginald, Earl of Cornwall; Richard de Humez, William fitz Hamo, Manasser Biset, Henry de Essex, William de Braose, and Walter fitz Robert.[4] Chinon.

c. Sept. K. Henry and Louis are reconciled at an interview which they had *apud Tociacum*, on the Loire, with Pope Alexander.[5] Touci (or Choisi), on the Loire.

Sept. 18. K. Henry supposed to have been at Deols.[6] (Deols).

A few entries on the Pipe-Roll of Michaelmas 1162 are here quoted as indicating something of Court history during the previous fiscal year.—

HAMPSHIRE. *Et ad conducendum thesaurum de Wintoniâ ad Hantonam et de Wintoniâ ad Londoniam pluribus vicibus* £1. 8*s*. 8*d*. *Et Nautis de Esnecâ* 20*s*. *per breve Regis. Et in liberacione Esnechæ ad festum Sanctæ Mariæ Magdalene* (July 22nd) *ad thesaurum transfretandum* £7. 10*s*. *Et pro cerâ ad Summoniciones faciendas et portandam Danegeldam* 14*s*. 4*d*. *Et ad conducendas damas Regis* 60*s*. *per Nicholaum de Sigillo.*

[1] Gervase, p. 1382. Diceto, p. 533.

[2] *In Sabbato Pentecostes.*—An expression which we believe has been quite exceptionally used elsewhere to denote the Saturday *before* Whit-Sunday. That, in this case, would denote May 26; but June 2nd or the Saturday *in* Whitsun-week is preferable.

[3] Godefridus Lanelvensis Episcopus (Gervase).

[4] Cartæ Antiquæ, T.

[5] Chron. Normann. p. 998. Choisi, near Blois, was probably the place. Vide S. T. C. iv. 223.

[6] Stubbs, quoting (with a mark of incredulity) Jaffé, p. 687. Deols was in Berri.

1162. WINCHESTER. *Et pro conducendis pannis filii Regis* 3*s*. 6*d*. *Et in liberacione Pagani probatoris* £7. 10*s*. 9*d*. *per Hugonem de Gundevill.*

SOUTHAMPTON. *In corredio filii Regis* 29*s*. 6*d*. *Et in custamento damarum* £7. 6*s*. 9*d*., *et item aliâ vice* £15. 1*s*. 4*d*. *Et in custamento thesauri . . . . ndi et locandarum navium* iii *vicibus* £4. 16*s*. *Et in liberacione Esnecæ filii Regis* £5. 10*s*. *Et in passagio falconariorum et austrucariorum* 51*s*.

MICHAELMAS, 1162, TO MICHAELMAS, 1163.

December. The King and Queen come to Barfleur, intending to cross over to England, but the wind is contrary, and— Barfleur.

Dec. 25. They pass Christmas at Cherbourg.[1] Cherbourg.

1163. Jan. 25. The King lands at Southampton. Becket, attended by Prince Henry, then his pupil, meets the King.[2] Southampton.

The following charge by the Sheriff of Hampshire is on the Pipe-Roll of Michaelmas, 1163. It refers probably to a period anterior to the King's arrival in England, and it indicates the Viceregal capacity of the Earl of Leicester.

Ad corredium equorum Regis £9 *per breve Comitis Legecestrie et Ricardi de Luci.*

The following charges by the same Sheriff indicate that the King came accompanied by the Queen and some of the Royal family, and that the Queen was resident in Hampshire after the King had left.

In corredio infantum Regis £16 *per breve Regis. In corredio Reginæ* £35 *per breve Regis. In corredio infantum Regis* £11. 10*s*. *per breve Reginæ.*

Again, the following charges by the Fermor of Southampton, probably allude to the arrival of the King's Treasure and of the Princesses Matilda and Elianor.

Vicecomitissa de Rothomago r. c. etc. In passagio thesauri 31*s*. 8*d*. *In custumento ad conducendas filias Regum* 7*s*. 4*d*.

c. Feb. In this month it would seem that the King visited Oxford.[3] Oxford. In the Pipe-Roll of the following Michaelmas the Sheriff of Oxfordshire charges—*In reparacione domorum Regis de Oxenfort* 10*s*.

A Charter, dated at Oxford, may well belong to this date. Thereby the King confirms to Warner de Lusoriis

[1] This is the statement of the Norman Chronicle (p. 999). Gervase (p. 1383) says, that the King landed at Southampton on December 20 (1162), and that Becket went to meet him, and, finding it impossible to get back to Canterbury by Christmas-day, celebrated mass at St. Paul's, London. We suppose that Becket *expected* the King and took the journey; but to no purpose.

[2] Diceto, p. 534, b.

[3] Hist. Abingdon, ii. 228–9.

1163. c. Feb. the land which he held in the time of King Henry, the King's grandfather. Witnesses, Thomas, Abp of Canterbury; Henry, Bp of Winchester; Reginald, Earl of Cornwall; Richard de Humez, Constable; Richard de Luci; Hugh Wach.[1] Oxford.

In the same month, probably, the King visited Salisbury.[2] Salisbury.

The Queen would seem to have been resident in Wiltshire about this time, for at Michaelmas the Sheriff charges payments, viz., *Johanni de Waurei et servientibus Reginæ ad faciendam soltam ipsius* £44. 8*s*. *per breve Regis. Et eisdem* £25 *ad faciendam aliam soltam ipsius per breve Regis.*

March 3. The King holds a Council in London.[3] London.

March 6. The King still in London. The business before the Council was concerning the vacant See of London.[4]

The residence of the Court in London is illustrated by the following charges in the Pipe-Roll of the year. The Sheriff of London and Middlesex had paid—

Ad corredium Regis et ad negocia pincernarum 118*s*. *per breve Regis. Ad corredium Ricardi filii Regis* £10. 6*s*. 8*d*. *per breve Regis. Et pro p'ca*[5] *in porcis et ovis et minutis rebus contra festum filii Regis* 100*s*. *Et Alnod pro domibus Regis mundandis et pro juncis* 10*s*.

March 8. The King is sitting *in Curiâ* at Westminster. Before him is decided a Suit-at-Law between Robert, Bishop of Lincoln, and Robert, Abbot of St. Albans.[6] The King's Assessors are— Westminster.

Thomas, Abp of Canterbury; Roger, Abp of York; Henry, Bp of Winchester; Nigel, Bp of Ely; William, Bp of Norwich; Hilary, Bp of Chichester; Josceline, Bp of Sarum; Walter, Bp of Rochester; Hugh, Bp of Durham; Gilbert, Bp of Hereford; Bartholomew, Bp of Exeter; Richard, Bp of Coventry; Godfrey, Bp of St. Asaph; Lawrence, Abbot of Westminster; William, Abbot of Ramsey; Gregory, Abbot of Malmesbury; Clement, Abbot of York; Reginald, Abbot of Pershore: Geoffry, Archdeacon

[1] Cartæ Antiquæ, N. 25.
[2] Chron. Abingdon, ii. 228–9.
[3] Palgrave's British Commonwealth. Appendix, p. xxii.
[4] Diceto; Imag. Hist. 534, b.
[5] Whatever word may be here intended its meaning will have been 'payment,' 'outlay.'
[6] Diceto, p. 533. M. Paris, vol. ii. p. 81.

1163. March 8. of Canterbury; Richard, Archdeacon of Poitiers; Robert, Earl of Leicester; Hugh, Earl of Norfolk; William, Earl of Arundel; Richard de Luci; Richard de Humez, Constable; Henry fitz Gerold, Chamberlain. Westminster.

The three following Deeds, all dated at Westminster, doubtless belong to the same occasion.—

(1.) To Kenilworth Priory, attested by Thomas, Abp of Canterbury; Geoffry, Archdeacon of Canterbury; Robert, Earl of Leicester; Richard de Humez, Constable; Henry fitz Gerold, Chamberlain; Manasser Biset, Dapifer; and Josceline de Baillol.[1]

(2.) To Sibton Abbey (Suffolk), attested by Thomas, Abp of Canterbury; Robert, Earl of Leicester; Richard de Luci; Richard de Humez; and Manasser Biset.[2]

(3.) To Eustace Cade, son of William Cade, giving ten librates of land in Navenebi, which were of the fee of Roger the Poitevin and of the honour of Lancaster. Witnesses, Geoffry, Archdeacon of Canterbury; Richard, Archdeacon of Poitiers; R., Earl of Leicester; Earl Geoffry (of Essex); Richard de Luci; Henry fitz Gerold, Chamberlain; Gosceline de Baillol; Richard de Canville; William Malet, Dapifer; and William de Cainneto.[3]

Perhaps also a writ addressed by the King to the Barons of the Exchequer, and dated at Westminster, belongs to the same occasion. It is in favour of the Nuns of Fontevrault, and is attested by Nigel, Bp of Ely; Robert, Earl of Leicester; Richard de Luci.[4]

March 17. The King is at Canterbury. He and Archbishop Becket attend the Monks' procession.[5] Canterbury.

March 19. The King and Prince Henry are at Dover, and are met by Theodoric, Comte of Flanders, and Comte Philip, his son. A treaty made between the respective parties embodies the military services which the Comtes of Flanders were bound to render to the Kings of England. The Sureties on the King of England's side, that he should observe his part of the treaty were— Dover.

Richard de Humez, Constable; Reginald de St. Walery;

[1] Monasticon, vi. 224. vii.
[2] Monasticon, v. 559. ii.
[3] Cart. Orig. In Offic. Ducat. Lancast.
[4] Monasticon, vii. 1085.
[5] Gervase, p. 1384. The day in question was Palm Sunday.

1163. March 19. Richard de Luci; Henry fitz Gerold, Chamberlain; Bernard de St. Walery; Manasser Biset, Dapifer; Roger de Cailli; Hugh, Earl of Norfolk; William, Earl of Arundel; Robert, son of the Earl of Leicester; Earl Geoffrey (of Essex); and Hugh, Earl of Chester. Dover.

Another and contemporary Charter settles the services which the vassals of the Comtes of Flanders owed to the King of England. This Charter is attested by—

Thomas, Abp of Canterbury; John, Earl of Ponthieu (*de Puntivo*); Reginald de St. Walery; Richard de Luci; Richard de Humez, Constable; Manasser Biset, Dapifer; Bernard de St. Walery; Henry de Essex; Walkeline Maminot; Henry fitz Gerold, Chamberlain; Joceline de Baillol, Hugh de Dovre, William de Crievequer, Roger de Cailli, Hugh, Earl of Chester; William, Earl De Ferrars; Hugh de Longchamp; William de Tracy; William fitz Aldelm.[1]

The Pipe-Roll supplies an entry illustrative of the King's visit to Dover.—The Sheriff of Kent, Hugh de Dover, charges—*In liberacione* v *militum de dominicâ familiâ Regis* £26.

March 19. Pope Alexander's letter to Gilbert, Bishop of Hereford, in approval of his translation to the See of London. Dated at Paris.[2]

King Henry's letter to the same, urging his acceptance of the See of London. Dated at Windsor and attested by Thomas, Archbishop of Canterbury.[3] Windsor.

March 24. Alleged day of Foliot's translation to the See of London.[4]

March 31. The King is at Windsor, and busied with the trial of Henry de Essex, who had been accused by Robert de Montfort of cowardice and treason, viz., that he, the said Henry, at the Battle of Counsylth (in July, 1157), being at the time Constable of England, had cast away the Royal standard and fled, proclaiming that the King was killed.[5]

A Royal Charter, dated at Windsor, may well belong to this occasion. It is attested by Richard de Humez, Constable (of Normandy); Richard de Luci; Henry fitz Gerold, Chamberlain; and Richard de Camville.[6]

c. April. From Windsor the King goes to Reading, where Henry Reading.

1 Rymer's Fœdera, i. 23. Hearne's Liber Niger i. 33.

2, 3 Gilbert Foliot's Epistles, 146, 147.

4 Hardy's Fasti, ii. 282.

5 Palgrave (ut supra). Appendix, p. xxii.

6 Monasticon, vii. 618.

1163. c. April. de Essex and Montfort try issues by 'Wager of Battle.' Essex, being defeated, is outlawed, and his estates confiscated. He is shorn a monk at Reading.[1] Reading

From Reading the King goes to Wallingford. Wallingford.

From Wallingford the King, accompanied by Richard de Luci, goes on an expedition against Wales. The English army ravages Carmarthenshire.[2] Wales.

The following charges on the Pipe-Roll of Michaelmas, 1163, are illustrative of this Welsh expedition :—

GLOUCESTERSHIRE. *In reparacione capellæ et domorum (Regis)* £15. 12*s*. 5*d*. *In liberacione Walteri de Clifford* £7. 5*s*. *Et pro anulis obsidum et corredio ipsorum* £8. 14*d*. *Et pro municione portatâ in Walliam* £31. 7*s*. 6*d*. *Et in liberacione militum et servientum in exercitu de Walliâ, per Willielmum de Bellocampo* £70. 9*s*. 1*d*.

WILTSHIRE. *Pro carectis locandis ad conducendos obsides de Bristol ad Wintoniam* 30*s*. 6*d*.

SHROPSHIRE. *In liberacione unius militis et* 310 *servientum et Walensium de Blanco monasterio (Oswestry)* £50. 13*s*. 8*d*.

c. June. After the Welsh expedition it is probable that the King went northwards, visiting Carlisle and York. The only evidence on the point is supplied by the Pipe-Rolls :—

CARLISLE. *In conductu venacionis Regis* 13*s*. *Et Gaufrido Monacho et Radulpho fil. Stephani* £100 *ad corredium Regis per breve ipsius*. Carlisle.

YORKSHIRE. *Bertram de Bulmer, r. c. etc. Et Radulpho filio Stephani et Willielmo de Ostilli* 100 *marcas per breve Regis, ad corredium ipsius. Et in conductu venacionis Regis de Eboraco ad Lundoniam et in custumento ipsius* £4. 4*s*. York.

SOMETHING SHOULD here be said as to the movements of Thomas, Archbishop of Canterbury, after the Treaty of Dover, on the 19th of March.

On the 28th of April, the Archbishop had recently left London, that being the most probable date for the enthronement of Gilbert, late Bishop of Hereford, in the See of London;[3] at which ceremony the

[1] Palgrave (ut supra), p. xxiii. Brakelond's Chronicle, p. 52. Hist. of Abingdon, ii. 229.

[2] Palgrave (ut supra), p. xxiii. The King's course through Wales is thus described by Giraldus.—*Per maritima de Guladmorgan* (Glamorgan) *et Gouher* (Gower) *viam versus Caermarthin et usque Pencadair intrando, et per Elenith* (Elvel) *et Melenith revertendo.*

[3] Diceto, (p. 535), gives this date. Other less weighty authorities, give March 24 as the day of the Bishop's translation. Gervase (p. 1384), placing it in January, must be altogether wrong.

1163. Bishop of Rochester, and Geoffrey Archdeacon of Canterbury, officiated as Becket's Vicars.

On May 19–21, the Archbishops of Canterbury and York attended Pope Alexander III. at the Council of Tours.[1] And this was after a proposal by, and with the full concurrence of, K. Henry in a Council of the Realm.[2]

July 1. The King is at Woodstock, where Malcolm, King of Scotland, Rese, Prince of S. Wales, and Owen, Prince of N. Wales, attend and do homage to him and his son.[3] Woodstock.

Becket opposes the King on the question of the Dane-geld.[4]

By Charter dated at Woodstock, and clearly on this occasion, K. Henry confirms the grants of Robert, Earl of Leicester, to Nun-Eaton (Warwickshire), a cell to the Priory of Fontevrault. There were witnesses of the King's Charter, Thomas, Abp of Canterbury; *William* (read Gilbert), Bp of London; Robert, Bp of Lincoln; M. (Malcolm), King of Scotland; William, the King's brother; Earl Reginald (of Cornwall); William, Earl of Gloucester; Richard de Humet, Constable; Richard de Luci; Henry fitz Gerold, Chamberlain; William de Crevequer, Hugh de Longchamp, William Malet, William de Hastinge, Simon fitz Peter, Peter de Mara, and John Mauduit.[5]

July 1-7. The Oxfordshire Pipe-Roll of Michaelmas, 1163, contributes its quota of evidence as to this Royal visit to Woodstock. The Sheriff charges the Crown with the following payments.—*In operacione vivariorum de Wudestoch £7 per breve Regis. Et pro feno conducendo ad Wudestoch* 60 *sol.* Woodstock.

c. July. The King and Becket are in London. Simon fitz Peter, a Justiciar recently in Eyre in Bedfordshire, complained to the King of having been insulted in Court at Dunstable, by one Philip de Broc (or Brois), a Canon of Lincoln, whom having been acquitted of homicide by the Court London.

[1] Pope Alexander III. was now a Refugee, and domiciled at Tours. He occurs there on January 9th of this same year (Monast. ii. 605).

[2] The Pope, in a letter dated at Paris on March 18th previous, acknowledges and accepts the proposal of the King in Council. The Pope further covenants, that the attendance of the English Bishops shall work no prejudice to the King or his successors, nor form ground for the introduction of a *new custom* in the realm of England. (Hearne's Liber Niger, i. pp. 41, 42).

[3] Palgrave (ut supra). Appendix, p. cccxxxv. Diceto, p. 535.

[4] Pontigny S. T. C. i. 113. Grim. S. T. C. i. 21.

[5] Old Monasticon, i. 318. The New Monasticon omits to notice the monastery of Nun-Eaton.

1163. c. July. Spiritual of the Diocese, the Justiciar had attempted to re-arraign, and had been resisted with insolence. London.

The King now insisted on a new Trial, while Becket carried the point that such new Trial should be in Court Spiritual. (De Broc was soon after tried at Canterbury by such a Court. He was acquitted of homicide, but heavily sentenced for contempt of a King's Officer).[1]

July 22. Summons returnable at Westminster in Becket's suit against Roger, Earl of Clare, relative to the Earl's tenure at Tunbridge.[2]

c. August. King Henry, at Windsor, makes an ungracious speech about Becket's having absolved William de Eynsford to gratify the King.[3] Windsor.

c. Sept. About this time, Gerard, Abbot of Vendome, sends two brethren to England to complain to the King about the extortions of one, Rodolf, Henry's Seneschal in Xantoigne. The King orders restitution to be made to the Abbot by hand of Stephen de Tours, Castellan ("Custos of the Tower") of Chinon.[4]

Sept. 4. Pope Alexander, at Bourges, exhorts Gilbert (Foliot), Bishop of London, to quicken K. Henry's attachment to the Church.[5]

MICHAELMAS, 1163, TO MICHAELMAS, 1164.

1163. Sept. 30. Pope Alexander III. comes to reside at Sens, where Hugh, Archbishop of Sens, entertains him for a year and half.[6]

Oct. 1. K. Henry holds a Council or Synod in London,—probably at Westminster. The "*Summa Causa Concilii*" is stated by one Writer to have been that the Archbishop of Canterbury should be formally acknowledged to be "Primate of All England." The Archbishop of York was present, and opposed the claim.[7] London. Westminster.

But it was at this Council of London that the afterwards famous question of the "Customs of the Realm" was first discussed by the King and the Bishops. The King complained of the venality and excesses of Archdeacons.

[1] S. T. C. Fitz Stephen, i. 214. Pontigny, i. 114. Grim. i. 22. Boseham, vii. 101.
[2] Diceto, p. 536. S. T. C. i. 208.
[3] S. T. C. Fitz Stephen, i. 209.
[4] Gallici Scriptores, xii. 488.
[5] S. T. C. vi. 85. Ep. GF., ccclix.
[6] Gallici Scriptores, xii. 285, 296.
[7] S. T. C. i. 111.

1163. Oct. 1. He also demanded that Clerks, accused of crime, should be tried and punished by lay-tribunals. Westminster.

Becket and all the Bishops, except Hilary of Chichester, opposed the King. At length Becket and the Bishops promised to observe the "Royal Customs," *salvo ordine suo;* while Hilary of Chichester promised to observe them *bonâ fide.*[1]

Oct. 2. The King deprived Becket of the Tutorship of Prince Henry, and of the custody of the Castles and Honours of Eye and Berkhamsted; and quitted London early in the day. London.

c. Oct. The King and Becket have an interview in a field near Northampton. Becket would concede nothing about the "Customs" without the saving clause—*salvo ordine nostro.* The King and Archbishop part in anger. Northampton.

About this time Arnulf, Bishop of Liseux, having offended the King in some matter, comes over to England, and succeeds in pacifying Henry as to the said offence.[2] He then advises the King to antagonize Becket by detaching the Bishops from his cause.[3] Within the last three months of this year, Bishop Arnulf and Richard, Archdeacon of Poitiers, are said by Diceto to have crossed the sea six times as Ambassadors of Henry, to confer with Pope Alexander, then at Sens, on the subject of *the Customs.*

King Henry, at Gloucester, obtains promises from the Archbishop of York and the Bishop of Lincoln that they will be prepared to confirm the Customs.[4] Gloucester.

Hilary, Bishop of Chichester, on behalf of the King, confers with Becket at Lentham (probably Lenham, Kent), but fails to persuade Becket to yield.[5]

Within the last three months of this year it is supposable that the King went Northward.—

At Michaelmas, 1164, the Sheriff of Derbyshire charges the Crown with a sum of £9. 8*s.* 2*d.* which he had expended by Royal Order. "*In corredio Regis apud Pech,*" that is, the King, within the previous fiscal year, had been at Peak Castle, in Derbyshire. Peak Castle.

Also the Sheriff of Lincolnshire alleges the following disbursement:—

"*In soltis per breve Regis Waltero de Amundevill* £7. 14 *sol.*

[1] S. T. C. ii. 251, ii. 88. Gervase, 1384.
[2] S. T. C. Pontigny, i. 117.
[3] S. T. C. Pontigny, i. 119 & ii. 6, correcting Hoveden (282, b), who says that Arnulf came to England professedly to mediate between the King and Becket.
[4] S. T. C. Pontigny, i. 120.
[5] S. T. C. Pontigny, ibidem.

1163. c. Oct. *qui liberati fuerunt Clericis Domini Papæ;*" that is, we suppose, the King had been followed northwards by certain Clerks, Envoys from the Papal Court at Sens, and Walter de Amundevill, then farming the City of Lincoln, had paid the said money to the said Clerks by the King's order, the King issuing a Writ or Warrant to the Sheriff of Lincolnshire to reimburse Amundevill. Lincoln.

Nov. 9. A letter from Pope Alexander to Gilbert, Bishop of London, dated at Sens, exhorts the Bishop to counteract the ill-feeling which had arisen between the King and the English Church.[1]

c. Dec. Pope Alexander sends Philip, Abbot of Elemosyna (L'Aumône) to England, as mediator between the King and Becket.[2] The Abbot of L'Aumône, having associated Robert de Melun, Bishop (it should be 'Elect') of Hereford, and John Comte of Vendome, has an interview with Becket at Herges. They present to Becket expostulatory letters of the Pope and Cardinals.[2]

King Henry is at Woodstock,[3] or more probably came over from Woodstock to Oxford,[3] where, in the Castle, he had an interview with Archbishop Becket, accompanied by the Abbot of L'Aumône, the Bishop (Elect) of Hereford, and the Comte of Vendome. The Archbishop now promised to obey the "Customs" and to obey the King *in bono* (*in what was right*; that is). Woodstock. Oxford Castle.

Sund. Dec. 22. Robert de Melun consecrated Bishop of Hereford, by Archbishop Becket at Canterbury.[4]

Dec. 25-31. King Henry seems to have held his Christmas Court at Berchamstede, the custody of which Castle and Honour he had in October previous taken from Becket. Berkhampstead, Hertfordshire.

At the close of the current fiscal year, the Sheriff of Hampshire charges—"*Et ad portanda vaisella Regis contra Natale de Wintoniâ ad Bercamsted 9 sol. et 3 den.*;" that is, the Royal plate had been sent from the Treasury at Winchester, anticipatory of the King's need thereof at Christmas last at Berkhampstead.

A Royal Charter, dated at Berchamstede, may well belong to the same date. It is attested by Earl Geoffrey de Mandeville, Richard de Luci, Reginald de St. Walery, and William Cade.[5]

[1] S. T. C. vi. 92.
[2] S. T. C. Pontigny, i. 121.
[3] S. T. C. Pontigny, i. 122; Boseham, vii. 113.
[4] Gervase, p. 1386.
[5] Monasticon, vii. 653. Reginald de St. Walery and Rotroc, Bishop of Evreux, were, in 1163,

Sometime in the year 1163, died Philip de Harcourt, Bishop of Baieux.[1]

A.D. 1164.

1164. c. Jan. At this period, Arnulf, Bishop of Liseux, and Richard de Ilchester, Archdeacon of Poictiers, were probably discharging the last of several embassies to the Papal Court at Sens. Their demands on the King's behalf were "the Legation of all England for Roger, Archbishop of York," and that a Papal Mandate should issue to Becket and the English Bishops enjoining the observance of the Ancient Customs and Dignities of the Realm. The Pope and Cardinals sent an answer moderative of the King's demands.[2]

Jan. 13-28. The King and his son Henry preside over the Council of Clarendon. (The boy was not nine years old). Clarendon.

The recognition of the "Customs" drawn up at this Council, is said to have had the assent of—

Thomas, Abp of Canterbury; Roger, Abp of York; Gilbert, Bp of London; Henry, Bp of Winchester; Nigel, Bp of Ely; William, Bp of Norwich; Robert, Bp of Lincoln; Hilary, Bp of Chichester; Joseline, Bp of Salisbury; Richard, Bp of Chester; Bartholomew, Bp of Exeter; Robert, Bp of Hereford; David, Bp of Menevia (St. David's), and Roger (Bishop) elect of Worcester.[3]

There were present, Robert, Earl of Leicester; Reginald, Earl of Cornwall; Conan, Comte of Brittany; John, Comte of Ewe; Roger, Earl of Clare; Earl Geoffrey de Mandeville; Hugh, Earl of Chester; William, Earl of Arundel; Earl Patric (of Wiltshire); William, Earl de Ferrars; Richard de Luci, Reginald de St. Walery, Roger Bigod, Reginald de Warren, Roger (Richer ?) de Aquila, William de Braose, Richard de Camvill, Nigel de Mobrai, Simon de Beauchamp, Humfrey de Bohun, Matthew de Hereford, Walter de Meduana, Manasser Biset, Dapifer; William Malet, William de

recognizors of the Royal revenues throughout Normandy (Chron. Normann. p. 999). We have other proof that about this time St. Walery was again in England.

William Cade was of the retinue of Queen Elianor (vide infra, p. 69).

[1] Chron. Normann p. 999. Vide supra p. 21. *n.*

[2] Gervase (p. 1385) gives January 13th as the date of the Council. M. Paris and Diceto (p. 536) give January 25th,—a more likely date, seeing that the 'Recognition,' as it was called, of the Customs was embodied in an Instrument expressly dated January 28th.

[3] This Prelate, according to the best authorities, was consecrated on August 23, 1164, and enthroned February 2, 1165 (Wharton's Anglia Sacra, i. 476). Diceto (p. 536), giving his consecration as on August 26, 1163, is manifestly in error.

1164. Jan. 13-28. Curci, Robert de Dunstanvill, Joseline de Lanvall,[1] William de Caisneto, Geoffrey de Ver, William de Hastinges, Hugh de Morvill, Alan de Nevill, Simon fitz Peter, William Maudut, Chamberlain; John Maudut, John Mareschall,[2] and Peter de Mara.[3] Clarendon.

Two Templars, viz. Richard de Hastings and Tostes de St. Omer, are noted as treating with the Archbishop in the course of the Council of Clarendon.

A Royal Charter, dated at Clarendon, seems to belong to this period. It is attested by Geoffrey, Archdeacon of Canterbury; Henry fitz Gerold, Chamberlain; Manasser Biset, Reginald de Courtenay, Josceline de Baillol, and William de Ostill.[4]

On January 30th, William the King's brother died at Rouen.[5]

February. In February, the King, having apparently received the moderative answer given by the Pope and Cardinals to the embassy of Arnulf, Bishop of Liseux, and the Archdeacon of Poictiers, was greatly dissatisfied therewith, and, according to one account, sent another embassy with still larger demands. South England.

This then was the Embassy conducted by Geoffrey Ridel, Archdeacon of Canterbury, and John of Oxford. They were charged by Henry to demand the "Legation of All England" for Roger, Archbishop of York. They were further to solicit from Alexander a Papal Confirmation of the "Constitutions of Clarendon." The latter solicitation had the concurrence of both the Archbishops, and the King is said to have forwarded letters of each in support of his request.[6]

One account is that the Pope now offered the Legation to Henry himself, with precautions against his misusing it. The Pope's subsequent statements were, that he had refused to confirm the 'Customs and Dignities' (as he calls the Constitutions of Clarendon), but that he had conceded to the King letters of Legation, to be granted to the Archbishop of York, provided that such letters were not to be handed to York, without Becket's knowledge and will.[6]

[1] Probably Josceline de Baillol was the witness; or possibly William de Lanvall; or perhaps both, the transcriber having omitted a portion of each name.

[2] It was John, the King's Marshal, whose complaints against Becket afterwards led to the Archbishop's attaint at Northampton.

[3] MS. Cotton. Claud. B. fo. 26.

[4] Monasticon, vi. 474. Num. i.

[5] Chron. Normann. p. 999. Rot. Normann. (Stapleton) ii. ccxv. At Michaelmas, 1164, the Sheriff of Norfolk and Suffolk accounts for half a year's revenues of the lands of William, the King's brother (then *in manu Regis*).

[6] S. T. C. iv. 2. Epist. cxcviii. cxcix.

1164. Feb. 27. Pope Alexander at Sens writes to Becket, telling him about K. Henry's two missions and his own replies to Henry.[1]

In another letter, undated, Alexander promises that in case the letters of Legatiou were handed (by Henry) to York, he, the Pope, would forthwith except Becket's person, church, and city from all Legatine authority whatever.[2]

c. March. K. Henry, receiving the above Letters of Legation, returned them to the Pope indignantly. The King's Ambassadors on this occasion are only described by the initial letters R. & H.— South England.

They write from Sens to the King, in terms which show that all idea of the Legation being granted to York was at an end. They tell the King that they had obtained from the Pope more for the monks of St. Augustine (Canterbury), than their predecessors (Ridel and Oxford) had obtained. The latter they accuse of having misled and misrepresented the King. Certain Cardinals, they say, have written to the King, to tell him of Ridel's and Oxford's *malice*. They tell how Becket's messengers to the Papal Court are always slandering the King. They enumerate three Cardinals (*Neapolis*, *Portuensis*, and *Papiensis*) as opposed to Becket.[3]

This letter is partly explained by another, written from Sens by Henry Pisanus, to Becket's most trusted friend John, Bishop of Poictiers. The Pope, it seems, advised by the Cardinals and wishing to satisfy Henry, had peremptorily ordered Becket to give the Benediction to Clarembald, that Abbot of St. Augustine's, who, backed by the King, had refused to make any profession to the Archbishop.

After the Council of Clarendon it is probable that the King remained for two months in the Southern or South Western Counties. The Queen would appear to have been resident in the same latitude most of the summer. The few indicia we have on the matter are contained in the Sheriff's accounts of Michaelmas, 1164.—

Thus the Sheriff of Devon had some time in the year paid £20 to Ralph fitz Stephen, in the *Camerâ Curiæ*, by the King's order. The same Sheriff had paid the Queen £51 by hand of William Cade, and £40 by hand of John de Waurei.

The Sheriff of Wiltshire, under the King's Order, had paid £13. 6*s*. 8*d*. on account of the Queen's expenses.

The Sheriff of Hampshire charges—*In corredio Reginæ*

[1, 2] S. T. C. iv. Epist. cxcviii, cxcix.

[3] Epistle (S. T. C.) ccclxix.

1164. c. March. *£40 per breve Regis. Et item in corredio Reginæ £70 per breve Regis, per Ricardum Archidiaconum Pictaviæ et Alanum de Neovill.* South England.

About this time the King appears to have visited Porchester.[1] This was to meet Rotrou, Bishop of Evreux,[2] who had in the previous year acted as Chief Commissioner in an inquiry into the King's Norman Revenues, and who now landed in England, probably with relation to political matters in France, and the expectation of a rupture with Louis. The Bishop's visit to England resulted in his attempting a compromise between the King and Becket. Porchester.

K. Henry had at this time an interview with Becket at Woodstock. Though there is authority for such a meeting,[3] it does not satisfactorily appear what passed thereat, and there may be some misapprehension on the subject. Woodstock.

However, a Royal Charter, dated at Woodstock, is good evidence of the King and Bishop having adjourned thither. It is attested by Rotrou, Bishop of Evreux; by John of Oxford; Richard, Chaplain; Henry fitz Gerold; and Josceline de Baillol.[4]

Immediately afterwards, the Bishop of Evreux, and Richard de Humez, Constable of Normandy, crossed the Channel, and, as will appear, their first business was an embassy to Louis. At the following Michaelmas, the Sheriff of Southampton makes the following charges in the Pipe-Roll:—

Et pro quatuor navibus ad transfretandos Episcopum Ebroicensem et Ricardum de Humet £6 per breve Regis.

Et in liberacione sciprorum ad portandum thesaurum cum Ricardo de Humet £7. 10s. per breve Regis.[5]

Another charge by the same Sheriff savours rather of concern with Henry's continental dominions than with the Court of Sens. It is—"*Pro navibus ad opus Archidiaconi Pictaviæ* (*Richard of Ilchester*) *et Vicecomitis de Casteldun* (*Château-Dun in the Orleannois*) *et Willelmi de Vernon £4. 10s.*"[5]

There is some ground for supposing that that Lieutenant of King Henry, whom John, Bishop of Poictiers, in his correspondence with Becket, nicknames *Luscus* (or, the one-eyed), was no other than the Bishop's own Archdeacon, Richard of Ilchester.

[1] Pontigny S. T. C. i. 128.

[2] Hoveden, (p. 282. b) calls Rotrou "Archbishop of Rouen" by mistake, or rather by anticipation. Hugh, Archbishop of Rouen, was living. He died in October, 1164. Rotrou de Newburgh was not translated to Rouen till 1165.

[3] Professor Stubbs, quoting Fitz Stephen, S. T. C. i. 218. Lyttelton, ii. pp. 366-7.

[4] Monasticon, iv. 92.

[5] Rot. Pip. 10 Hen II. Suthants.

1164. c. March. About this time, the said Bishop, writing to Becket, tells him the news that "Luscus had returned to Poictiers, but had issued no edicts;" and again, that "Luscus was summoning the army of Aquitaine to resist King Louis, if the latter should enter Auvergne;" and again, that "the result of the Bishop of Evreux,' and Richard de Humez' mission to Louis, to negociate peace (with Henry) was not known."

April 1. A letter from the Pope at Sens to Becket is curious, though importing no more than a date. The Pope has heard that Becket "*occasione cujusdam excessûs,*" is proposing "*a missarum celebratione cessare.*" The Pope excuses Becket's fault as involuntary, absolves him, and desires him to resume his ministrations.[1]

April 12. King Henry, it is probable, kept the feast of Easter in London. At the close of the fiscal year the Sheriff of Hampshire charges,— London.

"*Et ad conducendam archam thesauri ad Pascam de Wintoniâ ad Londoniam 5 sol. et 8 den.*"

Sun. April 19. King Henry was at Reading; and on that day Archbishop Thomas, attended by ten Suffragan Bishops, consecrated the Conventual Church of Reading in the presence of the King.[2] Reading.

In the same year as the consecration of Reading Church, there was according to one authority (Boseham)[3] a translation of K. Edward the Confessor's remains at Westminster, at which both the King and Becket attended. Other authorities,[4] placing this Translation in the year 1163, are less to be regarded than Boseham. But the day, which would probably still further determine the year, is nowhere given.[5]

April 22. Octavian (Victor IV. Antipope), died at Lucca.[6]

Guy of Crema elected in his place by title of Pascal III.

April 26. Pope Alexander consecrates the Church of St. Columba at Sens.[7]

May 16. John, Bishop of Poictiers, writes from that city to Becket, dating his letter "*in festo Sancti Albani animæ.*"—

The Bishop gladly understands from Becket's letter, that Becket's promise to observe the "Customs" was not absolute nor like that of others who had promised.—Reports Pope Alexander's regret about the "concession," such as it was, which the Pope had made to the Archbishop of York.—Omits to write about Octavian's death,[8] which was sure to have been reported to Becket by friends at the Papal Court.—States how he, the Bishop, abstains from the *Curia* (at Sens) advisedly,

[1] S. T. C. Epistle cci. Also S. T. C. i. 127, 218.
[2] M. Paris, vol. i. p. 102. Monasticon, iv. p. 31, note. Chron. Normann. p. 999. Boseham S. T. C. vii. 97.
[3] Boseham S. T. C. vii. 97.
[4] M. Paris, Annals of Waverley; Annals of Winchester.
[5] See Professor Stubbs' note to Benedictus Abbas II. cxxxiv; where it is shown that the only recognized day of K. Edw. Conf. Translation, viz. October 13, originated in the Ceremony of A.D. 1269.
[6] S. T. C. iv. 242.
[7] Gall. Script. xii. 288.
[8] See S. T. C. Epistle ccclxx as to the arrival of this news at Sens.

1164. the Poictevins reporting his attendance there to King Henry, as injurious to the King's interests. He, however, employs agents at the *Curia*.—Speaks of and suggests measures to be taken in contemplation of Becket's possible visit to Sens.—Recommends Becket to cultivate intimacy with the Abbot and Convent of Pontigny.—Proposes himself some day to take refuge at Pontigny.—Recommends Master Albert, Cardinal of St. Laurence, as trustworthy, like (Henry) Pisanus.—Has not yet learnt the result of the Bishop of Evreux' and Richard de Humez'[1] mission from K. Henry to K. Louis.—Speaks of John of Salisbury suffering exile for the Church's sake.[2]

A Council at Rheims concerning aid to be sent to the Holy Land.[3]

May. Of King Heury's movements during these three months we are unable to trace with precision a single item. One of the Chronicles speaks of Welsh insurrections under Rese and Owen during this summer.[4] Another reports Prince Rese's attack on the Welsh estates of Earl Roger de Clare, and the reconquest of Cardigan from the English.[5] Welsh Border.

May, June, July.

It is probable that King Henry visited Gloucestershire and other counties of the Border. The following extracts from the Pipe-Rolls suggest as much, and clearly allude to a troubled state of relations between England and Wales.

GLOUCESTERSHIRE. *In conductu venacionis Regis de Glocestriâ ad Wirecestriam* xix *den. Et pro securibus et picois et Beschiis ad opus Regis* xv *sol. et* vii *den.* Gloucestershire.

WORCESTERSHIRE. *Pro vino Regis* viii *Lib.* v *sol. Pro hostagiis remanentibus* xv *Lib.* xv *sol. et* ijd. *Pro compedibus latronum et obsidum* v *sol. et* vii *den. Idem Vicecomes (Willelmus de Bellocampo) reddit compotum de veteri firmâ de Gloucestria. In camerâ Regis Radulfo filio Stephani* cx *sol. per breve Regis.* Worcestershire.

HEREFORDSHIRE. *In corredio trium obsidum et pro careto thesauri de Herefordiâ ad Salopesburiam* xljs. *per breve Regis.* Herefordshire.

SALOPSHIRE. *Pro equis ad opus Regis* c *sol. per breve Regis. Et in operationibus Regis et aliis ejus serviciis in Salopescire, et in liberatione servientum* xc *Lib.* ix *sol. et* x *den.* Shropshire.

c. July 4. "*Paucis diebus post Natalem Apostolorum*" (June 29), "Luscus" and Simon de Turnebu, Constable of Thouars, and Henry Panetarius, came to Poictiers with a mandate for John, Bishop of Poictiers.

[1] In August following, De Humez is said to have taken Combort 'in Brittany' (?) by siege, (Chron. Normann.).

[2] Epistle (G. F.), ccccIxiij.

[3] Nicolas; Chron. Hist. p. 248.

[4] Chron. Normann. p. 999. "Rese and Owen, his uncle, *fidem non servantes*."

[5] Brut-y-Tywysogion. See also S. T. C. iv. 236,

1164. c. July 5. Bishop John set out for Tours, to meet and consult with Rotrou, Bishop of Evreux, Richard de Humez, and William fitz Hamo.

Bishop John arrived at Tours (70 miles North by East of Poictiers), but found that the aforesaid persons had left that day for Luches (Loches in Touraine, about 30 miles South of Tours), en route for Auvergne (180 miles S.E. of Tours).

Bishop John hastens to Loches, where he overtakes William fitz Hamo and Hugh de Claeris. From Loches he writes to Becket, to Rotrou, Bishop of Evreux, and to the Abbot of Pontigny. The Abbot he requests to meet him at Sens, whither he, Bishop John, now intends to proceed. He desires Becket to send Turstin de Buruns (to Sens, to meet him).[1]

August. Richard de Humez takes ('Combort, in Bretagne,' says the Norman Chronicle, but surely there was no disturbance in Bretagne at this period, and the place taken was) Comborn in the Limousin, a province adjoining Auvergne.

Sund. Aug. 23. Roger (son of Robert de Caen, first Earl of Gloucester) consecrated Bishop of Worcester, by Archbishop Thomas, at Canterbury.

c. Aug. 24–31. K. Henry at Woodstock. Archbishop Becket attempts to gain an interview with the King, but, being refused, returns to Canterbury.[2] Woodstock.

According to the most consistent account, it was now that Becket, alleging a wish to consult the Pope at Sens, made two ineffectual attempts to embark at Romney.[3]

c. Sept. 1–10. Whenever the attempt to quit England was made, it was followed by an interview at Woodstock, whereat the King reproached Becket for the said attempt.[4] Woodstock.

Sept. 14. K. Henry appears to have been in London. This was the day on which Archbishop Becket lay under summons to appear in the *Curiâ Regis* at Westminster, there to answer the complaint of John, the King's Marshal. The Archbishop "came not." He was ill at the time, says his biographer.[5] London.

c. Sept. 29. It seems that late in September, two of the Court Chamberlains reached Northampton in anticipation of the Council there shortly to be holden. Some entries on the Pipe-Roll of Michaelmas, 1164, suggest as much.—

CIVITAS WINTONIÆ. *Et ad portandam arcam Thesauri ad festum sancti Michaelis, de Wintonia ad Norhanton* vii. *sol. et* i *den.*

Et pro uno runcino ad portandum thesaurum Regis xxvii *sol. per Henricum filium Geroldi Camerarium.*

NORTHANTS. *In Camerâ Curiæ Radulfo filio Stephani* xx *Lib. per breve Regis.*

[1] S. T. C. Epistle cccclxij.
[2] S. T. C. Fitz Stephen, i. 218.
[3, 4] S. T. C. Bosham, vii. 131.
[5] S. T. C. Fitz Stephen, i. 219.

MICHAELMAS, 1164, TO MICHAELMAS, 1165.

1164. Sept. 30. Pope Alexander, having perhaps been absent from Sens for some days, is reported as on this day taking residence at Sens for the winter.[1]

Thursday, October 1. Mention of Pope Alexander as being at Sens.[2]

Tuesday, October 6. Summonses returnable for the Council of Northampton.[3] The King arrives late. Archbishop Becket is more punctual. Northampton.

Wednesday, October 7. Becket's complaint in Council against William de Courci.[4]

John Mareschall stated to be at the Exchequer in London.[4]

Thursday, October 8. The King gives sentence on Becket with regard to the affair of John Marescall.[4]

Friday, October 9. The King demands from Becket the repayment of monies advanced to the late Chancellor in the expedition to Toulouse [4] (five years before).

Saturday, October 10. Becket offers the King a fine of 2000 marks in composition of the alleged debt.[4]

Sunday, October 11. The day is devoted by the King to Councils. Becket does not leave his *Hospice*.

Monday, October 12. Becket is ill.[4] On this day died Hugh, Archbishop of Rouen.[5]

Tuesday, October 13. Becket says mass at the Altar of St. Stephen,[6] Northampton.

Wednesday, October 14. Becket is found to have clandestinely left Northampton. His retreat for about eleven days does not appear.

King Henry in Council treats on Welsh affairs.[4] (The King's sending at once an embassy to Sens, which embassy is further said to have been at Dover on Oct. 15, is certainly premature).

c. Oct. 20. The Council of Northampton broke up; the King pronouncing sentence against Becket. Northampton.

Such seem to us to be the outlines of the Council of Northampton, variously dated by the Chroniclers,[7] and whereof the general account, viz., that "the Archbishop of

[1] Rerum. Gall. Scriptores, xii. 288.
[2] S. T. C. vii. 69.
[3, 4] S. T. C. vii. 134, 136.
[5] Chron. Normann. p. 999. Nov. 10 is the date of the Archbishop's death on other authority (Monast. iv. p. 30).
[6] S. T. C. Fitz Stephen, i. 225. Boseham states that Becket said this Mass on "Natalicium Calixti," *i. e.* Oct. 14.
[7] Diceto dates the Council as opening Oct. 13th; Gervase on Oct. 12th; another writer on Oct. 11, (Sunday!)

1164. Oct. Canterbury, being condemned for perjury and treason, appealed to the Pope," seems both superficial and incorrect. The persons who took most active part on the occasion, were the Archbishop of York, the Bishops of Winchester, London, Lincoln, Exeter, Chichester, Rochester, Worcester and Hereford; the Earls of Leicester and Cornwall, and Hameline,[1] the King's brother. Northampton.

Oct. 6-20. A Royal Charter, dated at Northampton, seems to belong to the above occasion. It is in favour of Lenton Priory, Nottinghamshire. It is attested by Roger, Archbishop of York; William, Bishop of Norwich; Gilbert, Bishop of London; Richard de Humez (at this rate, recently returned from France), and by Richard Pincerna.[2]

c. Oct. 25-Nov. 2. Becket passes eight days at Eastry (S. W. of Sandwich).

Oct. 26. A dated letter of Pope Alexander, at Sens, indicates that the Pope had received Becket's appeal from the sentence passed at Northampton; but did not know of Becket's exact position. The Pope approves of the Appeal, and advises Becket to go and live quietly at Canterbury, and to "*travel in those parts*" as little as possible.[3]

Oct. 31. Walkeline, Abbot of Abingdon, died.[4]

Nov. 2. The King's Embassy, destined to the Pope at Sens, being now at Dover, Becket embarks (probably at Sandwich), and lands at Gravelines. His first resort is a barn. He writes to the Pope.[5]

c. Nov. 4. Becket goes to Clarus Mariscus,—a Monastery near St. Omer.

c. Nov. 6. Becket goes to St. Omer.[6] The King of England's ambassadors, both to Louis and to the Pope, are in St. Omer on the same night as Becket.

c. Nov. 7. Becket is received into the Monastery of St. Bertin (near St. Omer).[6]

While at St. Bertin, Becket has an interview with Richard de Lucy, then on an embassy from K. Henry to the Court of Flanders.

Becket, misdoubting the protection of the Comte of Flanders, leaves St. Bertin's and goes to Soissons.

November. At this period K. Henry had emissaries or ambassadors at several European Courts. Besides Richard de Lucy at the Court of Flanders, there was John Cumin at the Court of the Emperor Frederic; and of his numerous ambassadors into France, three at least were destined in the first instance to the Court of Louis VII. at Compeigne. These were Gilbert Foliot, Bishop of London; William, Earl of Arundel; and Richard de Ilchester, Archdeacon of Poitiers.[7]

c. Nov. 25. Henry's embassy to the Pope seems to have assembled at Sens about this date, being probably joined by the Deputation which had waited on King Louis at Compeigne and also by the two Norman Bishops of Liseux and Seez.

In addition to those already named, were Roger, Archbishop of York; Roger, Bishop of Worcester; Hilary, Bishop of Chichester; Bartholomew, Bishop of Exeter; Wido Rufus, Dean of Waltham; John of Oxford; Hugh de Gundevill; Bernard de St. Walery; Reginald de St. Walery, and Henry fitz Gerold.[7]

[1] Hameline (called by modern writers 'Plantagenet') was an illegitimate son of Geoffry, Comte of Anjou. His marriage with the Countess of Warren took place in this very year (Chron. Normann. p. 999).

[2] Monasticon, v. 112.

[3] S. T. C. iv. p. 4. Epistle CC.

[4] The Abbey was still *in manu Regis*, August, 1165. See below (pp. 81, 83).

[5] Gervase, Epistle ii.

[6, 7] S. T. C. i. 238, 239, 149.

[8] Hoveden, p. 284. Diceto, p. 330.

1164. *c.* Nov. 29. Becket arrives from Soissons at Sens on the fourth day after the arrival of K. Henry's ambassadors.

Nov. 30. After a conference with the Pope at Sens, Becket goes to Pontigny, a Cistercian Monastery about 12 leagues from Sens. There he remained nearly two years.

Nov. Dec. The movements of K. Henry's Court after the Council of Northampton, and during the last two months of the year 1164, are perhaps adumbrated in the following entries on the Pipe-Roll of September, 1165.—

Philip de Kime, Fermor of the Escheated Honour of Tickhill (Yorkshire), Fermor also of Doncaster until January, 1165, had paid £20 in the King's Chamber to Ralph Fitz Stephen, by the King's Order.[1] Yorkshire.

LONDON AND MIDDLESEX. The Sheriffs charge—*In conducendo crasso pisce de Londoniâ ad Nottingham,* xii *sol. et* vi *den.* Nottingham.

NOTTS AND DERBYSHIRE. The Sheriff charges—*In venacione Regis conducendâ de Peck ad Wudestock.*[1] Peak Castle. Woodstock.

OXFORDSHIRE. The Sheriff charges—*In operacione muri de Wudestoch circa parcum* xxx *Libr. In vino conducendo de Oxinford ad Wudestoch,* viii *sol. et* i *den. In corredio Abbatis de Sancto Germano de Pratis et Militum de Templo* xxx *sol. et* viii *den., per breve Regis quando venerunt de Rege Franciæ.*[1] (The Abbot of the French House of St. German de Preaux, with certain Knights Templars, had come on an Embassy to Henry from Louis of France, and had probably been entertained in Oxford Castle. Their Embassy was perhaps on Eastern affairs). Oxford.

WINDSOR. The Custos charges—*In conductu vini Regis de Windesorâ ad Oxinefort* xviii *den. Et pro vino Regis parando* xii *den. Et pro scicerâ Regis parandâ* ij *sol. et* ij *den.* Windsor.

SURREY. The Sheriff charges—*In Camerâ Curiæ Radulfo filio Stephani* xxxij *Lib.* xv *sol. in denariis et in vaisellâ, per breve Regis.*[1] Surrey.

GLOUCESTERSHIRE. *Pro Lardario Regis portando de Sancto Briavel' ad Merlberg,* xv *sol. et* ix *den.*[1] St. Briavell's.

Dec. 24. K. Henry's Embassy to the Pope at Sens, returning into England, finds the King at Marlborough.[2] Marlborough.

[1] Rot. Pipe, xi. Hen. II. TICHEHELLA, et passim. [2] S. T. C. (Fitz Stephen), i. 242.

1164. Dec. 25. K. Henry keeps his Christmas Court at Marlborough. Marlborough.

Pope Alexander says Mass in the Church of St. Columba at Sens.[1]

Dec. 26. K. Henry, in Council at Marlborough, sequestrates the See of Canterbury.

A King's Writ to the Sheriffs, enforcing such Sequestration, is extant.[2]

Also a Writ against the Archbishop's "Clerks," dated at Marlborough, and [2] attested by Richard de Luci. Marlborough.

Dec. 31. "*Solemnitate Sanctæ Colombæ.*" Pope Alexander saying Mass in the Church of St. Columba at Sens, King Louis of France and Comte Theobald (of Blois), his Steward (Dapifer), attend.[3]

A.D. 1165.

c. Jan. 25. K. Henry, after confiscating the See of Canterbury, drives the Archbishop's kindred into exile. Ranulph de Broc is appointed custos of the See.[4]

About this time the King, being at Westminster, gives Westminster. to Gervase de Cornhill the land of Chalk (Chalcha), which Roger, nephew of Hubert, held. Witnesses, Bishops Gilbert of London, and Josceline of Sarum; Archdeacons Geoffrey of Canterbury, and Richard of Poitiers; Robert, Earl of Leicester; Wm. d'Aubeiguy, Earl of Arundel; Richard de Luci; Roger, Earl of Clare; Manasser Biset, Dapifer; Reginald de Warren, and Alan de Nevill.[5]

c. Feb. In Lent (Feb. 17–April 3), K. Henry crosses the sea to Normandy.[6] He embarked perhaps from Southampton; Southampton. for in the Pipe-Roll of the following Michaelmas, the sub- Normandy. joined entry seems to relate to a period prior to Easter (April 4).

HAMPSHIRE. *In camerâ Regis per Radulfum fil. Stephani £44. per breve Regis.*

[1] Rerum Gall. Scriptores, xii. 288.

[2] S. T. C. Epistles (G. F.) cccclxxxij. cccclxxxj. See also S. T. C. iv. 187, for Nicholas de Monte's. Letter to Becket of about this date, wherein mention is made of the Empress, the Bishop of Liseux, John of Oxford, Ralph de Ardern, and Master Herbert.

[3] Rerum Gallic. Script. xii. 288.

[4] Gervase, p. 1398. Accordingly, at Michaelmas following, we have this entry on the Pipe-Roll.—*Archiepiscopatus Cantuariæ. Randulf de Broc, r; c; de £1562. 15s. 5½d. de firmâ terræ Archiepescopatûs Cantuariæ.*

[5] Ex. Orig. in Offic. Ducat. Lancastr.—This deed is most curious as an illustration of history. Except Manasser Biset, every one of the witnesses, as well as the grantee, was at some time distinguished for hostility or opposition to the Primate.

[6] Chron. Normann. p. 1000.

1165. c. Feb. Perhaps the King, on this occasion, embarked at Dover, (Dover). for the Kent Pipe-Roll charges—*In camerâ Curiæ* £35. 2*s.* *liberatæ Radulfo fil. Stephani per breve Regis.*

Feb. 17. The King said to have been at Mortimer.[1] (Mortimer).

c. April 4–11. Pope Alexander leaves Sens; his destination being Rome, but he was long in reaching Italy.[2]

April 11. An interview takes place between the Kings, Henry and Louis, at Gisors.[3] Gisors.

c. April 15. K. Henry, being at Rouen, receives Reginald, Archbishop of Cologne, and other ambassadors of the Emperor Frederick.[4] These ambassadors were to negotiate two marriages:—one between the King's eldest daughter, Matilda, and Henry Duke of Saxony; the other between the Princess Eleanor, and a younger son of the Emperor. The Empress mother appears to have refused an audience to these Ambassadors. Rouen.

The King was also visited at Rouen by Philip, Comte of Flanders.[5]

During the King's visit to Normandy, we suppose a charter to have passed in favour of the Canons of St. Mary of Gouffern. The Deed is dated at Argentan, and attested (Argentan). by Froger, Bishop of Seez; Richard, Archdeacon of Poictiers; Richard de Humet, Constable; Manasser Biset, Dapifer; William de Curci, Dapifer; Rob de Hasting; Robert de Brulcourt, and Hugh de Morvill.[6]

c. May 1. The King is joined in Normandy by Queen Eleanor, Prince Richard, and Princess Matilda. He sends Richard,

[1] Stubbs, quoting 'Alberic of Trois Fontaines,' p. 343, and indicating that if the transfretation were in Lent, which begun on Feb. 17, the King's presence at Mortimer on that day was impossible.

[2] Gervase, 1398. Chron. Norm. 1000.

[3] R. de Monte (Struve), 900. Diceto, p. 539.

[4] The Norman Chronicle it is that states Henry to have received the ambassadors in France. The far less accurate accounts of Diceto, (Ymag. Hist. 539), and M. Paris, represent the King as receiving them at Westminster. The truth seems to be that after his interview with Henry at Rouen, the Archbishop of Cologne was sent by the King to London, to confer with the Earl of Leicester (then Viceroy), and perhaps to visit the Queen and the Princess Matilda. Certain it is that the Archbishop crossed the sea and at the King's expense, for the Fermor of Dover charges his account with a sum of £69. 16*s.* 3*d.*, "*in passagiis et in corredio Archiepescopi Coloniæ,*"

The Archbishop, arriving at Westminster, was at first rebuffed by the Earl of Leicester, who looked upon him as an *Arch-Schismatic*, that is, as an instrument of a monarch who was then supporting the cause of the Antipope, Pascal.

The Archbishop seems to have passed onward from London into Berkshire, probably tending to the Queen's Court. The next step was that the Queen took her daughter Matilda to Henry's Court in Normandy, where the matrimonial negotiations were renewed, and whence Henry sent ambassadors to the Emperor.

[5] D'Anisy's Normandy Transcripts, iii. 296.

[6] Hist. Abingdon, ii. 223.

1165. c. May 1. Archdeacon of Poictiers, and John of Oxford as ambassadors to the Emperor Frederick. These emissaries were present at the Council of Wurtzburg on May 23. Normandy.

c. May 15. K. Henry, leaving the Queen at Angers, crosses the sea. He appears to have landed at Southampton from the following entry on the Pipe-Roll.— (Angers). (Barfleur). Southampton.

HANTONA. *In passagio esneccæ Regis quando Rex rediit de Normanniâ* £7. 10*s*. *Et in passagiis per brevia Regis* £18. 17. 4*d*.

And to have passed through Surrey.— Surrey.

SURREIA. *Et in corredio Regis quando rediit de Normanniâ* 5 *marcas per breve Regis*.

c May 15–31. On his arrival from Normandy the King found forces levied against Rese ap Griffith in pursuance of provisions made at the Council of Northampton in October, 1164.[1]

The King marches into Flintshire, where David, a son of Owen Gwyned, had been making depredations.

The King, arriving at Rhuddlan, finds that the Welshmen had retired with their booty to the vale of Clwyd in Denbighshire. Rhuddlan.

The King fortifies Besingwerk and all his Castles in Flintshire, and returns to England to augment his forces.[1] Basingwerk.

May 23. Richard, Archdeacon of Poictiers, and John of Oxford, Ambassadors of K. Henry to the Emperor Frederic, were present at the Council of Wurtzburg. The ostensible object of their embassy was to negotiate about the Princess Matilda's marriage, but they were among those who joined the Emperor Frederic in his oath never to recognise Pope Alexander.[2]

Sat. May 29. "Ordination" at Wurtzburg of the "Archbishop Elect" of Cologne.

Letter from Rotrou, Archbishop of Rouen, to the Cardinal Henry. The Archbishop promises to explain K. Henry's attitude at Wurtzburg and the Empress's sentiments. This he will do when *the Envoys shall have returned from Wurtzburg.*

[1] The sequence of K. Henry's movements during the two Welsh campaigns of 1165 has been clearly indicated, for the first time, by Mr. Bridgeman in his History of the Princes of South Wales (pp. 48, 49). Corrected by his statements, the author has rewritten the whole of this portion of the Itinerary.

A statement made by Carte is to the effect that on this occasion "K. Henry took Cardigan Castle and two sons of Prince Rese therein."—

The facts are that the King did not approach Cardigan; that Cardigan Castle was already in the hands of the English, and that Prince Rese ap Griffith besieged and gained it, not till November, 1165. And the same of Prince Rese's sons.—They were already among the hostages in K. Henry's hands, whose eyes he afterwards put out in retaliation for their father's breach of faith and rebellion.

[2] Nicolas' Chron. Hist. p. 248.—*Concilium Herbipolense.* The two Envoys accepted English Sees before Alexander's Papacy had expired.

1165. June and July. King Henry's preparations for a renewed attack upon Wales probably occupied most of these two months. The following extracts from the Pipe-Rolls, though fully indicative of such preparations and of the wide scope of Henry's invasion, and though specifying some of his chief Officers, tells little of the progress of his arms or of the King's personal movements. England.

OXFORDSHIRE. *Pro sagittis emptis et ipsis cum loricis conducendis ad Salopesburiam* 24*s*. 4*d*. *Et pro* 1000 *summis frumenti liberatis Willelmo de Bellocampo apud Wirecestriam* £45. 16*s*. 8*d*.

SHROPSHIRE. Guy Le Strange, who had ceased to be Sheriff of Shropshire about Christmas, 1164, renders account at Michaelmas, 1165, of certain balances which would seem to have been in his hand when quitting office, and which he had since expended as follows.—

Et Hugoni de Gundevill et Willelmo de Bellocampo 60 *sol. ad dextrarium ad opus Regis per breve Regis.*

The same Guy le Strange, being still (Sept. 1165) Custos of the estates of young William fitz Alan, Baron of Clun and Oswestry, charges the Crown.—"*In liberacione* cc *servientum apud Blancmost*" (Oswestry Castle), 103 *sol. et* 9*d*.

Geoffrey de Vere, stepfather of the same young Baron, having been Sheriff of Shropshire, from Christmas, 1164, to Michaelmas, 1165, charges his account with the following payments made on the King's behalf.—

Et cc *servientibus* £62. 7*s*. 5*d*. *Et* lx *servientibus apud Suewardin*[1] £6. *Et Carpentariis* £6. 14*s*. 9*d*. *Et Cementariis* £5. 4*s*. 5*d*. *Et in liberacione* xxv *obsidum* £4. 12*s*. *Et item* ccc *servientibus post pastiam* £69. 18*s*. 7*d*. *Et item in liberacione obsidum* 42*s*. *Et item eisdem* £4. 16*s*. *Et in ferro* 7*s*. 7½*d*. *Et Fabro* 31*s*. *Et Carbonariis* 12 *sol*. *Et pro Picois portandis in Walliam* 15*d*. *Et in custodia Castelli de Chirc*[2] £6. 19*s*. 8*d*.

GLOUCESTERSHIRE. The Sheriff charges an advance, viz., *Nicolao, Clerico Johanis de Oxinford* xx *marcas per breve Regis ad opus familiæ Regis de Salopiâ.*[3]

WORCESTERSHIRE. William de Beauchamp, the Sheriff, charges—*In liberacione obsidum remanentium* £13. 10*s*. 8*d*. *Et in liberacione servientum de Bergavenni* £34. 11*s*. 4*d*. *Et pro* DIX *summis frumenti portatis ad Salopesburiam* £19. 1*s*. 8*d*. *Et pro municione deferendâ de Wirecestriâ ad exercitum* £17. 9*s*. 6*d*. *Et in liberacione servientum de Mongomery* £14. 11*s*. 8*d*. *Et in servientibus de Chaus*[4] £14. 11*s*. 8*d*. *Et Willelmo filio Adelini*[5] £48 *ad liberacionem militum Regis apud*

[1] Shrawardine, like Oswestry, one of Fitz Alan's Border-Castles.

[2] Chirk Castle, Denbighshire.

[3] "Familiæ Regis de Salopiâ." The King's Staff or company when quartered at Shrewsbury.

[4] "Servientibus de Chaus."—Stipendiary soldiers, probably brought from Henry's continental dominions and put in garrison at Corbet's Border Castle of Caux.

[5] William Fitz Adeline, one of the King's Marshals. In the Feodary of 1166, he is expressly styled *Marescallus Regis*, and his Tenure in Hampshire is said to be "*De Marescalciâ Regis*," (Hearne's Liber Niger, i. 73, 74).

Salopesburiam. Et Thomæ et Nicholao clericis (of John of Oxford), *et Willelmo filio Adelini £24 ad liberacionem militum de Salopburia.*

1165. HEREFORDSHIRE. The same Sheriff, William de Beauchamp charges—

Et Radulfo de Grosmund £8. 5s. 6d. ad liberacionem Servientum de Grosmund, et Lantelio, et Schenefred. Et Waltero de Bellocampo £72. 4s. 8d. ad liberacionem familiæ Regis apud Bergeveni.[1]

BERKSHIRE. The Sheriff, Adam de Catmera, charges—

Pro 1000 summis frumenti liberatis Willelmo de Bellocampo apud Wirecestre £45. 16s. 8d. Et pro sagittis emptis, &c., et liberatis apud Salop 23s. 8d.

Abbas de Abendon r. c. de i *marc: de veteri scutagio.*[2] *In thro lib. E. Q. E. Nova Placita et Novæ Conventiones.* The same Sheriff of Berkshire accounts for a receipt as follows—*Idem reddit compotum de £76. 5s. de promissione servientum in Wallia. In thesauro £75. 11s. 8d. Et debet* i *marcam*[3] (13*s.* 4*d.*).

ABBATIA DE ABENDON. Ranulf de Catemera, Custos of the vacant Abbey of Abingdon, for the half-year ending May, 1165, renders account, at Michaelmas, 1165, of £87. 3*s.* 10*d.*, his receipts during the period of vacancy.—"*Ranulfus de Catemera reddit compotum de £87. 3s. 10d. de Abbatia de Abendon de dimidio anno.*—

In soltis per breve Regis pro debitis Abbatis (the late Abbot Walcheline) *Waltero filio Gerardi de Rothomago £33. 14s. 4d. Et in corredio Nuntiorum Imperatoris per Johannem de Oxineford £23 per breve Regis.*[4] *Et in liberatione septem militum qui fuerunt cum Rege in Waliâ £18. 18s. Et monachis qui perrexerunt in Normanniam in negotiis Ecclesiæ 118s. 6d.*[5]

July 10, 1165. Pope Alexander, now at Clermont in Auvergne, writes on this day to Gilbert (Foliot), Bishop of London, bidding him to associate with himself the Bishop of Hereford, and both to give admonition to K. Henry as to his relations with the Archbishop of Canterbury. Bishop Gilbert is also desired to collect the Peter-pence, and transmit the money to the Pope before August 1.[6]

[1] "*Familia Regis apud Bergeveni Servientes de Bergeveni.*" There will have been some concerted movement on the Monmouthshire Border to tally with this twofold introduction of Abergavenny. In that quarter Prince Rese's territory and interests would come more specially in question than in North Wales. However, we have no other hint that Henry himself operated against South Wales. His "familia," or corps of household officers at Abergavenny was probably under command of one of his Lieutenants.

[2] This Scutage was an arrear from the time of Abbot Walcheline, who died Oct. 31, 1164. The existing Pro Abbot (September, 1165), was Godfrey, Bishop of St. Asaph; but he was only Pro-Abbot, and that for the period of his expulsion from his See; which expulsion seems to have been caused by the Welsh commotion of which we are speaking. K. Henry gave him the vacant Abbey for his maintenance.

[3] Probably the Sheriff had received this sum extra to his receipts as a Sheriff and for the special purpose of forwarding the King's foreign Stipendiaries on their route towards Wales. And he had not spent it.

[4] This is with reference to the Archbishop of Cologne's visit to England in April or May, 1165. (Supra, p. 78). He probably passed through Abingdon, in his way from London to visit the Queen's Court, and to see the Princess Matilda.

[5] The Monks of Abingdon, who, I suppose about April, were summoned by, or went to, the King, then in Normandy, relative to filling up the Abbatial vacancy.

[6] S. T. C. Epistle cclxxxij. Bishop Foliot collected the Peter-pence as Dean of Canterbury.

1165. July. It is clear that when Bishop Foliot received this letter, the King was on his way to the Frontier, and that the Bishop at once determined on following him.

The King, if we may judge from the above extract from
c. July 31. the Pipe-Rolls, passed by way of Shrewsbury, and thence Shrewsbury.
to Oswestry, where Foliot overtook him and his army. The Oswestry.
Bishop of Hereford was with Foliot at the interview which ensued, and which one Record locates at the "Cross of St. Oswald."

We approximate to the date of this interview by the ascertainment that the Pope on August 22nd, being then at Montpelier in Lauguedoc, had received from the Bishop of London a report thereof.

August. King Henry now entered Powys-Land and advanced to Powys-Land.
the Valley and River of the Ceiriog. The Welsh, breaking The Ceiriog.
ground from Corwen in Edeyrneon, attacked the English vanguard, but without success, and Henry marched onward
to the foot of the Berwin, a high mountain-ridge in The Berwin.
Merionethshire. Here the King encamped. "The Welsh hung like a dark cloud on the crest and sides of the Berwin, waiting for an occasion to attack the King with advantage, who found it impracticable to approach them in the post they had taken, while flying parties of the Welsh cut off his provisions, so that his soldiers in camp were soon distressed by a scarcity of forage and provisions. The valley where the King was encamped was anon inundated by excessive rains and the torrents which followed from the mountain-gorges. Henry retired with great loss of men and ammunition, leaving his enemies in possession of the field."[1]

Henry now retired to Chester, where he awaited the Chester.
arrival of some Ships from Ireland which he had hired for the purpose of invading Wales by sea. The ships, when they arrived, were insufficient."[1]

This statement, derived we presume, from a Welsh Chronicle, is curiously supported by a piece of indirect evidence. King Henry was, it seems, encamped on a tract
of land, then called Wirhall. It was on the isthmus which Wirhall.

[1] See Princes of South Wales (by the Rev. the Hon. George T. O. Bridgeman), pp. 48, 49.

1165. August. divides the estuaries of the Mersey and the Dee, and has the City of Chester on its S. East, and the open sea on its N. West. Wirhall.

At Wirhall (apud Wirhalam) the King expedited a writ in favour of the Monks of Abingdon. The writ is attested singly by John of Oxford. It enjoins on the Sheriffs of London, of Hampshire, and of Gloucestershire, "*quod permittatis monachos de Abendon emere victualia et deferre ad Abbatiam &c., et quod non disturbentur (monachi) propter prohibitionem quam inde feci pro hoc exercitu meo Walliæ.*"[1] (There were, we suppose, some standing orders affecting the sale of provisions in certain districts, and necessary as regarded the commissariat of the army of Wales, which orders the King relaxed in favour of the Monks of Abingdon). The writ implies that his project of invasion was not yet abandoned.

August 22. (Sunday). Philip, son of Louis VII. of France, born.[2] Pope Alexander at Montpelier.[2] Pope Alexander, dating his letter, "*In gradu Mercurii,*" writes to the Bishop of London (Gilbert Foliot). He thanks the Bishop for having exhorted K. Henry, and for his letters touching Henry's devotion to the Church. The Pope wills that the Bishop of London, the Archbishop of Rouen (this will have been Rotrou de Newburgh,[3] recently promoted from the See of Evreux), the Bishop of Hereford (Robert de Melun), and the Empress-mother shall persevere in like monitions, tending to the restoration of Archbishop Thomas. London is to attend to the collection of the Peter-pence, and to transmit the same to the Pope by hand of the Abbot of St. Bertin.[3]

September. King Henry, on leaving Chester, is said to have gone to London. He probably passed through Staffordshire, and being at Brewood expedited a Charter to the Borough of Newport (Shropshire). It is attested by Geoffrey, Archdeacon of Canterbury; John Cumin; and Radulf de * am (perhaps Thamewood, or Tamworth).[4] Brewood (Staffordshire).

The following payment by Alexander Clerk, then Sheriff of Staffordshire, is possibly relevant to the King's passage through that county :—

Et Willelmo filio Adelini et Clerico Johannis de Oxinford per Ricardum de Luci £10 ad faciendas liberaciones familiæ Regis, per breve Regis.

[1] Hist. Abendon ii. 223.
[2] Gervase. Diceto.
[3] S. T. C. Epistle cclxxxiij. The date of Rotrou de Newburgh's translation is given as in 1165 (Chron. Norm. p. 1000).
[4] Harleian MSS. 1985, fo. 240.

1165. September. The Pipe-Rolls give small indication of Henry's arrival in London in September. At Michaelmas, the Sheriffs of London charge the Crown with 40 merks, which by order of the King they had advanced to Edward Blund, "*ad negotia Regis.*"[1] And the Custos of the Archbishoprick of Canterbury charged the Crown half a merk for carriage of fruit which the Lady Empress had sent to the King[1] (from Normandy). London.

On quitting London, the King perhaps visited, first Woodstock, and then Clarendon, for the Sheriff of Worcestershire, at Michaelmas, charges the Crown £2. 5*s.* 4*d.*, "*pro tonellis et pro vino portando ad Wudestoch, et ad Clarendon.*" Woodstock. Clarendon.

The following Royal Writs and Charters, all dated at Woodstock, probably passed during the King's stay there:—

A Writ, attested by John of Oxford, enjoins on the King's Bailiffs of Wich (Droitwich), or, they failing, on the Sheriff of Worcestershire, that the Monks of Abingdon do continue to have their salt as they had it in time of King Henry (the First).[2]

Another Writ, attested by William Fitz John, certifies that the same Monks have quittance of Toll for their own proper goods.[2]

A Royal Charter, also dated at Woodstock, confirms to Robert de Vaux (*Vallibus*), son of Hubert de Vaux, the land which his father held on the day of his death. Witnesses, Bartholomew, Bishop of Exeter; Henry, Elect of Baieux; Richard, Archdeacon of Poictiers; and Earl Geoffrey (of Essex).[3]

Another Royal Charter, dated at Woodstock,[4] mentions "E." (perhaps it should be C. for Clement), Abbot of Shirbourne, and Master Walter de Insula,[4] Clerk of the King. It is attested by Richard, Archdeacon of Poictiers;

[1] Rot. Pipe, xi. Hen. II.

[2] Hist. Abendon, ii. 234.

[3] Cartæ Antiquæ, D.D. Philip de Harcourt, late Bishop of Baieux, had died in 1163 (Chron. Norm. p. 999). It was in 1165 that Henry de Beaumont, theretofore Dean of Salisbury, was appointed his successor at Baieux. To the Deanery of Salisbury, thus vacant, John of Oxford soon succeeded, though his appointment was challenged by Archbishop Becket. (See Hardy's Le Neve, ii. 613.)

[4] Monasticon, i. 340, viii. Master Walter de Lisle (*Insula*) occurs in positions of Trust, 1165–1176. He was Incumbent of Stalbridge, Dorset; and a Canon of St. Paul's, London.

John of Oxford; Richard de Camvill; William de Caineto; William fitz Hamo; William de Hastings; and Ralph fitz Stephen, Chamberlain.

By a Charter, dated at Woodstock, the King confirms a quit-claim by Richard fitz Hildebrand to G. (perhaps it should be C. for Clement), Abbot of Sherborne. The Witnesses are Robert, Earl of Leicester; William, Earl of Arundel; Richard de Camvill; Master Walter de Insula; and William fitz Hamo.[1]

A Charter in favour of Wroxhall Monastery (Warwickshire), dated at Woodstock, is attested by Joceline, Bishop of Sarum; Richard de Luci; and the Archdeacon of Poitiers.[2]

A Royal Charter, dated at Clarendon, may possibly belong to this period. It is in favour of the Canons of Briweton (Bruton, Somerset), and is attested singly by Richard, Archdeacon of Poitiers.[3] Clarendon.

Sept. 29. At Michaelmas, 1165, there were sitting in the *Curiâ Regis* at Westminster, the following Justiciars and Officers of State, who attested a quit-claim by Robert, Abbot of St. Albans, and others, to Laurence, Abbot of Westminster. The said witnesses were Nigel, Bishop of Ely; Geoffrey, Archdeacon of Canterbury; Richard, Archdeacon of Poitiers; Wido, Dean of Waltham; Robert, Earl of Leicester; and Richard de Luci,—all Justiciars; also Henry fitz Gerold, Chamberlain; William fitz Adeline, Marshal; Richard, Treasurer; William Mauduit, Chamberlain; Simon fitz Peter, Marshal; Alan de Nevill, Marshall; Geoffrey Monk, Marshal; and Philip de Davenceester.[4]

HOUSEHOLD OF QUEEN ELIANOR and her Children.—We here insert a few notices of the Queen and other members of the Royal family which could not well be introduced in a diary treating more particularly of the Court and movements of the King:—

In February, 1165, when the King crossed the Channel to Normandy, the Queen and her younger children seem to have become resident for about three months at Winchester and elsewhere in Hampshire or the Isle of Wight, but at some interval visiting Sherborne Castle (Dorset).

Hence, at Michaelmas, 1165, Richard fitz Turstin, Sheriff of Hampshire, charges the Crown with these payments following:—

In corredio Reginæ £10. *In corredio Sororis Regis* £3.[5] *Et Gaufrido Monacho* £84. 2*s*. 3*d*. *ad faciendam soltam Reginæ et filiorum Regis. Et pro sellis et lorreis ad opus Marchisæ cognatæ Reginæ* 12*s*.

The same Sheriff, accounting for the Ferm of Ulferton,[6] charges:—*In corredio Reginæ* £18.

[1] Monasticon, i. 340, vii.

[2] Monasticon, iv. 92, ii. b.

[3] Cartæ Antiquæ, K.

[4] Madox's Formulare Anglicanum, p. xix.

[5] *Sororis Regis*. The King's half-sister, Emma, a natural daughter of Geoffrey le Bel, Comte of Anjou, by a woman of Maine (*Diceto, and Chronicon de origine Comitum Andegaviæ*). Contemporary Authors speak of her exceeding beauty, and declare, what we cannot credit, that she was the youngest child of the Empress. She married Guy V., Lord (*Toparcha*) of Val-Guyon (*Vallis Guidonis*). She married, perhaps secondly, David ap Owen, Prince of North Wales. This was in 1174.—

Aldewide, another natural daughter of Comte Geoffrey le Bel, is spoken of as wife of Ralph, junior Prince of Bourg-Deols.

[6] Perhaps Wolverton, in the Isle of Wight.

Hugh de Gundevill, Fermor or Custos of Sherborne, Dorset, charges—*In corredio Reginæ* £18. *In operacione domorum Regis* 40*s*.

In April, 1165, it seems that the Archbishop of Cologne, seeking an interview with the Queen and the Princess Matilda, passed from London through Abingdon on his way to the Queen's court.

In May, 1165, Queen Elianor, with the Princess Matilda and Prince Richard, joined K. Henry in Normandy; and about the middle of that month, the King, hastening to England, left the Queen at Angers, committing to her the Regency of the two provinces of Maine and Anjou.

Soon after this we may date a letter, written by John, Bishop of Poictiers, to Becket. The Bishop is staying at Le Mans with the Bishop of Le Mans. He reports the Queen as leaning entirely on Ralph de Faia, a well-known opponent of Becket, and, we believe, a relative of the Queen. The Bishop hints at a piece of Court scandal in connexion with this subject.[1]

At Michaelmas, 1165, Queen Elianor was still resident at Angers, where in the following month she gave birth to the Princess Johanna.

PRINCE HENRY, who on February 28, 1165, completed his tenth year, had in his ninth year, viz., in October, 1163, been taken from the tutelage of Archbishop Becket, and in January, 1164, still in his ninth year, joined his father in the so-called presidency over the Council of Clarendon.

When in February, 1165, the King quitted England, young Henry was not left under the tutelage or in the Household of the Queen. He had a separate establishment. Hence, at Michaelmas, 1165, the Custos of Winchester charges—"*In corredio Henrici filii Regis* £30 *per breve Regis.*"

And the Sheriff of Wiltshire (Richard de Wilton) charges—

In corredio Henrici filii Regis £22. 10*s*. *liberatas Ailwardo Pincernæ per breve Regis.*

Also the Sheriff of Berkshire (Adam de Catmera) charges—"*Et Willelmo filio Johannis* £20 *ad corredium Henrici filii Regis.*"

MICHAELMAS, 1165, TO MICHAELMAS, 1166.

Oct. Nov. Dec. The movements of Henry's Court for the last three months of the year 1165, and the first two months of 1166, may perhaps be indicated by the following quotations from the Pipe-Roll of 1166. The order in which the several localities were visited or revisited is of course as problematical as the exact month or day of visitation.

SURREY. *Et pro conducendo vino Regis de Lundon' ad* London.
Roffam 6*s*. *per breve Regis.* Rochester.

HAMPSHIRE. *Et pro conducendo vino Regis de Hantonâ* (Southampton) *ad Wintoniam; et pro vasis* 16*s*. 3*d*. *per* Winchester.
Hamonem Pincernam. Et pro conducendo thesauro Regis ad Hanton' et ad Clarendon' et ad Oxineford per totum annum 48*s*. 2*d*.

WINCHESTER. *Et pro conducendis sellis et scut' Regis de Winton' ad Lundon'* 18*d*.

WILTSHIRE. *Et in operacione Regis, de Clarendon,* (Clarendon).

[1] S. T. C. vi. 250, Epist. ccccl xv.

1165. Oct. Nov. Dec. £59. 17*s.* 6*d.* *per visum Warneri de Lusoriis. Et in restauracione manerii de Westcumba, &c.* (Clarendon).

LONDON AND MIDDLESEX. *Et pro conducendis piris Regis de Lundon' ad Wudestoch* 3*s.* *Et uxori Brightmari de Haverhell* £7 *pro aurifr' ad cappas Regis, per breve Regis. Et pro conducendo crasso pisce de Lund' ad Clarendon'* 6*s.* *per Edwardum Blundum. Et pro custamento probatorum et pro conducendis illis ad Clarendon'* 48*s.* (Salisbury.)

WILTSHIRE. *Et pro conducenda venacione Regis de Chepeham ad Wudestoch* 7*s.* 2*d.* *per breve Regis. Et pro conducendo vino Regis de Clarendon' ad Wudestoch* 78*s.* 8*d.* *per breve Regis.* (Chippenham).

SURREY. *Et in custamento probatorum Regis et pro conducendis illis ad Sarum* 5*s.* (Woodstock.)

SOUTHAMPTON. *Et pro vinis Regis et ipsis conducendis de Hantona ad Clarendon' et ad Wudestoch et ad Sarum et ad Chepeham* £24. 13*s.* 10*d.* *per brevia Regis per Hamonem Pincernam et Martinum de Hosa.* (Oxford.)

Oct. Nov. Dec. There are other evidences which associate the movements of the Court at this period with some of the same localities :—

A Royal Charter, dated at Westminster, is in favour of St. Catherine's Priory, near Lincoln. Among its *movent-clauses* are these, viz., '*pro statu regni mei,*' '*pro salute Alianoræ Reginæ,*' and '*pro animâ Matildæ Imperatricis matris meæ.*' It is attested by Roger, Abp of York; Hilary, Bp of Chichester; Hugh, Bp of Durham; Robert, Bp of Lincoln; Reginald, Earl of Cornwall; Roger de Moubray; and Reginald de Courtnay.[1] (Westminster.)

A Royal Charter, dated at Winchester, is in relation to Hertlands Abbey (Devonshire). It confirms a release by Geoffrey, son of Oliver de Dynham, to Richard, Archdeacon of Poictiers. It is attested by Geoffry, Archdeacon of (Winchester.)

[1] Monasticon, vii. 969. The date assigned to this Charter can only be proximate. It must have passed before March, 1166, the latest period at which any Deed of Henry II., expedited in England can have been attested by Robert, Bishop of Lincoln. But the movent clauses of the Deed are quite as suggestive, as to date, as the names of the witnesses.—The King was at this time (October, 1165) at variance with Louis VII. and with the Pope; he had failed in the Welsh expedition of August; there were troubles in Maine and Guienne, where Queen Elianor was acting as Regent; and at Angers in the month of October she gave birth to the Princess Johanna. The age and declining health of the Empress probably suggested the distinctive clause "*Pro animâ Matildæ Imperatricis,* etc.;" but she survived nearly two years, viz., till September, 1167.

1165. Oct. Nov. Dec. Canterbury; Geoffry, Chaplain of the King; Master Stephen de Fulgeriis; Nicholas, Chaplain; Master John Cumin; Master * * * * a priest of Hugh, Earl of Norfolk; Manasser Biset, Dapifer; Josceline de Baillol; William Malet; Alan fitz Jordan; and Richard Pincerna.[1] Winchester.

c. Oct. About this time we hear of a Synod of Bishops at Salisbury,[2] and which, if the King were present, was probably held in October. Salisbury.

A Writ, dated "*apud Clivum*" (King's Cliff, Northants), and addressed to Richard Basset, is in behalf of Abingdon Abbey, and relates to the monks' claim to four hides of land in Chedelesworth (Chelsworth, Wilts.). It is attested by William fitz John.[3] King's Cliff.

c. Oct. 14. Probable date of Becket's letter to Henry, beginning *Desiderio desideravi.*[4]

Nov. 21. Pope Alexander III. having left France, reaches Rome, where he remained till July, 1167.

Dec. 5. Death of Malcolm, King of Scots.

Dec. 25. The King probably kept Christmas at Oxford. About this time a Council or Synod, at which he presided, assembled at Oxford and took statutory cognizance of the heresy of the publicans or Girardists.[5] Oxford.

Dec. 31. The King probably at Woodstock. Woodstock.

A.D. 1166.

1166. January, February. Woodstock was now the usual place of K. Henry's resort, but in these two months he was at other places; at Feckenham, for instance, for the sake of hunting; at Salisbury and Clarendon on more important business; at Chippenham between whiles. Woodstock.

A Writ or Precept, dated at Woodstock, would make it seem that Godfrey, Bishop of St. Asaph, the Abbot Commendate of Abingdon, had some difficulty with the Abbatial tenants. The King addresses them all, "*tam Clericis quam*

[1] Monasticon, vi. 436.
[2] S. T. C. vi. 251.
[3] Hist. Abendon, ii. 224.
[4] S. T. C. (Fitz Stephen), i. 249; iii. 365; Epist. clxxix.
[5] Chron. Dunstable. Annals of Tewkesbury. Diceto, p. 539. See also Carte, i. 597, and Palgrave's British Commonwealth, Appendix, clxvii.

1166. January, February. *laicis tenentibus de Abbatiâ,"* with this command and threat, *" Intendatis Godefrido Episcopo cui commendavi Abbatiam tanquam Abbati, et nisi (feceritis) Vicecomites vos justicient."* This Writ is attested singly by " John, Dean of Salisbury,"[1] that is, by John of Oxford, who became Dean of Salisbury not earlier than 1165, when his predecessor, Dean Henry de Beaumont, was promoted to the See of Baieux, and not later than June, 1166, when Archbishop Becket excommunicated him for usurping the Deanery. Woodstock.

February. King Henry held in this month what now appears to have been a second Council of Clarendon.[2] Clarendon.

At this Council an Assize[3] '*pro pace servandâ et justiciâ tenendâ*' was enacted by the King, with the advice of the *Archbishops*, Bishops, Abbots, and Barons of his realm.

We refer in a note to our authority[2] for holding that the words *" Consilio Archiepiscoporum,"* used in the preamble of this Assize were a formal expression, and do not affect the question of the date of this Council; for, indeed, if the Council sat in 1166, it is certain that only one English Archbishop (Roger of York) was in attendance.

The same authority cites from the Pipe-Roll of Michaelmas, 1166, the following clauses, pertinent to the question of date.—

WILTSHIRE. The Sheriff had paid *" Rogero Ostiario*

[1] Hist. Abendon, ii. 235, 234. The learned editor dates this Writ, "November, 1164." The reasons for a later date are, to our minds, insurmountable.

[2] This discovery of a second Council of Clarendon is by no means our own. In his British Commonwealth (p. cxlviii), Sir Francis Palgrave remarked that "between the years 1165 and 1176 (but more probably between 1170 and 1176) there was a second Great Council at Clarendon, different to that at which the customs were mooted." The idea was unquestionably right, the narrower limitations of date (1170–1176) certainly wrong.

Professor Stubbs, in his Appendices to the Chronicle of Benedict of Peterborough (vol. ii. pp. cxlix–cliv.) has printed the text of this "Assize of Clarendon." In his notes thereon and in his Preface (pp. lix–lxiv.) he has given details and reasons which almost conclusively fix the Council and Assize of Clarendon as in the first two months of 1166. He has also met the objection to such date founded on the words *Consilio Archiepiscoporum.*

[3] The word 'Assize,' as used in the text, signifies a statute enacted by the King with the advice of his Council.

The noun-substantive, *Assisa*, belongs to mediæval Latinity, but was formed from the classical verb, *assidere.*

Assisa was originally a court or place where judges, councillors, or other assessors met, to hear, to consult, or to determine.

Secondarily, the word *Assisa* came to signify the act of so meeting, the cause, the subject, or the result of such meeting.

Hence the following tertiary uses of the term, viz. an ordinance or statute;—a trial or series of trials;—a tax or other assessment;—a power of assessing or of prescribing.

The *Assisa magna Regis*, the *Assisa Forestæ*, the *Assisa nummi*, the *Assisa per dominica Regis* (or Royal Tallage), the *Assisa panis et cervisiæ*, the *Assisa pannorum* (or statute regulating the cloth-trade), are expressions whose relation to one original idea is easily traced.

1166. February. (who was Usher of the King's Treasury) 13*s.* 4*d.* *ad portandas summoniciones* (viz., to the *Proceres* who were bidden to attend the Council): *et* 12*d.* *pro cerâ ad summoniciones* (for wax wherewith to seal the Writs of Summons). *Et pro pannis ad opus Henrici filii Regis* £16. 13*s.* 10*d.* (suggestive of the Prince's attendance at the Council). Other extracts, already given from the Pipe-Rolls, corroborate the the idea of some high occasion at Clarendon. Clarendon.

But there is another important subject associated with this second Council of Clarendon. We do not hesitate to say that at this Council the King issued to all the Barons and Military Tenants-in-capite, those letters which commanded each and all, by their fealty and allegiance, to make a return before the First Sunday in Lent (in this year, March 13th), of the constituents of their several Fiefs:—that is, how many Fees of *Old Feoffment,* how many of *New Feoffment,* and how many were in the *Demesne* of each Fief or Barony.

February. Moreover, the King's letters prescribed that these Returns were to contain the names of the knights and subtenants who were holding such old or new fees in each barony, so that, "if there were any who had not yet done allegiance to the King, and whose names were not yet entered on the King's Roll, they should do such allegiance before the first Sunday in Lent." Clarendon.

Before we quit this subject, it is well to say that we are quoting from a Record now called the "*Liber Niger Scaccarii,*" and that the said Record is a collection of the various Schedules returned in February or March, 1166, in obedience to the King's Precepts.[1]

By way of further fixing the date of the "Liber Niger," we note that Roger, Archbishop of York, styling himself "*Apostolicæ Sedis Legatus,*"

[1] These, our discovery and arguments as to the date of the Returns embodied in the Liber Niger, were apprehended before Professor Stubbs' work was written. They only constitute so much independent evidence in support of his view, and only add some little further precision to the date of the cognate "Assize of Clarendon."

The idea, or tradition, that the Returns embodied in the Liber Niger were made in contemplation of the marriage of the Princess Matilda needs some adjustment. The returns themselves contain no internal evidence whatever of having been provided for that specific occasion. But it so happened that at the time when the Returns were ordered the Princess's future marriage had been agreed upon; and it so happened that the *Auxilium,* collected in 1168 in *consequence* of her marriage, was grounded on these Returns, it being in fact the earliest *Auxilium* levied after these returns.

We may add that we have examined some score of minor indications as to the exact date of the Liber Niger Returns, and that the result in some cases is strongly confirmatory of, and in all cases consistent with the date we have assigned. We say nothing of certain supplementary matter, which in Hearne's printed Record is hardly distinguishable from the genuine Schedules of 1166. The two are quite discernible in the Queen's Remembrancer's Book, the nearest approximation to the original Schedules which is extant.

1166. February. hints in his return that he had used such diligence in the investigation necessary to the occasion, as the brevity of the time given had permitted, (*cum omni diligentiâ investigavi in tenemento meo, prout brevitas temporis passa est*).[1] Clarendon.

At Michaelmas, 1166, (12 Henry II.), the Sheriff of Wiltshire makes a charge on the King's exchequer, viz., "*Pro unâ huchiâ ad custodiendas cartas Baronum de Militibus*," that is, "for a hutch (or chest) wherein to keep the written returns of the Tenants-per-Baroniam concerning their knights-fees."

March 1-13. A Royal Charter, dated at Feckenham (Worcestershire), probably belongs to this period. It is in favour of Peter fitz William, and is attested by William Malet, Dapifer; John Marshall; William de Beauchamp (he was Sheriff of Worcestershire from 1155 to 1170); Geoffrey de Vere (he was Sheriff of Shropshire from January, 1165 to 1170); Hugh de Periers; and Walter de Dunstanvill.[2] Feckenham.

March 13. On or before this day, being the first Sunday in Lent, the barons' returns to the King's letters of February were due either at Salisbury or Clarendon. Also, all tenants by barony or military service, who had not previously done homage to the King, were to attend the Court, wherever it might be, for that purpose. Salisbury. Clarendon.

The King was about to cross the sea. His arms and accoutrements were to be shipped at Shoreham, Sussex. He himself designed to go from Southampton or Porchester. One of the last places of his visitation was Woodstock. At Michaelmas, 1166, the Sheriff of Oxfordshire charges—*Pro conducendis sellis et hernesio Regis de Wudestoch ad Shoreham* 13*s*. 4*d*. Woodstock.

And the Sheriffs of London and Middlesex charge—*Pro una hugiâ ad portandum hernesium, Regis ad Shorham et pro ipso hernesio* 8*s*. 10*d*. *Et pro* iij *palfridis ad opus Regis* £6. 13*s*. 4*d*. *per breve Regis*.

c. Mar. 15. Previous to the King's embarcation, we have a Charter dated at Porchester, whereby he grants the Stewardship of St. Edmundbury to William de Hastings, a Royal Steward (*Dispensatori Regis*). The Charter is attested by William Malet, Dapifer; Josceline de Baillol; Hugh de Gundevill; Hugh de Longchamp; Alan de Nevill; William de Lanval; Hugh de Piris (Periers); Walter de Dunstanvill; Porchester.

[1] Liber Niger, 303.

[2] Cartæ Antiquæ, T. dorso.

1166. c. March 16. Robert fitz Bernard; and Stephen, Chaplain and Præcentor (*Cantor*) of Moriton (Moretain).[1] Porchester.

c. March 16-23. "*Circa initium Quadragesima*," (the Chronicler's date for the King's embarcation) may perhaps mean the second week in Lent. The King embarked at Southampton. Southampton. Hence at Michaelmas, 1166, there is a charge on the Southampton Pipe-Roll:—*Et in liberacione Esneccæ* (the Royal yacht) *quando Rex transfretavit in Quadragesimâ* £7. 10*s*.[2]

It seems probable that the King was either accompanied or followed by the aged Earl of Leicester into Normandy. Being at Falaise, the King expedited a Charter Falaise. in favour of Henry de Beaumont, Bishop of Bayeux (who had become so in 1165). The Charter is attested by the said Bishop Henry; by Nicholas, Prior of Plessis-Grimoult; John, Archdeacon (probably of Seez); Robert, Earl of Leicester (who died in 1168); and William de Courci, Seneschal (of Normandy).[3]

King Henry was, according to some of the Chroniclers, accompanied, according to Hoveden, followed, into Normandy by William, King of Scots. The Southampton Pipe-Roll of Michaelmas, 1166, corroborates Hoveden in that it gives the cost of the King of Scots' transfretation distinctly from the cost of K. Henry's. It shows in addition that the former crossed at the expense of the latter.

HANTONIA. *Et in passagio Regis Scociæ £7. 10s. per breve Regis*.[3]

Various accounts of the King of Scots' motives in following Henry are alleged. His father, Malcolm IV., had deceased December 5, 1165, and one theory is that William must needs resort to the English court to do fealty for his realm of Scotland. But Cospatric, Earl of Northumberland, died at this very juncture; and another account is that William thought to gain that earldom by serving K. Henry. We must remember too that the existent Duchess of Bretagne was William's sister, and that her infant daughter, Constance, was, as will presently appear, the object of Henry's most considerate speculations.

About this time, a letter of Becket to the Chapter of Salisbury quashes the election of John of Oxford to the Deanery of Salisbury,[4] and a letter of Pope Alexander himself confirms Becket's cassation of the said appointment.[5]

[1] Soc. Camden (Brakelond), p. 120.
[2] Rot. Pip. 12 Hen. II. Hantonia.
[3] Stapleton's Rot. Normanniæ, i. clij.
[4, 5] S. T. C. Epistles, cxcix, ccxiii.

1166. c. March 23–31 and April. King Henry, on landing in Normandy, marched forthwith into Maine, where he reduced the two castles of Alençon and La-Roche-Mabile, held by William Talvas, Comte of Seez, John, his son, and John (son of Guy Comte of Ponthieu), his, William's, grandson. These had been rebelling against the authority of Queen Elianor, who had been left Regent of Maine and other provinces in the previous year.[1] Maine. Alençon. Roche-Mabile.

April 9. Sepulture of Waleran, Comte of Meulan. He was twin-brother of Robert, Earl of Leicester, above mentioned, and both, having been born in 1104, were now 62 years of age. Comte Waleran's successor was his son Robert.

April 24. Pope Alexander, in a letter dated at Lateran, and addressed to the Bishops, Abbots, etc., of all England, save the *Bishoprick* of York, appoints Archbishop Thomas of Canterbury to be Legate of all England except in the *Bishoprick* aforesaid.[2]

c. April 24. Another Papal Letter, probably of the same date, is to Archbishop Thomas himself; whom the Pope authorizes to deal justice on those who had done violence to the possessions and goods of the Church of Canterbury. The Pope will not *dictate anything about the King's person.*[3]

April 24. K. Henry kept the feast of Easter at Angers, and is said to have had conference with K. Louis.[4] Angers.

May 3. Pope Alexander, at Lateran, addresses by letter the Bishop of London and all Bishops Suffragan of the See of Canterbury. They are to compel restitution, under pain of anathema without appeal, by all those who, under Royal mandate, had accepted the Benefices theretofore held by Archbishop Thomas's Clerks.[5]

May 10. (Tuesday). King Henry holds a Council at Le Mans. It is attended by several Norman and French Bishops. They agree to a five years' tax in aid of the Holy Land. Le Mans.

May 16, (Monday). Pope Alexander, at Lateran, writes to Rotrode, Archbishop of Rouen. He expatiates on Henry's mission to Wurtzburg (May, 1165). Archbishop Rotrode is ordered to teach K. Henry more respect for Rome, and better treatment of Archbishop Thomas. If K. Henry persists, *the Pope will punish him.*[6]

May 17, (Tuesday). K. Henry holds another Council at Le Mans, on the same matters as the former one. Le Mans.

June 1. K. Henry holds a Council at Chinon, in Touraine. The Norman Bishops of Seez and Liseux are despatched to Chinon.

[1] Cartæ i. 598. Chron. Normann. Chron. St. Albin, sub anno, 1165.
[2] S. T. C. iv. 80. Epistle cclxx.
[3] S. T. C. Epist. ccx., ccxxxix.
[4] Stubbs, referring to S. T. C. Epist. cxliv., clxviii. and (for the conference) to R. de Monte, p. 901.
[5] S. T. C. Epist. cclxxxj.
[6] S. T. C. iv. 53, Epist. cclj.

1166. June 1. Pontigny to lodge (with Becket) (notice of) an appeal to Rome against the measures taken (or threatened by) Archbishop Becket. Chinon.

June 2. (Ascension Day.) The notice of appeal will have arrived at Pontigny too late. On Ascension Day (June 2), Becket left Pontigny. When Henry's messengers reached Pontigny, Becket was far away at Soissons, paying his celebrated visit to the Shrine of St. Dransius.

June 10. At this time K. Henry was ill, and probably lay at Chinon. Chinon.

A Royal Charter, dated at Chinon, is in favour of Robert, Abbot of Malmesbury, and is singly attested by Master Walter de Insula.[1]

c. June 11. K. Henry is purposing to march into Bretagne against the Vicomte of Porhoët and the Lord of Fougeres, who were in rebellion against Conan le Petit, Duke of Bretagne, K. Henry's ally.[2]

June 12. (Whit-Sunday.) Becket reaches Vézelay, a town on the river Cure, and on the borders of Nivernois and Burgundy. From the pulpit of Vézelay he uttered sentence of excommunication against the following persons.—Against *John of Oxford* for communicating with the schismatical and excommunicated Reginald of Cologne;—for usurping the Deanery of Salisbury in defiance of a Papal Mandate; and for taking 'that oath' in the Court of the Emperor.

Against *Richard of Ilchester*, for his commerce with Reginald of Cologne, and the German Schismatics; and for taking an oath in connection with the Saxon wedding.

Against *Richard de Luci* and *Joceline de Baillol*, for stimulating King Henry's tyranny, and fabricating the "heretical Customs."

Against *Radulf de Broc*, *Hugh de St. Clare*, and *Thomas fitz Bernard*, for usurping the goods and possessions of the Church of Canterbury.

One authority [3] adds Alan de Nevill to the list of the Vézelay excommunicates. Another intimates that about the same time Becket suspended the Bishop of Salisbury (Josceline de Bohun[4]) for instituting John of Oxford into the above Deanery.

c. June 16, 17. It is quite uncertain where K. Henry was when news of Becket's procedure at Vézelay reached him. It seems impossible that he should as yet have set out for Bretagne,

[1] Malmesbury Chartulary No. 56.

[2] See S. T. C. iii. 196. Rob. de Monte (Struve), 901; Diceto, 517; John Salisb. Epp. clxxvi. Chron. St. Albin, sub anno, 1165.

[3] Diceto, p. 539.

[4] Some authors have taken it for granted that Josceline de Bailleul was identical with Joceline, Bishop of Salisbury.

1166. c. June 16, 17. the nearest point of which would be more than 200 English miles distant from Vézelay, whilst Chinon would be about 140. (Chinon?).

The King despatched instant orders to England, and to Richard de Luci, that the Anglican Bishops should appeal to Rome against Becket's procedure.

On this the King set forward, we suppose, towards Bretagne. Bretagne.

c. June 24. The Anglican Bishops now appeal to Rome, fixing May 18, 1167, as the term of their appeal. It does not appear, however, that their appeal of this date touched any of the sentences pronounced at Vézelay. The present appeal was against Becket's having suspended the Bishop of Salisbury without the counsel of his Suffragans, and because Becket had threatened the King with a sentence (of excommunication).[1] Ralph de Hospital took news of the Bishops' appeal to Rouen. Geoffrey Ridel, Archdeacon of Canterbury, was at this juncture waiting in England for the King's license to cross to Normandy.[2]

June 28. The King was on march (*in exercitu*), and four leagues distant from Fougeres.[3]

July 6. Council of English Bishops and Abbots at Northampton.

July 7. Pope Alexander, at Lateran, certifies Archbishop Thomas and his Suffragans, that he, the Pope, has excommunicated Earl Hugh and William de Vals. The Pope cancels the exchanges made by the Prior of *Pantun* with Earl Hugh.[4]

July 12. The King and his army are before Fougeres. His presence there, or thereabouts, on this and two following days, is illustrated by a remarkable series of documents.—The first is— Fougeres.

The Quitclaim (*L'Abandon*) made by Rualon de Geneccio (perhaps Guaccio) to Robert, Abbot of Mont. St. Michael. And then follow these words,—

Acta est hæc Convencio assensu et consilio domini Regis Henrici Secundi,[5] *et actum* (sic) *publice in capitulo Montis*

[1, 2] S. T. C. iv. 196, vi. 185. Epist. (G. F.) ccccxxxvi. This same date (June 24) is mistakenly alleged as that on which K. Henry captured the Castle of Fougeres.

[3] S. T. C. iv. 196.

[4] This affair of the excommunication of Earl Hugh became indissolubly mixed up with the other national questions which were at issue between the Pope and K. Henry. As one writer (Lyttelton) assumed Earl Hugh to have been the contemporary Earl of Chester, much doubt and chronological difficulty has been added to these other questions. The root of the real story was this.—At Pentney (Norfolk) was a House of Austin Canons, whose Prior, without consent of his Canons, alienated certain possessions of his Church to Hugh Bigot, Earl of Norfolk, and to William de Vaux, by far the greatest of the Earl's feudal tenants of Norfolk. The Canons of Pentney complained hereof to the Pope. The Pope admonished Earl Hugh and William de Vaux to restore such possessions. The Earl and De Vaux refused. Hence the sentence of excommunication given in the text.

[5] The style of *Henricus Secundus*, rather than that of *Henricus Filius Imperatricis*, is unusual at this early date.

1166. July. 12. (the Chapter-House of Mont. St. Michael) 4to *idus Julii* (July 12), *anno Domini Incarnacionis* 1166, *regni vero Gloriosissimi Regis Angliæ* ix° (it should be xii°). There are witnesses—William de St. John, Gilbert de Camp', Radulf de Potterel, Richard de Venno, Radulf de Humeto, Hugh Bigot, and Richard Bosco (perhaps *de Bosco*).[1] Fougeres.

July 13. By a second Deed, K. Henry II. confirms the above and another convention, between the same Abbot and Gervase fitz Helias. The Witnesses of the King's Confirmation are Richard (of Ilchester), Archdeacon of Poictiers; Master John Cumin; Master Ralph de Tam̃; Richard de Humet, Constable; Jordan Teissun; William fitz Hamo; Fulco Paenell; and William de St. John. This Deed is furthermore dated *apud Fulgerias in exercitu*. And is expressed to be expedited (*datum*) *per manum Magistri Stephani*,[2] iii[io] *idus Julii* (July 13) 1166; *regni vero Henrici gloriosissimi Regis Angliæ* ix° (It should be xii°).[1]

July 14. By a third Deed, K. Henry releases to the Abbot and Convent of St. Michael "*operacionem quam facere consueverunt ad turrim meam de Guavreio.*" The witnesses are Richard, Archdeacon of Poictiers; Master John Cumin; William, Earl of Arundel; Comte Eudo (a Breton Comte); Richard de Humet, Constable; Jordan Teissun; Fulco Paenell; William de St. John; and Geoffrey Monk (Le Moyne). The words '*Apud Fulgerias*' follow, and then the date, viz., *Datum per manus Magistri Stephani* ij° *idus Julii* (July 14), *anno ab incarnacione Domini* MCLXVI; *præsidente universitati Catholicæ Ecclessiæ Alexandro Papâ* iii[io]; *regnante vero gloriosissimo Rege Angliæ et Duce Normanniæ et Aquitaniæ, et comite Andegaviæ, Henrico, anno* ix° (it should be xii°).[1]

Fr. July 22. Becket pronounced a Commination against King Henry, publicly and in Church.[3]

Fougeres at length fell before the arms of Henry. It afterwards appears that its defender and lord, Raoul de Fougeres, gave hostages to Henry, including one of his own daughters, in pledge of future fidelity.

[1] Chartulary of Mont St. Michael, (D'Anisy's Transcripts, ii. 291, 292).

[2] The Stephen de Fulgeriis of other charters.

[3] Gervase, p. 1400. See also S. T. C. iv. 195. The church where this took place is not stated. We can only conjecture that it was the Conventual Church of Pontigny, whither Becket retired after his demonstration at Vézelay.

1166. c. August. K. Henry now went to Rennes to take possession of Duke Conan's Dutchy of Bretagne, which Conan had ceded to Henry, under contract for a marriage eventually to be solemnized between Geoffrey, Henry's third surviving son (not yet eight years of age), and Constance, only child of Conan.[1] Rennes.

It was now, surely, that Prince Geoffrey was summoned from England to join his father in Bretagne. The Pipe-Roll of the year aptly illustrates the situation, and gives us the names of three officers who would seem to have been in charge of such of the Royal family as were left in England.

HAMPSHIRE. *Et in corredio Gaufridi filii Regis in transfretatione suâ £25 per Ailwardum camerarium et per testimonium Joscelini de Baillol et Willelmi filii Johannis. Et eidem Gaufrido filio Regis et hominibus ejus £25. 8s. 4d. ad pannos et equos per Alanum de Nevill. Et ad conducenda Regalia filii Regis in Normanniam, 8s.*

SOUTHAMPTON. *Et in passagio Domini Gaufridi filii Regis, Esneccæ et duabus aliis navibus £10.*

Aug. Sept. K. Henry at this period visited, but we know not in what order, the several Breton towns of Redon,— Redon.

Of Combort, and of— Combour.

Dol.[1] Dol.

The King also visited Mont St. Michael, and it was there probably that he was sought by William, King of Scots, by Ninian, King of the Western Isles, and by the Bishop of Man. The Bishop, it seems, had been sent onward to the King's Court by the Empress Matilda, then in Normandy.[1] Mont St. Michael.

King Henry received the homage of the Bretons at Thouars.[1] Thouars.

August 15. Meanwhile, 'the Archdeacon' (*i.e.* Geoffrey Ridel, Archdeacon of Canterbury), whom in the end of June we have seen waiting in England for the King's license to cross to Normandy, having so crossed, lodged, on August 15th, an appeal (the object of which is not specified) before the Archbishop of Rouen and others. The Archdeacon undertook at the same time to send an emissary to Becket (still at Pontigny) on the subject.[2]

August 25. Pope Alexander, at Lateran, confirms Comte Philip's (of Flanders) marriage with Elizabeth, daughter of the Comte of Peronne.[3]

[1] Chron. Normann. pp. 1000, 1001. King Henry's alleged visit to Jumiéges at this period is inexplicable. Professor Stubbs understands Genest to have been the locality intended by the Chronicle.

[2] S. T. C. iv. 185. Epist. ccexliv.

[3] S. T. C. iv. 146.

1166. August 31. Probable date of the death of Robert, Bishop of Bath.[1]

NOTICES OF THE QUEEN and of Prince Henry during the fiscal year ending *Michaelmas*, 1166, are as follows.—

At Michaelmas, 1165, Queen Eleanor had been left Regent of Maine and Anjou four months previously.

On October, 1165, being at Angers, she gave birth to the Princess Johanna. In March, 1166, she joined the King, then coming over from England.

At Michaelmas, 1166, she was probably still resident at Angers with five of her children, viz., Richard, Matilda, Geoffrey, Eleanor, and Johanna.

PRINCE HENRY, from Michaelmas, 1165, to Michaelmas, 1166, was continuously resident in England. The Pipe-Rolls will furnish the cost of his separate establishment, and the personnel of his suite, and will perhaps suggest that he was resident chiefly at Clarendon, Sherborne, or Winchester.—

WILTSHIRE. *Et in corredio Henrici filii Regis* £58 *per breve Regis. Et in corredio ejusdem* £30 *per Willm fil. Johannis per breve ipsius Willielmi.*

DORSETSHIRE AND SOMERSETSHIRE. *Et in corredio Henrici filii Regis* £56. 9*s.* 5*d. per breve Regis, per Willm filium Johannis.*

HAMPSHIRE. *Et in corredio Henrici filii Regis* £130 *per Willm filium Johannis de quibus idem Wills reddidit compotum. Et in corredio ejusdem filii Regis* £52. 4*s.* 2*d. per Willm fil. Johannis de quibus idem Wills debet reddere compotum.*

LONDON AND MIDDLESEX. *Et pro pannis ad opus Henrici filii Regis* £16. 14*s.* 10*d.*

Courts of Law and Justice.

From the year 1159 to the year 1165, the Pipe-Rolls supply us with scant evidence as to the persons who administered the Law or fulfilled other quasi-judicial functions in the provinces.

The "Assize of Clarendon," in February, 1166, was probably followed by a great exercitation of its powers in the County where it originated. The following extracts from the Pipe-Roll of the ensuing Michaelmas bear upon the point.—

LONDON AND MIDDLESEX. The Sheriffs charge—"*Pro custamento Probatorum et pro conducendis illis ad Clarendon* 48 *sol.*

SURREY. The Sheriff charges—*Et in custamento probatorum Regis et pro conducendis illis ad Sarum* 5 *sol.*

An extract from the Wiltshire Pipe-Roll will show still more forcibly how active had been the administration of criminal law during the previous six months. The Sheriff charges—*Et pro polis parandis ad Juisium latronum* 5*s. Et presbiteris pro benedicendis eisdem polis* 20*s. Et pro scutis probatorum et armaturis* 7*s. Et pro custodiâ probatorum* 22*s.* 5*d. Et pro ipsis conducendis* 25*s.* 3*d. Et pro reparacione gaiolæ de Sarum* 5*s.* 10*d. Et pro unâ gaiolâ faciendâ apud Malmesburiam* 27*s.* 9*d.*

Further, in the year ending Michaelmas, 1166, it is clear that nearly every county in England was formally visited by Justices-in-Eyre. Whatever of their duties resulted in fiscal gain to the Crown, was entered by the Sheriff of each County under the head of *Nova Placita et Novæ Conventiones.* In about twenty-one Counties (of the north, the east, the south-east, and the centre),[2] it appears that Earl

[1] This Prelate's death is usually (Annals of Burton, Annals of Winton) said to have taken place Aug. 31, 1165. But about February, 1166, we have him making a return, personally, of the Feodary of his See (Lib. Nig. i. 86), and on March 14, 1166, we have him actively and otherwise employed (Ecclesiastical Documents, p. 41, Camden Soc.). The earliest account of the Revenues of the vacant See is on the Pipe-Roll of Michaelmas, 1168, but it is *De anno præterito*, that is, of Revenues which had accrued previous to Michaelmas, 1167. The receipts (only £6. 16*s.* 8*d.*) would, *per se*, suggest that the Prelate's death took place on August 31, 1167. But it is possible that a whole year's account is missing in the Pipe-Rolls; and when we find the Pope, on Oct. 9, 1167, censuring K. Henry for maintaining this and other Vacancies we may be sure that the vacancy commenced earlier than August 31, 1167.

The only resource in such cases is to abide by the recorded day of *Obit.* (August 31), and to discover for ourselves the year which most consists with the general phenomena of the case. That year in this instance is the year 1166.

The date is the more important as being part of the collateral evidence in investigating the date of the returns embodied in the *Liber Niger.*

[2] Viz., the Counties of Northumberland, Cumberland, York,—Lincoln, Norfolk, Suffolk, Essex, Kent, Sussex, Surrey, Herts, Cambridge, Huntingdon, Bucks, Bedford, Northampton, Warwick, Leicester, Nottingham, Derby, and Stafford.

Geoffrey of Essex, and Richard de Luci were the Justices, by both or one of whom these Pleas were held. At Carlisle, and at Newcastle-upon-Tyne, Richard de Luci seems to have officiated singly. The Justices who visited the Counties of the west, south-west, and south, are not named.

In the same year very many counties were visited by Alan de Nevill, as Justice of the Forest. The fiscal results of his *iter* are in some instances entered on the Pipe-Roll as—*Nova Placita et Novæ Conventiones per Alanum de Nevill.*

1166. MICHAELMAS, 1166, TO MICHAELMAS, 1167.

Sep. 30. The King probably in Bretagne. (Bretagne).

Sun. Oct. 2. Peter, Archbishop of Bourges, consecrating the Church of Grammont, is attended by Bishops Gerald of Limoges, Gerald of Cahors (*Caturcensis*), and Roger (usually written *Froger*) of Seez.[1]

Oct. In this month, and again in May and in October, 1167, we find Robert, Earl of Leicester, acting as Grand Justiciar or Viceroy in England.[2]

Oct. 21. Geoffrey de Mandeville, Earl of Essex, died at Chester whilst associated with Richard de Luci in operations against Wales.[3]

The English refortifying Basingwerk, in Flintshire, are attacked by the Welsh, and suffer loss.

King Henry is at Caen. To this occasion belongs the story of the maniacal fury exhibited by Henry against the Constable, De Humez, whom the King denounced as a Traitor, because in negotiations then current, De Humez had testified to the deserts of William, King of Scots.[4] Caen.

The next day, at Caen, "in a meadow near the Chapel," the King prevented some Templars from saluting Richard of Ilchester (Archdeacon of Poitiers), because the latter was under sentence of excommunication.

c. Oct. 31. About this time died Robert de Chesney, Bishop of Lincoln.[5]

[1] Rerum Gallic. Scriptores, xii. 441.

[2] M. Paris, i. 107, Diceto (corrected), p. 547.

[3] This Earl's death is variously reported by Monastic Writers as on Oct. 21, 1165, and Oct. 21, 1167 (see Monasticon, iv. 140, and iv. 143). It took place on October 21, of the intermediate year, 1166. This new date is supported by some indirect evidence, such as his letter written to K. Henry in February or March, 1166 (Liber Niger, i. 228), and the fact that the Earl's death was known in Normandy in November of the same year. The date is further supported by the solid testimony of the Pipe-Rolls; which show Earl Geoffrey as receiving the *Tercium Denarium* of Essex up to Michaelmas, 1166, and Earl William, his successor, as receiving the same at Michaelmas, 1167. The date is most important.

[4] S. T. C. iv. 260. For the story of the King's demeanor, see Lyttelton, ii. 494-5.

[5] Diceto's date for this Prelate's death is January 26, 1167. Other authorities say January 8, 1167. Professor Stubbs, in a note to his Itinerary of Henry II. (Appendix to Benedict of Peterborough, p. cxxxvi.), shows that a Report of the Bishop's death, premature or not, had reached Normandy before November 30, 1166. Such report was not premature, for the Lincolnshire Pipe-Roll of 1167 shows that the Bishop died during the term which expired at Christmas, 1166, which neutralises the statements of Diceto and the other Chroniclers, and leaves us no alternative but to accept the date suggested by Professor Stubbs' note.

But, in further limitation of the date, 'before Nov. 30, 1166,' we observe that the death of Geoffrey, Earl of Essex, which took place (as above proved) on Oct. 21, 1166, was reported in Normandy by the same channel, and at the same time, as that of the Bishop of Lincoln. Probably then the latter event took place late in October.—

The entry on the Pipe-Roll of Michaelmas, 1167,

1166. c. Nov. 1. The King at Toques refuses the Bishop of Liseux' (Arnulf's) petition to quit Normandy on account of his debts.[1] Touques.

Nov. The King goes to Rouen, and while there arrests a Papal letter-carrier, a boy, it seems, who being put to torture, confessed that the letters which he brought were handed to him by 'Master Herbert.' Master Herbert escaped arrest. The Empress-mother demanded the release of the messenger, which K. Henry refused.[1] Rouen.

It would seem that on this occasion Henry had an interview, near Rouen, with Philip, Comte of Flanders, and promised an annuity of £1000 to Matthew, Comte of Boulogne.[1]

King Henry 'returns' to Rouen (apparently after his conference with Flanders), and has an interview with Rotrou, Archbishop of Rouen, and Arnulf, Bishop of Liseux. They reprove him for arresting the Papal letter-carrier, and for his wrath against Master Walter[2] (Geoffrey Ridel's clerk), who had failed to arrest the bearer (perhaps Master Herbert) of certain letters of Becket. The Archbishop of Rouen explains to Henry the purport of letters received by himself from the Pope. The King replies that he fears no threats.[1]

Reginald, clerk of the Dean of Tours, speaks in support of Rome, whereat Henry sneers.[1]

K. Henry *returns* to Caen, where he presents the Bishop of Liseux with 60 merks. Alfred, a clerk of the Bishop of Hereford (Robert de Melun), arrives at court and asks the King's leave for the Bishop and Sir Roger (*Dominus Rogerius*) to cross the Channel in obedience to a summons of Archbishop Thomas. The King says that they need not obey such a summons, an appeal being open to them; but that if they do obey, they will not be allowed to return to England.[1] Caen

There is a Charter of Confirmation to the Abbot of Mont St. Michel, granted by K. Henry II., and dated (according to the Transcript) *Apud Kadun'*. It undoubtedly passed in Normandy and probably at Caen (*Apud Kadomum*). If

which bears upon this curious question, should be given. It is as follows.—

EPISCOPATUS LINCOLNIÆ. *Ricardus Archidiaconus Pictaviæ et Ricardus de Ameri, custodes, reddunt compotum de* £699. 9*s*. 2*d*. *de firmis maneriorum et redditibus Archidiaconatuum ab eo termino quo Robertus Episcopus mortuus fuit, scilicet a Natali Domini* (Dec. 25, 1166) *usque ad festum Sancti Michaelis* (Sept. 29, 1167).—

This, of course, does not determine how long previous to December 25, 1166, the Bishop died.

[1] S. T. C. iv. 261, 262. Epist. ccclxxviii.

[2] "Master Walter" was clearly "Keeper of the Seal" on behalf of Geoffrey Ridel, then Vice-Chancellor. The King in his rage took the seal from Master Walter (S. T. C. iv. 185), but afterwards restored it to "the Archdeacon" (of Canterbury, that is) (S. T. C. iv. 261).

1166. Nov. so, we can assign it to no period but the present. It is attested by Geoffrey, Archdeacon of Canterbury; Richard, Archdeacon of Poitiers; Gilo, Archdeacon of Rouen; Waleran, Archdeacon of Bayeux; Clarembald, Abbot of St. Augustine's, Canterbury; Manasser Biset, Dapifer; Richard de Luci; William Malet; and Bertram de Verdon.[1]

Richard de Luci's presence in Normandy at this time is a surprise, but hardly a difficulty. News about him had reached Rouen, from England, not indeed that he had crossed the channel, but that he had taken the cross and was proposing to go to Jerusalem.[2]

Here then we come to a letter written, evidently at Rouen, by Nicholas de Monte, to Archbishop Becket. This letter tells (as above) about the deaths of Earl Geoffrey and the Bishop of Lincoln, about Richard de Luci, and about the affair of Basingwerk, all which was English news. The Rouen news was about K. Henry's conduct in regard to the Great Seal, and about the Papal letter-carrier, *still detained in prison*. The letter says that the Archbishop of Rouen and his Suffragans had not as yet *openly convened* King Henry in obedience to a Papal Mandate, (enjoining such a measure). It also says that a Master of a hospital (Magister infirmorum) from Canterbury had reported in Rouen, how that the Bishop of London had paid all his receipts of income belonging to Becket's clerks into the King's Treasury, and how the Prior of (Christ Church) Canterbury had imprisoned a monk for declaring in favour of Archbishop Thomas.[2]

The letter adds that King Henry was expected to be in Rouen on November 30.

Nov. 11. On this day Archbishop Becket quitted Pontigny, going, it would seem, first to Soissons, and then, under the auspices of Louis VII. of France, taking up his abode at St. Columba, near to Sens.[3]

This move of Becket was consequent upon a threat dealt by Henry against the Cistercian Order, of which Pontigny was a member, viz., that if that Abbey continued to harbour Becket, Henry would confiscate the possessions of every Cistercian house in England.

Nov. 18. King Henry, now at Tours, holds conference with Theobald, Comte of Blois, to whom he promises a pension of £500 per annum.[4] Tours.

It was clearly while the King was at Tours that a monk of Abingdon came to the Court to complain of a wrong done to his house by Turstin fitz Simon. The King's writ, dated at Tours, orders the Sheriff of Berkshire to do right to the Abbey in the matter of immediate complaint (a wrongful seizure of tithes), and likewise enjoins that 'when Turstin fitz Simon shall have returned to England, further

1 D'Anisy's Transcripts, ii. 289.
2 S. T. C. iv. 185, Epist. cccxliv.
3 Gervase of Canterbury, 1401. Diceto.
4 S. T. C. iv. 185, 262. Carte, vol. i. p. 599.

1166. c. Nov. process should be taken as to certain land which Turstin fitz Simon held (the Abbot said, wrongfully) under the Abbey.'[1]—

This writ and its exact date are of much chronological importance, seeing that it is attested, singly, by "Master John de Oxenford" (now, it seems, no longer entitling himself "Dean of Sarum").

At this very juncture and within a few days of each other K. Henry despatched two distinct missions to the Court of Rome. One Envoy was John of Oxford himself. The other embassy was conducted by John Cumin and Master Ralph de Tamworth. Its specific object is nowhere declared, but it was strongly antagonistic to Becket and was probably suggested by Becket's having put himself under the protection of Louis. The Pope, though he nowhere censures Becket directly for this step, blamed the Abbot of Pontigny and the Cistercian Order generally for their conduct in the matter, and (as will appear in due course) became much more tolerant of K. Henry's animosity towards Becket.

Nov. 20. King Henry is now at Chinon (in Touraine).[3] He holds conference with the Barons of Poitou, whom, says our authority, the King found the more tractable in that he had dealt first with their ally, the Comte of Blois. Chinon.

Nov. 30. This was the day on which it was previously expected that the King would be in Rouen. (Rouen.)

Dec. 1. Pope Alexander, dating from Lateran, apprises the Anglican Bishops that he has received their appeal, and will send *Legates-a-latere* "to hear and to decide."[4]

Dec. 7. The King (if our authority[4] be strictly correct) was still expected at Rouen, and (again) for a conference with Flanders, and to *promise* an annuity to the Comte of Boulogne. At such a conference, whatever its date, the King gave to Comte Matthew of Boulogne a pension of £1000 per annum in lieu of his claim (as husband of King

[1] Hist. Abendon ii. 225. Turstin Fitz Simon, of whom we shall hear again, appears in the Feodary of February, 1166, as holding half a knight's fee under the Abbey (Lib. Nig. i. 182).

[2] "Much more tolerant," we say; for the Archbishop of Rouen had previous to this, and by Papal directions, advised the King of impending interdicts if enjoined by the Pope, and told the King that such injunctions would be obeyed by the Archbishop himself (S. T. C. Epistle xcvii).

[3] S. T. C. iv. 263, 185.

[4] S. T. C. iv. 77. Epist. cclxviii.

1166 Stephen's eldest daughter) to the Comte of Moretain in (Rouen). Normandy.

Dec. 10. Pope Alexander, at Lateran, directs the clerks (Canons) of Bangor to elect a Bishop after consulting Archbishop Thomas, and to present the "Elect" for the said Archbishop's approval. Alexander abolishes the hereditary Archdeaconry (of Bangor).[1]

c. Dec. 15. Cumin and Tamworth, Henry's envoys to Rome, reaching Viterbo, seize certain letters of Becket from the person of his messenger, and also a letter of the Archbishop of Bourges.[2]

About this time the Pope absolved John of Oxford in person. The latter is said to have gained that end by abjuring "the customs," and by promising to procure peace between Henry and Becket.[3]

Dec. 20. (Tuesday). Pope Alexander, at Lateran, writes to K. Henry. The Pope has conferred with the King's messengers, John Cummin and Master Ralph de Tamworth. The Pope will attend to Henry's wishes;—will send *Legates-a-latere* to adjudicate between the King and the Archbishop of Canterbury, and between the latter and the Anglican Bishops in the matter of their appeal to Rome. The Legates, being ordered to set out before Christmas, will be able to do so in January. They will absolve. The Pope entrusts confidentially to Henry a power of quashing future sentences of Becket. The Pope has written to Becket, forbidding further molestation of Henry.[4]

Cumin, while at Rome, got sight of Becket's letters relative to his sentences of excommunication, and his threats against K. Henry.[5]

King Henry had other business with the Papal Court, relative to a dispensation to be obtained in regard to the projected marriage of his son Geoffrey and Constance of Bretagne.[6] This business seems to have been successfully negotiated with Alexander by John of Oxford.[7]

Dec. 24. Queen Elianor, now in England, gave birth to Prince John, at Oxford.[8]

Dec. 25. King Henry kept Christmas at Poitiers, where he is Poictiers. joined by Prince Henry, coming from England.[9]

1 S. T. C. iv. 91. Epist. cclxxvii.
2 S. T. C. vi. 253.
3 S. T. C. vi. 252. Epist. G. F. cccclxvi.
4 MS. Cotton Claudius, B. 2. fo. 142. S. T. C. iv. 136. Epist. cccix.
5 S. T. C. vi. 253.
6 There was consanguinity between the two children. Geoffrey was third in descent, and Constance was fourth in descent, from K. Henry I. Though the daughter of Henry I., through whom Constance's consanguinity arose, was illegitimate, that, we believe, would not affect such questions.

It is curious, and perhaps that was the point raised, that the two parties, Geoffrey and Constance, were of consanguinity in another and perfectly legitimate way. Each of them was fourth in descent from Margaret, sister of Edgar Atheling; that is, they were cousins in the third degree.

7 And it will have been the success of John of Oxford's diplomacy, and his consequent boasts about it that were subsequently alluded to in the Canterbury letters as being calculated to create dissatisfaction and annoyance to Louis and the French. His own absolution and recovery of the Deanery of Salisbury can have been no concern of Louis; but Louis will naturally have viewed with apprehension and dismay the possible coalition, and feudal combination of Bretagne, with those other powerful Fiefs, Normandy, Aquitaine, Anjou, Touraine, etc., which owed allegiance to France.
8 Matthew of Westminster. Carte.
9 Chron. Normann. p. 1001.

1166. SOME ENTRIES on the Pipe-Roll of 1167 will show Prince Henry's residence in England after Michaelmas, 1166, and the circumstance of his transfretation.

LONDON AND MIDDLESEX. (*De veteri firmâ*). *Pro pannis Henrici filii Regis* £8. 15*s*. 8*d*. *per breve Comitis Legecestriæ per Edwardum Blundum et Ailward Camerarium.*

WILTSHIRE. *In corredio Henrici filii Regis* £20 *per breve Comitis Legecestriæ.*

DEVONSHIRE. *Reginæ* £100,[1] *et Willo filio Johannis* 76*s*. *ad acquietanda corredia Henrici filii Regis per breve Comitis Legecestriæ.*

WINCHESTER. (*De veteri firmâ*). *In corredio Henrici filii Regis* £71. 11*s*. 8*d*. *numero pro* £68. 3*s*. 6*d*., *blancis* [2] *per breve Comitis Legecestriæ.*

SOUTHAMPTON. *In liberacione Esneccæ quando filius Regis transfretavit* £7. 0*s*. 10*d*. *Et pro* 6 *navibus quæ transfretaverunt cum ipso* £8. 15*s*. *per breve Regis.*

IN THE ABOVE YEAR died William, King of Sicily.[3]

A.D. 1167.

Jan. 1. K. Henry, leaving Poitiers soon after Christmas, goes into Guienne. Guienne.

Jan. 1. John Cumin and Ralph de Tamworth leave Rome.

John of Oxford, having been restored by the Pope to the Deanery of Salisbury, will have left Rome in December, and will have had an interview with K. Henry, if in January, by following the King into Guienne. Returning thence, and charged with a mission to England, he seems to have passed through Poitiers. John, Bishop of Poitiers notices his passage to England in a letter to Becket, and says that his object there is to collect evidence against Becket.[4]

Landing at Southampton, John of Oxford finds the Bishop of Hereford waiting there with the intention of crossing to visit Becket in France,[5] which it would seem was now abandoned. John of Oxford then has an interview with the Bishop of London at Winchester.

Jan. 25. Gilbert Foliot, Bishop of London, celebrates High Mass at St. Paul's Church on the feast of the Conversion of St. Paul. While officiating, he is served with letters from Becket, asserting the legatine powers vested in Becket by the Pope, and enjoining on all the Suffragan Bishops of England, that the deprived Clergy be reinstated.

Jan. 28. Pope Alexander, at Lateran, writes to the Anglican Bishops. They are not to intrude on the rights, dignities, or liberties of Canterbury without the Archbishop's consent, nor in virtue of their Appeal to the Pope now pending.[6]

Jan. 29. Pope Alexander, at Lateran, to Archbishop Thomas. He is to admonish the Clergy of Bangor that they elect a Bishop within two months after receipt of the Papal mandate. In their default the Archbishop is to nominate a Bishop in three months after receipt of this letter.[7]

Jan. 30. Pope Alexander, at Lateran, to Henry, Archbishop of Rheims:—commends and encourages the Archbishop's patronage of Becket.[8]

[1] The Queen had undoubtedly returned to England before Prince Henry left for Poitiers; but this payment to her by the Sheriff of Devon was not (as it would seem from the entry on the Pipe-Roll) on account of the Prince. It was a *constituted* charge in her favour on the Revenues of the County of Devon.

[2] This entry shows that the *blanch money* of the period was represented by as much current coin, with about 5 per cent. added, for the weight lost in the process of *dealbation.*

[3] Chron. Normann. p. 1000.

[4] S. T. C. vi. 253.

[5] S. T. C. iii. 215. The Bishop of Hereford had been cited by Becket, and the citation was for Feb. 2.

[6] S. T. C. iv. 76. Ep. cclxvii.

[7] S. T. C. iv. 36. Ep. ccxxxij.

[8] S. T. C. iv. 52. Ep. ccl. Note, that Henry, Archbishop of Rheims was brother of Louis VII.

Feb. 1. 1167. John Cumin and Ralph de Tamworth, returning from Rome, reach Tours, and on Feb. 2nd, they are apparently at Poitiers, for on that day they have an interview with John, Bishop of Poitiers. The Bishop could get nothing out of them, but from one of their Clerks he learnt of the promised Legation of William of Pavia and Otho; also that Cumin and Tamworth denounced John of Oxford's negotiations at Rome as traitorous to K. Henry in that they promised reconciliation between the King and Becket.[1] (It seems clear that Cumin and Tamworth thus passing from Tours to Poictiers were en route to Henry's Court further south).

Feb. 9. Pope Alexander, at Lateran, to the Canons, Clergy and people of Bangor:—Reiterates his precept to elect a Bishop and to present the Elect to Archbishop Thomas for Consecration.[2]

Sun. Feb. 26. King Henry's Commissioners come to Souterraine, apparently about the recent rebellion of William IV. (surnamed *Sector Ferri*), Comte of Angouleme, Adelbert IV., Comte of Marche, and Robert de Selit.[3] Gascogne.

Feb. 27. Robert de Melun, Bishop of Hereford, died.

At Michaelmas following, John Cumin answers as Custos for the Revenues of the vacant See arising in three quarters of the year. Out of the same he had paid the Dean of Hereford 50 shillings for "celebrating the late Bishop's funeral." [4]

March. In Lent (that is between Feb. 22 and April 9), K. Henry confers with the Comte of St. Geours (*Sancti Egidii*) at Mont de Marsan (*Magnum Montem*). Mont de Marsan, (in Gascony).

c. March. Becket writes to John of Canterbury, his Clerk at the Papal Court.[5]—

He complains of the Pope's alleged concessions to Henry, as reported by John of Oxford. He mentions the return to England of John of Oxford, and of the other King's messengers (meaning Cumin and Tamworth), from the Papal Court and what they give out. He also mentions John of Oxford's passage to England and his interview with the Bishops of Hereford and London.[5] He also deprecates the Pope's reported appointment of his, (Becket's), personal enemy, William of Pavia, to be Legate to Henry.

c. March 20–31. K. Henry sent ambassadors to Rome, we do not find for what purpose or with what diplomatic result. Some of them reached their destination by buying safe-conduct from the Senate for £20. These were back at Bologna and on their way to France on Sunday, May 21. Two others, viz. Roger, Bishop of Worcester, and Reginald, Archdeacon of Salisbury, would not trust Senatorial faith, and are presumed to have turned home again much sooner. Robert de Newburgh, whether one of those who reached Rome or not, took Gascogne.

[1] S. T. C. vi. 251. Ep. G. F. ccccIxvi.

[2] S. T. C. iv. 90. Ep. cclxxvi.

[3] Rerum Gall. Script. xii. 442. Geoffrey, of Vigeois was at Souterraine at the time. He tells how Robert de Selit, afterwards captured, was imprisoned by K. Henry, and died of starvation.

[4] Mag. Rot. Pip. 13 Hen. II. Herefordsh.

[5] S. T. C. iii. 214. Ep. xc. Becket, now at Sens, had evidently not heard of the Bishop of Hereford's death.

1167. c. April. the opportunity of being in Italy, to pass on to Sicily, purposing a visit to the King of Sicily and to his own relations (*parentes*).[1] Gascogne.

c. April 15. Soon after Easter (April 9), K. Henry leads an army into Auvergne, a province which Comte William of Auvergne held under Henry as Duke of Guienne, or Comte of Poitou. But William had recently, in a domestic dispute, invoked the King of France as his Suzerain and ally. Henry's attack on Auvergne provoked Louis VII. to an attack on Normandy; and the French King devoted four days to pillage in the Vexin frontier. Auvergne.

April 22. Pope Alexander, at Lateran, writes to Archbishop Thomas.—The Pope has authorised the Bishops of Winchester and Worcester to absolve Earl Hugh (of Norfolk), taking security that within 40 days the Earl restore to the Canons of Pentney what he had deprived them of (*ablata*). In case of the Earl's default, the said Bishops are to re-sentence him. If the Bishops fail to do so, then after 30 days added to the 40, the Archbishop is to re-sentence the Earl. If however the Earl repent within the said 30 days, then Becket is to provide for his absolution. If the Earl continue impenitent for a year after his original sentence (7th July, 1166), Becket is to lay all his lands under an interdict.[2]

April 23. Pope Alexander to the same. "The instant second Sunday after Easter lapsing, and Joceline, Bishop of Sarum, not appearing to his Appeal (terminating on that day), the Pope confirms Becket's sentence of interdict (the suspension *circa* June, 1166) on the said Bishop, and leaves him to Becket's discretion *sans appeal*.[3]

c. May. K. Henry marches from Auvergne into Normandy to confront Louis. Normandy.

c. May 1. The Cardinal Legates, William of Pavia and Otho leave Rome for France, but being delayed on their journey, do not seem to have accomplished it under five months.

May 7. The Pope, at Lateran, sends amended instructions after the Legates. The Pope has heard conflicting rumours about the conduct of John, Dean of Salisbury, and how John Cumin had shown the Pope's rescripts to Guy of Crema (the Anti-Pope). The Pope has received complaints from Archbishop Thomas and from K. Louis.[4]

May 18. Simon, dedicated Abbot of St. Alban's by Gilbert, Bishop of London, in presence of Robert, Earl of Leicester. On the same day expired the term of the English Bishop's appeal to the Pope.

May 21. The Abbot of Clairvaux at Piacenza on his way to Rome, to report to the Pope about the treaty and peace recently concluded between K. Louis and the Emperor.[5]

June 4. K. Henry and Louis VII. confer in the Vexin.[6] They come to no terms, and prepare for a further campaign. The Vexin.

Louis burns several villages of the Norman border between Mantes and Pacey.

[1] S. T. C. vi. 332. Epist. dxx. It is possible that these Ambassadors had charge of the Anglican Bishops' Appeal to the Pope, the term of which was to expire on May 18. The Archdeacon of Salisbury with equal probability was specially charged with the Appeal of his father, Bishop Josceline, which expired on April 23, when, no one appearing thereto, the Pope re-sentenced the said Bishop. The Anglican Bishops also failed in due appearance, but they and their clients were not immediately re-sentenced.

[2] S. T. C. iv. 23. Ep. ccxxi.

[3] S. T. C. iv. 13. Ep. ccxii.

[4] S. T. C. vi. 54. Epist. cccxxxi.

[5] S. T. C. vi. 332.

[6] Chron. Normann. p. 1101.

1167. c. July. K. Henry burns the castle of Chaumont, where the French had their military chest and stores.[1] Chaumont (in the French Vexin).

Louis burns the town of Andely (on the Seine), belonging to the See of Rouen.

The following extracts from the contemporary Pipe-Roll will serve to illustrate the above account of Henry's campaign.—

GLOUCESTERSHIRE. *Pro duobus tonellis, plenis sagittis et ingaignis, missis ultra mare* 116*s. per breve Regis.*

SOUTHAMPTON. *Et in liberacione esneccæ quando transfretavit cum Willo Maledocto Camerario*[2] *et thesauro* £6. 10*s*. *Et pro tribus navibus et apparatu eorum, scilz unâquâque centum hominibus armatis ad conducendum thesaurum in Normanniam* £27 *per breve Regis.*

During the month of July, Pope Alexander III. retired from Rome to Beneventum.

August. A truce, to endure till Easter (March 31, 1168), is concluded between Henry and Louis. The Vexin.

It was now doubtless that K. Henry visited Rouen and his mother, the Empress. In conjunction with her, the King expedites a charter to the Abbey of Valasia, or St. Mary de Voto, at Cherbourg. The charter is dated at Rouen, and certifies the King's and his mother's joint foundation of the said Abbey.[3] Rouen.

The witnesses are:—R. (Rotroc) Abp of Rouen; A. (Arnulf) Bp of Liseux; E. (Egidius) Bp of Evreux; Earl William de Mandeville; A. (Amalric) Comte of Evreux; Nicholas de Stoteville; Hugh de Longchamp; Reginald de Courtenay; Reginald de Paveillei, and Robert de Stotevill.

Another charter by the King to the same Abbey is dated at Rouen, and similarly attested.[4]

Perhaps too we may attribute to this occasion a Royal Charter which, though undated, probably passed at Rouen. It was in favour of the Monastery of St. Mary de Prè,[5] at

[1] Chron. Normann. p. 1001, and Gall. Script. xii. 483 (Chron. St. Albin.).

[2] Here we have William Mauduit of Hanslape (usually styled *Camerarius*) in his distinctive office of Chamberlain of the Treasury.—

The Pipe-Roll of 1168 contains a payment of 6*s*. 8*d*. to Odo de Falaise by the Sheriff of Bucks and Bedfordshire. The payment is expressed to be *pro ducendâ hugiâ thesauri de Hamaselapâ ad Norhanton' et inde usque London.* So then, portions of the Royal revenue were occasionally and temporarily lodged at the Chamberlain's own private residence. William Mauduit's pay as Chamberlain was not a third of the pay of the *Magister Camerarius*, or the *Dapifer*, or the *Thesaurarius*, but it is worth noting that he was allowed three sumpter-horses and their forage (vide Hearne, *Constitutio Domus Regis.* Lib. Nig. p. 352).

[3] Monasticon, vii. 1110, I.

[3] Neustria Pia, p. 852.

[4] *Sancta Maria de Prato*; also called *Notre Dame de Bonnes Nouvelles.*

1167. c. Aug. Rouen, in which the Empress was now domiciled.[1] The instrument is attested by Rotrode, Archbishop of Rouen; Richard de Humet, Constable; Robert, Comte of Mellent; Warino filio Giron (?) Comitis; Magistro Alveredo; Gosceline Crispin and his son, William; Hugh de Gornay; and Robert de Herecourt.[2] Rouen.

August 22. Pope Alexander at Beneventum, writes to the Legates William and Otho still *en route* for France. They are to labour for peace between Henry and the Archbishop, and not to enter England, nor meddle with consecrations till it was effected. The Pope notices John Dean of Salisbury's *advertisements* as likely to have disturbed the King and Realm of France.[3]

c. Aug. 31. The King now set out for Bretagne, and subdued the Comte of Leon whose Vicomte Guiomar, or Widomar, was in rebellion. Leon in Bretagne.

This rebellion was far from insignificant. The nobles of Aquitaine are said to have been sympathizers therein, and King Louis and the French were privy thereto.

The rebellion in Bretagne was headed by Eudo, Vicomte of Porhoet, calling himself Comte of Bretagne, and claiming sovereignty in virtue of his wife (now deceased), the Comtesse Bertha, mother by a previous husband of Duke Conan le Petit. The Vicomte of Thouars was another rebel.[4]

Sept. 10. The King being still in Bretagne, his mother, the Empress, died at the Priory of the Prè de Rouen. Geoffrey of Vigeois says that she died a Nun of Fontevrault. She gave 30,000 shillings to Grammont, and King Henry as much on her behalf *(pro ipsâ)*. Bretagne.

Sept. 29. The King was probably still in Bretagne.

THE MOVEMENTS of Queen Eleanor, during the fiscal year now ended, should here be traced.

The Queen, leaving Henry's Court in Normandy or Tourain, seems to have returned to England in October or November, 1166. An entry on the Pipe-Roll, already quoted, would imply that the Queen reached England before Prince Henry quitted it; for the Sheriff of Devonshire paid her £100 to discharge the Prince's corrodies.

At Oxford, on Christmas Eve (Dec. 24), 1166, the Queen gave birth to Prince John.

The Queen, it seems, when she came to England, as aforesaid, brought with her the Princess Matilda. Between July and September, 1167, Envoys from the Duke of Saxony arrived in England for the pur-

[1] The King grants *pro salute meâ et heredum meorum et pro animabus patris mei et matris meæ Matildæ Imperatricis et omnium ancessorum meorum.*

[2] Neustria pia, p. 612. The charters printed in this work seem to be most inaccurate as transcripts. The fourth witness we should suppose to have been *Warin filius Geroldi Camerarius;* but that functionary was dead before Rotrode became Archbishop of Rouen, and before the year 1166, when Robert became Comte of Mellent.

[3] S. T. C. vi. 57. Epist. G. F. cccxxxiij.

[4] Gall. Script. xii. 483 (Chron. Sti. Albini Andeg.).

pose of conducting the Princess (now but eleven years of age) to Saxony. The entries on the contemporary Pipe-Rolls fix and illustrate these circumstances.—

OXFORDSHIRE. *Et in corredio Saxonum* 43*s.* 4*d. per breve et testimonium Willi filii Baldwini.*

LONDON AND MIDDLESEX. *Et Simoni, nuntio Ducis Saxoniæ ad se vestiendum* 20*s. Et pro* 20 *paribus Bulgarum*[1] *et* 20 *paribus coffrorum*[2] *ad opus Matildæ filiæ Regis* £26. 13*s.* 4*d. per breve Regis. Pro auro ad deauranda vaisella*[3] *ejusdem filiæ Regis* £28. 14*s. Pro pannis ejusdem filiæ Regis quando missa est in Saxonium* £63. 13*s.* 7*d. per visum Edwardi Blundi et Willielmi Magni. Et pro tribus paribus coffrorum ad opus Reginæ* 33*s.*

SOUTHAMPTON. *In liberacione esneccæ quando ivit contra filiam Regis* £7. 10*s. Et in apparatu trium navium quâ iverunt cum esneccâ contra filiam Regis* £8. 10*s.* Also, the Sheriff of Sussex paid £11 for 'equipment of three ships of Shoreham which went with the King's daughter towards Saxony.'

The Princess, according to one account, was fetched from England in this year by the Elect of Cologne.[4] The same authority adds that the Princess embarked at Dover and that Queen Eleanor accompanied her, the first is probable enough, and we see thereby what the Pipe-Rolls mean by stating that ships of Southampton met, and ships of Shoreham accompanied the Princess. They sailed to Dover to attend her transfretation. The other statement, that the Queen went too, is very doubtful. All that can be concluded on the point is that the Queen went no further than Normandy, and returned to England very shortly and without any contemporary notice of the circumstance.

Diceto, with much more probability of correctness, states that the escort of the Princess consisted of the Earls of Arundel and Strigoil and many others.'

That the Princess's embarcation was late in September, 1167,[5] is suggested by part of the expenses not being charged till Michaelmas, 1168, viz:—

KENT. *Et ad passagium filiæ Regis quando missa fuit in Saxoniam* £15. 5*s.* 6*d. per breve Regis per Robertum Kentesium. Et pro navibus locandis ad opus peregrinorum* 51*s.* 8*d. per brevi Regis. Et item ad perficiendum passagium filiæ Regis ipsi Roberto* 62*s.* 4*d. numero, per breve Regis.*

IN THE YEAR ending Michaelmas, 1167, the administration of the Law in the provinces is not marked by any recorded *Itinera* of justices, if we except the *Iter* of Alan de Nevill, who held Pleas of the Forest in at least seventeen counties, and realized a large income to the Crown.

MICHAELMAS, 1167, TO MICHAELMAS, 1168.

1167. c. Oct 1. Early in this month the King probably returned from Bretagne into Normandy, where he expected the arrival of the Legates, William and Otho, and whither he had summoned several of the English Bishops.[6] Normandy.

[1] BULGA. *Papiæ; saccus scorteus;* Gallice, *Bouge; vas ex corio confectum* (Duchesne).

[2] COFFRUM. *Cista; arca* (Duchesne). A chest, box, or casket.

[3] VAISELLUM. *Vas quodvis; supellex* (Duchesne). Household utensils.

[4] Gervase (p. 1403). Lyttelton (by a natural but very false association of ideas) calls the envoy the "*Elector* of Cologne." Gervase probably means by the Elect of Cologne, Archbishop Reginald's successor. He calls him *Coloniensis electus et scismaticus.* It is not probable on other grounds that Archbishop Reginald came to England on this occasion, for he died in this very year.

[5] The year 1168 is named by several Chroniclers (Gervase, Bromton, and Robert de Monte) not so much as that of the Princess's transfretation as that of her marriage to Duke Henry. The date is doubtless correct. The great aid levied by the King on the occasion was among the *Nova Placita et Novæ Conventiones* of that year's Pipe-Roll.

[6] At Michaelmas, 1167, the Sheriff of Hampshire charges the King 3*s.* 4*d. pro summonitionibus portandis ad summonendos Episcopos.*

At the same time the Sheriff of Northumberland charges £13. 14*s.* 1*d. pro conducendo plumbo Regis de Novo Castello* (Newcastle on Tyne) *ad Cadomum* (Caen). Probably some building was in progress at Caen, where were the Exchequer and the Treasury of Normandy.

1167. c. Oct. In this month, most probably, the King was at Valognes, and attended by most of the Norman Bishops. At Valognes the King settled a dispute between Gilbert, Abbot of St. Martin, at Troarn, and Earl John, Lord of Montgomery, (*i.e.* John Comte of Ponthieu). There were witnesses of the transaction R. (Rotrou) Archbishop of Rouen; R. (Roger) Archbishop of York; Henry, Bishop of Bayeux; A. (Arnulf) Bishop of Liseux; R. (Richard) Bishop of Coutances; R. (Richard) Bishop of Avranches; H. (Henry) Abbot of Fecamp; R. (Radulf) Abbot of Montebourg; R. Abbot of Valasse; V. Abbot of St. George of Bocherville; Richard de Humet, Constable; William de Curci, Dapifer; (Fulk?) Paenell; William fitz Hamo; Richard de Canvill; and Seiher de Quinci.[1] Valognes.

Oct. 9 Pope Alexander, at Beneventum, to K. Henry;—censuring the King for the existing vacancies in the Sees of Lincoln, Bath, and Hereford, also for oppressing the Freedom of Election in the Sees of Bangor and Llandaff:—threatening trouble (*gravamen*) against Henry, and is determined to support the Church.[2]

c. Oct. 31. Later in the month the two Legates confer with K. Henry in Council, at Caen. Further consulting with the Prelates of Henry's court, the Legates send to Becket proposing a meeting on the 11th of November, at some place within the King of England's territory. Becket objects, and proposes November 18th as the day of the meeting. Caen.

Nov. 18. (Sat.) "Conference of Planches," a place between Gisors and Trie, on the day proposed by Becket. The Legates find Becket impracticable.[3]

Nov. 19. (Sun.) The Legates go to confer with K. Louis of France.[4]

Nov. 23. (Th.) The Legates arrive at the Abbey of Bec Hellouin (in Normandy).[5]

Nov. 24. (Fr.) The Legates reach Liseux.[6]

Nov. 25. (Sat.) The Legates reach St. Pierre-sur-Dive.

Nov. 26 (Sun) K. Henry, travelling two leagues, meets the Papal Legates at Argentan.[7] Argentan.

Nov. 27 (Mo) Chamber-Council of Argentan;—whereat were present the King of England, the Legates, William of Pavia and Otho; the Archbishops, Rotrou of Rouen and Roger of York; the Bishops of London, Worcester, Salisbury, Chichester, Baieux, and Angoulême; also several Abbots. No decision was arrived at. K. Henry expressed bitter disappointment in the action and views of the Papal Embassy.

[1] D'Anisy's Transcripts, iii. 345.
[2] S. T. C. iv. 124. Epist. ccciij.
[3] S. T. C. Epistles vii. ccclxxxij.
[4, 5] S. T. C. iv. 276, and 268.
[6] S. T. C. Epistles ccclxxxj.
[7] S. T. C. iv. p. 269. Ep. ccclxxxi.

1167. Nov. 28 (Tu.) The day consumed in messages carried to and fro, between K. Henry and the Papal Envoys, by the Bishops. Argentan.

Nov. 29. Wednesday. The King goes out hawking. The Legates confer with the Archbishops and Bishops above named. The Bishop of London renews the Appeal of All England against Becket's sentences, fixing Nov. 11, 1168, as the term of such renewed Appeal. The Bishop of Salisbury includes himself (he was under suspension), and the Bishop of Winchester (he was absent we presume), in the said Appeal. The Archdeacon of Canterbury (Geoffrey Ridel), or his Clerk, also appeals.

Nov 30, to Dec. 4. The King and the Legates continue at Argentan.[1]

The Legates seem to have ordered the absolution of some or of all the persons who had been excommunicated at Vézelay. We hear at least of some of them being absolved in England by Godfrey, Bishop of St. Asaph (then Abbot-Commendate of Abingdon); also of Alan de Nevill being absolved by the Bishop of London.[2]

Nov. 29. to Dec. 5. Very apposite to this date and occasion is a Royal Charter which passed at Argentan, whereby the King 'confirms the donation which Geoffry Ridell, Archdeacon of Canterbury, made to Robert de Insula, and Galiena his wife, daughter of William Blund, which donation, Matthew, Comte of Boulogne, had confirmed to them by his charter.' Witnesse R. (Roger) Abp. of York; A. (Arnulf) Bp. of Liseux; William de Curci, Dapifer; William fitz Hamo; and William de Caisneto.[3]

Another Royal Charter, dated at Argentan, is in favour of the Cluniac Priory of Ferley (Wiltshire). It is attested by Josceline, Bp of Sarum, Richard de Humetz, and Walter de Dunstanvill.[4]

Dec. 5. On this day the Papal Legates quit Argentan, intending to go to Paris.

William of Pavia sends as messenger to the Pope a Clerk, a cousin of Master Lombard. K. Henry sends, as messengers to the Pope, Master Henry Punchun (a clerk of the Bishop of London), and Reginald fitz Joceline (Archdeacon of Salisbury).

Dec. 9. The Legates, now at Evreux, *en route* for Paris, send Master Joceline of Chichester and the Præcentor of Salisbury to lodge notice of the Anglican Appeal on Becket. The Legates style Becket "Legate of the Apostolick See," but forbid him to pass interdicts on the realm or subjects of K. Henry.

c. Dec. 10. It would seem that immediately after the Council of Argentan, the King visited Le Mans. By a Charter, there dated, he concedes to the Church and Monks of Ferley land which Walter de Dunstanvill and Alan, his brother, had given for the soul's health of Robert de Dunstanvill, their uncle (*avunculi*). Witnesses, Rotroc, Abp of Rouen; (Le Mans).

1 S. T. C. iv. 269.

2 Compare Diceto, pp. 540, 548.

3, 4 Cart. Antiq. P. 10, and M. Ferley is Monkton-Furleigh, in Wiltshire).

Joceline, Bp of Sarum; Hillary, Bp of Chichester; Earl William de Mandevill; William Malet, Dapifer; William de Curci; and William de Hasting. *Apud Cenom.*'[1] Le Mans.

The Southampton Pipe-Roll of 1168 contains several consecutive entries which probably belong to the months of November and December, 1167, and to illustrate the supposed or ascertained history of Henry's Court.

HANTONIA. *Et pro* liii *modiis cervisiæ missis Regi in Normanniam et in conductu ejus* £7. 15*s.* 10*d. per breve Regis.*

Et in liberacione esneccæ quando Thesaurarius transfretavit ad festum Sancti Andreæ[2] £7. 10*s.* *Et in liberacione navis quæ portavit equos Camerariorum* 30*s.* *Et pro onerando et deonerando thesauro* 2*s.* 1*d.*

Et in liberacione esneccæ quando Regina tranfretavit £7. 10*s.* *Et sex aliis navibus quæ transfretaverunt cum Reginâ* £9. 5*s. per breve Regis.*

That the Queen had been resident at Winchester since Michaelmas, 1167, is further suggested by an entry on the Hampshire Pipe-Roll.—*Et in corredio Reginæ* £35. 12*s. per breve Regis.*

On the whole we conclude that in December, 1167, the Queen joined her husband in Normandy, and we have the best authority for stating that the Court kept the festival

Dec. 25. of Christmas at Argentan. The Court assembled on the Argentan.
occasion is styled *Magna Curia.*[3]

IN THE ABOVE YEAR, previous to September, died the Archbishop of Bourges, and was succeeded by Stephen, Bishop of Meaux, an ally of Becket, and brother of Adam, formerly Chamberlain of K. Henry of France.[4]

In the above year the Cardinal Jacinthus went as Papal Legate into Spain.[4]

A.D. 1168.

January. In this month K. Henry marches southwards to quell Poitou.
a rebellion which had arisen in Poitou and Guienne. The rebels enumerated are the Comtes of Angoulême and La Marche, the Vicomte of Thouars, Aimery de Lusignan, Robert de Silly, and Hugh de Silly.

The King takes the Castle of Lusignan (*Lezenninum* Lusignan, (Poitou).
Castrum) and achieves other successes. He is called away to treat with Louis of France, his truce with whom was to expire at Easter. He leaves his interests in Guienne to the care of Queen Eleanor, and returns to Normandy. Normandy.

[1] Cart. Harl. 43, C. 23. William de Mandeville became an Earl after October, 1166. Hilary, Bishop of Chichester, died in 1169. Knowing that that Prelate was at Argentan on November 26, 1167, we must connect his presence at Le Mans with the same period of transfretation.

[2] November 30, 1167.

[3] R. de Monte, p. 903. Another authority says that the King kept Christmas at Rouen.

[4] S. T. C. vi. 332, Ep. DXX.

1168. c. March. The Comtes of Flanders and Champagne had been treating with Louis at Soissons concerning a peace between the two kings. The last named Comte now sought Henry in Normandy, to get his ratification of the treaty of Soissons.

April 7. The King was at Pacey,[1] and held a conference with the Comte, but being called again southwards by troubles in Poitou, left Richard de Humet, Constable of Normandy, the Archbishop of Rouen, and Richard de Luci, Justiciary of England, to conclude peace for him on conditions already accepted by Louis. Pacey. Poitou.

K. Henry, suspecting Louis's sincerity, strengthens his dominions beyond the Loire with garrisons, and leaves the Queen in government thereof, associating with her Patric, Earl of Sarum, 'uncle of Rotroc, Comte of Perch.'[2]

April 7. Confereuce between Henry and Louis at a place on the Norman Frontier between Pacey and Mante. Proposal for the marriage of Prince Richard with a daughter of Louis. The peace, which was all but agreed upon, was exchanged for a truce till July 1st; and Henry, hearing of the murder of Patric, Earl of Sarum,[3] by Guy de Lusignan,[4] was hastening into Poitou, when his presence was demanded in Bretagne by the rebellion of Eudo, Vicomte of Porhoet,[5] and of Oliver de Dinan, and his cousin Roland. Near Pacey and Mante.

May 12. King Henry confers with Louis VII.,[5] but where we are not informed. He then goes into Bretagne. Bretagne.

c. May. K. Henry takes two castles of the Vicomte Eudo, viz., *Jocelin* and *Abrahi*. Castle Jocelin. *Abrahi* Castle (Aurai ?)

[1] R. de Monte (Struve), 904. Joh. Salisb., Ep. 244.

[2] Hoveden, 294, b. The mother of Rotrou, the existing Earl of Perche, was a sister of Earl Patric, and a daughter of Walter de Salisbury, and of Sibil (usually called de Chaworth).

[3] Patric, Earl of Salisbury, was slain on March 27. He was succeeded by his son (says the Chronicle), whose mother was a daughter of William, Comte of Ponthieu, and was also mother of the Countess of Warren (Chron. Normann.). The statement is quite correct. Ela, the double Countess, was widow, first of William Earl Warren, and then of Patric, Earl of Salisbury. So she was mother of Isabel, the heir-female of Warren, and also of William, the last Earl of Salisbury of the original male line.

[4] Guy de Lusignan fled from France and K. Henry's vengeance. It was he who afterwards became King of Jerusalem.

[5] *Porhoet.*—This Eudo, sometimes called 'Comte,' is said to have married *a niece of the Empress*; the meaning of which is that his wife Bertha (daughter of Conan, Comte of Upper Bretagne, and widow of Alan, Comte of Lower Bretagne), was born to Comte Conan by Maud, a natural daughter of K. Henry I. The ground of Eudo's present quarrel with his wife's cousin, K. Henry II., was said to be that the King had debauched a daughter of Eudo, the girl being at the time a hostage in the King's hand.

1168. c. May. K. Henry reduces Vannes and the country of Porhoet and half Cornouaille.[1] Vannes, Porhoet, Cornhouaille, (in Bretagne).

In apt illustration of Henry's warlike necessities at this period, we have an entry on the Southampton Pipe-Roll :—

Et in liberacione Esneccæ quando thesaurarius transfretavit post clausum[2] *Pentecostes* £7. 10*s*. *Et tribus aliis navibus quæ portaverunt equos Archidiaconi Cantuariæ et equos Camerarii* £4. 10*s*. *per breve Regis*. *Et pro onerando et deonerando thesauro in Castello de Hanton'* (Southampton) *et aliis locis* 6*s*. 11*d*.

At this juncture K. Henry's relations with the Papal Court, with the Courts of France and Germany, and with Archbishop Becket, were so complicated that a few parallel events will illustrate the main subject of Henry's feelings and subsequent conduct.

In March, 1168, the Pope being at Beneventum, the Emperor Frederick Barbarossa, the supporter of the Anti-Pope (Pascal III.), was forced by pestilence to renounce his occupation of Italy.

Previous to this, and probably under fear of an alliance between the Emperor and Henry, the Pope had written to the latter from Beneventum promising to repress Becket's Legatine authority and expected censures against the King, failing Becket's restoration to the King's favour.

Also the Cardinal, John de Neapolis, wrote to Henry, suggesting Becket's removal from Canterbury to some foreign See.

April 25. Pope Alexander writes from Beneventum to the Anglican Bishops. He censures their disobedience to the Archbishop of Canterbury. He has respect unto K. Henry's messengers (those sent from Argentan, we presume, circa 5 December, 1167). He releases the Bishops and their Sureties from prosecuting their appeal (made November 29, 1167, terminable November 11, 1168), against the Archbishop, the object of such appeal being that the Archbishop should be prevented from in any way harming the King, the bishops, or the realm of England ("*ne Regem aut vos vel regnum Angliæ in aliquo gravaret*)."[3]

May 18. Pope Alexander writes from Beneventum to Archbishop Thomas. He speaks of Henry's *recent* messengers and their threats; of the Church's danger arising in the Schism and in the Emperor Frederic's attitude. The Archbishop must not sentence Henry, his officers, or realm, without further advice from Alexander. If Henry so long continue obstinate, Alexander will restore Becket's power at Lent (March 5, 1169).[4]

On May 19th a Diet was assembled by the Emperor at Wurtzburgh, and attended by the Duke of Saxony, whereat all present took an oath to support the Anti-Pope, Pascal III., and, in case of his death, to support Calistus as his successor.

On May 22nd Pope Alexander, still at Beneventum, and not having heard of the events at Wurtzburgh, wrote two discrepant letters to Henry; one of which was styled *commonitory*, the other *comminatory*. These letters he intrusted to Commissioners who were, at their discretion, to use one or other.[5]

One of these letters (the *comminatory* one) we have. The Pope commends to K. Henry the forthcoming mission of the Prior of Mont Dieu and Bernard de Corilo. The Pope threatens to let loose Becket's powers in case of Henry's obduracy.[6]

The Pope's commission to these persons, bears date at Beneventum, May 25. The persons were more fully described as Simon, Prior of Mont Dieu, and Bernard de Corilo, Monk of Grammont. Their

[1] R. de Monte (Struve), 904.
[2] *i.e.*, May 26, 1168.
[3] S. T. C. vi. 79. Epist. cccliv.
[4] S. T. C. iv. 24. Epist. ccxxij.
[5] The plan of entrusting antagonistic powers to its several or individual correspondents was a feature of the Papal diplomacy of the period. The vast itinerant distance between Normandy and Italy suggested a process which seems to have sometimes answered its political ends very sufficiently, but which sometimes failed. And accordingly in this very instance, there was a failure. For the ambiguous policy of Pope Alexander set two antagonistic parties to rely upon promises which were irreconcilable, and which, being interchangeably unknown to each party, determined both in more persistent opposition.
[6] S. T. C. iv. 130. Epist. cccvi.

primary Charge was to effect a composition between K. Henry and Becket. (It will be seen that seven months elapsed before these commissioners attempted their task.)

The Commissioners were to go to Henry if he were in France (*citra mare*). The two forms of letter were to be entrusted to them, the *comminatory* form only to be used if the King did not repent before the beginning of Lent (March 5th, 1169), when also Becket's powers were to have full scope. This commission was only to proceed in case the Bishop of Beauvais and the Prior of the Carthusians should have failed to execute a previous commission.[1]

After the Pope's commission had left Beneventum, and probably after he had heard of the proceedings at Wurtzburgh (therefore, perhaps, in July or August), the Pope wrote to Becket, apologising for the promise which he had made to Henry of suspending Becket's Legatine functions, and undertaking that if Becket could not come to terms with Henry before Lent (*i.e.*, before March 5, 1169), Becket should then have full power of censure, not only on the Dignitaries of K. Henry's court but against his realm and person.

1168. June 1–23. K. Henry, still in Bretagne, reduces the country about Dinan and St. Malo, and takes the Castle of Heddé,[3] surrendered by Geoffrey de Montfort. *Dinan.*[2] *St. Malo.*[2] *Castle Heddé.*[2]

June 24. K. Henry takes Castle Becherell, in Little Brittany, and dismantles the Castle of Tiutiniac (or Tintigny). *Castle Becherell.*[2] *Tintiniac.*[2]

June 25. King Henry takes Leon,[4] and burns the Church, but, at the prayer of William fitz Hamon, spares Monastic churches and habitations. *Leon (in Bretagne.)*

Subsequently the King is said to have been at Dinan (again) and at Aleth. *Dinan.*[2] *Aleth.*[2]

The Pipe-Roll once more supplies evidence of the passing of treasure to Normandy, in support of the King's needs. After the feast of St. John (June 24th is meant) the Sheriff of Southampton, at a cost of £7. 10*s.*, had chartered a ship (*esneccam*) laden with treasure, and at a cost of 30*s.* more had chartered a ship (*navem*) to carry the horses of the Chamberlain; all in compliance with a Writ Royal.

June. Probably in this month, two messengers from the Pope and from Beneventum, reached Henry. They brought a letter from the Pope (a letter written, we suppose, four months previous), wherein the Pope undertakes to suppress Becket's legatine authority, and his problematical censures until and unless Becket should be restored to the King's favour.

[1] S. T. C. iv. 113. Epist. ccxcvij.

[2] The list of places given in the margin is chiefly from R. de Monte (Struve), 904.

[3] *Hecdæ castellum a Gaufrido de Monteforti redditum munivit* (Chron. Normann).

[4] *Cimiterium Lehonense combussit, ecclesiis et domibus Monachorum prece Willelmi filii Hamonis in pace dimissis.* (Gall. Script. xii. 560).

1168. c. July. K. Henry takes up his quarters at La Ferté Bernard, King Louis at Chartres, the River Huines dividing the two stations. The intended conference failed in some points of feudal form, but the real grievances probably were that the Comte of Flanders and ambassadors from Scotland and Wales were known to be in Louis's court, while Henry had received the Papal letter, promising to nullify Becket's legatine powers, and had with him William of Pavia, the Legate whose mission of the previous year had proved abortive. This failure of negotiations, as between the Kings of England and France, resulted in warlike demonstrations, which lasted till Advent (December 1). Ferté Bernard.

It would also seem that on this occasion, King Henry, being fortified by the Pope's letter (supposed to have been written four or five months previous), refused to negotiate with Becket, or even to speak with him.

K. Henry's capture of the French Castle of Bellomonte is recorded by one Chronicle[1] under this year. The only Castle on K. Louis's side of the frontier, that seems likely to be here alluded to, was that of Beaumont sur-Oise. Beaumont-sur-Oise.

c. Aug. K. Henry burns more than forty towns in Ponthieu,[2] whose Comte, John, had prevented Matthew, Comte of Boulogne, from sending forces through Ponthieu, to assist Henry against Louis in Normandy. Ponthieu. The Viemieu.

One authority next gives K. Henry at Brueroles.[3] Brueroles.

And then at Neufchâtel.[3] Neufchâtel.

At this time, the Comtesse of Boulogne (King Stephen's daughter) is giving Louis clandestine information about symptoms of Henry's negotiating with the court of the Emperor Frederick.

Contemporaneously Louis of France makes an inroad into Normandy and burns Chesnebrun, near Verneuil.

Hereupon, Henry returns to the Norman frontier, surprises the rear of Louis's army, and takes the seneschal of Flanders prisoner. Marches of Normandy.

c. Sept. K. Henry is visited by his son-in-law, the Duke of Saxony, and by others (viz., the Archbishops of Metz and

[1] Chron. St. Albin, (Gall. Script. xii. 483.

[2] The towns burnt by K. Henry were in the Vimieu (*Wimacensi pago*), a district of Ponthieu. The Comte of Boulogne managed to join K. Henry by sea (R. de Monte (ed. Struve), p. 905.

[3] R. de Monte, ibidem.

1168. c. Sept. Cologne, and the Bishop of Liege), coming as ambassadors from the Emperor. They offer an alliance against Louis and against the Pope. Henry temporizes. Marches of Normandy.

On September 21, the Sheriff of Southampton chartered a vessel (*esneccam*) at the cost of £7. 10*s*. to convey the King's treasure over sea; and a ship (*navem*) at the cost of 30 shillings, to transport the horses of Walter de Insula and of the Treasurers; all in compliance with a Writ of the King.[1]—

On September 20, Pascal III. (the Anti-Pope) died. John (called Calixtus III.) was nominated in his stead.

The Pipe-Rolls, made up at Michaelmas, 1168, supply a few items illustrative of an event of the previous year.—

The aid on marriage of the King's eldest daughter was at the rate of two merks for every knight's fee, and was in general process of collection.

Moreover, the King had enjoined on the Sheriffs of several counties, each to expend a sum of 36*s*. on the purchase of a palfrey and a greyhound (*fugatoris*), for the use of his daughter (*ad opus filiæ Regis*).[2]

At Michaelmas, 1168, Richard, Archdeacon of Poitou, and Richard de Ameri, Præcentor (*Cantor*) of Lincoln, accounted for the Revenues of the vacant See. Their receipts from the Episcopal Manors alone, were £1008. 9*s*. 8½*d*.

In the fiscal year ending Michaelmas, 1168, many counties were visited by Justices-in-Eyre. The persons so officiating stand on the Pipe-Roll variously grouped, but collectively we find no more than seven names. These were Richard, Archdeacon of Poitiers; Wido, Dean of Waltham; William Basset, Reginald de Warren, John Cumin, Gervase de Cornhull, and Henry fitz Gerold, Chamberlain. The results of their *Itinera* are in many cases not recorded before Michaelmas, 1169, which implies that they took place in Autumn, 1168. In 1168, Richard de Luci, singly, held *Pleas and conventions* at Carlisle. We ascribe to the same year a legal process, which it is worth while to introduce here from the names of the functionaries which it supplies.—

An arrangement between certain Suitors was arrived at before Justiciars of the King, to wit, Richard, Archdeacon of Poitiers, and Reginald de Warren, sitting at Dunstable (Bedfordshire). This agreement was embodied in a charter, which charter was subsequently sealed at the Exchequer *coram Domino Ricardo de Luci et aliis Baronibus de Scaccario*. There were witnesses of such sealing, viz., Reginald de Warren, Wido, Dean of Waltham, Henry fitz Gerold, William Basset, Ralph de Glanvill, Hugh de Beauchamp, Nicholas de Treilli, Simon the Cellarer, Robert de Haubeni, and others.[3]

MICHAELMAS, 1168, TO MICHAELMAS, 1169.

c. Oct. and Nov. About this time, as we may reckon, K. Henry was employed in overrunning the province of Perche.[4] Perche.

[1] Rot. Pipe, 14 Hen. II. Tit. Hantona.

[2] The Sheriffs of Essex cum Hertfordshire, of Norfolk cum Suffolk, of Northamptonshire, of Lincolnshire, Cambridgeshire cum Huntingdonshire, Staffordshire, Dorsetshire cum Somerset, Wiltshire, Hampshire, Sussex, and Kent, and the Fermor of William Peverel's Honour had each made this outlay of 36 shillings. The Sheriff of Buckinghamshire cum Bedfordshire, had been ordered to expend twice the sum, and to furnish *two* palfreys and *two* greyhounds. These contributions to the Princess's establishment were not a feudal exaction from the subject, as the *aid* was, but a present from the King, furnished out of his own revenues.

[3] Madox's Exchequer, 145, a.

[4] R. de Monte (Struve), p. 905.

The Pipe-Roll of Michaelmas, 1168, has a Post-Michaelmas entry which is worth noting in this place.—

HANTONIA. *Et in liberacione Esneccæ quando transfretavit cum thesauro post festum Sancti Michaelis* (Sep. 29, 1168), £7. 10*s*. *Et uni navi ad equos Camerarii* 30*s*. *per breve Regis. Et sex navibus quæ portaverunt cervos et damos Regis ultra mare et in custamento eorundem* £9. 2*s*. 2*d*. *per breve Regis.*

Sunday, Dec. 22. William, brother of Comte Henry (of Troyes) is consecrated Archbishop of Sens. His predecessor, Hugh, the friend of Becket, had died within the year. Archbishop William was afterwards translated to Rheims.[1]

Dec. 25. K. Henry kept his Christmas court at Argentan. Argentan.

Dec. 31. The King still at Argentan. Argentan.

THE ABOVE YEAR is given as that in which Richard, Earl of Pembroke and Strigoil, with Milo de Coggeham invaded Ireland.[2]

It is also the year, given by the best authorities, for the death of the Earl of Leicester, the Justiciar.[3]

Also for the death, in Palestine, of William (IV.) Comte of Nivernois.

In the said year died also Theodore, Comte of Flanders.[4]

A.D. 1169.

1169. Jan. 1. The King at Argentan.

It was perhaps while thus at Argentan that the King expedited two Charters in favour of Nicholas, Prior of Plessis-Grimould and of that House. This was seconded by a contemporary grant by Henry, Bishop of Bayeux. The witnesses were Rotrou, Archbishop of Rouen; Henry, Bishop of Bayeux; and the Bishops of Liseux, Seez, and Evreux; also by Thomas, Bishop of Rennes; Richard de Humez, Constable; Richard fitz Count; Jordan Taisson; Will de Courcy; and Archibald, Constable of Tinchebray.[5] Argentan

The two Papal Commissioners, appointed at Beneventum in May previous, are now in France, Engelbert, Prior of Val

Jan. 6. St. Pierre, being added to their number. On this day they assist at a conference between K. Henry and Louis, which was held at Montmirail, a town of Maine, near to the French frontier, and to the French town of Chartres. A treaty was concluded between the French and English Kings, the results of which seem to have been that K. Henry and his son Henry were to hold Normandy as heretofore, doing fealty to Louis and his son Philip;—that Prince Henry was Montmirail.

[1] Rerum Gallicarum Scriptores xii. 289.
[2] Hoveden, p. 293, b.
[3] Hoveden; Chronicle of Mailros: and Annals of Waverley.
[4] Chron. Normann. 1002.
[5] Archives de Calvados, ii. 111.

1169. Jan. 6. to hold Bretagne, Maine and Anjou, *sine medio*, of Louis, Montmirail. and also the Hereditary Seneschalcy of France;—that Prince Richard was to hold Poitou and Guienne, *sine medio*, of Louis, and should espouse Louis's daughter, Adelais; that Prince Geoffrey was to hold Bretagne under Prince Henry, as mediate between himself and Louis;—that K. Henry should hold Touraine under the Comte of Blois as similarly mediate; and that Louis should give up to Henry certain Breton and Poitevin hostages which Louis held as having been leagued with those provinces against

Jan. 7. the King of England. Accordingly we have it recorded that Prince Henry and Prince Richard did homage to Louis on the following day.[1]

At the above gathering at Montmirail the three Papal Envoys, secured the waiting attendance of Archbishop Becket. They delivered to K. Henry the *commonitory* letter of May, 1168, wherein the Pope exhorted the King to a reconciliation with Becket. Becket at first knelt to Henry, and threw himself on the King's mercy; but Becket afterwards insisting on certain salvos about the 'dignity of his church' and the 'Honour of God,' the negotiation broke off; Henry retired from the conference, angry;[2] and even Louis, in whose train Becket left Montmirail, was estranged from the Archbishop for a few days.

Jan. 7-26. Now, probably, the Papal Envoys delivered to Henry the *comminatory* letters[3] which they had in charge, whereupon Henry sent messengers to the Pope, first Reginald, Archdeacon of Salisbury, and afterwards Randulph, Archdeacon of Landaff.

The Envoys write to the Pope.

Feb. 2. Prince Henry, in person, attended Louis's table, and performed the office of Seneschal of France, already surrendered to him by the Comte of Blois.

[1] Gall. et Franc. Scriptores, xii. 536.

[2] S. T. C. iv. 175. Epist. cccxxxviii. is the report sent to the Pope by his Envoys, as to the meeting of Montmirail. Bernard de Corilo, monk of Grammont, does not join in the letter, because the Grandemontensian brethren were forbidden to write letters to any one. He joins in the report, by repeating orally before Master Lombard, the Papal nuncio who brought the Commission, the same matter as the Envoys, Simon and Engelbert, recorded by letter.

[3] See Hook's Lives of the Archbishops, ii. 468; and Lyttleton, ii. 505. See S. T. C. iv. 177, Ep. cccxxxix. These *Comminatory* letters were delivered to Henry at a second conference between Louis and Henry, of which we have no other Record than the Envoys' report to the Pope. They complained that they could not fix the King to any definite or uniform answer to their demands. Bernard de Co.ilo does not join in the letter; for reason as before, but makes public attestation of its correctness.

Feb. 28, 1169. Pope Alexander, at Beneventum, writes to K. Henry. The Pope has heard and now ignores the demands made by Reginald, Archdeacon of Salisbury, Henry's first messenger, and by Randulph, Archdeacon of Landaff, Henry's second messenger. Alexander accredits the forthcoming mission of Vivian and Gratian,[1] who are fully instructed as to the Pope's will and disposition, and as to things which will tend to Henry's honour, advancement, and satisfaction.

1169. c. March. Before Lent (March 5), K. Henry appears to have been at St. Germain en Laye.[2] St. Germain en Laye.

c. March 10. Early in Lent, that is soon after March 5, King Henry passes into Poitou and effects the submission of the Comte of Angoulême (William IV. surnamed *Sector Ferri*), and the Comte of La Marche (Adelbert IV.). Poitou. La Marche. Angoumois.

It will also have been in the very beginning of Lent that Archbishop Becket, relying on the Pope's permission of the previous year, and being still at Sens, pronounced sentences of excommunication against Josceline, Bishop of Sarum; Earl Hugh (of Norfolk), Ranulf de Broc, Thomas fitz Bernard; Robert de Broc, Clerk; Hugh de St. Clare; Letard de Norflete, Clerk (elsewhere called nephew of Archbishop Theobald); Nigel de Sackville: and Richard, *brother* of William de Hastings (elsewhere described as a Clerk, and as *nephew* of William de Hastings).[3]

Also, very early in Lent,[3] Gilbert Foliot, Bishop of London, and Josceline (de Bohun) Bishop of Sarum, fearing, but not as yet hearing of such censures, made *provisional* Appeals to the Pope, the term of which was to expire February 2, 1170.[3]

March 10, 1169. Pope Alexander writes to Archbishop Becket from Beneventum, aware only of the failure of the conference of Montmirail, and of Henry's subsequent embassy; but not aware of Becket's actions or intentions. The Pope says that he has refused the demands of Henry's ambassadors (the two Archdeacons). He enjoins moderation and conciliation on Becket. Becket is not to sentence Henry's person, realm, or officers, till the appointed Nuncios, Gratian and Vivian, shall have fulfilled their mission to to the King. Any sentence, already pronounced—a thing incredible to the Pope,—must be suspended until the same period.[4]

April 13, 1169. On Palm Sunday, Archbishop Becket, being at Clairvaux, and not having heard of the Bishop of London's provisional appeal,[5] excommunicated the said Bishop. He also referred to his previous sentences against the Bishop of Salisbury and others. He further announced his intention of excommunicating on Ascension day (May 29) Geoffrey Ridel, Archdeacon of Canterbury; Robert his Vicar; Richard de Ilchester, Archdeacon of Poictiers; Richard de Luci; William Giffard; and Adam de Cheringes. "Thomas Archbishop of Canterbury and Legate of the Apostolick See," certifies by letter the above acts and intentions to the clergy of London.[6]

He also certifies his excommunication of Earl Hugh to the Bishop of Norwich,[7] and Canons of Pentney; the latter are to notify the same to Nigel, Bishop of Ely.[7]

His concomitant letters to the Bishops of London and Salisbury, indicate that the sentences against themselves involved an interdict of their respective Dioceses.[8]

[1] S. T. C. iv. 122. Epist. cccij.

[2] Stubbs, quoting R. de Monte, 906.

[3] Diceto, p. 549. S. T. C. v. 287; iv. 284. Epist. ccclxxxvi. March 18 was the day of the Bishop of London's provisional appeal. It was made in St. Paul's Church; the Abbots of Westminster and Chertsey were present (S. T. C. vi. 218).

[4] S. T. C. iv. 20. Epist. cccix.

[5] The slow transit of messages and intelligences is remarkable; moreover the process was watched by both parties; envoys were searched and letters seized. Thus 26 days had elapsed, and Becket at Clairvaux had not yet learnt of London's appeal. *Vice versâ*, it took 46 days, before Becket's sentence, of April 13 could be served and published in St. Paul's, London, by his emissaries.

[6] S. T. C. iii. 298. This letter gives us a reason of the excommunication of Richard, brother of William de Hastings, that he had occupied the Archbishop's Church of *Manech*.

[7] S. T. C. iii. 309. Epist. cxlj. 353. Epist. clxx.

[8] S. T. C. iii. 297. Epist. cxxxvi. In these letters Becket says that the King's *impenitence* has now endured nearly six years; that is, he will have put its commencement at the Council of London, in October, 1163. (Vide supra, p. 64).

April 19, 1169. Pope Alexander, at Beneventum. A letter to Henry Bishop of Winchester.[1]

c. May. King Henry being now at St. Machaire, in Gascony, hears of Becket's proceedings on April 13. The King writes to the Pope, complaining bitterly of the excommunications of two of his Bishops, subsequently to their appeal; and of Becket's intention to sentence, without any provocation, certain of the King's confidential friends (*familiares*). The King beseeches the Pope to quash all Becket's sentences, pronounced after appeal, against the persons of his realm, whether clerks or laymen. The letter is attested by *G. Vasatur' Episcopo apud S. Macharium in Guasconiâ*.[2] St. Machaire (Gascogne).

The King writes also to Gilbert, Bishop of London, to say that he has heard of the wrongs done by "that Traitor, Thomas, mine enemy." The King will enlist both the Pope and the King of France in his struggle against Becket's injuriousness. The Bishop of London is to come to the King in *Normandy*, or to remain in England, as he shall deem most expedient for the King's interests and his own. If the Bishop should wish to go to *Rome* (sic), the King guarantees, at his own cost, to provide all necessaries for such a journey. The letter is attested by *G . . . . . Clerico apud sanctum Macharium in Gasconiâ*.[3]

Probably it was now that K. Henry sent Froger, Bishop of Seez, and Geoffrey Ridel, Archdeacon of Canterbury, to Louis, of France, desiring that Becket might be expelled the French territory, which request Louis instantly refused.

May 10, 1169. Pope Alexander, at Beneventum, writing to K. Henry says that from the latest messengers he learns that the King is softened towards Becket. The Pope (still ignorant it seems of Becket's acts or intentions), again recommends his Nuncios, Gratian and Vivian, to Henry. The King may attend to their instructions about a reconciliation with Becket, and as to other matters (sometime) certified to the Pope by Reginald, Archdeacon of Salisbury.[4]

May 11, 1169. Pope Alexander, at Beneventum, writes to Archbishop Thomas, Legate of the

[1] Adam of Domerham, ii. 325. The date of this letter is its important feature. It is, 13 *kalend. Maiæ. Indict.* ii. A.D. 1168. *Pontificatûs nostri anno* x^{mo}.—

The true Dominical year was 1169, which tallies with Indict. ii. and with 10 Alexander III. The date shows that Pope Alexander III. did, sometimes at least, adopt the Pisan calculation in his Rescripts, a calculation used occasionally by his predecessor, Adrian IV., and which reduced the number of the Dominical year by one. (Sir H. Nicolas, in his 'Chronology of History,' has not adverted to the use of the Pisan calculation by Pope Alexander III.).

[2] S. T. C. vi. 293. Epist. ccccxci. Professor Stubbs refers to Monasticon, vi. 818, for another Deed of K. Henry, dated *Apud Sanctum Macharium super Gerundam in Gasconiâ*. We ascribe that Deed to a later occasion.

[3] S. T. C. vi. 296. Epist. ccccxciij.

[4] S. T. C. iv. 119. Epist. cccj.

Apostolick See, suggesting that the Bishop of Salisbury's age entitles him to consideration.—The Pope's Nuncios (Gratian and Vivian) have now left Beneventum, and the Archbishop should exercise forbearance till the Nuncios should have visited and quitted (France).—If ultimately the Nuncios should fail in their mission and the Archbishop should renew his sentences, the Bishop of Salisbury is to be spared.—The Pope explains how that Prelate, in his conduct about the Deanery of Salisbury, had been overawed by King Henry.[1]

1169. May. K. Henry seems to have passed the whole of this month in Gascony or in some other Province of Acquitaine. Gascogne.

In this month Prince Geoffrey (not yet eleven years of age) receives the homage of his Breton subjects at Rennes.

c. May 20-29. About this time the Bishop of London, clearly aware that Becket's sentence, though not yet served on his Church and person, had been pronounced (viz., at Clairvaux on April 13), convoked at Westminster the following persons, viz., Bartholomew, Bishop of Exeter; Richard de Ilchester (Archdeacon of Poictiers); the Abbot of Westminster; Wido Rufus; the Bishop of Salisbury; and the Barons of the Exchequer.—

The Bishop of London's object, so far as it transpired, was to persuade the Bishop of Exeter to join in his *provisional* appeal. Exeter gave London "the kiss of peace," but determinately refused to join. Salisbury made a facetious speech, indicating his intention to disobey the Primate if the latter ordered him to do anything wrong (in allusion probably to Becket's as yet hypothetical injunction that Salisbury should promulgate an interdict in his Diocese).

May 29. On Ascension Day, Gilbert, Bishop of London, not being himself present, the officiating clergy of St. Paul's were served during mass, by Becket's emissary, one Berenger, with formal notice of the Bishop's excommunication by the Primate.[2]

May 29. On the same day the Primate, being in France, excommunicated not only the persons whom he had threatened on April 13th, but apparently many others.[3]

May 30. Death of Nigel, Bishop of Ely.

May 31. Convocation of the London clergy by Bishop Gilbert. He renews his appeal to the Pope, in which the Dean, Archdeacon, and Canons of the Church of London, and the London clergy, generally, join. But the Canons of St. Bartholomew, St. Martin's, and the Holy Trinity, refuse to make any appeal.[2]

[1] S. T. C. iv. 16. Epist. ccxvi.

[2] S. T. C. iv. 225. Epist. ccclxiv.

[3] S. T. C. iv. 284. Epist. ccclxxxvi. gives a nearly complete list of Becket's sentences on or before May 29. Wimar, a clerk of Earl Hugh, and other clerks of the said Earl, had been sentenced on some previous occasion, probably that of March previous.

The additional Excommunicates of May 29 seem to have been these following:—

Robert, brother of William de Einesforde;—

The Holders of the Churches of *Chere* and *Hele*;

William de Essedesforde (read Einesforde);—

Robert, Butler to (the late) Archbishop Theobald;

Alan de Reclinges;—

William de Becco;—

The Holder (not being the King himself) of the land of *Mundeham*, (parcel) of the Manor of *Pagaham*, which land the King took from the Church of Canterbury in the cause of (*propter*) John Mareschall;—

The Holder (not being the King himself) of the land of *Lese* (parcel) of the Manor of Otteforde, which John, brother of William de Eynesford, lately held;—

John Cumin;—

Wido Rufus, who was bound, like others abovementioned, to have restored to the Archbishop whatever he had received of the income (*redditibus*) of the Treasurer of Liseux;—

All others, if any, who had received by hand or by concession of the King any property (*possessiones*), whether lay or ecclesiastical, of the Church of Canterbury.

It further appears that the Bishop of London had been Receiver, by appointment of the King, of the confiscated incomes of several of Becket's Clerks. The Bishop was called upon by Becket to refund; and, though it does not transpire that this Receivership was the sole ground of his excommunication, it is clear that his so refunding was to be a condition of absolution.

Summarily, it would seem that all the Excommunicates of this year, except the Bishop of Salisbury, the Earl of Norfolk, and the Earl's Clerks, had participated in the fiscal spoils ensuant on the forfeiture and escheat of the Archbishop and his See, and that their excommunication was intended as a first step in the suit and process of recovery.

1169. June. K. Henry passes the whole of this month in Gascony. Gascogne.

June 19. Pope Alexander, at Beneventum, had now, it seems, heard of Becket's proceedings of April 13, at Clairvaux. The Pope writes to the "Archbishop and Legate," expressing his displeasure at the Archbishop's sentences, and that they should have been pronounced before the Archbishop's messengers to the Pope had returned to Sens. The Pope now trusts that the Archbishop will *suspend* the same till the Nuncios (Gratian and Vivian) shall have reported King Henry to be obdurate. In that case the Archbishop may renew the sentences, though the Nuncios be still in France.[1]

c. July 1. King Henry, with his army, is in the remoter parts of Gascony.[2] Gascogne.

The Nuncios, Gratian and Vivian, arriving in France, have a conference with King Louis at Sauvigny (apud Salviniacum) and present Papal letters. Louis advises them not to proceed into Gascony.[2]

The Nuncios go to Sens (where Becket was), and await K. Henry's return into Normandy. It was delayed longer than they expected.[2]

It was during the Nuncios' visit to Becket that they and he, in the presence of the Bishop of Troyes, made an arrangement as to the future absolution of Becket's Excommunicates. The Nuncios were so to absolve for a given period after exacting an oath from the Excommunicates that they would stand by Becket's subsequent mandates, or else by the like mandates of the Nuncios themselves. The Nuncios, for their part, promised that, if peace should not be restored between the King and Becket before the feast of St. Martin (Nov. 11), which feast was to be the limit of their stay in France, then the Nuncios would re-sentence the temporarily absolved parties, without benefit of appeal, unless indeed the Nuncios should be staying in France twenty days later than the said feast, and, during those twenty days, the Excommunicates should satisfy Becket as to the matters for which he had sentenced them. But if the Nuncios should be leaving France before Martinmas, then they were to re-sentence the absolved from the day of their said departure, unless satisfaction, as aforesaid, were first made to Becket.[3]

A letter from Josceline, Bishop of Salisbury, who is awaiting K. Henry's return at Le Mans, tells Gilbert Bishop of London, that the King, to whom he has sent messengers, will pass near Angiers on his road, and will probably summon Salisbury to meet him at that city, and will there instruct Salisbury as to what he is to do. The Bishop does incline to fall back to Argentan, a step which might entail on him a longer journey (than that from Le Mans to Angiers) when summoned to meet the King. Moreover, Salisbury is getting very good wine and plenty of it at Le Mans, whereas, at Argentan, he would only get bad beer, abhorrent to gentle folk, and very little thereof. The Bishop of Chichester (*Dominus Cicestrensis*), who is evidently with Salisbury, concurs in these views.[4]

c. Aug. 1-8. King Henry doubtless returned northwards by way of Angiers. In this very month he is said to have been engaged in the construction of an extensive embankment on the River Loire, above that city. Angiers.

Aug. 15, (Friday). On the day of the Assumption of the Virgin, King Henry being at Argentan, receives Papal letters, transmitted by the Nuncios. Argentan.

Aug. 16, (Saturday). The King sends John, Dean of Salisbury, and Reginald, Archdeacon of Salisbury, to meet the Nuncios.

[1] S. T. C. iv. 22. Epist. ccxx.
[2] S. T. C. iv. 217. Epist. cccl x.
[3] S. T. C. iv. 283. Epist. ccclxxxv.
[4] S. T. C. vi. 266. Epist. cccclxxi. Hillary, Bishop of Chichester, is said (Annals of Waverley), to have died in this very year.

1169. Aug. 23, (Saturday). King Henry is at Damfront. He and his son, Henry, appear to have gone out hunting, when the Nuncios, Gratian and Vivian, arrive in the town. Geoffrey Ridel, Archdeacon of Canterbury and Nigel de Sackville (because, as we presume, they were excommunicate) hurry from the place. The King returns late from hunting and visits the Hospice of the Nuncios. While he is conversing with them, young Henry and his party arrive at the Nuncios' Hospice. A stag which they had taken is presented to the Nuncios.[1] Damfront.

Aug. 24. (Sunday). The King, attended by the Bishops of Rhedon and Seez visits the Nuncios at their lodgings. He is followed by John of Oxford, Dean of Salisbury; and Reginald, Archdeacon of Salisbury; and soon afterwards by Ralph, Archdeacon of Landaff.[1] The conference which ensued lasted till near sunset. According to a correspondent of Becket, who of course only speaks from hearsay, the King's contention was that the excommunicate clerks should be absolved without first taking the oath prescribed by the Nuncios. High words passed, and the King quitted the council-chamber in a rage. After sunset an adjourned conference took place, to which the King summoned all the barons, all the White Monks, and nearly all the Royal Chaplains who were at Damfront, and called them to witness that he offered to the Nuncios the restoration of Becket's Archbishoprick and of Peace.[1] At length the King grew gentler, and left the conference, saying that he would give a definite answer to the Nuncios in a week.[1]

The Nuncio Vivian's account of this day's conference is of course more authentic. The King, having read the Papal letters which were now handed to him, begun to make the old charges against Becket, but being admonished by the Nuncios that he must rid himself of rancorous feeling and receive Becket into love and favour, he hinted a qualified assent, and said he would take counsel on the point. But first the King made a proposal about absolving the excommunicates. Vivian afterwards explains to the Pope, what was perhaps intimated at the time to Henry, viz., that the Nuncios' powers as to absolving the Bishops depended on the prospect of

[1] S. T. C. iv. 277, 278. Epist. ccclxxxiij.

1169. Aug. 24. (Sunday). ultimate peace, and on the Bishops taking a certain oath binding on themselves in case of the failure of such a prospect.[1] Damfront.

A week now elapsed, during which, as Vivian writes, the King was leading the Nuncios "through many windings both of road and speech," and thus detaining them for some time.[1]

Here we should parenthetically notice that these diplomacies were not occupying the whole of King Henry's time and attention. According to one chronicle, the King, after returning in peace to Normandy, built the frontier castle of Beauvoir-en-Lions.[2] Beauvoir-en-Lions.

Aug. 31, (Sunday). Conference of Baieux between Henry and the Nuncios. Baieux. Vivian writes that this conference took place in presence of the Archbishops of Rouen and Bordeaux; that the King proposed that the Nuncios should absolve those three of the excommunicates who were with him in Normandy; that then one of the Nuncios should cross to England and absolve all such excommunicates as he might meet with near the coast, while the other Nuncio should proceed to the Archbishop (at Sens). On these conditions K. Henry promised to permit the Archbishop (Becket) "to come securely, and, in good and firm peace and safety, receive his church in all integrity as it was before he left it, and hold it to the Honour of God, of the Church, of the King, and of the King's *sons*." The same restitution the King promised to those who were in exile with, and for, the Archbishop. The King also bound himself to reduce his promises to writing.[1]

Diceto describes the Conference of Baieux as attended by several English Bishops.[3] Becket's correspondent says that the Archbishops of Rouen and Bordeaux and all the Normandy Bishops were present; that by accident (not summons) the Bishop of Le Mans was there; that the Bishop of Worcester was expected, but did not arrive till the next day; that the Bishop of Poitiers (he was a great ally of Becket) excused his attendance, saying that he was holding a Synod, which, being over, he would attend forthwith.

[1] S. T. C. iv. 217, 218. [2] Chron. Normanniæ. [3] Diceto, 550.

1169. Aug. 31. (Sunday). Becket's correspondent mentions a speech made by K. Henry on this occasion to the effect that the King conceived himself to be laying the Pope under great obligations by his concessions in behalf of Becket.[1] Baieux.

Sept. 1, (Monday). On the following day, according to the Nuncio Vivian's account, the King affecting to repeat his promise, merely substituted the word *heirs* (*heredum*) for *sons* (*filiorum*). This was in the presence of the Archbishops of Rouen and Bordeaux, and of the Bishop of Liseux. Being asked about the Kiss (of Peace), the King replied that Peace should not remain abeyant for such a trifle as that. The Nuncios, well pleased, absolved the three excommunicates who were at Court; but, this being done, and the King again renewing his promises, he added to the previous formula the words "*Salvâ dignitate regni mei.*" This, says Vivian, much startled the Nuncios. They parted from the King, and, under escort of the Archbishop of Rouen, went to Caen.[2] Le Bur.

Sept. 2, (Tuesday).

(It seems that here, Vivian is epitomizing two days' proceedings, viz., September 1 and September 2. The account of the same conference, as given below by a correspondent of Becket, expresses only one day of actual date, but clearly indicates the proceedings of two days. The narrative of Becket's correspondent should be collated with that of the Nuncio.) Le Bur.

Sept. 1, (Monday). The meeting took place in the Park of Le Bur, near Bayeux, says Becket's correspondent.—

The King first proposed that the Nuncios should absolve his clerks, *sine juramento*. This was at once refused. The King mounted his horse and swore never to listen again to the Pope or anyone else as to 'Peace' with Becket.

The Archbishops and Bishops came to the Nuncios, and with much difficulty persuaded them to yield the point. The King dismounted and made a speech, promising peace and restoration to Becket and his co-exiles. This was about the ninth hour (3 P.M.).

The King then devoted some time to other matters, which, being concluded, he again raised the question about the Nuncios, or one of them, or at least one of their

[1] S. T. C. iv. 278-281. Epist. ccclxxxiij.

[2] S. T. C. iv. 218-19. Epist. ccclx.

1169. Sept. 1. (Monday). clerks, going to England to absolve the excommunicated there. Gratian refused. The King, again angry, told the Nuncios that he did not care a fig ('an egg' was the word he used) for them or their excommunications, and again mounted his horse, as if for leaving the conference. The Bishops followed and reproved the King for his language. He set the Bishops to write to the Pope, and tell how they had heard the King's promises of restitution to Becket and obedience to the Pope, and how the only obstacles to 'peace' were the Nuncios themselves. These letters could not be written in a moment; and the King seemed to chafe and to be at issue now with the Bishops. At last the Bishops told him plainly that they had seen Papal letters in the Nuncios' hands, commanding them, the Bishops, to do whatever the Nuncios might enjoin. "I see, I see," said the King, "they will interdict my land; but surely I, who can take the strongest of castles in any single day, shall I not avail to scotch a single clerk, if he should interdict my land?" Le Bur.

Sept. 1, (Monday).

The Bishops promised to act to a certain extent according to the King's wishes. He told them that unless they could manage to make peace *that night* they would never again reach the point already attained.

Finally the King repeated his promise as to the restoration of Becket and his co-exiles. At this the Nuncios and all rejoiced. The King said that if he had done in any respect too little that day, he would mend it on the morrow.[1]

Sept. 2, (Tuesday). On the morrow (which Becket's correspondent seems erroneously to call the Calends of September, but which was, according to the context, the 4th of the Nones), there was a meeting in the same place—the Park of Le Bur. The Nuncios absolved Geoffrey Ridel, Nigel de Sackville, and Thomas fitz Bernard, they promising, on the word of truth and laying hand on the Gospels, that they would obey the Nuncios' (subsequent) mandates. Le Bur.

It was then asked of the Nuncios that they would allow the properties of Becket's church to remain with the King's presentees; but it was settled that these properties were to revert to Becket absolutely (*libere*).

[1] S. T. C. iv. 278-281. Epist. ccclxxxiij.

1169. Sept. 2. (Tuesday). The Bishops were then set to write down the "Form of Peace" propounded by Henry: the King again urging one of the Nuncios to go to England. The Nuncios were leaving the assembly, and it was near midnight, when the King said that the words "*salvâ dignitate regni mei*" were to be appended to the '*Forma Pacis.*' Gratian said he would not allow it. Le Bur.

"And in that resolution" (adds Becket's correspondent) "the Nuncios persevere, and on the day of the Virgin's Nativity (September 8) they are to go to Caen to confirm the said resolution more fully. The Bishop of Liseux (during the preceding conferences) was bent on serving the King, the Archbishop of Rouen, on serving God and the Pope." [1]

Another authority points out Rotrou, Archbishop of Rouen, as the most strenuous mediator in the above diplomacy, and says that at one step of the altercation, William, Archbishop of Sens (he was Legate in France at the time), warned the Nuncios not to proceed without his advice.

Another authority states that the three excommunicates were absolved with the proviso that "peace" was to be restored between Henry and Becket before Martinmas (November 11). And such was substantively the fact.

Sept. 3, (Wednesday.) King Henry went to Rouen to meet the Comte of Flanders. He left the negotiation with the Nuncios to be conducted, on his part, by the Archbishops of Bordeaux and Rouen, the Bishops of Liseux, Worcester, Seez, Baieux, and Rhedon, and by the Archdeacons of Canterbury and Salisbury, and by his barons (*principibus suis*).[2] Rouen.

At Rouen the King is said to have conferred with several English Bishops.[3]

Sept. 8, (Monday.) The Nuncios go to Caen and confer with the King's Commissioners. The Nuncios agree to accept the proviso "*Salvâ dignitate regni,*" but require to add also the expression "*salvâ libertate Ecclesiæ.*" This, the Commissioners, alleging the King's disapproval, refuse. The agreement and promise remained then intact, as originally tendered by the King.[2]

c. Sept. 16, (Tuesday). The King summons the Nuncios to Rouen and informs them by messengers that he would not recede from the clause "*salvâ dignitate regni sui.*" [2]

And so the Nuncios quitted Rouen, but not without warning the Archbishops (of Bourdeaux and Rouen)

[1] S. T. C. iv. 281. [2] S. T. C. iv. 218, 219. [3] See Lyttelton, ii. 518.

on their allegiance to the Pope, that if Peace were not restored before the Nuncios should leave France, that both the King and the three absolved persons should be told that the latter were no longer to enjoy the benefit of absolution, but must observe the sentence originally pronounced against them by the Archbishop of Canterbury.[1]

1169. c. Sept. 20. King Henry now sends ambassadors to the Pope, viz., Reginald, Archdeacon of Salisbury; Randolph, Archdeacon of Landaff; and Richard Barre.[2] They were to gain the Pope's sanction of the King's saving clause, "*salvâ dignitate regni,*" in addition to former requirements (as to absolutions); and to say that, unless the Pope acceded, the King would provide for his honour and safety elsewhere (we infer by siding with the Emperor and Anti-Pope). Rouen.

September, 1169. The Nuncios now visit Becket, and tell him the state of things. He said he would gladly aid in "preserving the dignity of Henry's realm," "saving his own Order and his fealty to the Church of Rome."

c. Sept. 24. Later still, the Nuncios, by counsel of the Archbishops and Bishops, send Peter, Archdeacon of Pavia, to exhort the King to comply with the Pope's requirements. The Envoy was courteously received, but indecorously dismissed, and then robbed, on his way back, of certain effects. One of his attendants, too, remaining outside the town, was set on by ruffians, but released when a certain Knight passing by hinted that he would inform the Nuncios of the outrage.

Vivian now writes the above particulars to the Pope. He excuses Gratian for not joining in his letter. That Nuncio was in a hurry to leave France, and though he agreed in Vivian's statements he disapproved of their length. Both Nuncios concurred in begging the Pope not to accept any statements of Henry's ambassadors, till verified by the Nuncios themselves on their return to Italy.[3]

c. Sept. 29. The Bishop of London sets out for the Papal Court on the matter of his appeal. Having passed the Alps, and reached Milan, the Pope's Bull of absolution (directed to the Archbishop of Rouen and the Bishop of Exeter) meets him. He returns to Normandy and is absolved by the Archbishop at Rouen, on Easter Sunday (April 5), 1170.[4]

Of the Queen, or of any other member of the Royal family, we have scant mention in the records of the fiscal year now ended. The silence of the Pipe-Rolls indicates that both the Queen and her children were over sea.

The various Writs authorizing the Sheriffs' expenditure of Royal revenue during the year were one-while Writs of the King, one-while Writs of Richard de Luci.

A few further extracts from the Pipe-Roll indicate little more than the King's continued residence abroad:—

Civitas Winton'. *Et pro conducendo thesauro et hugiâ thesauri de Winton' ad Hanton' et in aliis minutis negociis thesauri per totum annum 25s. 2d.*

[1] S. T. C. iv. 219. Epist. ccclx.

[2] One account (M. Paris's) styles the Envoys "Reginald, Archdeacon of Salisbury," and "R. Barre."

Another names the Archdeacons of Landaff and Salisbury.

Another styles them "Ralph, Archdeacon of Landaff," and "Reginald de Salisbury."

Another names the "Archdeacon of Salisbury" and "Richard Barre."

Thus each account names but two of the three Envoys who actually went. The two Archdeacons had been each on distinct missions to the Pope previously.

[3] S. T. C. iv. 219, 220.

[4] Diceto, pp. 550-553.

HANTONIA. *Et pro perficiendis doliis cervisiæ, missæ in Normanniam 6s. 4d. Et pro locandis quinque navibus ad portandas damas Regis in Normanniam £4. 10s. Et in liberacione Esneccæ de tribus passagiis £22. 10s. per breve Ricardi de Luci. Et pro locandis tribus navibus ad equos Camerarii £4. 10s. per idem breve. Et item pro onerando thesauro duabus vicibus 6s. 4d.*

FROM VARIOUS SOURCES we get a tolerably full list of the persons employed during the above year in the administration of the law and the assessment of taxes :—

Richard, Archdeacon of Poitiers ; Guy, Dean of Waltham ; Reginald de Warren ; Oger, Dapifer ; William Basset ; and Alan de Nevill, junior ; had officiated either as justices in eyre, or assessors of the aid in marriage of the Princess Matilda on certain boroughs. Alan de Nevill (senior, we presume) had visited a few counties, and held pleas apparently of the forest.

On Michaelmas Day, clearly the Michaelmas of 1169, a certain suitor in the *Curiâ Regis* (at Westminster, it is evident) accepted the homage of, and executed a feoffment to, another suitor ; and this was in presence of ten "Barons of the Exchequer," viz., Richard de Luci ; Richard, Archdeacon of Poitiers ; Wido, Dean of Waltham ; Henry fitz Gerold, Chamberlain ; Richard the Treasurer ; William Mauduit ; Alan de Nevill ; Reginald de Warren ; William Basset ; and Adam de Gernemue. The said feoffment was also attested by Joceline, Bishop of Sarum ; Earl Hugh (of Norfolk), Earl William of Arundel, Geoffrey de Luci, Thomas Basset, Philip de Chimes, Radulf de Glanvill ; Gervase de Cornhill, Oger, Sheriff (of Norfolk and Suffolk),[1] Roger fitz Reinfred, Nicholas, Dean of Tilbury ;[2] and Stephen de Beauchamp, Sheriff of Essex ;[3] that is by twelve persons, of whom seven are known to have acted as justiciars on other occasions.[4] Moreover, four of the persons thus attendant at the Exchequer are known to have been among Becket's Excommunicates, of whom only the Bishop appears to have appealed to the Pope.

Oct. 1-31. King Henry probably at Rouen most of the month. Rouen.

c. Oct. The Nuncios Gratian, and Vivian, remind Geoffrey, Archdeacon of Canterbury, Nigel de Saccavill, and Thomas fitz Bernard, that they had previous to Michaelmas been apprised by the Archbishops of Rouen and Bourdeaux, that their absolution formerly conferred by the Nuncios would be cancelled if 'Peace' were not secured before Michaelmas ; and add that Becket, having in default of such Peace renewed their sentences of excommunication, they, the Legates, now order them to keep their promises and observe their sentences.[5]

Oct. 29. The Nuncio Vivian passing southwards, and intending to go to Italy with the Archbishop of Tours, halts at Tours. Here he is found by the Prior of Bec-Hellouin who brings him letters from K. Henry, from Rotrou, Archbishop of Rouen, and from Geoffrey Ridel, Archdeacon of Canterbury. Hereupon Vivian's resolution to go to Italy seems to have changed. He sends transcripts of the above three letters to Becket at Sens. Therewith he himself writes to Becket, telling him not to be persuaded by the Archbishop of Rouen, nor to defer to Gratian [6] (who at this rate would seem to be still in France).

Nov. 3, (Monday). Becket left Sens.[7]

Vivian writes again to Becket, inviting him to attend a conference between Louis and Henry, which was to take place at St. Denys on November 16 (Sunday) : also intimating that he, Vivian, was on his way to the French court.[8]

[1] Identical with Oger, Dapifer. He was Sheriff of Norfolk and Suffolk from Michaelmas, 1163, till Easter, 1170.

[2] Otherwise called *Nicholas Decanus* and *Nicholas Clericus*. He had served as Sheriff of Essex and Hertfordshire from Michaelmas, 1164, to Easter, 1169, when he was succeeded by Stephen de Beauchamp.

[3] Stephen de Beauchamp's tenure of the office only lasted a year, and consequently he was Sheriff only on one Michaelmas Day—that of 1169.

[4] Madox (Formulare cccxi. Exchequer, p. 744). Madox suggests *circiter* 16 *Hen. II.*, as the date of the transaction. It is wrong only by a year.

[5] S. T. C. vi. 127. Epist. cccxc.

[6] S. T. C. iv. 214. Epist. ccclviij.

[7] S. T. C. i. 158.

[8] S. T. C. iv. 215. Epist. ccclix.

1169. c. Nov. 10, (Monday). Becket writes to Vivian. Becket does not see why Vivian should urge his attendance at the conference of "*Sunday next*" (November 16). However, Becket will meet Vivian himself at Corboil Castle on "*Friday next*" (November 14). Becket's letter is high-toned, and discourages any prospect of effectual mediation between himself and King Henry.[1]

Nov. 14, (Friday).—The conference at Corboil Castle, between Becket and the Nuncio Vivian, probably took place.

1169. Nov. 16, (Sunday.) Conference of St. Denys between Louis VII. of France and Henry of England.[1] The Nuncio Vivian was present at the conference; but Archbishop Becket was in Paris. St. Denys.

The treaty made at St. Denys between Louis and Henry had nothing to do with Becket. It bound Henry to treat amicably with Raymond, Comte of Toulouse (or St. Giles), whose Fief was claimed by Prince Richard of England as Duke of Aquitaine.[2] Henry also covenanted to send Prince Richard (already affianced to Louis's daughter) to be educated in the French court.

Nov. 18, (Tuesday.) Conference of Montmartre (near St. Denys) on the differences between K. Henry and Thomas, Archbishop of Canterbury, who were both present.[3] The mediators were Louis of France; Rotrou, Archbishop of Rouen; and the Nuncio Vivian. Froger, Bishop of Seez, and Theobald, Comte of Blois, were also present. K. Henry is represented as yielding everything to Becket except the "Kiss of Peace,"—a feudal symbol which, if given, purported to disarm the giver of any covert intention against the peace or safety of the recipient. Montmartre.

Henry's refusal put an end to the conference and to all present hope of reconciliation. It was regarded by K. Louis and the Comte of Blois with such suspicion, that they advised Becket not to return to England without the symbol in question.

Vivian's letters to Pope Alexander and to K. Henry on this occasion are both extant.[4] In that to Henry he still urges the bestowal of the "Kiss of Peace," and speaks of the possibility of an interdict and of impending sentences of excommunication against Henry's most important officers. If Henry will not even in such a crisis listen to Vivian, Henry's repentance will be too late.[4]

The Nuncio after refusing a bribe from Henry took journey towards Italy.

c. Nov. K. Henry now again sent ambassadors to Benevento; viz., John of Oxford (Dean of Salisbury); Giles, Archdeacon of Rouen; and John, Archdeacon of Seez. Normandy.

[1] S. T. C. iii. 357. Epist. clxxxiij.

[2] Diceto, p. 551. Comte Raymond's son and apparent heir was Louis's nephew, son of his sister Constance, who after the death of her affianced husband, Eustace son of K. Stephen, had married Comte Raymond.

[3] S. T. C. iv. 220. Ep. ccclxj. Vivian describes the conference as '*Colloquium Regum*,' and (in loose terms) as taking place "at Paris."

[4] S. T. C. iv. Epistles ccclxi; ccclxij.

1169. Nov. It was now too that K. Henry transmitted to England the Edict known as the 'Ten Ordinances.' The King's object was to cut off from Becket or his agents all possibility of communication with England, so that if the Archbishop should have recourse to what Henry most dreaded, an interdict of the realm, its lodgment, publication, and efficacy could not be achieved without involving numbers of persons in the guilt of treason. One of these Ordinances, the tenth, was retrospective rather than precautionary.—The said Ordinance pronounced the Bishops of London and Salisbury to be *in misericordiâ Regis*; that is, liable to penalty at the King's discretion, in that they had disobeyed the Statutes of Clarendon by interdicting the lands and excommunicating the person of Earl Hugh[1] (of Norfolk). Normandy.

Various accounts are given about the promulgation of the Ten Ordinances.[2]—

It is probably correct that the King sent them over to England by the hands of Richard, Archdeacon of Poitiers, and Geoffrey, Archdeacon of Canterbury, with orders for the assemblage of a Synod in London.

Dec. 25. The King, attended by Prince Geoffrey kept Christmas at Nantes in Bretagne.[3] Nantes, Bretagne.

Dec. 31. The King still in Bretagne.

In the above year died Hilary, Bishop of Chichester,[4] and Nicholas de Stuteville founded *Ecclesiam de Vallo Monte*[5] (the Monastery of St. Mary de Valmont).

[1] Cotton Claud. B. II. p. 27.

[2] See Lyttelton, vol. ii. pp. 527, 532; vol. iv. 236. Lyttelton dates the Edict rightly no doubt, and says that it was disregarded by the Bishops of Winchester, Exeter, Norwich, and Chester. His idea that Earl Hugh of the 10th Ordinance was Hugh, Earl of Chester, was of course wrong.

Carte's notions (Hist. of England, pp. 596, 597) about this Edict are so wrong and also so plausible that they need not mislead us, and yet it is interesting to criticize them. He says that the Ordinances were sent "to the Chief Justiciars in England, viz., to Richard de Luci and the two Archdeacons;" and it is certain that De Luci was Chief Justice of England at the time, and it is probable that as recently as Michaelmas the Archdeacon Richard had been acting as a Justiciar in England. Carte says that the bearers of the letters to England were "Walter de Grimesby and Wimer, two High Sheriffs—the latter in Priest's Orders." Certainly Wymer was in Holy Orders, and these two persons were sometime Sheriffs, viz., of Lincolnshire and Norfolk, but their appointment as Sheriffs was not till Easter, 1170.

Carte, moreover, dates the Edict as A.D. 1165, which is utterly inexplicable,—the more so as it is subversive of all his other ideas.

[3] Benedictus, p. 1. At this time the Chronicle in question, variously attributed to Benedictus Abbas and Benedictus Petroburgensis, commences.

[4] Annals of Waverley, p. 160.

[5] Chron. Norm. p. 1003. Gall. Script. xii. 778.

A.D. 1170.

1170. Jan. 1. The King is still in Bretagne with Prince Geoffry. He remains there the whole month; and succeeds in bringing Eudo, Vicomte of Porhöet, to submission.[1] Bretagne.

Jan. 19. The Pope, at Beneventum, appoints and instructs a new commission to carry out the agreements of Montmartre between Henry and Becket. The Commissioners were Rotroc, Abp of Rouen, and Bernard, Bp of Nevers (to whom was afterwards added William, Abp of Sens). Their instructions were to lay an interdict on Henry's citra-marine dominions if he neglected forty days after notice to perform his undertaking as to a peace with Becket.[2]

Feb. 2. K. Henry is at Seez in Normandy.[1] Seez.

The following charter, dated *apud Moritonium*, is noticed in this place without any assumption as to the period of its issue other than that it was probably between the years 1166 and 1170. It is a general confirmation to the Abbey of White-Ladies of Mortain (*des Dame Blanches de Mortain*), in the Diocese of Avranches.[3] Its witnesses are—Geoffry and Roger, King's Chaplains; Hugh Murdac; Earl William de Mandeville; Radulf de Fulgeriis; Robert de Vitrei; Bernard de St. Valery; Fulco Paganell; William de Traci; Robert de Bricourt; and Rodolf fitz Stephen. Mortain (in the Avranchin).

Feb. 3. Incidentally we have notice of Richard de Humez and Bertram de Verdon being on this day at Stamford in Northamptonshire.[4]

Feb. 12. Pope Alexander, at Benevento, to Gilbert, Bishop of London.—Is sorry to withold the usual epistolary Benediction.—Has empowered the Archbishop of Rouen and Bishop of Exeter to absolve Bishop Gilbert conditionally, unless the latter should prefer to prosecute his appeal.—Becket has been instructed to keep such absolution secret till it might be safe to Bishop Gilbert that it should be advertised.[5]

Feb. 18. Pope Alexander, at Benevento, to all the French Bishops;—certifying the commission of the Archbishop of Rouen and the Bishop of Nevers. If they or either of them subject Henry's citra-marine dominions to an interdict, the

[1] Brompton, p. 1060, Vide supra pp. 94, 113 *n*.

[2] S. T. C. iv. 55. Ep. ccliii. Vivian, as well as K. Henry's messengers had conferred with the Pope before he issued this commission. The only outstanding difficulty was about the "Kiss of Peace," which, if the Commissioners failed to force upon Henry, they were, with Becket's consent, to compromise.

The question of the "Customs" was not to be urged at present, The Commissioners, when assured of "Peace," might absolve Excommunicates; but they were to sentence, *sans appeal*, those who had done violence to Peter, Archdeacon of Pavia. The Pope instructs the Commissioners to tell K. Henry that neither Gratian nor Vivian were to be blamed by the King. They could not, on their instructions, have acted otherwise than they had.

[3] D'Anisy's Normandy Transcripts, i. 90.

[4] Monasticon, iv. 261.

[5] S. T. C. iv. 93. Ep. cclxxx. The proviso about non-publication was, we presume, in avoidance of any possible displeasure on the King's part at Bishop Gilbert's submission to the Papal delegates.

French Bishops are to enforce and to cause the same to be enforced in all their parishes (*i. e.* dioceses).[1]

Feb. 18. Pope Alexander, at Benevento, to Roger, Archbishop of York, A.S.L.; to Hugh, Bishop of Durham, and to all Suffragans of the Province of York, certifying the same commission, and the order given thereupon to the citra-marine Bishops.—Now gives similar order to York, Durham, and Suffragans of York. In case Thomas, Archbishop of Canterbury, lay an interdict on his own province, York and his Suffragans are to publish and enforce it in their Province.[2]

Pope Alexander addresses contemporary and correlative injunctions, as to the enforcement of the threatened interdict, to the Archbishops of Tours, Bourges, Bourdeaux, and Auxerre, and to the Suffragan Bishops of each, as well as to the Suffragan Bishops of Rouen.[3]

c. Feb. 20. The Archdeacon of Landaff and Richard Barre, returning from Beneventum, reach Normandy. They are incorrectly said to have brought the Pope's commission, addressed to Archbishop Rotroc and Bp Bernard, and purporting to have been procured by John of Oxford's agency at Beneventum. They probably brought only the news that the Pope intended to issue such a commission.[4] They are also said to have brought a private letter from the Pope to Roger, Abp of York, authorizing him to crown Prince Henry as desired by the King.[5]

Another, not inconsistent, account is that at this time John of Oxford himself returned from Beneventum.[4]

1170. *c.* Feb. 20. K. Henry being at Caen, invites Becket to meet him there. Caen.

[1] S. T. C. iv. 42. Epist. ccxl. This precept is superscribed by some Rubricator, as addressed "*Omnibus Episcopis Cantiæ*," and so has been concluded by some to have been a precept to the Suffragans of Canterbury;—a great mistake and inconsistent with the letter itself. In another letter (S. T. C. iv. 60) the Pope himself alludes to it as addressed to the Archbishops and Bishops of Henry's citra-marine territory.—

Therefore we conclude to read *Franciæ* rather than *Canciæ* in the superscription.

[2] S. T. C. iv. 47. Ep. ccxlviii.

[3] S. T. C. iv. 73, 74. Epist. ccxliv.

[4] The mission of the Archdeacon of Landaff and Richard Barre had left Normandy *c.* Sept. 1169, that of John of Oxford *c.* Nov. 1169 (Supra pp. 129 and 131). Both missions will have quitted Benevento early in January, 1170. They brought news doubtless to Henry of the Pope's intention to issue a new commission; but the commission itself, being dated Jan. 19, 1170, can hardly have left Benevento under their care, neither is it probable that the Pope would have entrusted such a document to such conveyance.

The Pope's answer to Henry (S. T. C. iv. 131, Ep. cccvii.) is what the Envoys took back. It tells of an audience given by the Pope and his brethren to John, Dean of Salisbury; Giles, Archdeacon of Rouen; John, Archdeacon of Seez; and Reginald, Archdeacon of Salisbury at one and the same time. It tells also of the commission of Rouen and Nevers.

[5] There may be some doubt about the genuineness of this letter (S. T. C. iv. 45. Ep. ccxlv.), but no doubt that K. Henry entertained the scheme of the Archbishop of York's crowning the Prince, and that Becket had not as yet any notice of the King's intention. Becket's agents at Beneventum procured a Bull, dated Feb. 26, wherein the Pope forbids the Abp of York, the Bishop of Durham, and the English Bishops, from attempting, or assisting at, such a ceremony (S. T. C. iv. 47. Epist. ccxlvii.) Our own impression is that the Pope's license to York (Epistle ccxlv.) is genuine, though undated. It was perhaps obtained by John of Oxford (who was in Henry's confidence) early in January, and the Pope granted it solely with a view to gratify K. Henry's wish that his son should be crowned, and without dreaming of the grievance which such a license would constitute for Becket. The language of the Pope's inhibition of Feb. 26, is to the effect that the Archbishop of Canterbury's exclusive right to crown an English King had only recently dawned upon the Pope.

1170. c. Feb. 28. Becket, on his way from Seez to Caen, is stopped by a message announcing the King's intention of instantly going to England. Caen.

March 3. K. Henry lands at Portsmouth, after four years' absence from England. One of forty vessels which attended his voyage was wrecked, whereby were lost Henry de Agnis, a nobleman; Master Ralph de Bellomont, the King's Physician; and Gilbert de Suleny. Portsmouth.

c. March. By a Charter, dated at Edwardston (that is, Shaftesbury, Dorsetshire), the King confirms to certain Lepers the manor of Bradley,[1] which Manasser Biset had given and conceded to the said Lepers, for Alicia his wife, of whose inheritance it is. Witnesses, Fulk Paenell; William Malet, Dapifer; Reginald fitz Urse; Ralph fitz Stephen, Chamberlain.[2] Shaftesbury.

By a Charter, dated at Feckenham (Worcestershire), the King confirms to Bermondsey Priory Walcheline Maminot's gift of the Church of Berlyng.[3] Witnesses, Wido, Dean of Waltham; Thomas, Archdeacon of Bath; Richard de Luci; Manasser Biset, Dapifer; William de Courci; and Gilbert Malet.[4] Feckenham.

April 5. Pope Alexander, at Lateran, to the Archbishop of York and the English Bishops.—They are not to interfere in any coronation of a new king in derogation of the rights of Canterbury and of Archbishop Thomas, nor without his consent.[5]

April 5. At Easter, the King held a great Council at Windsor, and appointed a commission of enquiry into the conduct of all persons in authority (Archbishops, Bishops, Abbots, &c., Earls, Barons, Sheriffs, &c., Foresters, Citizens, Burgesses, &c.) during his late absence from England. Windsor.

The Commissioners for one circuit (Kent, Surrey, Middlesex, Berks, Oxfordshire, Bucks, and Bedfordshire), are named. They were the Abbot of St. Augustin, Canterbury; the Abbot of Chertsey; the Earl of Clare; Wm. de Abrancis; Manasser de Dammartin; Gerold fitz Ralph; Gilbert de Pinkeni; Wm. fitz Helt; Wm. fitz Nigel; William fitz Martin; Ralph de Hospital; and Ralph de Dene.[6] On another circuit, which included Warwickshire,

[1] Afterwards Maiden Bradley.

[2] Monasticon vii. 644.

[3] Walcheline Maminot's grant appears to have been in 1168 (Bermondsey Chronicle).

[4] Monast. v. 100, vi. Thomas, Archdeacon of Bath, occurs thrice in this year. In one case (c. May) he is called the *new Archdeacon*. His appointment was probably irregular and afterwards cancelled. In May, 1171, John was Archdeacon of Bath.

[5] S. T. C. iv. 45. Ep. ccxliv.

[6] Gervase, p. 1410.

1170. April 5. Walter de Insula and Eustace fitz Stephen were two of the Commissioners.[1] Windsor

On this same day (April 5) Gilbert, Bishop of London, is said to have been absolved at Rouen by Archbishop Rotrou. The Bishop would seem at once to have hastened to England, and to have reached Windsor before the King left it.[2]

William, King of Scots, and his brother David were present at the Council of Windsor.

A royal grant, dated at Windsor, is in favour of Swineshead Abbey. The movent clause is "*pro animâ avi mei Henrici Regis, et patris mei, et pro salute animæ meæ et matris meæ Imperatricis et pro salute Reginæ et filiorum et fratrum meorum.*" The witnesses are Roger, Archbishop of York; Gilbert, Bishop of London; William, Earl de Mandeville; Richard de Luci; Reginald de Curtenai; and Will fitz Radulf.[3]

c. April 10.[4] From Windsor the King went to London and there held a great Council about the proposed coronation of his eldest son Henry, and about the Statutes of the Realm. Now, also, the King deposed[5] almost all[6] the Sheriffs in the kingdom.[7] London.

c. May. Two Royal Charters to Haughmond Abbey (Shropshire) would appear to have borne date at Woodstock, and to have passed at this time. When collated, they seem both to be attested by Geoffry, Archdeacon of Canterbury, and Richard de Camvill.[8] Woodstock.

Another Charter, dated at Silveston (Northants), is in Silverston.

[1] Rot. Pip. 19 Hen. II. (Madox. Exchequer 96).

[2] To a date immediately subsequent to this is ascribed a chronologically important letter of Becket to the Cardinal Albert. It is the letter in which Becket speaks of the absolution of the Bishops of London and Salisbury, and in which he denounces so fiercely Reginald fitz Josceline, the Bishop of Salisbury's *bastard* son. (See Hook's Lives of the Archbishops of Canterbury, vol. ii. pp. 479, 480).

[3] Monast. v. 337, i.—This Charter proves how little we can gather of the life or death of persons named in a *movent clause*. The Empress and the King's brothers, whom we might suppose to be living at its date, were all three dead before William de Mandeville became an Earl.

[4] Neither Benedictus nor Gervase supply the exact date of this Council of London; but the King went thereto from Windsor. Moreover, the displacement of the Sheriffs, so far as we can judge from the changes of accountants on the Pipe-Roll, dates from Easter (April 5).

[5] *Deposuit* is the word used by Benedictus (i. 5). We understand it, both from the context, and from the statement of the Norman Chronicle, under June 11, to mean only *suspended*, *i. e.*, till the Commissioners appointed at Windsor should have made their reports.

[6] Of thirty-five counties accounted of by their respective Sheriffs at Michaelmas, 1169, only nine were accounted of by identical Sheriffs at Michaelmas, 1170; but out of the twenty-six cases of change, two were because the previous Sheriff was represented by deputy, and one (Shropshire) was accounted for by the clerk of a deceased Sheriff.

[7] Benedictus (Stubbs), i. 4, 5. Gervase, 1410.

[8] Haughmond Chartʸ. fo. 53, and Monast. vi. 108, iii.—

Alured, now Abbot of Haughmond, had so been appointed by the King during the minority of young William fitz Alan. Formerly Alured had been tutor to the King; "*qui me nutrivit*," says the King of the Abbot.

1170. c. May. favour of Tavistock Monastery, and was tested singly by Geoffry, Archbishop (read Archdeacon) of Canterbury.[1] Silverston.

c. May. Pope Alexander, to the Archbishop of Rouen and Bishop of Nevers.—Has heard of K. Henry's transfretation (on March 3) to England. The Commissioners are to go to the King within twenty days after receipt of this Letter. The Pope repeats his former instructions, and if the King delay to fulfil the Commissioners' injunctions, forty days after receipt thereof, they are to interdict his continental (*cis-marinam*) territory, as before prescribed. They are further to intimate to Henry that if he continue obdurate, the Pope will deal with him as with the Emperor Frederick, and sentence his person.[2]

The Commissioners, in virtue of the powers of absolution, primarily intrusted to them by the Pope, are not so to absolve Geoffrey, Archdeacon of Canterbury, or others, unless he or they shall first have surrendered the the Church of Otteford or other possessions of the Church of Canterbury.[2]

May. Prince Richard, to whom, by Queen Eleanor's wish, Henry had ceded Aquitaine, comes with the Queen to Limoges. They lay the foundation stones of the monastery of St. Augustine.[3]

May 31. Prince Richard, seated on the Abbot's throne in the Church of St. Hilary at Poictiers, is presented with the "lance" and "standard" (the insignia of the Poitevin Comtes) by Bertram, Archbishop of Bordeaux, and by John, Bishop of Poictiers.[3]

Afterwards Richard was received in procession at Limoges, was decorated with the Ring of St. Valerie, and proclaimed Duke.[3]

May 31. On the octave of Pentecost, David, brother of the King of Scots, was knighted by K. Henry. England.

King Henry sends Thomas, the *new* Archdeacon of Bath, to the Archbishop of Rouen, with what result, as regards the Archbishop himself, there is no record.

But Archdeacon Thomas persuaded the Bishop of Nevers to delay his passage to England till June 14, and proclaimed publicly that the King was immediately coming back to Normandy, which, says our authority, was an utter falsehood.[4]

June 5, Friday. Richard, Archdeacon of Poitiers, having been sent to Caen, where Prince Henry was, sets out with the Prince for England.[4] England.

Roger, Bishop of Worcester, being at Dieppe, obedient to a summons to attend the forthcoming Council of London, and having in charge certain prohibitory letters of the Pope to the Abp of York and others, touching the coronation of Prince Henry, is detained from proceeding to England by authority of Queen Eleanor and Richard de Humez, constable of Normandy, both then at Caen.

Bernard, Bishop of Nevers, having received the Papal commission of January, and in pursuance thereof seeking an early interview with Henry, happened to reach Caen on the same day, but the Prince, with the Archdeacon of Poictiers, and the Bishops of Bayeux and Seez had already started for the coast (Barfleur probably), *en route* for England.[4]

c. June 8. AMICUS, a warm partizan of Becket, resident at Caen, writes an important letter to Becket, who is still at Sens.—

Tells him of the Coronation to take place in England on "Sunday next," and that the Pope's prohibitory letters to York and others, though they had long since reached England, had never been delivered to the persons addressed: that, if the Archbishop of York should fear to crown young Henry,

[1] Monast. ii. 496, iii.
[2] S. T. C. iv. 59. Ep. ccliv. cclv.
[3] Rerum Gallicarum Scriptores, xii. 442.
[4] S. T. C. iv. 287. Epist. cclxxxix.

the "Butcher of Seez" was to do it. Dwells on the offence to Louis that his daughter should be left at Caen, and excluded from sharing in her husband's coronation. Tells, as above, about Thomas, Archdeacon of Bath; about the Queen and de Humez; the Archdeacon of Poictiers; and the two Norman Bishops. Reflects much on the supineness, or slothfulness, or credulity of the Bishop of Nevers, who was *creeping* about West Normandy affecting to seek, and yet careful to postpone his passage to England, which he might easily have accomplished had he stuck to his original plan of going by way of Sens and Flanders. Suggests that Becket would only stop K. Henry's design (of the Coronation) by going with the Archbishop of Sens to Louis, who would send a message to the Queen and De Humez, prohibiting the Coronation without his daughter's presence, which message would alarm the Queen and De Humez, and induce them to warn K. Henry. Further suggests that Becket, K. Louis, and the Archbishop of Sens, should send to the Bishop of Nevers, ordering him to demand at once, from the Queen at Caen, a passage to England; which passage being impracticable, Nevers would resort to Becket, and accomplish his object (of reaching K. Henry) with some celerity (*idem Episcopus ad vos revertatur facturus citius quod facturus est*.[1]

1170. June 11. The King holds a great Council at London, whereat the Commissioners, appointed at Windsor in April, make their reports, and whereat many Sheriffs and Officials are said to have been cashiered.[2] London.

June 14, (Sunday). Prince Henry crowned King, in presence of his father, at Westminster, by Roger, Archbishop of York, Legate of the Apostolic See. There were present and assisting two Norman and four English Bishops, viz., Henry of Baieux Froger of Seez, Hugh of Durham, Gilbert of London, Josceline of Salisbury, and Walter of Rochester.[3] Westminster.

June 15. William, King of Scots, and his brother David do homage to the younger King Henry.

c. June 20. The Bishop of Nevers, having been refused a passage to England by the Queen and De Humez, was now at Mantes, waiting the King's return to Normandy.[4]

King Henry, to cajole Louis, had sent orders for the Princess Margaret to hold herself in readiness to leave Caen on being summoned by the King to England.[4]

The Bishop of Worcester, staunch to Becket, had not yet effected a passage to England.[4]

c. June 24. King Henry embarks for Normandy from Portsmouth. Louis of France, in dudgeon that his daughter, Margaret, was not crowned with her husband, is threatening the Norman frontier. The King lands at Barfleur. Portsmouth. Barfleur.

[1] S. T. C. iv. 287. Epist. ccclxxxix.

[2] Chron. Normann. 1004, is the only authority for this Council of June 11th. The statement as to the receipt of the reports of the Commissioners on the Sheriff-Inquest is probably correct. We understand also that most of the Sheriffs, already suspended, were now cashiered.

[3] Chron Normann. 1004. Hoveden, 497. Benedictus, 4.—Giles, Bishop of Evreux, would seem also to have been present. One writer, resident in Normandy, says that young Henry was knighted by his father, and then anointed King by York, *transactâ Dominicâ*; but whether he meant on Monday or after sun-set on Sunday, we suppose neither was correct. (S. T. C. iv. 299).

[4] S. T. C. iv. 299. Ep. cccxcij.

SOME EXTRACTS FROM the Pipe-Roll of 1170 will here be pertinent, illustrating as they do K. Henry's visit to England, the coronation of his son, and the King's transfretation.—

WICUMBA.[1] *Et pro conducendâ vaissellâ Regis de Wudestokâ ad Windresor et inde ad Lundon* 3s. 6d. *Et pro hugiâ thesauri conducendâ ad Lundon* 18d. *Et pro quatuor carretis ad opus Regis* 23s. 7d. *per breve Regis.*

BERCHAMESTEDA. *Et in operacione quatuor galearum ad opus Regis* 41s. 4d. *per breve Regis.*

HANTESCIRA. *Et Willelmo filio Adelini* £10 *ad corredium Regis filii Regis per breve Regis. Et item Ailwardo camerario* £11. 13s. 4d. *ad corredium Regis per breve Regis. Et pro locandis navibus ad passagium Ricardi de Luci et aliorum Baronum* £11. 10s. *per breve Regis. Et in liberacione Esneccæ quando Rex ipse transfretavit* £7. 10s. *per breve Regis.*

CIVITAS WINTONIÆ. *Et in conducendis thesauro et hugiis et Regalibus et rotulis et taleis de thesauro septem itineribus* 63s. 5d. *Et pro locandis caretis ad portandum thesaurum . . . . . . ciis thesauri* 12s. 8d. *per Willelmum Picot et Godefridum Clericum.*[2]

LONDON AND MIDDLESEX. *Et pro* 4 *caretis ferrandis ad opus Regis filii Regis* 64s. 7d. *Et Edwardo Blundo* £12. 16s *ad emendos pannos sericos et unam pelliciam variam ad opus Regis et unum palefridum ad opus unius militis de Andegaviâ per breve Regis. Et fratri Ernulfo et nuncio Imperatoris et nuncio Ducis Saxoniæ et Martino de Capella* £16. *per breve Regis. Et pro pannis ad opus Reginæ per Edwardum Blundum* £6. 19s. 9d. *per breve Regis. Et pro robâ de viridi essaiâ et caligis et ocreis et tribus pannis sericis ad opus Regis filii Regis* £9. 15s. *per breve Regis per visum Edwardi Blundi. Et pro coffris et minuto harnesio ad capellam Regis filii Regis* 18s. 3d. *per breve Regis. Et pro robâ filiæ Regis Franciæ et familiæ ejus* £26. 17s. 5d. *per breve Regis et per testimonium Edwardi Blundi.*[3] *Et Willo de Hauvill* 24s. *ad emendos duos accipitres ad opus Regis filii Regis per breve Regis et pro uno accipitre ad opus Regis Scottiæ* 20s. *per breve Regis. Et pro auro ad deaurandam vaissellam Regis filii Regis et ad*

[1] This is High Wycombe (Bucks), a Lordship then *in manu Regis.*

[2] In this Pipe-Roll, the Southampton account is torn away, with the exception of the heading *Hantonia*, and a few scattered words, amongst which are *passagiis Esneccæ* £22.

[3] It does not follow from this that the Princess Margaret came to London during any part of the King's stay. An outfit was provided for her in case the King should summon her from Caen to join the Coronation festivities; but he never did summon her, and his intending it, or affectation of intending it, was only to appease Louis. "*Mandavit (Rex Henricus) Ricardo de Humes quod filiam Regis Francorum cum Reginâ Cadomi morantem vestibus, equitaturis, et familiâ decenter instrueret ad transfretandum quando ipse mandaret. Hoc autem factum est ut audiat Rex Francorum et ab indignatione quam de contemptu filiæ concepit, aliquantisper quiescat. Non enim mandatum est ut statim eat, sed præparari jubetur ut quando Rex miserit pro eâ ire non differat. Forte ergo consecrationem puellæ sicut et pueri furari nituntur.*" (S. T. C. iv. 300. Ep. cccxcij.).

On the whole we think that, had circumstances rendered it politic, Henry was really intending to send for the Princess. For though Humez' provision of an outfit at Caen may have been only intended as a sop for Louis's pride, Edward Blunt's outlay in London can have had no such object.

reparandos enses ad coronamentum Regis 24*s.* 9*d. per Ottonem fil' Willielmi et Willielmum fil' Ailwardi.*[1]

1170. c. June 30. King Henry is at Falaise[2] (100 miles from Barfleur). Falaise. On hearing of the King's landing in Normandy, the Archbishop of Rouen and Bishop of Nevers promptly sought his presence (*diligenter convenerunt regressum ejus*), and handed to him the Pope's *commonitory* letters containing the *form of Peace* which the commissioners were charged to negotiate between the King and Becket. After some conversation, the King undertook, at the Pope's bidding and pleasure, to restore to Becket his 'peace,' his church, and its entire possessions, and even the Royal favour; but the King still objected to give the "Kiss of Peace" because he had sworn in the presence of the French at Montmartre never to do so.[3]

July 2. Louis of France and Guy Comte of Nivernois destroy the castle of Donzi, Geoffry, its lord, being in rebellion.[4]

c. July 2. It was now perhaps that King Henry was at Argentan. Argentan. A Royal Charter, there dated, and in the year 1170, grants franchises to the Abbey of St. Sauveur le Vicomte (in the Diocese of Coutances). The Charter is attested by Richard de Hommet, William fitz Hamo and Jordan Taisson.[5]

July 6. (Monday.) King Henry confers with Comte Theobald of Blois at La Ferté Bernard (in the Pays Chartrain). La Ferté Bernard.

July 16, (Thursday). The Papal Commissioners (the Archbishop of Rouen and Bishop of Nevers) come to Sens and have an interview with Becket.[3] They are joined by William, Archbishop of Sens (then Papal Legate for France). Becket is pursuaded to attend a conference which was shortly to take place between the Kings, Louis and Henry. All four journeyed towards the frontier of the Chartrain, and reaching their destination on or before July 20, waited the pleasure of K. Henry as to an interview with Becket.[3]

July 20. (Monday). K. Henry is said to have met K. Louis at Vendome,[6] and Vendome. it is quite supposable that on this or on some preceding day Henry was at that place, but the meeting of the 20th between Henry and Louis took place in the open country,

[1] Under LONDON there are numerous other charges for household articles, clothing, plate, and provisions, for the King and royal family.

[2] S. T. C. i. 269 (W. fitz Stephen).

[3] S. T. C. iv. 301–306. Epist. cccxciij.

[4] Gall. Scriptores xii. 299. This shows that Louis was otherwise engaged than in threatening the Norman frontier.

[5] D'Anisy's Normandy Transcripts, iii. 36–37.

[6] "*Apud Wendoniam*," says our usual authority, Benedictus, by which we suppose Vendome to be meant. Vendome-sur-Loire was like La Ferté, in the Pays Chartrain, and not far from the frontier of Touraine (*Confer* S. T. C. i. 272, iv. 304).

1170. July 20. at a spot between La Ferté (in the Pays Chartrain), and Fréteval (a castle of Touraine).[1] Fréteval.

July 21. (Tuesday.) The conference between Henry and Louis continued. Henry explained the non-coronation of the Princess Margaret to Louis's satisfaction. The Kings parted amicably, without exchanging a word about Becket.[1]

July 22. (Wednes.) On the Feast-day of St. Mary Magdalene, as previously arranged by K. Henry, he and Becket met at the same place, near Fréteval, and arranged all their differences, exactly according to the terms prescribed by the Papal Commissioners.[2] Becket dispensed with the "Kiss of Peace," Henry promising that it should thereafter be given, when Becket should have been restored, and vouching the Archbishop of Sens as his surety that, in witholding the said symbol, he intended nothing insidious against Becket.[1]

The persons present, and assisting more or less at this conference, appear to have been K. Louis of France; Rotrou, Archbishop of Rouen; William, Archbishop of Sens, Legate of the Holy See; Bernard, Bishop of Nevers; Arnulf, Bishop of Liseux; Theobald, Comte of Blois, and Geoffrey Ridel, Archdeacon of Canterbury.

There were many episodes in this conference which, for the sake of chronological perspicuity, deserve some notice:—

Becket reproached the King with the injury done to his church of Canterbury by the recent coronation. Henry excused himself on the ground of political necessity (the *status regni* required it), and on the ground of his late anger against Becket, but he promised that Becket should crown the Princess Margaret and re-crown young Henry.

K. Henry proposed one-while, that he himself should take the cross, and leave his son Henry in Becket's care. Becket declined any secular office, but promised his counsel in case the King should entrust his son and his kingdom to the care of Hugh de Beauchamp.[1]

[1] S. T. C. iv. Epistle cccxciij.

[2] Dean Hook intimates that at this time Becket had in his hands Papal authority for fulminating an interdict against the King's dominions, of which authority neither the King nor the Papal Commissioners were cognisant till they met Becket at Fréteval (Lives of the Archbishops, ii. 480). We cannot think that the King or Commissioners were so entirely ignorant. Though the Pope's Letters of Feb. 18 to the Archbishop of York, extending this very power over the Province of York, were perhaps in Henry's hands by seizure *en route*, yet it was in manifest fear and forestalment of this possible exercise of Becket's powers that the King had issued the "ten Ordinances," had gone over to England, and had procured the coronation of his son. And as to the *Commissioners'* ignorance, why, they had in their own hands parallel powers for putting an interdict on Henry's continental dominions.

[3] S. T. C. iv. Epistle cccxciij.

1170. July 22. Becket's co-exiles fell at Henry's feet; the King restored Fréteval. to them his peace and favour, and their property.

Henry invited Becket to be his guest in a progress through Normandy, that thus they might exhibit their mutual concord. Becket begged some postponement of this plan, saying that self-repect did not allow him to quit France without leave of the French King and French Church.

Henry suggested that Becket should send a clerk over to England to take seizin of the possessions now restored to Becket and his kindred,—such clerk or legate to come first to the King and receive letters addressed to young Henry and to the other custodians of the realm, and so cross to England with security. To this business Becket appointed his clerk, Master Herbert.[1]

c. July 25. Becket writes to Pope Alexander an account of the reconciliation of Fréteval, and records his own impression that the King was sincere. In his private conference with the King, Becket had warned him against evil councillors, and had held a long argument to prove what the King at first denied, that the Archbishop of York's crowning young Henry was a flagrant wrong to the Church of Canterbury. The King had at last replied satisfactorily on each point;—he would, God helping him, give such answer to those who had hitherto betrayed both him and Becket, as traitors deserved;—he would, with Becket's counsel, take such measures for relieving the Church of Canterbury in the matter of the grievance in question as that its ancient dignity should in all points be restored. Becket had declined, by the Archbishop of Sens' advice, a proposition made by certain bishops on Henry's part, that Becket should refer ulterior questions to Henry's arbitration. Becket, not having the Pope's authority to demand restitution of arrears taken from him and his, had not urged that point, nor yet abandoned it, and he now gives the Pope a hint to make that injunction. Becket would remain in France till his nuncios, sent to take seizin of his church's possessions, should return. According to that restitution he would test the King's sincerity. Becket had promised due consideration of a proposal made by the Bishop of Liseux that he, Becket, should receive into favour all the King's partizans there present:—and when Geoffrey, the Excommunicate Archdeacon of Canterbury, the suggester of the proposal, gave a saucy answer to Becket's promise, the King had drawn Becket out of the crowd, and begged him not to regard the speeches of such persons.

Since the conference, Becket had been given to understand that the Bishop of Seez was going to England instructed by Rouen and Nevers as to the absolution of Becket's excommunicates, but Becket was doubtful whether those mediators had prescribed the exact form and condition of such absolution as dictated by the Pope, or, if they had, whether Seez would adhere to it. Becket suggests that power should be reserved to himself, on the part of the Pope, to correct any deviation from the Pope's order by subsequent process. Becket concludes with saying that he shall, as the Pope has commanded, still keep silence on the subject of recovery of arrears of damages; but he hopes that the Pope will listen to the bearer of his letter on that subject, and will also correct the injury done to Canterbury in the matter of the recent Coronation.[2]

(We would observe that, in this letter, Becket did not say a word to stimulate Alexander's anger against the Archbishop of York or the Bishops who had assisted at the recent Coronation. We shall also find that the Pope, when on receipt of this letter, he wrote to King Henry, attended only to Becket's overt requests).

[1] S. T. C. iv. Epist. cccxciij.

[2] S. T. C. iii. pp. 65-77. Epist. xxv.

c. July 25, 1171. About the same date, complaints certifying the actual Coronation by York will have reached Pope Alexander; and the first cognizance he will have taken of the offence is indicated in an undated letter to the Archbishop of Rouen, enclosing other letters to the Archbishop of York and to the English Bishops, which last letters do not seem to be extant.

The Pope states to Rouen that the offences of York and the Bishops, were their swearing to observe the Royal Customs (on which point the Pope's information was afterwards shown to be incorrect), and their assisting at the Coronation of the King's son.

Rouen was to forward these letters and cause them to be delivered. We suppose either that the Pope misdoubted Becket's ability to transmit them to their destination, or because he did not wish that Becket should be mixed up in the matter.

The Pope's special instructions to Rouen were that he should enquire whether the Bishops of Baieux and Seez were at the Coronation, and inform the Pope to the end that, if present, he, the Pope, should punish them. As to Seez, if it was true that he was acting the Courtier and serving the King in savage capacities, Rouen was to compel him either to renounce such offices or else his See.[1]

1171. c. Aug. 10. King Henry seized with serious illness at Gerni, or Mote-de-Ger (near Damfront), makes his will.[2] La Mote Garnier.

There is a Royal Charter, dated *apud motam de Ger*, whereby quittance of customs is granted to the Abbey of Lonlay, in the Diocese of Le Mans. It is attested by . . . de Oxenfort (probably John of Oxford), Richard de Canvill, and Symon de Turnebu.

c. Aug. 31. Pope Alexander, on receipt of Becket's letter, announcing the reconciliation of Fréteval, writes to congratulate K. Henry thereon. The Pope presses on Henry the distinct duties of restoration and compensation, that is, of restoring to the Archbishop and his Church all *ablata*, and also of repairing all damages and detriments done to the same. Henry is further exhorted to turn a deaf ear to the incentors of the late dissensions; to cause emendation of the omission made by young Henry in his late Coronation-oath, wherefrom the established clause, as to preserving the rights and liberties of the Church of Canterbury, had been excluded; finally, to leave *ordinations of churches* and other things which pertained to ecclesiastical persons to the Archbishop and to other such persons.[3]

(*Succeeding letters of Alexander here demand particular attention*).

Sept. 10. The Pope, now at Veruli, writes to the Archbishop of Canterbury;[4]—excuses himself for not coinciding entirely in Becket's wishes and suggestions; suspends from Episcopal functions Roger, Archbishop of York, and all other Bishops who had administered (to young Henry at his recent Coronation) an oath to maintain iniquitous "Customs" (those enacted at the first Council of Clarendon); renews the sentence of anathema (excommunication) against the Bishops of Salisbury and London, in case they were present or assistant at the said Coronation; leaves to Becket's sentence, *sans appeal*, these persons following, viz., the Bishop of Rochester, the Archbishop's Vicar; Geoffrey Ridel, Archdeacon of Canterbury, reported to be raging more than ever against that Church, "his mother," and to be contemning Becket's sentence of excommunication; Robert, the said Archdeacon's Vicar; Godfrey, Bishop of St. Asaph, despiser of a Papal mandate; and David, Archdeacon of St. Asaph. Whatever sentence Becket

[1] S. T. C. iv. 64. Epist. cclviii.

[2] "Ger," says Mr. Stapleton (Rot. Norm. i. lxvii). "was a place situate in the heart of the Forest of La-Lande-pourrie. The Comtes of Mortain had here a moated dungeon, whence the vill was usually called "Mota de Ger."

"King Henry" (continues Mr. Stapleton) "took the subsequent pilgrimage to Roque Madour, in consequence of a vow made during his sickness at Mote de Ger. Under a like obligation, he established a cell of the Priory of Plessis Grimould, in the adjoining hermitage of Yvrande."

[3] S. T. C. iv. 135. Ep. cccviii.

[4] S. T. C. iv. 32. Ep. ccxxx.

may pronounce will be ratified by the Pope; and if repentance does not follow, the Pope will resort to still stronger measures.[1]

The Pope, in this same letter, further alludes to troubles in France, and to the invasion of Maçon by foes of the Church. The Pope bids Becket to consult with K. Louis, and to forward to their destinations certain Papal letters entrusted to Becket, as Louis should advise.

Sept. 16. Pope Alexander's letter, suspending the Archbishop of York, was written at Ferentino on Sept. 16, and sent to Becket to be forwarded at the joint discretion of himself and Louis. The Pope's alleged grounds for this sentence are the Archbishop's Coronation of young Henry, out of York's Province, and in wrong of Canterbury; the omission in the Coronation oath then administered, of the usual clause as to preserving the liberty of the Church, and the insertion of a new clause binding the young King on his oath to preserve those "Customs, called ancient," which were in dishonour of the Church.[2]

Sept. 16. Pope Alexander's letter, suspending the Bishops of London, Salisbury, *Exeter*, Chester, Rochester, St. Asaph, and Landaff, bears even date with the last, and was sent to Becket for discretionary use. The grounds alleged by the Pope are the favours and assistance bestowed by the said Prelates at the recent coronation, and their complicity in the matters of omitting one part of the usual Coronation-oath, and of inserting a new clause about the "Customs of the Realm." In this letter the Pope repeats his judgments on the Bishops of London, of Salisbury, and of Rochester, on Geoffrey Ridel and his Vicar, Robert, as expressed in his letter of the 10th to Becket. The Pope further excommunicates Nicholas, Thomas, and William, Clerks of Earl Hugh, who, although excommunicated by Becket, had dared to "celebrate."[3]

Sept. 17. Another Papal Letter, dated at *Anagni, xx. kal. October* (probably xv. kal. Oct. or Sept. 17 was the date), formally restores to Archbishop Thomas and his Church of Canterbury the right of Coronation, as it had existed for forty years past, and in cancellation of its recent invasion by the Archbishop of York.[4]

1170. c. Sept. 29. K. Henry makes a votive journey to the shrine of St. Mary of Roque Madour (*De Rupe Adamatoris*) in the Quercy.[5] Roque Madour.

During the fiscal year ending Michaelmas, 1170.—

Queen Elianor seems to have been continuously in France. No particulars, further than have been indicated above, transpire in the Chronicles.

Between his coronation (June 14) and the same Michaelmas, K. Henry, junior, seems to have visited several parts of the kingdom. The Pipe-Roll supply such indications:—

Surrey. *Et in corredio Regis filii Regis per Ailwardum Camerarium £35 per breve Regis.*

Wiltshire. *Et Edwardo Blundo £9. 12s. ad adquietandam robam Regis filii Regis, et ejus familiæ.*[6] *Et in corredio Regis filii Regis, Radulfo filio Stephani et Ailwardo Camerario £60 per breve Regis.*

Dorset and Somerset. *Et in corredio Regis filii Regis per Ailwardum Camerarium £20 per breve Regis.*

Worcestershire. *Et in corredio Regis filii Regis per Radulfum fil' Stephani £20 per breve Regis.*

[1] S. T. C. iv. 32. Ep. ccxxx.

[2] S. T. C. iv. 48. Ep. ccxlix. The superscribed title of this letter includes the Bishop of Durham; but though the use of the word "vos" in the body of the letter indicates the suspension of more than one person, the Bishop of Durham is nowhere expressly named in the body of the letter.

[3] S. T. C. iv. 82. Ep. cclxxij.

[4] S. T. C. iv. 30. Ep. ccxxviii.

[5] Benedictus i. 7.

[6] This entry occurs in various Counties. It hardly suggests so much as a personal visit of the young King to each county. It was probably a draft on this or that Sheriff in discharge of the expences of the Coronation. In each case the item was charged on the Royal revenue.

STAFFORDSHIRE.—*Et Willelmo Rufo et Ailwardo Camerario £20 ad corredium Regis filii Regis, per breve Regis.*

THAT THE YOUNG KING, within four months of his coronation, was joined by his consort, Margaret of France, is suggested by the following entry under the "City of Winchester:"—*Et in procuratione filiæ Regis Franciæ et familiæ ejus £22. 17s. . . . . .*[1]

PRINCE GEOFFRY seems to have been brought to England by his father in March, and to have been domiciled at Northampton about the middle of April. At Michaelmas he was still there, as the following charge by the Sheriff of Northamptonshire suggests.—

Et in procuracione Galfridi filii Regis apud Northampton £36 de xxiv. septimanis per breve Regis. Et pro minutis utensilibus in apparatu hospitii ejus 23s. 1d. per breve Regis.

THE PIPE-ROLL of Michaelmas, 1170, mentions as having been in eyre several of the justices already noted at Michaelmas, 1168, and besides them Robert de Stuteville, Hugh de Morvill, Henry fitz Gerold the Chamberlain, Oger Dapifer, and Alan de Nevill, junior (the latter usually associated with William Basset).

But Alan de Nevill, junior, as well as Alan de Nevill, appear singly to have held Pleas of the Forest in some counties.

From another record we learn of a judicial committee, of date Sept. 11, 1169, wherein William Basset, Alan de Nevill, junior, and Robert de Gernemue, were associated with the three Sheriffs of Yorkshire, Lincolnshire, and Nottinghamshire.[2]

MICHAELMAS, 1170, TO MICHAELMAS, 1171.

1170. c. Oct. 1. King Henry leaving the Shrine of St. Mary de Roque Madour goes into Anjou and Touraine. The King occurs first at Tours.[3] — Anjou. Touraine. Tours.

In this month of October Pope Alexander seems to have recurred to the subjects mentioned in Becket's letter of the end of July.

(Oct. 8). On October 8, at Anagni, the Pope directs Archbishop Thomas and the English Bishops how to deal with priests, deacons, and sub-deacons, who had 'celebrated,' or who should hereafter 'celebrate,' in defiance of Papal or Episcopal mandate. They were to be deprived of their benefices till they had been with the Pope and received his award. If they further despised the Pope's mandate they were to be excommunicated, and if, being excommunicate, they persisted in officiating (*si excommunicati cantaverint*) they were to be arrested and confined for perpetual penance in monasteries.[4]

(Oct. 9). On Oct. 9, at Anagni, Pope Alexander instructs the Archbishop of Rouen and Bishop of Nevers how to deal further with such of Becket's excommunicates as they may have absolved according to the form already prescribed by the Pope. If the said persons, within 20 days after notice served upon them by Becket and his people, should not have resigned the churches and possessions of Canterbury, the Commissioners were to re-sentence them after 15 days from the date of any application (made by the aggrieved) to the Commissioners,—such re-excommunication to continue till the said resignations were completed. If, among the delinquents, any clerks had celebrated, the Commissioners were to deprive them of office and benefice, and publish such deprivation through the realm. If any of them, being laymen, had similarly neglected, or should neglect to resign the like property in their hands, the Commissioners were to visit them with severe commination, and a threat of still heavier punishment; but King Henry and his son were to be excepted from this last provision.[5]

A correlative letter to Becket himself, dated Oct. 9, at Anagni, gives him similar powers over the absolved who had not fulfilled the conditions of their absolution as imposed by Rouen and Nevers.[6]

[1] The Record is mutilated.—
That the Princess's arrival was about Michaelmas is suggested by most of the consequent charges appearing on the Pipe-Roll of 1171.

[2] Monasticon v. 420.

[3] S. T. C. vii. 307 (Herb. Bosham); i. 278 (Fitz Stephen).

[4] S. T. C. iv. 31. Epist. ccxxix.

[5] S. T. C. iv. 63. Epist. cclvii.

[6] S. T. C. iv. 28. Epist. ccxxvi.

(Oct. 9). A Papal letter, dated Oct. 9 at Anagni, instructs the Archbishops of Sens and Rouen how to deal with King Henry. Within 20 days after receipt of these instructions, the Archbishops were to approach the King, and warn him to complete by acts "the peace" which he had promised in words to Becket. They were to suggest to the King that presently he should restore all *ablata*, should compensate all damages, and should put an end to all wicked and hateful "customs." If the King should delay for 30 days to consummate the enjoined "peace," the Archbishops were to lay his cis-marine dominions under an interdict, *sans appeal*.[1]

(Oct. 11). A letter of Alexander to the Archbishop of Rouen is dated at Tusculanum on Oct. 11. It is an answer to enquiries as to the right theory and course of procedure in cases of appeal to an archbishop from the sentence of a suffragan bishop. It had no relevance to Becket's affairs, but shows the Pope's movements.[2]

1170. Oct. 12. King Henry and Becket meet at Amboise, near Tours. It was arranged that Becket should leave Sens on Nov. 1 and go to England, and that, on his arrival there, he should receive the 'kiss of peace' from young King Henry.[3] Amboise.

King Henry occurs next at Chaumont[3] (in Touraine). Here the King and Becket have their last interview. It is friendly. The King arranges to meet Becket at Rouen, when the latter should be there on his forthcoming journey to England.[3] Chaumont, near Blois.

Oct. 13. Pope Alexander, now at Segni, writes two letters. One to Archbishop Thomas congratulates him on his great patience, but adds, that if King Henry, so often exhorted by the Pope to complete his promises to Becket, should not have yet restored the possessions and honours of the church of Canterbury, the Pope hereby gives to Becket full authority to exercise his Legative powers both against individuals and places, excepting the persons of the King, the Queen, and their children, and this without appeal, though the Pope recommends that circumspection and caution which sacerdotal modesty demanded.[4]

The other Papal letter from Segni enjoins on all the Bishops of K. Henry's cis-marine dominions, that they observe, and cause to be observed in their dioceses, the interdict which the Legate Archbishop of Sens and the Archbishop of Rouen, or either of them, might happen to promulgate.[5]

c. Oct. 15. King Henry is next at Chinon. His writ to his son Henry, there dated, is significant of all good faith in regard to Becket. Chinon in Touraine.

Henricus Rex Angliæ Regi filio suo salutem. Sciatis quod Thomas Cantuariensis Archiepiscopus pacem mecum fecit ad voluntatem meam. Et ideo præcipio quod ipse et omnes sui pacem meam habeant; et faciatis habere ipsi et omnibus suis qui pro eo exierunt ab Angliâ res suas sicut habuerunt tribus mensibus antequam Archiepiscopus exiret ab Angliâ; et faciatis venire coram vobis de melioribus et antiquioribus militibus de Honore de Saltwude et eorum sacramento facias recognosci quid ibi habetur de feudo Archiepis-

[1] S. T. C. iv. 72. Epist. cclxiij.
[2] S. T. C. vi. 78. Epist. cccliii.
[3] S. T. C. vii. 308 (Herb. Bosham).
[4, 5] S. T. C. iv. 29 & 81. Epist. ccxxvii & cclxxi.

1170. c. Aug. 15. *copatûs Contuariensis et quod recognitum fuerit de feudo esse ipsi Archiepiscopo habere faciatis. Teste Rotrodo Archiepiscopo Rotomagensi, apud Chinum.*[1] Chinon.

To the same occasion we may safely refer a Charter, dated at Chinon, whereby K. Henry confirms to the Norman Abbey of Lyra the grant of Hinckley (Leicestershire) made by Robert (late) Earl of Leicester.

Witnesses—Geoffrey Archdeacon of Canterbury; John Dean of Sarum; Reginald Archdeacon of Sarum; Earl William de Mandeville; Reginald de Courtenay; and Reginald fitz Urse.[2]

c. Oct. 24, 1170. We have now to review a letter of Becket to the Pope,[3] as to the presumed date of which we would observe that it was written after the arrangement with Henry that Becket should return to England, leaving Sens on Nov. 1, and before that arrangement was altered;—that it was written after Becket had received from his agents in England unfavourable reports as to the practical fulfilment of the King's promises in respect of the claims of restitution which those agents had set on foot in the first half of October;—lastly, that it was written some days after Becket had been in receipt of the Papal rescripts dated at Veruli and Ferentino on the 10th and 16th of September.—

For Becket had consulted with King Louis on the matter of these rescripts, and it is clear that Becket had decided not to use them, probably because the Pope, in issuing them, had gone on the false averment that part of the Coronation-oath, administered to young Henry, had bound him to maintain the "Constitutions of Clarendon."

Becket then writes, distrustful of the King's promises, however fair, knowing of the failure of his agents, and yet determined to risk no rupture with the King by any impatience of his own. Becket requests the Pope to sentence York and the bishops, as before, for their share in the Coronation, but in so doing to repress all mention of "K. Henry's excesses," of the "enormity of the oath" tendered to young Henry, of the "perverse customs," and of the "caution" (in maintenance of the Church of Canterbury) "non-exacted" at the said Coronation.

Becket asks the Pope to entrust to him the suspension or excommunication of the bishops, leaving it to him to spare London and Salisbury, in case their punishment should seem to threaten a renewal of the present schism. Bartholomew of Exeter, Becket says, is wholely blameless as to the Coronation. Roger of York, 'the head and incentor of all the mischief,' he hopes the Pope will reserve to his own judgment.

Becket, by K. Louis's advice, having suppressed the former letters, now asks by the same advice for three further letters, one by which the Pope shall suspend York without offence (*læsione*) to the King; another excommunicating London and Salisbury; a third suspending the other bishops,—it being left to Becket to use each according to circumstances.

Becket further requests that the Pope will instruct the Bishop of Meaux and B. Prior of St. Crispin of Soissons, to approach K. Henry and threaten him and his land, unless he obey the Pope. And, if the King refuse, then Becket demands for himself that, or a still stronger power of coercing the King than had heretofore been given to Rouen and Nevers. He asks also that the Archbishop and Church of York should

[1] S. T. C. vi. 300. Epist. ccccxcvii. Diceto, p. 553.

[2] Monasticon, vii. 1030. Num. ii. Some of these attestations are remarkable. The Archdeacon of Canterbury having apparently been with the King ever since the Peace of Fréteval (July 22), soon left the Court for England. John Dean of Salisbury left the Court also, his destination being to meet Becket at Rouen. Within the next ten weeks Fitz-Urse also left the Court for England, with what purpose we shall see anon.

[3] S. T. C. iii. 77. Epist. xxvi.

be made obedient to the Primacy of Canterbury, in conformity with ancient precedent, and for the avoidance of future schisms. "*Credimus*," continues Becket, "*nos in Angliam profecturos, ad pacem, an ad pœnam, nobis incertum est, sed divinitùs ordinatum, quæ sors nos exceptura sit.*"

All the letters thus solicited by Becket were written by the Pope, and in the amended form suggested by Becket. They are all extant. Such of them as are dated bear date at Tusculanum or (which is the same thing) at Frascati, on Nov. 24, which satisfies us that Becket's application was (as we have dated it above) about a month earlier.[1]

1170. c. Nov. 1–10. King Henry was at Loches, on the borders of Touraine and Berri, and about to march eastwards to Bourges, the capital of Berri. Loches.

At Loches the King writes to Becket a letter excusing himself for not having kept his appointment with Becket, whom he was to have met at Rouen preparatory to Becket's passage to England, which, however, the King wished to accelerate. But the letter itself will best explain the situation.—

"*Thomæ Cantuariensi Archiepiscopo, Henricus Rex Angliæ. Sciatis quod obviam vobis Rothomagum venire non potui ad terminum quem prolocuti fuimus inter nos, quia significatum mihi fuit ab amicis meis Franciæ, Regem Francorum præparare se ad eundum in Alverniam* (Auvergne) *super homines meos, et ad male faciendum ipsis et terræ meæ. Ipsi autem homines Alverniæ idem mihi significaverunt rogantes ut eis succurrerem. Quapropter ad terminum quem statuimus inter nos, ad vos Rothomagum venire non potui* (the engagement was already broken then). *Sed mitto vobis Johannem Decanum Saresberiensem, familiarem clericum meum, vobiscum in Angliam iturum, per quem significo Henrico Regi*

[1] The Pope's amended letter to the Archbishop of York (S. T. C. iv. 102. Epist. cclxxxv.) reserves to the Pope himself the release of the sentence of suspension, as suggested by Becket.—

The Pope's amended letter to the Bishops of London and Salisbury (S. T. C. iv. 102. Epist. cclxxxv.) recites their standing *suspension*, and their obligation to appeal to the Pope in bar of the renewal of their excommunication, unless Becket should release them from such obligation. But if the two should satisfy Becket and the Church of Canterbury that their Penalty should be released, the Pope wished to commit to Becket the Papal authority requisite to that end.

The Pope's amended letter to the Bishops (S. T. C. iv. 85. Epist. cclxxiij.) is addressed to the Bishops of Chester, Rochester, St. Asaph, Landaff, and Durham; but not to Exeter. It pronounces their suspension on the ground of their share in the Coronation being in wrong of Canterbury. Their suspension will continue till they have either been with the Pope and satisfied him, or obtained a release of their penalties from Becket, whom the Pope appoints his Vicar in the matter.

The Pope's letter to Stephen, Bishop of Meaux, and to the *Abbot* of St. Crispin, at Soissons (S. T. C. iv. 102. Epist. cclxxxvi.) instructs those Commissioners to approach Henry, as Becket had suggested; only, if mild exhortation failed, the Commissioners are told to use language bitter and severe according to their discretion, but not expressly to threaten Henry's territory.

The date of these amended letters (viz. Nov. 24) is of the more importance, because, as will be seen, Becket did not wait for them, but on Dec. 1st caused to be served Papal rescripts of suspension on the Archbishop of York, and of re-excommunication on the Bishops of London and Salisbury. It follows that the rescripts actually served by Becket were those which the Pope had issued in September.

1170. c. Nov. 1-10. *Anglorum filio meo ut bene et in pace et honorifice habeatis omnes res vestras; qui, etiam emendari faciat, si quid minus actum est quam oportuerit de his quæ ad vos spectant. Et quoniam mihi et filio meo plura referuntur de morâ vestrâ quam facitis, quæ forsitan vera non sunt, vobis ut credo expediret ne ire in Angliam diutius differetis. Teste, Rege ipso apud Lokchas.*"[1] Loches.

Nov. 23. King Henry on St. Clement's day reaches Mount Luzzun (Mont Luçon in Berri, near the frontier of Auvergne).[2] Mont Luçon.

c. Nov. 26. King Henry arrives at Bourges (in Berri), and encounters the hostile array of Louis. The two Kings agree to a truce.[3] Bourges.

It does not appear that this affair developed into any attack upon Auvergne proper. King Henry was claiming Berri as an appendage of Guienne, and had sought to increase his power there by a recent purchase of Montmirail and the Castle of St. Agnan from Henry de Vienne. This transaction involved questions of feudal title which were contested both by Louis of France and by Theobald of Blois.

c. Nov. 24, 1170. Becket proceeds to Witsand *en route* for England.

Dec. 1. Becket lands at Sandwich.

On the same day the Archbishop of York, the Bishops of London and Salisbury and the Archdeacons of Canterbury and Poitiers are at Dover, waiting to go over to Normandy in compliance with the King's injunctions that they should attend him relatively to the filling up of the vacant Anglican Sees. At Dover the Archbishop and two Bishops are served with notices of the suspension of York, and the excommunication of London and Salisbury, which notices had been despatched by Becket from Witsand on the previous day.

c. Dec. 2. The Bishop of Salisbury and Geoffrey Ridel, Archdeacon of Canterbury, go to the young King's Court to tell of Becket's procedure. Becket refusing to release the suspension of the Bishops, York, London, and Salisbury cross to Normandy for the purpose of complaining to the King.

Dec. 1–15. During the first half of December Richard, Archdeacon of Poictiers, seems to have crossed to France and, whether with or without an interview with K. Henry, to have proceeded to the Papal Court, probably on the matter of his own excommunication.

It appears also that about Dec. 15, several persons left France for Italy to obtain from the Pope absolution and release for the Prelates of York, Durham, London, and Salisbury. King Henry sent John Cumin, who arrived at the Papal Court 15 days before Master David, the envoy of the Bishop of London, and before the Clerks of the Archbishop of York, and the nuncio of the Bishop of Durham.[4]

It further appears (though we have no Papal rescripts of this month extant) that the Pope, either knowing that Becket would be now in England or having some other ground of fear for Becket's personal safety after he should have left the protection of Louis, wrote amended instructions as to a "cis-marine Interdict" to the Archbishops of Sens and Rouen. They, or either of them, were to publish and enforce such an Interdict, in case of the arrest and imprisonment of the Archbishop of Canterbury (*si Cantuariensis Archiepiscopus captus teneretur*).[5]

[1] S. T. C. vi. 300. Ep. cccexcviii.

[2, 3] Benedictus (Stubbs), i. 9 & 10.

[4] S. T. C. vi. 260. Epist. coeclxix.

[5] S. T. C. iv. 207. Epist. cccliv. On Jan. 25, 1171, the Archbishop of Rouen denied the exigency of this mandate as regarded himself. *Mutatus est casus*, said he of Rouen at the Conclave of Sens. 'The case is altered; the Papal Letter is inoperative; the Archbishop of Canterbury has not been imprisoned; he has been killed.'

1170. Dec. 21. King Henry had, ere this, returned from Berri into Normandy. On this day there is some probability that he was at Bayeux. Bayeux.

Dec. 25. King Henry keeps the festival of Christmas at Bures or Bure (which we take to be Bur le Roi, near Bayeux, rather than Bure a Castle in the Pays de Caux). Bur-le-Roi or Bures.

At this time Henry had appointed the Earl of Essex, Saier de Quinci and Richard de Humez, commissioners for the personal arrest of the Archbishop of Canterbury. De Humez had sailed for England and, having landed, had sent orders to William Fitz John and Hugh de Gundeville, who were with the young King at Winchester, to bring a party of knights who should proceed to Canterbury for the purpose of effecting the said arrest. Humez himself proposed to make surveillance of the English ports so as to intercept Becket's escape, if attempted. William de Mandeville, Earl of Essex, and Saier de Quinci had it in charge to watch Witsand and the Continental ports, in case the Archbishop should reach any of them.

Dec. 26. Reginald Fitz Urse, William de Tracey, Hugh de Morville and Richard Brito, four knights of Henry's Court, left the said Court at Bur,[1] and reached Saltwood Castle, near
Dec. 28. Canterbury, on the second day following.

Dec. 29. Becket was assassinated in Canterbury Cathedral by Fitz Urse and his three associates.

Dec 31. King Henry was at Argentan [2] where news of Becket's murder had not yet reached him. The King is said to have remained at Argentan 40 days.[3] Argentan.

[1] The King's being previously at Bayeux, and subsequently at Argentan, makes it more probable that the intervening Christmas was spent at Bur le Roi, than at Bures. The latter place would not have been in question, were it not that one account indicates that the four knights performed the journey from Henry's Court to Saltwood Castle in a single day. It could hardly have been done, had the Court been at Bur le Roi. But take the alternative account, which gives two days for the journey, and Bur le Roi becomes supposable, as the point of departure.

[2] Professor Stubbs (quoting Benedict I. 11 and R. de Monte 909) supposes the King to have been still at Bur on Dec. 31, and after Jan. 1, 1171.

[3] S. T. C. vii. 203, viii. 34.

Court of King Henry the Younger.

(Oct. Nov. and Dec., 1170.)

The Royal status of the younger Henry was at any time little more than titular. The title of Viceroy had better fitted the realities of his position.

At the cost of something of recapitulation and something more of digression, we here give a formal account of a few months of his so-called reign. These months, following immediately on Michaelmas, 1170, happen to comprise what is known of Archbishop Becket's English diplomacy, consequent on the Reconciliation of Fréteval and the elder King's Writ of restitution, dated at Chinon. The same few months of young Henry's reign will comprise some further notice of the events which befel Archbishop Becket on his actual return to England.—

October 5, (Monday).[1] Becket's agents for recovery of his Church's possessions, having cited William de Einsford, William fitz Nigel, Turstin, and Osbert (Defendants, it seems), and assisted only by Robert, Sacristan of Canterbury,—others (witnesses) declining to stand with them,—and having consulted William Fitz Aldeline and Ralph Fitz Stephen (two English justiciars) appear with the King's letters before the 'Young King,' in his chamber at Westminster. The young King's assessors are Earl Reinald (of Cornwall), the Archdeacons of Canterbury and Poitiers, William de St. John, and many others. The Earl and some, but not all, present, express joy at the news of "peace." The agents read the King's letters.

The agents are desired to withdraw, while the Council consults with Walter de Insula (a Pro-Vice-Chancellor, it seems). On the agents' return, Geoffry Ridel (Vice-Chancellor, we believe), tells them that the young King decides to adjourn the Court till October 15th, to the end that it might have the evidence of Randulf de Broc and other "Ministers" and "Farmers" (who had the Archbishop's possessions in various quarters by the King's order) as to what stock pertained to each Archiepiscopal estate.

c. October 6. The Young King goes from London to Windsor, and returns a gracious acknowledgment to some of Becket's agents who met him on the way and offered humble salutations.

Subsequently it transpires, or is strongly suspected by Becket's agents, that Walter de Insula is in England, with Royal Letters to York, London, and Salisbury, instructing them to proceed with the election of Bishops to all the vacant Sees, so that such Bishops-elect should be forthwith forwarded to the Pope for consecration to the great discomfiture of Becket on his arrival. However, London was at the moment on a (pretended) pilgrimage to St. John's of Beverley.

c. Oct. 10. Becket's agents write to him the above particulars. They add their misgivings as to the issue of Oct. 15th, and the *bona fides* of the King's party. The bearer of their letter will communicate orally to Becket further ominous, yet true, particulars. Becket, they say, has not a friend in England who is sanguine as to "peace;"—nay, his once most trusted friends keep carefully aloof from his agents. His agents twice exhort him to stay near the King, and not to hasten to England till he is sure of the King's goodwill and more genuine favour.[2]

December 1 (Tuesday). Whilst Becket's messengers, expedited from Witsand on Nov. 30, were serving letters of suspension or excommunication at Dover, on the Prelates of York, London, and Salisbury, Becket himself was landing at Sandwich. Gervase de Cornhill, Sheriff of Kent; Reginald de Warren; and Ranulf de Broc, awaited Becket on the shore and proposed to search him for concealed letters, also to force an oath of fealty to K. Henry on Simon, Archdeacon of Sens, attendant upon Becket.[3] Both propositions were discouraged and withdrawn by permission of John of Oxford, escorting Becket by the King's permission.

[1] S. T. C. iv. 307. *Die Lunæ proximâ post festum Beati Michaelis*, that is Monday, Oct. 5, 1170. Carte gives the date as Monday, Oct. 1.

[2] S. T. C. iv. 306. Epist. cccxciv.

[3] It seems to affect the question of the elder King's good faith in getting Becket to England that these local officers had not been advertised of the "King's Peace" with the Archbishop. Their action was rather in consonance with the "provisions" or "ordinances" of December, 1169, than with any Royal sanction of Becket's return.

It is well to quote what duties these "Ordinances" imposed on the Officers of the Crown in the matter of searching suspected bearers of Letters.—

We give the purport of these "Ordinances" exactly as they were reported to Becket by an

Dec. 2, 1170. (Wednesday). Archbishop Becket enters Canterbury.

c. Dec. 3–6. Becket, by letter, instructs William, Bishop of Norwich, to absolve Earl Hugh.

c. Dec. 6–9. The Bishop of Norwich absolves Earl Hugh, and reports the fact to Becket, congratulating the Archbishop 'on the mercy shewn by Providence to the land' (in respect of Becket's return). Earl Hugh also writes to Becket requesting consideration for his interdicted (suspended) Clerks.

c. Dec. 9. Becket writes to the Bishop of Norwich;—rejoices in Earl Hugh's restoration to "the flock;" —praises God for His mercy shewn to himself; hopes to see the Bishop before his, the Bishop's, translation to heaven, that so some portion of the Bishop's spiritual graces may be imparted to and may strengthen his humble self;—cannot alter anything about Earl Hugh's Clerks till he shall have visited the Bishop and consulted with him on that and other Church matters, but allows the bearer of the Bishop's letter and of Becket's answer (evidently one of the Clerks in question), to preach, baptize, and administer the *viaticum in extremis*.[1]

Becket's Letter to Earl Hugh himself explains at greater length the cogent reasons of his refusal to absolve the Clerks, but hopes soon to visit the Earl and fulfil his wishes. This Letter expresses the same consideration for the bearer as that to the Bishop of Norwich, thus synchronizing the two. It has a further chronological import, in that it shows that the Earl's repentance and altered treatment of the Canons of Pentney had been consummated before Becket's arrival in England (*utpote qui in nostræ pacis initio ante etiam quam terram ingrederemur, mandatum nostrum et consilium non minus magnifice quam benigne consummastis, cæteris similiter faciendi vos ipsum præbens exemplar*).[2]

c. Dec. 9. Becket refusing to relax the Papal sentences on York, London and Salisbury, those Prelates cross to Normandy to complain to the King. (*c.* Dec. 10–12.) The Young King being at Woodstock. Becket sets out from Canterbury and passing through Rochester is received joyfully in London. Becket takes up his quarters in the Bishop of Winchester's Palace in Southwark. (c. Dec. 12–15.) Becket sends Simon, Abbot of St. Albans, to Woodstock to solicit an interview with the young King. (Dec. 18, Friday.) The young King is at Windsor.—Josceline de Louvain and Thomas de Tunbridge are sent thence to prohibit Becket's further progress to the Court, and to order his return to Canterbury. (*c.* Dec. 21, Monday). Becket goes to Harrow, but makes short stay there. (*c.* Dec. 23, Wednesday). Becket returns to Canterbury, where he finds that the Brocs have been committing violent trespass on his lands and effects. (Dec. 25, Friday). Becket officiates on Christmas-day in Canterbury Cathedral. During service he excommunicates Nigel de Sackville and Robert de Broc. The young King kept Christmas at Winchester. (Dec. 28, Monday). Fitz Urse and his associates reach Saltwood, having left K. Henry's Court at Bur on the previous Saturday. On the same day probably, the Emissaries of Richard de Humez arrive at Winchester to take order and aid for the arrest of Archbishop Becket at Canterbury.

Dec. 29 (Tuesday). Becket assassinated in Canterbury Cathedral. The Assassins go to Hugh de Morville's Castle of Knaresborough.

English correspondent, at the time of their first transmission to England.—

Sciatis hunc esse tenorem mandatorum quæ Henricus Rex in Angliam misit;—scilicet ut omnes portus cautissime custodiantur ne literæ interdictionis ullatenus illuc deferantur. Et si aliquis Regularis illas attulerit, pedibus truncetur; si Clericus, oculos et genitalia amittat; si laicus, suspendatur (the gallows is intended), *si leprosus, comburatur. Et si aliquis Episcopus ejus* (*Henrici, scilicet*), *interdictum metuens, recedere voluerit* (shall desire to quit England) *nihil secum deferat nisi baculum. Vult etiam* (*Rex*) *ut omnes Scholares* (Students at Foreign Universities) *repatriare cogantur aut beneficiis suis priventur; et qui remanserint* (staid abroad) *sine spe remeandi remanebunt. Et Presbyteri qui cantare noluerint* (should decline to officiate) *genitalia amittant; omnesque rebelles sibi* (*Regi*) *beneficiis priventur* (S. T. C. iv. 249. Ep. ccclxxii.

[1] S. T. C. iv. 311. Ep. cxlij.

[2] S. T. C. iii. 398. Ep. excv. Another letter of the Bishop of Norwich to Becket gives no internal proof of its place in the above sequence. It may have preceded, it may have followed, the other letter of the same Bishop. The Bishop says that, by Becket's order, he absolves those Clerks of Earl Hugh, who had celebrated in defiance of the Pope's veto: but they are pledged by oath to abide by Becket's judgment and their suspension is not removed. Two of them, Gilbert and Baldwin, Priests, bearers of this letter, are recommended to Becket's mercy (S. T. C. vi. 227. Epist. ccccلvi).

A.D. 1171.

Jan. 1. (Friday. King Henry is at Argentan, and hears of the murder of Archbishop Becket. Argentan.

The King spends three days in solitude. He remained at Argentan 40 days, according to one authority.

c. Jan. 1–5. William, Archbishop of Sens, Legate of France, writes to the Pope an account of Becket's murder. He sends Masters Alexander and Gunter, friends of the "Martyr," with the letter.[1]

Louis of France and Theobald Comte of Blois also write to the Pope expressing their horror at the recent event.[2]

c. Jan. 5. Richard de Ilchester, Archdeacon of Poictiers arrives at the Papal Court at Frascati. There he remained more than three months. He had quitted England since Dec. 1. He had perhaps seen the King on his way through France, but his business at the Papal Court was not as an envoy of the King.[3]

c. Jan. 13. John Cumin, K. Henry's Envoy to procure the relaxation of the sentences served Dec. 1, 1170, on the bishops, arrives at the Papal Court. He is kept waiting 15 days.

c. Jan. 30. Master David, Envoy probably of the Bishop of London, arrives at Frascati, and with or before him, clerks or agents of the Archbishop of York and the Bishop of Durham.

c. Jan. 31. John Cumin, giving or offering 500 merks, gains a hearing for himself and the other Appellants in the Papal Court. They plead in excusation of the prelates; and, in Richard of Ilchester's opinion, would have taken home the absolution of their principals, when—

c. Feb. 4. A rumour of Archbishop Becket's murder reached Frascati. All became dark, says Ilchester. The Pope forbade any Englishman to approach him. For eight days (c. Feb. 5–12) he would not converse even with his own people. All business was at an end.[3]

Meanwhile, that is between Jan. 10 and 20, a Papal Rescript had reached France, which, though only its outline is preserved, shows that Alexander viewed with the greatest apprehension what must, at the time when Becket wrote to him on the subject, have been only a prospect, viz., that Becket was going to England. The Papal Rescript, sent forthwith to the Archbishops of Sens and Rouen, was that in case Becket were arrested and imprisoned (*si Cantuariensis Archiepiscopus captus teneretur*), then Sens and Rouen, one or both, were to lay an Interdict, *sans appeal*, on Henry's continental dominions.

c. Jan. 20. The Archbishop summoned his Suffragans to Sens, that they might hear and carry out the intended sentence.

Jan. 25. (Monday). Synod of Sens;—whereat the Archbishop William pronounced the aforesaid Interdict. The Archbishop of Rouen attended, but opposed the publication on two grounds, first that the Papal commission was addressed to himself and Sens jointly; secondly, that the Pope's order was only exigent in case of Becket's imprisonment, not his murder. Sens replied that the Pope's commission was addressed severally as well as jointly, and that its execution was *a fortiori* incumbent on the commissioners, when the crime to be avenged was murder, added to sacrilege.—

However, the Archbishop of Rouen, the Bishops of Worcester, Evreux and Liseux; the clerks, Reginald, Lumbard, Richard Barre, and Master Henry de Northampton, appealed against the Interdict, which then and there became suspended till such time as the appellants had prosecuted their appeal at Frascati;—whither they all proceeded to set out.[4]

Jan. 28 (Thurs). King Louis of France set out for Mechisi (Metz?) where it was proposed that he and the Emperor should confer on Feb. 14, with a view to the restoration of the unity of the Church and other peaceful propositions.[4]

[1] S. T. C. iv.–162. Epist. cccxxx. The Legate gives the names of the four assassins. He denounces as chief instigators of the Tyrant (Henry's) madness, "Roger, the Archdevil of York, and the Apostates of London and Salisbury, the veritable, not figurative, slayers of the Pope's son, their brother Joseph."

[2] S. T. C. vi. p. 306. Epist. DIII. and iv. p. 211. Epist. ccclvi.

[3] S. T. C. vi. 260. Epist. cccclxix.

[4] S. T. C. iv. 206. Epist. cccliv. From William, agent of the Bishop of Durham, to the said Bishop.

c. Jan. 28, 1171. The Archbishop of Sens writes to the Pope an account of the Synod, sentence, and appeal of the 25th:—says that he was supported by all his Suffragans and by the Abbots of St. Denys, St. German de Preaux, Pontigny and two others:—that Rouen's alleged object at the Synod was lest he should increase the bitterness of K. Henry's exasperation (*exacerbationem Regi se nolle infundere acerbiorem*):—that Henry had acknowledged to a Carthusian monk sent to him by the Archbishop of Sens, that he, Henry, had supplied the primary cause of the Archbishop's murder, in fact had slain him (*significavit quod causam mortis ejus dederat, et quod eum occiderat*). Sens exhorts Alexander to ratify his sentence[1] (of Interdict).

c. Jan. 31. The Appellants of Jan. 25 (except Arnulf, Bishop of Liseux) may be supposed to have left France for Italy. They were joined by K. Henry's special Envoys, whose names will appear in the sequel. Richard Barre outstripped the whole party and got first to Frascati. The Archbishop of Rouen, when the rest were half way, turned homewards again.

c. Feb. 21. The main body got as far as *Senæ* (in Savoy ?) with much difficulty. There they were detained some days; "for Comte Machary was on all sides blockading the roads."[2]

Feb. 1-10. King Henry's abode at Argentan is quite problematically marked by two Royal Charters, dated at that place.— Argentan.

One is a Confirmation to the Abbey of St. André-en-Gouffern of the donations of William de Ponthieu and others.—Witnesses, Henry, Bishop of Bayeux, Froger, Bishop of Seez.[3]

The other Charter is in favour of Roger de Flamenville, and is attested by Froger, Bishop of Seez, Hugh de Cressi, and '*Goceline the Castellan, brother of the Queen.*'[4]

A Royal Charter dated at Falaise probably belongs to the same month of February. It is in favour of the Priory of Plessis Grimould, and is attested by Henry, Bishop of Bayeux, Froger, Bishop of Seez, and Hugh de Cressi.[5] Falaise.

c. Feb. 11-25. King Henry at Pont Orson, on the frontier of Normandy and Bretagne. There he abode 15 days.[6] Pont-Orson.

Feb. 20. Death of Conan IV (Le Petit), Duke of Bretagne, and Earl of Richmond.

March. April. King Henry's movements for two months are unrecorded. It is probable that Duke Conan's death necessitated his presence in Bretagne, a situation which is illustrated by the further phenomenon that Prince Geoffrey left his domicile at Northampton about the beginning of March.[7] (Bretagne).

[1] S. T. C. iv. 163. Epist. cccxxxj.

[2] S. T. C. vi. 198. Epist. ccccxl. From the King's Envoys to K. Henry.

[3] D'Anisy, Extrait des Chartes, vol. i. p. 407. John son of William, Comte of Ponthieu, had in the year 1168, confirmed his father's grants to the same Abbey.

[4] Cartæ Antiquæ, Y.—Josceline de Louvain, commonly called 'the Castellan,' was brother of Adeliza, Queen of Henry I., and afterwards Countess of Arundel, and was Ancestor of the House of Percy. Two months previous to the assumed date of this Charter, Josceline de Louvain was attendant on the young King at Windsor, (supra p. 151.)

[5] D'Anisy, Extrait des Chartes, ii. 62.

[6] Professor Stubbs' Itinerary quoting R. de Monte (Ed. Struve, p. 900).

[7] See extracts from the Pipe-Rolls, infra p. 162.

c. March 1, 1171. Four of Henry's messengers to the Pope, seeing that there was no chance of the whole party getting away from Senæ, abscond by night, and taking their course through a mountainous and well-nigh pathless country, pass forward with great doubt and danger towards Frascati. The four were R. Abbot of Valasse; Reginald fitz Josceline, Archdeacon of Salisbury; R., Archdeacon of Liseux; and Master Henry Pinchun. A Knight Templar, who had set out with them, here vanishes from their diary, but nevertheless reached Frascati with them. The rest of the Embassy, viz., Roger, Bishop of Worcester; Giles, Bishop of Evreux; Sir Robert de Newburgh, Dean of Evreux; and Master Henry de Northampton, seem to have been left at Senæ till the roads should be open.[1]

c. March 3. Richard Barre reaches Frascati. The Pope would not hear him. He met with no encouragement from others in his exertions on the King's behalf.

c. March 20 (Saturday). The Abbot of Valasse, the Archdeacons of Salisbury and Liseux, Master Henry Pinchun and the Templar reach Frascati. At first the Pope would not hear any of them; but at last the Abbot of Valasse and the Archdeacon of Liseux were, at the prayer of certain cardinals,[2] admitted to an audience.[1]

In their pleadings on behalf of K. Henry they were opposed by Becket's old clerks, Alexander of Wales and Gunter of Flanders.

c. March 22, 23. It was expected in Frascati that in a general Consistory, to be holden on Thursday, Alexander would sentence both the King and Realm of England.

March 25 (Thursday). A general Consistory at Frascati. King Henry's five envoys, viz., the Abbot of Valasse, the Archdeacons of Salisbury and Liseux, Richard Barre and Henry Pinchun swore that the King would abide by the Pope's decision, and, if bidden by the Pope, would take his own personal oath to the same effect.[1]

On this occasion (probably because the most influential of K. Henry's Nuncios had not yet arrived), the Pope only excommunicated generally the assassins of Becket, and all who had afforded them counsel or countenance (*assensum*), and all who should hereafter receive or entertain them on their lands.[1]

On the same occasion the Nuncios of the Archbishop of York and of the Bishops of London and Salisbury swore that their Principals should abide by the Pope's decision, and themselves take an oath so to do.

March 28 (Easter Sunday). King Henry's five Envoys despatch a letter to the King with the above particulars. They congratulate the King on the result of their mission. They add that they had heard nothing of the King's messengers to the Emperor since (their outset). One of them adds:—"*De vestro quod mihi per Reginaldum misistis secreto, coram Willelmo filio Hamonis et postmodum Abbate de Walace spem bonam concepimus, quod fiet*;" by which we infer that the King, in letters close, attested by Fitz Hamon and the Abbot of Valasse, had charged either Richard Barre or Master Henry Pinchun with some commission; that the letters had been delivered to the Commissioner by the Archdeacon Reginald, and that all had good hopes of accomplishing the King's object.[1]

March 29. K. Henry's five Envoys now probably left Frascati.

{ *c.* April 2. About this time the Princess Margaret of France sailed from Southampton, leaving her affianced husband, the young King, in England. She had not been crowned, though that was the pretended object of her coming. Of course she was still an infant. }

c. April 5. About this time, Roger, Bishop of Worcester; Giles, Bishop of Evreux; Robert de Newburgh, Dean of Evreux; and Master Henry de Northampton seem to have reached Frascati.—

They were more than fifteen days (*c.* April 6–21) before the Papal *Curia*. They agreed with the previous advocates of King Henry both in their *excusation* and *accusation* of the King, that is, that the

[1] S. T. C. vi. 198. Epist. ccccxl. and vi. 260. Epist. cccclxix. The secret commission probably related to some temporal scheme, such as the invasion of Ireland.

[2] The Cardinals and Curial friends of Henry were Portuensis, Papiensis, Hyacinth, Tusculanus, and Peter de Mirso. John, of Neapolis, was not at Frascati.

murder of the Archbishop had been committed without the King's order or wish; but they did not deny that the King had afforded a motive cause for the murder (*dedisset causam mortis*), nor that he had made use of words in which the assassins found an occasion for committing it (*aliquid dixisset unde malefactores illi occasionem interficiendi sumpserunt*.[1]

Whether these Envoys were asked to take the same oath as had been propounded by the former Envoys, Richard, Archdeacon of Poictiers, who had now been more than three months at Frascati, did not know. He only knew that they did not take any oath. A favourable decision was looked for from the Pope when at length the Envoys were called upon to hear it.[1]

c. April 21. Instead thereof Alexander confirmed the interdict pronounced by the Archbishop of Sens on Henry's continental dominions, and the sentences of excommunication and suspension which lay upon the Anglican Prelates. Alexander spared Henry's person, except that the King was forbidden to enter any Church; "and," concluded the Pope, "I will send my Legates to the King that they may see and know of his humility."[1]

The Archdeacon of Poictiers says that afterwards (*c.* April 22–to 24), by much pressure on the part of the Envoys, by much interposition of Cardinals, and, as was said, by a free flow of money, the Pope was induced to instruct the Archbishop of Bourges that if, within a month after the return of Henry's Envoys to Normandy, the said Archbishop had not learned that the Papal Legates had crossed the Alps (*transalpinasse*), that then the Archbishop might absolve the Bishops of London and Salisbury from excommunication, exacting an oath that "they and others remaining under suspension would abide by the Pope's mandate." [1]

We happen to be able to verify and supplement the Archdeacon of Poictiers' account by the actual instructions which Alexander was writing at the moment. His letter, dated at Tusculanum (Frascati) on April 24, commissions the Archbishop of Bourges, the Bishop of Nevers, and, failing the Archbishop's ability to act, the Abbot of Pontigny. To them the Pope delegates the power of absolution of London and Salisbury, because both those Prelates were so aged and infirm, and one of them so sick, that they could not come to the Pope's presence. The absolution was to be given at the time and under the conditions stated by the Archdeacon, except that the power was not to benefit other suspended Prelates. The suspension of London and Salisbury was not to be removed, but to remain in full force on the grounds which had originally provoked their excommunication. As to Salisbury, if he should be too ill to attend the Commissioners, they might go to him at a place approved by themselves; and, if unable to do so, they might delegate their powers to proper emissaries, who should receive his oath publicly in sight of the Church, and so absolve him.[2]

c. April 26. The Archdeacon of Poictiers concludes his history of K. Henry's embassies to Frascati, saying that the King's *Nuncii* had left, taking with them nothing more than he had stated. He did not think that the Cardinals knew when the Legates were to set out, nor who they were to be. But his correspondents need not fear an interdict on England if the King would only obey the Legates. The Pope had with great difficulty been persuaded to write to K. Henry, and was at that moment so writing and inviting the King to humility.[3]

1171. March and April. King Henry, as has been already suggested, spent the months of March and April in Bretagne. A Breton Chronicle, detailing the events of the year 1171, is in accordance with that idea, and is worth both quoting and explaining:— Bretagne.

"MCLXXI. *Thomas Cantuariensis Archiepiscopus jussu Regis interficitur.*" (This shows the general conception

[1] S. T. C. vi. 261, 262. Epist. cccclxix.
[2] S. T. C. vi. 59. Epist. cccxxxvi. Hoveden, p. 302.
[3] S. T. C. vi. 262. We cannot find the Pope's letter here spoken of.

1171. March and April. about Becket's murder. The event took place Dec. 29, 1170; but this Chronicler commenced his year with Christmas). Bretagne.

"*Haimo Leonensis Episcopus a consanguineis occiditur.*" (Hamo, Bishop of Leon, in Bretagne, is put to death by his kindred.)

"*Obiit Conanus, junior, Dux Britanniæ.*" (Conan le Petit is meant. He died Feb. 21, 1171).[1]

"*Hoc anno tota Britannia Henrico Regi Angliæ subjugata est*" (which we take to indicate Henry's assumption of the Duchy on Duke Conan's death, and in behalf of his son Geoffrey.)[1]

"*Castrum Jocelini incensum et habitores exules facti.*" (Chateau Jacquelin burnt, probably by K. Henry, and its defenders exiled). Château Jacquelin.

"*Et Eudo, Dux Britanniæ, a Ducatu sublatus et penitus propulsus est in exilium in Galliam.*" (Eudo, Vicomte of Porhöet, pretending to the Duchy in right of his deceased wife, Duke Conan's mother, was expelled by Henry, and took refuge in France).[1]

May 2-16. King Henry is again at Pont Orson,[2] (on the frontier of Normandy and Bretagne.) King Henry's movements during June & July. the next two months are only to be surmised from a series of Charters, the earliest of which indicate the return of certain of his Envoys who left Frascati in the end of April, while the latest further indicate his own intention of soon visiting Ireland. There is a Royal Charter in favour of the Abbey of Bec Hellouin.[3] It passed at Rouen. Roger, Bishop of Worcester, a witness, had been one of the Envoys in question. The witnesses are Rotroc, Archbishop of Rouen; Henry, Bishop of Bayeux; Froger, Bishop of Seez; Arnulf, Bishop of Liseux; Gilbert, Bishop of London; Roger, Bishop of Worcester; Geoffrey, Archdeacon of Canterbury; John, Dean of Salisbury; William, Earl Mandeville; Richard de Humet, Constable (of Normandy); Eudo fitz Pont-Orson. Normandy. Rouen.

[1] Rerum Gall. Script. xii. 560. Henry's original Treaty with Bretagne entailed the Duchy on his son Geoffrey only after the deaths of Duke Conan and the Vicomte Eudo, whose life-claim thereto arose on his marriage with Berta, the heiress of the Duchy and Duke Conan's mother. The Breton Chronicle points out the breach of treaty involved in Henry's seizure of the Duchy on Duke Conan's death; but it is probable that the Vicomte Eudo's right under the original treaty was held to have lapsed by his subsequent rebellion against Conan.

[2] Professor Stubbs, quoting R. de Monte (Ed. Struve, p. 909.

[3] Monasticon, vii. 1068.

1171. June and July. Ernise; William de Courci (Seneschal of Normandy); Rouen. Saher de Quinci; Richard de Camvill and Walter de Dunstanvill.

A Royal Charter, dated at *Chivilli*[1] (Chevaillec) is in favour Chevaillec. of Boxley Abbey (Kent), and purports to be attested by H. (read R.[2] *i. e.*, Rotroc), Archbishop of Rouen; Arnulf, Bishop of Liseux; Giles, Bishop of Evreux (he had been at Frascati); Earl William, of Albemarle; Roger, Earl of Clare; Earl William de Mandevill; Hugh de Beauchamp; Hugh de Cressi and Walter de Duustanvill.[3]

A Royal Charter, dated at *Chuell* (probably Chevaillec) is Chevaillec. to St. Paul's, Bedford, and is attested by Earl William de Mandeville.[4]

King Henry contemporarily confirms a Charter, dated at *Chivilly*, whereby Hugh, Earl of Chester, ensures to the Chevaillec. Abbey of St. Stephen (Bayeux Dioc.) the gifts of his ancestor, Ranulf, Vicomte of Bayeux (the Bessin). Both Charter and Confirmation are attested by the same witnesses, viz., Gilbert, Bishop of London; Richard, Archdeacon of Poictiers (he had been at Frascati January–April); Waleran, Archdeacon of Bayeux; Master Ralph de Than (probably Tamworth); William de Mandeville, Earl of Essex; William, Earl of Arundel; Hugh de Longchamp; Reginald de Curtenay; John de Waureio; Hoel de Ridefort; Ranulf de Glandivalle; Geoffrey de Constantine; Roger de Livet'; Ranulf de Glainvill (Glanvill); Germanus, the King's Scribe (*Scriptor Regis*); and William, the Earl of Chester's Clerk.[5]

July. In this month K. Henry summoned a Council of Barons to meet at Argentan.[6] He also summoned the young King Argentan. from England.

A Royal Charter, dated at Falaise, is relative to the Falaise. Abbey of St. Mary, Dublin, and its subjection, as a cell, to Buildwas Abbey, in Shropshire. It is attested by William de Courci, Dapifer; Roger de Newburgh; William de St.

[1] *Chivilli*, afterwards represented by Chevaillec, was a hamlet on the skirts of the Bois de Gonneville, near Honfleur (Stapleton's Rot. Norm. ii. xlvi. xlvii).

[2] This emendation rests on the sure fact that Hugh, Archbishop of Rouen, was dead before Giles became Bishop of Evreux.

[3] Cartæ Antiquæ. C.

[4] Monast. vi. 374, iii.

[5] D'Anisy's Normandy Transcripts, i. 177, 178. Another Confirmation by the King, gives somewhat different witnesses, including John, Archdeacon of Bath and Richard de Luci.

[6] Stubbs, quoting R. de Monte (Struve), 910.

1171. June and July. John; Hugh de Cressi; William de Stuteville; and William fitz Adeline.[1] Chevaillec.

Prince Henry, or rather the "young King Henry" is stated in one edition of Benedictus to have joined his father in Normandy immediately before the latter crossed the sea to England. If so, the meeting probably took place at Bur le Roy, near Bayeux.

We have a Charter of the young King, dated *apud Burum*, and which certainly passed before his father's court had left the place. In this remarkable deed the young King's style is "*Henricus Rex Anglorum, Dux Normannorum et Comes Andegaviæ Regis Henrici filius.*" The deed is in favour of the Monks of Montebourg, to whom the young King concedes all that Alicia de Redvers, mother of Earl Baldwin gave them out of her marriage-portion, and William de Vernon, Juvenis, conceded. The witnesses were, Geoffrey, Archdeacon of Canterbury; Richard, Archdeacon of Poitiers; Reginald (Archdeacon) of Salisbury; John, Dean of (Salisbury), Richard de Camvill; Reginald de Curtenay; Hugh de Cressey, and William de St. John.[2] Bur le Roy.

July. A Charter of the elder King dated *apud Burmoun*, (Burum probably), is in favour of Newstead Abbey, Lincolnshire, and makes mention of Stephen fitz Chamberlain. Its witnesses are Geoffrey, Archdeacon of Canterbury; Richard, Archdeacon of Poitiers; Reginald, Archdeacon of Salisbury; John, Dean of Salisbury; Richard de Humet, Constable; William de St. John; and William fitz Andeline.[3] Bur-le-Roy.

Another Charter of the elder King is dated *apud Burum* (Bur-le-Roy) and is in favour of Blanchelaunde Abbey, in the Diocese of Coutances. It is attested by Henry, Bishop of Bayeux; Froger, Bishop of Seez; Reginald, Archdeacon of Salisbury; Richard de Camvill; and Hugh de Cressy.[4] Bur-le-Roy.

c. July 30, 31. King Henry, approaching the coast, is now at Valognes. We still trace his course by Charters rather than Chronicles. By one Charter, dated at Valognes, the King gives to Richard de Luci the Vill of Grinsted. Witnesses Geoffry, Valognes

[1] Monasticon v. 363, ii. The years 1174 and 1175 have been variously suggested as the date of this Charter. Perhaps 1175 is as likely as 1171. See Antiquities of Shropshire, vi. 327).

[2] D'Anisy's Transcripts, ii. 181. Reginald de Curtenay and Hugh de Cressy, and perhaps Richard de Camvill, went with the King to Ireland in this same year.

[3] Monasticon Angl. vii. 966.

[4] D'Anisy's Normandy Transcripts, i. 60.

1171. c. July 30, 31. Archdeacon of Canterbury; Richard, Archdeacon of Poitiers; William Earl de Mandeville; William de St. John; Richard de Camvill; Reginald de Curtenay; William de Lanval; Hugh de Cressi; William de Stutevill; Reginald de Pavelli, and Thomas Bardulf.[1] Valognes.

Another Royal Rescript, dated at Valognes, is addressed to the People of Ireland, to whom the King accredits William fitz Adeline, his Dapifer, as Envoy to that Island, and promises his own speedy attention to its weighty affairs. This Deed is attested by the Archdeacons, Geoffrey of Canterbury and Richard of Poitiers; and by Richard the Constable (De Humez).[2]

Aug. 1. Gilbert Foliot, Bishop of London, attends the Papal Commissioners at Chaumont, near Gisors, within the French frontier. The Commissioners are the Bishop of Beauvais (apparently acting for the Archbishop of Bourges), the Bishop of Nevers, and the Abbot of Pontigny. They release Foliot's excommunication.[3] His suspension remains.[4]

Aug. 1. King Henry embarks for England, probably at Barfleur. Barfleur.

Aug. 3. King Henry lands at Portsmouth. Portsmouth.

Aug. 8. Henry of Blois, Bishop of Winchester, dies.

c. Sept. 8 (Wed.) K. Henry is either at Monmouth, or Strigoil (*i.e.* Chepstow), or Cardiff, or, more probably than either, on his march between some two of those places, when Res ap Griffith, Prince of South Wales, coming from his quarters at Llwyn-Danet, meets the King and engages to find him 300 horses, 4000 oxen, and (as a security we suppose) 24 hostages.[5] (Strigoil).

K. Henry marches into Gwent and takes Caerleon-upon-Usk from Jerwerth ap Owen ap Caradoc ap Griffith.[5] Caerleon.

Sep. 21 (Tu.) K. Henry enters Pembrokeshire, and makes over to Prince Res, Cardigan, Ystrad-Tywi, Arwistli, and Elvael. Pembrokeshire.

Sep. 25, (Saturday.)[6] Prince Res, coming from Aberteivi, confers with K. Henry at Pembroke Castle. Pembroke Castle.

Sept. 26. (Sun.) Prince Res returns to Aberteivi and selects 86 horses to be sent on the 27th to the King, but the King had gone from Pembroke.

Sept. 27, (Monday.) King Henry sets out for St. Davids,[5] where he makes

[1] Cartæ Antiquæ I.I.—
Courtenay, Cressy and Pavilli all went to Ireland with the King.

[2] Rymer's Fœdera I. p. 36

[3] Diceto C arte, 62.

[4] Foliot was relieved from suspension (*restitutus officio*) at Aumale on May 1, 1172 (Diceto, p. 560).

[5] These particulars are from Mr. Bridgeman's 'Princes of S. Wales,' pp. 51, 52, 53.

[6] This date is given by the Brut-y-Tywysogion as Saturday XII. kal. Oct., an impossible date, but easily corrected by the context, which shows that Saturday VII. kal. Oct. (Sept. 25) was the original reading.

1171. c. Sept. 18. votive offerings to the Church. Here the King was entertained by David fitz Gerald, Bishop of St. David's.[1] St. David's.

Sep 29 (Wed) King Henry returned from St. Davids to Pembroke. Hither Prince Res sent the horses he had selected, whereof the King accepted 36, as a matter of courtesy to the Prince rather than because he, the King, needed them. Pembroke.

The King, having Prince Res in his company, comes to Y-Ty-Gwyn (The White House), where the King releases to Res his son, Howel, of long time a hostage in Henry's hands. The King also respites, till his return from Ireland, the other hostages, and the tribute which Res had agreed to pay. Y-Ty-Gwyn.

The King continues weather-bound in Pembrokeshire for eighteen days.[1]

THE PIPE-ROLL of Michaelmas, 1171, gives abundant illustrations of King Henry's proposed invasion of Ireland.—

CIVITAS WINTONIÆ. *Et item in conductu thesauri qui venit de Normanniâ, de Hantonâ, ad Gloecestriam* 15*s*. *Et in conductu amigdalarum et ceræ Regis de Winton' ad Bristou* 7*s*. 1*d*. *Et in conductu vini Regis quod Stephanus de Turonis*[2] *illi misit, de Winton ad Bristou* 10*s*. 5*d*. *per breve Regis.*

HANTONIA. *Et Rogerio filio Leonardi quinque marcas ad ducenda victualia Regis in Hyberniam per breve Regis.*

LONDON ET MIDDELSEXA. *Et pro* 200 *summis frumenti missis in exercitum Hyberniæ* £15. 18*s*. *Et duobus servientibus missis ad Regem cum predictâ garnisione* 8*s*.

SALOPESCIRA. *Et pro* 286 *Baconibus* £19. 4*s*. 4*d*. *Et pro vecturâ eorundem Baconum de Salop' ad Glocestriam* 7*s*. 8*d*. *per breve Regis.*[3]

Some more general evidences about the King's affairs, as extracted from the same Pipe-Roll, here follow :—

HANTON. *Et in duobus aliis passagiis esneccæ cum thesauro* £15 *per breve Regis. Et pro duabus navibus ad equos Camerariorum* 60*s*. *per idem breve. Et pro onerando thesauro et in liberacione vigilum et pro lumine* 9*s*. 5*d*. *Et in liberacione duarum navium quæ portaverunt Comiti Flandriæ Damas* 110*s*. *per breve Regis.*

NORHANTESCIRA. *Et pro locandâ caretâ ad portandam Pavillonem Regis de Norhanton' ad Lundon'* 3*s*. 6*d*. *per breve Regis.*[4]

BUCHINGEHSCIRA ET BEDEFORDSCIRA. *Et in conductu hugiæ de thesauro per Odonem de Falesiâ* 3*s*. 4*d*.

MINARIA CARLEOLI. *Et in soltis per brevi Regis Ædwardo Blundo* £30 *ad Coronationem Regis filii Regis.*[5]

OXINEFORDSCIRA. *Et pro locandâ caretâ ad papitionem Regis deferendam de Oxeneford' ad Lundon'* 21*d*.[4]

---

[1] Bridgeman's Princes of S. Wales, pp. 52, 53.

[2] Stephen de Tours, Seneschal of Anjou.

[3] And from other counties large supplies of provision, &c. had been furnished in this year for the *Army of Ireland*.

[4] This does not imply any visit of the King to Northampton during his month's residence in England. The Royal Tent had probably lain at Northampton since the Council of October, 1164. It now went to London for repairs, preparatory to its shipment to Ireland. Another Tent-Royal, similarly stored at Oxford, was also sent to London.

[5] This account is retrospective. The item belongs to June, 1170.

HONOR BOLONIÆ. *In camerâ Curiæ* £313. 7*s. per breve Regis.*

LUNDON ET MIDDELSEXA. *Et pro oleo ad lampadem Reginæ* 30*s.* 5*d.*[1] *Et in conductu thesauri et hugiarum thesauri de Lundon' ad Winton',* 9*s.* 3*d. per Odonem de Falesiâ. Et pro reficiendis papilionibus Regis* £7. 13*s.* 2*d. per breve Regis.*

CIVITAS WINTONIÆ. *Et in conductu thesauri a Wintoniâ ad Hantoniam et Portesmuam in septem itineribus* 45*s.* 7*d. per Odonem de Falesiâ.*

The YOUNGER KING HENRY, as we have seen, joined his father at Bur-le-Roi in the end of July, just previous to the King's departure for England.

The younger King clearly remained in Normandy for a time.

An agreement, dated in 1171, passed probably at Caen. It was between the Abbey of St. Stephen in that city and William de Aboville, whose eldest son, Henry, was assenting. There were present in Court these following:—

Henricus Rex junior, Arnoldus Episcopus Luxoviensis, Frogerus Episcopus Sagiensis, et Joscelinus Episcopus Saresburiensis.

Also the following, who are called King's justices, *viz.*, William de St. John, William de Courcy, and Thomas Archdeacon of Bayeux, as representing Henry his Bishop.[2]

Afterwards, and while his father was in Ireland, the younger Henry and his wife clearly crossed from Normandy to England, and, as will be seen, were resident in England till the King's return from Ireland.

THE PIPE-ROLL of 1171 gives some evidence as to the household expenses of the PRINCESS MARGARET OF FRANCE, previous to her transfretation;—and also a hint as to the time of that transfretation, *viz.* April 2, 1171.

WILTSCIRA. *Et in corredio filiæ Regis Franciæ et familiæ ejus* £71 *per breve Regis.*

HANTESCIRA. *Et Margaretæ filiæ Regis Franciæ viginti marcas per breve Regis. Et in pannis servientum filiæ Regis Franciæ et pro duobus palefridis et uno summario et apparatu eorum ad opus ejusdem filiæ Regis* £15. 19*s.* 8*d. per breve Regis. Et in corredio ipsius apud Wintoniam et Portesmue in passagio suo* £10. 18*s.* 3*d. per breve Regis.*

CIVITAS WINTONIA. *Et in corredio filiæ Regis Franciæ a festo Sancti Michaelis preterito usque ad diem Veneris in Septimanâ Paschæ*[3] £58. 3*s. per breve Regis.*

HANTONIA. *Et in passagio esneccæ cum filiâ Regis Franciæ* £7. 10*s. per breve Regis. Et pro unâ navi ad equos ipsius* 30*s. per idem breve.*

PRINCE GEOFFRY was probably domiciled at Northampton for about 22 weeks of the fiscal year, commencing Michaelmas, 1170. The following extract from the Northamptonshire Pipe-Roll of 1171, when compared with the Roll of 1170,[4] suggests as much.—

Et in corredio Galfridi filii Regis apud Norhanton' £34 *per breve Regis.*

At that rate, Prince Geoffry will have quitted Northampton early in March, 1171.

Under the head of London and Middlesex, there are in the Pipe-Roll of 1171 numerous charges for apparel, &c. &c., *ad opus Regis filii Regis, ad opus Ricardi et Galfridi filiorum Regis, ad opus Reginæ,* and *ad opus filiæ Regis Franciæ.*

But these hardly amount to any presumption of the parties having been resident in London, within the previous year, unless we had other indications of such facts.

[1] This entry has nothing to do with Queen Elianor or her movements. It was a fixed charge on the Revenues of the City of London, for the purpose of maintaining the "undying lamp,' before the tomb of Matilda, Queen of K. Henry I.

[2] D'Anisy, Extrait des Chartes, i. 278.

[3] Sep. 29, 1170, to April 2, 1171.

[4] Vide supra, p. 145.

MICHAELMAS, 1171, TO MICHAELMAS, 1172.

1171. Sept. 30. The King probably at Pembroke. Pembroke.

Oct. 16. The King, having been more than a month assembling his soldiers and transports at Pembroke, embarks for Ireland at Milford Haven. Milford Haven.

Oct. 17, 18. The King lands at Croch, near Waterford, and proceeds to Waterford, where he is joined by William fitz Adeline and Robert fitz Bernard, who had preceded him.[1] Croch. Waterford.

The Pipe-Roll of Michaelmas, 1172, is full of allusions to the Irish expedition and its cost. *The scutage of Ireland*, was put in charge generally;[2]—also provisions and stores from nearly every county in England were sent *pro exercitu Hyberniæ*, or *in guarnisonem Regis in Hyberniá.* The following extracts will suffice to illustrate the point:—

BERKSHIRE. *Et pro duobus equis missis Regi in Hyberniam* £4 *per breve Regis.*

OXFORDSHIRE. *Et pro thesauro portando de Oxineford ad Glocestriam cum Ricardo de Luci* 2*s. Et pro locandis* v. *carretis de Oxineford ad Warewicam cum pannis familiæ Regis*[3] *de Yberniá* 17*s.* 8*d. per breve Regis.*

CARLISLE. *Et in conductu et liberacione navium quæ portaverunt victualia Regis de Everwicscirâ et de Northumberland et de Cumberland in Hiberniam* £27. 11*s.* 7*d.*

SEE OF WINCHESTER. *Pro* 569 *libris amigdal' missis Regi in Hiberniam* 118*s.* 7*d. Et pro* 12 *pannis sericis et* 5 *pellibus de Lutreis* £13. 19*s.* 2*d. per breve Regis filii Regis de computando sibi per fidem ballivorum suorum quicquid expenderat in rebus missis patri suo in Hiberniá.*

STAFFORDSHIRE. *Et pro* 2 *equis missis in Yberniam ad opus Regis* £4 *per breve Regis. Et pro locandis* 5 *caretis de Stafford ad Cestriam quæ portaverunt pannos familiæ Regis*[3] *missos in Yberniam* 15*s.* 11*d. per breve Regis. Et Radulfo Archidiacono de Stafford* £8. 6*s.* 8*d. ad locandas naves ad portandam Guarnisonem Regis in Yberniam per breve Regis. Et Radulfo Archidiacono de Stafford* £16. 13*s.* 7*d. ad faciendam liberacionem* 9 *navium apud Cestriam quæ portaverunt warnisionem Regis in Yberniam per breve Regis.*

GLOUCESTERSHIRE. *Et pro locandis navibus ad portandum Regis thesaurum in Hiberniam et vinum et pannos quos Stephanus de Turonis misit Regi. Et pro portando harnesio Regis de Striguil in Glocestriam* 16*d. per breve Regis.*

SHROPSHIRE. *Et pro* 400 *Baconibus missis in Hyberniam* £31. 15*s.* 2*d.*

Oct. 23, 1171. Pope Alexander, at *Tusculanum* (Frascati), instructs the Archbishop of Rouen and Bishop of Amiens as to the release from suspension of Roger, Archbishop of York, who had always stated his readiness and wish to come to the Pope for absolution, but had been refused safe-conduct by the Emperor Frederic. Alexander's trust in York, and wish to oblige K. Henry, induce him to dispense with York's personal attendance. Rouen and Amiens will convene York at some place in the Marches of

[1] Benedictus, i. p. 25 (Stubbs's edition). The dates given by Gervase and Diceto for the King's landing in Ireland, are not quite so accurate.
Mr. Bridgeman has it (Princes of S. Wales, p. 53) that the King embarked on Sunday, the Eve of St. Luke, that is Sunday, Oct. 17, and landed at Waterford on the 18th.

[2] Madox, Exchequer, p. 438.

[3] The term, *Familia Regis*, usually indicates the King's suit or staff; but any detachment of retainers or troops employed by the King's order on special services would be called *Familia Regis* irrespectively of the King's personal presence. Sometimes the King's personal staff and household is distinguished as *Dominica familia Regis.* (*Confer supra* [page 81, note 1.]).

Normandy and France. He is to bring with him two dignitaries of his Church, or two canons, or priors, or abbots of good repute, and before them to swear on the Gospels (1), that he never swore, or promised to observe, or hereafter to observe, the "depraved customs;" (2), that he never, by letter, word, or deed, incited K. Henry to violence against Becket; (3), that he never received the Archbishop of Rouen's letters prohibiting him from the coronation of the young King, nor had knowledge of such letters; nor had hindered their presentation.

On his so swearing (which it seems he did), Rouen and Amiens were to restore him to the full plenitude of his office.[1]

Another, and probably contemporary, letter instructs the same Commissioners that York's repeated attempts to avoid the necessity of crossing the Channel for his absolution were inadmissible. The ascertainment of the truth, and the expedient publicity of the process, required that Pope Alexander's method be implicitly followed.[1]

Oct. 18. Nov. 1. K. Henry remains at Waterford fifteen days.[2] Waterford.

Nov. 6. K. Henry having sent Nicholas, his chaplain, and Ralph, Archdeacon of Landaff, to summon the Irish Bishops, the latter meet the King at Cashel.[2] Cashel.

At the Council of Cashel Canons were enacted remediative of the evils existing in Ireland.

Nov. 11. King Henry's Court is at Dublin,[2] where it seems to have remained nearly three months. Dublin.

While at Dublin the King expedited a Charter to his "men of Bristol," whereby he gave *his* city of Dublin to the said men, to inhabit and to hold as they held Bristol. Witnesses—William de Braose; Reginald de Curtenai; Hugh de Gundeville; William fitz Aldeline; Ranulph (Qy. Richard ?) de Camvill; Hugh de Cressi; and Reginald de Pavilli.[2]

Dec. 1-31. The King was at Dublin and kept Christmas there.[3] Dublin.

Mon. Dec. 13. On Monday after *Gandete Sunday*, being the Feast of St. Lucia, Roger, Archbishop of York, appeared before the Papal Commissioners at Aumale, and achieved compurgation by the process prescribed in the Papal Rescript of October 23, 1171. The Commissioners who absolved him and removed his suspension were Rotrou, Archbishop of Rouen, and the vicars of the Bishop of Amiens. There were witnesses of the ceremony, Giles, Bishop of Evreux, and abbots, priors, and other religious persons.[4]

The Archbishop writes of the event to Hugh, Bishop of Durham, to R. the Dean, William Canterbury, and the Chapter of York; to the Canons of Southwell, Beverley, and Ripon, and to the abbots, priors, clergy, and people of his Province of York.[5]

The Archbishop of York writes also to Pope Alexander, thanking him for his goodness, and begging that he would similarly favour the pious and excellent Bishop of London, now broken down with age, who had so often, in York's presence, tried to mollify K. Henry's wrath against Becket.[6]

In this month of December, the Pope seems to have despatched his Legates who were to ascertain, verify, and adjudicate on K. Henry's complicity in, and contrition for, the death of the Archbishop of Canterbury. The Legates so sent were Albert, Cardinal of St. Laurence in Lucina, and Theodwine, Cardinal of St. Vitalis.

[1] S. T. C. iv. 65, 67. Epist. cclix. cclx.
[2] Lyttelton, vol. iv. Appendix (1).
[3] Benedictus (Stubbs), i. pp. 25–29.
[4, 5] S. T. C. iv. 173. Epist. ccccxxv. R. Dean of York, is probably Robert Botivelein. He died in 1186. No extant list of the dignitaries of York includes the name of William Canterbury.
[6] S. T. C. iv. 171. Epist. ccccxxiv.

A.D. 1172.

Jan. 1-31. Henry the whole month at Dublin.[1] Dublin.

In January, probably, the Cardinal Legates reached Normandy, but the King does not seem to have heard of their arrival there, before February.

Feb. 1-29 Henry is still in Dublin for the whole month.[1]

Feb. 28. Pope Alexander, at Frascati, writes to the Archbishop of Rouen and Bishop of Amiens.—The Bishop of London's messengers have been with the Pope, viz. R. Archdeacon,[2] and Masters Richard and Hugh, clerks, their object being to clear the Bishop, himself too infirm for the journey, of all complicity in the murder of Becket. The Pope now directs that the said compurgation be taken by Rouen and Amiens in the Marches between Normandy and France, after citing London with six others, abbots, priors, monks, or regular canons of good repute, and not likely to perjure themselves. London is, in the presence of all, to swear upon the Gospels that he had neither by letter, word, or deed incensed the King in any way calculated to result in Becket's death or personal injury. The Commissioners, or one of them (the other being unavoidably absent, is to be represented by religious and influential persons of his province), are then to restore to London, on the Pope's authority, the full plenitude of his office.[3]

March 1. Pope Alexander, having been certified by letter of his Legates, Albert and Theodine, of the miracles (*de mirabilibus*) of Thomas, late Archbishop of Canterbury, canonizes the said saint as a martyr in full Consistory of the Church.[4]

March 10. Pope Alexander, at Segni, writes to certify his Legates, Albert and Theodine, of the said canonization.[5]

March 12. Pope Alexander, at Segni, writtes letters to the Chapter of Canterbury, and to the people of England, certifying the said canonization.[5]

March 1. King Henry, probably having heard of the arrival of the Papal Legates in Normandy, moves to Wexford, where he Wexford.
March 1-31. remains, apparently weather-bound, the whole month.[6]

While at Wexford the King expedites a Charter, whereby he gives to Hugh de Lacy the land of Meath (theretofore held by Murchard Hu-Melachlin) for service of 50 knights. The Charter also speaks of knights'-fees in the vicinity of Dublin, and of the King's city of Dublin, and of Hugh de Lacy as being, *pro tempore*, bailiff thereof. It is attested by Earl Richard fitz Gilbert (of Strigoil and Pembroke) and by William de Braose.

March 26. The King, himself remaining at Wexford, sends his army to Waterford to cross the Channel, but it would seem that the wind was contrary.[6] Wexford.

[1] Benedictus (Stubbs), i. pp. 25–29.

[2] If the 'Archdeacon' here spoken of was 'of London,' he was no other than Ralph de Diceto, the historian. He held the dignity in 1163 and 1168; but when, in 1181, he was promoted to the Deanery of London (*i.e.* St. Paul's), he is styled Archdeacon of Middlesex. Possibly he exchanged the higher but poorer dignity of London for the richer Archdeaconry of Middlesex; but Mr. Hardy's view (Fasti, ii. 307) seems to be that an Archdeacon, though occasionally styled 'of London,' might the while have been merely of Middlesex.

[3] S. T. C. iv. 69. Epist. cclxi.

[4] S. T. C. vi. 58, 59. Epist. cccxxxv.

[5] S. T. C. iv. 75, 39. Epist. cclxvi. ccxxxvii.

[6] Benedictus (*ut supra*). Carte talks of a Council at Cashel on March 25. We cannot verify or suppose such an incident.

March 30. A letter of Pope Alexander to Joceline, Bishop of Salisbury, bears date on this day at Beneventum. If we date it correctly as to year, it shows that that prelate had not availed himself of the acilities of compurgation proposed in the Papal Rescript of April 24, 1171. Now, the Pope, considering the Bishop's age and infirmities, will allow him to purge himself of all complicity in the death of Becket by sending five, or at least four, religious persons of his diocese to the Pope's presence, who shall so excuse and purge him of the matters for which he had been suspended and excommunicated. The Pope had been moved to this concession by the frequent solicitations of Robert, Dean of Evreux; of Reginald, Archdeacon of Salisbury; of William, King of Sicily, and Queen *Matilda* his mother; and also by his, the Pope's, consideration and love for his dearest son in Christ, Henry, King of the English.[1]

1172. April 1-16. K. Henry at Wexford, still waiting apparently for a fair wind.[2] **Wexford.**

April 16 (Easter Sunday). The King's household embarks at Waterford, and lands at Milford Haven the same day.

April 17 (Monday). The King himself crosses the Channel[3] and lands at Portfinnan, near St. David's. He leaves Hugh de Lacy as his Justiciar in Ireland, holding Meath and Dublin as a tenant-in-capite of 100 knights' fees. He also entrusts the custody of Waterford and Wexford to Robert fitz Bernard, and leaves the Earl of Strigoil in possession of Leinster. **Portfinnan.**

c. April 19. From St. David's the King goes to Haverfordwest.[3] **Haverfordwest.**

YOUNG KING HENRY and his wife, now styled Queen, during some months of the elder King's residence in Ireland, seem to have been in England. Hence the following entries on the Pipe-Roll of Michaelmas, 1172.—

BERKHAMPSTEAD. *Pro x ollis Galearum ad opus Regis filii Regis* 30*s. per breve Regis.*

BUCKS AND BEDFORDSHIRE. *Et in corredio Regis filii Regis* £20 *per breve Regis et per Robertum de Ansgervill.*

HIDE ABBEY. *In corredio Regis filii Regis* £25 *per breve Regis.*

HAMPSHIRE. *Et in expensâ Reginæ, filiæ Regis Franciæ,* £20 *per breve Regis filii Regis. Et in corredio Regis filii Regis per Robertum de Ansgervill* £33. 6*s.* 8*d. per breve Regis. Et item in corredio ipsius per eundem Robertum* £30 *per breve Regis. Et Ailwardo Camerario* 10 *marcas ad negocia Cameræ per breve Regis. Et in corredio Regis filii Regis per Robertum de Ansgervill* £28 *per breve Regis.*

NORTHAMPTONSHIRE. *Et pro robâ Reginæ filiæ Regis Franciæ ad equitandum* £9. 11*s.* 10*d. per breve Regis.*

WINCHESTER. *Et Ailwardo Camerario* £20 *ad emendam Robam Regis filii Regis in Nundinis Wintoniæ per breve Regis. Et pro uno Summario et Coffris et uno Tapeto et pro* 2 *Urceolis et una pixide*

[1] S. T. C. iv. 104. Epist. cclxxxviij. There is much that is marvellous about this Epistle, but it is unquestionably genuine. William, King of Sicily, was at this time under the tutelage of his mother, usually called *Margaret*, a Princess of the House of Navarre. Robert de Newburgh, Dean of Evreux, whom the Pope calls Bishop Joceline's "beloved son," is known to have gone to visit his relations in Sicily after this embassy to Frascati (accomplished April, 1171). Reginald, Archdeacon of Salisbury, whom the Pope delicately styles his own son (*dilectus filius noster*), was, in fact, Bishop Joceline's son after the flesh; only there was a question about his legitimacy.

[2] Benedictus (Stubbs), i. p. 29.

[3] Giraldus Exp. Hib. i. pp. 37-39. Brut-y-Tywysogion, 219.

Mr. Bridgeman (Princes of S. Wales, p. 53) quotes another diary, which makes the King to reach Pembroke on Good Friday (April 14), and so renders the preceding and succeeding dates a week earlier than is stated in the text.

et duobus candelabris et 2 pelvibus et uno thuribulo et uno Texto, et his omnibus argenteis ad obsequium capellæ Reginæ filiæ Regis Franciæ. Et pro uno palefrido ad opus Willielmi Clerici ejusdem Reginæ £14. 17*s.*

1172. April 21, The King reaches Pembroke. Pembroke.

Friday. April 22. The King at Cardiff. Cardiff.

April 23. The King goes to Newport from Cardiff.[1] Newport.

April 24. The King is met on his road to England by Prince Res at Talacharn. Soon afterwards the King appointed Res his Justiciary for South Wales. Talacharn.

The King, after his return from Ireland and leaving Wales, seems to have stayed about eighteen days in England. Hence the following charges on the same Pipe-Roll.— England.

WINCHESTER. *Et in conductu thesauri per totum annum et pro thesauro onerando et exonerando et in aliis minutis negociis thesauri per Odonem de Falesia et Waleranum de Crickelada et alios servientes thesauri* 48*s.* 6*d.* *Et pro* 2 *equis ad opus Regis* £4 *per breve Regis.*

SEE OF WINCHESTER. *Et pro* XXV *ulnis de rubeâ escarlet' ad opus Regis* £6. 17*s.* 6*d.* *Et pro uno opertorio ad opus Regis* 13*s.* 4*d.* *Et pro* 26 *ulnis viridis* £3. 3*s.* 8*d.* *Et pro* 10 *paribus ocreorum* 15*s.* *Et in speciebus et electuariis per Josephum medicum* £10. 7*s.* *Et Osberto clerico de Camerâ et Camerariis Regis* £200 *ad portandum cum Rege quando rediit ab Hibernia, per breve Regis.* (Winchester).

c. May 12. The King, embarking from Portsmouth,[2] lands at Barfleur, Prince Henry goes with him. The following charges on the Pipe-Roll are pertinent.— Portsmouth. Barfleur.

HAMPSHIRE. *Et item in corredio Regis . . . . in transfretatione suâ per Robertum de Angersvill* £50 *per breve Regis. Et in liberacione* XXV *navium in transitu suo* £36. 14*s.* *per breve Regis. Et pro uno palefrido ad opus Reginæ* 40*s.* *Et pro* VI *carettariis ad opus Regis liberatis Roberto Malduit et Hugoni de Kewilli* £8 *per breve Regis. Et in liberacione navis Willielmi Tirevache in transitu Regis* 40*s.* *per breve Regis.*

May 16. The King is at Gorram [3] (in Maine). Gorram.

May 17. Henry meets the Cardinal-Legates, Theodine and Albert, at Savigny, S.W. of Caen. They cannot agree. Savigny.

[1] Giraldus Exp. Hib. i. pp. 37–39.

[2] Benedictus (the authority usually relied upon at this period of our Itinerary) does not date this transfretation precisely as to day. Both he and Gervase say, *circa ascens onem domini.* That would be "about May 25;" but we know that the King was in Normandy many days earlier.

[3] Stubbs, quoting S. T. C. i. 372.

1172. May 17. K. Henry quitted the conference of Savigny, the Legates thought with the intention of retnrning to England. Probably the King went to Caen. Caen.

May 19. The Legates being informed by the Bishop of Liseux and two Archdeacons sent by Henry that the King would agree to their demands, went to Avranches to meet the King.[1]

May 21. Council of Avranches (on *Vocem Jucunditatis* Sunday), wherein K. Henry was absolved from the murder of Thomas à Becket, after he and his son had sworn to the Cardinals that he would abolish all the unlawful customs established during his reign, and after the King had made other large promises and professions. Avranches.

c. May 22. From Avranches the King appears to have gone to Caen; and from Caen into Bretagne. At Caen he publicly reiterated his professions made at Avranches.[1] Caen. Bretagne.

c. May 23. Great Council of Caen, held by the Cardinals, with the Norman Archbishop and Bishops, at which certain Decrees were made.[1]

c. Aug. 24. Prince Henry and his wife, Margaret, land at Southampton, being sent by the King for the purpose of another Coronation. Rotrode, Abp of Rouen, Giles, Bp of Evreux, and Roger, Bp of Worcester, accompany them.

Aug. 27. They are crowned at Winchester, the said Prelates performing the ceremony. The following notes from the Pipe-Roll of 1172 are pertinent.—

HIDE ABBEY. "In corredio Regis filii Regis et Reginæ in coronatione suâ apud Wintoniam £30 per breve Regis."

SEE OF WINCHESTER. "Et in corredio Regis filii Regis de tribus diebus ante coronationem suam £12. 11s. 5d. per breve Regis. Et item in corredio ejus in ipsâ coronatione £55. 11s. 2d. per Robertum de Ansgervill et Willielmum Ruffum et Robertum Monachum. Et item ipsi Roberto et sociis ejus £18. 10s. 9d. ad portandum cum Rege filio Regis per idem breve."

LONDON AND MIDDLESEX. "Et in soltis per breve Regis pro Robâ Regis filii Regis et Reginæ suæ in coronacione eorum apud Wintoniam £88. 10s. 4d. per breve Regis et per testimonium Edwardi Blundi. Et item pro robâ Regis filii Regis ad equitandum et tribus pannis sericis £8. 8s. per breve Regis."

At this time K. Henry was in Bretagne, while the Cardinal-Legates were visiting the Norman Abbeys. Bretagne.

Sept. 8. The Archbishop of Rouen and the Bishops of Evreux and Worcester return to Normandy from England.

On this same day (Sept. 8) a return was made to the Curia Regis at Caen, which, for Normandy, was equivalent to the return of 1166 for England, now known as the *Liber Niger*. On this day all the Barons of Normandy met at Caen, by command of King Henry II., and each Baron acknowledged before the King's Justiciars how many knights'-service he owed to the King, and how many he could command for his private occasion. And each Baron returned two writs, one sealed, which expressed the amount of his knights'-service to the Crown, the other, not sealed, which expressed the names of his knights,

[1] S. T. C. vi. p. 122. Epist. ccclxxxvii. and p. 125. Epist. ccclxxxviii.

and the proportions (*partes et divisiones*) of their feudal tenures. And these writs were carried to, and deposited in, the Treasury at Caen. An example of the return will show its nature,—"Robert, Abbot of Mont St. Michel, acknowledged that he owed the service of seven knights to the Crown, viz., three in the Avranchin, three in the Cotentin, and one in the Bessin (Abrincatino, Constantino, et Baiocasino). And of those of the Avranchin, the Earl of Chester was responsible for half a fee *in Bacilleio*; and William de St. John, for half a fee, for the fief of St. John," &c. &c.[1] Abstracts of these returns are preserved, but none of them giving the names of the knight-tenants.

Pope Alexander's three letters to King Henry, to the Hierarchy, and to the Kings and Princes of Ireland, sanctioning, rejoicing in, and stimulating Henry's conquest of Ireland, bear date at Frascati, Sept. 20. We will say nothing of their matter more than that they name Christian, Bishop of Lismore, as Legate of the Holy See, and the Archbishops Gel', of Armagh; Donatus, of Cashel; Laurence, of Dublin; and Catholicus, of Tuam; and that they speak of reports as to the barbarity and profligacy of the Irish people, furnished to the Pope after personal inspection by R., Archdeacon of Landaff.[2]

Sept. 21. K. Henry was again in Normandy.[3] Normandy.

MICHAELMAS, 1172, to MICHAELMAS, 1173.

October. November. The King is not recorded to have quitted Normandy during any part of these two months. Normandy.

c. Nov. 1. The young King and Queen are sent for by Henry into Normandy.[4] The following entries on the Pipe-Roll of 1173 are pertinent to the period of the young King's residence in England and his transfretation to Normandy.—

LONDON AND MIDDLESEX. *Et Edwardo Blundo* £42. 12*s*. 6*d*. *ad emendam Robbam Regis filii Regis et Reginæ Matris ejus et Reginæ uxoris ejus, per breve Regis. Et Edwardo Blundo* £3. 6*s*. 8*d*. *pro panno serico ad opus Regis filii Regis per breve Regis.*

WINCHESTER. *Et Waltero Vitulo* £7 10*s*. *de liberacione esneccæ de* xv *diebus ultimis quibus fuit in servicio Regis quando Rex filius Regis novissime tranfretavit in Normanniam per breve Regis.*

It is clear that Richard de Luci was now acting as Chief Justice of England. The following entry on the same Pipe-Roll will illustrate that point.—

SOUTHAMPTON. *Et in liberacione Esneccæ quando transfretaverunt cum thesauro quem Andreas clericus thesauri duxit* £7. 10*s*. *per breve Ricardi de Luci.*

c. Nov. 7. The young King and Queen visit her father, the King of France. The counsels of Louis led to the subsequent rebellion.

c. Dec. The young King and Queen return into Normandy, to K. Henry's Court, by his desire. Normandy.

Dec. King Henry, on quitting Normandy for the South, occurs first at Le Mans. Here he decrees immunities for the Church Le Mans.

[1] D'Anisy's Transcripts, ii. 270.
[2] Hearne's Liber Niger, i. 42–48.
[3] Benedictus (Stubbs), i. 31. The same authority gives Sept. 27 and 28 as the dates of K. Henry's compurgation, and of the Council of Avranches. It is probably a mere mistake as to date, though Robert de Monte seems to have shared in it.
[4] Hoveden, p. 304.

1172. Dec. of *Beata Maria de Aquilone* (Loc Marie, in Bretagne). The Diploma is consistently dated. "*Actum Cenomannis, Anno* 1172. *Concurrente VI. Epactâ IV.*[1] Le Mans.

Dec. 25,—Dec. 31. King Henry and Queen Elianor are at Chinon, in Anjou, and the young King and Queen in Normandy.[2] Chinon (in Anjou).

In the above year the outlawry and forfeiture of Adam de Port took place.[2]

A.D. 1173.

1173. c. Jan. Feb. 2. The King sends for his son Henry to join him; and father and son go into Auvergne. At Mont Ferratz (Montferrand le Fort, near Clermont) they negotiate with Hubert, Comte of Maurianne.[3] He contracts to give his eldest daughter Aalays in marriage to Prince John. The Commissioners, who swore to keep the convention on King Henry's part, were Earl William de Mandeville, William Earl of Arundel, Ralph de Faia, William de Curci, William de Humez, Fulco Painel, Robert de Brivecurt, William de Mangat, Theobald Chabot, William de Munlufzun, Peter de Muncasson, and Geoffrey Forester. Reginald (fitz Joceline) Archdeacon of Salisbury, was also named among the referees in case of disputes.[4] Chinon. Montferrand (in Auvergne).

c. Feb. From Auvergne it seems probable that the King went into Gascony.

At St. Machaire, on the Garonne, the King expedites a Charter, granting the Church of St. Clement Danes, London, to the Order of the Temple. Witnesses, Earl William de Mandeville; William de Curci, Dapifer; and Fulk Paenell.[5] Gascogne. St. Machaire.

Feb 18. As showing the reputed co-royalty of the younger Henry at this period, we quote the date of a deed which passed on this day in the Archbishop of York's Court at Ripon, viz., *Data apud Ripon in Curiâ Archiepiscopi* xix°. *anno Henrici nepotis Henrici Senioris, et tertio anno regni Henrici filii ejusdem Regis Dominicâ ante Cathedram Beati Petri Apostoli.*[6]

Feb. 21-28. Council of Limoges, attended by the King, Queen, Prince Henry, Prince Richard, and many other magnates. Limoges.

Thither came the Comte of Maurianne; in negotiating

[1] Gall. Script. xii. 560.
[2] Benedictus (Stubbs), i. 35.
[3] Maurianne was a district of Savoy.
[4] Hoveden, p. 304 b. Fœdera, i. 28. Benedictus (Stubbs), i. 35. R. de Monte (Struve), 911.
[5] Monasticon, vii. 818. Dated "*Apud Machariam super Gerundam in Gasconia.*"
[6] Monast. vi. 1191, lxxxviii.

1173. Feb. 21-28. with whom K. Henry proposed to give up Chinon, Mirabeau, and Loudon, as a portion for Prince John, which thing gave great offence to young Henry.[1] Limoges.

Thither came Raymond, Comte of Toulouse and St. Giles, and undertook to do homage to the elder and younger Henry, and also to Prince Richard, as Comte of Poitou, for Toulouse.[1]

Feb. 25. (*"Invocavit me" Sunday*). William le Templier, Abbot of Reading, consecrated Archbishop of Bordeaux at Limoges, the King being present.[1] One authority names the same day as that on which the Comte of St. Giles did the aforesaid acts of homage.

Coincidently the Comte of St. Giles revealed to King Henry that the Queen and Princes were forming a plot against him.[2]

c. Feb. 26, Mond. The King and the Comte of St. Giles, affecting to go out hunting, devoted themselves to the fortification of the cities and castles of the threatened district.[2]

Feb. 28, Wed. The Council of Limoges, having lasted seven days, was quitted by the magnates (*heroes*) who were there assembled.[2]

The King and the Comte of St. Giles leaving the neighbourhood of Limoges pass through Vigeois (*Vosias*).[2] Vigeois.

March 5 Mond.) The King and his son are at Chinon, but the Prince leaves before night, and the next day (March 6) arrives at Alençon.[3] Chinon.

March 7. The Prince reaches Argentan; the King, following him, sleeps at Alençon. Alençon.

March 8. The Prince absconds to the Court of Louis (then at Chartres), the Comte of Perche allowing him to pass by way of Mortagne (Mortagne en Perche).

March. K. Henry goes to Gisors, and strengthens that fortress. He then passes throughout Normandy, causing all Castles to be put in a state of defence. Gisors.

The young King goes into Aquitaine. Queen Elianor sends his brothers, Geoffrey and Richard, to join him. She herself, endeavouring to abscond in disguise, is arrested by K. Henry and committed to prison.

The partisans of the Prince, or those who shared his treason, were Arnulf Bishop of Liseux, Robert de Ble, Saher Quinci the younger, and Ralph de Fayo (uncle to Queen Elianor). Those whom he

[1] Gall. Script. xii. 443. Joseph, who succeeded William as Abbot of Reading died, in 1180. Archbishop William was arrested within the year of his consecration by the King's sons, then in rebellion. He died 25 Feb. 1182.

[2] Rerum Gallicarum Scriptores (ibidem).

[3] Diceto gives March 23 as the day of the Prince's elopement.—We follow J. Bromton and Benedictus Abbas, who are more circumstantial.

associated to his cause by promises or gifts were, Philip, Comte of Flanders; Matthew, his brother, Comte of Boulogne; Theobald, Comte of Blois; William, King of Scots; David, his brother (whom the Prince affected to create Earl of Huntingdon); and Hugh Bigot, Earl of Norfolk.[1]

The following numbers of the Prince's household forsook their offices and joined his father, viz., Walter, the Chaplain; Ailward, the Chamberlain; William Blund, his Usher (*Hostiarius*); and Richard Barre, keeper of his seal.

1173. April 4. King Henry at St. Barbe in the Lieuvin.[2] St. Barbe.

April 5, (Thurs.) *Quintâ feriâ Majoris Hebdomadæ.* Whilst Giles, Bishop of Evreux was consecrating the Holy Chrism in the Church of the Blessed Mary at Rouen, a fire broke out which destroyed thirteen churches and parishes of that Metropolis.[3]

April 8. K. Henry held his Easter-Court at Alençon.[4] Alençon.

April 15. This is the date given for the outbreak of Prince Henry's matured rebellion. More of his English partisans are named, viz., Hugh, Earl of Chester; Robert, the young Earl of Leicester;[5] Robert, Earl Ferrers; Roger de Mowbray; Thomas de Muscamp; Robert de Lund; Richard de Morvill; and Gervase Paynel.[6]

The most notable of the King's supporters, now and afterwards, were Richard, Archbishop-elect of Canterbury; Roger, Abp of York; Rotrode, Abp of Rouen; Geoffrey, Bishop-elect of Lincoln (the King's natural son); the Earls of Cornwall, Essex, Strigoil, Albemarle, Arundel, Warren, Gloucester, and Salisbury; Richard and William de Albini, Ranulf de Broc, Hugh de Beauchamp, Hugh de Lacy, John, Constable of Chester; Richard de Luci; Richard de Humez, Constable of Normandy, with his sons and brethren; Thomas Bardulf, Humphrey de Bohun, Walter de Dunstanvill, Everard de Ros, Geoffrey Trussebut, Philip de Chime; William de Vesci, Odonell de Umfraville, Robert de Stuteville, with his sons and brethren, Robert de Brus, Adam Brus, Richard Luvetot, Bertram de Verdon, Wido de Vere, and David and Evayn (Owen) Kings of Wales.

[1] The Pipe-Roll of Michaelmas, 1173, shows that the Earl of Norfolk only received the *Tertium Denarium* of his county for half the year, viz., the half-year ending at Easter. This suspension of income, from Easter to Michaelmas 1173, was doubtless a result of his rebellion.

[2] R. de Monte (Struve), 912.

[3] Chron. Rothom. (Gall. Script. xii. 786.)

[4] J. Bromton, p. 1085.

[5] The Dorset Pipe-Roll of Michaelmas, 1173, shows that the Earl of Leicester's manor of Kingston (now Kingston Lacy) had been confiscated four months previously (Hutchins iii. 233).

[6] To these Benedictus (vol. i. p. 45), adds many foreigners, viz., John, Comte of Ponthieu; the Comtes of Ewe and Mellent; the Chamberlain of Tankerville; William Patric, senior; Robert de Munford, Thomas de Caluncis, Amauri Turellus, William de Tibovill, Eudo fitz Ernise, William fitz Ernise, Robert and Oliver fitz Ernise, Ralph de Haye, Hasculf de St. Hilaire, Robert de Angervill, Robert de Sablul, Robert de Tresgorce, William Mareschall, William de Diva, Hugh de Diva, Geoffry and Guy de Lusignan, William Talwazs, Ralph de Chainai, Gerald Talbot, William de Tintiniac, and more than thirty others.

1173. April to July. The King made Rouen his head-quarters till near August. Rouen.

Diceto[1] describes the King, during his residence at Rouen in the summer of 1173, as maintaining an aspect of supreme equanimity and devoting more time than usual to the pleasures of the chase. The Southampton Pipe-Roll for Michaelmas, 1173, has some entries which illustrate Diceto's statement,—*Et pro locandis* 2 *navibus ad portandas damas Regis ultra mare et in apparatu navium* 59*s.* 2*d. per breve Regis. Et in passagio Petri de Sandiacrâ et aliorum Austrucariorum in liberacione* 2 *navium et pro hugiis ad aves* 74*s. per breve Regis.*

It would further appear, from the same Pipe-Roll, that the King was at one time intending to visit, or actually visited, England; and that a transport ship went from Southampton to meet him.—

Et item in liberacione Esnaccæ quando transfretavit in Normanniam contra Regem £7. 10*s. per breve Regis. Et in liberacione* XX *hominum qui fuerunt missi de cremento in Esnacchâ* 40*s. per breve Regis. Et in liberacione, quatuor navium quæ transfretaverunt cum Esnacchiâ* £7. 10*s. per idem breve. Et pro locandis carretis ad reportandum thesaurum de Hantoniâ ad Wintoniam duabus vicibus* 9*s. Et pro unâ carretâ locandâ ad portandas Bulgas Regis ad Winton'* 9*d.* (Southampton.)

The above charges, from their position on the Roll, would seem to have been incurred after July 15, and, from other evidence, before August.

It is very remarkable that an entry on the Northamptonshire Pipe-Roll of this very year speaks almost conclusively of a short visit to England, paid by the King within the year.—*Et in corredio Regis apud Norhanton per quatuor dies* £32. 6*s.* 5*d. per breve Regis.* And then follows, *Et in conductu thesauri missi in Hyberniam per Godefridum clericum.* And again the Sheriff of Northamptonshire (Robert fitz Sewin), accounting for the ferm of the borough of Northampton, makes this charge against the Crown, viz., *Et in soltis, per breve Regis, ipsi Vicecomiti* £72. 11*s.* 9*d. pro robbâ quam invenit Regi.* (Northampton.)

[1] Diceto, Ymag. Hist. p. 571.

1173. April to July. This is the year in which the King is said to have made one Ralph de Venneville or Varneville, his Chancellor.[1] It is further stated that the said Ralph, not liking the routine duties of the office, appointed a deputy, viz., Walter de Constanciis, to perform the same. Rouen.

It is probable that the two following Charters passed in the summer of 1173. Both are dated at Lillebone (Julia Bona);—a place which the King would easily be visiting during a normal residence at Rouen. Lillebone.

(1). To the Abbey of St. George at Bocherville. Witnesses Radulph de Wadnevill, Chancellor; Sehar de Quenci; Robert de Stutevill; and Reiner de Pavilli.[2]

(2). To the Abbey of St. Victor en Caux. Witnesses, Radulph de Wannevill, Chancellor; Master Walter de Constantiis; Seiher de Quenci; Hugh de Cressey and Reginald de Pavilley.[3]

It is evident that Richard de Luci was in the spring and summer of 1173 acting as Regent or Viceroy of England. The Pipe-Roll (of Southampton) registers £7. 10*s*. as the livery of a ship which had crossed the sea in Lent (after Feb. 21) with treasure, *by writ of* Richard de Luci.

On the outbreak of the rebellion in Normandy it would seem that the King summoned Hugh de Lacy from Ireland, and Richard de Luci and other faithful persons from England. It would also seem that the last summons was not fulfilled to the letter. Such is the apparent meaning of an entry on the Southampton Pipe-Roll,—*Et in liberacione* ix *navium quæ debuerunt transfretare cum Ricardo de Luci, et Ricardo Pictaviæ Archidiacono, et Gaufrido Cantuariensi Archidiacono et aliis Baronibus, precepto Regis* £13. 15*s*. *per breve Ricardi de Luci*.[4] Rouen.

[1] On Becket's resignation of the Chancellorship in 1162, K. Henry, it seems, suspended the use of the official title. For eleven years then, we have no authentic mention of a Chancellor, nor even of a Vice-Chancellor. The question (hitherto untouched, we believe) arises, as to who was Keeper of the Great Seal during so many years. Possibly there was more than one, but the one of whom alone we have evidence, was Geoffrey Ridel, Archdeacon of Canterbury. Our own impression is that Ridel, as he succeeded Becket in the Archdeaconry of Canterbury, succeeded him also in his functions as Chancellor, and held the office continuously till the year 1173, when he being nominated to the See of Ely, the King appointed his successor, De Varneville, with the full title of Chancellor. In one year (1166) we have Ridel clearly designated as keeper of the Seal (*supra*, p. 100, *n*. 2), and we have several Royal Charters attested by Ridel singly in the interval between 1162 and 1173. It would seem however that as on one occasion (that of 1166); so on many, Ridel, being absent from Court, was represented by Deputy. On the said occasion Walter de Insula was his Deputy.

[2] Monasticon, vii. 1067, III.

[3] Monasticon, viii. 1106, I.

[4] It is impossible to say in what particular the King's precept was not carried out. The charge of £13 and the word *liberacione* indicate that the ships made the voyage. The two Archdeacons would also go to Normandy in prospect of their elections to Bishoprics. Our idea is that the word *debuerunt* means no more than that Richard de Luci did not cross the sea. Apprehending disturbances in England, he probably thought it wise to adhere to his post of Viceroy.

On May 1, 1173. Richard, Archdeacon of Poitiers, was elected Bishop of Winchester.

And about the same time, Geoffrey, Archdeacon of Canterbury, was elected Bp of Ely, and Geoffrey Archdeacon of Lincoln, Reginald Archdeacon of Salisbury, Robert Archdeacon of Oxford, and John Dean of Chichester, were respectively elected to the Sees of Lincoln, Bath, Hereford, and Chichester.[1]

The two first-named Prelates were enthroned on May 17, though yet unconsecrated.

There are entries on the Southampton Pipe-Roll which specify this date (May 17), and point out the extra precautions which were taken in transmitting money to Normandy,—*Et in liberacione Esnaccæ, quando transfretavit cum thesauro ad Ascensionem quem Baldwinus Clericus duxit, £7. 10s. per breve Regis. Et in liberacione navis ad equos Camerariorum quæ abiit ad Oistirham 40s. Et in liberacione* xv *hominum armatorum de* xv *diebus qui fuerunt missi in navi Camerariorum de cremento ad custodiendam Esnaccham 38s. 6d. per breve Regis.*

June 3. Richard, Prior of Dover, elected Archbishop of Canterbury.[1]

June 29. Philip, Comte of Flanders, breaks into Normandy and takes the castle and town of Albemarle. Earl William of Albemarle becomes a prisoner, and surrenders his other castles.[2]

c. July 6. Prince Henry and his brothers, aided by the Comtes of Flanders and Boulogne, lay siege to Driencourt. Its constables and defenders were Doulf Bardolf and his brother Thomas. It surrendered before July 21 ,but the Comte of Boulogne died of a wound he received during the siege.

c. July 9. King Louis invests Verneuil, a town on the river Eure, S. W. of Evreux. Hugh de Lacy and Hugh de Beauchamp defend it.

July 11. Death of Amalric, King of Jerusalem.

July 22. Reginald, Earl of Cornwall, and Richard de Lucy, having summoned the army of England to the siege of Leicester, take that city and reduce it to ashes. The Pipe-Rolls of this year are full of charges for garrisoning and victualling castles throughout the kingdom. Mention also is frequently made of the "War in Leicestershire" and the "Army of Leicester;" *e.g.*—

Shropshire. *In liberacione 325 servientum de 8 diebus qui ituri erant in exercitu Legrecestriæ £9. 13s. 8d. per breve Regis. Et in liberacione eorundem et 100 præter illas quorum quatuor fuerunt cum loricis de* xv *diebus £24. 10s. per idem breve. Et in liberacione 10 Arcuariorum de 15 diebus £1. 6s. 10d. per idem breve. Et item in liberacione aliorum servientum per comitatum de Salopscira dum Vicecomes* (*Guido Extranus*) *fuit in exercitu Legecestriæ £40. 2s. 5d. per idem breve. Et in liberacione 80 servientum peditum qui missi sunt ultra mare ad Regem £4 de 6 diebus per breve Ricardi de Luci.*[3]

London and Middlesex. *Pro locandis carretis ad deferendum thesaurum ad Wintoniam et ad Legecestriam et ad Colecestriam 39s. 3d. per Odonem de Faleisâ.*[3]

The contemporary disbursements of the Fermor of Southampton relate rather to the rebellion in Normandy;—*Et in liberacione Esnacchæ quando transfretavit cum thesauro ad festum Sti Suitthuni* (July 15), *quem Andreas clericus thesauri duxit, £7. 10s. per breve Regis. Et in liberacione* xv *nautarum qui fuerunt missi de cremento in Esnacchiâ pro custodiâ thesauri £1. 17s. 6d. per breve Ricardi de Luci. Et in liberacione navis ad equos Camerariorum 30s. Et in custamento thesauri 18d. Et in liberacione navis quæ portavit thesaurum cum Roberto Malduit ad Oistreham 40s. per breve Ricardi de Luci. Et in liberacione* x *hominum qui fuerunt missi de cremento in eâdem nave ad custodiendum thesaurum 18s. 9d. per idem breve. Et item in liberacione Esnacchiæ quando transfretavit cum thesauro, quem Decanus Saresburiæ duxit, £7. 10s. per breve Regis. Et in liberacione navis ad portandos equos suos ad Oistreham 40s. per idem breve.*[3]

[1] The dates of six of these seven elections are indicated by the Pipe-Roll as having taken place after Easter (April 8), 1173. The same memorandum shows that the revenues of a See accrued to the Bishop-Elect from the commencement of the half year during which he was elected. The memorandum in question is to the effect that the officers of the Exchequer had not, up to Michaelmas, 1173, received account of the revenues of the vacant Archbishoprick of Canterbury, nor of the vacant Bishoprics of Lincoln, Winchester, Ely, Chichester, and Hereford, *de dimidio anno ante electionem*, that is for the half-year, ending at Easter, in which the said revenues were due to the Crown. (See Madox's Exchequer, p. 211).

[2] The Earl of Albemarle's surrender is said by one authority to have been collusive.

[3] Rot. Pip. 19. Hen. II. *passim.*

1173. Aug. 6. The King of England advances to Conches, purposing to relieve Verneuil.[1] Conches.

Aug. 7. The King, at Conches, awaits further reinforcements.

Aug. 8. The King advances to Bréteuil, offers Louis battle, but is persuaded to an amnesty till the morrow, and retires to Conches. Bréteuil. Conches.

Aug. 9. Verneuil surrendered to Louis, according to a previous stipulation with the besieged. Louis fires the town and retreats. K. Henry follows him with great slaughter; but returns to Verneuil before night, and gives orders for re-fortifying the place. Verneuil.

Aug. 10. The King, leaving Verneuil, takes Damvill, the Castle of Gilbert de Tylers, and then passes to Rouen.[2] The King's Generals in the above campaign were Earl William de Mandeville, William Earl of Arundel, Richard Earl of Strigoil, John Comte of Vendome, Richard de Humez, Constable (of Normandy), Richard fitz Count,[3] Richard de Vernun, Jordan Teisun, and Henry de Newburgh. Damville. Rouen. Fougeres.[2]

Aug. 20. Henry's Brabantine mercenaries defeat the Earl of Chester and Raoul de Fougeres, near Dol, in Bretagne. The King hastens thither from Rouen, by way of Tenchebray. Rouen. Tenchebray. Dol.

Aug. 26. Dol is surrendered to his arms, the Earl of Chester and Raoul de Fougeres becoming prisoners.

Sept. 8–15. The King was at Le Mans. Le Mans.

Sept. 25, 26. The Kings, Henry and Louis, come to a conference near Gisors (between Gisors and Trie). The King of England's three elder sons, and Robert Earl of Leicester, were present with Louis. The negotiation failed. Gisors.

The Pipe-Roll of Michaelmas, 1173, exhibits the Justiciars, Law Officers, and Clerks of the Crown as having been largely employed during the previous year.

An *assize* had been charged on the King's demesnes by the following persons, acting in groups of two, three, or four, viz.—(1) Siffrid, Archdeacon of Chichester; Wimer, Chaplain; Adam de Gernemue; and Robert Mantel. (2) Nicholas de Sigillo, Archdeacon of Huntingdon; Reginald de Warren, and Richard, the Treasurer. (3) Wido, Dean (of Waltham); Richard de Wilton; Hugh de Bochland, and William Rufus. (4) John Cumin, Walter Map, and Thurstin fitz Simon. (5) William Basset, John Mauduit, and John Clerk. (6) John de Dover and his colleagues.

[1] Benedictus is here the principal authority.

[2] According to Professor Stubbs (quoting R. de Monte, 913), the King's stay at Rouen was interrupted by a visit to Fougeres.

[3] Richard fitz Count, noticed so seldom except at this period of History, was a son of Robert de Caen, the great Earl of Gloucester, who had supported the cause of the Empress, his half-sister, in the reign of Stephen. Richard fitz Count was therefore brother to William, the existing Earl of Gloucester, and to Roger, Bishop of Worcester; Richard fitz Count had several sons, viz., Robert, apparently the eldest; Roger, called de Croilleio, a benefactor to the Norman Abbey of Longues; also Philip, Richard, and Henry (D'Anisy's Transcripts, ii. 91).

MICHAELMAS, 1173, TO MICHAELMAS, 1174.

Sep. 29, 1173. Robert, Earl of Leicester, lands at Walton, in Suffolk, with a body of Flemings; is received by Hugh Bigot at his Castle of Framlingham; and (Oct. 13) besieges and takes the Castle of Hagenet, defended by Randal de Broc on behalf of the Crown.

At this juncture, Richard de Luci, the Viceroy, and Humphrey de Bohun, the Constable, of England, are operating against the King of Scots, and devastating the Lothians. They hurry southwards and are reinforced near Bury St. Edmunds by the Earls of Cornwall, Gloucester, and Arundel.

Oct. 17. The armies engage at Fornham St. Genevieve. The Earl and Countess of Leicester are taken prisoners. The Earl is sent to Normandy and imprisoned at Falaise,

Hence the following, on the Southampton Pipe-Roll of the year.—*Et item in liberacione Esneccæ quando transfretavit cum Comite Legrecestriæ et aliis prisonibus* £7. 10*s*. *per breve Ricardi de Luci. Et in liberacione navis Radulfi Vituli* 50*s*. *quæ transfretavit cum eo in eodem itinere per idem breve. Et in liberacione navis Sansonis Wascel' in eodem itinere* 35*s*. *per idem breve. Et in liberacione navis Herbert filii Geldewini in eodem itinere* 40*s*. *per idem breve.*

1173. c. Nov. 11. K. Henry marches into Anjou. The Castles of *Haia* (Haye), *Pruilli* (Prulli), and *Campani* (Campenni) are surrendered to him. Anjou. Haye. Prulli. Campenni.

Nov. 30. K. Henry takes Vendome on the Loire. Vendome.

c. Dec. About this time, Richard, Bishop-elect of Winchester, and John (of Oxford) Dean of Salisbury seem to have crossed to Normandy. Hence the following entries on the Southampton Pipe-Roll.—*Et in custamento venacionis Regis missæ in Olnam* 3*s*. 6*d*. *Et pro duabus navibus locandis ad opus Ricardi Wintoniensis electi* £4 *per breve Ricardi de Luci. Et pro duabus navibus locandis in duobus passagiis Decani Saresburiæ* £4. 5*s*. *per breve Ricardi de Luci.*

Dec 25. K. Henry kept his Christmas Court at Caen. To this occasion may be referred a Royal Charter, dated at Caen, whereby the King grants to Richard de Hommet, his Constable, Stamford, and other lands in England and Normandy. Witnesses Rotrou, Archbishop of Rouen; Henry, Bishop of Baieux; Arnulph, Bp of Lisieux;[1] Froger, Bp. of Seez; Richard, elect of Winchester; John, Dean of Salisbury; William de Curci, Dapifer; Jordan Tesson; Fulk Paenel; John de Subligny; Robert Bertram; Hugh de Gornai; Richard fitz Count; Hugh de Cressy, and Robert de Brucourt.[2] Caen in Normandy.

Another Charter, dated at Caen, is in favour of the Nuns of St. Mary of Liseux, otherwise known as the Convent of *Notre Dame de St. Désir*. It is attested by Arnulf, Bishop of

[1] The appearance of the Bishop of Liseux in this testing clause may seem inconsistent with the date which we assign to the Deed, as he was a partisan of the Prince. We can only suggest that at this period his treason had not become manifest.

[2] Stapleton's Rot. Norman. ii. p. clxxxiii. There is a version, not a duplicate, of this Charter in D'Anisy's Normandy Transcripts (vol. i. p. 6). Hugh de Gundeville, is the witness instead of Hugh de Gornai, Rob. Brito instead of Robert de Brucourt, and Robert de Stutevill is added to the list.

1173. c. Dec. Liseux; Giles, Bishop of Evreux; Stephen, Bishop of Redon; Earl William de Mandeville; Richard de Humetis, Constable; William de Curci, Dapifer; Alvered de St. Martin; and Hugh de Lacy[1]. Caen.

A writ, dated at Caen, in favour of Malmesbury Abbey is attested singly by John de Solineio (Subligny).[2].

IN THE ABOVE YEAR,—Prince Richard, now sixteen years of age, was knighted by Louis VII. of France, as being his Suzerain in respect of Acquitaine and Poitou.

A.D. 1174.

c. Jan. 1, 1174. Prince Henry, and the Comtes of Blois and of Perche, attack Seez, but to no purpose.

c. Jan. 13. K. Henry agrees on a truce with Louis till the close of Easter, (March 31). Normandy.

Hugh, Bishop of Durham agrees on a like truce with William King of Scots. Roger de Mowbray fortifies the Castle of *Kinard-Ferry*, in the Isle of Axholm, against the King. The garrison of Leicester Castle chooses David Earl of Huntingdon as its chief.

Jan. 20. William Bishop of Norwich died.[3]

April 2. Richard, Archbishop-elect of Canterbury, and Reginald, Bishop-elect of Bath, after waiting long in Rome, prevail on the Pope to confirm the Archbishop's election.[4]

April 8. Archbishop Richard consecrated at Rome, or at Anagni.

April 10. Archbishop Richard receives the *Pallium*; and soon afterwards the Primacy, and then, after an interval, is appointed Legate in his own province.

c. April. William King of Scots besieges Carlisle, then in custody of Robert de Vaux. His army also ravages Northumberland.

About the same time, David, brother of the King of Scots, takes the English King's Castles of Knaresborough and Appleby, then in custody of Robert de Stuteville.

April 30. Guy, Comte of Nivernois, defeated and captured by Hugh, Duke of Burgundy. The question between them was of Guy's homage and the castles he had built.[5]

April 30. K. Henry, accompanied by Alured de Vavaci and Geoffrey Esturmi, goes out of Normandy to Le Mans. Le Mans.

c. May 4. Thence the King goes into Anjou. Anjou.

May 5. The men of Lincoln, commanded by Geoffrey the King's son, their Bishop-elect, destroy Kinard Ferry Castle.

Reginald, Bishop-elect of Bath, writes from Rome to K. Henry, with an account of his and the Archbishop's proceedings. They were purposing to leave Rome on their journey home forthwith.

1 D'Anisy's Transcripts, i. 148.

2 Malmesbury Chartulary (*Penes Remem. Reginæ*).

3 Gervase of Canterbury:—But the date of this *Obit*, given by Diceto, and adopted by Hardy in his Fasti (Vol. ii. p. 459), is January 16, 1175.

4 Richard, Prior of Dover, had been elected Archbishop by the Monks of Christ Church, Canterbury, on June 3rd, 1173. The Bishops, assembling at Westminster, at about the same time, either originated a similar election or confirmed that of the Monks. K. Henry in due course, approved the election, several or joint, but the younger King objected, on the ground that his consent was wanting. The younger King appealed to Rome; and to the *Curia Romana* there were sent Procurators of the elder King, virtually making the Pope an Umpire in the case. Hence, and very sagaciously, the Pope undertook, not merely to decide the question, but to consecrate the new Archbishop himself.

As to the revenues of the See of Canterbury, it is worthwhile observing that they accrued to the Archbishop-elect from and after Easter, 1173.

5 Gall. Script. xii. 299.

1174. May 12. K. Henry is at Poitiers. Thence he goes into Santonge, and relieves Saintes, which was attacked by Prince Richard's followers. Poitiers. Saintes.

Anskettll Mallore, Constable of Leicester Castle, defeats the King's Burgesses of Northampton.

William, King of Scots, ravages Northumberland; takes Warkworth and four other castles; lays siege to Odonel d'Umfravill's castle of Prudhou (which is relieved by the men of York); and lastly, forms the siege of William de Vesci's castle of Alnwick.[1]

May 31. On this day we have incidental notice that Richard de Humez, "Constable of the King of England," was, with his three sons, William, Enguerran, and Jordan, at Beaumont (*apud Bellam Montem*), that is, at Beaumont in Maine.[2]

June 11. K. Henry takes Ancenis (on the Loire); lays waste the country about St. Florant (Saumur); builds a castle at Ancenis, which he entrusts to Maurice de Creun. Ancenis in Anjou.

June 14. Some chosen Flandrian knights (318 in number), sent by Philip, Comte of Flanders, land at Airewell. They place themselves under Earl Hugh of Norfolk, and, on June 18, sack the city of Norwich.[3]

June 23. Reginald, Bishop-elect of Bath, is consecrated by Archbishop Richard on their return from Rome, viz., at St. John's, a town of Maurienne in Savoy.

Richard de Luci (the Chief Justice), having been employed since May 8 in the siege of Huntingdon, proposes to make over the town to Simon, Earl of Northampton, who is assisting at the siege.

c. June. The burghers of Limoges are busy building a town-wall. *Et quia seditio erat inter Regem et filios, opus accelerabant, ne quandoque, redditâ pace, Dux fieri prohiberet; quod ita postmodum contigit evenire.* Peter Abbot of St. Martial, was pressed to join in the work, and his inability to do so provoked the burghers to cut off the water-supply from the castle. Abbot Peter was ill of dropsy, and died on Sept. 10 following.

June 24. Henry is holding a Council at Bonneville sur Touques, where Richard, Bishop-elect of Winchester, sent to summon him to England, finds the Court. Bonneville sur Touques (in Normandy).

July 7. K. Henry first embarks a body of Brabantine mercenaries at Estreham (Ostrea), and then sails himself from Barfleur; taking with him his family, viz. Prince John and the Princess Joan, and his prisoners, viz. Queen Elianor, the young Queen Margaret, the Earl of Chester, the Earl and Countess of Leicester, and (as one author adds) the *wives* of the Princes Richard and Geoffrey. Barfleur.

July 8. K. Henry lands at Southampton, and consigns his pri- Southampton.

[1] The state of things in the North during this year is curiously illustrated by Robert de Stuteville's statement on the Pipe-Roll, excusing himself from accounting for the Shrievalty of Yorkshire.—

Robertus de Stutevill non reddidit hoc anno compotum de firmâ Comitatûs de Everwichsira neque de debitis Regis in eodem Comitatu quia nondum habuerat warantum Regis de expensâ quam fecerat tempore werræ in servitio Regis. The Sheriff it seems, in cases of emergency, was allowed to act on his own responsibility, and the *brevia Regis*, which should be produced at the Exchequer to justify any outlay, might be obtained *after* such outlay had been incurred.

[2] D'Anisy's Transcripts, iii. 21.

[3] This is not what another Chronicle (Gall. Script. xii. 285) describes as 'Flanders threatening to invade England.' For that episode see July 13.

1174. July 8. soners to safe custody. The Pipe-Roll of Michaelmas, 1174, has many good illustrations of these events, *e.g.*— Southampton.

SOUTHAMPTON. *Et in corredio Regis apud Hantoniam* £1. 3*s.* 4*d.* *per breve Regis.*

WINCHESTER. *Et pro equis locandis ad opus nautarum ad sequendum Regem Londoniam* 4*s.* *per breve Regis.* London.

WILTSHIRE. *Et Roberto Malduit* £10 *ad procurationem Reginæ per breve Regis.*—(So that Queen Elianor was imprisoned in Wiltshire,[1] and Robert Malduit[2] was her gaoler.)

GLOUCESTERSHIRE. *Et in procuratione Reginæ junioris et obsidum apud Divisas per Eustachium filium Stephani.* (This makes Queen Margaret, and the other State prisoners, to have been sent to Devizes Castle.)

July 9. K. Henry sets out for Canterbury.

July 12. The King does penance at Becket's tomb at Canterbury.[3] Canterbury.

July 13. The King, after concluding his penance, and hearing mass at Canterbury, sets out for London.

The same day a party of Royalists, after a forced march, captured William, King of Scots, employed in the protracted siege of Alnwick. The Royalists concerned were Robert de Stuteville, Sheriff of Yorkshire; Ranulf de Glanvill; William de Vesci; Bernard de Bailiol; Ralph de Tilli; and Odonell d'Umfravill.

The same day saw the dispersion of Prince Henry's fleet off the coast of Holland. He and Ralph de la Haie had been waiting some time at Whitsand (or Gravelines), intending to cross the sea and invade England.

[1] Geoffrey of Vigeois indicates Salisbury as the place of Queen Elianor's confinement. (*Rex*) "*conjugem propriam, matrem filiorum, apud Angliam in turre de Salisberi per plures annos inclusit.*" This writer, a native of Souterraine, and, at this time, a monk of St. Martial's Abbey at Limoges, was likely to inquire, and to learn, what had befallen his former suzeraine, the Duchess of Aquitaine.

[2] Robert Malduit was second son of William Mauduit, noticed already (p. 107 *n.*) as Chamberlain of the Treasury.

[3] The story of K. Henry's penance at Canterbury is so quaintly exaggerated by Geoffrey of Vigeois (G. S. xii. 443), that we cannot forbear giving it.—

Patre ac filio per biennium in alterutrum sævientibus, adeo Rex, multis thesauris exhaustis, nauseatus est ut Brabantionibus qui ei parebant, pro mercede spatham Regiæ coronæ in gagium mitteret. Locutus denique cum quodam Normanniæ Episcopo, a quo pro consuetudine pœnitentiam accipere solet, ab eo tale responsum Rex accepit.—

"*Si fieres humilis peregrinus Thomæ Cantuariensis, credo tibi pacem a Domino dari.*"

Qui ait illi, "*Si digneris venire mecum pergerem libenter.*" *Respondet Episcopus*—"*Ibo gaudenter.*"

Mare transmeato condictum expetit locum. Cumque devote vigilias celebraret jejunus, coram se signo a Sancto Martyre Archiepiscopo patrato exhilaratus est. Missâ finitâ, ab Ecclesiâ procedenti (*Regi*) *occurrunt nuntii, dicentes.*—

"*Jucundare, Rex Angliæ, nam de cælo tibi datur triumphus. Filius*" (*inquiunt*) "*tuus, Manzer, Regem Scotorum hostem tuum, cum multis millibus, hesternâ die captum, carceri mancipavit.*" *Exultanti animo Rex adstantibus ait.*—"*Pacem mihi redditam noveritis per meritum Archiepiscopi Thomæ cujus sedulus auxilium imploravi.*"

Vigeois did not know the distance between Alnwick and Canterbury, nor that the day of penance at the later was the day of victory at the former. The news reached the King, not at Canterbury but at London, two, perhaps three or four, days after the battle. Who may have been in Vigeois's mind when he makes the messengers attribute the success at Alnwick to the King's son "Manzer," is another question. The Editors of the Chronicle in question suggest "William Longespee" in the margin. That, afterwards renowned, son of Henry was perhaps not as yet ten years of age. There is no mention of him in any public capacity during K. Henry's lifetime. It was about this very time that the King began to live in open adultery with Rosamond Clifford, Longespee's mother. (See Antiquities of Shropshire, v. 148–150, for errors as to the age of William Longespee. See also the Preface to this work for a partial correction thereof).

1174. July 14. The King reaches London, where he is confined till the 17th by illness. News of the capture of the King of Scots reaches him while sick. The following from the Pipe-Roll is pertinent:—LONDON AND MIDDLESEX. *Et pro bulgis et alio harnesio Summariorum Regis et in aliis minutis negotiis Cameræ Curiæ 38s. 6d. per breve Regis.* London.

It must have been while he thus lay sick that the King expedited a Charter to Herbaldown Hospital, near Canterbury. The Charter is dated at Westminster, and is attested by G. Bp of London; R. Bp of Worcester; R. elect of Winchester; R. elect of Hereford; Master William de Insula; Earl William de Mandevile; William fitz Andrew (probably Audelm should be read for Andrew); and Hugh de Cressi.[1] Westminster.

July 19-21. The King goes to the siege of Huntingdon. Concerning this fact the Pipe-Rolls bear their evidence.—

LONDON AND MIDDLESEX. *Et pro uno palefrido et uno Summario ad opus Ricardi Carpentarii filii Wiching' qui missus fuit Regi ad Huntindonam, et pro apparatu equorum 55s. 3d. per breve Regis.* Huntingdon.

BUCKS AND BEDFORDSHIRE. *Et Yvoni Ingeniatori unam marcam ad locandos Carpentarios ad faciendas machinas quando Rex venit ad Huntindonam per breve Regis.*

July 21. Huntingdon surrenders to the King. The King marches thence towards Hugh Bigot's castle of Framlingham.

July 22. Louis of France, Prince Henry, and Philip, Comte of Flanders, invest Rouen. With the besiegers were Hugh (III.), Duke of Burgundy; Theobald, Comte of Blois; and Henry, the young Comte (of Champagne).

July 24. K. Henry encamps for a night at a place called Seleham, near Framlingham. Hence the Sheriff of Norfolk and Suffolk, in his next account, charges "£3. 6s. 8d. for conducting 500 carpenters to the King at *Sileham*." Seleham.

July 25. Hugh Bigot comes to the King at Seleham and surrenders[2]

[1] Monasticon, vii. 654.

[2] Hugh Bigot's surrender seems to have procured an immediate reversal of his attainder. There is a very remarkable entry on the Norfolk Pipe-Roll of Michaelmas, 1174 (20 Hen. II.), which proves, not only that, as a general rule, the Pipe accounts were balanced up to Michaelmas, but what was the practice in the case of an Earl's attainder in regard to his claim on the *tertium denarium* of his county.

In the present instance, Bartholomew de Glanvill, Wimar the chaplain, and William Bardulf, Sheriffs of Norfolk and Suffolk, enter the following disbursement on their accounts.—

ET COMITI HUGONI £16. 13s. 4d. (*sic*), 111s. 1d. (*sic*) DE IX. SEPTIMANIS POST PACEM FACTAM CUM REGE DE TERCIO DENARIO COMITATûS.

Now the *tercium denarium* of Norfolk was £33. 6s. 8d. The Sheriffs, it would seem, were about to allow Earl Hugh £16. 13s. 4d. or exactly half a year's proportion of this item of revenue; but the entry was corrected, and they only allowed him £5. 11s. 1d. for the nine weeks, which they

1174. July 25. his castles of Bungay and Framlingham.—His Flandrian soldiers are permitted to return home without any effects. The King met with an accident.—A horse belonging to Tostes de St. Omer, a Templar, kicked him on the thigh. Seleham.

July 26. The King went from Seleham. Perhaps he visited Brampton on his road westward; for the Pipe-Roll of Cambridge and Huntingdon charges,—*In corredio Regis apud Branton'* £18. 4*s*. *per breve Regis*. Brampton.

About this time Rese, Prince of South Wales, as an ally of the English King, besieges Robert Earl Ferrers' castle of Stutesberie (Tutbury); Geoffrey, Bishop-elect of Lincoln, takes Malesart (or Malesberde), a castle of Roger de Mowbray, and entrusts it to Roger, Abp of York. On the other hand, Robert, Earl Ferrers, had sacked the castle and town of Nottingham, of which Reginald de Lucy was custos. Geoffrey, elect of Lincoln, builds Topclyve Castle, and consigns it to the care of William de Stuteville.

July 31. K. Henry is at Northampton. There he receives the fealty of Hugh, Bishop of Durham, who, with intentions not quite definite, had brought over his nephew, Hugh, Comte of Bar, with 40 knights and 500 Flandrian soldiers. The Bishop surrenders the castles of Durham, Norham, and Alverton (Northallerton) to the King, and dismisses his nephew. Northampton.

Roger de Mowbray also appears at Northampton and surrenders his castle of Tresk. The Earl Ferrers also comes and surrenders Tutbury and Driffield. Anketill Malore and William de Diva, constables of the Earl of Leicester, surrender the castles of Leicester, Mount Sorrel, and Groby. The King of Scots is also brought a prisoner to Northampton. William, Earl of Gloucester, and Richard, Earl of Clare, whose loyalty had been somewhat doubtful, also come to the King at Northampton.

About this time King Henry gave his half-sister, Emma,[1] in marriage to David ap Owen, Prince of North Wales. Hence the following, on the Pipe-Roll of 1174.—

LONDON AND MIDDLESEX. *Et pro pannis et apparatu sororis Regis quam David filius Oeni duxit in uxorem* £28. 17*s*. *per breve Regis et per visum Edwardi Blundi.*

DORSET AND SOMERSET. *Et in procuratione sororis Regis quam David filius Oini duxit uxorem* £8. 7*s*. *per breve Regis et per Willielmum filium Johannis.*

considered to have elapsed since the reversal of his forfeiture. And it may be remarked further, that £5. 11*s*. 1*d*. was not the exact proportion for nine weeks, nor yet for the nine weeks and three days, which elapsed between July 25 and Sept. 29. It was less than either, and was, in fact, the proportion for two calendar months.

[1] See page 85, note 5, for a previous allusion to the King's half-sister, Emma, now probably the widow of Guy de Val-Guyon.

1174. c. July. STAFFORDSHIRE. *Et in procuratione sororis Regis quam David duxit uxorem* £12. 9*s*. 6*d*. *per breve Regis*. Northampton.

The King's stay at Northampton and journey to the coast are further illustrated by the following entries.—

NORTHAMPTONSHIRE. *In robis domini Regis quas Vicecomes liberavit in camerâ curiæ per breve Regis* £168. 7*s*. 7*d*. *numero, pro* £160. 7*s*. 3*d*. *blanc'*. *In robâ Regis quam* (*Vicecomes*) *liberavit per breve* (*Regis*) £10. 5*s*. 8*d*.

LONDON AND MIDDLESEX. *Et pro ducendo thesauro tribus vicibus semel ad Windresor', bis ad Winton'* 16*s*. 6*d*. Windsor. Winchester.

c. July. While the King was in England, Maurice de Creoun, to whom in June, he had entrusted the castle of Ancenis, was acting strenuously in command of the Army of Anjou. Under Maurice de Credonio says our authority, that army destroyed Castellum Celsum, and Sabloil, and St. Lupus, and St. Brictius, near Sabloil.[1]

Aug. 8. The King sails from Portsmouth, taking with him as prisoners the King of Scots, the Earls of Chester and Leicester, and (Gervase adds) the Earl Ferrers. Hoveden says that he took back to France his Brabantine troops and a thousand Welsh soldiers. The Pipe-Rolls add some particulars.— Portsmouth.

HEREFORDSHIRE. *In corredio Reis et aliorum Walensium qui venerunt ad Regem in expedicionem* £4. 18*s*. 11*d*.

WINCHESTER. *Et in custamento et conductu thesauri in multis itineribus ad Hantoniam et ad Portesmue et ad Porcestr' per totum annum* 41*s*. 2*d*. *per Andream clericum cameræ et Johannem de Wicha et Willielmum Picot* (*ser*)*vientes de thesauro. Et Comiti Willielmo* (*de Mandevill*) £9. 10*s*. *ad properandam transfretacionem suam cum familiâ Regis, per breve Regis.*

SOUTHAMPTON. *Et in passagio Comitis Willielmi de Mandevill et familiæ Regis ad festum Sancti Laurentii* (Aug. 10) *quando missus fuit ad Rothomagum* £60. 9*s*. 6*d*. *in liberacione* xxxvii *navium per breve Regis. Et in liberacione* xi *navium quæ transfretaverunt cum Brabantinis et Flandrensibus quos Robertus Puherus et Petrus Picot custodiebant* £20. 17*s*. *per breve Regis. Et pro duabus navibus locandis ad transfretandam Comitissam Britaniæ*[2] *et prisones Regis qui erant apud Porcestriam* £4. 7*s*. *per breve Regis et per Osbertum de Camera et Ricardum Giffard. Et in passagio Episcopi Sagiensis et Willielmi Ruffi pro unâ nave per breve Ricardi de Luci.*

[1] Chron. St. Albin. (Gall. Script. xii. 483.

[2] Constance of Bretagne, Prince Geoffry's wife.

1174. Aug. 8. The King lands at Barfleur, and proceeding coastwise towards Rouen, bestows his prisoners at Caen; (they were c. Aug. 9. afterwards removed to Falaise). On the coast, near Caen, the King meets the Archbishop of Canterbury and the Bishop of Bath, on their journey homeward from Rome. He desires them to pass on to England. Barfleur. Caen.

Aug. 10 or 11 to 15. King Henry arrives before Rouen, then besieged by Louis. His Welsh troops meet with some success in capturing a convoy of French provisions. Rouen.

Aug. 15. At this date the Southampton Pipe-Roll speaks of treasure having crossed the Channel. *Et in liberacione Esneccæ* £7. 10*s*. *quando Radulfus clericus Cameræ transfretavit cum thesauro circa Assumptionem Stæ Mariæ per breve Regis. Et in liberacione navis Roberti de Baion* 40*s*. *quæ transfretavit cum thesauro, quam Walterus de Constantiis et Willielmus Picot et Hugo filius Hervei, homines Cameræ duxerunt,* 40*s*. (*sic*.) *per breve Regis. Et pro unâ nave ad opus Austurcariorum et Falconariorum* 30*s*. *per idem breve. Et pro hugiis ad aves* 8*s*. 6*d*. *per idem breve.*

Aug. 21. King Louis decamps from Rouen by night, under cover of a truce, and retreats across the frontier.[1]

Sept. 8. K. Henry and Louis confer at Gisors. A truce agreed upon, from which Prince Richard is excluded. Gisors.

Sept. 21 or 23. K. Henry forces Prince Richard to submission in Poitou. They go to Poictiers together. Poictiers.

It is probable that the King now visited Beauvoir, a town on the coast, N.W. of Poictiers. A Charter, dated *Apud Beauvoir super Moiram,* grants to Richard de Lucy (whose services in the late rebellion had been so conspicuous), the Hundred of Ongar in Essex. Witnesses, John, Dean of Sarum; John, Archdeacon of Bath; Earl William de Mandevill; Reginald de Courtenay; William de Lanval; and Robert de Briwecourt.[2] Beauvoir sur Mer.

The great feature in the Law and Finance of the fiscal year now ended was the Tax, levied on the King's Demesnes and on the lands of the late rebels (*Assiza super dominica Regis et super terras eorum qui recesserunt*). And it is to be noticed that, in each county, the person levying the said tax was usually the Contemporary Sheriff, but that in very many instances the said Sheriff had one or more assessors.—

Thus, William fitz Ralph, Sheriff of Notts and Derbyshire, had for his assessor, Reginald de Luci.

William de Braose, Sheriff of Herefordshire, had for his assessor, Milo de Mucegros.

Ralph fitz Stephen, Sheriff of Gloucestershire, had for his assessors, Philip fitz Ernise and Alexander Pincerna.

Richard de Wilton, Sheriff of Wiltshire, was associated with Robert de Luci.

[1] *The Chronicon Rothomagense* (Gall. Script. xii. 786) puts Louis's retreat from Rouen on the 'Vigil of the Assumption of our Lady;' that is, on August 14; adding that it was effected with loss. Though our usual authorities as to date (Diceto, Hoveden, and Benedictus) are not always in agreement with each other; their more circumstantial account of Louis's retreat recommends the later date given in the text, viz. August 21.

[2] Palgrave's Brit. Commonwealth. Appx. p. xii. *n*.

Hugh de Bochland, Sheriff of Berkshire, was coupled with Leonard, a knight of Thomas Basset.

Alured de Lincoln, Sheriff of Dorset and Somerset, had for his assessor Walter de St. Quintin.

Hugh de Gundevill, Sheriff of Hampshire, had for his assessors, Hamo Morgan, Wm. Bastard, and Matthew de Escuris.

Alard Banastre, Sheriff of Oxfordshire, had for his assessor the Constable of Oxford.

Robert Mantel, Sheriff of Essex and Herts, had for his assessor, Walter de Hadfeld.

William fitz Richard, Sheriff of Bucks and Bedfordshire, had for his assessor, Richard fitz Nigel.

Randulf de Lenchis, Sheriff of Worcestershire, had as assessors, Hugh Puher and Osbert de Ahitot.

And again, Guy le Strange, Sheriff of Shropshire, having found apparently but one renegade in that loyal county, taxed the said delinquent's (Robert fitz Walkeline's) lands in a sum of fifty-one shillings and fourpence, and, so doing, acted without an assessor.

Again, Gervase de Cornhull and Reginald de Warren, neither of them being Sheriff of Surrey, mulcted the lands of the disaffected in that county; as did William Basset and John Malduit the lands of the Lincolnshire rebels. And lastly, Richard de Luci himself, returning from Scotland (*in redditu ejus a Scotiâ*), and being at York (*in civitate Eborum*), set an Assize on that city; and Reginald de Warren, Sheriff of Sussex, took due cognizance of the disaffected in that county.

It was either in this or the previous year that William Rufus, Gilbert Pipard, and Gilbert de Columbarii held Pleas in Wiltshire; and that Bertram de Verdon, William fitz Ralph and William Basset, held Pleas in Gloucestershire and Staffordshire.

MICHAELMAS, 1174, TO MICHAELMAS, 1175.

1174. Sept. 30. K. Henry, Louis, and the Princes, Henry, Richard, and Geoffrey, confer and come to terms at Mont Louis (Mons Laudatus), between Tours and Amboise.[1] Mount Louis.

By a Charter, dated *Apud Sanctum Laudinum*, the King grants freedom from toll and other customs, whether in England, Normandy, Wales, or Ireland, to his Burgesses of Dublin. Witnesses, Richard de Humets, Constable; Reginald de Courteney; Richard de Camvill; and William de Lanelleys (Lanvall, probably).[2] (St. Laud?).

Oct. 6. The Bishops of Winchester, Ely, Chichester, and Hereford, were consecrated by Archbishop Richard at Canterbury.

Oct. 8. Geoffrey, Bishop elect of Lincoln, crosses to Normandy by command of the King, who purposes to send him on to Rome to have his election confirmed.

c. Oct. 10. The Royal Family seems to have been all assembled at Falaise, where the State-prisoners then were, and where the recent agreement was embodied in a written manifesto. This document was attested by R., Abp of Rouen; Henry, Bp of Baieux; Roger (Froger) Bishop of Seez; R., Bishop Falaise.

[1] Diceto (p. 582) mentions this meeting between Tours and Amboise, but places it on 5 id. Oct. (*i.e.*, Oct. 11). Diceto has it that a peace between K. Henry and his sons was negotiated by Louis of France and the Comte of Flanders.

[2] Lyttelton, iv. Appendix (2).—The date of this charter is quite problematical; both as to time and place.

1174. c. Oct. 10. of Nantes; Stephen, Bp of Rhedon; G., Elect of Lincoln; John, Dean of Sarum; Richard de Humez, Constable; Richard de Bellomonte, Sheriff;[1] Reginald de Curtenay; Morice de Creon; William Malvoisin; W. de Humez; Geoffry de Perch; William de Curci; Fulk Saenell (read Paenell); John de Soliney (*alias* Subligny); Saher de Quinci; Richard de Canvill; W. fitz Audell', Seneschal; Alured de St. Martin, Dapifer; Gosbert de Sisseney; Robert fitz Ernise; Eudde fitz Ern'; Walter de Ypra; William Marescall; Robert de Ble; and Eimer fitz Eudon.[2] Falaise.

Oct. 13. The Bishop of Ely enthroned at Ely.

Oct. 24. Archbishop Richard visits St. Paul's as Legate. Thence he goes to Waltham, and finding Wido, the Dean, absent, suspends him. He then visits Gloucester and Winchester.

Nov. 24. The Archbishop is present at the enthronization of Reginald, Bishop of Bath.

c. Dec. 1. William, King of Scots, though imprisoned at Falaise, came to terms with K. Henry. The instrument of pacification is dated at Falaise, and attested by Richard, Bp of Avranches; John, Dean of Salisbury; Robert, Abbot of Malmesbury; Radulph, Abbot of Montisburgh; Herbert, Archdeacon of Northampton; Walter de Constanciis; Roger, the King's Chaplain; Osbert, Clerk of the Chamber; Richard, son of the King and Comte of Poitou; Geoffrey, son of the King and Comte of Bretagne; Earl William, of Essex; Hugh, Earl of Chester; Richard de Humez, Constable; the Comte of Mellent; Jordan Teison; Humphrey de Bohun, Constable; William de Curcy, Seneschal; Gilbert Malet Seneschal.[3] Falaise.

Dec. 8. The above agreement is embodied in another Charter at Valoins, which has additional witnesses, viz., William fitz Adelm, Seneschal; Alured de St. Martin, Seneschal; Reginald de Curtenai; Fulco Painell; Geoffrey de Pertico; William de Humez; Jordan de Humez; Engelram de Humez; Radulf Teisun; Roger, his brother; Robert Bertram; Richard de Vernun; William Vavasur; Robert de Mortimer; Robert fitz Bernard; Ranulph Puher; Bertram de Verdun; and Roger Bacun.[4] Valognes.

Dec. 11. William, King of Scots, obtaining his release, sails to England.

[1] Vicomte of Beaumont le Roger.
[2] Fœdera, i. p. 30.
[3] Fœdera, i. pp. 30–31. Brompton substitutes William fitz Adelm, seneschal, for Gilbert Malet, seneschal. Probably both were present.
[4] Hearne's Liber Niger, i. 40.

1174. c. Dec. About this time we may venture to date a Charter of the King to the Abbey of Bec, given at Vaudreuil (*Vallem Ruelii*), and attested by R., Abp of Rouen; Richard, Bp of Winchester; John, Dean of Salisbury; Hugh de Cressi; Secher de *Canems* (*Quinci?*); and Alured de St. Martin.[1]— Vaudreuil.

Also a Writ, dated at Vaudreuil (*apud Vallem Rodolli*), addressed to Alan de Nevile and the King's Foresters, on behalf of Hugh de Hameslape, and attested by John, Dean of Sarum, and Robert Malduit.[2]

Also a Charter, inexplicably dated, in favour of Winchcombe Abbey (Gloucestershire), attested by Giles, Bishop of Evreux; John, Dean of Sarum; and Alured de St. Martin.[3]

Also a Charter, dated at Rouen, to the Abbey of Jumieges, belongs to this period. It is attested by Rotrold, Abp of Rouen; Henry, Bp of Baieux; Egidius, Bp of Evreux; Earl William de Mandeville; Richard de Humet, Constable; Reginald de Courtenay, Robert Marmion; Richard de Camvill; Hugh de Cressi; Seiher de Quinci; Reginald de Pavilli; William Malvoisin; Richard de Vernone; Hugh de Lacy; Hugh de Longchamp; Robert de Stuteville; Alured de St. Martin; Gilbert Malet; and Gerard de Camville.[4] Rouen.

Again, a Charter dated at Chivilli,[5] in favour of William fitz Walkeline, may be noticed here. It is attested by Earl William de (Mandeville probably); Richard de Humez, Constable; Unfrey de Bohun; Reginald de Curtenay; Richard de Camvill; Robert Marmium; Hugh de Cressi; Alvered de St. Martin; Robert de Stutevill; Bertram de Verdon; Gerard de Camvill; Guido de . . . .; Martin de Hosa; and Ailward, Chamberlain.[2] Chevaillec.

Dec. 25. K. Henry spent Christmas at Argentan (in Normandy). Argentan.

At Argentan, about this time, the King confirms to the Abbey of St. Andrew-en-Gouffern the grants of William, Comte of Ponthieu, its founder. Witnesses, Henry, Bishop of Bayeux; Froger, Bishop of Seez; William de Curci, Geoffrey de Lucy, and John de Solinges.[6]

The year 1174 is given as that in which Eudo, Vicomte of Porhoet, called 'Duke of Bretagne,' returned from exile into Bretagne and began to recover his territory.[7]

[1] Neustria Pia, p. 485. This deed most certainly passed between Oct. 6, 1174, and May 9, 1175. It would suggest that the Bishop of Winchester crossed to Normandy soon after his consecration.

[2] Cartæ Antiquæ, N.

[3] Rot. Pat. 1 Hen. IV. p. 8, m. 18. Dated *Apud Clum'*, which, if read *Clivum*, meant King's-Cliff, in Northamptonshire. At that rate the Charter did not pass at this period.

[4] Monast. vii. 1088, i.

[5] Chevaillec, a hamlet near Gonville-sur-Honfleur (see Stapleton's Rot. Norm. ii. xlvi. n.)

[6] D'Anisy's Transcripts, ii. 30.

[7] Gall. Script. 560, 565.

A.D. 1175.

c. Jan. 1. The King goes into Anjou. Anjou.

Feb. 2. The King was at Le Mans, with the Princes, Henry, Richard, and Geoffrey. The two latter renew their oaths of fealty. Le Mans.

The Hampshire Pipe-Roll speaks of treasure being sent to the King at this period,—*Et in liberacione Esnacchæ ad transfretandum thesaurum quem Andreas Clericus duxit in Purificacione* £7. 10*s*. *per breve Ricardi de Luci. Et in custamento thesauri illo itinere et quodam alio* 3*s*. 3*d*.

Feb. 24. The King and Prince Henry confer with Louis at Gisors. Gisors.

Feb. 26. The King at Rouen. Rouen.

The King then goes into Anjou, Prince Henry to Rouen.[1] Anjou.

Mar. 25. The King returns to Caen, and intending shortly to cross to England, summons Prince Henry to accompany him. Caen (in Normandy).

The Prince refuses.

The following entries on the Southampton Pipe-Roll relate to this period,—*Et item in liberacione Esnacchæ quando tranfretavit in quadragesimâ contra Regem* £7. 10*s*. *per breve Regis. Et in liberacione navis Willielmi de Baion, quæ portavit thesaurum quem Walterus de Constantiis et Henricus de Aven' duxerunt ultra mare* 25*s*. *per breve Ricardi de Luci. Et eidem Henrico* 20*s*. *de liberacione suâ per idem breve. Et in custamento ducendi eundem thesaurum de Windresor' ad Sudhanton'* 18*d*. *per idem breve. Et pro locandâ unâ Sornet' ad significandum Regi rumores Angliæ unam marcam per breve Regis.*

A Royal Charter, dated at Caen, undoubtedly belongs to this period. It confirms to Montebourg Abbey the chapel of St. Maglorius, in the Isle of Sark, as given by William de Vernone. Witnesses, Geoffrey, Bishop of Ely (consecrated Oct. 6, 1174); Master Walter de Constanciis, Archdeacon of Oxford (mentioned above as crossing to Normandy); Richard de Vernone;[2] Fulk Paienell; Richard de Canvill (ob. 1176); Reginald de Curtenay; Hugh de Cressy; and William de Vernone,[3] junior.[4] Caen.

[1] Stubbs, quoting Bened. Peterb. i. 82.

[2] Son and heir of William de Vernon, senior, whose grant is confirmed.

[3] Nephew of Wm. de Vernon, senior, and younger brother of Richard de Redvers, late Earl of Devon, on failure of whose issue in 1193 this William became Earl.

[4] D'Anisy's Normandy Transcripts, ii. 182.

April 1. The King and Prince Henry meet at *Bures*,[1] and are reconciled. Perhaps we may ascribe to this period two Charters, dated *apud Burum*,[1] and attested by Earl William de Mandeville, William de St. John, Richard de Canvill, Hugh de Creissi, and Philip de Kime. By one of these Charters, the King confirms to Roger de Beningeurth the land which the father and grandfather of William de Romare had given him; by the other, the King confirms an agreement made at *Bures* between Wm. de Roumare and Robt. de Calceis.[2] Bur-le-Roi.

From other authority it appears that the following persons were present at Bur on this occasion, viz., the Archbishop of Rouen; the Bishops of Baieux, Avranches, and Rhedon; and Earl William de Mandeville.[3]

c. April 2. The King goes to Valoins; the Prince pays a visit to the Court of Louis. Valognes.

A Royal Charter, dated at Valognes, passed either now or in December previous. It is in favour of Blanchelande Abbey, and is attested by William de Curci, Dapifer; Gilbert Malet, Dapifer; Robert Marmion; Maurice de Crona (Creon); Hugh de Lacy, and Philip de Hastings.[4]

April 13. The King is at Cherbourg, keeping the festival of Easter. Prince Henry has joined him. Hence, perhaps, at Michaelmas following, the Sheriffs of London charge,—*Pro locandis carretis ad portandam carnem quater viginti Damorum missorum Regi ultra mare apud Hantoniam* 15*s. per breve Regis.* Cherbourg.

A Royal Charter, undated as to place, but which may possibly belong to this period is in favour of *Notre Dame de Voeu*, at Cherbourg. It is attested by Maurice de Creis (probly Creon); Hugh de Lacy; and Osbert de Hosa.[5]

April 22. The King and Prince Henry are at Caen. They are visited by Philip, Comte of Flanders, who, on Good Friday previous (April 11), had taken the Cross. Caen.

Prince Richard now goes into Poitou, and Prince Geoffrey into Bretagne, their object being to reduce the castles of those provinces to the same condition as before the civil war. The Southampton Pipe-Roll of Michaelmas, 1175, charges,—*In liberacione navis quam Abbas de Reddon' et nuncii Ricardi et Gaufridi filiorum Regis et Herveus Panetarius habuerunt* 25*s. per breve Regis.*

1 The place thus variously written as Bures or Bura, or Burum, is more usually Bur-le-Roi, in the Bessin, than Bures in the Pays de Caux. Bur-le-Roi was a favourite residence of Henry II. Mr. Stapleton describes it as in the parish of Noron, on the confines of the Bois-du-Vernai, and says that the Royal Chapel there is known in its ruins as St. Catherine's.

2 Cartæ Ducatûs Lancastriæ.

3 Benedictus (Stubbs), i. 82.

4 D'Anisy's Transcripts, i. 69.

5 D'Anisy's Transcripts, i. 102.

1175. c. May 1. A Royal Charter, dated *apud Barbefluctum,* confirms to Hugh fitz Osbert the grant which Henry, Bishop of Bayeux, made him. Witnesses, William de Curcy, Dapifer (ob. 1176); William de Humet; Gilbert Malet, Dapifer; Roger Bacon; Benedict de Angervill; and Hamo Pincerna.[1] Barfleur.

May 8 or 9. The King and Prince Henry embark at Barfleur, and land at Portsmouth. The young Queen came with them. The following entries on the Pipe-Roll are pertinent:— Barfleur. Portsmouth.

LONDON AND MIDDLESEX. *Pro robâ ad opus Reginæ junioris* £26. 5*s.* 2*d.* *per breve Regis, per Ricardum Ruffum et per visum Edwardi Blundi.*

HAMPSHIRE. *Et Willielmo de Sancto Mauro et Godman Armigeris Regis* i *marcam ad procurandos equos Regis apud Wintoniam quos Thesaurarius duxit secum de ultra mare per breve Regis. Et Gern' filio Stigandi* 3*s.* *ad emundandas domos Regis contra adventum Regis per breve Regis.* Winchester.

SOUTHAMPTON. *Et in liberacione Esnacchæ quando Rex filius Regis transfretavit* £7. 10*s.* *per breve Regis.*

May 18. The Council, or Synod, of Westminster, convened by the Archbishop of Canterbury, was attended by the King and Prince. The Archbishop of York, without sending any excuse, was absent from this Synod. According to Gervase all the Suffragans of Canterbury were present, except the Bishop of Worcester, whose excuse was infirmity; but Benedictus says expressly that that Bishop was present, as also the Bishop of St. David's, and the Abbots of St. Albans, St. Edmundbury, Ramsey, and Boxley. At this Synod Geoffrey, Bishop of St. Asaph, being enjoined to reside, relinquished his See. His successor (Adam) was nominated. Westminster.

We have a Charter to Gloucester Abbey, dated at London, and which certainly passed about this time. It is attested by Richard, Archbishop of Canterbury; Richard, Bp of Winchester; R. Earl of Cornwall; W. Earl of Gloucester; and Richard de Humez, Constable.[2] London.

May 28. The King and Prince Henry paid a joint visit to the shrine of Thomas à Becket. Canterbury.

It would seem that the young Queen went, either with them or alone, for the Sheriff of Surrey charges,—*In procuratione Reginæ junioris de* ii *diebus* £3. 5*s.* 2*d.* *per breve Regis;* and the Sheriff of Kent charges,—*In procuracione Reginæ junioris de* iiii *diebus quando ivit Cantuariam causâ orationis* £9. 0*s.* 8*d.*

[1] D'Anisy's Transcripts, iii. 24.

[2] Cartæ Antiquæ, Q. Q.

1175. June 1. The King and Prince hold their Court, on Whitsunday, at Reading. The King sends Roger de Hoveden,[1] his clerk, to Norwich, and to all vacant Abbeys, to summon the proper persons to attend the Court at Oxford, on June 24 following, for the purpose of the prospective elections. At this period the King commenced that wide-spread system of prosecutions, which appear on the Pipe-Rolls of the next year as "*Misericordia Regis pro forestâ;*" that is, he prosecuted the abettors of the late rebellion, throughout England, for the overt act of trespass on the Royal Forests. Reading.

c. June 15. In this month the King was probably resident a good deal at Woodstock. The Sheriffs of London charge,—*Pro* xxx *modiis vini missi Regi ad Wudestoch', et in custamento ducendi* £16. 19*s*. 4*d*. *per breve Regis*. Also a Charter to Cerne Abbey must have passed in this month. It is dated at Woodstock, and attested by Richard, Bp of Winchester; William, Earl of Arundel; and Reynald, Earl of Cornwall.[2] Woodstock.

June 24. The King, Prince Henry, and Archbishop Richard, were at Oxford, touching the business of the elections. William, Earl of Gloucester, surrenders Bristol Castle to the custody of the Crown. A Charter, in favour of the Canons of Malton, is dated at Oxford, and attested by William fitz Adelm, Dapifer; John Dean, of Sarum; Master Walter de Custanciis; William de Mandevile; and William Mareschal.[3] Oxford.

June 29. A Royal Charter, tested singly by Geoffry, Bishop of Ely, at Oxford, defines the Forest-rights of the Shropshire Priory of Bromfield.[4]

It appears, too, that during this year a Royal Exchequer was established at Oxford, for the Sheriff of the county charges,—*Pro scannis scaccarii apud Oxinford* 12*d*.

The King held a Council at Gloucester relative to the affairs of Wales. Rese ap Griffin was there. William, Earl of Gloucester, and William de Braose were enjoined to defend the King's subjects against the Welsh. It was in this year that William de Braose, junior, slaughtered a host of unarmed Welshmen in Abergavenny Castle, in revenge for the murder of his uncle, Henry de Hereford. Gloucester.

[1] This was Roger de Hoveden, the Historian, to whose authorship, however, has been attributed much more than he ever wrote.

[2] Cartæ Antiquæ, R. and Q.

[3] Great Coucher of the Duchy of Lancaster.

[4] Monasticon, iv. 155.

1175. June 29. The King's visit to Gloucester is illustrated by the Pipe-Roll of 1175:—OXFORDSHIRE. *Et pro locandis equis ad portandum thesaurum ad Glocestriam* 16*d*. Gloucester.

LONDON AND MIDDLESEX. *Et pro locando uno summario ad portandum thesaurum a London' ad Gloceestriam post Regem* 3*s*. 1*d*.

Reginald, Earl of Cornwall, died at Chertsey on July 1st,[1] and was buried at Reading. Hence at Michaelmas, 1175, the Sheriff of Shropshire accounts 47 shillings "*de firma de Fordâ postquam rediit in manum Regis post mortem Comitis Reginaldi.*"

July 1-8. The King and Prince Henry were now at Woodstock, where a Council was held concerning ecclesiastical vacancies. The Archbishop of Canterbury and the Bishops of Winchester, Bath, Salisbury, Worcester, Ely, Chichester, Rochester, Exeter, and Durham were present. Woodstock.

The following Royal Charters, dated at Woodstock, may be referred to this period.—

(1) Confirmation to Alexander de Barentin (the King's *serviens*) and Margaret his wife, of the lands of William, son of Durand le Naine, cousin of the said Margaret. Witnesses, R. Abp of Canterbury; R. Bp of Winchester; G. Bp of Ely; Herbert, Archdeacon of Northampton; Earl William de Mandevill; Richard de Luci; Richard de Humet, Constable; Seer de Quinci; Reginald de Curtenai; William de Lanvaloi; Thomas Basset; Hugh de Creissi; Robert de Stutevill; and Richard fitz Walkeline.—[2]

(2) Confirmation of Simon Earl of Huntingdon's Charter to Roger fitz Reinfrid. Witnesses, Richard, Bp of Winchester; Geoffrey, Bp of Ely; John Dean of Sarum; Richard de Luci; Maurice de Creon; John de Suligny; Reginald de Curtenai; Reginald de Pavilli; Robert de Estutevill; and Girard de Canvill.[3]

(3) Charter to Newenham Priory (Bedfordshire). Witnesses, Geoffrey and Nicholas, Chaplains of the King; John fitz Luce, Canon of Rouen; Wm. fitz Audelm, Dapifer; Hugh de Creissi; Robert Marmion; Randulf de Gla vile; Gerard de Canvill; Ralph fitz Stephen, Chamberlain; and Eustace his brother.[4]

[1] This is Diceto's date. Benedictus says that the Earl died "shortly before Christmas." The Pipe-Roll decides the question in Diceto's favour; and the point is worth noting, for the two authorities, Diceto and Benedictus, are often in like discrepancy.

[2] Formulare Anglicanum, p. 295.

[3] Fœdera, vol. i. p. 46.

[4] Monasticon, vi. p. 374. Num. iii. b.

1175. c. July 7. Perhaps the King visited Shrewsbury about this time. Shrewsbury. Being there, he expedited a Charter to Roger Mussun (*servienti suo*). It is attested by Osbert, Clerk of the Chamber; Richard de Humet, Constable; William de Curci, Dapifer; Richard Giffard; Wido de St. Walery; Randulf Poer; Hugh Pantulf; Eustace fitz Stephen, Chamberlain; Robert Mauduit, Chamberlain; Thomas fitz Odo; and Robert Monk, son of Henry de Damfront.[1]

July 9. The election of Geoffrey fitz Roy to the vacant See of Lincoln is confirmed by the Archbishop of Canterbury, and by the Bishops of London and Worcester, at Woodstock.

July 9. The King was now at Lichfield, *en route* for Nottingham. Lichfield. Gilbert, a Royal forester, had been killed.

While the King was in Staffordshire, there were Pleas Staffordshire. held in that county, which are expressed to have been held by William fitz Ralph, Bertram de Verdon, and William Basset *in curiâ Regis*. These Pleas are merely fines, viz. one, *pro benevolentiâ Regis*; another, that a suitor *non mittatur in placitum de tenurâ suâ nisi coram Rege*.

July 18. Geoffrey, Bishop-elect of Lincoln, comes into England.
Aug. 1. He is received in procession at Lincoln; but the King will not have him consecrated, and eventually sends him to Tours to study.

Aug. 1. The King is at Nottingham, impleading persons for forest-trespass. Nottingham. A Royal Charter to Welbeck Abbey, dated at Nottingham, is very pertinent to this occasion. It is attested by R. Abp of York; H. Bp of Durham; G. elect of Lincoln; William fitz Audelm, Dapifer; Reginald de Curtenai; Henry de Laci; William de Lanvalei; Thomas Basset; Hugh de Cressi; Randulf de Glanvill; Walter de Dunstanvill; William Basset; and William fitz Radulf.[2]

Aug. 10. The King and Prince Henry are at York. William, King York. of Scots, his brother David, and the Bishops, Abbots, and Nobles of Scotland, attend the Court, and do homage to both father and son.

Roger, Abp of York, and Hugh, Bp of Durham, are specially mentioned as attending the Court at York.

To this period may be assigned a Royal Charter in favour of St. Clement's Nunnery at York.

The said Charter is dated at York, and is attested by G. Bp of Ely; H. Bp of Durham; John, Dean of Sarum; Earl

[1] Antiquities of Shropshire, viii. 153–4.
[2] Monasticon, vii. 875. Num. xiv.

1175. Aug. 10. William de Mandeville; Richard de Luci; Richard de Humet, Constable; William fitz (Adelm), Dapifer; Ranulph de Glanvill; Reginald de Curtene; William de Lanvall; Thomas Basset; Hugh de Creissi; and Thomas Bardulf.[1] York.

While at York the King held Pleas of the Forest.[2]

Perhaps also, while the King was in the North, he expedited a Charter to St. Bartholomew's Nunnery at Newcastle-upon-Tyne; attested by William de Mandevill (Earl of Essex); Reginald de Curtnay; William de Stutevill; Thomas Bardulf; Robert de Stutevill; and Richard Gosfard (probably Giffard).[3]

c. Aug. 12. In passing southwards from York, perhaps the King halted at Stamford. There he ratified an agreement which the Monks of Rivaulx had made with the Monks of Malton. Witnesses, William fitz Adelm, Dapifer; John, Dean of Sarum; and William de Ous.[4] Stamford.

In his journey further south from York, the King was probably at Northampton. There the three Justiciars who had attended him in his special *curiâ* in Staffordshire and at York, negotiated a fine by Robert de Nevill, viz. of £30, *pro rehabendâ saisinâ de Uppetona quæ fuit Radulfi de Walter-villâ*.[5] Northampton.

Also a Royal Charter bears date at Northampton, and is granted at request of Richard Peche, and Matildis his wife. Witnesses, Geoffry, the King's son; Hugh de Lacy; Hugh de Cressi; William de Lanvall; Thomas Basset; Robert fitz Bernard; (Gerard ?) de Canvill.[6]

From York the King and Prince went to London. London.

About this time Prince Richard is engaged in the siege of Chatillon in Guienne, which he takes after a siege of nearly two months, commencing with Midsummer (June 24).[7]

[1] Monasticon, iv. 325. Num. v.

[2] The Forest-Pleas held by the King at York are not entered on the Pipe-Roll of Michaelmas immediately following, but on that of Michaelmas, 1176. But the Pipe-Roll of 1175, after duly recounting the results of the ordinary Assizes, held by William de Lanvall and Thomas Basset (who appear to have visited York while the King was there), contains the following (in regard to a different kind of judicature than that at which the two Justiciars presided), and which probably took place in a Court of which the King in person was president.—

Placita et convenciones per Willielmum fil. Radulphi, Bertram de Verdon, et Willielmum Basset in curiâ Regis. These *Placita* are apparently nothing more than fines with the Crown: one is to compound for a charge of false imprisonment; another is for a composition of £100 chargeable on the county of York, *pro recordacione duelli;* another is an absolute penalty on the Canons of York, *quia non venerunt ad summonicionem Regis ad Eboracum* (because they had not attended to the King's summons to York); and another is where a suitor pays 5 merks to transfer his cause into the *curiâ Regis* (*ut habeat placitum suum in curiâ Regis*).

[3] Monasticon, iv. 488. Num. ii.

[4] Great Coucher of the Duchy of Lancaster.

[5] Rot. Pipe, 31 Hen. II.

[6] D'Anisy's Transcripts, i. 106.

[7] Castelloneum supra Agiens (Bened. i. 101).

WITHIN THE FISCAL YEAR, ending Michaelmas, 1175, there were two famous *Itinera* of Justices.

The *Iter* of William de Lanvall and Thomas Basset extended to Kent, Surrey, Berkshire, Gloucestershire, Warwickshire, Leicestershire, Staffordshire, and Shropshire; and to other counties west and south-west of the same.

The *Iter* of Ranulph de Glanvill and Hugh de Cressi extended to Essex, Herefordshire, Bucks, Oxfordshire, Northamptonshire, Lincolnshire, Notts, Derbyshire, Yorkshire, and Cumberland; and to other counties east and north-east of the same.

MICHAELMAS, 1175, TO MICHAELMAS, 1176.

1175. c. Sept. 25. Envoys from the King of Connaught find the King at Windsor. Windsor

Oct. 6. On this day the King held a great Council at Windsor,[1] and came to an agreement with the Envoys of Roderick, King of Connaught. The agreement was attested by Richard, Bp of Winchester; Geoffrey, Bp of Ely; Laurence, Archbishop of Dublin; Geoffrey, Nicholas, and Roger, King's Chaplains; William, Earl of Essex; Richard de Lucy; Geoffrey de Perche; and Reginald de Curteney.[2]

Augustine was appointed Bishop of Waterford, and sent to Ireland.[3]

With reference to the King's visit to Windsor is a charge by the Sheriffs of London on the Pipe-Roll of 1175.—*Pro* vi *tonellis musti et* iiii *tonellis rubei vini missi Regi ad Windresoras* £10. 10*s. per breve Regis. Et item pro ducendâ vassellâ et thesauro post Regem per Andream clericum* 12*s.*

Perhaps the King went from Windsor to London.[3] London.

Oct. 13. Adam, Bishop of St. Asaph, was consecrated at Westminster by the Archbishop of Canterbury.

c. Oct. About this time the King visited Marlborough. Hence on the Pipe-Roll of 1175 the Sheriff of Hampshire charges *pro* iiii *doliis vini optimi missi Regi apud Merleberg' et pro carriagio eorum* 77*s. per breve Regis.* Wine was also sent from Southampton to Marlborough in the year ending Michaelmas, 1176. Marlborough.

We have also a Royal Charter, dated at Marlborough, to the Monks of Christ Church, Canterbury. It is attested by R. Bp of Winchester; G. Bp of Ely; J. Bp of Salisbury; Henry, Bp of Baieux; R. Bp of Bath; A. Bp of St. Asaph;

[1] Benedictus, i. 101.

[2] Fœdera, vol. i. p. 31.

[3] It would seem probable that after the appointment of Augustine, and before that Prelate left for Ireland, the King paid a visit to London. A Royal Charter, dated at Westminster, and in favour of Clerkenwell Nunnery, is attested by Richard, Bp of Winchester; G. Bishop of Ely; A. Bishop of Waterford; and Humphrey de Bohun, Constable (Monast. iv. 85).

1175. c. Oct. John, Dean of Sarum; Richard de Luci; Earl Richard of Striguil; William fitz Aldelm, Dapifer; Gilbert Malet, Dapifer; Randulf de Glanvill; and Philip de Hastings.[1] Marlborough.

c. Oct. Also, about this time the King visited Ludgershall (in Wiltshire). A Charter, dated '*apud Lutegareshole*,' is in favour of the Norman Abbey of Mont St. Michel. It is attested by Josceline, Bishop of Sarum; Henry, Bishop of Baieux; Reginald, Bishop of Bath (enthroned Nov. 24, 1174); Earl Hugh Bigot; Earl William of Arundel (ob. Oct. 12, 1176); Richard de Humet, Constable; William de Humet, his son; William de Trussebot; William de *Stuton* (read Stutevill); William fitz John; John de Malherbe; and Ralph fitz Stephen.[2] Ludgershall.

About this time too, if not in this very month of October, the King visited Feckenham[3] in Worcestershire. The following Charters are dated at that place:— Feckenham.

(1) Charter giving to Ranulph, Abbot of Buildwas, the Cell of St. Mary's, Dublin, in subjection. Witnesses, Richard de Luci; Earl Richard of Strigoil; William fitz Andelm, Dapifer; Hugh de Laci; Hugh de Longchamp; Wm. de Stuteville; Hugh de Creissi; and William fitz Radulf.[4]

(2). Charter confirming William Earl of Gloucester's grants to the Priory of St. James at Bristol. Witnesses, Richard, Bishop of Winchester; G. Bp of Ely; Richard de Lucy; Reginald de Courtenay; Hugh de Creissy; William de Lanvall; Thomas Basset; Geoffrey de Perche; Robert de Stuteville; William de Stuteville; Michael Belet; William fitz Radulph; William Basset; and Ralph fitz Stephen, Chamberlain.[5]

(3). Charter to Haughmond Abbey, attested by William fitz Andelm, Dapifer; Hugh de Laci; Hugh de Longchamp; William fitz Radulph; and William Basset.[6]

Oct. 27. The Cardinal Huguzon lands in England as Legate.

Oct. 30. Archbishop Richard deposes William de Waterville, Abbot of Peterborough.

Oct. 31. The King and Prince Henry meet Huguzon at Winchester. Winchester.

The King persuaded the Cardinal to allow the prosecution

[1] Cartæ Antiquæ, F. T.

[2] D'Anisy's Normandy Transcripts, ii. 282.

[3] Some of the King's wine was sent from Southampton to Feckenham during the current year (Rot. Pip. 22 Hen. II. Tit. Hanton).

[4] Monast. v. 363. ii.

[5] Monast. IV. 335. Num. I (corrected.)

[6] Haughmond Chartulary. Tit. Longmunde.

1175. c. Oct. 31. of clerks, accused of forest-trespass, in Courts temporal. Winchester. He also endeavoured to obtain the Papal consent to his divorce from Queen Elianor.

The said Queen Elianor was a prisoner at the time.—

In the Pipe-Roll of Michaelmas, 1175, the Sheriff of Wiltshire charges,—*In corredio Reginæ* £128. 13*s*. 6*d*. *per breve Regis per testimonium Roberti Malduit.*

Again at Michaelmas, 1176, the same Sheriff charges,—*In corredio Reginæ* £77 *per breve Regis et per testimonium Roberti Malduit.* Also the Custos of Winchester charges,—*Et Roberto Malduit* 56*s*. *ad acquietandum corredium Reginæ apud Wintoniam per breve Regis.*

A Royal Charter, dated at Winchester, is of safe conduct for the Abbots and Monks of St. Michel de Monte, in Normandy. It is attested by Richard, Bishop of Winchester; Henry, Bishop of Bayeux; Richard de Humet, Constable; William fitz Audeline, Dapifer; William de Lanvall.[1]

While at Winchester, and possibly on this occasion, the King expedited a Charter to Whitby Abbey. The witnesses are Richard, Abp of Canterbury; Richard de Luci; Joceline de Luvain; and Hugh de Cressi.[2]

c. Nov. From Winchester the King went to Windsor. Windsor.

Nov. 26. The King being at Eynsham appoints John of Oxford, Dean of Salisbury, to be Bishop of Norwich. Eynsham.

c. Nov. 30. The King was again at Winchester. He there ratifies a grant made to William Turpin, his Chamberlain, by Roger, Abbot of Abingdon. Witnesses, G. (it should be J.), Bishop elect of Norwich; Adam, Bishop of St. Asaph; Richard de Luci; William fitz Aldelm, Dapifer; and Radulph fitz Stephen, Chamberlain.[3] Winchester.

Dec. 14. John of Oxford consecrated Bp of Norwich by Abp Richard, at Lambeth.

Dec. 25. The King and his son Henry keep Christmas at Windsor. Windsor.

Huguzon is now at York with Archbishop Roger.

Dec. 31. The King still probably at Windsor.

In the above year died Roger Earl of Clare.[4]

Also Henry, Archbishop of Rheims, brother of Louis VII. He was succeeded in the Primacy of France by William, heretofore Archbishop of Sens, the friend and champion of Becket.

[1] D'Anisy's Transcripts, ii. 283.

[2] Cart. Antiq. DD.

[3] Historia de Abingdon, ii. 237.

[4] This date of the death of Roger, Earl of Clare, seems to be given in some Norman MS., or else to be quoted from Robert de Monte by the Compilers of Neustria Pia (p. 478). Usually the year 1178 is given as that of the Earl's death.

A.D. 1176.

Jan. 1. We suppose the King to have been still at Windsor. Windsor.

c. Jan. About this time, probably, the King visited Shropshire and Staffordshire, for the purpose of holding Forest-Pleas. Being at Bridgnorth (Bruges), he confirms the Will of Bridgnorth. Hugh de Periers, bequeathing the reversion of the Manor of Ditton to Wenlock Priory, after the death of Aelicia de Caineto, widow of the said Hugh. The King's Charter is attested by Richard de Luci; William fitz Andelm, Dapifer; Reginald de Curtenai; William de Lanval'; Robert Marmion; Secker de Quinci; Thomas Basset; Wido le Strange; William fitz Ralph; and Randal Broc.[1]

At the same time the King visited Shrewsbury, and, being Shrewsbury. there, expedited four several Charters to Haughmond Abbey. These are, one or other, or all of them, attested by R. Bishop of Chester; A. Bishop of St. Asaph; Richard de Luci; William fitz Adelm, Dapifer; Hugh de Laci; Robert Marmion; William Malvoisin; Bertram de Verdon; Saher de Quinci; Walter de Dunstanvill; Gerard de Camvill; William fitz Ralph; and Wido le Strange.[2]

A Charter by which the King gives Weston to Guy le Strange (he was now Sheriff of Shropshire), certainly passed within a year after Michaelmas, 1175. It may well have passed during his visit to Shropshire. It is attested by Richard de Lucy, Bertram de Verdon, and William fitz Alan[3] (who had livery of his inheritance in June, 1175).

Jan. 26. The King and Prince Henry held a great Council at Northampton. Northampton, whereat several statutes were passed.

William, King of Scots, attended this Council, as did several Scottish Bishops, and the Archbishops of Canterbury and York. A quarrel about the subjection of the Scottish Bishops (whether to York or Canterbury) was the result, and also an appeal to the Pope.

At this Council of Northampton, the King divided his kingdom into six circuits, and appointed three Justiciars to go on each circuit.

[1] Monasticon, v. p. 73. Note 3. From the Shropshire Pipe-Roll of 1176, it would appear that Hugh de Pirariis died about Christmas, 1175. (See Eyton's Antiquities of Shropshire, vol. iii. 330).

[2] Haughmond Chartulary at Sundorne Castle.

[3] Cartæ Antiquæ, Roll E.E. Num. 13.

1176. c. Jan. The names and circuits of the Justices appointed at Northampton were as follows.[1] Northampton.

1. Hugh de Cressi, Walter fitz Robert, and Robert Mantel, to Norf. Suff. Cambr. Huntingd. Bedf. Bucks. Essex, and Herts.[2]

2. Hugh de Gundevill, William fitz Radulph, and William Basset, to Linc. Notts. Derb. Staff. Warw. Northants, and Leicestershire,

3. Robert fitz Bernard, Richard Giffard, and Roger fitz Reinfrid, to Kent, Surrey, Hants, Sussex, Oxon. and Berks.

4. William fitz Stephen, Bertram de Verdun, and Turstan fitz Simon, to Heref. Glouc. Shropsh. and Worcestershire.

5. Ralph fitz Stephen, William Rufus, and Gilbert Pipard, to Wilts. Dorsetsh. Somerset. Devon, and Cornwall.

6. Robert de Vaux, Ralph de Glanvile, and Robert Pikenot, to Yorksh. Lancash. Westmoreland, Cumberland, and Northumberland.[3]

c. Feb. It is probable that the King was about this time at Geddington (Northamptonshire), and at Woodstock. The following entries on the Pipe-Roll of Michaelmas, 1176, show those and other places of his sojourn during the year. Geddington. Woodstock.

SOUTHAMPTON. *Pro 100 modiis vini quod Alexander de Barentin elegit ad opus Regis £35 per breve Regis. Et in custamento et cariagio ducendi vinum quod Alexander de Barentin ei (scil. Vicecomiti), dixit ex parte Regis, quod missum fuit usque ad Fekeam (Feckenham), et ad Nottingham et Gattintune et Wudestoke et Merleberge et Titegrave et Lutegareshall et Clarendon £11. 16s. 4d. per breve Regis.* (Feckenham) (Nottingham) (Geddington) (Marlborough) (Titgrave) (Ludgershall) (Clarendon)

NORTHAMPTON. *Pro ducendo thesauro ad Wudestoc' et Gaitenton et London' 7s. per Waleramnum et Odonem de Falesia.*

[1] It is worth noting that of the Eighteen Justices of this list, exactly one half were Sheriffs of Counties, viz.—

Robert Mantel of Essex and Herts; Hugh de Gundevill of Northants and Southants; William fitz Ralph of Notts and Derby; Robert fitz Bernard of Kent; William fitz Stephen of Gloucestershire; Bertram de Verdon of Warwicksh. and Leicestersh.; William Rufus of Devonshire; Robert de Vaux of Cumberland; and Ranulf de Glanvill of Yorkshire and Westmoreland.

[2] The Justices of the Circuit (1) also visited Rutland, according to the Pipe-Roll 22 Henry II.

London and Middlesex are omitted both on the above list and on the Pipe-Roll.

[3] The Pipe-Roll of 1176, fully bears out the accuracy of this list. Before Michaelmas in that year, every county had been visited by the Justices respectively nominated to that duty.

But it is curious that Gilbert Pipard (who certainly went his appointed circuit in the West of England) is found on July 10th in the *Curia Regis* at Lincoln, where a fine was levied before Geoffrey Bp of Ely, Nicholas Archdeacon of Coventry, Gilbert Pipard, then Justices of the King and other Barons and Lieges (Vespas E. xx. fo. 42). The solution is that the fine in question is misdated. It probably passed in 1179. (*Vide infra.*)

1176. Feb. Other evidence of the King's being at Geddington, about this time, is a Charter to Tinmouth Priory (Northumberland), dated *apud Gaititon,* and attested by R. Bishop of Winchester; G. Bp. of Ely; Richard de Luci, William fitz Adelm, Dapifer; Alured de St. Martin; Robert Marmion; Hugh de Cressy; Radulph de Glanvill; and Robert de Stuteville.[1] Geddington.

Another Charter, dated "*apud Gentinton,*" is to Pipewell Abbey, and is attested by William fitz Aldelm, Dapifer; Hugh de Cressi; Hugh de Gundeville; William de Stutevill; Robert de Stutevill; Ralph fitz Stephen, Chamberlain; William Basset; and William fitz Ralph.[2]

Feb. 24. Cardinal Huguzon, dissatisfied with his reception at Westminster Abbey, suspends the Abbot Walter, from the use of the mitre.

March 14. A great Council, convened by Huguzon, assembles at London. The Archbishops' quarrel about precedence ends in a riot; Geoffry, Bishop of Ely, being accused of taking a leading part therein, is for a season in disgrace with the King. At this time Prince Henry appoints Geoffrey, Provost of Beverley and Archdeacon of York, to be his Chancellor. London.

A Royal Charter to Rivaulx Abbey, bears date at Westminster, and passed, perhaps, at this time. It is attested by Roger, Archbishop of York; Richard, Bp. of Winchester; Roger, Bp of Worcester; Hugh, Bp. of Durham; Robert, Earl of Leicester; Hameline Earl Warren; Earl Simon; Richard de Luci; Reginald de Curtenai; and Wm fitz Aldelm, Dapifer.[3] Westminster.

Prince Henry and his wife now go to Portsmouth, and are waiting at Porchester for a fair wind to cross the channel. The Pipe-Rolls make the following allusions to the young Queen's movements and Court since Michaelmas, 1175.—

NORTHAMPTON. *In corredio Reginæ Junioris* 29*s.* 6*d. per breve Regis.*

WINCHESTER. *Et pro* iiij *ulnis et dimidiâ Escarlatæ et pro unâ penâ variâ et pelliceâ et unâ Sabelinâ et* xxxij *ulnis lineæ telæ ad opus filiæ Regis Franciæ contra Pascha* £4. 5*s.* 6*d. per breve Regis. Et pro* iii *ulnis de Biso ad opus cujusdam Pucri sui* 3*s.* 6*d. per idem breve.*

c. March 30. The King comes to Winchester and holds a Council there for the purpose of adjusting the Archbishops' quarrel. Winchester.

[1] Monasticon, iii. p. 314. Num. xi. Glanvill was Sheriff of Yorkshire at this period.

[2] Cartæ Antiquæ, OO. The third, seventh, and eighth witnesses were the three justices appointed to visit Northamptonshire in this year.

[3] Great Coucher of the Duchy of Lancaster. The Earl of Leicester's attestation would incline us to date this deed as later than January, 1177, when he was restored to his Honours, but there are other and stronger objections to so late a date. If the Earl was at Court in March, 1176, it was probably as a prisoner rather than a peer.

1176. c. March 31. Geoffrey, Bp of Ely, is present, and dispels the accusation which lay against him. The King sends for Prince Henry to join him. The latter complies, leaving his wife at Porchester.[1] Winchester.

April 2. The Princes Richard and Geoffrey land at Southampton.

April 3. They join their father at Winchester.

April 4. The King and his three sons keep Easter-day at Winchester. Winchester.

It was perhaps on this occasion that a Royal Charter, dated at Winchester, passed. Thereby the King confirms an agreement made between William de Roumare and Burgeise, and Emma, sisters of William Bruere. Witnesses, R. Bp of Winchester; G. Bp of Ely; Earl William de Mandeville; Earl Alberic; Roger de Stuteville; and Hugh de Creissi.[2] Also a Charter, giving to the Burgesses of Preston (Lancashire) the same franchises as were enjoyed by the men of Newcastle-under-Lyme, is dated at Winchester, and attested by Geoffrey Bishop of Ely, John Bp of Norwich, Earl William de Mandevill, Ranulf de Glanvill; Hugh de Creissi; Ralph fitz Stephen; Bertram de Verdon; and Hugh de Laci.[3]

Another Winchester Charter which we more confidently assign to this occasion is a confirmation by K. Henry of a grant made by Conan Comte of Bretagne to the Abbey of Mont St. Michel. The witnesses are, Richard Archbishop of Canterbury, Geoffry Bishop of Ely, John Bishop of Norwich; Reginald Bishop of Bath; Bartholomew Bishop of Exeter; Geoffry fitz Roy, Comte of Bretagne; Richard de Luci; Humphrey de Bohun, Constable; William fitz Adeline, Dapifer; William de St. John; Ranulf de Glanvill; and William fitz Radulf.[4]

The Hampshire Pipe-Roll of this year records a payment of 100 merks to Ralph fitz Stephen in the *Camera Regis*, and another payment of 40 merks, *in camerâ Regis, per breve Regis*. Also the Winchester Pipe-Roll charges,—*In corredio Regis ad Pascha pro* xii *multonibus* 12*s. per breve Regis*.

[1] So says Benedictus (i. 114). But it is probable that the young Queen joined the Court at Winchester before Easter-day. In the Pipe-Roll of the year the Custos of Winchester charges for attire *ad opus filiæ Regis Franciæ contra Pascham*.

[2] Duchy of Lancaster muniments.

[3] Great Coucher of the Duchy of Lancaster.

[4] D'Anisy's Transcripts, ii. 286.

On April 4, 1176, Cardinal Huguzon is said to have been at Canterbury, (it was Easter Sunday).

April 5. Richard Earl of Strigoil, the conqueror of Ireland, died. The King appointed William fitz Adelm to succeed the Earl officially.

April 19. Prince Henry joins his wife at Porchester, and embarks for Normandy.

April 20. They land at Barfleur and proceed to the Court of Louis.

At this time also, Prince Richard crossed to Normandy. Hence the following entries on the Pipe-Roll of the year.—

SOUTHAMPTON. *Et in liberacione Esneccæ quando Rex Junior transfretavit £7. 10s. per breve Regis. Et in liberacione quatuor navium quæ transfretaverunt cum eo scilicet navis Radulfi Vituli et navis Hugonis Palmer et navis Samsonis Wascel' et navis Berengerii de Hanton £7. 15s. per breve Regis. Et item in passagio Esneccæ quando Ricardus filius Regis transfretavit £7. 10s. per breve Regis. Et in liberacione quatuor navium quæ transfretaverunt cum eo £6 per breve Regis. Et item in liberacione unius navis ad portandum thesaurum Regi juniori quod Adam de Yrebuef duxit 40s. per breve Regis.*

May 8. David Fitz Gerald, Bishop of St. David's, died.

1176. c. May 20. About this time ambassadors from William, King of Sicily, came to England to ask the hand of the Princess Joan for their Master.[1] The Archbishop of Rouen came with them out of Normandy. The Pipe-Rolls refer to this event as follows.— (London.)

HIGHAM (NORTHANTS). *Et Magistro Waltero de Constantiis Archidiacono de Oxineforde* viii *marcas ad procurandos nuntios Regis Siciliæ, per breve Regis.*

CORNWALL. *Et servientibus Episcopi Wintoniæ quater-viginti marcas ad corredia nuntiorum Regis Siciliæ, per breve Regis.*

WINCHESTER. *Et servientibus Episcopi Wintoniæ £6.7s. 11d. ad procurandos nuntios Regis Siciliæ per breve Regis.*

Et Magistro Waltero de Constanciis Archidiacono de Oxenford ad procurandos nuntios Regis Siciliæ, &c.

May 25. The King holds a Council at Westminster, and gives a favourable answer to the Sicilian Ambassadors. Cardinal Huguzon is present. The King appoints four Ambassadors to Sicily, viz., John, Bishop of Norwich; Paris, Archdeacon of Rochester; Baldwin Buelot (or Beluot); and Richard de Camvill. Westminster.

Whilst thus at Westminster, the King expedites a Charter, confirming to Alexander de Barentin, his butler, all the property which Alexander had acquired from various sources.[2] Witnesses, Richard, Bp of Winchester; Geoffrey, Bp of Ely; John, Bp of Norwich; Herbert, Archdeacon of

[1] The ambassadors were Elias, elect of Troja; Arnulf, Bishop of Capaccio; and Florius de Camerotâ (Stubbs's note on Benedict, i. 115).

[2] Formulare Anglicanum, p. 47.

1176. c. May. Canterbury; Earl William de Mandevill; William fitz Andelm, Dapifer; Gilbert Malet, Dapifer; Reginald de Curtenai; Richard de Canvill; Robert Marmion; William de Lanvalei; William Malvoisin; Thomas Basset; Geoffrey de Perche; Gerard de Canvill; Radulf fitz Stephen, Chamberlain; and Eustace, his brother. Westminster.

A Charter to Ranulf de Glanvill, dated at Westminster, may well have passed at the same time. It is attested by Richard de Luci, Hugh de Cressi, Robert de Stutevill, Roger de Stutevill, and William de Stutevill.[1]

Again, a Royal Charter, dated at Westminster, confirms, at request of Maurice, son of Geoffry de Tiretei, that which the said Maurice had granted to the Church of St. John the Baptist at Wodeham (Woodham-Ferrers, Essex). Witnesses, Gilbert, Bp of London; Richard, the Treasurer; Richard de Luci; Reginald de Curtenai; William de Lanval; Thomas Basset; William de Humet; Roger fitz Reinfrid; and Robert Mantel.[2]

Another Charter, also dated at Westminster, is in favour of Earl William de Mandeville, and is attested by Geoffrey, Bishop of Ely; Richard de Luci, and Ranulf de Glanvill.[3] Two Royal Charters to Clerkenwell Nunnery are undated as to place, but probably passed at London, or Westminster, and at this time. One is attested by R. Bp of Winton; G. Bp of Ely; Richard de Luci; Earl William de Mandevill; Gilbert Malet, Dapifer; Hugh de Cressi; William de Lanvall; and Hugh de Beauchamp.[4] The other confirms (*inter alia*) grants of William, Earl Mandeville, and of his father, Geoffrey. It is attested by G. Bishop of London; R. Bp of Winchester; G. Bp. of Ely; William, Earl of Gloucester; Richard de Luci; Reginald de Curtenai and Alured.[5]

Another Royal Charter, to the Knights Hospitallers of Clerkenwell, is dated *Apud Westminster ad Scaccarium*, and is attested by R. Bp of Winchester; G. Bp of Ely; and Richard de Luci.[6]

Two Charters, without date, may well have passed at Westminster, and at this period. Both are in favour of Whitby Abbey (Yorkshire). Both are attested by Walter

[1] Monasticon, vii. 880. Num. iii.
[2] Cart. Antiq. G G. (See also Monast. v. 625, and vi. 446).
[3] Cartæ Antiquæ, OO.
[4, 5] Monasticon, iv. 84. Numm. xxii. xxiij.
[6] Cartæ Antiquæ, CC.

1176. c. May. de Constantiis, Archdeacon of Oxford. The second witness (Westminster.) of one is William, Earl de Mandeville; of the other, William de Humez.[1]

c. May 31. After the Council of Westminster, but before his Ambassadors left England, it is evident that the King visited Winchester, where the Princess Joan was residing. He (Winchester.) there expedited two Charters to the Abbey of St. Alban's, which have the attestations of Rotroc, Archbishop of Rouen; Richard, Bp of Winchester; Richard, Bp of Coventry; Richard, Bp of *Naumur* (probably Nantes); Wm. fitz Aldelm, Dapifer; Richard de Camvill; Gilbert Malet, Dapifer; Alured de St. Martin; William de Albini;[2] Richard de Aufai[3] (elsewhere Alfai); and Girarde de Camvill.[3]

The King's Ambassadors, of whom Richard de Camvill and Baldwin Buelot never lived to return, now set out for Sicily.[4] They reached Panormus about August 5.

About this time Prince Richard wins a battle at Buteville (Botville in Saintonge) and meets with other successes.

c. June. About this time the King paid a visit to Clarendon. The (Clarendon.) Pipe-Roll of the year has the following entries, probably pertinent to the summer quarter.—

DEVONSHIRE. *Et in camerâ Curiæ Radulfo filio Stephani,* XXX *marcas per breve Regis.*

CORNWALL. *Et in camerâ Regis* 154 *marcas per breve Regis.*

HAMPSHIRE. *Et pro vino quod Stephanus de Turonis misit Domino Regi ponendo in cellario apud Hantoniam et ducendo apud Clarendon' et Winton' et London'* 67*s.* 2*d. per breve Regis et per visum Magistri Walteri de Insulâ et Galfridi Monachi junioris.*

[1] Monast. i. 413, xiii. & 415, xx. It was now (according to Benedictus, i. 116) that the King sent Richard, Archbishop of Canterbury, and Geoffry, Bishop of Ely, as Ambassadors to Flanders about the crusade. But the Pipe-Rolls show that those Ambassadors went many months later. The embassy, which came and left in May, 1176, is described with greater probable accuracy in the text beneath (see page 205, *infra*).

[2] Probably the son and apparent heir of that William de Albini, Earl of Arundel, who died in October, 1176 (*Vide infra*, page 208).

[3] Monasticon, ii. 228, xiv. xv. Richard de Aufai or Alfai appears as Richard de "Ansei" in a nearly contemporary, but undated deed, wherein he follows William fitz Adelim, and precedes William de Stuteville as witness of a Royal Charter to Kingswood (Wiltshire). (*Vide* Monast. v. 427).

[4] Their outset is thus marked on the Southampton Pipe-Roll of Michaelmas, 1176. *In passagio Archiepiscopi Burdigaliæ et Episcoporum Norwicensis et Nannetensis et Capuacensis et Paris* (sic) *Archidiaconi Roffensis et Ricardi de Canvill, et Baldwini Buelot et Clericorum Domini Legati* 105*s. per breve Regis.* Of these, the Bishop of Capuacia was the returning ambassador of Sicily; the Archbishop of Bourdeaux and the Bishop of Nantes had probably been in England on some other Embassy; the Legatine Clerks, who contemporaneously left England, were of course those of Cardinal Huguzon, who probably needed their attendance no longer, or sent them with despatches for Rome.

1176. June. There was also in this year wine sent from Winchester to Clarendon. Clarendon.

Another proof of the King being at Clarendon about this time is his Charter to Stamford Nunnery (Lincolnsh.) dated at Clarendon, and attested by R. Archbishop of Rouen; Jordan, Dean of Sarum; Roger, Chaplain; Master Osbert de Camera; Roger le Bigod; Hugh de Cressei; Roger de Stutevill; and Roger (Qy. Reginald?) de Pavilli.[1]

c. May. Conjecturally at this time the arrival of ambassadors from the Court of Flanders and their return home, accompanied by ambassadors from K. Henry, are indicated by the following charge in the Dover Pipe-Roll[2] of Michaelmas, 1176.—*Et in passagio Advocati de Bettonâ*[3] *et Castellani de Curtrai*[4] *et Walteri de Constanciis Archidiaconi de Oxenford et Ranulfi de Glanvill* £7. 10*s*. *per breve Regis.*

c. June 20. The feast of the Nativity of John Baptist (June 24) being near, the Cardinal Huguzon leaves England.

c. July 1. Prince Henry joins his brother Richard, campaigning in Poitou. At Poictiers Henry punishes with ignominy his Vice-Chancellor, Adam de Chirchedune, who had betrayed his affairs to the elder King.

c. July 15. About this time Earl William de Mandeville and other nobles went on some continental embassy. At Michaelmas the Fermor of Dover charges,—*In minutis passagiis Comitis Willielmi et aliorum Baronum qui transfretaverunt cum eo per preceptum Regis* £6. 16*s*. *per breve Regis.*

c. July 15. The Cardinal Vivian, appointed Legate to Scotland and Ireland, lands in England.

July 22. Vivian, reaching Northampton, is stopped by the Bishops of Winchester and Ely, the King being enraged at his landing in England without license of the Crown. He agrees to certain stipulations of the King, and then is allowed to proceed northwards.

Aug. 15. This is the date given for another Council at Winchester, whereat the subjects of discussion were the recent quarrel of the Archbishops and the Princess Joan's marriage. Winchester.

Probably it was now that Peter de Lee, Prior of Wenlock, was elected Bishop of St. David's by the Canons of that Church, and in the King's chamber at Winchester.[6]

August 23. This is the date of a letter written by the King of Sicily to K. Henry. It is probable that the Bp of Norwich left Panormus therewith and sailed to Saint Gilles (at the mouth of the Rhone), there to await the arrival of the Princess Joan.

About this time Prince Richard is successful in subduing the rebels of Angoulême.

[1] Monasticon, iv. 261. Num. v.—We know of no other visit to England, made by Rotrou de Newburgh, Abp of Rouen, except this in connection with the Sicilian marriage. The Newburghs were akin to the royal family of Sicily (*supra*, p. 106).

Jordan, Dean of Sarum, succeeded John of Oxford in that preferment.

[2] The entry precedes that relating to the departure of Huguzon in June. It is very singular that Benedictus (i. 133, 136) says that embassies, constituted precisely as the above, arrived at and left the Council of Northampton in January, 1177. We may conclude that there were two exchanges of negotiation between England and Flanders at an interval of some months; and perhaps on the same subject (*de quo vide infra*, p. 210). Our idea is that Benedictus has transposed the two.

[3] "Robert V. of Bethune, Advocate of Arras" (says Professor Stubbs).

[4] "Roger, Castellan of Courtrai at this time" (says the same authority).

[5] Benedictus (Stubbs), i. 117.

Hence, on the Pipe-Roll of Michaelmas, 1176, the Warden of Dover charges,—*Et in passagio Hugonis Legati*, 70*s*. *per breve Regis.*

"The Cardinal left on July 3rd," says another authority.

[6] Anglia Sacra, ii. 536.

1176. Aug. 27. On this day (according to Matthew Paris) the King crossed to Normandy, but this is probably a mistake. (Normandy ?)

It was the same day on which, according to Diceto, the Princess Joan left England for Sicily; but that is also a mistake, for it is certain that the Bishop of Ely, who went with her, was in England two days later August 29), and then came to an agreement with the Order of Templars.[1]

c. Sept. 8. This is the date given by Gervase and Bromton for the departure of the Princess, her outfit and suite having been provided by the care of Richard, Bp of Winchester. The Pipe-Rolls illustrate the event as follows.—

WINCHESTER. *Et pro xl ulnis de Canevaz tinguendis ad Cameram Regis et aliis minutis apparatibus quando filia Regis ivit in Siciliam 42s. per breve Regis.*

SOUTHAMPTON. *Item in liberacione esneccæ quando filia Regis transfretavit itura in Siciliam* £7. 10s. *per breve Regis. Et in liberacione* vii *navium quæ cum eâ transfretaverunt* £10. 13*s. per breve Regis.*

The Princess Joan's escort consisted, in the first instance, of Richard, Abp of Canterbury; Rotroc, Abp of Rouen; Geoffrey, Bp of Ely; Earl Hameline, of Warren (her uncle); Giles, Bp of Evreux; Henry, Bp of Baieux; Hugh de Beauchamp, Osbert de Camera, and Geoffrey de la Charre. The Princes, Henry and Richard, were enjoined to insure her safe conduct through Normandy and Poitou.

Sept. 21. The King, still at Winchester, grants a pardon to certain state-prisoners who had been sent over by his sons from Angoulême. Winchester.

Sept. 28. The King holds a Court at Windsor. William, Earl of Gloucester, attends, and makes Prince John his heir. Windsor.

At the same time, in consequence of the death of William de Courci, Seneschal, or Chief Justice of Normandy, the King sends Richard, Bishop of Winchester, to discharge that office. Hence, on the Pipe-Roll of 1176, we have the Fermor of Southampton charging,—*In passagio*[2] *Episcopi Wintoniæ et Simonis de Turnebu et Adam de Ykebuef et eorum qui cum Episcopo transfretaverunt* £6. 18*d.*

At this time the King seizes upon Richard de Lucy's Castle of Angra (Ongar, Essex), and on other castles throughout England, some of which are destroyed.

AN ENTRY on the Pipe-Roll of Michaelmas, 1176, relates to QUEEN ELIANOR, and probably indicates, her imprisonment at Winchester.—

The Fermor of that city charges,—*Et Roberto Mauduit 56s. ad acquietanda corredia Reginæ apud Wintoniam.*

---

[1] New Monasticon, volume i. page 485.

[2] A MATTER WORTH NOTING in the records of the year now ended is the number of EMBASSIES OR MISSIONS which (beside the important ones already mentioned and dated) the King sent over-sea. The Fermor of Southampton charges the Crown at Michaelmas, 1176, for the following vessels chartered from that Port.—A ship for the use of Hugh de Cressi, Peter fitz Wido, and Alured de St. Martin. Two ships for the use of Geoffry Monk and Radulf de Hispania. One ship for Jordan de Humez. One ship for Peter de Lardario, Ralph Frasier, and other King's messengers. One ship for the wife of John de Solignei. One ship for Richard de Humet (the Constable of Normandy). One ship for Wido de Lanvall. One for William de Solariis. One ship for Robert de Briucurt. One ship for Robert Marmion.—Besides what are termed *minuta passagia,* that is unimportant freights, and which cost £4. 13*s.* in the whole.

THE PIPE-ROLL of the year, ending Michaelmas, 1176, is full of matter, CURIAL, FISCAL, AND JUDICIAL.

It was the year in which the King in person traversed the kingdom, holding everywhere a Forest-Court, and amercing all those who in the recent disturbances had trespassed on his forests. We may safely conclude that every county under which the said Roll gives a list, entitled *Misericordia Regis pro Forestâ*, was so visited by the King within the previous fifteen, if not the previous twelve months.

Of the said counties there are four (viz., Staffordshire, Nottinghamshire, Yorkshire, and Northamptonshire), which it is supposable that the King may have visited in this relation previous to Michaelmas, 1175, though the penalties inflicted at such visitation are not recorded till Michaelmas, 1176.

Again, in the year ending Michaelmas, 1176, we can trace the King's course through several counties on evidence parallel with that of the Pipe-Rolls. These counties are Berkshire, Wiltshire, Worcestershire, Hampshire, Oxfordshire, and Shropshire. We may safely add to the list other counties, the King's presence in which is only evidenced by his *Misericordia pro Forestâ* recorded on the Pipe-Roll. The latter counties are those of Essex, Herts, Bucks, Bedford, Cambridge, Huntingdon, Rutland, Derby, Warwick, Leicester, Lincoln, Hereford, Gloucester, Somerset, Dorset, Devon, and Surrey; while the amercements recorded under Kent and Sussex were not due to a visitation of the King, but had been transferred from other counties.

Again, in this year (1176), under Wiltshire, there are entries entitled, *Nova Placita et Novæ Convenciones in Curiâ Regis*. This indicates that, sometime during the year, the King presided over a *Curia* in Wiltshire, distinct from any Forest-Court, and distinct from any such Court as was held by Itinerant Justices.

And as to the CIRCUITS OF THE JUSTICES, it appears that the Justices nominated at Northampton in January, had discharged their respective *Itinera* nearly according to the programme already set forth.[1] The lists of their amercements, combined with those inflicted by the King for his forest, swell the Pipe-Roll of 1176 to unusual dimensions.

Quitting now the subject of the administration of the law, by the King or his agents, we observe that the Pipe-Roll of this year (1176) furnishes us with materials for estimating the extent of another source of Royal Revenue, and with a list of persons, not necessarily Sheriffs, who were entrusted with the ferm, custody, or wardenry, of boroughs, or of vacant ecclesiastical fiefs, or of what were more generally termed, THE KING'S DEMESNES AND ESCHEATS. In the said year the following ferms or escheats were accounted of at the Exchequer, and by the following Trustees; viz.—

Dover, by Robert fitz Bernard; Mienes, by Richard de Humez; Boseham, by Geoffrey de Boseham; Windsor, by Richard de Luci; Tickhill, by Robert Pikenot; Lincoln City, by Warner fitz Turstin;

[1] The exceptions are (1) that Rutlandshire was visited as in the second, or Lincolnshire, Circuit; (2) that Surrey was not included in the third circuit, but was visited abnormally by Robert Mantel and William fitz Radulf, who belonged to, and discharged their duties on, the first and second circuits respectively; (3) that Lancashire, Westmoreland, and Cumberland do not appear to have been visited at all; and (4) that the visitation of Essex and Hertfordshire seems to have taken place after Michaelmas, so as not to have been enrolled till the following year (or 23 Hen. II.).

Gloucester Borough, by Osmund Provost; Oxford, by Bartholomew de Glanvill; Winchester City, by Hugh de Gundevill: Southampton, by Robert de St. Laurence; the Mines of Carlisle, by William fitz Grenbald; the Honor of William de Curci, by Wm. Puher and Hugo Pincerna; the lands of Earl Richard, in Devonshire, by William fitz Stephen; the ferm of Wicumb, in the Honor of Wallingford, by Thomas Basset; the Honor of William Peverel, by William fitz Ralph; the Honer of Earl Conan, by Ranulf de Glanvill; the Honor of Eye, by Geoffry, Bishop of Ely; the Abbey of Thorney, by Rob de Jakesley.

MICHAELMAS, 1176, TO MICHAELMAS, 1177.

1176. Sep. 30. The King may be supposed to have been still at Windsor. Windsor.

c. Oct. 9. The King visits Feckenham (Worcestershire). William, King of Scots, meets him there, bringing Gilbert fitz Fergus, who had slain his brother Uctred, King William's relation (*cognatum*). Feckenham.

Perhaps King Henry was also at Kinver (Staffordshire) about this time. A very late entry on the Winchester Pipe-Roll of 1176 is a charge of 22*s.* *in custamento ducendi Willielmum de Berewich a Wintoniâ ad Kenefaram.*[1] Kinver.

Oct. 12. William de Albini, Earl of Arundel, dies at Waverley, and is buried at Wymundham on the 19th.

Oct. 17. The Church at Cirencester is consecrated by Bartholomew, Bishop of Exeter, the King attending. Cirencester.

Nov. 7. Peter, Bishop of St. David's, having made due profession to the Church of Canterbury, is consecrated there. The Archbishop being absent, the Bishop of London (as Dean of Canterbury)[2] officiates as his Vicar. Walter, Bp of Rochester, and Roger, Bishop of Worcester, attend.

Nov. 9. The Princess Joan leaves St. Gilles for Sicily. The Abp of Canterbury, and the Bps of Ely and Norwich, with some others of her suit, set out for England. The Bishops of Evreux and Baieux, Hugh de Beauchamp, Osbert de Camera, and Geoffrey de la Charre continue their attendance.

Nov. 12. The King and his Court are at Westminster. Various foreign Ambassadors are in attendance, viz. from Constantinople, from Castile, Navarre, and Saxony, from the Emperor of Germany, the Archbishop of Rheims, and the Comte of Flanders. The Pipe-Roll of 1177 contains some illustration of this: *e.g.* Westminster.

BOSEHAM. *Pro unâ navi ad passagium nuntiorum Regis Navarræ 40s. per breve Regis. Et in passagio nuntiorum Regis Castellæ 50s. per breve Regis.*

[1] The Bishop of London was *ex-officio* Dean of Canterbury, a matter not noticed by Hardy in his *Fasti*. It was this condition of things that brought Archbishop Becket, when in exile, into such constant collision with his Dean, viz., Foliot, Bishop of London.

[2] If the King visited Kinver, as supposed, then this is perhaps another instance of the Pipe-Roll of a given fiscal year containing a Post-Michaelmas entry. (We have noticed this elsewhere in the present work, and may refer also to Antiquities of Shropshire, ix. p. 42; xi. 160 *n.*).

SURREY. *Et Galfrido de Haia xx marcas ad adquietanda vadia nuntiorum Imperatoris Constantinopolitani per breve Regis.*

DOVER. *Et in procuracione Nunciorum Imperatoris Constantinopolitani* 5s. 5d. *per breve Regis.*

c. Nov. 25. The Archbishop of Canterbury and Bishop of Ely reached England, before Advent (Nov. 28), says Benedictus.[1]

Dec. 24. The Cardinal Vivian, having discharged his legatine duties in Scotland, embarked at Witern (in Galloway), for the Isle of Man.

Dec. 24. The King is at Nottingham. John, Bishop of Norwich, reaches the Court on this day, returning from St. Gilles. Nottingham.

Dec. 25. The King and his two younger sons, Princes Geoffrey and John, keep Christmas at Nottingham.

Young Henry and his Queen are at Argentan.
Prince Richard is at Bourdeaux.

A Royal Charter to Lenton Priory, in Nottinghamshire, bears date at Nottingham, and has a testing-clause of very remarkable relevance to this occasion. It is attested by *John Bishop* of Norwich; G. son of the King;[2] Randulf de Glanvill; Hugh de Creissi; Geoffrey de Perche; Robert de Stuteville; William fitz Ralph; and Ralph fitz Stephen, Chamberlain.[3]

Some writers give the above year as that in which K. Henry gave Ireland to his son John, and married his daughter, Elianor, to the King of Castile.

A.D. 1177.

1177. Jan. 1. The King probably at Nottingham. Nottingham.

Jan. 6. The Cardinal Vivian leaves the Isle of Man for Ireland. After landing, he meets John de Courci at the head of an army going to besiege Dun. William fitz Adelm (now in office as Viceroy of Ireland) had prohibited De Courci's proceeding.

In this month an Assize, or Trial, wherein William, Dean of Bayeux, was a party, was taken at Caen, before Richard, Bishop of Winchester, Simon de Turnebu, Robert Marmion, and William de Glanvill, (evidently acting as Justiciars of the King). Their assessors appear to have been Henry, Bp of Bayeux Arnulf, Bp of Liseux; Richard, Bp of Coutances; Stephen, Abbot of St. Severe; Richard de Humet, Jordan Taisson, Fulk Paganell, Wm. de Ferrars, Wm. de Solers, Roger d'Arry, Hamo Pincerna, Ran. de Grandwal, Jordan de Landa, Simon de Tenchebray, and Robert de Agnellis.[4]

c. Jan. 15. The King holds a great Council at Northampton. Robert, Earl of Leicester, and Hugh, Earl of Chester, are restored in blood and honours. William de Albini, son and heir of Northampton.

[1] John Bromton says that these Prelates came later, that is after December 24, and the arrival of John, Bishop of Norwich.

[2] Geoffrey, Bishop-Elect of Lincoln.

[3] Cartæ Antiquæ, T.

[4] D'Anisy's Transcripts, i. p. 50. The Assize is said to have been taken in January, 1176; but the year 1177 must be understood, the new year in this instance having been taken to commence on March 25, or else at Easter.

1177. c. Jan. 15. the late Earl of Arundel, is created Earl of Sussex.[1] Guy, Dean of the Church of Waltham, resigns that dignity, and the King appoints Walter de Gaunt, first Abbot of the new foundation of Waltham Abbey. The Comte of Flanders sent an embassy to this Council, touching the marriage of his nieces, the daughters of Matthew, late Comte of Boulogne, and touching a certain agreement with regard to the Crusade which the Abp of Canterbury and Bp of Ely (who we know had come home from Saint Gilles) had made with him.[2] Northampton.

In connection, perhaps with the King's visit to Northamptonshire, is the following charge by the Fermor of Peterborough Abbey, on the Pipe-Roll of 1177,—*Et Radulfo filio Stephani in camerâ Curiæ* £40 *per breve Regis. Et in corredio Johannis filii Regis* £4. 6*s.* 8*d. per breve Regis. Et pro* ij *palefridis ad opus ejusdem Johannis* 52*s. per breve Regis.*

It was doubtless at this Council of Northampton that the following Charters, there dated, passed.—

(1) Charter confirming to Thomas, son of Robert fitz Noel, the several grants of Richard, Bp of Coventry; Laurence, Prior of Coventry; Anselm, Abbot of St. Edmundbury; and Robert de Stafford. Witnesses, G. Bp of London; G. Bp of Ely; John, Bp. of Norwich; Hugh, Chaplain; Earl William de Mandevil; Hugh, Earl of Chester; Richard, Earl of Clare; William de Aubini;[3] Randulf de Glanvill; Bertram de Verdon; Geoffrey de Feu (?); Wido le Strange; and William fitz Ralph.[4]

(2) Charter to the Order of Lepers of St. Lazarus of Jerusalem. Witnesses, Geoffrey, the King's son; William, Earl of Albemarle; Walter fitz Robert, Hugh de Creissi, William de Lanval, Thomas Basset, Roger de Stuteville, William de Stutevill, and Gerard de Camvill.[5]

[1] The Honour, and, presumptively, the Earldom of Arundel, were never allowed to this Earl in Henry II.'s lifetime. The Earl is usually entitled as 'of Sussex,' or as 'of Chichester.'

[2] The Earl of Flanders' Ambassadors were the Advocate of Bethune and the Castellan of Courtrai. So says Benedictus (Stubbs, i. 133).—

The King's answer to the Earl was despatched by hand of Walter, Archdeacon of Oxford, Keeper of the Seal (Sigilliferi), and Ranulf de Glanvill. So says Benedictus (Stubbs, i. 136); but Benedictus has confused this embassy with that of May, 1176. The Pipe-Roll of Michaelmas, 1177, clearly proves that the persons who responded to this Flandrian Embassy were those whom Benedictus has represented as responding to the former one. The entry on the Pipe Roll is as follows. Doura. *Et in passagio Ricardi Archiepiscopi, et G. Elyensis Episcopi et Comitis Willielmi de Mandevill ad Comitem Flandriæ* £14. 4*s. per breve Regis.*

And, *vice versâ*, the Ambassadors described by Benedictus as coming and returning in January, 1177, came and returned in or about May, 1176 (*supra*, p. 205).

[3] Probably the Earl of Sussex, but without his dignity yet recognised.

[4] Dodsworth's MSS. vol. 130, fo. 119 b.

[5] Cartæ Antiquæ, K K. (corrected) and C.

1177. Jan. 20. The King is at Windsor, and sends Richard, Abp of Canterbury; Geoffrey, Bp of Ely; and Gilbert, Bp of London, as Commissioners to Waltham Abbey. He also sends Bartholomew, Bishop of Exeter, and Roger, Bp of Worcester, to Amesbury, whence the Convent of Nuns was to be expelled. Windsor.

Feb. 2. The King is at Marlborough. There he issues a summons to all the Prelates of the realm to meet him in Council at London, on March 13 following. Marlborough.

Feb. 13. The Princess Joan was married, and was crowned Queen of Sicily at Panormus. Giles, Bp of Evreux; Henry, Bp of Baieux,[1] Hugh de Beauchamp, Osbert de Camera, and Geoffrey de la Charre waited in Sicily to witness the ceremony. They then returned home, and reached England before Ascension-day (June 2).

Feb. 22. The King is at Winchester. He issues a summons to the army of Normandy to muster on the *octaves of the close of Easter* (*i. e.* May 8). Winchester.

c. March 1. The King being at Windsor, and Hugh Bigot, Earl of Norfolk, having died in Palestine, Roger Bigot, his son, comes to Court concerning some dispute which he had with his step-mother, the late Earl's widow.[2] Windsor.

March 9. The King is at Windsor. The Ambassadors of Sanctius, King of Navarre, and Alfonso, King of Castile, reach the Court.

March 13. The King holds a great Council at London, and there makes arbitration of the various matters which were in dispute between the aforesaid Spanish potentates. The King's award was dated at Westminster, and attested by Richard, Abp of Canterbury; Hugh, Bp of Durham; Geoffrey, Bp of Ely; Roger, Bp of Worcester; Bartholomew, Bp of Exeter; Gilbert, Bp of London; Walter, Bp of Rochester; Reginald, Bp of Bath; John, Bp of Norwich; John, Bp of Chichester; Robert, Bp of Hereford; the Bp of St. David's (Peter); Adam, Bp of St. Asaph; the Bishop of Bangor;[3] Christian, Bp of Whitherne (*Candidæ Casæ*); Geoffrey fitz Roy, Comte London. Westminster.

[1] There must be a mistake about the Bishop of Bayeux. Either he was not in the *Curiâ* at Bayeux in January, 1177, or he was not in Sicily on Feb. 13, 1177. The first negative is the most supposable.

[2] Benedictus (Stubbs), i. 143, 144.—where it is said that Earl Hugh Bigot died in 1177, *ante caput jejunii* (before March 9). But the Earl died in Palestine, according to other authority. If so, and the news reached Windsor before March 9, the Earl must have died in 1176. The allusion of Benedictus to the dispute between Roger Bigot and his step-mother is but a glance at a very extraordinary genealogical problem, which, however, is beyond the scope of our present undertaking.

[3] It should be the *Bishop-elect* of Bangor. His name was Guy.

Roger, Abp of York, excused his attendance on the plea of infirmity. The Bishops of Chester and Salisbury were unable to attend. Richard, Bp of Winchester was, we know, in Normandy.

1177. March 13. of Bretagne; Wm. Earl of Albemarle; Robert, Earl of Leicester; Wm. de Mandevill, Earl of Essex; William, Earl of Gloucester; *William de Arundel*, Earl of Sussex; the Earls of Chester and Ferrers; Richard de Luci; William de Vesci; Odonell d'Umfravill; Robert de Vaux; Roger de Mowbray; Robert de Stutevill; Philip de Kime; and Roger Bigot.[1] Westminster.

While the Court was in London, a brother of the Earl De Ferrers was murdered in his lodgings by certain citizens.

It was now, probably, that the King, by a Charter dated at Westminster, confirmed an agreement, between G. Bp of Ely, and Richard de Hastings, Master of the English Knights-Templars. Witnesses, G. Bp of London; Richard, the (King's) Treasurer; Geoffrey fitz Roy, Comte of Bretagne; Richard de Luci; William de Vesci; Hugh de Gundevill; Hugh de Cressi; Bertram de Verdon; and Ralph fitz Stephen.[2]

c. March 20. The King was at Marlborough. Thence he sends Ambassadors to Spain, viz. John Comyn, Bertram de Verdon, and Robert of Shrewsbury. On the Pipe-Roll of 1177, the Sheriff of Wiltshire charges,—*In camerâ Curiæ* xl *marcas per breve Regis*. It appears also that treasure was despatched to Clarendon during the year. Marlborough. (Clarendon).

A Charter to Kenilworth Priory, dated at Marlborough, is attested by Bartholomew, Bp of Exeter; Geoffry, the King's son; Geoffry de Perche; Richard de Vernon; and Bertram de Verdon.[3] Marlborough.

April 17. The King keeps Palm Sunday at Reading. He hears that the Comte of Flanders is at Witsand, intending to cross, and visit the shrine of St. Thomas at Canterbury. Reading.

It was perhaps on this occasion that the King expedited a Charter to the Abbey of Mellifont. It is dated at Reading, and attested by Ralph, Treasurer of (the Church of) St. Hilaire at Poitiers; Earl William de Mandevill; Earl Hameline of Warren; Gilbert Malet, Dapifer; Hugh de Laci; William Malvoisin; Reginald de Pavilli; Gerard de Camvill; Ralph fitz Stephen, Chamberlain; and Eustace his brother.[4]

April 20. Philip, Comte of Flanders, lands at Dover, and proceeds to Canterbury.

[1] The last eight witnesses are styled of baronial rank (*de Baronibus Angliæ*). It is singular that five of the eight should be North-country men.

[2] Monasticon, i. 485. Num. xxv.

[3] Cartæ Antiquæ, U. U.

[4] Cartæ Antiquæ, P.

1177. April 21. The King, the Comte of Flanders, and William, Earl Mandeville, are at Canterbury, the Comte and Earl with a joint intention of going on a Crusade. The King offers a Charter (dated at Marlborough)[1] on the tomb of Becket. Canterbury.

April 21, Thursday. (In the evening of *Cœna Domini.*) Battle of Malamort, near a place called Baufort between Brives and Malamort (in the Limousin), wherein Gerald, Bishop of Limoges; Isembert, Abbot of St. Martial (Limoges); Ademar V., Vicomte of Limoges; Archambald, Vicomte of Comborn; Oliver de Turribus, and Eschivard de Chapanes, defeat and slay 2000 *Brabansons*[2] (Brabantines, serving probably against K. Henry's cause).

April 22. The King is at Dover keeping Good-Friday. Dover.

April 23, 24. The King goes to Wick,[3] and so passes Easter Day (April 24) in the diocese of Canterbury. The Archbishop attends the Court, and celebrates mass. Wick (Wye ?)

c. April 26. The King goes to London. London

May 1. The King is at St. Edmundbury on Sunday in the close of Easter. St. Edmundbury

May 2. The King is at Ely. Roger, Abp of York; Reginald, Bp of Bath; John, Bp of Norwich; and Adam, Bishop of St. Asaph, meet him, and confer on the state of the realm. Ely.

c. May 4. The King, at Gayton, receives the homage of certain Welshmen. Gayton (*i.e.* Geddington).

About this time William de Mandevile, Earl of Essex, Henry de Lacy,[4] Robert Pirdu (or Pirou), a Templar, and other English, join the Comte of Flanders in a Crusade.

c. May 8. From Gayton the King, with the Abp of York, and Bishops of Bath, St. Asaph, and Norwich, goes to Windsor, where he is met by the Barons (*cum equis et armis*), ready to perform military service of what kind soever the King might direct.[5] The King, on this occasion, redisposed of many Castles throughout the kingdom. Allerton Castle was destroyed, its builder, the Bishop of Durham, compounding for his inactivity in the late civil-war by payment of 1000 merks. The Earl of Chester has all his castles in Windsor.

[1] Whereas the King had been at Marlborough about a month before, one might be led to think that the Charter had passed on that occasion. But the internal evidence of the Deed itself proves it to have passed about Oct. 1175 (*vide supra*, pp. 195–6).

[2] Gall. Script. xii.

[3] Benedictus writes the place *Wi*, or *Wie*, in different MSS. We understand it to be Wye in Kent, about 20 miles N.W. of Dover, and 10 miles S.W. of Canterbury. One authority places it (erroneously, we think) in Surrey.

[4] Benedictus (according to one MS.) names *Hugh* de Lacy as the Crusader. It is clearly incorrect. Henry de Lacy died, it was supposed, in Palestine. The day of his obit. was Sept. 25. The place of his sepulture unknown. The year (unrecorded) will have been 1177.

[5] The summonses for the army of Normandy were returnable on May 8. It would seem as if that muster had been now postponed to June 2nd.

1177. c. May 8. Normandy and England restored, the King requiring him Windsor. to go to Ireland for the conquest thereof, for the behoof of Prince John. The King entrusts Roxburgh Castle to William de Stutevill; Edinburgh Castle (*Castellum puellarum*) to Roger de Stuteville; Norham Castle to William de Neville; Scarborough Castle to Roger, Abp of York; Berwick Castle to Geoffrey de Neville; and Durham Castle to Roger de *Comers* (Qy Coniers).[1]

The King holds a great Council at Oxford, whereat, by Oxford. the authority of Pope Alexander, he constitutes his son, John, King of Ireland. Rese ap Griffin, Prince of S. Wales; David ap Owen, Prince of N. Wales; Cadwallon, Prince of Delvain (Dynmael, Denbighshire); Owen de Kevelioc, and Griffin de Bromfield (Princes of Powys); and Madoc ap Gervetrog,[2] attend at Oxford and do fealty to the King.

c. May. The King now gives Meath for 100 knights'-fees to Hugh de Lacy; Cork (except the town) to Robert fitz Stephen and Milo de Cogham, for 60 fees;[3] Limerick (except the town) to Herbert fitz Herbert, to William,[4] brother of Earl Reginald, and to Joel de Pomerai, their nephew, for 60 fees; Wexford city to William fitz Adeline, his Dapifer, as *Custos*; Waterford city to Robert le Poer, his Marshal, as *Custos*; and Dublin to Hugh de Lacy, as *Custos*.

It was doubtless on this occasion, that a Royal Charter, dated at Oxford, was granted to the Priory of St. Thomas at Dublin.[5] It is attested by William fitz Adelm, Reginald de Courtenay, Hugh de Lacy, Thomas Basset, and Robert le Poer.

May 22. The King, accompanied by Richard, Abp of Canterbury; Amesbury. Bartholomew, Bp of Exeter; John, Bp of Norwich; Regi-

[1] Hoveden, 323-b. Benedictus is silent about Durham Castle. He names Roger de Cuneriis (Conyers) as the displaced Castellan of Norham.

[2] Benedictus has this name as *Madacus* (or *Maddocus*) *filius Gervet Chone*. The individual was doubtless Madoc, eldest son of Gervase Goch, third son of Meredyth ap Blethyn, Prince of Powis. Of him, and his descent, and how his family were the hereditary interpreters (*Latimarii*) between the Kings of England and Princes of Wales, more may be seen in the Antiquities of Shropshire (vol. ii. pp. 108–120), under Sutton Maddock,—a place whose name is a still existing record of this its early possessor.

[3] This Charter is actually preserved. It is dated at Oxford. It gives to Robert fitz Stephen and Miles de Cogan the kingdom of Cork (except the city and the Hostman's Cantred, of which the grantees are to have custody during the King's pleasure); to hold under the King and his son John, and their heirs, by service of 30 knights from each grantee. Witnesses, Bishops John of Norwich, Adam of St. Asaph, and Augustine of Waterford; Richard de Luci; William fitz Aldeline, Dapifer; Hugh de Lacy; Hugh de Barid (?); Roger fitz Reinfrid; Maurice de Prendergast; Robert Dene (?); Robert fitz Eliodere; Geoffry Poer; and Hervey de Montemarisco (Lyttelton, vol. iv. Appendix (3).

[4] As *Willielmus frater Comitis* he appears in 1166, and as holding 4 knights'-fees in the Barony of Earl Reginald of Cornwall.

[5] Monasticon, vii. p. 1141.

1177. May 22. nald, Bp of Bath; Adam, Bp of St. Asaph; and Guy, Bp-elect of Bangor, is at Ambresbury, and there introduces a fresh Convent of Nuns from Fontevrault.[1] The Prioress of Fontevrault seems to have come over in charge of the Nuns, for at Michaelmas the Custos of Southampton charges,—*In liberacione navis Rogeri de la Wicha ad opus Priorissæ de Fonte Ebroldi 50s. per breve Regis.* Amesbury.

On the same day Archbishop Richard consecrated Guy Bishop of Bangor.

May 29. The King, now at Winchester, appoints Richard, Prior of Kirkby, to be Abbot of Whitby; and Benedict, Prior of the Church of the Holy Trinity at Canterbury, to be Abbot of Peterborough. The latter receives the benediction from Archbishop Richard. Winchester.

About this time the Cardinal Vivian returns from Ireland to England. The King allows him safe-conduct into Scotland. He holds, about August 1, a Council at Ediuburgh (*Castrum Puellarum*), and suspends the Bishop of Whitherne for not attending.

c. June 1. Henry, Bishop of Bayeux; Hugh de Beauchamp; Osbert, Clerk of the King's Chamber; and Geoffry de la Charite (? Charre), having been present at the Princess Joan's marriage at Panormus, on February 13, return to England.

June 2. Muster of the Barons, *cum equis et armis*, at Winchester, and of a fleet of transports at Portsmouth and Southampton. The King orders their re-assemblage on July 1. Winchester.

c. June 3. The King is still at Westminster, which Vivian now quits. The King sends (appoints) Geoffry, Bp of Ely; Henry, Bp of Bayeux; and Walter de Constanciis, Archdeacon of Oxford (his Vice-chancellor), ambassadors to Louis. The Abp of Rouen and the Bishop of Winchester were to join them in their passage through Normandy. Hence the following charge on the Pipe-Roll of the year.—

SOUTHAMPTON. *Et in passagio unius navis ad opus Episcopi Elyensis 60s. per breve Regis. Et in liberacione navis Radulfi Vituli junioris ad opus Walteri Archidiaconi Oxineford' 50s. per breve Regis.*

c. June 4. The King, at Winchester, appoints Roger, a Knight-Templar, to be his Almoner.

c. June 6. The King goes to Marlborough, and there gives the kingdom of Limerick to Philip de Braose; the former grantees having declined the same. Marlborough.

[1] Benedictus (Stubbs), i. 165.
Diceto puts this visit to Amesbury a week earlier, viz., on May 15.
Bromton puts it on Sunday, July 1st, the inaccuracy of which is self-evident, for, in 1177, July 1st fell on Friday.

1177. c. June 10. The King arrives in London, and gives the Abbacy of Thorney to the Prior of Ely. **London.**

June 11. The King goes to Waltham Abbey, and with him the Bishops of London, Norwich, Rochester, and Durham, the Abp of Canterbury being unable to attend. The regular Canons were inducted, and Ralph, a Canon of Cirencester, was appointed Prior, and enthroned. **Waltham.**

A grant by Geoffry de Scalariis to Waltham is without date, but may well belong to this occasion. It is attested by the King himself, John his son, Earl Alberic, and Alberic his son, and Ralph de Heford.[1]

June 12. The King keeps Pentecost in London. **London,**

Perhaps the King was in Hertfordshire about this time. The Sheriff charges,—*In camerâ Curiæ £9 per breve Regis. Et pro equis ad opus Regis* 5 *marcas per idem breve.* **(Hertfordshire.)**

c. June 14–18. The King is at Woodstock, waiting the return of his messengers from Normandy. They come with unwelcome messages from Prince Henry. **Woodstock.**

The Sheriff of Hampshire charges,—*Pro vassellâ Regis ducendâ a Winton' ad Wudestoch'* 18*s.* 2*d. per breve Regis.*

About this time the King sends Henry, Bishop of Baieux, and Richard Giffard, as Ambassadors to Louis of France. Hence the Southampton Pipe-Roll charges, *In liberacione navis Sansonis Waszelini ad opus Henrici Episcopi Baiocensis* 35*s. per breve Regis.*

About this time Margaret, the young Queen, was delivered of a son at the Court of her father at Paris. The infant survived its birth long enough to be named William.

July 1. The King holds a great Council at Winchester. The summonses, which he had issued for the army of Normandy, were returnable. William, King of Scots, came as the King's liege; but the King deferred the expedition, waiting till his messengers to Louis should return. **Winchester.**

July 9. The King is at Stokes, near Portsmouth, waiting a fair wind to cross the Channel. The following charges on the Pipe-Roll may have place here.— **Stokes.**

HAMPSHIRE. *Et in camerâ Curiæ Ricardo Britoni clerico Regis* 40 *marcas per breve Regis. Et servientibus Regis ad corredium ipsius* 117*s.* 9*d. per breve Regis. Et servientibus Gaufridi filii Regis* 40*s. per idem breve.*

[1] Monast. vi. 66. Number x.

1177. c. July. WINCHESTER. *Pro ducendo thesauro multis itineribus a London' ad Winton' et a Winton' ad Clarendon et item a Winton' ad Porcestre et item a Winton' ad London', Baldwino et Ricardo et Andreæ clericis* 116*s.* 6*d.* (Porchester ?)

SOUTHAMPTON. *Et pro lumine ad custodiendum thesaurum apud Portesmudam* xl *noctibus* 20*d.*

July 10-17. The King at Stanstede, in Sussex (on the borders of Hampshire), waiting a fair wind. An old wound in the thigh breaks out afresh, and affects his health.[1] A Charter, whereby the King gives the Church of Wicumbe to Godstow Nunnery, is dated *Apud Stanestede,* and attested by G. Bp, of Ely; B. Bp of Exeter; John, Bp of Norwich; Richard de Luci; Ranulf de Glanvill; Hugh de Gundeville; Reginald de Pavilli; W. Basset; William fitz Ralph; and Ralph fitz Stephen.[2] Stanstede.

July 12. The King, at Stanstede, restores to Bartholomew, Bishop of Exeter, the Royal Chaplaincy of Boseham, surrendered by Arnulf, Bishop of Liseux, the previous and wrongful Incumbent. Witnesses, Richard Abp of Canterbury, Geoffry Bp of Ely, and John Bp of Chichester.[3]

The King being at Stanstede, John de Rainewill, a Templar, arrives there, bringing a message from Richard Giffard, Robert Pikenot, and Robert fitz Bernard, who were in France.—Peter, the Cardinal Legate, had arrived in France, and was threatening an interdict against Henry's dominions unless he permitted the consummation of Prince Richard's marriage with Alice, daughter of Louis of France, which Princess was in Henry's custody.[4] The King consults the Abp of Canterbury and the Bishops of Ely, Exeter, and Chichester. They appeal to the Pope, thus forestalling the Legate's supposed intention. The King directs the Abp of York to appeal also.

The King's residence in Sussex is illustrated by the Pipe-Roll of that county,—*Et in camerâ Curiæ* £17. 15*s.* 7*d.* *per breve Regis. In camerâ Curiæ* £9. 10*s.* *per predictum breve.*

BOSEHAM. *In camerâ Curiæ* £13*s.* 8*s.* 3*d.*

[1] The result of a horse's kick received three years before (*vide supra*, p. 182). The thigh-bone had probably been injured. A mere flesh-wound would not be likely to re-open after such an interval.

[2] Godstow Chartulary, fo. 152 b.

[3] Benedictus (Stubbs) i. 181, 182.

[4] The Legate's threat, the perpetual diplomacy with France on the subject of the Princess Alice, and the persistent, nay aggravated, disaffection of Prince Richard, support the suspicion and allegation that Henry had debauched the affianced bride of his son.

1177. c. July 17. The King's illness obliges him to go to Winchester. Winchester.

July 25. Pope Alexander and the Emperor Frederic are reconciled at Venice. A Papal Rescript of August 6, announces the fact to Richard, Archbishop of Canterbury.

Aug. 15. The King has been for about a month ill at Winchester.

It was at Winchester, and probably while thus lying ill, that the King made a grant of lands to Richard Rufus, one of his Chamberlains. It is attested by G. Bp of Ely; B. Bp of Exeter; J. Bp of Norwich; Richard de Luci; Ranulf de Glanvill; Hugh de Gundevill; William Basset; William fitz Ralph; Ralph fitz Stephen, Chamberlain; William Ruffus; Eustace fitz Stephen; Robert Malduit and Ailward, Chamberlains.[1]

Aug. 18. The King embarks from Portsmouth for Normandy. Portsmouth. Hence the Southampton Pipe-Roll charges,—*In liberacione Esneccæ quando Rex transfretavit* £7. 10*s. per breve Regis. Et in liberacione navis Sansonis Wascelini ad ducendam harnasiam Regis in Normanniam* 35*s. per breve Regis.*

Aug. 19. The King lands at Capewike (*Caplevic*). He sends Caplevic. Prince Geoffrey into Bretagne to subdue his opponents.

c. Sept. 1. Ivri is surrendered to King Henry's arms by Walleran de Ivri. Ivri.

Sept. 11. The King meets the Legate, Peter, at Rouen. The young Rouen. King is present at the interview. The Legate postpones the threatened interdict, till the King should have conferred with Louis.

About this time a Royal Charter to St. George's Abbey at Boscherville, bears date at Rouen, and is attested by Henry Bp of Bayeux, Froger Bp of Seez, Reginald Bp of Bath, Master Walter de Constanciis, and Richard Guiffard.[2]

Another Charter, dated at Rouen, is to Lincoln Cathedral. It mentions Roger Archbishop of York as contemporary, and is attested by J. Bishop of Chichester.[3]

c. Sept. It was probably about this time that "the young King," as Prince Henry was usually called, being at Argentan, expedited a Charter to Waltham Abbey. In this remarkable Argentan.

[1] Fœdera, I. 41.

[2] Monasticon, vii. 1066. Num. ii. The Bishop of Bath was certainly in France about this time. The next year he and John, Bishop of Poitiers, were among the Missionaries appointed to preach down the so-called Arian heresy in Toulouse.

[3] Ibidem, viii. 1276. Num. lix. John, Bishop of Chichester was consecrated Oct. 6, 1174.

1177. c. Sept. document his style is "*Henricus Dei gratiâ Rex Angliæ Dux Normanniæ et Comes Andegaviæ, Regis Henrici filius.*" He speaks of his living father as *inclytæ recordacionis,* recites how he had changed the old Canons of Waltham into Regulars. He commends the new body; and for the health of his father and himself concedes, and by his "regal authority" confirms the grants already made, and the franchises which his father is thereafter about to give, to the said House. The Deed is attested by Richard Bp of Winchester; F. Bp of Seez; H. Bp of Baieux; Master Walter de Constanciis; Master Osbert de Camerâ; Nicholas, a Chaplain; Ranulf de Glanvill; Geoffrey de Perche; Hugh de Creissi; Gerard de Camvill; William the Grantor's Chaplain; William Marescall; and William fitz Roger.[1] Argentan.

The testing-clause suggests that the elder King was at Argentan at the time.

A Charter of K. Henry, dated at *Driencurt,*[2] to St. James's of Bristol, speaks of Robert, Earl of Gloucester, the King's uncle, as lying buried in that Church. It is attested by R. Bp of Winchester; Hugh de Creissi; William fitz Ralph; Alured de St. Martin; and William Rufus.[3] Driencourt.

Sept. 21. Henry meets Louis at, or near, Ivri. Nothing was settled as to the Princess Alice, but both monarchs swore to take the cross, and made various mutual stipulations. There were present the Cardinal Legate, Peter; R. Bp of Winchester; J. Bp of Chartres; H. Bp of Baieux; F. Bp. of Seez; Egidius Bp of Evreux; the young King Henry; Theobald Comte of Blois; Robert Comte of Meulan; Simon Comte of Evreux; Peter de Courtenai; and William de Humez. Ivri (or perhaps) Nonancourt (or perhaps) Gué St. Remy.

Sep. 25. A written agreement, between Henry and Louis, bears date at Nonancurt, on this day (Sept. 25). Nonancourt.

King Henry the younger, now goes into Berri.

Sept. 27. Geoffrey, the younger King's Chancellor, with three hundred others, were drowned in crossing from England to Normandy. Geoffrey was Provost of Beverley, and nephew of Roger, Abp of York. This catastrophe happened near St. Valery.

[1] Cartæ Antiquæ, M.

[2] Drincort, otherwise called Neuf-Chatel-en-Brai, was N.E. of Rouen. It is still called Neuf-Chatel.

[3] Cartæ Antiquæ, K. and OO.

IN THE FISCAL YEAR, ending Michaelmas, 1177, the JUSTICES ITINERANT, grouped as in the previous year, repeated most of their circuits; and Essex, Hertfordshire, and Surrey, were visited by their appropriate Justices.[1]

There was an *Auxilium*, or *Tallage*, set upon Boroughs in this year, the Assessors of which were Justiciars grouped in another fashion. Thus Ralph fitz Stephen, Turstin fitz Simon, and William Rufus were the Assessors in Shropshire, Herefordshire, Worcestershire, Gloucestershire, Hampshire, Berkshire, Oxfordshire, Wiltshire, Dorsetshire, Somersetshire, Cornwall, and Devonshire; William fitz Ralph, William Basset, and Michel Belet were the Assessors in Staffordshire, Warwickshire, Leicestershire, Notts, Derbyshire, Northants, Lincolnshire, Yorkshire, Lancashire, and Northumberland;—Robert Mantel and Ralph Brito in Norfolk, Suffolk, Essex, Herts, Cambridgeshire, and Huntingdonshire; and Roger fitz Reinfrid, with Gervase de Cornhull, in Sussex, Kent, Bucks, and Bedfordshire.

In this year too, Richard de Luci, held *New Pleas* in Hampshire and Middlesex; and Thomas fitz Bernard held *Forest-Pleas* in some counties.

MICHAELMAS, 1177, TO MICHAELMAS, 1178.

1177. c. Oct. 1. The King is at Verneuil. With him are Richard Bp of Winchester; H. Bp of Baieux; Egidius Bp of Evreux; Froger Bishop of Seez; Simon Comte of Evreux; and Robert Earl of Leicester. Verneuil.

The King issues summonses for the army of Normandy to muster at Argentan. He also passes an ordinance concerning Debtors, at instigation of the "Good men of Grandmonte."[2]

c. Oct. 2. The King, at Alençon, sends Prince Richard into Poitou. Alençon.

The King holds a Council at Argentan, and then marches into Berri to assist his eldest son. Argentan. Berri.

Oct. 9. The King besieges and takes Châteauroux (Castellum Radulfi), theretofore the possession of one Raoul de Déols. Châteauroux.

The King proceeds to La Châtre (*Castre*), the Lord of which town surrenders the daughter and heir of Raoul de Déols, custody of whom was claimed by the King. (She was afterwards given in marriage to Baldwin de Redvers). La Châtre.

[1] The Justices who visited Devonshire were perhaps the same as had visited the County in the previous year, though their causes in that County are in this year entitled *Nova Placita et Novæ conventiones per justiciarios ad scaccarium*; but the Justiciars are not named. They had, probably, rendered their accounts at the Exchequer on coming off Circuit.

And it should also be noted that, in this year, Ralph fitz Stephen, William Rufus, and Gilbert Pipard, the Justices proper to Wiltshire, Dorsetshire, Somersetshire, Cornwall, and Devon, held no *new pleas* in the four first-named counties. Perhaps this was because two of their number were actively engaged as assessors of the *Auxilium Burgorum* levied during this same fiscal year.

[2] The Priory of *Grandmonte* or *Bellaria* was in the Forest of Beaumont le Roger, N. of Verneuil and W. of Evreux. It was probably an off-shoot of the greater House of Grammont in Limousin. There is a Charter of K. Henry II. to the first-named House (Monasticon, vii. 1089. Num. i.) It probably passed while he was thus at Verneuil, though the date is lost. It is addressed to the Abp of Rouen, and to the King's sons, Henry, Richard, Geoffrey, and John. It is attested by Froger, Bishop of Seez; Robert (Comte) of Meulan; Henry de Newburgh; Fulk de Duno; Fulk Poumelli (probably Paganell); and Richard Guiffart.

1177. October. The King passes onwards into Limousin, and there prosecutes the persons who had opposed him during the civil war. Limousin.

The King passes back into Berri. Berri.

c. Nov. 15. Conference between Henry and Louis at Graszay (or Graserai), where they are met by the Proceres of Auvergne. The point in dispute (viz. what seigneurial rights over Auvergne pertained to the Duchy of Aquitaine) was referred to arbitration. Graszay.

King Henry visits Grandmont (in Limousin). There Albert, Count of Marche, meets him, and sells the province of La Marche to the King for £15,000 (Angovin money), 20 mules and 20 palfreys. The Abp of Bordeaux, and John Bp of Poitiers, attested the transaction. Grandmont.

Nov. 26. The Comte of Flanders and Earl of Essex fight a great battle with the Saracens at Rames, in Palestine.

Dec. 26. The King keeps Christmas at Angiers, with the Proceres of Anjou. Angiers.

IN THE ABOVE YEAR Roland de Dinan is named as Justice of Bretagne.

In the above year died Nicholas de Estoteville (Stuteville).[5]

In the above year John of Salisbury, the friend of Becket, being appointed to the Bishoprick of Chartres, excommunicated John, Comte of Vendôme, apparently for his persecution of the Monks of Vendôme, who suffered fourteen months' exile in the Priory of *Aquarium* (at Angiers). Comte John got absolution from Peter, Cardinal of St. Chrysogon, the Papal Legate, but conditionally on the approval of the Bishop of Chartres, which approval the Comte failed to obtain, and so remained excommunicate for three years.[2]

A.D. 1178.

1178. Jan. 1. The King may be supposed to have been still at Angiers. Angiers.

Perhaps the King was in Normandy.—

c. Feb. A Royal Charter, dated *apud Burum* (Bur le Roy, near Bayeux) is in favour of the Abbey of *Longues*, or *De Longis*, in the Diocese of Bayeux. It is attested by Richard, Bishop of Winchester; Henry, Bishop of Bayeux; Master Walter de Constantiis; Geoffry de Lucy; Hamo Pincerna; and William fitz Radulf.[3] Bur le Roy.

Feb. 10. Sebrand was elected Bishop of Limoges in succession to Gerald. The election was secret, because expected to be displeasing to King Henry.[4]

March 19. On this day, being Midlent Sunday, the Church of Bec was dedicated. The King, the young King Henry; Rotroc, Bec Hellouin.

[1] Chron. Sti. Taurini (Gall. Script, xii. 777).
[2] Gall. Script. xii. 488.
[3] D'Anisy's Normandy Transcripts, ii. 89.
[4] Gall. Script. xii. 446 *e*.

1178. March 19. Abp of Rouen; Henry, Bp of Baieux; Richard, Bp of Avranches; and Giles, Bp of Evreux, were present.[1] Bec Hellouin.

On the same day, by Charter, dated *apud Beccum*, the King presents the Abbey with an annuity of £100, chargeable on the revenues of the Vicomté of Rouen. Witnesses, R. Abp of Rouen; Henry, Bp of Baieux; Egidius, Bp of Evreux; Richard, Bp of Avranches; Comte Robert of Mellent; Comte Henry of Ewe (*de Augo*), and Henry de Novo-burgo.[2]

Mch. 21. Richard, Bishop of Winchester, having been in Normandy a year and half now returns into England. He is succeeded as *Dapifer* or Grand Justiciary of Normandy by William fitz Ralph. The Southampton Pipe-Roll of 1178 alludes to the Bishop's return,—*Et in passagio Episcopi Wintoniæ et Simonis de Turnebu* 57*s. per breve Regis.*

About this time Geoffrey, Bishop Elect of Lincoln, and Prince John were sent from England into Normandy by Richard de Luci, now acting as Viceroy of England. This and other entries, indicative of the King's absence from England, may here be cited from the Pipe-Roll of 1178.—

SOUTHAMPTON. *Et in passagio Esneccæ in transitu Galfridi Lincol' electi et Johannis fratris sui* £7. 10*s. per breve Ricardi de Luci. Et item in* (*liberacione*) *Esneccæ ad portandum thesaurum ultra mare per Alexandrum de Barentin et Eudonem Pil'* £7. 10*s. per breve Ricardi de Luci. Et pro onerando thesauro et deonerando* 11*d. Et in passagio thesauri in navi Radulfi Vituli propter absentiam Esneccæ* 50*s. per breve Regis.*

OXFORDSHIRE. *Et pro ducendâ papilione Regis a Wudestochâ ad Hantoniam* 2*s.* 6*d. per breve Regis.*

LONDON. *Pro ducendo thesauro tribus vicibus a London' ad Winton,* 77*s.* 6*d. per Odonem de Falesia et Ricardum de Windr' et Andream Clericum.*

WINCHESTER. *Et pro duobus magnis hugiis, et ostio thesauri Wintoniæ reficiendo et pro ducendo thesauro pluribus vicibus per Andream et Ricardum clericos et alios servientes thesauri* 25*s.* 2*d.*

April 9. The King keeps Easter Day at Angiers. Angiers.

c. April 15. The King goes into Normandy. One authority[3] places him at Nonancourt on April 9th, but that seems improbable. Normandy (Nonancourt).

April 17. Bull of Pope Alexander III. ordering Roger, Bishop of Worcester, to give the benediction to Roger, Abbot-elect of St. Augustine's, if the Archbishop refused to do so.

June 11. Richard de Luci lays the foundation-stone of the Abbey of Westwood, or Lesnes, in honour of St. Thomas the Martyr.

June 18 (Sunday). Martin, Prior of Vigeois, died at Limoges. On the same day Geoffrey, a Monk of St. Martial (Limoges), succeeded to the Priorate of Vigeois.[4] This was Geoffrey of Vigeois, the Historian.

July 15. The King having sailed from Normandy, lands at *Dighesmut.*[5] The Hampshire Pipe-Roll charges,—*Et nautis Normanniæ qui detulerunt harnasium Regis a Normanniâ in Angliam* £6. 10*s. per breve Regis.* Dighesmut.

[1, 2] Neustria Pia, pp. 460, 485. Stapleton's Rot. Norm. i. cxi. *n.*

[3] Rob. de Monte (Struve), p. 922.

[4] Gall. Script. xii. 446.

[5] *Apud Dighesmutam* (Benedict, i. 207. Ed. Stubbs). Bromton says, '*ad portum optatum.* Hoveden altogether omits the place of the King's landing. In default of all evidence as to where *Dighes-mouth* was, we presume it to have been in Hampshire.

1178. c. July 18. The King visits Becket's shrine at Canterbury. Canterbury.

The King goes to London. London.

July 27. William, Archbishop of Rheims, visits Becket's shrine.

c. July 28-31. The King entertains the said Archbishop for three days at London.

Perhaps it was now that the King visited Waltham in Essex. A Charter there dated is in favour of the Canons of St. Osyth, at Chich (Essex). It is attested by G. Bp of London; G., Bp of Ely; Ralph, Prior of Waltham; Earl Alberic; Hugh de Cressi; William de Vere; Richard, the Treasurer; and Roger Bigot.[1] Waltham.

Aug. 6. The King is at Woodstock, and there knights Prince Geoffrey. The latter goes forthwith into Normandy. In the Pipe-Roll of Michaelmas following the Sheriff of Kent charges 104*s*. *in procuratione Galfridi filii Regis per breve Regis*. Woodstock.

About this time also the King probably visited Reading, for the Fermor of Hampshire charges 20*s*. *ad deferendum harnasium Regis a Portesmudâ usque Rading'*. Reading.

c. Sept. He also, perhaps, visited Worcestershire; for the Sheriff of that county charges, *In camerâ Curiæ* 100 *marcas per breve Regis*. Worcestershire.

About this time, too, the King sent Ambassadors to the Pope;—for the Sheriff of Hampshire charges,—*Et Goscelino Archidiacono Cycestriæ et Osberto clerico de Camerâ et Waltero Map quos Rex misit ad Dominum Papam* lx *marcas per breve Regis*.

Sept. 1. Sebrand, Bishop-Elect of Limoges, and the Canons of Limoges, were exiled, by order of K. Henry, on publication of the said election.[2]

Sept. 13. Record of an Eclipse of the Sun, nearly total, at Saumur, and lasting from four to six o'clock (*ab intitio missæ usque refectorium*), on the Vigil of the Exaltation of the Holy Cross.[3]

In the fiscal year, ending Michaelmas, 1178, we have—

Wm. Basset, Michael Belet, Robert de Vaux, and Bertram de Verdon, or some three of them, making Eyre in Lincolnshire, Yorkshire, and the North.[4] We have also—

Roger fitz Reinfrid, Ralph fitz Stephen, William fitz Stephen, Robert Mantel, Robert fitz Bernard, and Richard Giffard, or some three of them visiting, other parts of the kingdom;[4] and Thomas fitz Bernard holding Forest-Pleas in diverse quarters. In the same year we have an indication of Richard de Luci; Geoffrey, Bishop of Ely; John, Bishop of Norwich; and William Basset, sitting at the Exchequer.[5]

[1] Cartæ Antiquæ, E. No. 23.

[2] Rerum Gall. Script. xii. 447, c.

[3] Ibidem xii. 285, 287, 491. The Records are verified by scientific calculation, say the Editors.

[4] Both these *Itinera* are perpetuated in the Roll of 1179, under the head of *Nova Placita*. We conclude that they were in process when the Pipe-Roll accounts of Michaelmas, 1178, were finally made up.

[5] Monasticon, vol. iii. p. 25.

MICHAELMAS, 1178, TO MICHAELMAS, 1179.

Oct. 8. William de Mandevill, Earl of Essex, returns from the Crusade.[1]

1178. Oct. Nov. Dec. About this time the King is said to have visited several parts of the kingdom. He is also said to have revoked his plan of having six circuits and eighteen justiciars, and to have appointed five justiciars only (two clerks and three laymen) who were always to attend the Court.[2] England.

Albert de Suma, Cardinal Legate in Normandy and England, and Peter de St. Agatha, Legate in Scotland and Ireland, are summoning all Bishops, &c., to attend a General Council at Rome in the beginning of Lent.

Dec. 25. King Henry kept Christmas at Winchester. With him were the Princes Geoffrey (who had returned from Normandy) and John. The young King is in Normandy, and Prince Richard in Poitou. Winchester.

The King's great Charter to the Abbey of Waltham (in Essex) passed on this occasion. It is attested by Richard, Abp of Canterbury, and Legate of the Apostolic See; Gilbert, Bp of London; Josceline, Bp of Salisbury; Walter, Bp of Rochester; Bartholomew, Bp of Exeter; Roger, Bp of Worcester; Richard, Bp of Winchester; Geoffrey, Bp of Ely; John, Bp of Chichester; John, Bp of Norwich; Reginald, Bp of Bath; Hugh, Bp of Durham; Adam, Bp of St. Asaph; Geoffrey, Bishop-elect of Lincoln; Geoffrey, the King's son; William, Earl of Gloucester; Richard de Luci; Humphrey de Bohun, Constable; Roger Bigod, Reginald de Curtenai, William de Lanval, Thomas Baseth, William fitz Ralph, William Baseth, Ralph fitz Stephen, Chamberlain; and Eustace his brother; and Ailward, Chamberlain.[3]

[1] Diceto, Bromton.— But we do not find that the Earl returned at once to England.

[2] Benedictus, ii. 207.—It is remarkable that the Pipe-Roll of Michaelmas, 1179, records several *Itinera* of Justices within the year then ended. One was that of William Basset, Robert de Vaux, Michael Belet, and Bertram de Verdon, in Lincolnshire. Now, since part of their Iter is recorded on the Pipe-Roll of Michaelmas, 1178, we may conclude that it was then in progress, and that it was concluded before the King's ordinance of October came into operation. (To this subject we shall recur in the sequel).

[3] Monasticon, vi. 63. Num. iv. The way in which the date of this important Charter may be proved is worth stating. It passed after May 21, 1177, when the Regular Canons were inducted at Waltham, for it speaks of that event as past. At that time, Richard, Bishop of Winchester, had been eight months absent from England; nor did he return to England till March, 1178. From March, 1178, to July 15, 1178, the King himself was absent from England. Between July 15 and August 6, 1178, the King was not at Winchester at all, certainly not in Council, as at the time of this Charter. On August 6, 1178, Geoffry Fitz Roy (Comte of Bretagne) went to Normandy, and did not return till Christmas, when he was at Winchester with his father; and when also the Charter passed. For Richard de Luci retired from public life at Easter, 1179, and though the King and Prince Geoffrey were at Winchester in the interval, viz., on April 1, 1179, the Deed cannot have passed on the latter occasion, inasmuch as it is attested by three Prelates (Norwich, Bath, and Durham), who, from March 15 to March 19, were in attendance at the Council of Lateran, and could not have returned to England so early as April 1.

1178. c. Dec. A Royal Charter in favour of Godstow Nunnery is without (Winchester). date as to the place of its issue, but belongs to this period. Its witnesses are—Geoffry, Bp of Ely; Hugh, Bp of Durham; Geoffry, Elect of Lincoln; Walter, Archdeacon of Oxford, and Roger, King's Chaplains; Richard de Luci; and Reginald de Curtenai.[1]

A.D. 1179.

1179. Jan. 1. The King probably at Winchester. Winchester.

c. Jan. 1. Laurence Abp of Dublin, Catholicus Abp of Tuam, five or six Irish Bishops, several Scotch Bishops, and other Dignitaries from both countries, pass through England *en route* to the Council of Lateran.

In the Pipe-Roll of Michaelmas, 1179, the Custos of Dover charges,—*Et in passagio Petri Legati Hiberniæ et Laurencii Archiepiscopi Duvelin' et B. Episcopi de Limerich* 15*s. per breve Regis.*

c. January. About this time the King is said to have been at Windsor. Windsor, and there to have received complaints from Ireland about the conduct of William fitz Adelm and Hugh de Lacy.

Jan. 28. The Pope bestows the benediction on Roger, Abbot of St. Augustine's, Canterbury.

Feb. 26. Prince Henry, after three years' absence from England, embarks at Witsand, and visits his father's Court.[2]

March 5–14–19. These are the three days of the eleventh general Council of Lateran. It was attended by four English Bishops, viz., Durham, Norwich, Hereford, and Bath, to whom some add a fifth, viz., Worcester. The Abp of Canterbury set out, but got no further than Paris.

c. March. About this time the King must have visited Gloucester. Gloucester. The Pipe-Roll has the following entries.—

GLOUCESTERSHIRE. *Et pro 200 summis bladi et custamento ducendi ad Bristowam quas Rex misit familiæ suæ in Hiberniâ per servientes Hugonis de Laci* £19. 2*s*. 8*d*. *per breve Regis. Et pro ducendâ venatione Regis a Bikenaur*[3] *usque* (Bicknore.) *ad Wintoniam* 36*s*. 1*d*. *per breve Regis.*

But a better proof of the King's visit to Gloucester at Gloucester. this time is a Charter, there dated, whereby, at the petition of Richard de Luci, the King confirms that Baron's foundation of Westwood Abbey.[4] The Charter is attested by Earl

[1] Godstow Chartulary, fo. 14.

[2] Hoveden and Benedictus Abbas place this at, or about, Midlent (March 11).

[3] Bicknore, on the Wye, in Gloucestershire, where the King had apparently been hunting.

[4] Monasticon, vi. 457. Num. ii.

1179. c. March. William de Mandeville; William de Albini, Earl of Sussex; Rannulph de Glanvill; William de Braose, junior; Gilbert de Monemue; Geoffrey; Thomas Bardulf; Gerard de Canvill; Richard de Canvill his brother; Roger de Porte; and William fitz Stephen. Gloucester.

Young King Henry during his short stay in England would seem to have visited Worcestershire. The Sheriff of that county charges,—*Et Henrico Regi filio Regis* 50 *marcas per breve Regis . . . D . . . ad quietanda vadia egis Franciæ* 20 *marcas*.

April 1. The King and Prince Henry keep Easter at Winchester. Winchester.

Richard de Luci retires from public life immediately after. The King sends Prince Geoffrey, Comte of Bretagne, to Bretagne. Hence, on the Pipe-Roll of the year, the Custos of Dover charges,—*Et in passagio Gaufridi filii Regis* 114*s*. *per breve Regis*.

The King's residence in Hampshire is further evidenced by the following extracts.—

Hampshire. *Et in camerâ Curiæ, Turpino* 140 *marcas per breve Regis. Et Willielmo Franceis* 20*s*. *quos expendit in equis domini sui Johannis filii Regis in Angliâ et in Normanniâ per breve Regis. Et in camerâ Curiæ* 20 *marcas per breve Regis. Et in corredio Regis apud Titegrave* 63*s*. 6*d*. *per breve Regis. Et in custamento ducendi thesaurum a Winton' usque ad London'* 6*s*. 1*d*. *per breve Regis*. Titgrave.

April 10. The King holds a great Council at Windsor, and divides the kingdom into four circuits, appointing justices to each as follows.— Windsor.

(1) Richard, Bp of Winchester; Richard, the King's Treasurer; Nicholas fitz Torold; Thomas Basset, and Robert de Witefeld for Hants, Wiltshire, Gloucestershire, Dorset, Somerset, Devon, Cornwall, Berks, and Oxfordshire.

(2) Geoffrey, Bp of Ely; Nicholas, the King's Chaplain;[1] Gilbert Pipard; Reginald de Wisebec, a Clerk of the King; and Geoffrey Hosee;—for Cambridge, Huntingdon, Northants,

[1] In wonderful confirmation of the names given for the second Circuit, we discover a fine levied at Coventry (Warwickshire) on July 30, 1179 (25th Hen. II.), before Geoffry, Bp of Ely; Nicholas Archdeacon of Coventry; Master R. de Weseby, Geoffrey Hose, and Gilbert Pypard, King's Justices (Lilleshall Chart^y. fo. 85).

So then we get the probable and proximate date of the appointment of Nicholas, the King's Chaplain, to the Archdeaconry of Coventry, viz., between April 10 and July 30, 1179.—

We also infer that a fine in the Bardney Chartulary, which purports to have been levied at Lincoln, on Saturday, July 10, 1176, was levied on Saturday, June 30, 1179; for it was levied before "Geoffry, Bishop of Ely; Nicholas, Archdeacon of Coventry; and Gilbert Pipard, King's Justices and others." Now these justices were not *in Eyre* in the alleged year (1176). (*Vide supra*, pp., 199, 207, and Cotton MSS. Vesp. E. xx. fo. 42).

1179. c. March 10. Leicestershire, Warwickshire, Lincolnshire,[1] Worcestershire, Herefordshire, Staffordshire, and Shropshire. Windsor.

(3) John, Bp of Norwich; Hugh Murdac, a King's Clerk; Michael Belet, Richard del Pec, and Ralph Brito, for the counties of Norfolk, Suffolk, Essex, Hertford, Middlesex, Kent, Surrey, Sussex, Buckingham, and Bedford.

(4) Godfrey de Luci, John Cumin, Hugh de Gaerst, Ranulf de Glanvill, William de Bendings, and Alan de Furnellis, for the counties of Nottingham, Derby, York, Northumberland, Westmoreland, Cumberland, and Lancaster.[2]

April 20. The King and his son, Henry, keep Pentecost together; but where is not stated.

c. April 22. Prince Henry crosses to Witsand.

May 1. Prince Richard besieges the castle of *Taileborch*.[3]

May 10. Taileborch Castle surrenders and is demolished.

c. June 1-10. Prince Richard returns to England.[3] He crossed to France again before Michaelmas; for then the Fermor of Southampton charges,—*In passagio Esnaccæ quando Ricardus Comes Pictaviæ transfretavit* £7. 10*s*. *per breve Regis.*

June and July. The Court seems to have been very stationary during this summer. The only evidences of its movements [3] are supplied by the Pipe-Roll; and those are not very decided: *e.g.*

LINCOLNSHIRE. *Et Ailwardo Camerario Regis in camerâ Curiæ* £13. 1*s*. 7*d*. *per breve Regis.*

ESSEX AND HERTFORD. *Et Turpino in camerâ Curiæ* £130 *per breve Regis.*

LONDON AND MIDDLESEX. *Et in custamento ducendi thesaurum pluribus itineribus et pro hugiis et saccis et aliis minutis rebus* 49*s*. 10*d*. *Et pro papilione Regis ducendâ ad Wudestoc'* 18*d*.

Perhaps two Charters which the King granted to Nutley (Bucks) passed about this time. One is dated at Woodstock, the other at *Bruhull*; both are attested by Ralph de Glanville, Hugh de Cressy, Gilbert Pipard, and William de Jarponville.[4] Woodstock. Brill.

[1] Hoveden p. (337) omits Lincolnshire. Benedictus rightly includes it in the second Circuit.

[2] The six Justices of the fourth Circuit, besides their *Eyre*, are said to be "constituted in the *Curiâ Regis* to hear the plaints of the people."

[3] Taillebourg in Saintonge. Benedictus (i. 213) places the siege of Taillebourg in May, 1178.

Benedictus, we should observe, after reciting Prince Richard's campaign, concludes with the submission of the Comte Angoulême, *statim post Pentecosten*, which day in 1179 fell on May 20). "*Et postea*" (says Benedict) "*transfretavit* (Dux Aquitaniæ) *in Angliam ad patrem suum*,"

We may therefore confidently assume that Richard, Duke of Aquitaine's arrival in England was early in June; but we are not told where he found his father's Court.

[4] Monasticon, vi. 278. Nums. ii. iii.

In July 1179. Richard de Lucy died in cloister, at Westwood-in-Liesucs, whither he had in retired in April previous.

July 30. Geoffrey, Bp of Ely; Nicholas, Archdeacon of Coventry;[1] Master R. de Weseby,[2] Geoffrey Hose, and Gilbert Pypard, occur as Justices-in-eyre at Coventry.[3]

Aug. 9. Roger, Bishop of Worcester died at Tours, and was buried there.

Aug. 20. William, Earl of Albemarle, died and was buried at Thornton Abbey (Lincolnshire).[4]

1179. Aug. 22. Louis VII.; Philip, Comte of Flanders; William, Earl Mandeville; Henry, Duke of Louvain; and Baldwin, Comte of Guisnes, land at Dover from Witsand, for the purpose of visiting the shrine of Becket. King Henry meets them at

Aug. 23. Dover, and accompanies them to Canterbury. In the Pipe-Roll of Michaelmas, the Sheriff of Kent charges,—*In corredio Regis Franciæ* £28. 2*s*. 5*d*. *per breve Regis*. Dover. Canterbury.

Aug. 26. The King accompanies Louis and his companions to Dover, where they re-embark. At Michaelmas the *Custos* of Dover charges,—*In passagio Comitis Flandriæ et Comitis de Gisnis* 68*s*. *per breve Regis*. Dover.

Aug. 27. The King is at Westminster, where the Justices Itinerant, and the three president Bishops (called Arch-Justiciars), give an account to him of their conduct. Westminster.

Perhaps it was now that a Royal Charter to Furness Abbey passed. It is dated at Westminster, and attested by R. Bp of Winchester; G. Bp. of Ely; J. Bp of Norwich; Godfrey de Luci; Rannulf de Glanvill; Reginald de Curtenai; William de Lanval; T. Basset; Robert fitz Bernard; and William de Bending.[5]

Sept. Perhaps the King was at Winchester in this month. The Sheriff of Hampshire paid 2*s*. *pro locandâ carettâ ad reportandam Vaissellam Regis a Cantuariâ ad Wintoniam*. Winchester.

Sept. 22. Cadwallon, a Prince of S. Wales, was killed while returning home from the English Court and under Henry's *safe-conduct*. Many persons were implicated; among the rest, Roger de Mortimer of Wigmore.[6]

The Pipe-Roll of Michaelmas, 1179, records a visit of Thomas fitz Bernard, as Justice of the Forest, to several counties. The *Itinera* of other justices, recorded in the same Roll, probably took place either before the Ordinance of October, 1178, came into operation, or else in lieu of the said Ordinance.

One of these *Itinera* has been already noticed,[7] as that of Wm. Basset, Michael Belet, Rob. de Vaux, and Bertram de Verdon. It extended to Lincolnshire, Nottinghamshire, Derbyshire, Rutlandshire, Staffordshire, and Northamptonshire.

Again, as in the year ending Michaelmas, 1178, Ralph fitz Stephen, Roger fitz Reinfrid, Robert Mantel,

[1] Evidently identical with Nicholas the King's Chaplain in the foregoing list of Justices.

[2] Called Reginald de Wisebec (*supra*, p. 226).

[3] *Supra*, p. 226, note 1.

[4] Benedictus, ii. 243. But the Chronicle of Thornton (Monast. vi. 326) says he died in 1180.

[5] Inter Cartas Ducatûs Lancastriæ.

[6] Eyton's 'Antiquities of Shropshire,' vol. iv. pp. 205, 206.

[7] *Supra*, p. 223.

and William fitz Stephen, or some of them, had visited the counties of Sussex, Surrey, Kent, Norfolk Suffolk, Essex, Hertford, Cambridge, Huntingdon, Buckingham, and Bedford.

And lastly, Richard, the King's Treasurer, Nicholas fitz Turold, and Robert de Witefeld, had visited Somersetshire and Dorsetshire; but this was in pursuance of the Royal Ordinance of April, 1179, and shows, what we have other reasons for concluding,[1] that the Justices, then appointed, went *in eyre* forthwith, though the chief results of their Circuits are not registered till Michaelmas, 1180.

MICHAELMAS, 1179, TO MICHAELMAS, 1180.

1179. October. In this, or the previous month, the King visited Windsor and Worcester. If in this month, then an entry on the Pipe-Roll of 1179 is postscriptive to Michaelmas. The Sheriff of Herefordshire charges the King 2½ *merks pro prisonibus rettatis de morte Cadewill* (Cadwallon) *ducendis ad Curiam apud Windresor' et apud Wigorniam, per breve Regis.* Windsor. Worcester.

Nov. 1. Prince Henry attends the coronation of Philip of France at Rheims[2]. Louis VII. was unable to attend by reason of a paralytic attack.

c. Dec. 15. About this time the King was at Northampton, as indicated by some entries on the Pipe-Roll of Sept. 1180.—

> NORTHANTS. HIGHAM. *Pro unâ hûgiâ ad reponendum thesaurum in turri Norhantoniæ* 6*s. per breve Regis. Et in careagio thesauri a Norhant' usque ad Notingeham per Willielmum Malduit Camerarium et Johannem Cumin* 5*s. per breve Regis. Et in carreagio thesauri a Norhant' usque ad Notingeh'* 7*s.* 6*d. Et item pro unâ hugiâ ad thesaurum portandum et carragio ejusdem thesauri* 6*s. per idem breve. Et Alardo filio Willielmi* 20 *marcas ad procuracionem Johannis filii Regis.*

Dec. 25. The King kept Christmas at Nottingham, where William, King of Scots, met him. The Pipe-Rolls illustrate the matter.— Nottingham.

HAMPSHIRE. *Et in ducendâ vassellâ Regis a Wintoniâ usque ad Notingeham contra Natale* 33*s.* 4*d. per breve Regis.*

LONDON. *Et in carreagio thesauri ad Wincestre et Nottingeham et alibi per Angliam per totum terminum* 39*s.* 3*d.*

[1] The allusion is to the Lilleshall Chartulary (fo. 85), which preserves a fine, levied at Coventry, in Warwickshire, on July 30, 1179, before Geoffry, Bishop of Ely; Nicholas, Archdeacon of Coventry; Master Reginald de Weseby (Wisebec); Geoffrey Hose; and Gilbert Pypard, Justices of the King. These, it will be observed, are the five Justices nominated, in April previous, to hold pleas in Warwickshire. And yet the results of the Warwickshire *Iter* do not appear on the Pipe-Roll of 1179, but among the *Nova Placita* of Michaelmas, 1180. Moreover, the Justices who were appointed in April, 1179, are expressly said to have accounted of their duties at Westminster, on Aug. 27, 1179. The inference is that these *itinera* were accomplished at the latter date, but the whole of their written accounts were not admissible into the next month's Pipe-Roll.

[2] The original summons for Philip's coronation stood for Aug. 15 (Benedictus, ii. 240); but the youth's sickness, and his father's visit to Canterbury, had caused a postponement.

1179. c. Dec. 25. A Royal Charter to Haughmond Abbey bears date at Nottingham, and is attested by Geoffrey, Bishop-elect of Lincoln; and Godfrey de Lucy.[1] Nottingham.

IN THE ABOVE YEAR, as is recorded, Henry, Comte of Troyes and Peter de Courtenay went to Jerusalem and conducted to Constantinople K. Louis's daughter, to become the wife of the Emperor's son.[2]

A.D. 1180.

1180. c. Jan. 1. From Nottingham the King, probably, went to Newark, and from thence to Doncaster, and from thence to York. Hence the following charges on the Pipe-Roll.— Newark. Doncaster. York.

NOTTS AND DERBYSHIRE. *Et pro ducendo thesauro a Niweherch* (read *Niwewerch*) *usque Donecastr'* 5*s. per Johannem Cumin et Willielmum Malduit. Et item pro ducendo thesauro a Notingeham usque Norhanton'* (Northampton.) *per Ricardum et Andream clericos* 4*s.*[3]

DONCASTER. *Et ad ducendum thesaurum Regis a Danecastrâ usque Everwick' per Willm. Malduit Camerarium* 5*s.*

YORKSHIRE. *Et pro thesauro ducendo a Notingeham ad Eve ich' et serris et aliis minutis rebus ad custodiam ejusdem thesauri* 8*s.* 6*d.*

After his northward journey, the King is at Woodstock. Woodstock.

The Sheriff of Northamptonshire charges,—4*s.* 10*d. pro thesauro portando a Notingeham usque ad Wadest'.* Also the Sheriff of Oxfordshire charges, *pro thesauro ducendo et reducendo multis itineribus per totum hoc annum.* 27*s.* 2*d.* Also the Sheriff of London charges, *pro unâ hugiâ ducendâ ad Wudestoc' cum thesauro* 3*s.*

Jan. 14. William de Mandeville, Earl of Essex, married Hawyse, eldest daughter and coheir of William, Earl of Albemarle, at Plashy Castle (Essex). He thus became Earl of Albemarle as well as of Essex.

c. Jan. About this time the King, sitting in his *Curiâ* at Oxford, decided on the issue of a new coinage.[4] He also confirmed Fulk Paynel's gift of Renham to Gilbert de Vere.[5] Oxford.

To this matter of a new coinage the Pipe-Roll of the year has many references, *e.g.*—

HAMPSHIRE. *Et pro locandis caretis et emendis tonellis ad thesaurum qui fuit missus Londoniam ad faciendam novam monetam* 27*s. per breve Regis. Et item pro locandis caretis ad portandum thesaurum ad Oxinford' mittendum Monetariis de Everwick'* 19*s.* 6*d. per idem breve. Et in carreagio thesauri missi Norhanton' ad monetam faciendam* 14*s. per idem breve.*

[1] Haughmond Chartulary.

[2] Rerum Gall. Script. xii. 285.

This was Henri le Libéral, Comte Palatine of Champagne, Troyes, Meaux, etc., and elder brother of Theobald, the contemporary Comte of Blois. He had married Mary, one of the two daughters of Louis VII. by Elianor of Aquitaine. He had been in the Crusade of 1146–7, and went again in 1179. He lived to return, but died 14 Feb. 1181.

Peter de Courtenay was a brother of Louis VII. His niece, named Agnes, was the destined bride of the above Record. Her destined husband was Alexius, son of the Emperor Emmanuel.

[3] It is evident that part of the monies sent to Nottingham was not to go further north, but was sent back in charge of two ordinary Clerks of the Treasury.

[4] *In assisâ apud Oxoniam quando consideratum fuit ut secunda moneta curreret.*

[5] Abbreviatio Placitorum, p. 98. Essex.

WINCHESTER. *In custamento ducendi archam Monetariorum cum cuneis, primo apud Oxineford' et postea Norhanton' et reducendi Wintoniam* 7*s.* 10*d.*

March 5. Richard, Bishop of Winchester, and Walter de Constanciis, keeper of the seal (*sigillifer Regis*) go on an embassy to Louis VII. The Pipe-Roll alludes to the fact.—

DOVER. *Et in passagio Episcopi Wintoniæ et eorum qui cum eo transfretaverunt* £4. 16*s. per breve Regis.* And so does the Roll of the Norman Exchequer allude to the Bishop's return;[1] for the Fermor of Barfleur charges,—*In passagio Episcopi Wintoniæ et Cambiatorum Regis, de Turonis et de Cenomanniâ* £10. 10*s. per breve Regis.*[2]

1180. c. April 5. The King being at Reading, Prince Henry comes over to England, swears to the observance of his father's will and pleasure, and consults his father about the aggressions made by the young King, Philip, in conjunction with the Comte of Flanders, on the rights of Philip's mother, and other French nobles. Reading.

c. April 10. About this time the King was probably at Winchester. Winchester. The Sheriff of Hampshire charges,—*In Camerâ Regis, Willielmo clerico et Turpino* £7. 13*s.* 4*d. per breve Regis.* A Royal Charter to the Canons of Legh (Devonshire) bears date at Winchester, and is attested by Master Walter de Constanciis, Godfrey de Lucy, and Ranulf de Glanvill.[3]

c. April 15. The King embarks at Portsmouth, the Prince at Dover, Portsmouth. both for Normandy. The Pipe-Roll has the following charge:—

SOUTHAMPTON. *Et in passagio Esneccæ quando Rex transfretavit* £7. 10*s. per breve Regis.*

Before he quitted England the King appointed Ranulf de Glanvill, High-Justiciar, or Viceroy, of England. The King's absence and Glanvill's position are illustrated by a few entries on the Pipe-Roll of Michaelmas, 1180.—

HAMPSHIRE. *In carriagio thesauri ultimo missi Londoniam et pro forellis et aliis necessariis thesauri* 22*s.* 3*d. per breve Rannulfi de Glanvill.*

SOUTHAMPTON. *Et in liberatione navis Radulfi Vituli Junioris qui portavit harnasiam Regis in Normanniam* 50*s. per breve Rannulfi de Glanvill. Et in liberatione navis quam Willielmus Anglicus et Willielmus de Bendinges habuerunt in transitu suo ad Regem in Normanniam* 25*s. per breve Regis.*

DOVER. *Et in passagio falconarionem et austrucariorum Regis per Willielmum de Gerponvill* £6. 15*s.* 3*d. per breve Randulfi de Glanvill.*

QUEEN ELIANOR, of whom a word should now be said, was probably a prisoner all this time at one of the King's Wiltshire residences. The Wiltshire Pipe-Roll charges,—*In procuratione Reginæ* £121. 15*s.* 8*d. per breve Regis. In corredio Reginæ* £12 *per idem breve.*

[1] The Bishop's return was not, perhaps, immediate on the discharge of his embassy. He probably awaited the King's arrival in Normandy, and remained there with the King till July (*infra*, p. 233). On Oct. 23 we have evidence of his being at Westminster (*infra*, p. 237).

[2] So that the King had Money-changers from Tours and Mans over to England, to assist in the new coinage. Diceto tells a story about Philip Aymari, a Mintman from Tours, who came over at the King's order, "*et numismatis innovandi procurationem suscepit.*" Philip was accused of fraudulent practices, and went home in disgrace.

[3] Monasticon, vi. 334. Num. i.

1180. c. April 16. On Henry's landing in Normandy, the Queen of France and Comte Theobald, of Blois, solicit his aid against Philip. Normandy.

c. April 17. The King at Alençon.[1] Alençon.

April 17. "*In Cœnâ Domini.*" Oliver de Turribus dies at Jerusalem.[2]
April 19. "*In Sabbato Sancto.*" Burial of Oliver de Turribus at Jerusalem, attended by Audebert, Comte of La Marche; Ademar, Vicomte of Limoges; and Bernard de Turribus (a relation of the deceased).[3]

April 20. The King keeps Easter at Le Mans. Hence perhaps, on the Norman Exchequer-Roll of this year, the Fermors of Alençon charge,—*Pro thesauro Regis portando de Alencon ad Cenomanniam* 16*s*. *per breve Regis*. Le Mans.

c. April 30. It is probable that about this time the King visited Angiers, and Chinon (in Touraine). Hence, in the Norman Exchequer-Roll of 1180, the Fermor of Falaise charges,—*In robâ Regis portandâ de Falasiâ ad Andegavum* 19*s*. *per breve Regis*.[3] Also, Roger fitz Tiold, Provost and Fermor of Caen, charges,—*Pro thesauris portandis de Cadomo in Andegav' et in plura loca per Normanniam* £6. 13*s*. 6*d*. *per breve Regis*.[3] Also, Herbert fitz Bernard, Fermor of the Forest of Goufern, charges,—*Pro portando hernesio Regis ad Chinon*.'[3] Angiers. Chinon. Chinon.

May 29. Margaret, Queen of the younger King, Philip,[4] is crowned at St. Denis by the Archbishop of Sens.

June 28. Conference between K. Henry and Philip of France at a place between Gisors and Trie.[5] The Comte of Flanders is present, and makes an agreement with Henry. Henry and Philip renew the treaty of Ivri, and appoint referees in case of future disputes, viz., on Philip's part, the Bishops of of Clermont, Nevers and Troyes, Comte Theobald, Comte Robert (of Dreux, probably), and Peter de Cortenai; on Gisors.

[1] Stubbs, quoting Rot. Normann. p. 81, where there is a charge for conveying royal treasure, *de Alenceon ad Cenom'* (from Alençon to Le Mans), as in the text.
[2] Gall. Script. xii. 447.
[3] Rot. Normanniæ pp. 50, 56. 17.
[4] Margaret, sometimes called Isabella, sometimes Elizabeth, was daughter of Baldwin, Comte of Hainault, by a sister of Philip, Comte of Flanders. This marriage of the young King Philip was displeasing to his mother, Queen Adela, of the House of Blois, and had thrown her and 'her brothers' (says the Record Gall. Script. xii. 298) into rebellion. Which of Queen Adela's brothers, beside Comte Theobald, is here meant, seems problematical. She had four living, viz., Henry, Comte of Champagne and Troyes (who was now in the East), Theobald, Comte of Blois; Stephen, Comte of Sancerre; and William, Archbishop of Rheims, whose non-appearance in the matter of the Coronation seems indeed abnormal.
[5] On the Norman Exchequer-Roll of 1180 (Rot. Norm. i, 77) the Fermor of the Roumois charges 3*s*. *pro Vassellâ Regis portandâ ad Gisortium*. It is impossible to say whether this refers to the meeting of June or to that of September,

1180. June 28 Henry's part, William, Bp of Le Mans; Peter, Bp of Perigueux (*Petragoritensis*); Robert, Bp of Nantes; Maurice de Creoun, William Maingot, and Peter de Mont Rabel.[1] Gisors.

It would seem that the Duke of Burgundy and the Comte of Bar were entertained by Henry in the Castle of Gisors on this occasion. In the Exchequer-Roll the Fermor of Rouen charges,—*In corredio Ducis Burgondiæ et Comitis de Bar apud Gisortium* £14. 1*s. per breve Regis. Pro* xxx *marcatis vassallæ quam Rex dedit Duci Burgondiæ et Comiti de Bar* £79. 7*s. per breve Regis.* (Rouen).[2]

June 30. Death of Hugh, surnamed De Kevelioc, Earl of Chester.[3]

c. July. About this time Richard de Hommet (or Humez), High Constable of Normandy, resigned office, and became a Monk in the Abbey of Aunay.

The King forthwith (as we must needs suppose), in a Charter dated at Caen, "gives to William de Humez the office (*Constabulariam*) which his father, Richard de Humez, used to hold (*habebat*) of the King. Witnesses,[4] R. Bp of Winchester; H. Bp of Baieux; Nicholas, Chaplain; Walter fitz Robert; Ranulf de Glanvill; Hugh de Creissi; Fulk Painell; Bertram de Verdon; Richard Giffard, Robert de Stutevill and Gilbert Pipard.[5] Caen.[2]

July 20. Sebrand, Bishop of Limoges, was received in that City, but soon retired for fear of K. Henry.[6]

July, Aug. In the Norman Exchequer-Roll of 1180, there is a charge for conveying the King's wine from Caen to Valognes and to Cherbourg, and again for conveying Royal treasure from Valognes to Cherbourg.[7] Valognes. Cherbourg.

A Writ of *safe-conduct* for the Monks of Mont St. Michel is dated *apud Valonias*, and attested singly by Brother Roger, the Almoner[8] (appointed June, 1177).[8]

[1] Fœdera, vol. i. p. 36.

[2] Stubbs (quoting Rot. Normann. i. 77) puts the King as going from Rouen to Caen, after June 28. The passage is merely a charge, *pro ducendo hernesio Regis a Rothomago ad Cadomum.*

[3] Monasticon iii. p. 218. But Benedictus would seem to date the Earl's death *c.* April, 1181.

[4] Some of these witnesses were holding important offices in Normandy at this very time, as we learn from the Exchequer-Roll of the year, *e.g.*—Hugh de Cressy was Custos of the Tower of Rouen, with a salary of £200 per annum; Fulk Paynell was Custos of the Castles of Alençon and Roche-Mabile and Fermor of the Royal demesnes in the Avranchin; Richard Giffard was Bailiff of the Oximin, and Custos of the Castle of Falaise; Robert de Stoteville was Fermor of Lillebone, and Custos of the Castles of Lions la Forêt and Arques; and Gilbert Pipard was Custos of the Castle, and Fermor of the Vicomté of Exmes.

[5] Cartæ Antiquæ DD. Glanvill's presence in Normandy on this occasion is not accounted for. Nevertheless, he was doubtless there.

[6] Gall. Script. xii. 489.

[7] Rot. Normann. i. 31.

[8] D'Anisy's Transcripts, ii. 289. See p. 215 *supra.*

1180. c. July. A Royal Charter, dated at Rouen, is probably of this period. It confirms to Roger Barr that which Richard de Humez, the Constable, had given him. It is attested by William fitz Ralph, Seneschal of Normandy, and Bertram de Verdon.[1] Rouen.

The accounts of the *Fermors* of Rouen contain several entries, which indicate the King's occasional presence at the capital during this summer, *e.g.*—

Pro venatione Regis portandâ de Rothomago ad Parisias £10 *per breve Regis. Pro bolgis et bahurdis et sellâ summarii et frenis et capistris ad Capellam Regis* 70*s.* 2*d. Pro bolgis et bahurdis et sellis et aliis necessariis ad summarios de Camerâ Regis et quadrigis* £14. 3*s. Pro summario et hernesio ejusdem ad portandam vaissellam Regis* £11. *Pro presentis Regis portandis de Rothomago ad Parisias ad Regem Franciæ* £4. *Ricardo Crasso pro robâ ad opus Regis* £17. 14*s.* 8*d.*

Also the Fermor of the Roumois charges,—*Pro faillatâ Regis faciendâ ante turrim Rothomagi* 58*s.* 2*d. per breve Regis. Et Falconariis Regis qui remanserunt post cum* 20*s. per idem breve.*

July, Aug. Sept. The Norman Exchequer-Roll gives evidence, more or less complete, of the King having visited a number of other places during the course of this summer and autumn.[2] We quote the Roll without an attempt at placing the entries in any chronological sequence.—

The Fermors of Alençon charge,—*Pro vinis Regis adducendis de Andegavi ad Argent', et pro duobus tonellis ejusdem vini portandis de Argent' ad Valonias* £17. 2*s. per breve Regis.* Argentan. Valognes.

The Fermors of Argentan charge,—*Pro ducendis* xxxiiij *tonellis vini de Andegavi ad Argenten' et inde ad Burum et Cadomum et Valonias et Cesarisburgum, et Tenerchebraium, et Danfront et Moritonium et Gorran et Falesiam* £55. 4*s. Pro portando thesauro Regis de Falesiâ ad Argent'* 10*s.* Bur le Roy. Caen. Cherbourg. Tenchebray. Damfront. Mortain. Gorron. Falaise.

The Fermor of Caen charges,—*Pro pastu gantarum quæ venerunt de Angliâ et pro* lx *de illis ducendis ad Argentom' et* lx *ad Burum* £6. 3*s.* 9*d.*

The Fermors of Rouen charge, *Pro tribus tonellis vini missis in Leons ad opus Regis* £19. *Pro duobus tonellis vini portandis a Rothomago ad Bonamvillam* 32*s.* Lions la Fôret. Bonneville sur Touque.

The Fermor of the Roumois charges,—*Pro hernesio Regis ducendo a Rothomago ad Cadomum* 40*s. Et pro thesauro Regis ducendo ad Drincort* 6*s.* 6*d. per breve Regis.* Drincort.

The Fermor of Ste Mére Eglise charges,—*Pro robâ Regis portandâ de Kileboto ad Bonamvillam* 3*s.* 2*d.*[3] Quillebœuf.

Some Charters, which perhaps passed between June and September of this year, will coincide therefore with the probability of the King having visited one or other of the above localities.—

[1] Cartæ Antiquæ, OO.

[2] As Mr. Stapleton well remarks, we have here ten chief places of the King's abode, all in Lower Normandy, and west of the River Dive.

[3] Professor Stubbs (quoting Rot. Normann. i. 68) supposes the King to have been at Dieppe between June and October; also at Bur, in October (quoting Rot. Normann. i. 39); also at Gorram (quoting Rot. Normann. i. 39); also at Falaise (quoting Rot. Normann. i. 50, 56); also at Angers (quoting Rot. Normann. i. 50, 56); also at several other places indicated in the text, but with the suggestion of somewhat different limits of chronology.

1180. June-Sept. (1) One, dated at Argentan, confirms to the Abbey of Argentan. Montmorel, in the Diocese of Avranches, the grants of John de Subleiguey, his wife Alice, and his son, Hasculf. Witnesses, Henry, Bishop of Bayeux; Froger, Bishop of Seez; William de Humet, Constable; Ranulf de Glanvill; Hugh de Cressi; Geoffrey P . . .; Gerard de Camvill; Robert de St. John; and William fitz Ralph.[1]

(2) Another, dated at Valognes, is in favour of the Abbey Valognes. of St. Mary de Longues (near Bayeux), and is attested by Richard, Bishop of Winchester; Henry, Bishop of Bayeux; Master Walter de Coutances; Godfrey de Luci; William fitz Ralph, Seneschal of Normandy; Alvered de St. Martin; Osbern de Hosa; and Hamo Pincerna.[2]

(3) A third, dated at Bur (*apud Burum*) is in favour of the Bur-le-Roy. same Abbey, and is attested by Henry, Bishop of Bayeux; Roger de Array; Robert de Sacy; William de Curtguidone (Courvandon), and Hamo Pincerna.[3]

(4) A fourth, dated at Bur, confirms an agreement made in the presence of Henry, Bishop of Bayeux, and is attested by M. Abbot, of Curzai; P. Abbot, of Caen; Master Walter de Coutances; Master J. (Josceline) Archdeacon of Chichester; Master Peter de Blois; William fitz Ralph, Seneschal of Normandy; Fulk Painel; Richard d'Aufay; Rob. de Brucourt; and Hamo Pincerna.[4]

(5) A fifth, dated at Gorron (*apud Gorham*), is to the Gorron. Abbey of Savigny, in the Diocese of Coutances, and is granted at request of Isabella, daughter of Walleran, Earl of Mellent. Its witnesses are, Master Walter de Constanciis; William, Archdeacon of Avranches; Maurice de Creon; Stephen de Turonis, Seneschal of Anjou; William de Humet, Constable; and Fulco Paganell.[5]

(6) A sixth, dated at Caen, is in favour of the Abbey of Caen. the Holy Trinity at Caen, and is attested by Henry, Bishop of Bayeux; William de Humet, Constable; William fitz Ralph, Seneschal of Normandy; Hugh de Cressy; Alvered de St. Martin; Robert de Brucourt (*Bruecuria*); Richard de Canvill; and Gilbert fitz Reinfrid.[6]

1 · 4 · 5 D'Anisy's Normandy Transcripts, ii. 107; iii. 77; iii. 195.

2 · 3 · 6 D'Anisy's Extrait des Chartes ii. 41; ii. 438. With reference to the first witness at Valognes, it may be stated that Richard, Bishop of Winchester, crossed from Barfleur to England before Michaelmas, accompanied by the King's money-changers of Tours and Le Mans. (Rot. Nor. i. 38.)

Aug. 10, 1180. Baldwin, Abbot of Ford, was consecrated Bishop of Worcester by Archbishop Richard at Lambeth.

Aug. 29. Audebert IV. Comte of La Marche died at Constantinople.[1]

Sept. 18. Louis VII. King of France, died.[2]

1180. c. Sept. 29. King Henry and Philip Augustus meet near Gisors, and renew the treaty of June 28. Gisors.

Hence, perhaps, on the Norman Exchequer-Roll of 1180, the Fermor of the Roumois charges,—3*s.* *pro vaisellâ Regis portandâ ad Gisortium.*[3] (Rouen).

Sept. 29. Presuming that the Roll of the Norman Exchequer is mainly an account of the fiscal year ending Michaelmas, 1180, it contains a few entries which are of some chronological importance. For instance—

William de Humez is in full office as Constable, though his father is alive :—*Willielmus de Hom' Constabularius debet compotum pro patre suo de vinagio Abrincassini et Ballivæ de Virâ.* And again, *In liberatione Willielmi de Hommet Constabularii* £100 *pro custodiâ Castri de Virâ.* And again, *In liberaacione Willielmi de Hommet Constabularii* £100 *pro custodiâ Castri de Ponte Ursonis.* And again, *Wills de Homet Constabularius reddit compotum de firmâ terræ Peurel.*

Ralph de Varneville, whom we have seen made Chancellor in 1173, still held that office, though Walter de Constanciis, the acting Chancellor, usually appears as Keeper of the Seal. The Roll mentions the Chancellor repeatedly, *e.g.*, *Radulfus Cancellarius r. c. de* £29 *de reguardo forestæ de Bort. Radulfus Cancellarius habet Vallem Rodolii et debet inde compotum de septem annis.*

Touching the Law-Proceedings in England during the fiscal year now ended :—

The Pipe-Roll of Michaelmas, 1180, gives the main results of the *Itinera* of the four Committees of Justiciars who had been appointed in April, 1179. It seems that nearly every county had been visited by a quorum of these justices, but the two Bishops are in no case recorded to have been *in eyre*, and the fourth Committee of six persons had divided itself into two committees of three persons each, and also re-arranged the counties it was to visit.

It would further seem that these *Itinera* had been accomplished early in the fiscal year now ended ; and that some of the justices had changed either their colleagues or their counties, or both. Thus we have notice of the exceptional *Iter* of Alan de Furnellis and Robert de Witefield in Berkshire, while that of Gilbert Pipard, and Geoffrey Hosee in Lincolnshire, &c., and that of Ranulf de Glanvill, Godfrey de Luci, and Hugh de Gahurst in Yorkshire, were according to the programme of April, 1179.[4]

In 1180, as has been already said, Ranulf de Glanville was appointed Chief Justiciar in or about the month of April.[5] It would seem too that his provincial *Iter* was ere then ended, and that the newer appointment did not prevent his accompanying or following the King to Normandy.

[1] Gall. Script. xii. 448.

[2] The Annals of Waverley (p. 161), placing Louis VII's. death on April 29, must not be regarded. Hoveden, Benedictus, and the Editors of Gall. Script. (xii. 448 *n*), all agree on Sept. 18. The Chron. St. Maxent (Ibm. p. 418), gives Sept. 20 and the 24th day after the death of Comte Audebert, as the date of Louis's death ; but the two items of date are inconsistent with each other.

[3] Rot. Normann. i. 77.

[4] In another instance, Ranulf de Glanvill, Godfrey de Luci, and Hugh de Gaherst, three members of the fourth Committee, visited Yorkshire, which was one of their proper counties ; but John Cumin, William de Bendinges, and Alan de Furnellis (the other three members of the fourth Committee) visited Gloucestershire, a county which belonged primarily to the members of the first committee. In short the justiciars were the same, but their circuits had been re-arranged.

[5] Hoveden, p. 600, Madox's Exchequer, p. 24. The appointment, we think, made him Viceroy, and did not work any material alteration in the administration of law in the provinces, though the *Itinera* certainly became less frequent, and the Justices who were subsequently employed were oftener Sheriffs than before. However, this remark demands its

MICHAELMAS, 1180, TO MICHAELMAS, 1181.

1180. c. Oct. 1. Henry, Duke of Saxony, being dethroned by the Emperor Frederick, takes refuge at the Court of his Father-in-law, Henry, King of England. Normandy.

Oct. 23. The Justiciars sitting at the Exchequer at Westminster, on this day, were Richard, Bp of Winchester, Geoffrey, Bp of Ely, John, Bp of Norwich, Ranulf de Glanvill, Richard the Treasurer, William Basset, Alan de Furnellis, and Robert Mantel.[1]

They made Record of the purchase by William Briwere of half a knight's-fee in Ilesham (Devon) from his own tenants thereof, viz., Hawyse de Ilesham, Ralph, her husband, Roger, her son and heir, and Anger his brother.

Nov. 4. The new coinage issued in England (according to Gervase). The Pipe-Roll of Michaelmas, 1181, illustrates the matter.—

Notts and Derbyshire. *Et in custamento ducendi thesaurum a Notingeham usque Norhanton' et pro forulis et aliis minutis negotiis Cambii* 21*s.* 2*d. per breve Regis.*

Worcestershire. *Et in carragio thesauri a London usque Wirecestr' ad cambium faciendum et item a Wirecestr' usque London; et pro forulis et tonellis ad eundem thesaurum deferendum* £8. 8*s.* 10*d. per breve Regis.*

Yorkshire. *Et in custamento ducendi thesaurum ab Everwich' usque Niwewerch* (Newark) *et pro domo cambii reficiendâ et in minutis necessariis Cambii* 71*s.* 3*d. per breve Regis.*

Lincolnshire. *Et in custamento deferendi thesaurum Regis a Lincol' usque Notingeham ad faciendum ibi cambium. Et item a Lincol' usque London' ad reponendum ibi in thesauro* 20*s. per breve Regis.*

Norfolk and Suffolk. *Et in carragio thesauri per ballivam (Vicecomitis) ad faciendum cambium et item thesauri missi London' multis vicibus* 39*s.* 5*d.*

London. *Et pro conducendo thesauro a London' usque Hereford' per Brunburdin et socios ejus* 21*d. per breve Regis. Et item pro conducendo thesauro misso a London' usque Norhanton' et Notingeham ad faciendum cambium* 16*s. per breve Regis.*

Nov. 16. Seffrid (II.) consecrated Bishop of Chichester at Canterbury.

Dec. 25. The King keeps Christmas at Le Mans. The Archbishop of Bordeaux, with many Bishops, Earls, and Barons, are present. Le Mans.

The King enacts a statute of arms for his transmarine dominions.

Dec. 25. Audomar (V) Comte of Limoges, returning from the Crusade, is received at Limoges.[2]

c. Dec. 31. The King is at Angers. Angers.

qualification, for among the Sheriffs of 1180, we count no less than thirteen who were or had been justices-in-eyre. These were William fitz Ralph (Sheriff of Notts and Derbyshire), Robert Mantel (of Essex and Herts), William Rufus (of Bucks and Bedfordshire), Gervase de Cornhull (of Surrey), William fits Stephen (of Gloucestershire), William Basset (of Lincolnshire), Roger fitz Reinfrid (of Sussex), Thomas fitz Bernard (of Northants), Bertram de Verdon (of Warwicksh. and Leic.), Michael Belet (of Worcestershire), Ranulf de Glanville (of Yorkshire), Alan de Furneaux (of Cornwall), and Robert fitz Bernard (of Kent).

[1] Madox, Exchequer, p. 146. Dugd. Baronage, p. 700. It need occasion no doubt as to Glanvill's being Chief Justice at the time. that even in the Court of Exchequer he is made to succeed three Bishops. The latter often took precedence of even Princes of the blood.

[2] Gall. Script. xii. 448.

In the year 1180 died Giles, Bishop of Evreux;[1] Richard, Bishop of Coutances; R. Bishop of St. Andrews; John, Bishop of Chichester; and Joseph, Abbot of Reading;[2] also in Lent (March 5–April 16) Garin, Archbishop of Bourges.

Also, in the same year, Philip, Comte of Flanders, gave in marriage his two nieces (daughters of Matthew Earl of Boulogne) viz., Ida, the eldest, to (Gerard), Comte of Gerres (Gelders); and (Matilda) the youngest, to (Henry the Warrior), the son of the Duke of Louvain (and afterwards Duke of Lorrain).[3]

Also in the same year, John of Salisbury, Bishop of Chartres, at the prayer of K. Henry II, released John, Comte of Vendome, from his sentence of Excommunication. The Bishop, formerly a staunch servant and friend of Becket, begins and ends his diploma of absolution as follows:—"*Johannes divinâ dignatione et meritis Sancti Martyris Thomæ, Carnotensis Ecclesiæ Minister humilis,*" *&c.* *Actum public anno Gratiæ* 1180.[4]

A.D. 1181.

1181. c Feb. 5. The King is in Normandy. Laurence, Archbishop of Dublin, comes to him bringing a hostage, a son of the King of Connaught. Normandy.

The said Archbishop dies at Ewe. Geoffrey de Haye, a Clerk of the King, accompanied by a Clerk of the Legate Alexius, is sent to Ireland to seize the vacant see in *manu Regis.* Also John, Constable of Chester, and Richard Peche, are sent to hold Dublin, in Hugh de Lacy's place, the latter having married a daughter of the King of Connaught without King Henry's licence.[5]

Feb. 14. Henry, Comte of Troyes and Champagne, died in France, or his return from the Crusade.

c. March. Geoffrey, Bishop Electof Lincoln, being already Chancellor, renounces his election to Lincoln. This was evidently in Normandy. Geoffrey consulted the King (his father), his three half-brothers, Henry, Richard, and Geoffrey, and the Bishops, Reginald of Bath, Froger of Seez, Henry of Baieux, and Seffrid of Chichester, before he wrote to Archbishop Richard to announce his resolution.[6]

About this time the King being at Ivry, we have the first appearance of William, son and heir of Patric, Earl of Salisbury. The evidence is a Charter to Wenlock Priory,[7] dated at Ivri, whereby the King ratifies an agreement made in 1180, between Geoffrey de Say and his wife Adeliza (widow of Hugh de Periers), and the said Priory. The witnesses of the King's confirmation are William, Earl Ivry.

[1] Benedictus (Stubbs) i. 269. Hoveden puts the death of Bishop Giles in 1181. John fitz Luke, his successor, was appointed according to Benedictus (vol. i. 278), in July, 1181; but in other passages (pp. 278, 290, 291), Benedictus places the death of Bishop Giles, and the appointment of Bishop John, in 1181, and in 1182.

[2] Joseph was succeeded in the Abbacy of Reading by Hugh II., who in 1199, became Abbot of Clugni.

[3] Benedictus (apud Stubbs) i. 269.

[4] Gall. Script. xii. 489.

[5] This is from Hoveden. The Staffordshire Pipe Roll of the year is in wonderful consonance.—*Et in acquietando passagio Johannis Constabularii Cestriæ, Ricardi de Pech, Galfridi de Haia, et Widonis Clerici Legati in Hiberniam, per breve Ranulfi de Glanvill, &c. &c.*

[6] Rymer's Fœdera, i. p. 37. Benedictus i. 271.

[7] Monasticon, v. 73. Note.

1181. c. March. Mandeville; William, Earl of Salisbury; Richard Dufay,[1] Richard de Lucy,[2] Hugh de Cressi, Reginald de Luci, Robert de Stuteville, Gilbert Pipard and Girard de Canville.[3] Ivry.

March 5. The King at Valasse.[4] Valasse.

c. March. The King at Grandmont.[5] At prayer of the Monks, he allows to Saibrand, Bishop of Limoges, the fief which he held of the Duchy of Aquitaine. Saibrand had already been a second time to Limoges by grace of both King and Duke. Grammont.

April 5. The King keeps Easter at Chinon. Chinon.

At Chinon is dated a Royal Charter to the Abbey of St. Martin at Marmontier, near Tours. It is attested by Master Walter de Constanciis, Archdeacon of Oxford; William Paynel; Gervase Paynel; Ambric, Archdeacon; Stephen de Turri (Qy. Turonis), Seneschal of Anjou; Hugh Bardulf, Dapifer; Geoffrey fitz Piers; Ernise de Nevill.[6]

A Charter to Walter, Usher (Ostiario) of the King's chamber, is also dated at Chinon, and attested by "Geoffrey my son and my Chancellor," Richard de Humez,[7] Maurice de Creon, William Marescall, Gilbert Pipard, Gilbert fitz Reinfrid, and William Dean of Moriton.[8]

c. April 10. The King goes into Normandy. Normandy.

April 27. Henry confers with Philip at the Ford of St. Remigy, near Nonancourt. The Templars and Hospitallers present letters of Pope Alexander, dated on January 16th previous, urging the Crusade. The two Kings promise to assist the enterprise. Gué St. Remy (near Nonancourt).

April 28. K. Henry moves towards the coast. Hugh, Comte of Bar, meets him and asks leave to attack the Saracens in Spain.

[1] Read *De Alfai*. Richard De Alfai occurs in the Norman Roll of 1180 (p. 67), as holding land of the King's gift at Frenaie-sous-Bellencombre.

[2] Not the great Justiciar, who was dead; but one who appears in the above Roll as tenant of certain land at Gorron (in Maine) (Ibm. p. 23).

[3] In 1180 the King excused Gerard de Camvill £800 of his father's debts in Normandy (Ibidem, p. 63).

[4] R. de Monte, p. 926.

Stubbs (quoting Geoff. Vigeois, 326). Another way of stating the same thing is that the King being at Grammont Abbey, in Lent, (Feb. 18–April 4), restored the previously forfeited temporalities (*feuvum quod auferebat*) of Saibrand, Bishop of Limoges, as he already held them by favour of the Duke (Richard). See Gall. Script. xii. 418.

[6] Monasticon, vii. p. 1097.

[7] Not the constable of Normandy, who died in this year, and who if living at the date of the above was a monk of Aunay. His grandson, the above witness, was eldest son of Wm. de Humez, the existing Constable; but he appears early in life at Court, in consequence of his marriage with a great heiress.

[8] Cartæ Antiquæ, DD.

1181. c. April. William, King of Scots, lands at Barfleur, to consult Henry about Matthew and John, Bishops of Aberdeen and St. Andrews, whom he had banished. King Henry is on the point of embarking for England when he hears that the Comte of Flanders had invaded Philip's territory. Barfleur

This derangement of the King's plans is perhaps connected with the following charge on the Southampton Pipe-Roll,—*Et in liberacione Esneccæ quæ missa fuit contra Regem*[1] £7. 10*s. per breve Randulfi de Glanvill.*

In or about this month of April, Hugh, Earl of Chester, is said to have died.[2]

c. June. John fitz Luce, a clerk of Master Walter de Constantiis, becomes Bishop Elect of Evreux.[3]

Arnulf, Bishop of Liseux, resigns his see, having never been reconciled to the King since the rebellion of 1174. He is succeeded by Ralph de Warneville (or Varneville), lately Chancellor to the King, Treasurer and Archdeacon of Rouen, and Treasurer of York.

June 24. The walls of Limoges levelled by order of Duke Richard.[4]

c. July. K. Henry at Gisors, reconciles the King of France and the Comte of Flanders. William King of Scots and the young King Henry were present. Gisors.

Quite hypothetically the following charters of the King are noticed in this order of time.—

(1) Charter dated at Caen, to Monteburg Abbey. Witness, Geoffrey Bp of Ely.[5] Caen.

(2) Charter dated at Cherbourg in favour of St. Mary de Voto at Cherbourg, attested by Geoffry, Bp of Ely; R. (Richard) Bishop of Avranches; and Stephen de Turri (read Turonis), Seneschal of Anjou.[6] Cherbourg.

(3) Charter dated at Cherbourg, confirming to L'Essay Abbey (Coutances Dioc.) the grants of Richard de Haia. Witnesses, Henry, Bishop of Baieux; John, Bishop of Evreux; William fitz Ralph, Seneschal of Normandy; Saer de Quinci; and Hugh de Cressi.[7]

July 26. The King, with William of Scotland, embarks at Cherbourg, and lands at Portsmouth. Soon afterwards the King sent some hawks to his son Henry, and other presents to his daughter, the Queen of Castile. Certain charges on the Pipe-Roll show these facts, as also that Queen Elianor had remained in England while Henry was abroad.— Cherbourg. Portsmouth.

[1] *Contra Regem* means "to meet the King;"—"against the King's coming," as we say colloquially.

[2] Benedictus. But see June 30, 1180, for a various date.

[3] The year 1182 is also given as the date of this (compare Hoveden, p. 350, and Benedictus Abbas (Hearne) pp. 364, 380.)

[4, 5] Gall. Script. xii. 448. Monasticon, vii. 1097.

[6] Neustria Pia, p. 852.

[7] D'Anisy's Normandy Transcripts, ii. 63.

HONOUR OF ARUNDEL. *Et Ricardo de Wada et sociis suis unam marcam ad portandos nisos ultra mare Regi Regis filio per breve Regis.*

LONDON. *Et Fierebrachio* 39*s.* 6*d. ad faciendas malas et alia minuta vasa ad portandam vassellam et pannos quos Rex misit filiæ suæ in Hyspania per breve Regis et per visum Edwardi Blundi.*

DORSET AND SOMERSET. *Et Radulfo filio Stephani* £32. 6*s.* 8*d. ad acquietandum corredium Reginæ per breve Ranulfi de Glanvill.*

HAMPSHIRE. *Et Radulfo filio Stephani ad procuracionem Reginæ* £60 *per breve Randulfi de Glanvill. Et item eidem Radulfo ad procuracionem Reginæ* £18 *per breve Randulfi de Glanvill.*

1181. c. August. First, after his landing in England, King Henry occurs as at Canterbury.[1] Canterbury.

On leaving Canterbury it is evident that the King took a journey northwards in company with the King of Scots.

The following entry by the Fermor of Higham (Northants) may possibly relate entirely to the circulation of the new coinage; but it may also be possibly connected with the movements of the Court.—*Et pro deferendo thesauro a Norhanton' usque Lincol' per Brimburd et Manse Cambitores Regis; et item a Norhanton' usque London' et item a Norhanton' usque Notingeham, et item a Norhanton usque Winton' per Johannem Cumin et Willielmum Malduit Camerarium* 35*s. per breve Regis.*

c. August. We are expressly told of the King being at Nottingham.[2] Nottingham. With him were the Archbishops of Canterbury and York, the King of Scots, and the Bishops of Durham, Ely, Norwich, and Chichester. The Abp of Canterbury proceeded from Nottingham to Lincoln; the King probably kept on to the North. Another evidence of the King's visit to Nottingham is that Michael Belet (Sheriff of Worcestershire) sent wine thither from Feckenham.

A Charter to the order of Lazarites, bearing date at Clipston, very possibly belongs to this period. It is attested by Geoffrey the King's son, Fulk Painel, Reginald de Curteneye, Robert de Stuteville, Ralph fitz Stephen, Bertram de Verdon, Michael Belet, and William de Bendinges.[3] Clipston.

A Charter, dated at Pontefract, is some evidence of the King's northward journey. It is a confirmation to one Reiner de Wextonesham, at the prayer of Ranulf de Glanvill. It is attested by Hugh Murdach, John Cumin, Bertram de Verdun, Michael Belet, William de Bendinges, Hugh de Cressi, and Robert fitz Bernard.[4] Pontefract.

[1] Diceto, 612.
[2] Benedictus Abbas (Stubbs), i. 280.
[3] Cartæ Antiquæ, KK.
[4] Cartæ Antiquæ, P.

1181. c. August. From a Charter, too, dated at York, we infer the King's onward progress. It is a grant to Kirkeham Abbey, and is attested by R., Abp of York; Hugh, Bp of Durham, Hugh Murdac, Ranulf de Glanvill, Reginald de Curtenai, William de Lanval, Thomas Basset, Michael Belet, and William de Bending.[1] York.

A Charter dated at Knaresborough is to Finchale Chapel (Durham), and is attested by Hugh, Bp of Durham, John Cumin, Hugh Murdac, Ranulf de Glanvill, Michael Belet, and William de Bending.[2] Knaresborough.

And a Grant to Marrick Priory (Yorkshire), dated at Richmond, is the furthest point to which we can trace this northern journey, (unnoticed by any of the Chroniclers). It is attested by Hugh Murdach, Ranulf de Glanvill, Michael Belet, and William de Bendinges.[3] Richmond.

c. August 15. Prince Richard leads an army into Gascogne. He occupies Lectoure (Lactoram). Vivian, Vicomte of La Lomaque, surrenders to him, and receives the belt (of knighthood) at St. Sever (Stm. Severum).[4]

August 30. Pope Alexander III. died.

September 1. Lucius III. elected Pope; crowned September 6.

c. Sept. 1. The King appears next at Lichfield, and granting to Wombridge Priory (Shropshire). The Deed is attested by Godfrey de Lucy; Master Joceline, Archdeacon of Chichester; Humphrey de Bohun, Constable; Roger Bigod; Robert fitz Bernard; Ralph fitz Stephen, Chamberlain, and Michael Belet.[5] Lichfield.

Another Charter to the same house, and attested by the same witnesses, is dated at Feckenham (Worcestershire), and shows the course of the Royal progress.[5] Moreover the Pipe-Roll shows Michael Belet, Sheriff of Worcestershire, sending venison of the King's to Marlborough. Feckenham.

Sept. 6. The King is at Evesham. It is Sunday. He approves the nomination of John Cumin to the Archbishoprick of Dublin, the electors being the Prelates and clergy of England, and certain clerks of Dublin Province. Evesham.

Probably the King's journey southward lay through Marlborough. Marlborough.

[1] Cartæ Antiquæ, V.

[2] Collectanea Topographica et Genealogica, vol. iv. p. 80.

[3] Monasticon, iv. 245.

[4] Gall. Script. xii. 449.

[5] Wombridge Chartulary, Nos. 491, 506.

1181. Sept. 12. The King is at Winchester. William, Archbishop of Rheims, who had visited Becket's shrine early in the month, finds the King at Winchester, and, leaving him there, returns to France by way of Dover.[1] Winchester.

Sept. 20. Robert, Comte of Mellent, died.

An Interdict was laid about this time on the realm of Scotland. It was pronounced by Roger, Abp of York, as Legate, and Hugh, Bp of Durham.

While at Winchester, and probably on this occasion, the King made a grant to Elycia, daughter of Arnald the Goldsmith. Witnesses, R. Bishop of Avranches; Godfrey de Luci; John Cumin; Earl William de Mandeville;[2] Ranulf de Glanvill; Stephen de Turris (Qy. Turonis), Seneschal of Anjou; Peter fitz Gwido; Ralph fitz Stephen, Chamberlain; and William de Bending.[3]

---

c. July–Sept. The autumn of this year was marked by a Crusade against the Albigenses, led by Henry, Bishop of Albano.[4]

Sept. 29. FOR THE FISCAL YEAR, now ended, the Pipe-Roll of 27 Hen. II. gives us scant record of the *Itinera* of Justices. Ranulf de Glanvill had held *Nova Placita and Novas Conventiones* in Norfolk, Suffolk, Lincolnshire and Yorkshire. Under the title *Nova Placita et Novæ Conventiones :—De Placitis Curiæ*; there had been an *Assize* in Kent, but the president justices are not named.

MICHAELMAS, 1181, TO MICHAELMAS, 1182.

c. Oct. About this time the King was much in Wiltshire, and probably at Salisbury. One proof of this is that, at Michaelmas, 1182, the Sheriff of Wiltshire charges 34*s*. 5*d*. for taking treasure many times from Sarum to Winchester, and from Winchester to Sarum; also the Sheriff of Hampshire (as we shall see below) charges for taking treasure to Salisbury. Salisbury.

[1] The Dover Pipe-Roll of 1181, gives us no account of the return to France of the Archbishop; probably because his passage was not at K. Henry's charges. But nearly at the same time an embassy from Louis returned by way of Dover, and for its passage K. Henry was at charges with the Warden of Dover. The entry on the accounts of the latter runs thus,—*In passagiis Comitis de Dammartin et nuntiorum Regis Franciæ* 20*s*. *per breve Regis*.

[2] It seems that about this time, Earl William de Mandeville either went on, or had returned from, some continental embassy. His going is distinctly marked on the Dover Pipe-Roll as previous to Michaelmas, 1181. — (DOURA.—*Et in passagio Comitis Willielmi de Mandeville* 100*s*. *per breve Regis*). We presume that the Earl's embassy was that recited by Benedictus (i. 287), as indefinitely previous to certain other events of March, 1182. Benedictus's story is that the Earl (here styled *D'Aumale*) was ambassador to the Emperor Frederick to obtain a remission of the sentence of seven years exile pronounced on the Duke of Saxony. The Earl and other envoys from France and Flanders got six of the seven years to be taken off. The Duke hereupon went into exile for a year. He reached Normandy in May, 1182.

[3, 4] Cartæ Antiquæ, C. 23. Gall. Script. xii. 448.

1181. Oct.-Dec. A number of Royal Charters belong probably to the last three months of 1181. These we arrange without any assumption as to their proper sequence.— Winchester.

(1.) Charter to St. Giles's Hospital at Wilton, dated at Clarendon, and attested by Master John Cumin, Hugh Murdach, Brother Roger the Almoner, Ralph fitz Stephen, Chamberlain; Michael Belet, and William de Bending.[1] Clarendon.

(2.) Charter to Shaftesbury Nunnery, dated at St. Edward (*i.e.*, at Shaftesbury), mentioning Mary, the King's sister as Abbess there, and attested by Master Laurence Archdeacon of Bedford; Master Joceline, Archdeacon of Chichester; Roger, the King's Chaplain; Ralph fitz Stephen, Chamberlain; Thomas fitz Bernard; and Eustace fitz Stephen.[2] Shaftesbury.

(3.) Charter to Derley Abbey (Derbyshire), dated at Woodstock, attested by Geoffrey the King's son; William de Humez, Constable; Reginald de Courtenay; Richard de Aufre (probably Aufai), Wydo de St. Wallery; and William de Curtmorlimer.[4] Woodstock.

(5). Charter to the Canons of Waltham (Essex), dated at Westminster, and attested by Bishops, Richard of Winchester, Geoffrey of Ely, and John of Norwich; also by Geoffrey, the King's son and Chancellor; by Master Walter de Constantiis; Master Laurence, Archdeacon of Bedford; Ranulf de Glanvill; Reginald de Curtenay; William de Humez, Constable; and Walter fitz Robert.[5] Westminster.

Nov. 22. Roger, Archbishop of York, dies at York. Hugh, Bishop of Durham, buries him. William, King of Scotland, still under an Interdict, sends Joscceline, Bp of Glasgow, and Arnulf, Abbot of Melrose, to Pope Lucius.

c. Nov. 29. The Comte of Flanders attacks the French territory. King Philip's uncles, viz., William, Archbishop of Rheims, and Comtes Theobald and Stephen, are with Flanders. Philip is assisted by young King Henry.

[Dec. 1. The following justiciars were sitting in the *Curia Regis* at Westminster, viz., R. Bishop of Winton; G. Bp of Ely; and Ranulf de Glanvill, "Justices of the King;" Richard the Treasurer; Godfrey de Luci; Roger fitz Reinfrid; Michael Belet; Gilbert de Colevill; Ranulf de Gedding; Gervase de Cornhill; and Osbert fitz Hervey.[6]]

Dec. 25. "The King keeps Christmas at Winchester; and after- Winchester.

[1] Journal of the Archæol. Institute (1861), p. 312.
[2] Monasticon, ii. 484, Num. xx.
[3] Cotton MS. Vespas, E. xxii. fo. 3.
[4] Monasticon, vi. p. 359.
[5] Cartæ Antiquæ, M.
[6] Fines (printed), vol. i. p. xxii. This Fine is entered on the Pipe-Roll of Michaelmas, 1182, but it is dated as on December 1, 28 Henry II. (1182). We rather incline to adhere to the date given on the Fine, and consequently repeat the quotation a year later (*Infra*, p. 249).

1181. Dec. wards remains about the southern coast waiting a fair wind to sail to Normandy." This statement of Benedictus is well supplemented by a charge on the Hampshire Pipe-Roll.— Winchester.

Et pro locandis caretis quæ detulerunt thesaurum a London' usque Winton' et partem ejusdem thesauri ad Salesburiam et item Porcestriam et pro multis negotiis thesauri dum Rex moratus fuit in maritimis £6. *Et in liberacione Clerici Thesaurarii et Camerariorum dum moram fecerunt apud Portesmue ante transfretationem Regis* £7. 10*s. per breve Regis.*

While at Winchester and surely on this occasion, the King expedited a Charter to Godstow Nunnery.

(1.) It is attested by Richard, Bp of Winchester; Geoffrey, Bp of Ely; B. Bishop of Worcester; Geoffrey the King's son and Chancellor; Master Laurence, Archdeacon of Bedford; Master Walter de Constanciis; Roger, the King's Chaplain; Ranulf de Glanvill; Reginald de Curtenai; William de Humez, Constable; Roger le Bigoth; Gilbert Pipard; Bertram de Verdon; Ralph fitz Stephen, Chamberlain; William fitz Adelm, Dapifer; Alan de Furnellis; Hugh de Morewyk; Robert de Witefeld; William de Bending; William Rufus; Richard, Rufus; and Durandus de Ostill.[1]

(2.) Another Charter, dated at Winchester, is to Hugh Esturmi; and is attested by Ric. Bp of Winton; Geoffrey Ridel, Bp of Ely; Reginald de Curtenai; and Hugh de Morewic.[2]

(3.) Another, also dated at Winchester, is to Stratford Abbey (Essex); and is attested by Rich. Bp of Winton; G. Bp of Ely; B. Bp of Worcester; S. Bishop of Chichester; Geoffrey the King's son and Chancellor; Master Laurence, Archdeacon of Bedford; Master Walter de Constanciis; Godfrey de Luci; Richard the Treasurer; Rannulf de Glanvill; Roger Bigot; Reginald de Curtenai; Walter fitz Robert; Hugh de Cressi; Hugh de Beauchamp; and Reginald de Paveilli.[3]

(4.) Another, dated at Winchester, is to Dureford Abbey[4] (Sussex); and is attested by R. Bishop of

[1] Godstow Chartulary, fo. 165.

[2] Cartæ Ducatûs Lancastriæ.

[3] Cartæ Antiquæ, X.

[4] Monasticon, vii. 938. Num. ii.

1181. c. Dec. Winchester; P. Bishop of St. Davids; Geoffrey the Chancellor, the King's son; Master Walter de Constanciis; Ranulf de Glanvill; Gilbert Pipert; Bertram de Verdon; Robert de Wytefeld, and Michael Belet. Winchester.

(5.) Another, also dated at Winchester, is to Stratfleur Abbey (Cardiganshire); and is attested by Richard, Bishop of Winchester; Geoffrey, Bishop of Ely; Seffrid, Bp of Chichester; Peter, Bp of St. Davids; and Geoffrey the Chancellor, the King's son.[1]

A.D. 1182.

1182. Jan. 1. The King probably at Winchester. Winchester.

Jan. 6. The King is at Marlborough. Geoffrey the Chancellor, in presence of the King, the Archbishop, and many Bishops, renounces his election to the See of Lincoln.[2] Marlborough

A Royal Charter to Dureford Abbey (Sussex), bears date at Marlborough, and is attested by William de Humet, Constable; Roger Bigot, and William fitz Aldelm.[3]

c. Feb. While the King was waiting on the Coast, he probably visited Aruudel. A Charter to the Burgesses of Beverley (Yorkshire), bears date at Arundel, and is quite in keeping with the fact that the See of York was vacant at the assumed time of its passing. It is attested by R. Bp of Winchester; G. Bp of Ely; J. Bp of Norwich; Geoffrey the King's son and Chancellor; John the King's son; Master Walter de Custanciis; G. de Lucy; R. de Glanvill; Reginald de Courtenay; R. Bigot; Hugh de Cressi; Hugh de Morewic; Alan de Furnellis; Robert de Witefeld; Michael Belet; and William Rufus, Dapifer.[4] Arundel.

Feb. 21. The Prior of St. Edmundsbury, finds the King at Bishops Waltham (Hampshire.)[5] Bishops Waltham.

Feb. 22. The King holds a Council at Bishops Waltham and makes his Will. He addresses the four Princes, his sons, and appoints trustees for various bequests, viz., the Abps of Canterbury and Rouen, and the Bps of Winchester, Worcester, Ely, Norwich, Baieux, Avranches, Seez,

[1] Monasticon, v. 633. Num. ii.

[2] Diceto. Ymag. Hist. p. 613. This we take to have been a second, and more formal renunciation. (*Vide supra*, p. 238).

[3] Cotton MS. Vespas. E. xxii. fo. 3.

[4] Fœdera, vol. i. p. 40.

[5] Chronicle of Josceline de Brakelond (Camden Soc.), pp. 15, 47.

1182. Feb. 22. Evreux, Le Mans, and Angiers, and also Ranulf de Glanvill, "Justiciar of England." The witnesses of the Deed are R. Bp of Winchester; John, Bp of Norwich; G. the Chancellor, "my son"; Master Walter de Constanciis, Archdeacon of Oxford; Godfrey de Lucy, Archdeacon of Derby; Ranulf de Glanvill; Roger fitz Reinfrid; Hugh de Morewic; Radulf fitz Stephen, Chamberlain; and William Rufus.[1] Bishops Waltham.

c. March 10-11. The King embarks at Portsmouth,[2] and lands at Barfleur. Portsmouth.

It is evident that while the King was absent in Normandy, the Queen remained in England, and that Ranulf de Glanvill was left as Viceroy. The following from the Pipe-Roll of Michaelmas, 1182, will suffice on both points.— Barfleur.

DORSET AND SOMERSET. *Et Radulfo filio Stephani £20 ad corredium Reginæ per breve Ranulfi de Glanvill.*

BUCKS AND BEDFORDSHIRE. *Et Willielmo de Gerpunvilla ad liberaciones* vi *austrucariorum qui transfretaverunt ad Regem £4 per breve Ranulfi de Glanvill.*

March 11. Pope Lucius, at Velletre, releases William of Scotland from the Interdict.

March 13. John Cumin, already a Cardinal, is ordained Priest by Pope Lucius at Velletre.

March 21. John Cumin is consecrated Archbishop of Dublin by the Pope.

K. Henry has a conference at Senlis with Philip of France, and Philip Comte of Flanders. Henry the young King; Henry Bishop of Albano, Pope's-Legate; and William, Archbishop of Rheims, were present. Senlis.

April 29. The following persons were sitting in the *Curia Regis* at Westminster, viz., *R. Bp of Winchester; John, Bp of Norwich;* and Rannulf de Glanvill, "Justiciars of the King;" Richard, the Treasurer; Roger fitz Reinfrid: William Rufus; *Thomas fitz Bernard;* William Basseth; Michael Belet; *William Torel;* Osbert de Glanvill; *William de Albervill*; Rannulf de Gedding; and *Gervase de Cornhill*[3]

May 1. The first, second, seventh, tenth, twelfth, and fourteenth of the above-named, together with Walter fitz Robert, were sitting in like manner, in the *Curia Regis* at Westminster.[4]

About this time the King was in Poitou.[5] Poitou.

c. May 20. The King is at Grandmont,[6] in La Marche. Grandmont.

Then at St. Yriez, in Limousin.[6] St. Yriez.

[1] Rymer's Fœdera I. 47. Diceto, p. 613.

[2] Diceto (p. 613), puts the King at Portsmouth on March 3, and at Barfleur on March 4. But Benedictus (i. 285) says, that the King was delayed some time on the English coast, and that his transfretation was not till after Midlent, which fell on March 7th.

[3, 4] Printed Fines, vol. 1. pp. xxi. and 60.

[5] Benedictus (Stubbs), i. p. 288. It is evident that, from May to August, Benedictus knew nothing whatever of the King's movements.

[6] Geoffrey of Vigeois (Gall Script. xii, 330).

1182. c. May.	After St Yriez, the King appears at Pierre Buffiere.[1]	Pierre Buffiere.
June 24.	The King is at Grandmont.[1]	Grandmont.
July 1.	Then at Perigueux.[2]	Perigueux.
c. July 1–8.	And then at Limoges.[2]	Limoges.

In the summer of 1182, Radulph Puher (called erroneously Sheriff of Gloucestershire) was, with many others, while employed in building a border castle, slain by the Welsh. Ranulf de Glanvill attacks the Welsh, but suffers some loss while rebuilding the said castle.[3]

c. July. Hugh, Bishop of Durham, offends K. Henry by refusing to give up a legacy which had been left to him by Roger, late Archbishop of York.

Rolland, Archbishop-elect of Dol, and Selvan, Abbot of Rivaulx, are Legates from Pope Lucius to negotiate between William, King of Scots, and John and Hugh, rival Bishops of St. Andrews.

July 26. Walter, Bishop of Rochester, died.

c. Aug. When the King returned into Normandy,[4] he found the Duke and Duchess of Saxony taking shelter during their banishment. The Duchess remains with her father, and soon afterwards gives birth to a son at Argentan. The Duke, meantime, had gone on a pilgrimage to Compostella. (Normandy. Argentan.)

c. Sept. The King was wishing to return to England, but the discontent and waywardness of his son Henry, who had gone into the French territory, detained him.

In the fiscal year now ended, we notice the *Iter* of Godfrey de Luci, Alan de Furnellis, Hugh de Morewic, Robert de Witefeld, and Michael Belet, who, some or all of them, visited Yorkshire, Staffordshire, Shropshire, Herefordshire, Worcestershire, Gloucestershire, Somersetshire, Dorsetshire, and Wiltshire.

Also the County of Oxfordshire had been visited by Robert de Witefeld, but, in this instance, his associates *in eyre* were Roger fitz Reinfrid, William Basset, and Michael Belet. Also the County of Southampton had been visited by Ranulf de Glanvill and his associates, who are unnamed.

The Dover Pipe-Roll of the above year gives a curious list of persons who crossed the Straits at the King's cost, and in pursuance of the King's Writs. *In passagio Willi de Yerpunvill et Austrucariorum Regis* £4. 17*s*. *per breve Regis. In passagio Johannis electi Ebroicensis et Bertrami de Verdon* 48*s*. *per breve Regis. In passagio Episcopi de Sto. David et Abbatis de Dereford et Wigani clerici Regis filii Regis* 47*s*. *per breve Regis. In passagio Episcopi Norwicensis* 46*s*. *per breve Regis. In passagio Advocati de Bettun* 46*s*. *per breve Regis. In soltis per breve Regis Absolon de Doura* 20*s*. *pro passagio Hugonis de Morewich.*

[1] Geoff. Vigeois (Gall. Script. xii, 330.)

[2] Geoff. Vigeois (Ibidem p. 331.)

[3] Benedictus (Stubbs), i. 288–9. The Welsh version of this story is that "Randulf *De* Poer, and many knights with him, were killed by the youths of Winchester (*Caer Wynt*). (See Brut y Tywysogion, pp. 230–1). This extraordinary statement probably arises in some transcriber choosing to write 'Caer Wynt,' where he found 'Caer Went.'

The Pipe-Roll somewhat elucidates the matter. Randulf Puher was Sheriff of Herefordshire, not Gloucestershire. He accounted for the ferm of the former county up to Easter, 1182, charging among his expenses for custody of the well-known Welsh castle of *Camerium*, and for works at the castle of *Crichteton* (Knighton). At Michaelmas, 1182, two *Custodes* (Milo de Mucegros and Roger fitz Maurice) account for the ferm of Herefordshire for the last half of the fiscal year then ended. Of course this arrangement was owing to the death of the Sheriff.

[4] Benedictus (Stubbs), i. 288. See p. 247, note 5, as to the previous hiatus in Benedict's Chronicle,

MICHAELMAS, 1182, TO MICHAELMAS, 1183.

Oct. 6. Richard Peche, Bishop of Coventry, died at St. Thomas's Priory (Stafford), whither he had retired.[1]

Oct. 9. Waleran, Archdeacon of Baieux, a Clerk of Archbishop Richard, elected Bishop of Rochester in the Chapter of Rochester, before the said Archbishop and the Justiciar.

Nov. 13. The Abp of Canterbury crosses from Dover to Normandy.

Dec. 1. On this day a fine was levied in the *Curia Regis* at Westminster, before R. Bishop of Winchester; Geoffry, Bishop of Ely; and Ranulf de Glanvill, 'Justiciars of the Lord King;' Richard the Treasurer, G. de Luci, Roger fitz Reinfrid, Michael Belet, G. de Coleville, R. de Geddings, Gervase de Cornhull, Osbert fitz Hervey, and others.[2]

Dec. 4. The Archbishop of Canterbury ordains Walleran, Bishop-elect of Rochester, a Priest.

Dec. 5. The Archbishop consecrates the said Bishop at Liseux.

Dec. 25. The King kept Christmas at Caen. With him were the Princes Henry, Richard, and Geoffrey; also Henry, Duke of Saxony; Richard, Abp of Canterbury; and John, Abp of Dublin. Caen.

During the year now ended, Ranulf de Glanvill is said to have founded the Abbey of Leystone, in Suffolk. It is also said that the King, on quitting England in March, left Prince John under the tutelage of Ranulf de Glanvill, an arrangement which will have endured till August, 1183, when both Glanville and the Prince followed the King into Normandy. Ranulf de Glanvill's Foundation-charter of Leystone—may well have passed in 1182, and is an illustration of his alleged tutorship of Prince John. It is attested by "John, son of the Lord the King"; William de Aubervill; Ralph de Ardern; Roger de Glanvill; Osbert de Glanvill; William de Valoines; Ralph Murdac; Ralph de Gedinge; Alard fitz William; Theobald Walter; Thomas de Ardene, and many others.[3]

A.D. 1183.

1183. Jan. 1. Prince Henry takes a solemn oath of allegiance to his father. Le Mans.

Jan. The King, being at Le Mans, desires the Princes Richard and Geoffrey, to do homage to their elder brother. Richard refuses, retires into Poitou, and fortifies the Castle of Clairvaux. Geoffrey does homage to his elder brother at Angiers. Angiers.

[1] Chesterfield says that this Bishop died Oct. 7, 1181. The Annals of St. Werburgh put his death on "Wednesday, Oct. 6, 1182;" the Annals of Waverley say he died in 1182; Hoveden and Benedictus in 1183. The Pipe-Roll of 29 Henry II. proves that he received no revenues from his See after Michaelmas, 1182; that, between his resignation and his death, he had a daily *procuration* assigned him by the King, and that the amount of such procurations only reached £2. The best inference, on the whole, is that he retired about Michaelmas, 1182, and died on Oct. 6, 1182.

[2] Rot. Pipe 28 Hen. II. Oger fitz Oger, a party to the above fine, paid half a merk to have it enrolled on the Pipe-Roll. If correctly dated, the entry was quite supplementary, inasmuch as the accounts of the said Roll would ordinarily close at Michaelmas previous. (See p. 244, note 6.).

[3] Monasticon, vii. 881. The Manor of Leystone, which Glanvill here gives for the foundation of a Præmonstratensian Abbey, he had previously given to the Canons of Butley. His Charter recites how the said Canons had resigned the same in presence of John, Bishop of Norwich, of Glanvill himself, of Archdeacon Walkeline, of Hubert Walter, Geoffry fitz Piers, and Alan de Valoins.

In the beginning of the year 1183, Prince Henry took part with the Poitevin Barons against their Duke, Richard, whose occupation of Clairvaux Castle was an encroachment on the fief of Anjou, and so on the elder brother's heritage. Prince Geoffrey joined his brother Henry in opposing Richard. Richard placed Clairvaux Castle at his father's disposal.

1183. Feb. King Henry is at Limoges.[1] Limoges.

Then at Aixe.[1] Aixe.

March 1. Then again at Limoges.[1] Limoges.

March 8. The King is at Poictiers. Richard, Abp of Canterbury, and Roger, Abbot of St. Augustine's, Canterbury, come to an agreement in his presence. The Bishops of Baieux and Rochester were at Court. Poictiers.

About this time money was sent from England to the King. The Sheriff of Southampton charges,—*In liberacione Esneccæ quando transfretavit cum thesauro in Quadragesimâ* £7. 10*s*. *per breve Regis. Et in liberacione navis quæ transfretavit* (*item*) *cum esneccâ* 40*s*. *per idem breve. Et pro locandis* xx *servientibus ad custodiam ejusdem thesauri in ipsâ tranfretacione* 100*s*. *per idem breve. Et pro eodem thesauro onerando et deonerando et pro aliis necessariis* 9*s*. 5*d*.

The three Princes meet their father at Angiers. They make peaceable arrangements among themselves, and swear allegiance to him. Angiers.

A conference was held at Mirabel between the King and his sons to settle further particulars. Prince Geoffrey being sent to summon the Barons of Aquitaine to the conference, encourages them in their disaffection. Mirabel.

Prince Henry for a time joins his father in attempts to reconcile Prince Richard with the nobles of Aquitaine.

Prince Henry, after sending his wife to the Court of her brother Philip, goes to Limoges, ostensibly with the purpose of reclaiming his brother, Geoffrey, and the nobles of Aquitaine; but eventually he joins their rebellion.

April 17. The King at Easter is before Limoges.[2] He is treasonably attacked by the garrison of the castle. He retires thence accompanied by Prince Richard. Limoges.

The King, proposing to confer with his two rebellious sons, is again attacked by the Castellans of Limoges.

Prince Henry twice counterfeits attempts to bring the Aquitaine Barons to their allegiance; and twice pretends to be reconciled with his father.

While Maurice de Creoun, and other envoys of the King, are conferring with Prince Henry concerning a truce, their followers are attacked and slain.

1, 2 Geoff. Vigeois, pp. 332–334, 336, as quoted by Professor Stubbs (Itinerary, p. cxlv).

1183. c. April 10. A few days later, and Oliver fitz Ernise and Gerom de Musterol, going with a flag of truce from the King to Prince Geoffrey, were assaulted. Limoges.

c. April. About this time the Earls of Gloucester and Leicester were arrested and imprisoned in England.

May 8. The King having having sent to Lincoln an Order for the election of a Bishop, the Chapter on this day elected Walter de Constanciis. Their choice displeased the King.

May 9. A fine was levied in the Court of Exchequer, at Westminster, before R. Bp of Winchester; G. Bp of Ely: J. Bp of Norwich; and Rannulf de Glanvile, Justiciars;—Roger fitz Reinfrid, Wm. Basset, Alan de Furnellis, Robert de Witefeld, Gervase de Cornhull, Rannulf de Gedding, Gilbert de Colevill, and other Barons.[1]

May 26. Richard, Archbishop of Canterbury; Henry, Bishop of Baieux; John, Bishop of Evreux; Ralph, Bishop of Liseux; Roger (Froger), Bishop of Seez; and Walleran, Bishop of Rochester, meet in the Church of St. Stephens at Caen, and (excepting Prince Henry) they excommunicate all who foster the existing dissensions between the King and his sons.

c. June 1. Prince Henry commits a sacrilegious attack on the Church of St. Mary de Roquemadour (De Rupe Adamatoris), in the Quercy.

June 5. Nicholas, Bishop of Landaff, died.

June 5. More treasure was sent from England to the King. The Sheriff of Southampton charges,—*In liberacione esneccæ quando transfretavit cum thesauro in festo Pentecostes* £7. 10*s*. *per breve Regis. Et item in liberacione esneccæ de* viii *diebus* 75*s*. *dum moram fecit apud Portesmutham per idem breve. Et Clerico thesaurarii et duobus hominibus camerariæ* 40*s*. *de liberacione suâ per breve Ranulfi de Glanvill. Et in liberacione unius navis in quâ equi Episcopi Wigorniensis*[2] *et servientum de thesauro transfretaverunt* 35*s*. *per breve Regis predictum.*

June 11. The younger King Henry, having been attacked with dysentery, dies at Martel.[3] William Marescall, being in attendance on him, was entrusted with his cross to be borne to Jerusalem. His remains, being intended to be carried for burial at Rouen, are stopped at Le Mans, and buried there.[4]

On this same day, being Saturday in Whitsun-week, John, Bishop of Evreux, ordained Walter de Constanciis (Bishop-elect of Lincoln, and Archdeacon of Oxford) a Priest, by order of Richard, Archbishop of Canterbury, then in France.[5]

June 24. The King at length reduces Limoges. Limoges.

The King, accompanied by the Archbishop of Canterbury, goes to Le Mans, orders the disinterment of his son's corpse, and attends it to Rouen, where it is buried. Le Mans.

[1] Harl. MS. 2110, fo. 108.

[2] Baldwin was the existent Bishop of Worcester.

[3] Martel, the scene of Prince Henry's death, is variously described by the Chroniclers as in Turenne, as in Gascony, and as near Limoges. It is a village lying a little to the east of the road, which leads from Brives to Cahors.

[4] The body was afterwards removed to Rouen, and buried on the north side of the High Altar of the Cathedral. The translation was effected by Robert de Newburgh, then Dean of Rouen, who proved that the young King had during life selected his own place of sepulture (Gall. Script. xii. 539).

[5] The ordination of Walter de Coutances took place, according to Benedictus, at Evreux. But the date and place of this Prelate's *consecration* are uncertain. Diceto says that it was soon after his ordination (*postmodum*), and in the Church of St. Laud, at Angiers, the Abp of Canterbury consecrating. Benedictus agrees as to the place. Other statements name Caen, and one (that of Florence's Continuator) names Rouen as the place of the ceremony. A day also is named, viz., June 25, but not with probability, as it fell on Saturday. The consecration of John, Bishop of St. Asaph, is put by the Annals of Waverley on June 25, at Caen.

1183. c. June 30. The King holds a conference with Philip of France, probably at Gisors. They agree as to the dower of Prince Henry's widow, Margaret. (Gisors).

July 3. The King and Prince Richard go to Angiers, where they come to terms with Prince Geoffrey.[1] Angiers.

Aug. 11. The Archbishop of Canterbury returns to England, having, whilst in France, consecrated three Bishops, viz., Rochester, Lincoln, and (the third) John, Bishop of St. Asaph.

Aug. 19. A Chapter is held at Canterbury, whereat Waleran, Bp of Rochester, does fealty to the Prior and Convent of Christ Church. There were present the Archbishop Richard; Gerard, Bishop-elect of Chester; Benedict, Abbot of Peterborough; Moses, Prior of Coventry; Alan, Prior of Canterbury; Peter, Archdeacon of Bath; and William, Archdeacon of Gloucester.

Aug. In this and the following month the Southampton Pipe-Roll indicates the transmission of money to Normandy:—*Et item in liberacione navis Samsonis Wascel' quando transfretavit cum thesauro mense Augusti* 50s. *per breve Regis. Et in necessariis illius thesauri* 3s. 6d. *Et pro locandis uno Gubernatore et nautis ad transfretandum cum illo thesauro* 1 *marcam per predictum breve Regis. Et item pro navi Hunfridi Hai ad transfretandum thesaurum circa festum Sancti Egidii* (September 1) 30s. *per idem breve. Et pro locandis decem nautis ad custodiam thesauri illius in transfretatione* 50s. *per idem breve. Et pro onerando et deonerando eodem thesauro* 2s.

About this time the King sends to England for Prince John and for Ranulf de Glanvill, who was acting as his Guardian (*magister ejus*). They sail from Dover to Witsand. This statement is curiously confirmed by the Dover Pipe-Roll.—*Et in passagio Johannis filii Regis et Rannulfi de Glanvill et sociorum suorum* £15. 4s. *per breve Regis. Et in passagio Episcopi de Acra* 15s. *per breve Regis.*

The King requires Prince Richard, to yield up Aquitaine to Prince John. About this time also the King sent for the Queen, who was in prison. She had apparently been domiciled in Berkshire under the custody of Ralph fitz Stephen. Hence the Sheriff of that County charges,—*Et Radulfo filio Stephani* £20 *ad corredium Reginæ per breve Rannulfi de Glanvill.*

Prince John, while in Normandy, seems to have been chiefly at Rouen. Hence the Norman-Roll of Michaelmas, 1184, charges,—*In corredio Johannis filii Regis apud Rothomagum* £20 *per breve Regis.*[2]

Sept. 19. Gilbert Assaili, Master of the Knights Hospitallers, was drowned, with many others, passing from Dieppe to England.

Sept. 21. Gerard la Pucelle, Bishop-elect of Chester, was ordained a Priest.

Sept. 25. The said Bishop was consecrated at Canterbury by the Archbishop, assisted by the Bishops of Bath, Worcester, St. David's, and Rochester.

To this period we may assign a Royal Charter, confirming to Henry de Marisco, the grant of Gerard, the Prior of Norwich, made by consent of John, Bishop of Norwich.

The Charter is dated at Gorham (Gorron in Maine), and is attested by R. Archbishop-elect of Dol; Hugh Murdach; John de Constanciis, Treasurer of Liseux; Ranulf de Glanvill; Hugh Bardulf, Dapifer; Adelm de Fontibus; Ralph de Ardern; Geoffrey fitz Peter, and Gilbert fitz Reinfrid.[3] Gorron.

[1] R. de Monte (Struve), 933.
After Angiers, Stubbs (quoting Rot. Normann. i. 121) puts the King at Evreux: then (quoting Rot. Normann. i 116) at Gisors: then (quoting Rot. Normann. i. 116) at Rouen, conferring with Philip of Flanders. But the Roll quoted is that of 1184, not of 1183; and we have preferred to consider its evidence of the Royal visits in question to indicate a later date than Michaelmas, 1183. (See pp. 253, 255.)

[2] Rot. Normann. (Stapleton) i. 120.

[3] Cartæ Antiquæ, S.

IN THE YEAR ENDING Michaelmas, 1183, we may note the *Iter* of Thomas fitz Bernard, Alan de Furnellis, and Robert de Witefeld, in Herefordshire, Staffordshire, and Shropshire.

MICHAELMAS, 1183, TO MICHAELMAS, 1184.

c. Oct. About this time we may date a Royal Charter, which passed at Leon (Lyons-la-Forêt). It was in favour of Croxden Abbey (Staffordshire), and was attested by Walter, Bp of Lincoln; Ranulf de Glanvill; William fitz Ralph, Seneschall of Normandy; Hugh de Morewich, Dapifer; Hugh Bardulf, Dapifer; Radulf de Arderne; Geoffry fitz Peter and Gilbert fitz Reinfrid.[1] Lyons-la-Forêt.

A Writ Royal, dated *apud Bonam Villam*, is addressed to the Constable of Cherbourg, on behalf of the Canons of *Notre Dame de Voeu*, and is attested by Hugh Bardulf, Dapifer.[2] Bonneville sur Toques.

Oct. 30. Richard, Bp of Winchester; Geoffrey, Bp of Ely; John, Bp of Norwich; Godfrey de Luci; Richard, the Treasurer; Roger fitz Reinfrid; William Basset; Ranulf de Gedding; Robert de Wytefeld; and Michael Belet, were the Justiciars sitting at the Exchequer at Westminster.[3]

c. Nov. About this time the King appears to have been at Rouen. A Royal Charter to the Abbey of Barbery, is dated at Rouen, and attested by Seffrid, Bishop of Chichester; Ralph, Bp of Liseux; Richard Brito, Clerk; William, Clerk of the Chamber; Earl William de Manneville; Robert, Comte de Meulan; Rannulph de Glanville; Wm. fitz Ralph, Seneschal of Normandy; Hugh de Creissi; Walcheline de Ferrières; Hugh de Gurnai; Roger de Mortimer; William de la Mare; Richard Selvein.[4] Rouen.

Nov. 23. William, Earl of Gloucester, died.
Nov. 25. Rotrou, Archbishop of Rouen, died.

Dec. 6. K. Henry holds a Conference with Philip at the usual place, between Gisors and Trie. Henry does homage for his continental dominions. This event is illustrated by the following from the Norman-Roll of 1184.—Alvered de St. Martin, Fermor of the Prepositure of Drincourt, had paid to Hugh de Morwic and Hugh Bardulf "for corrody of the King at Gisors £100, by order of the King." [5] Gisors.

[1] Monasticon v. 662. Num. iii.
[2] D'Anisy's Transcripts, i. 102.
[3] Madox's Exchequer, p. 144. Glanville's absence is remarkable. He was doubtless still with the King in Normandy.
[4, 5] Rot. Normann. ii. ci. and i. p. 116.

Dec. 11, 1183. Walter, Bishop of Lincoln, having come into England, was enthroned at Lincoln by Herbert, Archdeacon of Canterbury. Baldwin, Bishop of Worcester, was also at Lincoln.

About this time John, Comte of Mortain, by Writ, dated *apud Verundiun*,[1] petitions his father to grant a right of Fair and Market to Abbot Peter, of Blanchelaunde. Witnesses, Walter de Ver, Roger de Amondevill, and Henry de Clare.—

1183. c. Dec. The King's reply is, perhaps, a mere renewal of a Charter (Valognes). which he had granted twenty-six years before. But the renewal is dated as passing in his twenty-ninth year, and apparently passed at Valognes.[2] Valognes.

Perhaps at this time passed a Royal Charter to St. Lo, an Augustine Abbey in the Diocese of Coutances. It is dated *apud Valonias*, and attested by William de Humet, Constable; William de Aubigney, Earl of Sussex; William de St. John; Bertram de Verdon; William de Moyun; Richard de Canvill, and Stephen de *Turno* (Turonis).[3]

About this time Walter de Constanciis, Bp of Lincoln, was elected to succeed Rotrou, Abp of Rouen.

Dec. 25. King Henry kept Christmas at Le Mans. Prince John was with him. Le Mans.

A.D. 1184.

1184. Jan. 1. King Henry probably at Le Mans. Le Mans.

Jan. 13. Gerard la Pucelle, Bishop of Chester, died. The Pipe-Roll of Michaelmas, 1184, notices his death; Master Thomas de Husseburn and Thomas Noel account therein for the ferm of the Episcopal Manors from Easter (April 1) to Michaelmas, 1184.

About this time died Thomas fitz Bernard, who had succeeded Alan de Nevill as Chief Justice of the Forests. The Pipe-Roll shows that Thomas fitz Bernard's fermorship of Kinver Forest ended previous to Easter (April 1), 1184. At Thomas fitz Bernard's death the King divided the Forests into several districts, appointing four justices (two clerks and two knights) to preside over each district.

Feb. 17. Richard, Archbishop of Canterbury, died.[4]

1184. Jan. Feb. Mar. Apr. The movements of the King's Court during the first four months of this year are quite uncertain. He seems to have been at Limoges; for, at Michaelmas, the Fermor of the Limoges. escheated lands of Henry de Essex charges,—*Pro penis et pelliciis missis Domino Regi apud Lemovicum* xvi *marcas per breve Regis*.[5]

[1] Probably the original had *Vernolium*, *i.e.*, Verneuil; or perhaps *Valonias*, *i.e.*, Valognes.

[2] D'Anisy's Transcripts, i. pp. 64,65. (*Vide supra*, p. 23, note 7.)

[3] D'Anisy's Transcripts, ii. 82.

[4] Gervase says that the Archbishop died xiv *kal. Martii, feriâ sextâ, i.e.* on Friday, Feb. 16. But Feb. 16 fell on a Thursday in 1184. So we have adopted the date given by Benedictus.

[5] Rot. Pipe, 30 Hen. II.

1184. Jan. Feb. Mar. Apr. Other extracts, from the Norman Exchequer-Roll, show that the King visited Evreux; for instance, the Fermor of Liseux charges,—*In corredio hominum et equorum Regis apud Ebroicas* £6. 10*s. per breve Regis.*[1] And another Accountant charges,—*In minuto hernesio ad opus duorum militum Ducis Sauxoniæ qui perhendinant in Abbatiâ de Bernaio* £4 *per breve Regis. In corredio hominum et equorum Regis apud Ebroicas* c *solidos per idem breve.*[1] Evreux.

That the Duke of Saxony, after sojourning with his father-in-law, paid a visit to his dominions about this time, is proved by a charge of Alvered de St. Martin, Fermor and Castellan of Drineurt:—*In corredio Ducis Saxoniæ apud Drincort quando ivit in Saxoniam* £21. 11*s.* 11*d. per breve Regis.*[2]

c. May. In this month the King was probably at Rouen, and was visited by the Comtes of Flanders and Hainault. Rouen.

At Michaelmas the Fermor of Drincurt charges as follows:—

In corredio Comitis Flandriæ apud Drincort in veniendo Rothomagum ad Regem et redeundo £132. 7*s. per breve Regis. In corredio Comitis de Hanoû ibidem in veniendo ad Regem et redeundo* £51 *per breve Regis.*[3]

These visits to the Court of Rouen were probably connected with other events. The Comte of Flanders had been at issue with the King of France concerning the inheritance of the Comte's deceased and childless wife, which Philip claimed, as Suzerain. King Henry had supported the Comte, and, not only that, but had negotiated a second marriage for him with a daughter of Alphouso, King of Portugal. The said Princess landing at La Rochelle had had safe conduct through the King of England's French territories till she reached the frontier of Flanders, and was married to the Comte. K. Henry's interest in the affair is manifested by a number of entries on the English Pipe-Roll, viz.—

HAMPSHIRE. *In emendacione Esneccæ Regis et pro funibus at aliis necessariis quando transfretavit in Hyspaniam pro Comitissâ Flandriæ* £169. 15*s.* 9*d. per breve Ranulfi de Glanvill.*

SOUTHAMPTON. *Et Alano Trenchem' ad procuracionem nautarum qui venerunt ad Sudhanton' ad transfretandum in Hyspaniam in servicio Regis* 40*s. per breve Rannulfi de Glanvill. Et pro* ii *anchoris ad navem Willielmi de Braiose quando transfretavit in Hyspaniam* £4 *per predictum breve Regis. Et Alano Trenchem' et sociis suis ad procuracionem suam dum fecerunt moram apud Sudhanton' et ad warnisturam emendam ad portandam secum in Esneccâ et aliis* ii *navibus quas Rex misit in Hyspaniam pro Comitissâ Flandriæ peticione Comitis* £78. 4*s.* 2*d. per breve Rannulfi de Glanvill.*

SUSSEX. *Et pro conducendis nautis ad transfretandum in Hyspaniam in servicio Regis per breve Ranulfi de Glanvill.*

c. June 5. The King is noticed as holding a conference at Choisi, and arbitrating between the King of France and the Comte Choisi.

[1] Rot. Normann. vol. i. pp. 118, 121.

[2] Rot. Normann. vol. i. p. 116.

[3] Ibidem, p. 116.

There is a fragment of a Royal Charter (Cartæ Antiquæ, EE.) which passed perhaps in 1181, but more probably in 1184. We quote thus much of it without further comment.—

It is in favour of Baldwin de Betun.

It is attested by Earl William Harundell; William * * * *, William Marescall, Philip de Columbariis, Geoffry *Ostorio*, Geoffry de la *Cele* (?), and Hugh Bardulf.

1181. c. June 6. of Flanders as to Vermandois, which the Comte had conditionally promised to Philip.[1] Henry's arbitration procures a peace between the disputants from June 24 to the end of the year. Choisi.

June 10. King Henry, having negotiated the said truce, passes through the territory of the Comte of Flanders, embarks at Witsand, and lands at Dover. Witsand. Dover.

June 12. The Duchess of Saxony follows the King and lands at Dover. Hence an Accountant on the Norman Exchequer Roll of this year charges,—*Pro equis ad opus Ducissæ Sauxoniæ quando transfretavit* £35. 10. *per breve Regis.*[2] Also the Fermor of Dover, on the English Pipe-Roll, charges—*In corredio Ducissæ filiæ Regis* £6. 7*s.* 4*d.* *per breve Regis.*

The Duchess remained in England, and shortly gave birth to a son, at Winchester. Her stay is indicated by the following entry on the Pipe-Roll.—

London. *In corredio Ducissæ Saxoniæ* £8. 12*s.* 10*d.* *per breve Regis.*

c. June 13. The King visits the shrine of Becket, and then proceeds to London. But the King's alleged visit to Waltham, and appointment of Walter de Gant to be Abbot there, seem doubtful at this date.[3] Canterbury. London. (Waltham?).

Simon, Earl of Huntingdon, dies about this time.
The King sends an expedition into Wales.

July 22. The King is at Worcester. Sir Gilbert de Plumpton, condemned to death at the instigation of Ranulf de Glanville, is rescued by the interference of Baldwin, Bishop of Worcester, (because the day was Sunday), and finally reprieved by the King. Worcester.

Rese ap Griffin, Prince of S. Wales, comes to Worcester and arranges a treaty of pacification with the King. From Worcester the King probably went to Gloucester. Rese ap Griffin comes thither, but neglects his undertaking to bring his son as a hostage. Gloucester.

July 25. The Duke of Saxony lands at Dover and proceeds to Winchester, where the King meets him. About this time the King sends a commission to the Monks of Christ Church, Canterbury, desiring them to elect an Archbishop. They name the Abbot of Battle and four others. The Royal Commissioners were Ranulf de Glanvill, John Bp of Norwich, Waleran Bp of Rochester, Herbert Archdeacon of Canterbury, (Godfrey) Archdeacon of Derby, and Hubert Walter. Winchester.

[1] Benedictus (Stubbs). i. 312. Professor Stubbs places the Conference of Choisi, in May, but the King's immediate transfretation, spoken of by Benedictus, suggests the beginning of June. Choisi, here spoken of, was in Picardy, and would lie in K. Henry's route from Rouen to Witsand.

[2] Rot. Normanniæ, vol. i. p. 122.

[3] Vide supra pp. 210, 216, 223.

1184. August 5. The King holds a Council at Reading about the See of Canterbury. John Archbishop of Dublin, and the Duke of Saxony, were present. The King discountenances the Nominees of the Prior and Convent of Canterbury. Reading.

August 16. The King convenes the Bishops to a Council at Woodstock, about the Metropolitan See. An appeal to the Pope resolved upon. Woodstock.

August 18. Clement, Abbot of St. Mary's, York, died.

c. August 21. The King goes to Dover to meet the Comte of Flanders, and the Archbishop of Cologne, who came to visit Becket's shrine at Canterbury. The King goes with them to Canterbury and thence to London, but endeavours in vain to reconcile the said Archbishop to the Duke of Saxony. It was perhaps at this time, or soon after, that the King sent Hugh de Novant, Archdeacon of Liseux, as Ambassador to Pope Lucius, to induce his Holiness to effect a reconciliation between the said Duke and the Emperor. Dover. Canterbury. London.

Aug. 29. Waleran, Bishop of Rochester, dies there while preparing to go as the King's Ambassador to the Pope about the Primacy.

THE FOLLOWING EXTRACTS from the Pipe-Roll of the fiscal year now ended, will show something about several members of the Royal family and their recent movements.

OXFORDSHIRE. *Et Radulfo filio Stephani ad corredium Reginæ a Paschâ* (April 1), *usque ad festum Sancti Johannis Baptistæ* (June 24), £32. 14s. *per breve Ranulfi de Glanvitle.*

BERCHAMSTED. *Et in procuracione Reginæ et Ducis et Ducissæ Saxoniæ* £104 *per breve Regis.*[1]

DOVER. *Et in liberacione navium quæ venerunt cum filio Ducis Saxoniæ et in corredio ejus apud Douram* 47s. 2d. *per breve Regis.*

KENT. *Et in corredio filii Ducis Saxoniæ* 14s. *per breve Regis.*

DEVONSHIRE. *Et Ricardo de Rupe et aliis hominibus Johannis filii Regis* 40s. *ad transfretandum cum canibus predicti Johannis per breve Ranulfi de Glanvilt.*[2]

SOUTHAMPTON. *Pro unâ navi quæ transfretavit in Normanniam cum filiâ Hunfridi de Bohun*[3] 30s. *per breve Regis. Et in passagio nuntiorum Galfridi Comitis Brittaniæ et Stephani de Turonis et Præpositi de Luchis*[4] *et sociorum suorum et decem avium Regis* 15s. *per predictum breve Regis.*

[1] The date of this will have been after July 25th, when the Duke landed at Dover.

[2] Prince John's hounds were probably shipped for Normandy before June, when the King came to England, because it was done by order of the Viceroy, Glanvill.

[3] The transfretation of Humphrey de Bohun's daughter is not easily accounted for. He himself died about this time. The Duchess Constance of Bretagne was his *Stepdaughter*. She was born and betrothed to Prince Geoffrey in 1166, and was now about 18. Their daughter, Eleanor, was born *c.* 1185, and their son Arthur born March 29, 1187. It is probable that in this year (1184) Constance joined her affianced husband, and that she is the person called "Humphrey de Bohun's daughter."

And it is certain that the said Humphrey had by the Duchess Margaret of Bretagne no daughter, but only a son, and that that son was only eight years of age in 1184. (Vide Rot. de Dominabus, pp. 33, 44.)

[4] *Luchæ* must be Loches in Touraine.

During the year, ending Michaelmas, 1184, we have little record of the persons employed in administration of the Law. The Pipe-Roll of 1185, speaks of Pleas held in Worcestershire, by Geoffry de Luci, Hugh Bardulf and William Rufus; and, as these are not termed *Nova Placita*, we conclude them to have belonged to a previous year;—probably, 1184. It was certainly in the year 1184, and probably while the King was in England, that we find the following persons sitting at the Exchequer in England.—

Ranulf de Glanvill, Justiciar of the Lord King; Geoffry of Ely, John of Norwich, Bishops; Richard Dean of Lincoln, King's Treasurer; William English (Anglicus) brother of the Treasurer; Hubert Walter, Clerk; Hugh Murdac, Clerk; Ralph Murdac; Ralph de Worcester; Hugh de Morewic; and William Malduit, Chamberlain.[1]

MICHAELMAS, 1184, to MICHAELMAS, 1185.

1184. Oct. 21–23. The King holds a Council at Windsor about the Primacy. Windsor. Reginald Bp of Bath, Gilbert Bp of London, Alan Prior of Canterbury, and Ranulf de Glanvill, were present.

Nov. 18. Josceline de Bohun, Bishop of Salisbury, died, having previously assumed the Cistercian habit.

c. Nov. 25. Philip, Comte of Flanders, and the Princes Geoffrey and John, having leagued themselves against Prince Richard in Normandy, the three Princes are recalled by the King to England. They come,[2] and with Queen Elianor, the Duke and Duchess of Saxony, Walter Bishop of Lincoln, Richard Bishop of Winchester, and Alan Prior of Canterbury, meet the King at London, whither a Council was convened con- London. cerning the Primacy. Hugh Bishop of Durham, and the Canons of York, were also summoned thither to elect an Archbishop of York.

Nov. 30. The Council of London assembles.

Dec. 2. The English Bishops elect Baldwin, Bishop of Worcester, to the Primacy.

The Monks of Canterbury return home, denying the validity of such a nomination.

Dec. 5. The King sends messengers to Canterbury to negotiate with the Monks.

Dec. 10. The Prior of Canterbury returns to the Court at London, and makes proposals as to the election.

[1] Madox' Exchequer, p. 146 (d).

[2] It would appear from the Pipe-Roll of Michaelmas, 1185, that Prince John came to England accompanied by the Comte of Flanders, and that the twain landed at Dover.

The extract runs thus.—

Doura. *Et in passagio Comitis Flandriæ et Johannis filii Regis £7 per breve Regis.*

1184. Dec. 13. The King again sends messengers to Canterbury, viz., the Princes Geoffry and John, and the Abbot of Peterborough. Westminster.

Dec. 14. The King himself visits Canterbury. Canterbury.

Dec. 15. The King returns to London. London.

Bartholomew, Bishop of Exeter, dies on this day.

Dec. 16. The Monks of Canterbury elect Baldwin, Bishop of Worcester, to the primacy, in the Chapter-House at Westminster, the King being present. Westminster.

It was probably while the King was in London on the above business, but certainly before Dec. 18, and in the year 1184, that Matthew, son and heir apparent of Robert Mantel, made a certain recognition at the Exchequer, in favour of the Dean and Chapter of St. Paul's, represented by two Canons, viz., Master Richard de Storteford, Master of the Schools of London, and Osbert de Camera. The persons presiding in the Court of the Exchequer, were Ranulf de Glanvill the King's Justiciar; Geoffrey Bp of Ely; John Bp of Norwich; Richard, Dean of Lincoln, the King's Treasurer; William Anglicus, the Treasurer's brother; Hubert Walter, Clerk; Hugh Murdac, Clerk; Ralph Murdac; Ralph de Worcester; Hugh de Morewic: William Mauduit, Chamberlain; and Roger de Glanvill.[1]

c. Dec. A Royal Charter, to St. Giles' Hospital, without London, bears date at Westminster, and probably belongs to the year 1184. It is attested by Richard Bishop (of Winchester), G. Bp of Ely, John Bp of Norwich, Earl William de Mandeville and Ranulf de Glanvill.[2] Westminster.

Another Charter to Plympton Priory (Devonshire) is also dated at Westminster. It passed at request of Robert de Ponte-Arch, and is attested by the same three Bishops, and by Richard, the Treasurer.[3]

In this year, and probably at the same time, in the Chapel at Westminster, and in the King's presence, William de Mandeville, Earl of Essex, made a grant to the Knights Hospitallers.[4] At the close of the year the said William de Mandeville went into Flanders to assist his Suzerain, the Comte of Flanders, against the Comte of Hainault.

About this time the King dispatched Prince Geoffry into Normandy, in the capacity of Custos of that Dominion. The Princes, Richard and John, were detained in England.[5]

Dec. 25. The King kept Christmas at Windsor. Queen Elianor, the Princes Richard and John, the Duke and Duchess of Saxony, with their sons and daughters; Hugh, Bishop of Durham; Walter, Bishop of Lincoln, and David, brother of the King of Scots, were at Court.[6] Windsor.

[1] Madox' Exchequer, p. 744.
[2] Monasticon, vii. p. 636, ii.
[3, 4] Monasticon, vi. p. 54, iv. and vii. p. 833 a.
[5, 6] Benedictus Abbas, pp. 415, 431.

1184. c. Dec. 31. The King goes to *Geldeford*. Prince Richard sails from Dover to Witsand.[1] Guildford.

IN THE ABOVE YEAR died Froger, Bishop of Seez (whose successor was Lisiard), and William de Newburgh, Earl of Warwick. Two writers (Benedictus and Hoveden) say that William, Prior of Bristol, was appointed to the See of Bangor in the above year, but this is doubtful.

A.D. 1185.

On January 1st died Gilbert fitz Fergus of Galloway. Custody of his son and heir, Duncan, is given by K. Henry to Hugh de Morewie.

1185. Jan. 1-6. The King is at Winchester. Hugh de Novant, Archdeacon of Liseux, returns from Rome with tidings of a reconciliation having been effected between the Emperor Frederick and Henry, Duke of Saxony. King Henry, much delighted, sends for Queen Elianor, and for the Duke and Duchess of Saxony, who were still at Windsor.[2] Winchester.

It was now probably that Hugh de Novant was elected to, or rather forced upon, the See of Chester.[3]

The King sends Messengers to mediate between Philip, K. of France, and Philip of Flanders. The messengers are Walter, Bishop of Lincoln; John, Bishop of Norwich, and Godfrey de Luci, Archdeacon of Richmond. The Bp of Lincoln, being now Archbishop-Elect of Rouen, is not to return to England, but to remain at his Archiepiscopal See.[2]

Leaving Winchester, the Court was little stationary from January to March, as indicated by the following charge on the London Pipe-Roll of 1185.—*Et pro ducendo Thesauro Regis a London' ad curiam et usque Winton' et per diversa loca Angliæ* 77*s.* 2*d.* And under Surrey, there is a charge of 6*s.* *pro conducendo thesauro a London usque Winton'.*

Jan. 25. The King was at Melkesham. A fine was levied in his Court which divided the inheritance of the two daughters of William de Say, viz., Beatrice, wife of Geoffry fitz Piers, and Matilda, wife of Hugh de Bochland. The Justices present were Ranulf de Glanvill, Melkesham.

[1, 2] Benedictus (Stubbs) i. 333-4.

[3] *Electus est hoc anno, immo intrusus, ad regimen Cestrensis ecclesiæ Hugo de Nunant.* (Gervase, p. 1475). Novant seems to have had the revenues of the See from Christmas, 1184. (Rot. Pipe, 31 Hen. II.).

1185. Jan. 25. Robert Marmion, Ralph fitz Stephen, Chamberlain; Hugh de Morewic, Dapifer; Hugh Bardulf, Dapifer; Robert de Witefeld; Ranulf de Geddinges; and Gilbert fitz Reinfrid.[1] Melkesham.

A Royal Charter, dated at Melkesham, and expressing that the above settlement was made in the King's presence, and with his assent, is attested by the first three of the above Justiciars, and also by Wm. de Gerpunvill, Amaur' Dispenser; Durandus de Ostilli, Chamberlain; and Walter, son of Turstin fitz Simon.[2]

Heraclius, Patriarch of Jerusalem, arrives on January 29, at Canterbury, as Gervase says, '*orandi gratiâ*.'[3] With him was the Grand Master of the Hospitallers,—Roger de Moulin.

c. Feb. About this time the King appears to have been at Clipston. Of two Charters there expedited, one is to Thurgarton Abbey (Notts), the other to Barling's Abbey (Lincolnshire). The testing clause of the latter, when corrected by the former, gives witnesses common to both, viz., Hugh, Bishop of Durham; William, Earl of *Arundel*; Ranulph de Glanvill; Bernard de St. Wallery; Roger de Stutevill; William de Stutevill; Hugh Bardulf, Dapifer; and Ranulf de Guddinges.[4] Clipston.

Feb. The King is at Nottingham, and intending to proceed to York, but hearing of Heraclius's arrival, turns southwards. Nottingham.

March 17. The King meets Heraclius at Reading. Reading.

March 18. The King will have been in London. London.

The King presides over a great Council held at Clerkenwell (London), whereat it was decided that the King could not expediently go on the Crusade.[5] Clerkenwell.

William, King of Scots; David, his brother; Ranulf de Glanvill; Baldwin, Abp (elect) of Canterbury; Walter, Abp of Rouen; and Hugh, Bp of Durham, attended the Council.

[1, 2] Madox's Form. Angl. No. ccclvii. Madox's Exchequer, p. 744. Printed Fines, vol. i. p. lx. The Fine is dated as of January 25, 1184, (viz., on the Conversion of St. Paul, 30 Hen. II.). but that is impossible. Neither in January, 1184, nor January, 1183, was the King in England. We unhesitatingly adopt the equivalent day of 1185, as the date of the Fine. The law-clerk who dated it as of the 30th year of K. Henry, merely forgot that the King's thirtieth year had expired about a month previous (viz. on Dec. 18, 1184). And indeed there never was much account taken of regnal years in Henry II.'s reign; nor any absolute and technical concordance as to when his reign commenced. It is curious, if not relevant, that, in one instance, we know of the above Fine taking effect on Oct. 13, 1185 (Rotulus de Dominabus et Pueris et Puellis, p. 26).

[3] Gervase, p. 1474.

[4] Monasticon, vi. 192, and vii. 916.

[5] Hoveden (359 a.) gives March 10th as the date of this Council. Benedictus and Diceto say March 18; and this is most compatible with the probability arising from Ranulf de Glanvill's being at Woodstock on the 12th (*vide infra*, p. 265). M. Paris's date (March 23) needs no consideration.

1185. March. The King restored to William of Scotland the Earldom of Huntingdon. Also Heraclius consecrated the Conventual Church of the Hospitallers at Clerkenwell. London.

A Royal Charter, in favour of the Canons of Butley, bears date at Westminster, and doubtless belongs to this occasion.[1] It is attested by *B. Cantuar' electo, Wigorn' Episcopo;* [2] *J. Norwic', G. Elyens', H. Dunelm', R. Bathon'* and *S. Cycestr' Episcopis*; Herberto, Cantuar' Archidiacono; Godefrido de Luci, Richemond' Archidiacono; Huberto Walteri; (Hamelino) Comite de Warren; Willelmo Comite Sussex; Comite Albrico; Ricardo, Comite de Clare; Bernardo de St. Walerico; et Waltero fil. Roberti.[3] Westminster.

About this time the Archbishop of Auxerre seems to have visited England. At Michaelmas, 1115, the Fermor of Dover charges,—*In passagio Episcopi* (sic) *Altisiodorensis et suorum* 21*s. per breve Regis.*

March 31. On Midlent Sunday, the King being at Windsor, knights Prince John (aged 18 years and 3 months) preparatory to the Prince's going, as King, to Ireland.[4] The London Pipe-Roll charges 3*s.* 1*d. pro duabus hugiis et duobus tonellis ad thesaurum qui portatus fuit a London usque Windresor'.* Windsor.

c. April 1. Queen Elianor released, after nearly 12 years' imprisonment, "by advice of Archbishop Baldwin."[5]

It would seem that, if the King did not accompany Prince John as far as Gloucester, on the Prince's journey to Ireland, the King was at least at Chipping Campden, about this time. The following entry on the Pipe-Roll of 1185 would suggest as much.—

TERRA COMITIS GLOECESTRIÆ.—*Et pro duobus tonellis vini missis Regi apud Campeden 7s. 8d. per breve Regis.* Chipping Campden.

[1] Cartæ Antiquæ, W.

[2] That is, Baldwin, Bishop of Worcester (and Archbishop) elect of Canterbury.

[3] There is another Royal Charter, dated at Westminster, and in favour of Glastonbury Abbey, which, having been burnt, while *in manu Regis* the King proposes to rebuild with much splendour '*magnificentius reparare decrevi*'). This Charter is unquestionably a forgery. It is specially attested by Heraclius, the Patriarch of Jerusalem, which would fix its date as between January 29, 1185, and April 16, 1185. The attestations of Richard Bishop of Winchester, Reginald Bishop of Bath, William Earl Mandeville, and Ranulf de Glanvill are equally plausible. But then we have the attestations of Baldwin, Archbishop of Canterbury (he was only Archbishop elect at the time), of William, Archbishop of Rheims (whose implied visit to England is improbable and nowhere else recorded), and lastly by Bartholomew, Bishop of Exeter, who died Dec. 15, 1184 (as proved not only by the Chroniclers, but by the Pipe-Roll, which at Michaelmas, 1185, shows his See to have been vacant nearly a year).

This charter should be studied, if only to note its strange form and abnormal provisions as evidences of monkish fabrication. It is printed Monasticon, i. 63, cxxxvii.

[4] Hoveden, Benedictus Abbas, and the Annals of Waverley say that Prince John was knighted at Windsor; the Annals of Margan say at Gloucester.

[5] At that rate we must interpret certain previous notices of the Queen's movements as consisting with a state of surveillance.

1185. April 10. The King, accompanied by the Patriarch Heraclius is at Dover intending to confront Prince Richard, who had attacked his brother Geoffry's territories in Bretagne. With the King, at Dover, are also,—Richard, Bp of Winchester; John, Bp of Norwich; Herbert, Archdeacon of Canterbury; Hubert Walter; John, Prior of Winchester; Roger de Molins, Master of the Hospitallers of Jerusalem; Garnier de Neapolis, Prior of the same house in England; Ranulph de Glanvill; Herbert, brother of the Temple; Master Stephen of Rheims; Master Hamon, Physician; Master Richard, Physician; Master Robert de Buketorp; Master Thomas Griffin; Jordan de Turri; Thomas de Gaiherst; Hugh de Gaiherst; Thomas de Tornaco; Joceline de Risendon; Geoffry de Niuport; Robert de Cicester; and Ranulf de Gedding.[1] Dover.

April 15. The Annals of Waverley, and other authorities, note a terrible earthquake on this day.

On the day following.—

April 16. The King, accompanied by the Patriarch Heraclins, and by Hugh, Bishop of Durham, sails from Dover to Witsand. Witsand. The Pipe-Roll of the year illustrates this transfretation of the King.—

London and Middlesex. *Et pro vassellâ Regis deferendâ a London' usque ad Schorham* 5*s. per breve Regis.*

Sussex, Boseham. *Et pro locandâ nave ad transfretandum thesaurum Regis* 35*s. per breve Regis. Et pro onerando eodem thesauro* 12*d.*

Kent. *Et Willielmo filio Helt* £11. 11*s.* 6*d. quos posuit in locandis navibus et aliis necessariis in transfretatione Regis, ultra quod acceperat de firma de Dourâ, per breve Ranulfi de Glanvill.*

Archiepiscopatus Eboracensis. *Et pro avibus missis Regi ultra mare.*

April 21. The King, according to Diceto, kept Easter at Rouen.[1] Rouen.

April. Prince John tarried some days at Gloucester, on his way to Ireland.

April 24. Prince John sailed from Milford Haven.

April 25. Prince John landed at Waterford.

[1] Collectanea Topogr. et Geneal. vol. iii. 176.—The transaction which shows the King thus attended at Dover was supplemented by a Royal Charter, dated *apud Maredon'm*, (Ibm. p. 177.) The said charter clearly passed long afterwards, and will be noticed in due course.

PRINCE JOHN'S MISSION TO IRELAND is well illustrated by the contemporary Pipe-Roll of K Henry II.[1]

CHESHIRE. *Et in passagio hominum Johannis filii Regis in Hyberniam* £30. 6s. 8d. *per breve Regis. Et pro quinque navibus conducendis quæ portaverunt harnasiam sociorum Johannis filii Regis, qui remanserunt post ipsum pro defectu navium* £12. 6s. 8d. *per breve Regis.*

WARWICKSHIRE AND LEICESTERSHIRE. *Et in passagio militum et servientum Johannis filii Regis in Hyberniam* £34 *per breve Regis.*

GLOUCESTERSHIRE. *Et ad perficiendas predictas* MDC (1600) . . . *suras quas Rex dedit Johanni filio suo ad ducendas secum in Hyberniam* £9. 12d. *per breve Rannulfi de Glanvill. Et in corredio predicti filii Regis et familiæ ejus dum moram fecit apud Gloecestriam,* £40. 14s. 14d. *per breve Regis.*

LONDON AND MIDDLESEX. *Et pro ducendo thesauro quem Rex misit Johanni filio suo a London' usque Bristol'* 8s. 1d. *per breve Regis.*

1185. May 1. The King and Philip of France confer with Heraclius at Vaudreuil. They both decline to join the crusade in person, but promise large subsidies of men and money. Heraclius reached Jerusalem before the 1st of August. Vaudreuil.

c. May. The King now sends to England for Queen Elianor, in order that she may assume the sovereignty of Guienne in place of her son, Richard, who is recalled to the King's Court. The Queen goes, accompanied by her daughter, the Duchess of Saxony, and (according to other accounts) by the Duke.

The Pipe-Roll notices the Queen's transfretation and other incidents of the King's being over sea.

SOUTHAMPTONSHIRE. *Et Radulfo filio Stephani* £13 *ad procurationem Reginæ et Ducis Saxoniæ apud Porcestriam et Portesmuam per breve Regis. Et in custamento ducendi thesaurum multis vicibus, et pro doliis, et locandis caretis* 79s. 8d.

SOUTHAMPTON (HANTONIA). *Et in liberacione Esneccæ quando Dux Saxoniæ et Regina transfretaverunt* £7. 10s. *per Ranulfum de Glanvill. Et in liberacione septem navium quæ transfretaverunt cum hernesio predictorum* £12. 10s. *per breve Regis et per visum Radulfi filii Stephani.*

LONDON AND MIDDLESEX. *Et pro ducendo thesauro Regis a London' usque Hanton'* (Southampton) 20s. 6d.

May 19. Baldwin Archbishop of Canterbury collated, or enthroned.

c. June. Nothing seems to be known of the King's movements in Normandy during this summer. It is evident from certain charges on the Southampton Pipe-Roll that at one time he contemplated a return to England.— Normandy.

[1] A Charter, expedited by Prince John, is also noteworthy.—

It is to an Irish Monastery styled *Sancta Maria de Valle Salutis.* The Prince's title is "Johannes filius Domini Regis Angliæ et Dominus Hiberniæ." The witnesses are Hugh de Lacy, Constable (of Ireland, we presume), Bertram de Verdon, Seneschal (of the same), and Gilbert Vipard. (Monast. vii. 1136). We assume of course that the deed passed while the Prince was in Ireland (Apl. 25–Dec. 31, 1185). And the third witness's name may perhaps be corrected *Pipard,* though Gilbert Pipard was, during part of the year, employed as a Justice in England.

1185. June, July, August. *Et item in liberacione Esneccæ quando transfretavit in æstate contra Regem £7. 10s. per breve Ranulfi de Glanvill.* Normandy.

Then follow two entries further suggestive of the King's remaining in Normandy.

Et in passagio Mauricii de Creon et Ivel' de Ma'en[1] *et uxoris ejus, neptis Regis, 70s. per breve Regis.*

Et pro locandis strenuis nautis ad transfretandum cum thesauro 26s. 8d. per breve Regis.

And the Fermor of Dover charges,—£10. 1s. 6d. *in passagio Willelmi de Yerpunvill et avium Regis* (the King's hawks.)

At Michaelmas, which closes the fiscal year, the King is
Sep. 29. still over sea. Normandy.

On Sep. 29 Gilbert de Glanvill was consecrated Bishop of Rochester at Canterbury, the Bishops of Bath, St. David's, and Chichester, assisting the Archbishop.[2]

SOME EVIDENCES as to the persons presiding over the Law-Courts during the fiscal year now ended are here subjoined.—

March 12. On this day sat judicially at Woodstock these persons, viz. :—Ranulf de Glanvill; Hubert Walter; James,[3] Archdeacon of Chichester; Master Robert de Inglesham; Gilbert Pipard; Hugh de Morewic, Seneschal; Wm. Vavasour; Rannulf de Geddinges; and Ernise de Nevill.[3]

May 31. On this day a fine was levied in the *Curia Regis* at Westminster before John, Bp of Norwich, and Rannulf de Glanvill, Justiciars of the King; Richard the Treasurer; Godfrey de Luci; Hubert Walter; Wm. Basset, and Nigel fitz Alexander.—

Walter, Abbot of Westminster, was concerned in the business which occupied the Court.[4]

In the course of the year the following Justices in Eyre, viz. :—

Josceline, Archdeacon (of Chichester), William de Vere, Roger fitz Reinfrid, William Rufus, Otho fitz William, and Richard Peche, or some of them, visited, and held pleas in, the following counties, viz., Essex, Herts, Norfolk, Suffolk, Surrey, Cambridgeshire, Huntingdonshire, Lincolnshire, Warwickshire, Leicestershire, Derbyshire, Nottinghamshire, Buckinghamshire, and Bedfordshire.

Also Gilbert Pipard, Wm. fitz Stephen, Michael Belet, Roger (Clerk of Hereford), and Walter Map, or some of them, visited Gloucestershire, Worcestershire, Shropshire, Herefordshire, and Staffordshire.

Also Godfrey de Luci, Hugh de Morewich, Robert de Vaux (Sheriff of Cumberland), and Hugh Murdach, or some three of them, visited Northumberland, Cumberland, and Yorkshire.

Also Richard, Archdeacon of Wiltshire, Gosceline Archdeacon, Hugh Bardulf, Ralph fitz Stephen, and Geoffry fitz Azo, visited Wiltshire, Somersetshire, Dorsetshire, and Devonshire.

Also Geoffrey fitz Piers held pleas at Northampton; and Ranulf de Glanvill at Oxford.

Also Robert de Haselee, Nicholas le Bret, Robert del Broc, Roger Musson, and William de Stanton, or some of them held Forest-Pleas in Herefordshire, Shropshire, Staffordshire, and Gloucestershire.

Also Geoffrey fitz Piers, held Forest-Pleas in Sussex, Surrey, Berks, Oxfordshire, Wiltshire, Hampshire, Buckinghamshire, Bedfordshire, Worcestershire, Nottinghamshire, Derbyshire, and part of Yorkshire.

Similar Pleas were held by Peter de Lincoln, Ralph de Hanton, Ralph de Hospital, and Ralph Hose,

[1] Joel de Meduana (Mayenne), is meant.

[2] Gervase, 1477. Diceto, No. 629.

[3] Haughmond Register (British Museum). But the Christian name of the Archdeacon of Chichester was Josceline, rather than James.

[4] Madox's Form. Angl. ccclviii.

in Devonshire; by Robert Belet and Ralph de Hospital, in Somerset and Dorset; by Robert fitz Thomas, Robert Belet, and Peter de Lincoln in Cornwall; by Arnisius de Nevill and Nigel fitz Alexander, in Northumberland; and by Roger de Hoveden, Geoffry de Haia, Richard de Hug'ford and Henry Norreis in Yorkshire.

MICHAELMAS, 1185, TO MICHAELMAS, 1186.

Sep. 30. The King is still beyond sea, probably in Normandy. Normandy.

Oct. 6. John, Precentor of Exeter and Subdean of Salisbury, is consecrated Bishop of Exeter, by Archbishop Baldwin.

Oct. 22. The Bishops Geoffrey of Ely and John of Norwich, with Ranulf de Glanville, are noticed as Justiciars, sitting in the *Curiâ Regis* at Westminster.[1]

Nov. 1. At this time the King must have entertained and abandoned a design of returning to England. A ship left Southampton to meet him, probably at Barfleur. The extract from the Pipe-Roll of Michaelmas, 1186, is as follows: HANTON. *Et in liberacione Esneccæ quando transfretavit contra Regem in termino Omnium Sanctorum* £7. 10*s per breve Ranulfi de Glanville.* (Barfleur).

Nov. 7. The King at Albemarle. Aumâle *alias* Albemarle.

A conference between France and Flanders attended by K. Henry, and by the Archbishops of Rheims and Cologne, leads to a peace between the two first potentates.[2]

Nov. 9. The King, lying ill at Belvoir, is visited by Philip of France.[3] Belvoir.

Nov. 23 or 24. Pope Lucius III. died and was buried on the 25th.

Nov. 25. Urban III. elected Pope, and was crowned Dec. 1st.

c. Nov. 30, Granville's Viceroyalty in England and the transmission of treasure to Normandy are evidenced by the Southampton Pipe-Roll: *Et pro locandâ navi Herberto Geldwin quæ portavit thesaurum Regis circa festum Sti Andrea* 40*s per breve Ranulfi de Glanville. Et pro onerando thesauro et deonerando* 16*d.*

c. Dec. Prince John leaves Ireland, and is replaced in the government thereof by John de Courcy.

Dec. 25. King Henry keeps Christmas at Danfront.[4] Damfront.

Dec. 31. King Henry, at the end of the year, was probably still on the frontier of Normandy.

THE YEAR NOW ENDING was productive in Bretagne of the enactment called the ASSIZE OF RENNES, which regulated the descent of Fiefs according to the Norman custom of primogeniture.[5]—

It was issued by Prince Geoffrey, whose style is—*Galfridus filius Henrici Regis, Dux Britanniæ et Comes Richemundiæ.* His wife Constance joins in the manifesto. It specially provides for the case of Roland de Dinan's Fief. Its witnesses are *Radulfus de Fulgeriis; Comes Eudo; Alanus de Rohan; Alanus filius Comitis; et Henricus filius alterius* (*Comitis?*).

[1] Salop Chartulary, 281.
[2, 3] Diceto, 629.
[4] Benedictus (Stubbs) i. 343.
[5] Gall. Scriptores, xii. 567 *n.*

A.D. 1186.

1186. c. Feb. Before Lent (Feb. 26) the King confers at Gisors with Philip of France, and agrees that Prince Richard shall marry Philip's sister, here called 'Adelais.'[1] Gisors.

c. Feb. 26. The London Pipe-Roll supplies evidence of the transmission of money to Normandy. *Et in liberacione Clerici Thesauri et hominum Camerariorum quando transfretaverunt cum thesauro in capite jejunii £4 per breve Regis. Et pro locandis carretis ad eundem thesaurum portandum 8s.* Normandy.

March 10. The King confers again at Gisors with Philip of France, touching the dower of Margaret the young Queen.[2] Gisors.

c. March 25. The King, still in Normandy, despatches Hugh Bishop of Durham into England. There were eight episcopal Sees now vacant. These seem to have been York, Lincoln, Chester, Salisbury, Hereford, Worcester, Exeter, and Carlisle.[3] Normandy.

Bishop Hugh reaches Durham before the 6th of April.[4]

Perhaps it was now that certain persons crossed from Dover to Normandy by the King's order. ' The Dover Pipe-Roll says thus:—*Et in passagio Gilberti Episcopi Roffensis et Ranulfi de Glanville et Bernardi de Sto Walerico et aliorum qui cum eis transfretaverunt precepto Regis* £4. 16*s.* 10*d.* *per breve Regis.*

March 17, William Fitz Adeline, styled *Dapifer Regis*, is in London, and makes a grant to the Hospitallers.[5]

c. April 13. The King is still in Normandy. Money forwarded to him both before and after Easter (April 13) is indicated by consecutive entries on the Southampton Pipe-Roll.—

HANTON. *Et pro locandâ navi Sansonis Wascelini ad transfretandum cum thesauro* 50*s.* *per breve Rannulfi de Glanvill. Et pro onerando et deonerando thesauro* 18*d.* *Et item pro locanda unâ navi ad transfretandum thesaurum post Pascham* 50*s.* *per breve Regis. Et pro onerando thesauro et deonerando* 15*d.*

April 26. The King probably at Barfleur. Barfleur.

April 27. The King and Queen pass the sea, and land at Southampton. They bring with them their granddaughter, Matilda, the daughter of Henry Duke of Saxony.[6] Southampton.

[1] Benedictus, p. 444. Hoveden, 360.

[2] Benedictus. Diceto, 630. Queen Margaret soon afterwards married Bela, King of Hungary. The negotiations for the marriage are alluded to on the Pipe-Roll of Winchester thus,—*Et in corredio nuntiorum Regis Hungriæ* 13*s.* 5*d.* *per breve Regis.*

[3, 4] Benedict. (Stubbs) vol. i. pp. 344, 345.

[5] Monasticon, vii. 808, 833.

[6] Benedictus (Stubbs), ii. 345. Diceto, 630. The latter calls Southampton *Hamonis Portum.*

1186. c. April 28. The King at Merewell,[1] visiting the Bishop of Winchester. Merewell.

c. April 30. The King goes to Winchester[2] where he rests a night. Winchester.

May 25. The King is at Eynsham, and forthwith presides over a great Council at Oxford. At this Council, William King of Scots is present; and it is arranged that he shall marry Ermengarde, daughter of Richard, Vicomte of Beaumont le Roger.[3] K. William, for his part, undertakes to reduce Roland son of Uctred son of Fergus, which Roland, on the death (Jan. 1, 1185) of his uncle, Gilbert son of Fergus, had seized upon Galloway to the disinheritance of Duncan, son and heir of Gilbert, which Duncan was in ward to the King of England. Eynsham. Oxford.

At the same Council of Oxford William de Vere was elected Bishop of Hereford, and Hugh is said to have been elected Bishop of Lincoln.[4] Baldwin, Archbishop of Canterbury was in attendance.

The Oxfordshire Pipe-Roll of the current year has two entries, probably connected with the King's presence in the County.—*Et pro denariis ducendis a London usque Gloceestriam ad negocia Regis facienda* 18*d.* *per breve Regis. Et pro ducendis* £200 *ab Oxineford usque London* 12*d.* *p. b. R.*

The King at Woodstock.[5] Woodstock.

June 1. It is conjectured that during this month the King was in Kent; it is plausibly certain that during the course of the summer he passed by sea from Gravesend up the river to London. The Sheriff of Kent makes the following charge on the year's Pipe-Roll;—*Et nautis de Gravesent qui duxerunt Regem per Tamisiam usque London' unam marcam per breve Regis.*[6] Kent. London.

1, 2 Diceto, 630. Benedictus (Stubbs), II. 285.

3 The King of Scots was to have married K. Henry's grandaughter, Matilda of Saxony, but their consanguinity was alleged as a bar. The Chroniclers make a meaning allusion to the supposedly equal consanguinity of Ermengarde and William; for her father, Richard, was son of Roscelin, Vicomte of Beaumont le Roger, by Constance, a natural daughter of K. Henry I. But here the Chroniclers were too critical. The Vicomte Richard was descended from Henry I, but not from Malcolm III. K. William was descended from Malcolm III, but not from Henry I.

4 There had been three other nominees to the vacant See of Lincoln, viz.,—

(1) Richard, the Treasurer Royal, and Dean of Lincoln.

(2) Godfrey de Lucy, Clerk of the King, Canon of Lincoln; and Archdeacon of Derby.

(3) Herbert, Clerk of the King, Canon of Lincoln, and Archdeacon of Canterbury (Diceto, p. 631. Benedictus, i. 446). Diceto puts the election of Bishop Hugh on May 25, at Eynsham.

5 Stubbs, quoting *Vita Sancti Hugonis*, 102.

6 It is a further and still more hazardous conjecture that this almost unrecorded journey of the King was for the purpose of doing penance at the tomb of Becket, at Canterbury.

1186. July 1. The King was at Northampton. Godfrey de Luci was elected Bishop of Exeter in the presence of the King and of Archbishop Baldwin. Godfrey renounced the election. John, Subdean of Salisbury, was eventually substituted.[1] Northampton.

The King's being at Northampton was relevant to his journey further north, and to the military preparations against Galloway. The Pipe-Rolls, besides their frequent reference to the "Scutage of Galwey," put in charge this summer, give the following hints as to the King's presence and business at Northampton.

CIVITAS WINTONIA. *Et pro ducendis armis Regis a Winton' usque Norhanton 2s. per breve Regis. Et pro ducendis papilionibus Regis a Winton' usque Norhanton' 5s. 10d. per idem breve.*

NORHANTESCIRA. HECHAM. *Et pro ducendo thesauro a Norhanton' usque Merlebergam et item de Norhanton' usque Notingeham 10s.*

The King is presumed to have passed northwards by way of Nottingham. Nottingham.

The King occurs next at Carlisle, whence he sends William of Scotland and his brother, David, to summon Roland fitz Uctred to Court. Hugh, Bishop of Durham, and Ranulf de Glanvill, despatched on the same mission, bring the said Roland to the King at Carlisle. Roland gives satisfactory promises of submission to the King's judgment, the King and nobles of Scotland, and Joceline, Bishop of Glasgow, undertaking to compel him to performance. Carlisle.

It was now that Paulinus de Ledis, master of St. Leonard's Hospital at York, being elected to the See of Carlisle, renounces such election. Again, while the King was at Carlisle, Robert de Boutevelin, Dean of York, died;—to whose Deanery succeeded Hubert Walter, heretofore mentioned as a Justiciar, and who was in fact nephew of Ranulf de Glanvill's wife. A Charter Royal to the Cumberland Abbey of Holm-Cultram seems to belong to this period. It is tested by two Royal Chaplains,—Nicholas and Roger.[2]

It is possible that the King in his journey southward from Carlisle, halted at his Staffordshire hunting-lodge at Kinver, Kinver.

[1] Monasticon, ii. 515, note *o*.

[2] Monasticon, v. 594.

1186. c. June 13. and there gave orders for its repair. The Sheriff of Stafford- shire charges,—*Et in claudendâ Curiâ Regis de Kenefara circa domos Regis 42s. per breve Regis.* Kinver in Staffordshire.

July 15. On Tuesday, before the feast of Margaret the Virgin in the 32nd year of K. Henry, a fine was levied in the King's presence at *Fekeham* between the Prior of Dunstable on the one part, and Amalric, the King's *Dispensator*; and Amabilia his wife, on the other part.[1] Feckenham in Worcestershire.

A Royal Charter in favour of Haughmond Abbey (Shropshire), is dated at Feckenham,[2] and attested by Ranulf de Glanville, Brother Roger the Almoner, and Hugh Pantulf.[3]

c. July. About this time the King seems to have sent money in aid of Prince Richard, and of his contest with the Comte of St. Giles.[4] The entries on the Pipe-Roll are,—

WILTSHIRE. *Et pro ducendo thesauro a Sarum usque Sudhanton 2s. 7d.*

WINCHESTER. *Et pro onerando thesauro qui missus fuit Normanniam et in liberacione vigilum et pro lumine 2s. 4d.*

HANTON. *Et pro locandâ navi Sansonis Wascelini ad portandum thesaurum missum Ricardo Comiti Pictav' 50s. per breve Regis. Et pro onerando thesauro et deonerando 8d. Et pro uno cado ad reponendum thesaurum 6d.*

On July 25th, in this year Hugh de Lacy was assassinated at Durrow in Ireland.[5] The King hears of it in August, and is glad.[6]

c. Aug. 1. The King, on hearing of this event, despatches Prince John to Ireland for the purpose of seizing De Lacy's Irish fief into the King's hand.

The Pipe-Rolls indicate the aid tendered to Prince John in relation to this business.—

STAFFORDSHIRE. *Et pro ducendo thesauro a Burton usque Cestriam 6s. 11d.*

HONOR CESTRIA. *Et in passagio Willmi Cun.in et hominum suorum in servicio Regis et Johannes filii sui in Hyberniam 6s. per breve Regis.*

It will be seen presently that the Prince himself did not cross the Channel.

Aug. 10th is the day given for the consecration of William de Vere to the See of Hereford, also of Reiner to the See of St. Asaph, and (by some authorities) for the election of Hugh, Prior of the Carthusians, to the See of Lincoln.

Aug. 19th. Prince Geoffrey, aged 28 years, was killed in a tournament at Paris, where he was plotting with Philip of France against his father and his brother, Richard. He left an only child, and at the moment presumptive heir, Elianor. He was buried in the Church of Notre Dame. His posthumous son, Arthur, was born on March 29, 1187.

[1] Harl. MSS. 1885 fo. 22.
[2] Haughmond Chartulary, fo. 16.
[3] Hugh Pantulf was Sheriff of Shropshire in 1186.
[4] Benedictus (Stubbs) i. 347.
[5] Stapleton (Rot. Normann. i. lxxi), places this event erroneously in 1185. The Herefordshire Pipe-Rolls give the exactest evidence that custody of the Honor and Castles of Hugh de Lacy accrued to the Crown on and about August 1st, 1186.
[6] Benedictus (Stubbs) i. 351.

1186. c. Aug. 25. K. Henry, hearing of Prince Geoffrey's death, recalls Prince John from the coast, where he was waiting to embark for Ireland. Woodstock.

Sept. 5. A great Council held by the King at Woodstock. Thereat Richard, Vicomte of Beaumont le Roger gives his daughter Ermengarde in marriage to William King of Scots.

There were present at this Council—David, Earl of Huntingdon; Baldwin, Archbishop of Canterbury; and the Bishops, Joceline of Glasgow, John of Norwich, Geoffrey of Ely, and Reginald of Bath.

Sept. 9. The King goes to Marlborough, accompanied by William, King of Scots. Marlborough.

Sept. 14. The King holds a great Council at Marlborough, at which are present,—Baldwin, Archbishop of Canterbury; the Bishops, John of Norwich, Geoffry of Ely, Henry of Baieux,[1] Hugh of Durham, William of Worcester,[2] and Hugh, Bishop-elect of Lincoln.—

The business in hand was the elections to the vacant Sees of York, Salisbury, and Exeter.—

The Canons of York presented five nominees, all of whom were rejected by the King. They were Hubert Walter, Dean of York; Hamund, Præcentor of York; Master Laurence, Archdeacon of Bedford;[3] Bernard, Prior of Newburgh; and Master Roger Harundel.[3]

To the election of Herbert, Archdeacon of Canterbury, to the See of Exeter, the King assented; but an appeal was lodged against the nomination, on account of Herbert's illegitimacy.

John, Subdean of Salisbury, was appointed to the See of Exeter.

A Royal Charter, dated at Marlborough, is in favour of the Carthusian Priory of Witham (Somersetshire). It was undoubtedly solicited by Hugh, the first Prior of that house, now in process of elevation to the See of Lincoln.[4] The Charter is attested by the Bishops Hugh of Durham, Geoffrey of Ely, John of Norwich, and Reginald of Bath; by

[1] The Southampton Pipe-Roll supplies a curious corroboration of the Bishop of Baieux having been in England, and returning to Normandy before Michaelmas.—*Et item pro locandâ navi Sansonis Wascelini ad transfretandum Henricum Episcopum Baiocensum* 50*s. per breve Regis. Et pro locandis duobus nautis armatis ad transfretandum cum thesauro unam marcam per breve Regis.*

[2] Benedictus (Stubbs), i. 352. But it should be William, *Elect* of Worcester.

[3] These two were, at the time, among the Fermors of the vacant See of York (Madox, Exch. 211).

[4] The Deed promises that the Monks of Witham shall always elect their own Prior.

1186. September. Prince John, Earl William of Sussex, Ranulf de Glanvill, Walter fitz Robert, Reginald de Curtenay, Hugh Bardulf, Hugh de Morewic, Seneschal; Ralph fitz Stephen, Chamberlain; Gilbert fitz Reinfrid, Geoffry fitz Piers, Robert de Whitefeld, and Michael Belet.[1] Marlborough

Another Charter, dated at Marlborough, is in favour of Osbert, Prior of Dodford (Worcestershire). It is attested by Baldwin, Archbishop of Canterbury; Herbert, Archdeacon of Canterbury; Ralph, Archdeacon of Hereford; William, Earl Mandeville, Ralph fitz Stephen, Thomas fitz Bernard, and Master Silvester.[2]

On Sept. 21, Hugh (late Prior of the Carthusians), and William de Northale (late Archdeacon of Gloucester), were consecrated to the Sees of Lincoln and Worcester by Archbishop Baldwin at Westminster.

On Sept. 29, Bishop Hugh arrived at Lincoln, and was inducted by Gilbert, Bishop of Rochester, and Herbert, Archdeacon of Canterbury.

Sept. 29. The King was probably at Woodstock. Woodstock.

WE FIND NO EXACT DATE of an embassy which the King will have received from Flanders between May and September. All that we can say on the subject is that, within those limits, the authorities at Dover provided, at the King's charges, a ship for "Arnald, Chamberlain of the Comte of Flanders, and his fellows."

SOMETHING SHOULD be said of the *Itinera* of the King's Justices during the fiscal year ending Michaelmas, 1186.

Hugh de Morewich, Ralph Murdach, William Vavasour, and Master Thomas de Husseburn, or some of them, had visited the several counties of Lincolnshire, Norfolk, Suffolk, Essex, Hertfordshire, Cambridgeshire, Huntingdonshire, Buckinghamshire, Bedfordshire, Northamptonshire, and Rutland.[3]

William de Vere, Ralph fitz Stephen, Robert de Ynglesham, and Milo de Musgroz, or some of them, had visited Berkshire, Gloucestershire, Herefordshire, Shropshire, Staffordshire, and Worcestershire.[4]

Robert fitz Bernard, Richard Giffard, and Roger fitz Reinfrid had visited Berkshire.[5]

Josceline, Archdeacon of Chichester, William Rufus, Henry de Cornhill, and Oto fitz William had visited Dorsetshire, Somersetshire, Devonshire, Hants, and Wiltshire.

Richard, Archdeacon of Coventry, and Hugh Bardulf had visited Northumberland.

[1] Monasticon, vi. 2.

[2] Monasticon, vii. 944. Thomas fitz Bernard, Justiciar of the Forest, died in 1184 (Benedictus, i. 323), that is, at least a year before Baldwin became Archbishop of Canterbury.—

Whereas Thomas fitz Bernard left no son old enough to attest any deed of Henry II., we must presume the above testing-clause to be inaccurate, or else the whole Charter a forgery.—

If the former be the case, then the real witness will have been Robert fitz Bernard.

[3] The Record entitled "*Rotulus de Dominabus et Pueris et Puellis*" was a result of enquiries made in this *Iter*.

[4] This *Iter* evidently took place before May, 1186, when Wm. de Vere was elected to the See of Hereford.

[5] This *Iter* was abnormal, probably the result of Berkshire not having been visited in the previous year.

Ranulf de Glanvill; Josceline, Archdeacon; and Godfrey de Luci had held pleas in Hampshire, Southampton, Winchester, and Berkshire.

Geoffry fitz Piers had held Forest-pleas in Northamptonshire, Derbyshire, Warwickshire, Leicestershire, and Hampshire.

TOWARDS THE CLOSE OF the above and the beginning of the next, fiscal year, we observe a quorum of Sheriffs acting as Justiciars in several counties; for instance, Robert Marmion, Ralph de Ardern, Hugh Pantulf, William fitz Stephen, and Thomas Noel,[1] seem to have commenced a Circuit in Staffordshire, and to have sat at Litchfield, on August 13, 1186; but the rest of their *Iter* extending into Staffordshire, Shropshire, Herefordshire, and Worcestershire is not recorded on the Pipe-Roll till Michaelmas, 1187.

HERE IS ADDED a list of persons who, in the above or some recent year, appear to have been grantees of the Crown in respect of marriages, wardships, ferms, or other trusteeships, such as implied the favour of the King, or the deserts of the recipient.—

Ranulf de Glanvill, Thomas Basset (deceased), Gilbert Basset, Nigel fitz Alexander, Robert de Stutevill (deceased), Robert de Burun, Hugh de Morewich, Hugh Bardulf, Hugh de Cressi, Joceline de Evermue, Wido de Croun, Ralph Murdac; Laurence, Archdeacon of Bedford; Master Roger Arundel, William le Vavassour, Robert de Saucei, Ralph de Wircestre, William de Diva, Thomas fitz Bernard (deceased), Geoffry fitz Piers, Reginald de Curtenai, Henry de Pinkeni, William de Jarponville, Richard Rufus, Ralph de Hanville; Eugenia, late wife of Thomas fitz Bernard, Robert de Lucy, Eustace fitz Stephen, Gilbert de Vere, Osbert de Glanvill; Geoffry, Bishop of Ely; Gilbert de Coleville (deceased), Ralph de Dena, Picot de Tani, Robert le Poher, Godfry de Lucy, Stephen de Glanvill, Henry de Cornhill, Durand de Ostilli.[2]

MICHAELMAS, 1186, TO MICHAELMAS, 1187.

1186. Sept. 30. At this time we take the King to have been at Woodstock, but to have gone to Winchester early in the month of October.— Woodstock.

Certain Charters, dated at Woodstock, belong proximately to this period. One in favour of Stanley Abbey (Wiltshire) is attested by—Hugh, Bishop of Lincoln; Roger, Richard, and Nicholas, Chaplains; Hugh de Morwich, Dapifer; Hugh Bardulf, Dapifer; Ralph fitz Stephen, Chamberlain; Robert de Witefeld, and Michael Belet.[3]

Another Charter, in favour of St. Mary's, York, and its Abbot, Robert, is attested by Geoffry, Bp of Ely; Hugh, Bp of Durham; William, Earl Mandeville, and Hugh Bardulf.[4]

c. Oct. 2. In this month we suppose the King to have visited Winchester, where it will presently appear that Queen Eleanor was residing. Winchester.

A Charter, there dated, is in favour of the Church of St. Peter at York, and is attested by Ranulf de Glanvill; Hubert (Dean of) York; Hugh de Morewic, Dapifer; Hugh Bardulf, Dapifer, and Will. Vavasore.[5]

[1] Sheriffs of Worcestershire, Herefordshire, Shropshire, Gloucestershire, and Staffordshire respectively.

[2] Rotulus de Pueris et Dominabus, *passim*.

[3] Monasticon, v. 564.

[4] Monasticon, iii. 552.

[5] Cartæ Antiquæ, P.

1186. c. Oct. 2. Another Royal Charter to the Church of York is dated at Winchester, and attested by Bishops Hugh of Durham, John of Norwich, and William of Worcester; Hubert, Dean of York; Ranulf de Glanvill; Hugh de Morewich and Hugh Bardulf, *Dapiferi*; Robert de Whitefeld; and Michael Belet.[1] Winchester.

A third Charter, dated at Winchester, is to St. Leonard's Hospital, York, and is attested precisely as the last.[2]

c. Oct. 5. About this time King Henry accredits three ambassadors to France, viz., Ranulf de Glanvill; William de Mandevill, Earl of Essex and Albemarle; and Walter, Archbishop of Rouen. They were to pacify K. Philip, who was demanding the wardship of Elianor, the presumed heiress of Bretagne.

Oct. 9. Henry's ambassadors procure a truce with Philip until the feast of S. Hilary (January 13, 1187), and landing in England on the eighteenth of October,[3] find King Henry at Reading. Reading.

c. Oct. 20. The King consults with Baldwin, Archbishop of Canterbury, and then orders the Ambassadors to return forthwith to Philip, substituting Robert, Archdeacon of Nottingham, for Ranulf de Glanvill. They are to procure a prolongation of the truce till Easter (March 29, 1187).

The issue of this embassy was not immediately pacificatory. Philip of France was highly exasperated because Henry de *Veir*, Constable of Gisors, and kinsman of the Earl of Albemarle[4], had recently slain Ralf, son of Richard de Vaus, a French Knight.[5]

Nov. 30. K. Henry goes from Reading to Amesbury (in Wiltshire), Amesbury. and there introduces a number of Nuns, brought from the Abbey of Fontevrault, to the new buildings which he had caused to be erected.

c. Dec. 10. The King sends Glanville to negotiate with Rese ap Griffin, and to pacify the Welsh Border; also to secure Welsh soldiers for the troubles anticipated with France.

Benedictus notes certain King's clerks as returning from Rome about this time, having lodged a complaint against Savaric, Archdeacon of

[1, 2] Cartæ Antiquæ, D D. Monasticon, vii. 612.

[3] We follow the chronology indicated by Diceto, who (p. 631), says that the Archbishop of Rouen, had an interview with Philip, on Oct. 9, and landed at Dover on Oct. 18.

[4] The mother of Earl William de Mandeville was a daughter of Aubrey de Vere (Stubbs, quoting Monast. Angl. iv. 102).

[5] Son of Hugh de Vaus, says Diceto (p. 632). Diceto dates the catastrophe as on Nov. 28, which would make the second embassy to have been in France near a month.

Nottingham (it should be Northampton). It would seem that the Archdeacon's revenues, being forfeit to the Crown, had been previously assigned by the Pope to the payment of the Archdeacon's private debts. The Pope now allows that the Sequestrator (the Archbishop of Canterbury) shall collect and retain in his custody the said revenues. The Pope also entreats the King's clemency towards the Archdeacon.

Before Christmas, Octavian, the Papal Legate, and Hugh de Novant, Bishop-elect of Chester, reached England, and were at Canterbury. The latter was returning from a mission to Rome, but is said to have been associated in Octavian's legation, the objects of which were to determine all Papal appeals in England, and to visit Ireland. This legation was opposed by Archbishop Baldwin and his Suffragans, he himself being Legate in his province.

Dec. 25. The King kept Christmas at 'Gildeford.'[1] With him were Prince John, John Archbishop of Dublin, Geoffry Bishop of Ely, and David Earl of Huntingdon; also the Earl of Leicester,[2] the Earl of Arundel,[3] and Roger Bigod,[4] each of whom performed his respective household service at the Royal Table. Guildford.

We should here quote several consecutive entries from the Southamptonshire Pipe-Roll, which will serve to illustrate what has gone before.—

Et in negociis Reginæ in recessu suo a Wintoniâ 40*s*. *per breve Regis. Et ad faciendam soltam Reginæ apud Wintoniam* £38. 7*s*. 11*d*. *per breve Regis. Et in custamento numerandi et ponderandi thesaurum apud Wintoniam post Natale, et pro forulis novis ad reponendum eundem thesaurum et pro aliis minutis negociis ad predictum opus per Archidiaconum Cantuariæ*[5] *et Hugonem Bardulf et Radulfum filium Stephani*, £6. 19*s*. 7*d*. *Et pro carriando thesauro a Wintoniâ ad Saresburiam et ad Oxinford' et ad Geldeford' et ad plura loca per Angliam* £4. 8*s*. 3*d*.

Dec. 26. The King, still at Guildford, hears of the arrival of Octavian in England, and sends Prince John[6] and Ralph Archdeacon of Hereford to meet him.

c. Dec. 28. The Legate Octavian, either at Canterbury or Westminster, is met by the King's messengers.

[1] Benedictus (as printed by Hearne) says 'Bedford,' but it is an error, corrected in Stubbs' edition.

[2] The Earl of Leicester's household office was that of a Dapifer. He inherited it from his ancestor, Earl William fitz Osborne, Dapifer to King William the Conqueror.

[3] The Earl of Arundel (or rather Sussex) was hereditary Chief-Butler in the Royal Household.

[4] Roger Bigod was another of the Dapiferi Regis,—an office derived to him from his father and grandfather (*Vide supra*, p. 3 for the descent).

[5] Viz. Herbert (*Vide supra*, pp. 202–3, 256).

[6] Benedictus puts John, Archbishop of Dublin, instead of Prince John, on this mission.

A.D. 1187.

Jan. 1. King Henry receives the Legate Octavian, and Hugh de Novant, Bishop-elect of Chester, at Westminster Abbey.[1] Westminster.

Feb. 9. Octavian, now again at Canterbury, is visited by John Bishop of Norwich, William, Bishop of Worcester, and Hugh, Bishop-elect of Chester.[2]

Feb. 10. The King is at Chilham, where the above three Prelates, leaving Canterbury, find him.[2] Chilham.

A Royal Charter, bearing date at *Chileham*, and addressed to the Justices, Sheriffs, &c., of Norfolk and Suffolk, is attested singly by Hugh de Morewic. Thereby, the King, at request of Ranulf de Glanvill, and for the service of Ranulf de Geddinges, quit-claims and releases one Roger, son of William Curtpeil (to whom the King has given Geddinges' daughter to wife) from all Jew-debts which were owing by William (Roger's father), on the day of his (William's) death.[3]

Feb. 11. The King is at Canterbury on Ash-Wednesday (*quartâ feriâ cinerum* or *3cio id. Feb.* as two several authorities state the same date).[4] With the King are Baldwin, Abp of Canterbury, the Bishops of Lincoln, Norwich, Durham, and Worcester, and three Abbots. Canterbury.

On February 18th died Gilbert Foliot, Bishop of London.

The King and Prince John are stated *now* to have visited Clarendon, in Wiltshire.[5] That they were there together, and about this time, is quite clear.— Clarendon.

A fine levied in the *Curia Regis* at Clarendon, is dated

[1] Benedictus (Stubbs) ii. 4. Diceto, 634.

[2] Gervase, 1489.

[3] Cartæ Antiquæ, R.

[4] Viz. Brakelond (p. 37) and Gervase (p. 1489). There can be no doubt about the fact or the date. Benedictus says nothing about this visit to Canterbury, which is *primâ facie* evidence against his accuracy.

Benedictus' account would indicate—

(1) That the King sent Prince John to Normandy soon after his (the King's) meeting (Jan. 1), with Octavian.

(2) That the King reached Dover about Feb. 9 or 10), and, halting there a few days *post paucos dies* embarked on Feb. 14.

(3) That the King's ship sighted Witsand, but was obliged to put back to Dover, which it reached at nightfall of the 14th.

(4) That the King remained three days at Dover, and re-embarked on the 17th.

[5] Brakelond (pp. 47, 134) clearly intends to place the visit to Clarendon after that to Canterbury. That the two visits followed one another closely there can be no doubt, but there is a doubt as to the priority. It arises in this way.—There was hardly time between Feb. 11 and Feb. 17 for the King to get from Canterbury to Clarendon and back to Dover; and there is a question whether Prince John had not been sent to Normandy before the 11th of February. On the other hand there is a question whether the King's transfretation was not on the 27th rather than the 17th of February, and whether Prince John did not sail with him rather than precede him.

1187. February. as of the 33rd year of the King, and expressed to be *Coram ipso Domino Rege et Johanne filio ejus.* It was a fine between Robert Abbot of Ramsey, and Geoffry Peche. The Court was attended by Ranulf de Glanvill, Roger fitz Reinfrid, Michael Belet; Robert de Inglesham, Archdeacon of Gloucester; Ralph, Archdeacon of Hereford; Hubert, Dean of York; Robert de Witefeld; Josceline, Archdeacon of Chichester; and Master Thomas de Husseburn.[1] Clarendon.

Again, a Royal Charter, dated at Clarendon is in favour of Ranulf de Glanvill, and is attested by Hubert, Dean of York; Hugh de Morewic, and Hugh Bardulf, *Dapiferi;* Michael Belet, and Stephen de Thurnham.[2]

Another Royal Charter, dated at Clarendon, is in favour of Wombridge Priory (Shropshire), and is attested by Hugh Bishop of Durham; Peter, Bishop of St. David's; Hubert, Dean of York, Ranulf de Glanvill; Brother Roger, the Almoner; and by Hugh de Morewich and Hugh Bardulf, *Dapiferi.*[3]

Feb. 27. The King, accompanied by Octavian, and Hugh de Novant, embarks from Dover, and lands at Witsand.[4] Dover. Witsand.

As to this transfretation, and as to whether Prince John preceded or accompanied the King, the Pipe-Rolls speak equivocal language. They contain the following charges.—

London et Middelsexa. *Et Johanni filio Regis quinquaginta marcas ad perficiendas centum marcas, quas Rex dedit ipsi Johanni in transfretacione suâ per breve Ranulfi de Glanvill.*

Sudhantescira. *In liberacione navium et Esneccæ Regis cum thesauro et harnasio Regis quando ipse transfretavit apud Douram* £19 7*s. per breve Regis.*

Hantona. *Et pro onerando et deonerando thesauro et pro lumine dum thesaurus moram fecit apud Hantonam ante transfretacionem Regis* 7*s. Et pro locandis tribus navibus ad passagium Hugonis Episcopi Lincoln' et Willi de Stæ Mariæ Ecclesiâ et Willi Turpin cum harnasio et equis Regis* £6 *per breve Ranulfi de Glanvill.*

[1] Spelman, Archæol. *sub voce* Finis, p. 228. See also Hunter's Fines, vol. i. pp. lx. lxi.

[2] Cartæ Antiquæ, N. 36.

[3] Wombridge Chartulary, No. 423.

[4] The date (Feb. 27) is Brakelond's. Benedictus says *Die Martis post caput jejunii*; and Diceto says 13 *kal. Mart*, which are consistent, and mean Tuesday, Feb. 17. Gervase of Canterbury says 15 *kal. Mart.* or Feb. 15;— which day was Sunday.

We have preferred Brakelond's authority because his date is part of a consistent and circumstantial narrative of events which came under his own observation. And yet it must be owned that Benedictus, stating that the embarcation of the 17th was a second attempt, seems to have had some knowledge of contemporary circumstances.

1187. Feb. 27. CHENT. *Et in passagio Regis et Johannis filii sui et Ranulfi de Glanvill £49. 0s. 12d. per breve Regis. Et pro batellis ad portandos regem et socios suos ad magnas naves in ipsâ transfretacione 8s. per idem breve.*[1] Dover.

c. Feb. 28. The King, landing at Witsand, is met by the Comtes of Flanders, Blois and Guisnes, and convoyed by them, *viâ* Hesdin and Driucourt to Aumâle in Normandy,[2] where the King is met by his sons Richard and John, by Walter, Archbishop of Rouen, and William de Mandeville, Earl of Essex and Aumâle. c. March 1. Witsand. Hesdin. Driencourt. Aumâle.

March 29. On Easter-day the Duchess Constance, of Bretagne, gives birth to a posthumous son, Arthur, at Nantes.

In the same year Constance remarries with Ranulf (styled *junior*), Earl of Chester.

April 5. K. Henry and Philip of France confer at Gué St. Remi (*ad vadum Sancti Remigii*). They do not accord, and both sides prepare for war. Gué S. Remy.

It was ere this, we are told, that Ranulf de Glanvill, hired Welsh mercenaries, anticipatory of a war with France. The statement is well supported by the Pipe-Rolls, which also give evidence of the constant transmission of money in this year, from England to Normandy.

SHROPSHIRE. *Et in liberacione 250 servientum peditum qui abierunt precepto Regis ultra mare* £16. 13s. 4d. *per breve Regis. Et in liberacione 38 servientum equitum qui similiter abierunt ultra mare* £7. 12s. *de eodem termino. Et tribus magistris predictorum servientum 20s. de eodem termino per idem breve.*

HEREFORDSHIRE. *Et item in liberacione 250 servientum peditum et 4 servientum equitum de octo diebus qui missi fuerunt ultra mare ad Regem* £17. 6s. 8d. *Et item in liberacione servientum retentorum post Pascham* (*March* 29) *in servitio Regis in eadem provinciâ* 47s. 9d.

OXFORDSHIRE. *Et pro ducendo thesauro de Oxineford'*[3] *ad London' ad faciendas liberaciones Walensibus transfretaturis in Normanniam ad Regem* 2s. 10d.

LONDON AND MIDDLESEX. *Et quatuordecim servientibus de Marchis Waliæ qui transfretaverunt ad Regem tresdecim marcas de præstito super liberacionem suam a secundâ dominicâ mensis Junii* (*June* 14), *per breve Ranulfi de Glanvill.*

SOUTHAMPTON. *Et item in liberacione Esneccæ quando transfretavit post Pascham* (March 29) *cum thesauro* £7. 10s. *per breve Ranulfi de Glanvill. Et pro locandâ navi Sansonis Wascelini ad ducendum harnasium Clericorum Thesaurarii et Camerariorum qui transfretaverunt cum thesauro 50s. per idem breve. Et item in laberacione Esneccæ quando transfretavit cum thesauro circa festum Sti Johannis*[4] £7. 10s. *per breve*

[1] The Pipe-Roll says nothing about the great catastrophe which befell the King's household in his transfretation. The majority of the staff (*magna pars de familiâ Regis*) took the route between Shoreham and Dieppe, carrying with them the bulk of the confiscated wealth of Aaron, a Lincoln Jew, deceased. Both men and treasure were lost at sea (Benedictus, *apud* Stubbs, vol. ii. p. 5).

[2] Diceto's narrative (p. 634) implies the King's arrival at Witsand on Feb. 17, and indicates his arrival at Hesdin on the night of the 18th, and at Driencourt on the 19th. This sequence of localities is adopted in the text as exceedingly probable. The errors, if any, are of date; an error in the second and third instances resulting naturally from the supposed error in the first.

[3] A branch of the Treasury was at Oxford. Hence the London Roll of this very year charges *pro conducendâ hugiâ thesauri cum Rotulis et Taleis a London' usque Oxineford 2s.*

[4] The sequence of entries would indicate St. John Port-Latin (or May 6). Otherwise, when the day is thus baldly mentioned, the Nativity of John Baptist (or June 24) is usually meant.

Ranulfi de Glanvill. Et pro locandâ unâ navi Vitalis ad deferendum harnasium Willi de Glanvill [1] *et clericorum Thesaurarii et Camerariorum qui transfretaverunt cum eodem thesauro* 50*s. per idem breve. Et pro locandâ navi Herberti Geldewin ad deferendum thesaurum in Normanniam* 40*s. per breve Regis. Et item pro locandâ navi Hugonis de Hanton ad deferendum thesaurum in Normanniam* 50*s. per breve Ranulfi de Glanvill. Et item pro locandâ navi Godefridi Mansell ad deferendum thesaurum in Normanniam* 50*s. per breve Regis. Et item in liberacione Esneccæ quæ transfretavit cum thesauro post festum Sti Barnabæ* (June 11) £7. 10*s. per breve Ranulfi de Glanvill.*

1187. c. May 1. King Henry divides his army, appointing his sons Richard and John to command in two quarters, the Earl of Albemarle in another, and Geoffrey, his natural son and his Chancellor, in a fourth.[2]

On May 1st (as was afterwards reported) the Master of the Hospitallers and sixty knights Templar were slain near Jerusalem.

King Henry's frontier fortresses of Yssoudun and Fretteval are betrayed to Philip, by Urso de Fretteval and the Comte de Nevers, to the latter of whom Henry had recently given custody of Yssoudun, together with the relict of Eudo de Yssoudun, in marriage,[3] and the wardship of Eudo's heir.

c. May 20. Philip invades Berri and besieges Châteauroux (*Castrum Radulphi*), which was defended by the Princes, Richard and John.

June 23. K. Henry, having marched to the relief of Châteauroux, confronts the army of Philip on Midsummer eve. An engagement is prevented by mediation of the Legate Octavian and of the prelates and peers on either side. A truce of two years, being agreed upon, leaves Yssoudun and Fretteval, for that term, in the hands of Philip.[4] Châteauroux.

Prince Richard, already suspected of treachery by his father, becomes Philip's guest at Paris.

On July 3rd Saladin took Tabaria (Tiberias).

On July 4th Terrencius, præceptor of the Templars in Palestine, writes to other præceptors in Europe relative to the straits of the Christians.

On July 6th Guy de Lusignan, Roger de Moubray, and William de Marchis are taken captive by the infidels, and Hugh de Beauchamp is slain.

This will be the place to notice certain transactions in England which show, not only the Justiciar Glanvill, in discharge of his high function as Viceroy, but also indicate the King's attitude in respect of Papal ascendancy. Archbishop Baldwin, having a dispute with the Monks of Christ Church, (Canterbury),

[1] William de Glanvill occurs on more than one occasion as a messenger between the King and the Viceroy.

[2] Benedictus (Stubbs) ii. 6.

[3] Maud, Comtesse of Nevers, had had three husbands previous to the one mentioned in the text, who was Robert II. Comte also of Dreux, and cousin of King Philip. Her previous husbands were, first, Eudes de Yssoudun, secondly Guy Comte de Nevers, thirdly Peter of Flanders. (Stubbs.)

[4] *Ita quod Rex Franciæ haberet Ysoudun et Ursum de Freteval, &c.* (Benedictus ii. 7), meaning the homage of Ursus de Freteval, which of course implied the command of his castle, Fréteval in Beauce.

had suspended the said Monks for appealing (in defiance of the law) to Pope Urban III. That Pontiff in turn required the Archbishop to restore the Monks, and in case the Archbishop refused, a commission of three Abbots (of Battle, Feversham, and St. Augustine's) was appointed by the Pope, not only to relax the Monks' suspension, but to cite the Archbishop to Rome.

Archbishop Baldwin thereupon communicated with the King, then over sea. The King issued a precept to Ranulf de Granvill, which was attested by, and carried by, William de Glanvill to the Justiciar. The Justiciar's consequent Writ is preserved. It cites the King's authority '*de ultra mare*,' and prohibits the Abbot of Battle, on his allegiance, to proceed in the premises without first conferring with the Justiciar. It cites the Abbot to appear before the Justiciar in London on Saturday after the feast of St. Margaret the Virgin (Sat. July 25), so to confer.[1] The Viceroy addresses a similar writ and citation to the Monks of Christ Church.[2]

1187. Aug. 28. K. Henry confers with Philip at Alençon. Alençon.

On Sept. 3rd Prince Louis of France was born.

About the same time Prince Richard having been vainly invited to his father's Court, seizes the King's treasure at Chinon[3] from the custody of Stephen de Turonis, and proceeds to fortify his Castles in Poitou and Guienne.

c. Sept. K. Henry recalls Prince Richard, and, being reconciled to him, receives his homage at Angers. Angers.

K. Henry now goes into Bretagne, while Prince Richard receives the cross at the hands of the Archbishop of Tours. Bretagne.

The King takes the castle called *Mons Relaxus*, captured, since the death of Prince Geoffry, by Hervey de Leuns. Montreleis.

Of Queen Eleanor, during the whole of the fiscal year now ended, we have no mention, save in the Pipe-Rolls, and those indicate her residence in England. Besides the entry already quoted from the Southamptonshire Pipe-Roll,[4] and which speaks of her residence at, and departure from, Winchester, we have these further notices of the Queen.—

Dorset and Somerset. *Et Eustachio filio Stephani £24. 12s. 2d. ad faciendam soltam Reginæ a die Mercurii proximâ ante festum Sti. Georgii usque ad diem Veneris proximam ante festum Stæ. Trinitatis*[5] *per breve Ranulfi de Glanvill.*

London and Middlesex. *Et in soltis per breve Regis Jordano Clerico Reginæ £84 ad faciendam soltam ejusdem Reginæ.*

Moreover, the Sheriffs of London had supplied various articles of attire, or use, to the Queen and the Duke of Saxony's daughter, preparatory to Easter (*contra Pascham*), and to the Queen and her damsels (*puellis*), against the feast of St. Michael. Other persons similarly clothed at the King's charges, and under writs of Ranulf de Glanvill, were William, son of the Duke of Saxony, the son of the Earl of Gloucester, and the daughter of the King of France (probably the Princess Alice, the destined wife of Prince Richard).

Lastly, the Southampton Pipe-Roll intimates that the Princess of Saxony left England during the year. It charges, under a Writ-Royal, fifty shillings, for the ship hired '*ad passagium Reginaldi de Luci cum filiâ Ducis Saxoniæ.*'

[1] *Mecum inde locuturus;* a phrase which Dean Hook (Lives of the Archbishops) has rendered somewhat too magisterial by translating it 'to make answer in the premises.'

[2] Epist. Cantuar. lix. lx. (pp. 46, 47).

[3] The Treasury of Touraine was at Chinon, as that of Normandy was at Caen, and as that of England was at Winchester.

[4] *Supra*, p. 275. The said entry probably refers to a period previous to Christmas, 1186.

[5] From Wednesday, April 22, to Friday, May 22, 1187.

THE FISCAL YEAR ending at Michaelmas, 1187, was one in which the resources of Royal Revenue were worked with much activity. Taking, as a sample, the exactions levied in a particular district, we observe how closely the administration of provincial law was associated with the assessment of provincial taxes.—

The Justices-in-eyre, who held *Pleas and Conventions* in the several counties of Worcestershire, Herefordshire, Shropshire, Staffordshire, and Gloucestershire, were in each case a quorum of the Sheriffs of those counties, the said Sheriffs being Robert Marmion, Ralph de Arderu, Hugh Pantulf, Thomas Noel, and William fitz Stephen.

In the same year, and in the same counties, those same five officers constituted a committee which assessed a *Tallage* on the King's *Demesnes and Escheats.*

There were also *Pleas of the Forest* held in the same counties; the Justices presiding over which were Robert de Broc, William de Stanton, and Robert de Heselege.

In the same year we may note that the *Assessors of Tallage* in Cornwall, Devonshire, Wiltshire, Berkshire, Surrey, and other counties, were Hugh Bardulf, Dapifer; Master Thomas de Husseburn, and William Briwere; in Sussex, Kent, Cambridgeshire, Huntingdonshire, and other counties, were Ralph, Archdeacon of Colchester, Roger fitz Reinfrid, Michael Belet, and Robert de Witefeld; and that in Northumberland Cumberland, Yorkshire, and Lincolnshire, Godfrey de Luci presided over the said assessment. And, it may be added, that of the eight *Assessors of Tallage* thus mentioned, each one was an active Justiciar of the period; and all of them either Sheriffs of counties, or farmers of extensive fiefs and escheats, then in the King's hands.

In the same year, the afterwards amous Geoffry Fitz-Piers seems again to have acted as *Chief-Justice of the Forest*, and to have held Forest-Pleas in Cornwall, Wiltshire, Berks, Surrey, Hertfordshire, Essex, Cambridgeshire, Huntingdonshire, etc. Also Arnisius de Nevill, Wm. le Vavassour, Rob de Batuent, Roger de Hoveden, and Geoffrey de Haye held Forest-Pleas in Yorkshire. Also the same four Justices who assessed a tallage in Sussex, held *Pleas and Conventions* in that county.

MICHAELMAS, 1187, TO MICHAELMAS, 1188.

Sept. 30. The King was perhaps at this time in Bretagne. Bretagne.

In the course of the autumn, treasure was shipped at Southampton, as evidenced by the Pipe-Roll of Michaelmas, 1188.—

HANTON'. *Et item in passagio navis Prepositi quando transfretavit anno preterito cum equis et harnasio clerici Thesaurarii et camerariorum transfretantium cum thesauro 50s. per breve Regis.*[1] *Et item in liberacione esneccæ quando transfretavit cum thesauro in autumpno £7. 10s. per breve Regis. Et pro unâ navi ad opus clerici Thesaurarii et camerariorum transfretantium cum eodem thesauro 50s. per idem breve.*[2]

On Oct. 11th or 19th, in this year, Pope Urban III. died.

On Oct. 20th Gregory VIII. was elected Pope.

On Oct. 29th we hear of William, Bishop of Landaff, as consecrating an altar in Margan Abbey.[3]

On Dec. 17th Pope Gregory VIII. died. Clement III., elected to the Papacy Dec. 19, 1187, was crowned on Dec. 20th.

c. Nov. The King is supposed to have been at Caen.[4] (Caen.)[6]

c. Nov. 1-10. And then at Bure (Bur le Roy, near Bayeux).[5] Bur Le Roi.

1 · 2 These entries refer probably to two shipments of Royal Treasure, one before and the other after Michaelmas, 1187.

3 Annals of Margan, *sub anno*, 1187.

4 Stubbs's Itinerary, quoting Gervase, 1510. Gervase, speaking of letters of Pope Urban, carried by three monks to Archbishop Baldwin, at Caen, speaks of other letters carried by other monks to the King, who, it is inferred, was also at Caen.

5 Stubbs, quoting Epp. Cant. 106. The King's visit to Bur was before Nov. 18. While there, he executed a mandate to Ranulf de Glanvill, attested by William fitz Ralph, Seneschal of Normandy. The mandate was sent to England, and transmitted by Glanvill to the Sheriff of Kent, for execution on Nov. 18 following.

1187. c. Nov. 1–10. A Royal Charter, dated *apud Burum*, is in favour of the Norman Abbey of St. Stephen, at Caen (Bayeux Dioc.), and is attested by Henry, Bishop of Baieux; John de Constantiis, Archdeacon of Oxford; William de Humet, Constable; William fitz Ralph, Seneschal of Normandy; Thomas Bardulf; Gilbert fitz Reinfrid, and Hamo Pincerna.[1] Bur Le Roi.

Another Charter, dated *apud Burum*, is in favour of the Abbey of St. Mary de Longues (near Bayeux). It is attested by Walter, Archbishop of Rouen; Henry, Bishop of Bayeux; William, Bishop of Coutances; John, Bishop of Evreux; M. Abbot of St. Stephen's (at Caen); P. Abbot of Cerisy; William de Hommet, Constable; William fitz Ralph, Seneschal of Normandy; Hugh de Cressy; Thomas Bardulf; William de Mara; John de Mara; and Hamo Pincerna.[2]

Dec. 25. The King kept Christmas at Caen, in Normandy. Caen.

Dec. 31. The King still probably at Caen.

A Royal Charter, dated at Caen, is in favour of the Abbey of St. Peter, at Preaux. Its witnesses are Hugh, Bishop of Durham; Hugh, Bishop-elect of Coventry; Walter, Archbishop of Rouen; Henry, Bishop of Baieux; Robert fitz William, Archdeacon of Nottingham; John de Constanciis, Archdeacon of Oxford; William, Earl Mandeville; William, Earl of Salisbury; William fitz Ralph, Seneschal of Normandy; William de Humez, Constable of Normandy; William de Mara; Gilbert fitz Reinfrid; and Alured de St. Martin.[3]

Another Royal Charter, dated at Caen, is in favour of the Canons of St. Mary de Voeu (*Stæ Mariæ de Votis*), at Cherbourg. It is attested by Walter, Archbishop of Rouen; William, Earl Mandeville; and William de Mara.[4]

A.D. 1188.

c. Jan. 1. It was now probably that the King, being at Cherbourg, expedited a Charter to the Abbey of L'Essay.—Witnesses, H. (Hugh), elect of Coventry; Henry, Bp of Baieux; John, Bp of Evreux; Robt. de Newburgh, Dean of Rouen; Robert fitz William, Archdeacon of Nottingham; William fitz Ralph, Seneschal of Normandy; Wm. de Humez; Saher Cherbourg.

[1] D'Anisy's Transcripts, i. 180–1.

[2] D'Anisy's Extracts, ii. 41. This Charter is quoted in Gallia Christiana, xi. 83, and assigned to the year 1168.

[3] Monasticon, vii. 1027.

[4] Monasticon, vii. 1111.

1187. c. Jan. 1. de Quenci; Hugh de Cressi; Thomas Bardolf; and Alured de St. Martin.[1] Cherbourg.

Another Charter, dated at Cherbourg, is attested by Walter, Archbishop of Rouen, and Henry, Bishop of Baieux.[2]

A third Charter is witnessed by the same two Prelates, and by Wm. de Humez, Constable.[3]

c. Jan. 4. King Henry goes to Barfleur, intending to cross the Channel for England; but he gives up the design in consequence of Philip threatening to invade Normandy unless his sister Adelais were forthwith married to Prince Richard, or else the fortress of Gisors restored to France. Barfleur.

The following charges on the Southampton Pipe-Roll belong apparently to this occasion.—*Et in apparatu Esneccæ Regis scilicet teldis et loro et aliis necessariis* £7. 7*s.* 2*d. per breve Ranulfi de Glanvill. Et in liberacione Esneccæ quando transfretavit cum thesauro circa festum Hylarii* (Jan. 13) £7. 10*s. per breve Ranulfi de Glanvill. Et pro una navi ad opus clerici Thesaurarii et camerariorum transfretantium cum thesauro* 50*s. per breve Ranulfi de Glanvill. Et pro lumine et pro thesauro illo onerando et deonerando* 3*s.* 11*d.*

Jan. 13-21. A protracted conference between the Kings of England and France at the usual rendezvous, between Gisors and Trie. Both Kings agree to merge their differences in a Crusade, and this in deference to the preaching of the Archbishop of Tyre, who brings accounts of the capture of Jerusalem, and of other misfortunes, from Palestine. The Kings are joined in their vow by Philip, Comte of Flanders. A subsidy of *one-tenth*, in aid of the crusade, is voted by each of the three potentates, to be levied on their respective dominions. Between Gisors and Trie.

Prince Richard was present at this conference.

Jan. 23. K. Henry holds a Council at Le Mans, at which he orders the tax aforesaid to be levied on his continental dominions. There were present at this Council—Richard, Comte of Poitou (the King's son); Archbishops,—William of Tours,[4] Baldwin of Canterbury, and Walter of Rouen; Bishops,—John of Evreux, Ralph of Angiers, Reginald of Le Mans, Matthew of Namur; and Bishops-elect,—Hugh of Chester, and Lisiard of Seez. Le Mans.

1·2 Monasticon, vii. 1081, and vii. 1115.

3 Cartæ Antiquæ, M.

4 The name of the Archbishop of Tours was Bartholomew, but Benedictus always calls him 'William,' possibly a confusion with William, Archbishop of Tyre.

1188. c. Jan. 25. The King would seem to have been at Alençon (in his way to the coast), and there to have expedited that extraordinary Charter, whereby 'he conceded the Priory of Coventry to Hugh de Novant.' The testing-clause of this Charter runs as follows.—*B. Scti Angli Diacono Cardinali et Apostolicæ Sedis Legato;*[1] *B. (Baldwino) Cantuariæ Archiepiscopo; Radulfo Archidiacono Hereford'; Willo de Sanctæ Mariæ ecclesiâ, clerico de Camerâ.*[2] Alençon.

About January 27, Archbishop Baldwin and Hugh de Novant, Bishop-elect of Chester, returned to England; and the latter was consecrated by the former on January 31st.

Jan. 29-30. King Henry embarks from Dieppe, and lands at Winchelsea.[3] The Pipe-Rolls allude, as follows, to this voyage.— Dieppe. Winchelsea.

SUDHANTESCIRA. *Et in liberacione Alani filii Alani et nautarum de navi Willmi de Braiose quando missa fuit precepto Regis ab Hantonâ usque Depam contra Regem* 100*s. per breve Regis. Et in liberacione Esneccæ quando missa fuit contra Regem apud Depam* £7. 10*s. per breve Ranulfi de Granvill.*

HANTON'. *Et item in liberacione Esneccæ, quando transfretavit contra Regem* £7. 10*s. per breve Regis. Et pro thesauro onerando et deonerando qui transfretavit in nave Braiosi* 2*s.* 2*d. per idem breve.*[4]

c. Feb. 3. The King is said to have been at Otford.[5] Otford.

c. Feb. 6. The King goes to Northamptou, avoiding Canterbury, where it would seem that he was expected.[6] Northampton.

At this point the Pipe-Roll, making allusion to an embassy from Castile to England, may be quoted.—
HONOR COMITIS GLOECESTRIÆ. *Et in liberacione nuntiorum Regis Hyspaniæ* £8. 6*s.* 8*d. per breve*——. *Et in reparacione duarum longarum navium et apparatu earum quas Rex misit Regi de Castellâ* £40. 7*s.* 1*d. per breve*——[7] *et per visum Constabularii de Bristou. Et in liberacione Adamæ et Guncelini nuntiorum Regis Castellæ* 40*s. de* 40 *diebus per breve Ranulfi de Glanvill. Et item in liberacione eorundem nuntiorum*

[1] This will have been some Papal Legate after Octavian and before Henry, Bishop of Albano, but of whose mission we find no other Record.

[2] Lichfield Register.

[3] Brakelond says on the 28th; Gervase on the 30th.

[4] It is quite supposable that this vessel, chartered to meet the King, had gone to Barfleur early in January; otherwise there seems to be a redundancy of vessels to meet him later in the month. It is hardly needful to say that William de Braiose, the oft-mentioned ship-master of Southampton, had nothing more to do with the contemporary Baron than that each had his name originally from the same locality in Normandy.

[5] Stubbs (quoting Epp. Cantuar, 162). Otford was in Kent, near Sevenoaks. The Epistle, quoted by Professor Stubbs, is one of Henry II. to Pope Clement III., and was written in February, 1188. It is attested by Hugh (de Novant), Bishop of Coventry, and dated *Apud Otheford.* We cannot doubt that the King was either on that journey to Canterbury, which he afterwards abandoned, or else that, having already abandoned it, he passed through Otford on his way north.

[6] Gervase, 1520.

[7-7] Sic;—blank spaces left in the Record.

a crastino Apostolorum Simonis et Judæ usque ad Purificationem Stæ Mariæ[1] *48s. per breve Ranulfi de Glanvill. Et item eisdem nuntiis decem marcas per breve Regis.*

1188. Feb. 11. The King holds a great Council at Geddington, (Northamptonshire), at which Archbishop Baldwin and Gilbert, Bishop of Rochester, preach the Crusade. A tax, viz., *a tenth of rents and moveables*, to be collected in the course of a year, is assessed on all England.[2] Hugh, Bishop of Durham, is despatched to William, King of Scots, to press him to raise a like *tenth* in his dominions.[3] Geddington.

While at Gedington the King expedited two Charters.—

One to Studley (Warwickshire) is attested by the Bishops, John of Norwich, Geoffrey of Ely, and William of Hereford, and by Waleran, Earl of Warwick, and Ranulf de Glanvill.[4]

The other, to Bungay Nunnery (Suffolk), is attested by the Bishops, John of Norwich, and Hugh of Durham; also by Earl David (of Huntingdon), brother of the King of Scots; William, Earl of Sussex; Ranulf de Glanvill; Stephen de Turneham; Richard de Camvill; William Marescall; William de Humez, Constable of Normandy; Saher de Quinci; Geoffry fitz Piers; Roger de Glanvill, and Walter fitz Robert.[5]

Before the beginning of Lent (March 2), Archbishop Baldwin undertook to preach the Crusade through Wales.[6]

King Henry, with John, Bishop of Norwich, appears next at St. Edmunds.[7] St. Edmundbury.

Feb. 29– K. Henry is at Clarendon.[8] Clarendon.

March 1. And then at Cirencester.[8] Cirencester.

[1] Oct. 29, 1187, to Feb. 2, 1188.—Altogether, these ambassadors would seem to have been in England 136 days, or more than four calendar months. No contemporary Record accounts for the circumstance.

[2] The English tax realised £13,000. Of which £6000 was extorted from Jews.

[3] King William assented to the impost; but his *Proceres*, in Council, refused it.

[4] Monasticon, vi. 186.

[5] Monasticon, iv. 338. This charter confirms to the Nuns, at request of Roger de Glanvill and the countess Gundred, his wife, the church of Bungay, *quæ sita est in libero maritagio ejusdem Gundredæ.*

[6] Bridgeman's Princes of South Wales, pp. 59, 60.

[7] Brakelond (*apud* Soc. Camden) p. 39.

[8] Gervase. 1527. Epp. Cantuar. 221. Gervase's story says nothing about Clarendon, but is suggestive as to the intended movements of the Court at this period. It is as follows.—Four Monks of Christ Church, Canterbury, set out towards the Court on Feb. 25. On their arrival they were ill-received by the King and some of his courtiers (*a quibusdam auliciis*). They left the Court on the same day. They were first told to await the King's return from Wales (whether he does not seem to have eventually gone) at Winchester. Afterwards, the King changing his mind (*rege resiliente*), they were ordered to meet both the King and Archbishop Baldwin, at Cirencester. A meeting subsequently took place, but when or where, Gervase does not particularize.

It seems clear from the Canterbury Epistles (Stubbs, p. 221) that the King was at Clarendon on Feb. 29 and March 1., and that it was there that the Monks first found him. In his Court were Ranulf de Glanvill, Roger the Almonor, Prince John, Hugh Bardulf, William de St. Mary-Church, William de Glanvill, and William de Haubervill, an opponent of the Monks' negociations.

1188. March, April, May. The following extracts from the Pipe-Roll of the year 1188, suggest that the King visited other places (noted in the margin) in the course of the next three months.— Winchester.

HANTON'. *Et in custamento ducendi venationem Regis quæ allata fuit de ultra mare ab Hanton usque Wintoniam* 11*s.* 6*d. per breve Regis.*

GLOECESTRESCIRA. *Et pro ferro ad operaciones Regis in itinere Iherosolem'* £8. 16*s.* 3*d. per breve Regis. Et pro eodem ferro carriando a Gloecestriâ usque Wintoniam* 40*s. per idem breve.*

SUDHANTESCIRA. *Et in camerâ Regis apud Wintoniam viginti marcas per breve Regis. Et pro carriando harnasio Regis de Kingeston usque Wintoniam* 40*s. per breve Regis.* Kingston on Thames. *Et in custamento carriandi venacionem Regis quæ venit de ultra mare a Wintoniâ usque Wudestocham* 26*s.* 10*d. per breve Regis.* Woodstock.

OXINEFORDSCIRA. *Et pro feno parando et conducendo ad Wudestocham* 60*s.*

SURREYA. *Et pro ducendo thesauro a London usque Wintoniam* 10*s.* 2*d.*

HONOR COMITIS GLOECESTRIÆ. *Et pro lineâ telâ ad papiliones Domini Regis* £6. 13*s.* 4*d. per breve Regis. Et pro ducendâ eâdem telâ a Wilton usque ad Wudestocham* 28*s. per breve Regis. Et in emundacione domorum Regis de Clarendon et operacione unius Cameræ* 25*s.* 4*d. Et pro unâ magnâ hugiâ ad reponendum thesaurum in Castro de Sarum* 21*s. per breve. Et in procuracione duodecim equorum apud Wintoniam per sex dies* 8*s.* 8*d. per breve.* Clarendon. (Salisbury).

WINDLESORES. *In operiendis cameris Regis de Windlesores* 69*s.* 2*d. numero per breve Regis. Et in emendacione sedium Regis et Reginæ in Capellâ Regis de Windlesores et aliis operationibus domorum Regis* 52*s.* 3*d. per breve Regis.* Windsor.

c. April 24. King Henry intended to have been in London [1]; but we have no record of his actual presence there, nor of the Conference which he proposed to hold there. (London).

June 5. The King was certainly in London,[2] for the Sheriff charges on the Pipe-Roll a sum of 25*s.* paid by the King's order to London.

[1] Gervase, 1530. The King *desired* to be in London, *post Octavas Paschæ* (after April 24), for the purpose of conferring privately with such as wished to contribute more than two merks in aid of the Holy-Land.

[2] Gervase (p. 1532) corroborates this evidence of the Pipe-Roll; for he tells us how Archbishop Baldwin, returning from his visitation of Wales, found the King in London and had conferences with him at an interval of two or three days.

1188. June 5. the Clerks who sang *Christus vincit*[1] before the King on the day of Pentecost. In the same account there are a variety of charges *pro pelliciis et penulis et pannis laneis et sericis et pro galeis et auro et jocundiolis ad opus Regis.* London.

June 14. On Tuesday after Trinity Sunday, King Henry was again at *Gaitinton*, where a fine was levied before him between the Abbot of Lilleshall on the one part, and William de Boterell, Ysabella his wife, and Philip de Stepelton of the other part. There were present on this occasion, the Bishops Hugh of Durham and John of Norwich; also Godfrey de Luci; Ranulf de Glanvill; Wm. de Humez, Constable; Bertram de Verdon; Geoffry fitz Piers and Hugh Pantulf. Geddington.

June 16. The King sends Baldwin, Archbishop of Canterbury, Hugh, Bishop of Lincoln, and Hugh, Bishop of Chester, ambassadors to France, to learn the meaning of Philip's hostile attitude, and to demand restitution of certain fortresses taken recently by Philip.[2]

This embassage related by the Chroniclers to have embarked at Winchelsea, is supported by the Pipe-Roll of the year;—under Dover.—*Et in passagio Archiepescopi Cantuar' et Episcopi Lincoln et aliorum nuntiorum Regis, pro quatuor de melioribus navibus de Doura* 112*s.* 8*d. per breve Regis.*[3]

To account for the apparent breach of faith on the part of Philip of France, we must here revert to the proceedings of Prince Richard, who soon after the Council of Le Mans (Jan. 23), went into Guienne and subdued the rebellion of Aymer, Comte of Angoulême, Geoffrey de Rancone, and Geoffrey de Lusignan.

The Prince then marching against Raimond, Comte of Toulouse[4] captured Peter Seilun who had instigated the Comte to arrest some Guienne merchants. The Comte in revenge arrested Robert Poer and Ralph Fraser, two English knights who were returning through his territories from a pilgrimage to the Shrine of St. James at Compostella.

Philip of France neglected to mediate effectually between the Comte and Prince Richard, whereupon the latter took the castle of Moissa, seventeen other castles near Toulouse, and the town of Cahors, and subdued the whole province of Querey. Raimond then applied for succour to the King of France, who complained of Richard to K. Henry, then in England. Henry replied that the Archbishop of Dublin[5] had

[1] With respect to the Anthem or Chant styled *Christus vincit*, we can only refer to Sir Thomas Hardy's introduction to the Patent-Rolls of K. John; where, (at p. xxxv), it will be seen that the said Monarch was wont to hear the same sung at various periods of the year.

[2] Benedictus (Stubbs) ii. 40. Gervase. Hoveden.

[3] The Archbishop's embassy to Philip was countered by one from Philip to Henry. The return of Philip's embassy to France is thus indicated on the Pipe-Roll :—

Doura. *In passagio Gerardi de Chartuse et Dapiferi Lugdon'-super-Rodonum et in procuratione eorum dum moram fecerunt in transitu* 24*s.* 10*d. per breve Regis.*

Whether we have here a person named Gerard de Chartres, or a Carthusian Monk; and why the steward of Lyons should have been selected as Ambassador to England, we cannot suggest.

[4] Raimond V. sometimes styled Comte of St. Géours, or St. Giles (Sancti Egidii).

[5] The Pipe-Roll supplies curious evidence of the Archbishop of Dublin having visited France during this year, and at the King's charges.—

Doura. *Et in passagio Archiepiscopi de Duvelin pro unâ navi* 25*s. per breve Regis.*

brought him word from Richard that all the latter had done against Toulouse was with Philip's connivance, and because Comte Raimond had declined the Crusade. Philip, his breach of faith thus exposed, threw off the mask, and having been already in correspondence with the malcontents of Auvergne and Berri, attacked the latter province. He gained Châteauroux, Argenton, and Levreux, nothing being left in Berri to Henry but Loches and his demesne-castles.

Philip then mastered Auvergne in like manner, and fell into Touraine, where he took Mont Richard and Buzançais, and obtained possession of Vendome by the treason of Bouchard, its Comte.

K. Henry then, discerning that all these proceedings of Philip were in hitherto veiled complicity with Prince Richard, and now with the pacified Comte of Toulouse, sent the above Embassage to Philip.

Philip, it appears, refused even to give audience to the ambassadors.

K. Henry now sends Prince John as ambassador to Philip.[1]

It would seem that Prince John embarked at Shoreham, in Sussex, and landed at Dieppe. The Fermor of Boseham charges in the Pipe-Roll.—

In passagio Johannis filii Regis £15. 8*s*. *per breve Ranulfi de Glanvill.*

July 10. K. Henry, having levied forces both in England and Wales, embarks from Portsea[2] for France, leaving Salisbury[3] perhaps for Portsea.[3] Salisbury. Portsea.

The Pipe-Roll evidences of this transfretation are as follows.—

SHROPSHIRE. *Et in liberacione* 300 *servientum peditum de octo diebus qui venerunt Londoniam ad transfretandum in servitio Regis* £20 *per breve Regis. Et item in liberacione* 150 *servientum peditum et* 15 *equitum qui similiter venerunt Londonias* £13 *per idem breve.*

HONOUR OF ARUNDEL. *Et Prepositus de Boseham* £20 *de prestito ad passagium familiæ Regis per breve Regis.*

HONOUR OF GLOUCESTER. *Et pro carriando thesauro Regis a Sarum usque Portesmuam* 20*s*. 5½*d*. *Et in liberacione Alani Trenchemere in passagio Regis* 55*s*. *per breve.*

DOVER. *Et in minutis passagiis per brevia Regis* £15*s*. 11*s*. 6*d*. *Et in defaltâ passagii propter prohibicionem Regis* £15. 12*d*. *per breve Regis.*[4]

[1, 2] Benedictus, ii. 40.

[3] Besides the Pipe-Roll indications of the King having been at Salisbury and Clarendon (*supra*, p. 286) in the spring or summer of 1188, there is a composition made in his presence and in his Court, which probably was made in Wiltshire, and at about this time. It is expressed to be between R. Proctor of (the Nuns of) Mayden Bradley, and G. Prior of Brumore. It notices Henry Biset, as Lord of certain land (*dominum fundi*), contemplated in the arrangement.

There were present, besides the King, Ranulf de Glanvill, Godfry de Luci, William de St. Mary-Church, Hugh de Cressi, Ralph fitz Stephen, Hugh Bardulf, Geoffry fitz Piers, William Marshall, Gerard de Camvill, Richard de Camvill, and Gerard Talbot. (Madox. Form. Angl. p. 22.).

[4] We conclude that the King had ordered a number of ships or transports, which, after they had been outfitted, he countermanded.

1188. July 10. HAMPSHIRE. *Et in corredio et passagio quatuor equorum Regis quos precepit duci ultra mare 13s. 4d. per breve Ranulfi de Glanvill. Et nautis Esneccæ Regis 55s. de arreragio liberacionis suæ per breve Regis.* Portsea.

SOUTHAMPTON. *Et pro unâ navi ad Opus Matthei Turpin et Petri de Lincoln' Falconariorum Regis 35s. per breve Regis. Et Alano Trenchemere de liberacione Esneccæ £7. 10s. per breve Regis. Et eidem 19s. 3½d. ad preparandam eandem esneccam contra Regem per idem breve. Et pro transfretando harnasio Regis et pro uno batello ad opus esneccæ 50s. per breve Regis. Et pro vino empto ad opus Regis et pro carriagio et passagio ejusdem vini £45. 11s. 6d. per breve Regis.*

July 11. King Henry lands at Barfleur, and proceeds thence to Alençon, a town on the Norman frontier of Maine. The barons and knights of England, and Glanville's Welsh mercenaries, followed the King over sea. Barfleur. Alençon.

The Bishop of Beauvais now burns the two Norman towns of Blangy and Aumâle.

Aug. 16–18. K. Henry confers with Philip[1] between Gisors and Trie. (Gisors).

c. Aug. 28. K. Henry sends Walter, Archbishop of Rouen, John Bishop of Evreux, and William Marescall, with demands and threats to Philip. The ambassadors bring back a message of defiance.

Aug. 30. K. Henry now invades the French territory;[2] and advances to Mantes where he expects to encounter Philip's army. A skirmish only ensued, wherein William des Barres, a French knight, being taken prisoner by Prince Richard, escapes by breach of parole. The Earl Mandeville is mentioned as being with K. Henry. Mantes.

Aug. 31. Sept. 1. K. Henry marches to Ivry, whence his Welsh troops invade the French frontier, and burn Danville, Dreux, and other towns, while William, Earl Mandevill burns St. Clare-sur-Epte. Prince Richard, promising fidelity to his father, now goes into Berri. Ivry.

[1] Diceto (p. 639) is the only authority for this conference. His statements, that it lasted three days, that the Kings disagreed, and that Philip forthwith burnt the 'Gisors elm,' induce one to suspect that Diceto was thinking of the confereuce, mentioned below, as of date Sept. 30.

[2] Diceto's story of the Gisors conference, on Aug. 16, 17, 18, intimates that on the 19th K. Henry left Gisors. *In crastino recedens Gisortio transit per Vernonem, Franciam invadit hostiliter, et usque Medantum omnia demolitus est.*

The King's coming to Mantes brings the narratives of Diceto and Benedictus (adopted in the text) again into consonance (Vide Benedictus (Stubbs), ii. 46).

The district, called *Vernon* by Diceto, was, we presume, on the frontier between Gisors and the Seine. If so, it was in the Norman Vexin.

1188. Sept. 29. When Michaelmas came, it found Henry committing havoc on the French frontier, while Philip's resources had been weakened by many of his nobles having gone home for the vintage. The French Frontier.

About this time then, Philip appears to have made overtures of peace.

September, 1188, was the third of five months, most part of which was spent by King Henry in Normandy, or on the Norman frontier. We attribute to this period several charters of the King, which we have no means of dating with any precision, and the readings of which are more or less doubtful.

(1) A Charter, dated at Tenchebray, is to Lonlè Abbey. Witnesses, William de Humet, Constable; William fitz Ralph, Seneschal of Normandy; William de Soliars; Radulph de *Domo* (probably Duno); Nigel de Moriton; and Remigius Talliator.[1] Tinchebrai (near Mortain).

(2) A Charter, dated at Rouen, is to the Abbey of St. Mary, at Cormeilles. Witnesses, Stephen de *Curia* (read Turonis), Seneschal of Anjou; Albered de St. Martin; Geoffry fitz Peter; Eustace, son of *Peter* (read Stephen), Chamberlain.[2] Rouen.

(3) A Charter, dated *Apud Selvi Castrum*, to Vallemont Abbey. Witnesses, *Bartholomew* (Qy. Ralph ?), Bishop of Liseux; Geoffry, the King's son; Fulk Painel; Reginald de *Eurchen* (perhaps Curtenai); Ralph fitz Stephen; William de *Budaicq* (perhaps Bendinges); and Michael Belet.[3]

A FEW EXTRACTS from the Pipe-Rolls will serve to supplement the events of the fiscal year now ended.—

The Fermor of the vacant Abbey of Selby (Yorkshire) charges 35*s.* 7½*d.* *in custamento equorum Regis et hominum missorum ad custodiam eorum.* This was by order of the King.

Earl William (de Mandeville), having custody of the honour of the Comte of Flanders in England, has by order of Ranulf de Glanvill, paid £122. 11*s.* 1*d.* to the King himself, in the Treasury of Normandy.

Reginald, the hearth-keeper (*focarius*) of the King's chamber, has a grant of 25*s.* 4*d.* rent, in Shrivenham, Berks.

The Custos of Windsor has, by the King's order, paid 118*s.* 4*d.* for repairs of the palisades (*palicii*) of the Royal Castle of Pevenesel (Pevensey, Sussex); and by order of Ranulf de Glanvill has paid two merks to one Osbert for keep of the King's hounds.

The Sheriff of Oxfordshire, by the King's order, and at a charge of £6. 8*s.* 9*d.* has sent five hundred ells of linen (*lineæ telæ*) to the King.

1 · 2 · 3 Neustria pia, pp. 427, 601, 852. The last Deed is so ill transcribed that its date is the more problematical. Quite possibly it passed in 1180 or 1181.

The Sheriff of Hampshire charges the Crown three shillings for furbishing the Treasury-swords (*pro Gladiis thesauri furbiandis*). The same Sheriff makes several charges shewing that the King's grandson, William of Saxony, was domiciled in England, probably at Winchester. *Et in soltâ Willielmi filii Ducis Saxoniæ* £6. *per breve Ranulfi de Glanvill. Et item in corredio Willielmi filii Ducis Saxoniæ et amiliæ suæ a Pascha* (April 17) *usque ad festum Sti Michaelis* (Sept. 29) £11. 4*s.* 4*d. per breve Ranulfi de Glanvill. Et pro pannis ipsius Willielmi et servientum suorum et aultricum et latricis suæ* 73*s.* 4*d.*

Queen Elianor, during the whole past fiscal year, was probably under strict surveillance, if not actual imprisonment.

Other events of the same fiscal year, not specially dated, were,—

(1.) King Henry's sending embassies to Hungary and Constantinople to advocate the crusade.

(2.) The surrender of Durham Priory to the care of the Prior and Monks by Hugh, Bishop of Durham, who took the cross.[1]

(3.) The death at Rome, in August, of Henry, Archbishop-elect of Dol. He was a son of Robert fitz Harding, and had been Dean of Moretain. He was at Rome for the purpose of his consecration.

(4.) An instance of Scotch procedure, shewing the limits of ecclesiastical submission accorded by that kingdom to the Pope.—The outline of the case was, chronologically, as follows.—

On January 16, 1188, Pope Clement III, then at Pisa, expedited a Bull, deposing Hugh, Bishop of St. Andrews, and recommending the appointment, in Hugh's place, of John, Bishop of Dunkeld. The latter, charged with the said Bull, reached Scotland after February 2nd, when he was accepted as Bishop of St. Andrews.[2]

Hugh, the deposed Bishop, went to Rome for absolution, and died there, in August, 1188.

Between January and April, 1189, William, King of Scots, held a Council at Perth, and gave the See of St. Andrews to his Chancellor, Roger, son of Robert, Earl of Leicester,—John, Bishop of Dunkeld, not objecting, though he had before been consecrated to St. Andrews.[2]

During the fiscal year, which ended Michaelmas, 1188, we notice that the five Justices-in-eyre and the three Officers of Forest-Law, who had made circuits in Worcestershire, Herefordshire, and other Western Counties in the previous year (ending Michaelmas, 1187), had either continued or renewed their respective *itinera* in the year, now (Michaelmas, 1188) concluded.

During the same fiscal year there were three *Itinera* of regular Justices, viz.—

(1.) Roger fitz Reinfrid, Michael Belet, Robert de Witefield, and Ralph, Archdeacon of Colchester, or some three of them visited Kent, Sussex, Middlesex, Essex, Hertfordshire, Cambridgeshire, Huntingdonshire, Buckinghamshire, Bedfordshire, Northamptonshire, Warwickshire, Leicestershire, and Oxfordshire.

(2.) Godfrey de Luci, William le Vavasseur, and Josceline, Archdeacon of Chichester, visited Northumberland, Yorkshire, Nottinghamshire, and Derbyshire.

(3.) Hugh Bardulf, William Briwere, and Master Thomas de Husseburne visited Surrey, Berkshire, Wiltshire, Somersetshire, Dorsetshire, Devonshire and Hampshire.

And moreover, Geoffry fitz Peter, as Justice of the Forest, visited the counties of Essex, Hertford, Cambridge, Huntingdon, Surrey, Berks, Somerset, Devon, and Dorset.

MICHAELMAS, 1188, TO JULY 6, 1189.

c. Sept. 30. Oct. 1, 2. Three days conference between Henry and Philip, near Gisors[3]. It seems that Philip's demands were unreasonable, for, immediately afterwards, the Comtes of Flanders and — Gisors.

[1] Benedictus, ii. 60. The Bishop had been two years in possession of the Priory.

[2] Benedictus, sub annis, 1188, 1189.

[3] The conference was perhaps identical with that which Diceto dates on August 16. If there were two, the present one was of most importance. The spot of meeting was probably the usual one, under the shade of a gigantic elm which grew between Gisors and Trie. Accordingly, Philip's chagrin at the issue of this conference was so great that he burnt the elm. (See Benedict II. 47, and Professor's Stubbs's notes).

1188. c. Oct. 1, 2. Blois, declined to serve longer under Philip, or against any foes but the Infidels of Palestine. Gisors.

Oct. 7. Another conference between Henry and Philip '*apud Castellum*' (as Hoveden has it). Philip engages to restore all his acquisitions since the truce.[1] Prince Richard engages to make a like restitution to the Comte of Toulouse. Hereupon, Philip demands the Castle of Pacey as a pledge of Henry's good faith. Henry's indignant refusal puts an end to the negociation. Châtillon.

Oct. Henry regains the homage and fealty of Neulon, son of Urso de Fretteval, and, recommencing to negotiate hopefully with Philip, incautiously sends home his Welsh mercenaries.

In the month of October, 1188, Jerusalem was taken by Saladin.[2]

Nov. 18. Conference between Bonmolins and Soligny, at which were present K. Henry, K. Philip, and Prince Richard. Philip (in collusion with the Prince), adheres to his promised restitutions, but demands the immediate marriage of Richard with Adelais of France, and also that Henry should cause all his subjects to take an oath of allegiance to Richard. Henry rejects the latter proposition. Thereupon Richard sides openly with Philip and does him homage for Normandy and all other Provinces held of the French Crown. Philip gives Richard investiture thereof, and promises him Châteauroux and Yssoudun, and all that Philip had recently taken in Berri.[3] Bonmoulins.

On another day of conference, Henry proposes to leave alone the question of restorations of places taken in time of truce, and to negotiate on a permanent peace. Richard now opposes any compromise, declaring that having mastered Cahors, and reduced all Quercy, and so obtained a demesne revenue of 1000 merks per annum, he will not now exchange those advantages for the fief of Châteauroux and the Castles of Yssoudun and Graçay (both in Berri), in which his interest would be only mediate between the respective Tenants and the French Crown. The results of the conference were a truce till Hillary (Jan. 13), and the retirement of Philip and Richard in each other's company.[3]

[1] We presume the truce which was implied by the treaty of January, 1188 (*Vide supra*, p. 283).

[2] Gall. Script. xii. 276.

[3] Benedictus, Hoveden, etc.

1188. c. Nov. Dec. About this time, as we infer, the Cardinal Legate, Henry of Albano, sent by Pope Clement to promote peace between the two Kings, and so to further the crusade, excommunicates Prince Richard as the chief hinderer of both projects, and, shortly afterwards, dies.[1] Normandy.

Dec. 1. King Henry sends Geoffry, his natural son, and still his Chancellor, to care for his interests in Anjou.

The King himself goes into Guienne. Guienne.

The alliance between Philip and Richard is strengthened by the adherence of Ralph de Fougeres and the nobles of Bretagne.

On Dec. 21, Richard de Ilchester, Bishop of Winchester, died.

Dec. 25. King Henry kept Christmas at Saumur in Anjou. Saumur.

Queen Elianor at this time was in England, and apparently under surveillance of Ralph fitz Stephen and Henry de Bernevall.[2] Bernevall.

Dec. 31. The King still, probably, at Saumur. Saumur.

Problematically of the year 1188, is a Royal Charter, dated *Apud Maredonam*, and attested by R. (Ralph) Bishop of Angers; G. (Geoffrey) the King's son and Chancellor; William, Clerk of the Chamber; Hugh de Cressi; Roger fitz Reinfrid; and Alured de St. Martin.[3]

[1] 'He died in July at Arraz,' says Professor Stubbs, intimating however that one authority Alberic de Trois Fontaines) dates the Legate's death on January 1.

[2] Rot. Pipe, 1 Ric. i. pp. 5 & 6.

[3] Coll. Topographica et Genealogica iii. 177.—

This Charter is confirmatory of one which we have already noticed as having passed at Dover, in April, 1185 (Supra p. 263, note).

There is a question whether it passed in England or Normandy. If the former, then *Maredona* may possibly be Merden (Sussex), on the borders of Hampshire, and K. Henry may have visited that locality while going to or from Winchester in 1188. If the latter, then *Maredona* was probably the place, then called *Mar-és-dans*, near Pont de L'Arche and N. W. of Vaudreuil, which place became in Richard I.'s time, the site of the Abbey of Bonport.

As to the witnesses, they afford little light on the topographical question, for we can as little account for the Bishop of Angers being in England as for Roger fitz Reinfrid being in Normandy, at this period.

It is remarkable that we have a Charter of K. Henry I., dated *Apud Marendonam*, and that it passed in the same week or month as other charters which that King expedited at Fareham (Hants), and at Eastbourne (Sussex), when about to cross to Normandy.

A.D. 1189.

1189. Jan. 1. King Henry was probably still at Saumur. Saumur (in Anjou).

Revolt of the Bretons against Henry as soon as the truce had expired with Philip.[1]

Prince Richard also makes incursions into his father's territory.

K. Henry and Philip are persuaded by the Cardinal-Legate, John of Anagni, to refer their disputes to his judgment, and to that of the Archbishops of Rheims, Bourges, Rouen, and Canterbury.[1]

These mediators negociate a prolongation of the truce till after Easter (April 9th), and Archbishop Baldwin is sent by the King to reclaim Prince Richard. The experiment fails.

Feb. 1–3. The King was at Le Mans, where also were Baldwin, Archbishop of Canterbury; Hugh, Bishop of Lincoln; Hubert Walter, Dean of York; and Roger, the King's Almoner.[2] Le Mans.

c. Mch. 1–20. K. Henry was perhaps at Tours. A Charter Royal, there dated, is attested by Ranulf de Glanvill and Stephen de Tours (Seneschal of Anjou).[3] Tours.

March 20. K. Henry is at Le Mans. Messengers despatched by him to England arrive at Canterbury on March 24th. They are Ranulf de Glanvill; Gilbert, Bishop of Rochester; Hubert Walter, Dean of York;[4] and the Dean of Lincoln. The Bishop of Ely (Geoffry Ridel) also left Le Mans in their company.[5] Le Mans.

The Cardinal of Anagni, arriving at Le Mans, brings a letter dated at Lateran, March 12th.[5] The letter is from Pope Clement III. to Baldwin, Archbishop of Canterbury.

April 23 (or, according to other authority, on May 11), the Emperor Frederick's army marched from Regensburg for the East. Hereupon Henry, Duke of Saxony, declining the crusade, goes to England, and thence to the Court of K. Henry, in Normandy.[6]

c. May. K. Henry was apparently at Montfort[7] (near Le Mans). Montfort.

[1] Benedictus (Stubbs), ii. 61, 62.

[2] Epist. Cantuar. (Stubbs), pp. 281-283.

[3] Monasticon, vii. 1028. The Charter is in favour of Allerton Maleverer, a religious house in Yorkshire.

[4] On April 24 we find the Dean of York sitting in *Curiâ*, at Westminster (*infra*, p. 298).

[5] Gervase. 1540, 1543.—John de' Conti di Segni, of Anagni, Cardinal Priest of St. Mark.

[6] Benedictus, ii. 56. See also the note by Professor Stubbs.

[7] Montfort, N. E. of Le Mans.

1189. c. May. A Royal Charter, dated *Apud Montem fortem*, is in favour of the Norman Abbey of Bec. It is attested by John de Constantiis, Archdeacon of Oxford; William, Clerk of the Chamber (*Clerico de Camerâ*)[1]; William fitz Ralph, Seneschal of Normandy; William de Mara; Eudo and Roger de Fontibus.[2] Montfort.

May 19. The Cardinal Legate and the Archbishop of Canterbury were at Le Mans. In all probability the King was there also.[3] Le Mans.

June 4–9. K. Henry and Philip confer at La Ferté, near Le Mans. The Archbishops of Canterbury, Rouen, and Rheims; the Bishops, Hugh of Lincoln, Geoffry of Ely, Gilbert of Rochester, and Hugh of Chester, are there. Philip adds to his former demand (viz. that Prince Richard should marry Adelais and receive the homage of Henry's subjects) another, viz., that Prince John should accompany his brother Richard to Palestine. Richard urges the same stipulation. K. Henry rejects it.[4] La Ferté. Bernard.

The conference breaks off with the Cardinal Legate, John of Anagni, threatening to lay Philip's kingdom under an interdict, and being therefore threatened with personal violence by Prince Richard.

King Henry returning to Le Mans, now sends Ranulf de Glanvill, who was with him, to England for military reinforcements. Le Mans.

After the conference, Philip and Richard returned to their forces, which lay at Nogent-le-Rotrou.

Advancing thence they storm La Ferté Bernard, Montfort, Maletable, Beaumont, and Ballon, where they rest three days. Then, feinting to take the road to Tours, they turn suddenly short on Le Mans, where—

June 12. K. Henry was, with seven hundred knights. Stephen de Tours, Seneschal of Anjou, being with K. Henry, set the suburbs on fire as a measure of defence; but the flames reached the city. Geoffry de Bruillon also distinguished Le Mans.

1 William de St. Mary-Church was Clerk of the King's Chamber, or "Clerk of the Closet" (as we should now term the office).

2 Monasticon, vii. 1067, ii.

3 Canterbury Epistles, p. 290. A Papal letter was handed to the Archbishop on St. Dunstan's day at Le Mans.

4 Benedictus (ii. 66, 67) is the chief authority here, but he dates the Conference in ebdomadâ Pentecostes, *i.e.*, between May 28 and June 4, and omits all mention of Prince Richard's conduct to the Legate.

Hoveden dates the Conference of La Ferté on the octaves of Pentecost (June 4). But Gervase is most circumstantial as to date, placing the Conference on June 9, and adding that Philip took Le Mans, *infra tertium diem.*

Diceto partly accounts for the variety of date by telling us that there were two conferences (*bis habitum colloquium prope Feritatem Bernardi*). We have supposed them, in the text, to have taken place on June 4th and 9th.

1189. June 12. himself by endeavouring to destroy a bridge over the Sarte, but was made prisoner. The city was taken.[1] Le Mans.

K. Henry retreats towards Frenelles,[2] leaving thirty knights in the castle of Le Mans, which surrendered within three days (viz. on June 15). Frenelles.

June 13. King Henry, going himself with a small train from Frenelles towards Angers, sends William fitz Ralph, Seneschal of Normandy, and the Earl of Essex and Albemarle to Normandy. His son Geoffry, with the bulk of his army, he sends to Alençon.

June 18. K. Henry is rejoined by Geoffry at Savigny.[2] Savigny.

Philip and Richard, acting in conjunction, gain the submission of the chiefs of Mont-doubleau, Trou, Roches l'Evêque, Montoire, Chartre, Château du Loir, Chaumont, Amboise, and Rochecorbon; and, on Friday, June 30th, come in sight of Tours.[3]

They take Tours on Monday, July 3rd.

On July 28, Matilda, Duchess of Saxony, died.

On another part, and on June 30, at Azay, there was a conference between Philip, Comte of Flanders; Hugh, Duke of Burgundy; and Wm., Archbishop of Rheims; who agreed to provisional articles of peace, to be proposed to the belligerents.

On July 1st these negociators visited Philip, then before Tours. On July 2nd they found—

July 2. King Henry at Saumur, and in a very desponding state. Saumur.

c. July 3. The King, at Azay,[4] writes to the Convent of Canterbury, William de St. Mary Church attesting the Epistle. Azay.

July 4. King Henry is brought on a litter, extremely ill, to negotiate with Philip,[5] at Azay, or (as another Chronicler better expresses it) at a place *between Tours and Arasic*.[6] Colombières (between Azay and Tours).

[1] Benedictus and Diceto agree in naming June 12 as the day when Le Mans was taken; but Benedictus says that Philip had been halting at Ballon since June 9, and he implies that the capture of La Ferté Bernard and the three other places (named in the text, p. 295) had occupied four previous days.

[2] Giraldus de Inst. Principum, iii. 25 & Vita Galf. Ebor. i. 4.

[3] Benedictus, ii. 69.

[4] Canterbury Epistles, p. 297. The letter, if the chronology of the text be correct, must have been written between July 2 and 5. It is dated *apud Aczai*. It assures the Monks of Christ Church that John, Cardinal of St. Mark, is on his way to Canterbury to adjust the Monks' grievances. It speaks of the King's hoped-for return to England, and is deprecatory of the blame which the Monks throw upon the King, but it says not a word of his illness or misfortunes.

It appears from another letter (p. 295, Epistle cccxi.) that a deputation of Canterbury Monks had waited on the King, and elicited his letter to their Convent. They too write home to give an account of their interview with the King. They say that they had approached him in the midst of arms (*per medios enses*). They say that, at the interview, his *Magnates*, standing-by, told him that his troubles were due to his treatment of the Christ-Church Monks, while the King seemed disposed to attribute his present shame and ignominy to the same Monks. After their interview with the King, the monastic deputation went to Rouen, where were the Legate and Archbishop. It is clear that they wrote home, not having yet heard of the King's death.

[5] Diceto (p. 645) places the Treaty of Azay on June 28th; Giraldus places it on June 30. In the text we follow the chronology of Benedictus, which, as to the day of the Treaty, has been adopted by Rigord.

[6] The actual place of conference was Colombières, near Villandri, on the Cher. (Stubbs's note to Benedictus, ii. 69.)

1189. July 4. At this conference the King agreed to the articles of peace already propounded and settled by the negotiators. Colombières.

They were—1. That Henry should do homage to Philip, and put the Princess Adelais in the hands of one of five persons to be named by Prince Richard, in order to her marriage with the said Prince when he should return from Palestine.

2. That Henry's vassals should take an oath of fealty to Richard as his successor, and that previous revolters to the cause of Prince Richard should do no fealty to Henry till a month after Midlent, 1190, when the Crusade was to set forth.

3. That Henry was to be restored to his possessions in Berri, as before the war, but to pay 20,000 silver merks to Philip, for Philip's alleged outlay in fortifying Châteauroux.

4. That Philip was to keep Le Mans, Tours, the castle of Trou, and Château de Loir (unless Henry would exchange them for Gisors, Pacey, and Nonaucourt), till all the articles were fulfilled.

5. That the burgesses of Henry's demesne-towns should be free in France, paying only their due customs.

c. July 5. K. Henry is carried from the conference of Azay, in a dying state, to Chinon, where he learns that his son John has been beguiled to the allegiance of Philip. Chinon.

A Royal Charter, dated at Chinon, confirms a grant by Walleran fitz Robert to Theobald Walter's nascent foundation at Swainby (Lincolnshire). It is attested by William, Dean of Moretain; Ralph, Archdeacon of Colchester; William, Earl of Arundel; Ranulf de Glanvill, Theobald Walter, Stephen de Turnham, Ralph fitz Stephen, Gilbert fitz Reinfrid, Dapifer; Walleran fitz Robert, Henry de Cornhill, and Gilbert d'Aumari.[1]

Another Charter, in favour of the Monks of Robertsbridge (*De Ponte Roberti*), is dated at Chinon, and attested by Stephen de Turonis.[2]

July 6. On Thursday, July 6th, King Henry died at Chinon. His corpse was attended to Fontevrault by his natural son Geoffry, walking all the way on foot. Chinon.

[1] Monasticon, vii. 920. The sixth witness's name is clearly Turneham; written *Turneh'* in Cart. 22, Edw. III. No. 39.

[2] Cartæ Antiquæ. S. We see that Professor Stubbs (note to Benedictus, ii. 71) identifies Stephen de Turonis, *alias* de Marzai, the Seneschal of Anjou, with Stephen de Turnham, an English Baron. The error is a common one. We know of nothing so suggestive of the identity of Stephen de Turneham and Stephen de Tours, as the occurrence of the two names in the above Charters. Nevertheless, we take the said identity to be wholly imaginary.

SOMETHING SHOULD BE SAID of the Justices and Administrators of the Law during the last year of the King's life. The following extracts will afford a tolerably full list of those functionaries.—

On Jany 20, 1189, a Fine was levied in the *Curia Regis* at Oxford, before John, Bishop of Norwich, and Ranulf de Glanvill, Justiciars of the King; and Godfry de Luci; Richard, the Treasurer; Ralph, Archdeacon of Colchester; Roger fitz Reinfrid, Michael Belet, and Robert de Witefeld.[1]

On Feb. 8, 1189, a Fine was levied in the *Curia Regis* at Shrewsbury, before Ralph de Ardern, Maurice de Berkeley, William fitz Alan, Thomas Noel, Hugh Pantulf, Master Robert de Salop, Robert de Hasel' and Nicholas Britton, all styled "Justiciars of the Lord King."[2]

On April 24, 1189, a Fine was levied in the *Curia* at Westminister, before Hubert, Dean of York; Richard, the King's Treasurer; William, Archdeacon of Totness; Hugh Bardulf, Dapifer; William Rufus, Dapifer; Roger fitz Reinfrid; and Osbert de Glanvill.[3]

In the same fiscal year, Hugh Bardulf, William Briwere, Ralph fitz Stephen, Richard Brito, Archdeacon of Coventry; Robert de Yuglesham, Archdeacon (of Gloucester); and Ralph, Archdeacon of Colchester, or some of them, held Pleas, and sanctioned *Conventions*, in the counties of Cornwall, Devon, Dorset, Somerset, Wiltshire, Oxfordshire, Berkshire, and Hampshire.[4]

Also, John, Bp of Norwich; Gilbert, Bp of Rochester; Ranulf de Glanvill, and Roger fitz Reinfrid, held Pleas in Surrey, Sussex, Kent, Norfolk, Suffolk, Essex, and Hertfordshire.[4]

Also, Geoffry fitz Piers, Ralph Murdac, Michael Belet, Nigel fitz Alexander, Geoffry, Bishop of Ely; Josceline, Archdeacon (of Chichester); Robert de Hardr', and Henry de Norhanton, or some of them, held *Pleas and Conventions* in Warwickshire, Leicestershire, Northamptonshire, Nottinghamshire, Derbyshire, Lincolnshire, Cambridgeshire, Huntingdonshire, Buckinghamshire, and Bedfordshire.[4]

Also, Hugh, Bishop of Durham; William fitz Adeline, Peter de Roos, William le Vavassour, William de Stutevill, and Master Roger Arundel, held *Pleas and Conventions* in Yorkshire, Cumberland and Northumberland.

Lastly, Ralph de Ardern, William fitz Alan, Hugh Pantulf, Maurice de Berkeley, William fitz Stephen, Ralph, Archdeacon of Hereford, Thomas Noel, Robert de Haseleg, Nicholas Brito, Robert de Witefeld, and Master Robert de Salop, or some of them, held *Pleas and Conventions* in Gloucestershire, Herefordshire, Shropshire, and Staffordshire.[4]

And of the above Justiciars it should be noted that the following were contemporaneously Sheriffs of Counties, viz.—

Hugh Bardulf, of Dorsetshire, Somersetshire, and Wiltshire; William Briwere, of Devonshire; Ralph Murdac, of Nottinghamshire and Derbyshire; Michael Belet, of Warwickshire and Leicestershire; Nigel fitz Alexander, of Lincolnshire; William fitz Adeline, of Cumberland; Ralph de Ardern, of Herefordshire; Hugh Pantulf, of Shropshire; William fitz Stephen, of Gloucestershire; and Thomas Noel, of Staffordshire.

[1] Fines, vol. i. p. xxiii.

[2] Lilleshall Chartulary, fo. 82. An Assize taken at Salop (probable of the same date) gives Ralph, Archdeacon of Hereford, as a Justice acting with Robert de Witefeld, Robert of Salop, and Robert de Haselee (Abbrev. Placitorum, p. 25).

[3] Fines, vol. i. p. xxiii.

[4] Rot. Pipe 1, Ric. I. *passim.*

INDEX OF PLACES.

*** The name of each Place of the King of England's visitation is printed in Capital Letters.
Reference to the page or pages which mark such visitation is made by the larger figures.
The prefix ‡ signifies Country, County, Province, or District.
The suffix I. stands for Island; the suffix R. stands for River.
The abbreviation Abb. stands for Abbey; Cast. for Castle or Château; Eccl. for Church; Hosp. for Hospital; Mon. for Monastery; Nunn. for Nunnery.
The abbreviation *al.* stands for *alias*; *n.* for "note"; *v.* for *vide*.

A.

B.

T.

U.

INDEX OF PERSONS.

*** In the following Index, Names which belong to Official Lists, or seem to have any Genealogical relation, are generally classified in order of succession, not alphabetically.

Dates expressed in the Index are usually those established by the evidences of the Text; but where the Author is aware of an earlier or later occurrence of the Individual under notice, he has not hesitated to give the corresponding date.

The signs and abbreviations used in the Index are as follows.—

L. N. denotes the *Liber Niger Scaccarii*, and the numbers which follow the said sign denote those pages of Hearne's edition whereon the individual under notice occurs, the date indicated by such occurrence being uniformly *c.* February, 1166. (See page 90 of the Itinerary.)

R. D. denotes the *Rotulus de Dominabus et Pueris et Puellis;* and the numbers bracketed with the said sign, denote those pages of Grimaldi's transcript of that Record, whereon the individual under notice occurs; the date of such occurrence, if the individual be then alive, being uniformly the summer of 1186.

J. denotes that the individual, to the notice of whom this sign is affixed, sometimes acted as a Justiciar of the King. Similarly—

S. denotes that the individual under notice sometimes acted as a Sheriff. Similarly, the two letters—

J. S. indicate that the same individual sometime acted in each capacity.

T. stands for *Testis*, and is only used for witnesses of Royal Charters, who appear in no other capacity.

The abbreviation *al.* stands for *alias*;—c, for *circa*;—*def.* for *defunctus*;—*n.* or n. for note;—*ob.* for *obiit*;—*s. p.* for *sine progenie*;—*v.* for *vide*;—*v. p.* for *vitâ patris.*

The abbreviation *cons.* stands for *consecrated*;—*el.* for *elected*;—*enthr.* for *enthroned*;—*occ.* for *occurs*;—*tranl.* for *translated.*

C.

D.

F.

I.

J.

N.

O.

Q.

R.

Sheriffs of Counties *tem.* Hen. II.; viz. of—
Bedfordshire and Buckinghamshire.—
Henry de Essex (Mich. 1155–Mich. 1156)
Simon fil. Petri (Mich. 1156–Mich. 1160)
Gaufr. fil. Radulfi, Ricard. fil. Osberti (Mich. 1160–Mich. 1161)
Ricardus fil. Osberti (Mich. 1161–Mich. 1163)
Hugo de Lalega (Mich. 1163–Mich. 1165)
Hugo de Lalega, Ricard. fil. Osberti (Mich. 1165–Mich. 1169)
Hugo de Lalega, Wills fil. Ricardi fil. Osberti (Mich. 1169–Easter 1187)
David Archidiaconus, Wills fil. Ricardi (Easter 1170–Mich. 1179)
Wills fil. Ricardi (Mich. 1173–Mich. 1179)
Willelmus Rufus (Mich. 1179–Easter 1187)
Oger fil. Ogeri (Easter 1187–Mich. 1189)
Berkshire.—
Ricardus de Camvill (Mich. 1155–Mich. 1157)
Gilb. de Pinchigni (Mich. 1157–Xtmas 1160)
Adam de Catmera (Xtmas 1160–East. 1170)
Hugo de Bochland (East. 1170–Mich. 1176)
Hugo de So Germano (Mich. 1176–Mich. 1185)
Uxor ejusdem pro eo (Mich. 1185–Mich. 1186)
Rog. fil. Reinfridi (Mich. 1186–Mich. 1189)
Buckinghamshire, *v.* Bedfordshire
Cambridgeshire & Huntingdonshire.—
Paganus (Mich. 1155–Mich. 1163)
Hamo Peche (Mich. 1163–East. 1166)
Philip de Davintre (East. 1166–East. 1170)
Ebrard de Beche, Warin de Bassingeburn (Easter 1170–Easter 1177)
Walt. fil. Hugonis (East. 1177–Mich. 1182)
Radulf Bardulf (Mich. 1182–Mich. 1185)
Nich. fil. Roberti (Mich. 1185–Mich. 1189)
Cornwall.—
Eustace fil Stephani (Mich. 1175–Mich. 1179)
Alan de Furnellis (Mich. 1179–East. 1186)
Hugo Bardulf (East. 1185–East. 1187)
Wills de Bochland (East. 1187–Mich. 1189)
Cumberland (or Carlisle).—
Robert fil. Troite (Mich. 1157–Mich. 1172)
Adam fil. Robi Troite (Mich. 1172–Mich. 1174)
Robert de Vaux (Mich. 1174–East. 1185)
Hugh de Morewich (East. 1185–Mich. 1186)
Nicholas frater ejusdem (Mich. 1186–Mich. 1188)
Wills fil. Adelini (Mich. 1188–Mich. 1189)
Derbyshire and Nottinghamshire.—
Rob. de Perario (Mich. 1154–Mich. 1156)
Rand. fil. Engelram (Mich. 1156–Mich. 1165)
Robs fil. Randulfi (Mich. 1165–East. 1170)

Sheriffs of Counties *tem.* Henry II; viz. of—
Derbyshire and Nottinghamshire (*continued*).
Wills fil. Radulfi (East. 1170–Mich. 1180)
Radulf Murdach (Mich. 1180–Mich. 1189)
Devonshire.—
Ricardus Comes (Mich. 1155–Mich. 1156)
The same, but called 'Richard de Redvers' (Mich. 1156–Mich. 1157)
Wills de Botcrell (Mich. 1157–Mich. 1160)
Hugo de Ralega (Mich. 1160–Mich. 1167)
Robs fil. Bernardi (Mich. 1167–East. 1173)
Comes Reginaldus (East. 1173–June 1175)
Pagan Capellanus, et Alan de Furnellis pro Comite Reginaldo (June–Mich. 1175)
Wills Rufus (Mich. 1175–East. 1177)
Hugo de Gundevill (East. 1177–Mich. 1179)
Wills Briewerre (Mich. 1179–Mich. 1189)
Dorset and Somerset.—
Richard de Raddon (Mich. 1155–Mich. 1157)
Warner de Lisoriis (Mich. 1157–Mich. 1161)
Rob. de Bellocampo (Mich. 1161–Mich. 1163)
Gerbert de Perci (Mich. 1163–Easter 1166)
Robs Pucherel (Easter 1166–Easter 1170)
Alured de Lincoln (East. 1170–Mich. 1175)
Rob. de Bellocampo (Mich. 1175–East. 1182)
Wills de Bendeng' (East. 1182–Mich. 1184)
Robs fil. Pagani (Mich. 1184–Mich. 1188)
Hugo Bardulf (Mich. 1188–Mich. 1189)
Essex & Hertfordshire.—
Rics de Luci (Mich. 1155–Mich. 1157)
Maurice de Tiretei (Mich. 1157–Xtmas 1160)
Rad. de Marci (Xtmas 1160–Mich. 1161)
Maurice de Tiretei (Mich. 1161–Mich. 1163)
Otuel de Bovill (Mich. 1163–Mich. 1164)
Nicholas Decanus (Mich. 1164–Easter 1169)
Steph. de Bellocampo (East. 1169–East. 1170)
Robs Mantell (Easter 1170–Mich. 1181)
Oto fil Willelmi (Mich. 1181–Mich. 1189)
Gloucestershire.—
Walter de Hereford (Mich. 1155–Mich. 1157)
Wills de Bellocampo (Mich. 1157–Mich. 1163)
Wills Pipard (Mich. 1163–Mich. 1167)
Gilbert Pipard (Mich. 1167–Mich. 1171)
Rads fil. Stephani (Wills frater ejus pro eo) (Mich. 1171–Mich. 1175)
Wills fil. Stephani (Mich. 1175–Mich. 1189)
Hampshire, or Southampton.
Turstinus (Michaelmas 1155–Mich. 1159)
Ricardus fil. Turstini pro patre suo (Mich. 1159–Mich. 1160)

Sheriffs of Counties *tem.* Henry II; viz. of—
Hampshire, or Southampton (*continued.*—
Ricardus fil. Turstini (Mich. 1160–East. 1170)
Hugo de Gundevill (East. 1170–Mich. 1179)
Galfs fil. Azonis (Mich. 1179–Mich. 1189)
Herefordshire.—
Walter de Hereford (Mich. 1155–Mich. 1159)
Mauricius (Mich. 1159–Mich. 1160)
Wills de Bellocampo (Mich. 1160–Mich. 1169)
Walterus Clericus pro eodem } (Mich. 1169–Mich. 1170)
Wills de La Lega (Mich. 1170–Mich. 1171)
Gilbert Pipard (Mich. 1171–East. 1173)
Wille de Braose (East. 1173–Mich. 1175)
Randulf Puher (Mich. 1175–East. 1182)
Milo de Mucegros, Roger fil. Mauricii } (Easter–Mich. 1182)
Milo de Mucegros (Mich. 1182–East. 1183)
Wills Torel (Easter 1183–Easter 1185)
Rads de Ardene (Easter 1185–Mich. 1189)
Huntingdonshire, *v.* Cambridgeshire, and Huntingdonshire (*supra*, p. 337)
Kent.—
Radulf Picot (Mich. 1155–Xtmas 1160)
Hugo de Doura (Xtmas 1160–East. 1168)
Gervase de Cornhull (East. 1168–Mich. 1174)
Robs fil. Bernardi (Mich. 1174–Mich. 1183)
Wills fil. Nigelli, Wills fil. Philippi } (Mich. 1183–Mich. 1184)
Alan de Valoins (Mich. 1184–Mich. 1189)
Lancaster.—
Gaufr. de Valoins (Mich. 1164—East. 1166)
Wills de Vesci (Mich. 1166–East. 1170)
Rog. de Herleberg (East. 1170–East 1173)
Ranulf de Glanvill (East. 1173–East. 1174)
Ranulf de Glanvill, Rads fil. Bernardi } (East. 1174–Mich. 1174)
Rads fil. Bernardi (Mich. 1174–East. 1185)
Gilbert Pipard (East. 1185–Mich. 1189)
Leicestershire & Warwickshire.—
Robs fil. Hugonis (Mich. 1155–Mich. 1158)
(L) Robs fil. Harnulfi, (W) Wills de Bellocampo } (Mich. 1158–East. 1159)
Rads Basset (East. 1159–Mich. 1162)
Wills Basset pro Rado fratre suo } (Mich. 1162–Mich. 1163)
(L) Wills Basset, (W) Robs fil. Gaufridi } (Mich. 1163–Mich. 1164)
Wills Basset (Mich. 1164–East. 1170)
Bertram de Verdun (East. 1170–East. 1185)
Michael Belet (East. 1185–Mich. 1189)

Sheriffs of Counties *tem.* Hen. II; viz. of—
Lincolnshire—
Jordan de Blossevill (Mich. 1155–Mich. 1157)
Walt. de Amundevill (Mich. 1157–Mich. 1163)
Peter de Golsa (Mich. 1163–Mich. 1165)
Wills de Insula pro Petro de Golsa } (Mich. 1165–Mich. 1166)
Alured de Poilton (Mich. 1166–Mich. 1167)
Philip de Kime (Mich. 1167–East. 1170)
Walt. de Grimesby, Alured de Pointon } (East. 1170–Mich. 1174)
Walt. de Grimesby (Mich. 1174–Mich. 1175)
Drogo fil. Radulfi (Mich. 1175–East. 1177)
Wills Basset (Easter 1177–East. 1185)
Nigel fil. Alexandri (East. 1185–1189)
Middlesex & London.—
Johs fil. Radulphi (Oct. 1154–Mich. 1155)
Gervase and John (Mich. 1155–Mich. 1156)
Reiner fil. Berenger, Wills fil. Isabel } (Mich. 1156–Mich. 1157)
Reiner fil. Berenger, Gaufr. Bursarius, Josce Vinitarius, Ricardus Vetulus } (Mich. 1157–Mich. 1158)
Reiner fil. Berenger, Johs fil. Radulfi et socii } (Mich. 1158–Mich. 1159)
Reiner fil. Berenger, Wills fil. Isabel } (Mich. 1159–Mich. 1160)
Johes fil. Radulfi (Mich. 1160–Mich. 1161)
Ernald Scutarius, Vitalis Clericus } (Mich. 1161–Mich. 1162)
Reiner fil. Berenger, Wills fil. Isabel } (Mich. 1162–East. 1169)
Johes Bucuinte, Baldwin Crispus, David de Cornhill, Roger Blund } (East. 1169–Xtmas 1172)
Rads Aurifaber, Rads Vinitor, Andr. Bukerell, Aelardus } (Xtmas 1172–June 1174)
Brichtmer de Haverhill, Peter fil. Walteri } (June 1174–Juoe 1176)
Wills fil. Isabel (June 1176–Mich. 1177)
Walerannus, Johes fil. Nigelli } (Mich. 1177–Mich. 1178)
Wills fil. Isabel, Ernulf Buzell' } (Mich. 1178–Mich. 1179)
Wills fil. Isabel, Reginald le Viel } (Mich. 1179–Mich. 1181)

Sheriffs of Counties *tem.* Henry II; viz. of—
Middlesex and London (*continued*).—
Wills fil. Isahel (Mich. 1181–East. 1187)
Henry de Cornhill, Rics fil. Reineri (East. 1187–Mich. 1189)
Norfolk and Suffolk.—
(N) Wills de Nevill, (S) Wills de Fraxineto (Mich. 1155–Mich. 1156)
Wills de Caisnei (East. 1157–Mich. 1163)
Oger Dapifer (Mich. 1163–Easter, 1170)
Barth. de Glanvill, Wimar Capellanus, Wills Bardul (East. 1170–Mich. 1175)
Wimar Capellanus (Mich. 1175–East. 1187)
Willis fil. Hervei (East. 1157–Mich. 1189)
Northamptonshire.—
Simon fil. Petri (Mich. 1155–Xtmas 1160)
Hugo Gubiun (Xtmas 1160–Mich. 1163)
Simon fil. Petri (Mich. 1163–East. 1170)
Robs fil. Sawini (East. 1170–Mich. 1174)
Hugo de Gundevill (Mich. 1174–East. 1177)
Thos. fil. Bernardi (East. 1177–Mich. 1183)
Rads Morin pro eodem (Mich. 1183–Mich. 1184)
Galfs fil. Petri (Mich. 1184–Mich. 1189)
Northumberland.—
Wills de Vesci (Mich. 1157–Easter 1170)
Roger de Stutevill (East. 1170–East. 1185)
Roger de Glanvill (East. 1185–Mich. 1189)
Nottinghamshire, *v.* Derbyshire
Oxfordshire.—
Henr. de Oilli (Mich. 1155–June 1161)
Manasser Arsich (East. 1161–Mich. 1163)
Thomas Basset (Mich. 1163–Mich. 1164)
Adam de Catmera (Mich. 1164–East. 1170)
Alard Banastre (East. 1170–Mich. 1175)
Robs de Turevill (Mich. 1175–Mich. 1179)
Galfrid. Hosatus (Mich. 1179–East. 1182)
Robs de Witefeld (East. 1182–East. 1185)
Alan de Furnellis (East. 1185–East. 1187)
Robs de la Mara (East. 1187–Mich. 1189)
Rutland.—
Rics de Humez (Mich. 1155–Mich. 1157)
Robs fil. Gubolt (Mich. 1157–Mich. 1159)
Rics de Humez (Mich. 1159–Mich. 1161)
Robs. fil. Gubolt (Mich. 1161–Mich. 1163)
Rics de Humez (Mich. 1163–Mich. 1164)
Robs fil. Gubolt (Rics de Humez pro eo) (Mich. 1164–Mich. 1166)
Rics de Humez (Mich. 1166–Mich. 1178)
Simon Basset pro Rico de Humez (Mich. 1178–Mich. 1179)

Sheriffs of Counties *tem.* Hen. II; viz. of—
Rutland (*continued*).—
Wills Malduit Camerarius (Mich. 1179–June 1188)
Amalric Dispensator (June 1188–Mich. 1189)
Shropshire.—
Wills fil. Alani (June 1155–Mich. 1159)
Wido Extraneus (Mich. 1159–Xtmas 1164)
Gaufridus de Ver (Xtmas 1164–Mich. 1169)
Wills Clericus, pro eo (Mich. 1169–Mich. 1170)
Wido Extraneus (Mich. 1170–Mich. 1179)
Hugo Pantulf (Mich. 1179–Mich. 1189)
Somerset, *vide supra* Dorset
Southampton, *vide supra* Hampshire
Staffordshire.—
Robs de Stafford (Mich. 1154–Mich. 1160)
Alexander Clericus (Mich. 1160–East. 1166)
Herveius de Stratton (East. 1166–Mich. 1184)
Thomas Noel (Mich. 1184–Mich. 1189)
Suffolk, *vide supra* Norfolk
Surrey.—
Paganus pro Willo Martell (Mich. 1155–Mich. 1156)
Paganus (Mich. 1156–Mich. 1163)
Gervase de Cornhill (Mich. 1163–Mich. 1182)
Henricus fil. Gervasii de Cornhill pro eo (Mich. 1182–Mich. 1183)
Henricus de Cornhill (Mich. 1183–Mich. 1189)
Sussex.—
Mauger de Malcuvenant (Mich. 1155–1156)
Ricardus de Humez (Mich. 1156–Mich. 1157)
Radulfus Picot (Mich. 1157–Mich. 1160)
Hilary, Bishop of Chichester (Mich. 1160–Mich. 1162)
Henry, Archdeacon of Chichester (Mich. 1162–Mich. 1163)
Rogerus Hai (Mich. 1163–East. 1170)
Reginald de Warren (East. 1170–Mich. 1176)
Roger fil. Reinfrid (Mich. 1176–East. 1187)
Willelmus Rufus (East. 1187–Mich. 1189)
Warwickshire, *v. supra* Leicestershire
Westmoreland.—
Rand. de Glanvill (Mich. 1174–Mich. 1179)
[*Elsewhere treated as part of Yorkshire.*]
Wiltshire.—
Comes Patricius (Mich. 1155–Mich. 1160)
Ricardus Clericus (Mich. 1160–Mich. 1162)
Milo de Danteseia (Mich. 1162–Mich. 1163)
Richard de Wilton (Mich. 1163–Mich. 1179)
Robert Malduit (Mich. 1179–Easter 1187)
Hugo Bardulf (Easter 1187–Mich. 1189)